THE WORLD ENCYCLOPEDIA OF
FLAGS AND HERALDRY

THE WORLD ENCYCLOPEDIA OF
FLAGS AND HERALDRY

AN INTERNATIONAL HISTORY OF HERALDRY AND ITS CONTEMPORARY
USES TOGETHER WITH THE DEFINITIVE GUIDE TO NATIONAL
FLAGS, BANNERS, STANDARDS AND ENSIGNS

STEVEN SLATER AND
ALFRED ZNAMIEROWSKI

LORENZ BOOKS

This edition is published by Lorenz Books, an imprint of Anness Publishing Ltd, Hermes House, 88–89 Blackfriars Road, London SE1 8HA; tel. 020 7401 2077; fax 020 7633 9499

www.lorenzbooks.com; www.annesspublishing.com

If you like the images in this book and would like to investigate using them for publishing, promotions or advertising, please visit our website www.practicalpictures.com for more information.

UK agent: The Manning Partnership Ltd; tel. 01225 478444; fax 01225 478440; sales@manning-partnership.co.uk
UK distributor: Grantham Book Services Ltd; tel. 01476 541080; fax 01476 541061; orders@gbs.tbs-ltd.co.uk
North American agent/distributor: National Book Network; tel. 301 459 3366; fax 301 429 5746; www.nbnbooks.com
Australian agent/distributor: Pan Macmillan Australia; tel. 1300 135 113; customer.service@macmillan.com.au
New Zealand agent/distributor: David Bateman Ltd; tel. (09) 415 7664; fax (09) 415 8892

Designers: Nigel Partridge and Mike Morey, cover design: Adelle Morris
Illustrations: flag artworks: Alfred Znamierowski. Heraldic Artworks:
Antony Duke: p438tr,m & mr. Dan Escott: pp482, 493br. David Hubber:
p484b. Marco Foppoli: pp279tr; 281b; 298 & 317tl; 317tr & br; 327tl;
333 all; 335tl & br; 341br; 348 & 357tr; 351tr; 353t; 383tl,tm,tr & m;
398bl & br; 399tl; 444b all; 445 all; 447tm,tr & br; 448tl; 449t; 461mr;
462b; 468 all; 492bl,bm & br. Roland Symons: p287 all. Alfred
Znamierowski: pp260tr; 267br; 281m; 284br; 297 all; 303tl; 305b &
box; 306br; 309m & t; 311tl; 312ml; 314bl; 315tl & bl; 316bm & br;
320 all; 321t & m; 323 all; 324 all; 325t; 326; 328 all; 329 all; 330 all;
331 all; 334tl & m; 336bm & br; 337tr, mr & br; 338tr & br; 339tr;
340mr & br; 342tl,tr,bl,bm & br; 343ml,bl,tr, & tm; 344tl,tr & br; 345
all; 346bl,bm & br; 347tl,tm, tr & br; 350mr; 351bl & br; 352br; 353b;
354t; 355 all; 356ml,bl & bm; 359tr & bl; 362tr & bm; 365br; 367;
368t; 369t; 370 all; 371bl,bm,br; 397tr; 402bl & bm; 409tl; 413tm & tr;
427tl; 437 all; 458tr & br; 463b; 472b; 473t,m & br; 474 all; 475tl &
mr; 477mr; 493ml & mb.

ETHICAL TRADING POLICY
At Anness Publishing we believe that business should be conducted in an ethical and ecologically sustainable way, with respect for the environment and a proper regard to the replacement of the natural resources we employ. As a publisher, we use a lot of wood pulp to make high-quality paper for printing, and that wood commonly comes from spruce trees.

We are therefore currently growing more than 500,000 trees in two Scottish forest plantations near Aberdeen – Berrymoss (130 hectares/320 acres) and West Touxhill (125 hectares/305 acres). The forests we manage contain twice the number of trees employed each year in paper-making for our books. Because of this ongoing ecological investment programme, you, as our customer, can have the pleasure and reassurance of knowing that a tree is being cultivated on your behalf to naturally replace the materials used to make the book you are holding.

Our forestry programme is run in accordance with the UK Woodland Assurance Scheme (UKWAS) and will be certified by the internationally recognized Forest Stewardship Council (FSC). The FSC is a non-government organization dedicated to promoting responsible management of the world's forests. Certification ensures forests are managed in an environmentally sustainable and socially responsible basis. For further information about this scheme, go to www.annesspublishing.com/trees

© Anness Publishing Ltd 2007

Previously published in two separate volumes, *The World Encyclopedia of Flags* and *The Complete Book of Heraldry*

Illustration on page 1: The arms of the Old Town of Belgrade,
page 2: The impaled arms of bride and groom at the marriage of Charles VI of France and Isabeau of Bavaria.

CONTENTS

INTRODUCTION

Throughout the ages flags have been a means of cultural and national identity, and the development of heraldry in the medieval period had a similar purpose: a means by which to identify a person or a group. This book brings flags and heraldry together in a remarkable volume that shows how each have been created, displayed and administered. The first section of the book provides an exhaustive history of the flag from the earliest Egyptian standards of 3100BC to ensigns of 21st-century maritime nations. It then provides an up-to-date summary of world flags from the smallest states to the largest countries. With special sections on Emperors, Sovereigns and Presidents, Government Flags, Military Signs, Naval Ensigns and Flags, and Flag Families, no aspect of this fascinating subject is left uncovered. Learn how flag shapes were developed, as well as the techniques of making flags, flag terminology is explained, as well as flag usage and the intricacies of flag etiquette.

A product of the medieval battlefield and tournament, heraldry has been called both the "shorthand of history" and "the noble science". It is best defined as a hereditary system of colours and symbols, borne on the medieval war shield, for personal identification. The second section of this book deals with this system, tracing its history, looking at how and why it evolved, and then surveying the many different uses that have been found for it, by individuals and institutions all over the world. The book takes a comprehensive look at the way heraldry has been used and applied throughout up to the present time. Diverse heraldic traditions are compared, through the way it is used by monarchs, politicians, the military, the police, corporations, educational and medical establishments, and finally by the individual.

Heraldry and the art of flags have long excited the imagination and enthusiasm of historians, artists and anthropologists, and still inspires admiration and pride in its modern usage. The arcane languages may make the subjects seem difficult to grasp, yet the words are both precise and evocative. Some see flags and arms as a quaint pleasantry, others as an anachronism, or a symbol of nationalism, but both art forms have survived through the centuries, and still retain the power to evoke a noble past.

▶ *A knight bearing heraldic arms receives his trophy from the Queen of the Tournament.*

SIAM.

Ensign.

Merchant.

Officer's Pennant.

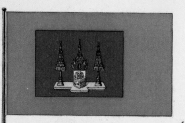

Royal Standard.

"Chakr,"
or White Wheel.

To be used as distinctive
mark for Vice-Admiral
and Rear-Admiral.

Coat of Arms.

Jack.

The same Flag is flown at the Main Top for Admiral.
The same Flag with one white Wheel in Upper Corner near Staff for Vice-Admiral.
The same Flag with two white Wheels, one in Upper and one in Lower Corner, near Staff for Rear-Admiral.
The same Flag with Swallow-Tail is used for Commodore.

Diplomatic Service Flag.

Note. The same Flag with Crown over Shield omitted
for the Consular Service Flag.

FLAGS OF THE WORLD

———

FLAGS HAVE ALWAYS APPEALED TO EVERY SECTION OF SOCIETY,
FROM THE PROUD TO THE HUMBLE, THE ROMANTIC TO THE
PROSAIC, THE RICH TO THE POOR. AS A STANDARD OF HONOUR
AND ALLEGIANCE THE FLAG WAS AN INTRINSIC PART OF THE
PAGEANTRY OF ROYALTY, BUT HAS ALSO BEEN ADAPTED TO SERVE
ARMIES, RELIGIOUS FOUNDATIONS, CITIES AND PROFESSIONS.
IN THE MODERN AGE DISTINCT NATIONAL STYLES HAVE BEEN
DEVELOPED, AND FLAGS HAVE BEEN ADAPTED TO CHANGING TIMES
AND NEW USES. A FLAG CAN BE AN ELABORATELY STITCHED
MEDIEVAL BANNER, OR A HAND-DRAWN EMBLEM ON A SCRAP OF
PAPER WAVED IN A SCHOOL PARADE, BUT WHATEVER ITS
MANIFESTATION THE FEELING OF IDENTIFICATION AND
BELONGING THAT A FLAG ENGENDERS IS THE SAME.

◀ *An illustration of Thai flags and arms from the*
album Flags of Maritime Nations *published in*
Washington in 1899

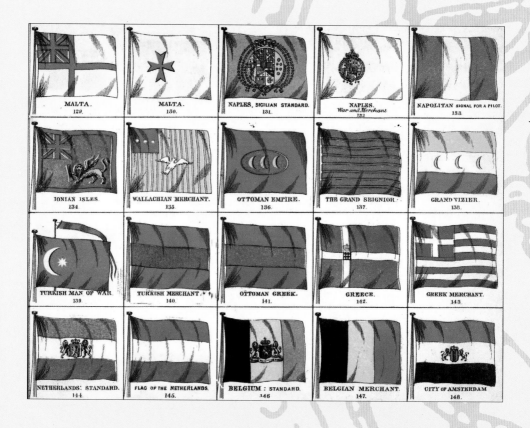

MALTA. 129.	MALTA. 130.	NAPLES, SICILIAN STANDARD. 131.	NAPLES. War and Merchant 132	NAPOLITAN SIGNAL FOR A PILOT. 133.
IONIAN ISLES. 134.	WALLACHIAN MERCHANT. 135.	OTTOMAN EMPIRE. 136.	THE GRAND SEIGNIOR. 137.	GRAND VIZIER. 138.
TURKISH MAN OF WAR. 139.	TURKISH MERCHANT. 140.	OTTOMAN GREEK. 141.	GREECE. 142.	GREEK MERCHANT. 143.
NETHERLANDS: STANDARD. 144.	FLAG OF THE NETHERLANDS. 145.	BELGIUM : STANDARD. 146.	BELGIAN MERCHANT. 147.	CITY OF AMSTERDAM 148.

FLAGS THROUGH THE AGES

The fascinating story of flags is closely interwoven with historical

events, reflecting the aspirations and lives of people over many centuries.

The eagle-topped standards of the Roman legions, the flame-edged flag of Genghis

Khan and the heraldic banners carried by medieval knights in tournament are

all part of a continuing development that has led to the flags we know today.

This chapter describes the physical characteristics of flags, various types of flag,

flag usage and etiquette, each with its own glossary for ease of reference. A discussion

of the flags of emperors, sovereigns and presidents and of government is

followed by military signs from battle banners to war ensigns, including

the flags of the armed services. A final section on Flag Families

shows how the flags of a few countries have influenced

those of the rest of the world.

◄ *Among flags presented on this plate from Colton's* Delineation of Flags of All
Nations *(1862) are royal standards of Naples, the Netherlands and Belgium, the civil
ensigns of Turkey and Greece introduced at the end of the 18th century, and the flag of
the Ionian Islands under British rule (1817-1864).*

The Origin and Development of Flags

*Symbols are sacred things, and one of the chief that every man holds
dear is the national flag. Deep down in our nature is the strong emotion that swells the
heart and brings the tear and makes us follow the flag and die round it rather than let it
fall into the hands of an enemy. This is no new emotion, no growth of a few generations,
but an inheritance from the ages before history began.*

W.J. GORDON, *FLAGS OF THE WORLD*, LONDON, 1915

The origin of flags lies in our remote prehistoric past. When people started to form large groups to live and hunt together, they appointed a leader to rule them and settle disputes. As a mark of office the leader wore a ceremonial head-dress and held a long decorated staff, rod or spear, topped with an ornament or emblem. The staff was also used as a visible sign to rally around, or to point out the direction of a march or attack. This proto-flag is known as a vexilloid.

Later in China, a different tradition developed when silk was invented. This strong, light fabric was ideal for making banners, which were much easier to carry than vexilloids and are easier to see from a distance. From China the use of fabric flags spread to Mongolia, India and Persia, and finally they arrived in Rome and the rest of Europe.

The first vexilloids and flags were military and ceremonial signs. But by the 12th century they began to serve as a way of identifying rulers and their domains, and nationality at sea. During the next two centuries cities and guilds adopted their own flags, and the 17th century saw the introduction of standardized regimental colours, war ensigns, jacks and the house flags of the trading companies. The first national flags on land appeared in the last quarter of the 18th century, as did the flags of yacht clubs. During the 19th and 20th centuries a host of other flags also appeared: flags of government agencies and officials; provincial flags; rank flags in all branches of the armed forces; and flags of schools, universities, scientific institutions, organizations, political parties, trades unions and guerrilla movements. There are also flags of nationalities and ethnic groups, flags of business corporations and sporting clubs, and occasionally flags for fun. It seems that you have no identity unless you have a flag.

▲ *ABOVE Standard of West Egypt, on the sarcophagus of Khons-mose (1000 BC).*

▲ *ABOVE Detail of the palette of Narmer, 3000 BC.*
▼ *BELOW LEFT Detail of the Osiris' misteria stela (2000 BC).*

▼ *BELOW Standard of the Two Falcons nome.*

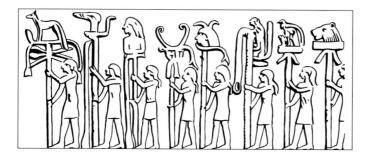

VEXILLOIDS

The original vexilloids were made of wood, feathers and the horns, tails, hooves and skins of animals. Later ornaments or emblems on top of the staff were made of carved and painted wood or metal. We know this from the well-documented Aztec vexilloids, and those of societies that 100 years ago still lived in Stone Age conditions. The characteristic feature of the Aztec vexilloids was extensive use of green quetzal feathers, metals such as gold, silver and copper, and precious stones. The vexilloids still used today by tribes in New Guinea are ancient Melanesian; the way they are made and their symbolism reveal no influence from other cultures. They consist mostly of wood, dried grass and feathers, with emblems of painted wood, feathers and pieces of cloth.

The oldest known vexilloids appear on Egyptian pottery of the Gerzean period (3400 BC) and on the reverse of the King Narmer palette (3000 BC). They were the signs of *nomes*, the provinces of pre-dynastic Egypt. The *nomes* were named after things or animals (Two Falcons, Sceptre, Ibis, Double Feather, and so on), which were depicted as highly stylized emblems on the vexilloids. Some provincial vexilloids displayed the emblems of local gods. They were made of wood, and the emblems were painted.

There is very little evidence of Assyrian, Babylonian and Persian vexilloids, although the oldest vexilloid still in existence was carried in Persia 5000 years ago. It has a metal staff, with a finial in the form of an eagle, and a square metal "flag" covered with reliefs. Two primitive vexilloids appear on a stela of Naramsin, King of Babylonia (c.3000 BC). At Alacahöyük, in north-central Turkey, archaeologists have found Hittite standards dating from c.2400–2200 BC. The metal emblems show a stag, a stag with two bulls and a sun disc.

The Romans copied the use of vexilloids as well as the eagle emblem from Persia. The military standard (*signum*) of the Roman legions consisted of a lance with a silver-plated shaft, topped with a crosspiece carrying figures of various beasts. The most important was an eagle

▲ *ABOVE Standard of the Double Feather nome.*

▲ *ABOVE Dragon standard from Psalterium Aureum (9th century).*

▼ *BELOW Vexilloids: (left to right) Assyrian, Roman, Aztec, Mongolian, Japanese.*

(*aquila*). Attached to the shaft were several metal rings in the form of a laurel wreath, and medallions with the eagle of Jupiter or with portraits of the emperor and members of the imperial house. According to Pliny the Elder:

Gaius Marius in his second consulship (103 BC) assigned the eagle exclusively to the Roman legions. Before that period it had only held the first rank, there being four others as well – the wolf, the minotaur, the horse and the wild boar – each of which preceded a single division.

Popular in the Roman Army from the 2nd century was the *draco* (dragon flag), borrowed from the Parthians or Sarmatians, who used this kind of flag several centuries earlier. A hollow bronze dragon's head sat at the top of the staff with a serpent-shaped silk windsock attached. When the wind blew it moved like a serpent and a device in its head made a whistling noise.

The dragon flag was used in Britain during the Dark Ages, and in the 6th century was adopted by the Saxon conquerors. It was borne in front of the armies of the Anglo-Saxons and Normans at least until the 12th century.

The Mongols also had an instantly recognizable vexilloid consisting of a staff topped with a metal ball or spear, with a horse's tail attached to it. These spread quickly among the Turkish people; in the Turkish Army they became the sign of a commander and in the 17th and 18th centuries they were carried before the commanders-in-chief of the Polish Army.

EARLY FLAGS

Long before flags appeared in Europe they had been used in China. Written sources even mention the flag of the Yellow Emperor, a mythological ancestor of the Chinese. The oldest iconographic information on the shape and function of flags in China dates from about 1500 BC. A bamboo staff was topped with a metal trident, to which were attached small rings holding tassels made of horses' tails. The number of narrow ribbons attached to the outer edge denoted the social rank of the flag-bearer, ranging from twelve for the Emperor down to just one for a functionary of the lowest rank. A long, wide, swallow-tailed ribbon was attached to make it into a signal for battle.

The Chinese, who first made cloth out of silk, were the first to make flags out of fabric and attach them sideways to the staff to form a banner. The hierarchy of Chinese society was reflected in a large number of different types of flag for use by the emperor, nobility, commanders of the imperial army, and governors of the provinces and counties. The most common flag symbols were a dragon, tiger, hawk, turtle and snake. The emperor had five chariots, each flying a different flag in yellow, blue, red, white and black. In the course of history the shape of Chinese flags changed to square or triangular with "flammules" (flame-shaped edges), but the hierarchy reflected in the number of flags was maintained. For example, in the 19th century there were nine classes of mandarins and the

army used some 50 different flags; there were also special flags for eleven ranks of envoys.

After the Mongols under Kublai Khan conquered China in 1279 they also began to use triangular flags with flammules, mounted sideways on a staff that was topped with the Chinese trident. The Mongols added flames to the trident and attached horses' tails to its base. This was the shape of the flag of Genghis Khan, which carried an image of a gerfalcon (gyrfalcon) and had nine yaks' tails attached to the nine flammules.

The earliest accounts of a flag in Europe are those of Greek writers, who mention a purple flag as the sign of the admiral's ship in the Athenian navy at the end of the 5th century BC. Two Samnite flags from 330 BC appear on frescoes from Paestum (now in the National Museum in Naples), which are the oldest known illustrations of flags in Europe. In the same museum there is a huge mosaic from Pompeii, depicting Alexander the Great defeating the Persians. It shows a Persian standard, an almost square piece of cloth hanging from a crossbar fastened underneath the spear-top of the lance; the bottom edge of the cloth is fringed. According to sketches made when the mosaic was discovered in 1831, the red field carried an image of a golden cock, the Zoroastrian symbol known as *parodash*.

A flag of exactly the same shape and mounted on the staff in the same way was adopted by the Romans for their cavalry and named *vexillum*.

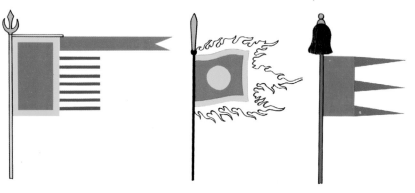

◀ *FAR LEFT
Reconstruction of the earliest Chinese banner.*
◀ *CENTRE LEFT Flag of Kublai Khan's armada, (13th century).*
◀ *LEFT Mongol banner (c.1310).*

▶ *RIGHT AND FAR RIGHT*
*Samnite flags on frescoes
from Paestum, 330 BC,
are the oldest flags in
Europe known to date.*

The cloth was red, sometimes carrying the name of the unit, an emblem or a portrait of the emperor. There was a heavy fringe on the bottom edge, and the cloth was fastened so that it always looked draped.

Another similar flag was the *labarum* adopted by Constantine the Great after his victory over his rival Maxentius in AD 312, won in the name of the Christian cross. The purple cloth carried the gold monogram of Christ, formed of the

▶ *RIGHT* Roman
*vexillum. Bas-relief from
Hadrian's temple in
Rome (AD 145).*

first two letters of the Greek word for Christ, ΧΡΙΣΤΟΣ. The shaft was encased in beaten gold, and bore medallions with the portraits of Constantine and his two sons. It seems that there were two forms of *labarum*; the other one displayed Christ's monogram at the top of the staff and the portraits appeared on the cloth.

In the 6th century the Byzantine army replaced the Roman *vexillum* with a square or rectangular banner, with one or two triangular tongues extending from the top edge. In the 8th century they spread to Hungary and Central Europe. Also in the 8th century the Arabs began to use triangular flags that were plain black or white. Later they increased the range of colours and the flags carried religious inscriptions and geometric ornaments (because of the religious ban on representational art).

One of the oldest flags in Europe was not a flag at all. It was the blue cape of St Martin, found in his grave by Clovis I of France (who reigned AD 481–511) and adopted as his banner. It was later carried in battle by French kings. In peacetime the cape was kept in a specially built oratory, which became known as a "chapel" (from the Latin word *cappa*). Another non-flag was the royal standard of the Persians, which for several hundred years until the Muslim conquest in the 7th century was a blacksmith's leather apron.

The very beginning of the 9th century saw the introduction of a new form of flag, the gonfanon. It is first seen in a mosaic that Pope

Leo III (AD *c.*750–816) had placed in the Triclinium of the Lateran Palace in Rome in about AD 800. On the right-hand side the mosaic shows Christ handing the keys of the Church to Pope Sylvester and a flag to Constantine, while on the left St Peter presents a cloak to Pope Leo and a flag to Charlemagne. The mosaic commemorates the crowning of Charlemagne as emperor, when he received from the Patriarch of Jerusalem the keys of that city and a flag. The original mosaic has not survived but contemporary sources tell us that the green field of the gonfanon was sprinkled with gold and bore six concentric rings of red, black and gold. This event started a tradition of ceremonial presentations of flags by ecclesiastical authorities to rulers or leaders of expeditions approved by the Church. Emperors also ceremonially handed flags to their subjects. The

▲ *ABOVE* Labarum *of Constantine the Great.*

form of the gonfanon was for several centuries reserved for rulers, but after the 11th century it prevailed in the army and from the 12th to the 14th centuries was used by cities.

From the late 8th century, northern European waters were the realm of the Vikings, whose longships sailed as far as Greenland and North America. They raided coastal towns and villages in Britain and France, sometimes settling and intermarrying with the local people. They were the first Europeans to use flags at sea, mounted on vertical staffs. The flags were triangular, with a slightly rounded outer edge; those mounted on the high bows of ships were probably vanes. A gilded vane dating from the 11th century, in the Historiska Museet in Stockholm, has several holes along the curved edge to which rings with tassels could be attached to make the exact shape of the Viking flag. The Vikings had various flags, but the most important seems to have been the raven flag. Both the flag and the raven on its own also appear on Northumbrian coins of the first half of the 10th century.

The Bayeux Tapestry, made in about 1077, contains more than 70 embroidered scenes of the Norman Conquest of England in 1066. It illustrates a very similar flag to the Viking flag, carried immediately behind the Duke of Normandy, William the Conqueror and shows that by that time flags were already being made of cloth. Among the many banners depicted, most of the Norman ones bear a cross, which in pre-heraldic times was the main emblem used by both the military and seamen. More banners with the sign of the cross appeared during the First Crusade (1096–9). One is shown on the seal of Bohemund III, Prince of Antioch. The oldest known account of flags with crosses, the *Gesta Regis Henrici Secundi* by Benedict Abbas, tells us that on 13 January 1188 the Kings of England and France (together with their men) received a white and red cross respectively, while the Count of Flanders received a green cross. We do not know whether these banners were used exclusively on land or also at sea.

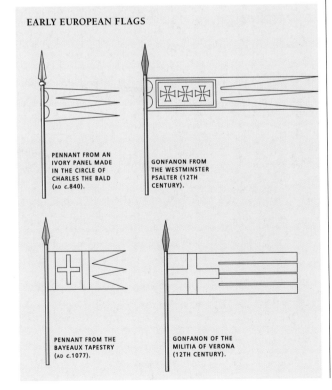

EARLY EUROPEAN FLAGS

PENNANT FROM AN IVORY PANEL MADE IN THE CIRCLE OF CHARLES THE BALD (AD c.840).

GONFANON FROM THE WESTMINSTER PSALTER (12TH CENTURY).

PENNANT FROM THE BAYEAUX TAPESTRY (AD c.1077).

GONFANON OF THE MILITIA OF VERONA (12TH CENTURY).

From the 9th to the 12th centuries merchant ships on the North Sea and the Baltic Sea carried a metal gridcross, a symbol of the king's protection, at the top of the mast. From at least the 12th century the same symbol, in the form of a staff topped with a cross, was used on land, mainly by princes and cities in the territories dependent on the German Empire. A second symbol of the king's protection also appeared in the 12th century: a gonfanon without any emblems, attached to a spear or to a staff topped with a cross. This is the *vexillo roseum imperiali* or the *Blutbanner* (blood banner), a red banner presented by the emperor to princes and counts. The *Blutbanner* gave them the right of judicial power over life and death in their domains, and imposed the obligation to contribute men for the imperial army. The *Blutbanner* was awarded also to the cities that became free imperial cities in the 12th and 13th centuries, and to the freed peasants of Schwyz in 1240.

At the beginning of the 13th century merchant ships in northern Europe began to fasten single-coloured gonfanons to the mast, topped with a cross. Those of the Hanseatic cities and of Denmark were red; the English gonfanon was presumably white, later to carry the red cross of St George. In the second half of the 13th century port cities began to differentiate their flags either by dividing them into different coloured areas or by adding simple emblems, the most common of which was the Christian cross. New flags in banner form were placed at the stern, while the mast still carried the single-coloured gonfanons, later replaced by pennants or banners. The oldest is the plain red flag of Hamburg; the date of its adoption is not known, but it was in use from at least the middle of the 13th century. A little later Riga and Lübeck adopted their flags, followed by Stralsund, Elbing, Danzig, Bremen and Rostock in the 14th century, and Königsberg and Wismar in the 15th century.

The oldest flag on record in the Mediterranean region is that of Genoa; the earliest illustration, dated 1113, shows it as

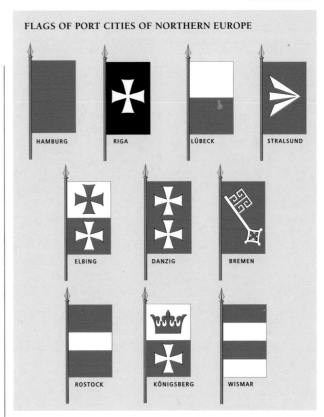

FLAGS OF PORT CITIES OF NORTHERN EUROPE

HAMBURG RIGA LÜBECK STRALSUND

ELBING DANZIG BREMEN

ROSTOCK KÖNIGSBERG WISMAR

▲ *Above Raven flag (9th century).*

white with a red cross. Pisa received the red imperial banner in 1162. Both flags are much older than those of England or Hamburg, which they resemble. Even in the 13th century, when all of these flags were in existence, merchant vessels did not travel very long distances so it was impossible for an English ship to meet a vessel from Genoa or a vessel from Pisa to meet a ship from Hamburg, so the flags could not be confused. Nevertheless Pisa later added a distinctive white cross to its red flag, and the red flag of Hamburg was given a white shield with a red castle (since 1751 the white castle has been located directly on the red background).

In the 14th century the flags of Savoy and Denmark were also identical, but the Danish ships did not venture as far as the Mediterranean. When, 400 years later, they did sail there they adopted especially for that purpose the Danish merchant flag, which had a white square in the centre carrying the royal cipher.

THE AGE OF CHIVALRY

The invention of a helmet to cover and protect the face of a warrior, and thus hide his identity, was one reason why it became necessary to develop signs of identification. The other reason was the widespread use of the cross by all armed forces in Western Europe. The similarity between the banners of friend and foe could cause major misunderstandings on the battlefield.

The basic rules of heraldry were adopted during the Second Crusade (1147–9) and the returning knights took them back to their countries. In the Middle East they had seen the traditional stylization of natural and mythological beasts, and they decided that simple figures on contrasting backgrounds would make excellent signs of identification. The shield was the ideal background. The number of heraldic tinctures was limited to seven: five colours (red, blue, green, black and purple) and two metals (gold and silver). To achieve the best possible identification from a distance the rule of alternation was adopted, which forbade putting colour on colour or metal on metal. A "fimbriation", or border, of metal was used to separate adjacent areas of two colours. The only pre-heraldic device incorporated into the arms was the Christian cross, and to distinguish the crosses that appeared in many arms a great number of different shapes were invented. Other popular heraldic emblems included the lion, eagle, griffin, horse, fleur-de-lis, rose and various weapons.

The invention of heraldry not only helped to distinguish flags denoting ducal, princely or civic domains, but also led to a rapid growth in personal flags. As well as a coat of arms, each qualified person carried an armorial banner, which now became the principal kind of flag. It was either square or much wider than it was long, and sizes varied according to the rank of its owner. According to one medieval source, the banner of an emperor should be 1.8 m (2 yd) square, that of a king 1.5 m (5 ft) square, that of a prince or duke 1.2 m (4 ft) square, and that of an earl, marquis, viscount or baron 90 cm (3 ft) square.

The personal heraldic badges of rulers, unrelated to their coats of arms, appeared on their standards, banners and the flags of their retainers. The most famous ones still remembered are the white and red roses of York and Lancaster, the white boar of Richard III, the salamander of Francis I, the porcupine of Louis XII and the radiant sun of Louis XIV.

A distinct type of armorial flag, designed to indicate the rallying point or headquarters of the arms-bearer, or "armiger", was the standard. It was a long, tapering flag with a rounded swallow-tail, and it bore the livery colours arranged horizontally. The hoist carried either the national mark (for example, the cross of St George, the cross of St Andrew or the cross of Burgundy) or a coat of arms in the form of an armorial banner. Next appeared the heraldic badge of the arms-bearer with his motto, and then another badge or crest, and around the edge was a border of pieces in the livery colour.

▼ *BELOW Banners of Swiss troops, 15th century.*

CIVIC BANNERS IN THE 14TH CENTURY

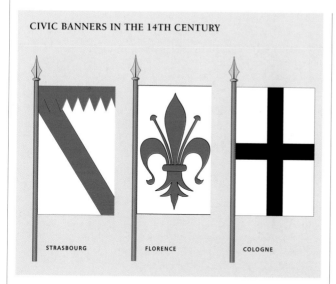

STRASBOURG   FLORENCE   COLOGNE

obtain charters from the crown and were granted arms. An even greater impact was created by the steady growth in the number of towns that adopted arms. Civic armorial banners became the real national flags for the burghers, as the symbols of their rights and privileges.

Not all banners in the Age of Chivalry were armorial. There was also extensive use of Christian symbols in non-heraldic form, including representations of the Holy Trinity, the Holy Ghost, the vernicle (veronica) and scenes of the Crucifixion. As well as banners with symbols of the saints, such as the cross of St George or the lion of St Mark, there were banners displaying the painted figures of saints with their attributes. The most popular were St Peter with his keys, St Andrew with a diagonal cross, St George (mounted) slaying the dragon, St Michael overcoming the Devil, St Paul with a book and sword, and St Catherine with the wheel. The lion of St Mark became the emblem of the Republic of Venice in the pre-heraldic period, the eagle of St John was adopted by the monarchs of Spain, St Peter's keys became the emblem of the papacy, and St Andrew's cross was adopted as the national symbol of Scotland and, in a slightly different form, by Burgundy and later by Spain. Banners with the figures of saints or the Virgin Mary were used until the 17th century as military signs, and also as the ceremonial banners of towns.

Only the arms-bearer could carry his banner or standard, so three other types of flag were used by his retainers: the guidon, pennon and badge-flag. The guidon was a simpler version of the standard. It was also tapered but was shorter with a descate outer edge (see *Flag Design*), bore the national device on the inner edge and had one badge on the livery colours. It was used on horseback, and was a precursor of the cavalry guidon. The pennon was a swallow-tailed flag carried on a mounted warrior's lance. In most cases it bore the badge on a background in the livery colours. The badge-flag was a rectangular flag with the background divided in the livery colours, bearing the heraldic badge or badges.

From the beginning of the heraldic period arms were also adopted and used by ecclesiastics and military orders such as the Knights Templar, the Knights of St John of Jerusalem, great Spanish and Portuguese orders and the Teutonic Knights. The arms and armorial banners of bishops and the abbots of monasteries did not represent them but the orders they temporarily represented; they were also signs of their domains. The rise of the guilds and universities also contributed to the increase in the use of arms and armorial banners as they began to

▶ *FAR RIGHT* Italian portolano, *1544.*

Even before the heraldic age, as early as the 11th century, peculiar vehicles called *carroccio* appeared in northern Italy which were designed to carry huge civic flags. In France *carrocci* appeared a century later, and German versions by the 13th century. They were the centre of all civic festivities and served as a rallying point during battle. The most ceremonial were made of fine wood, inlaid with gold, silver and ivory. According to the *Chronicle of Charlemagne* in the late 9th century, the Saracens used a *carroccio* "which eight oxen bore, upon which their red flag was elevated". From other sources we know that a *carroccio* appeared on the battlefield at the Battle of the Standard near Northallerton, Yorkshire, in 1138: indeed, the battle was named after it. In this the English displayed not only the banners of their patron saints, but also the consecrated Host. In 1191, during a battle with the Saracens near Acre, the banner of Richard I was flown from a *carroccio*. An eye-witness described the vehicle:

It consists, then, of a very long beam, like the mast of a ship, placed upon four wheels in a frame very solidly fastened together and bound with iron, so that it seems incapable of yielding either to sword, axe or fire. Affixed to the very top of this, the royal flag, commonly called banner, flies in the wind.

He explains that "because it stands fast as a sign to all the people, it is called the Standard". In the Battle of Bouvines in 1214 the *carroccio* of Emperor Otto IV was topped by a golden eagle. In the 12th and 13th centuries *carrocci* were in general use in the armies of western Europe and the transference of its original Italian name was completed in the 13th century.

Displays of banners were not limited to the battlefield. Tournaments were enormously popular from the 13th to the 16th centuries. Announced by heralds in many countries, they were an opportunity for knights from all parts of Europe to meet and exhibit their proficiency in handling a horse and weapons. During the tournament the heralds presented the personal coats of arms of the participants.

The main sources of information about medieval flags are coins and medals, grants of arms, illustrations in chronicles, mosaics and paintings in numerous churches. Especially valuable are some of the armorial rolls. The oldest is the *Zürcher Wappenrolle* (1340), which presents 28 flags of German, Austrian and Bohemian cities and bishoprics; the flags of Strasbourg and Cologne illustrated are taken from this document. The flag of Florence is taken from illustrations in the *Cronaca del Sercambi* (end of the 14th century).

Important information about flags used at sea from the 14th to the 16th centuries can be gleaned from *portolanos*. These are navigational charts depicting coastlines and ports, some rivers and mountain ranges, and flags and coats of arms. Often the flags are very small and their design simplified, but the *portolanos* still contain valuable data. These and the manuscript of a Franciscan friar, a native of Spain, are the oldest sources depicting the flags of North Africa and the Middle East. The manuscript, written and illuminated in about 1350, has a long Spanish title that translates into English as the *Book of the Knowledge of All the Kingdoms, Countries, and Lordships that there are in the World and of the Ensigns and Arms of Each Country and Lordship; also of the Kings and Lords Who Govern Them.* Although the friar claimed to have visited all the places he described, from Spain to China and

▲ *ABOVE LEFT Banner of Brandenburg, wood engraving from the Arms Book of Master IK, 16th century.*
▲ *ABOVE RIGHT Banner of Chur, wood engraving by Conrad Schmidt, first half of the 16th century.*

▲ *ABOVE Banner of Brandenburg from Banderia Prutenorum, 1448.*

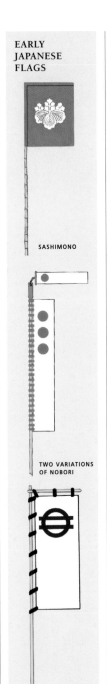

SASHIMONO

TWO VARIATIONS
OF NOBORI

from Norway to Egypt, some of his accounts are not very reliable; nevertheless the text has great value as the earliest account of flags of all nations, with illustrations of nearly 100 flags.

The first authoritative vexillological work was by the Polish historian Jan Dlugosz in 1448. Entitled *Banderia Prutenorum*, it contains detailed descriptions and measurements, as well as large and exact colour illustrations, of all 56 banners captured by the Polish-Lithuanian troops at Tannenberg in 1410.

From the end of the 15th century, banners were often depicted on stained-glass panels, mainly the Swiss *Standesscheiben*. In later centuries woodcarvings in numerous books show banner-bearers with banners of various domains and cities. Especially valuable are a print with representations of the Julius Banners, published in 1513 in Zürich; the *Arms Book of Master IK* (1545), with 144 banners of the cities and territories of the Holy Roman Empire; and the woodcarvings of Conrad Schmidt.

Although the use of symbols was universal among civilized communities, it is only in Europe and Japan that comprehensive heraldic systems developed. The Japanese *mons* are the equivalent of the heraldic badge rather than the heraldic figure. They do not appear on a shield, but in other respects they play the same role as the arms in Europe. The *mon* is a hereditary symbol, and since the 17th century there has been a legal requirement of registration. Like arms, the *mon* is used on banners, armour and the clothes of the retainers of great lords. It decorates castles, carriages, lanterns and the belongings of the individual and his family. *Mons* are usually symmetrical, simple and stylized representations of flowers (mallow, apricot, wisteria), birds (crane, wild goose) or everyday objects (fan, arrow, hatchet) or geometric designs. The banners used in Japan since the Middle Ages differed from both the Chinese and European ones. They were attached to the staff in the same way as Chinese banners but the shape of the cloth was different, the width being several times greater than the length. The *mon* was often repeated several times on the banner. These banners, like the much smaller *sashimono* banners, were fastened into a socket attached to the back of a cuirass, a piece of chest armour. Modern Japanese banners are rectangular, with the *mon* in the centre. Recently the *mons* have come to represent not only families but also cities and provinces.

► *RIGHT* Mons *appear on flags of all Japanese and noble families, as we see on this plate from* Herold, *1909.*

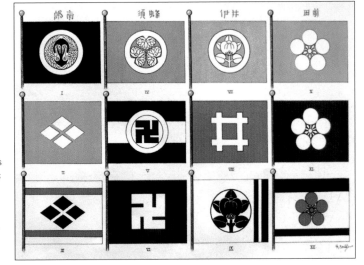

MODERN FLAGS

In the 16th century the general use of armorial banners ended. Although the monarchs of a few countries such as Great Britain retained their armorial banners, most of the royal flags displayed at sea after this date were single-coloured and bore the whole achievement of arms, i.e. with helmets, mantlings, crests, supporters, collars of orders and mottoes.

The first modern flag was the Dutch revolutionary *Prinsenvlag*, composed of simple stripes instead of heraldic devices, followed by the flags created after the revolutions in America and France. The design of these newly created flags reflected the idea that, with the abolition of monarchy, the heraldic system of identification was also rejected. The colours and designs acquired symbolic meaning and flags began to carry ideological and political messages. Flags were based on simple shapes and in most cases only very simple emblems were used. The most popular emblem was the five-pointed star, a symbol of liberty and independence.

This trend has survived to the present day. Even when thousands and even tens of thousands of flags exist at the same time, it is possible to create quite simple yet very distinctive designs. Some recent, but now obsolete, flags are illustrated below. At the time that the Chinese flag was adopted, consisting only of simple stripes, there were many other striped flags, especially in Europe. Nevertheless, since they were bicolours or tricolours, the Chinese flag with its five colours was still very distinctive. The flag of Malaya had different colours and bore the tiger badge. The flag of Manchukuo displayed the same colours as the earlier Chinese flag, but because of the canton it was distinctively different. The thin stripes in the flag of South Vietnam were the only device of this kind among all the world's flags, and the emblems on the flags of Lesotho and Surinam were also very distinctive. The flag of Congo for most of the time was the only flag to display a large star in its centre.

The best insight into the development of modern flags is provided by numerous charts and albums. The first collections of flags used at sea are in Dutch manuscripts of 1667 and 1669, and in a manuscript from 1670 ascribed to J. Moutton of France. The first English collections of flags for use at sea appeared in the notebook of William Downman (1685) and in *Insignia Navalia*, a manuscript by Lieutenant John Graydon dated 1686. The most thorough flag book of this period was *Nieuwe Hollandse Scheeps-bouw* by Carl Allard, published in Amsterdam in 1694 and reprinted several times; it was also extensively copied by other authors. The best were Cornelius Dankerts, who produced the first flag chart *c.*1700 entitled

MODERN FLAGS

CHINA (1912–1923)

FEDERATED MALAY STATES (1905–1948)

MANCHUKUO (1932–1945)

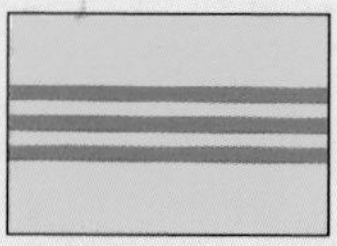

SOUTH VIETNAM (1948–1975)

BELGIAN CONGO (1885–1960)

SURINAM (1959–1975)

LESOTHO (1966–1987)

RHODESIA (1968–1979)

TABLE. DES PAVILLONS, QUIL'ON ARBORE Dans toute les Parties du Monde Connu. Cousernant la Marinne.

NIEUWE TAFEL VAN AL DE ZEE. Vaarende VLAGGE des Weerelts.

▲ **ABOVE** *Dutch flag chart by C. Dankerts (c.1700).*

▶ **RIGHT** *Page from the book by Jaques van den Kiebom,* La Connaissance des Pavillons ou Bannières, que la Plûspart des Nations Arborent en Mer, *1737.*

Table des Pavillons quil'on arbore dans toute les Parties du Monde Connu, Consernant la Marinne, and Jaques van den Kiebom, who in 1737 published the book *La Connaissance des Pavillons ou Bannières, que la Plûspart des Nations Arborent en Mer*. In the 19th century most charts were folded in handbooks. The best are *Plates Descriptive of the Maritime Flags of all Nations*, published by J.W. Norie in 1819, and *Three Hundred and Six Illustrations of the Maritime Flags of all Nations*, originally compiled by J.W. Norie and considerably augmented by J.S. Hobbs in 1848. The first official handbook on flags was compiled by Captain Le Gras and published in 1858 by the Secretary of State for the French Imperial Navy under the title *Album des Pavillons, Guidons, Flammes, de toutes les*

PAVILLON DE St. GEORGE

PAVILLON de l'ISLE de MAN

PAVILLON DES INDES ORIENTALES D'ECOSSE

PAVILLON de DIVISION des VAISSEAUX ECOSSOIS

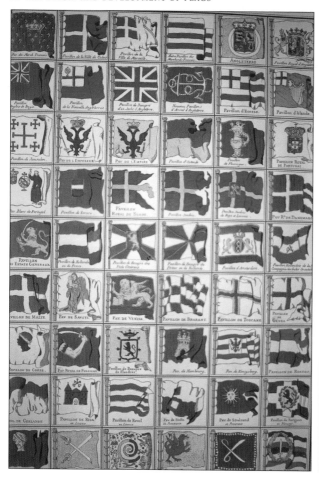

◀ LEFT *A fragment of the French flag chart from*
Tableau des Pavillons que la Plûspart des Nations
Arborent à la Mer, *1756.*

Puissances Maritimes. Ten years later the
American Bureau of Navigation published the
album *Flags of Maritime Nations from the Most
Authentic Sources.* In 1874 George Hounsell
with the approval of the British Admiralty
produced *Flags and Signals of All Nations*, and in
1905 the German Admiralty followed suit with
the *Flaggenbuch*, the best flag book of all.
Although the French and British naval
authorities published several updated versions,
even after World War II, they never approached
the perfection of the *Flaggenbuch*, edited by
Ottfried Neubecker and published in 1939.

Since the late 19th century manufacturers of
cigarettes, tea and chocolate have made a real
contribution to the popularization of national
flags and ensigns throughout the world. In the
United States, Great Britain, Germany, the
Netherlands and other countries cards or pieces
of silk with pictures of various flags have been
added to cigarette or cigar packets, boxes of tea
and wrappers for sweets. Collectors could send
for an album with additional information and,
although some of the pictures were inaccurate,
they were still of great documentary value.
Worth mentioning are the sets produced in the
1900s by Players in Great Britain and the
German sets produced in about 1930 by

▶ OPPOSITE PAGE
▶ TOP *Pages from the
book by J.W. Norie and
augmented by J.S.
Hobbs, 1848.*
▶ BOTTOM LEFT *Plate
from the album J.H.
Colton's Delineation
of the Flags of all
Nations, 1862.*
▶ BOTTOM RIGHT *Plate
from* Flags of All
Nations *presented by
J. & G. Stewart 1897.*

▶ RIGHT *Page from
the album* Pavillons
des Puissances
Maritimes, *1819.*

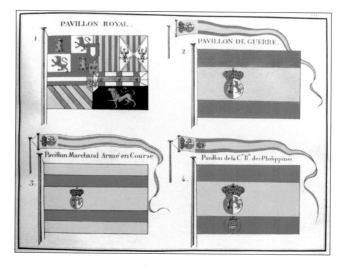

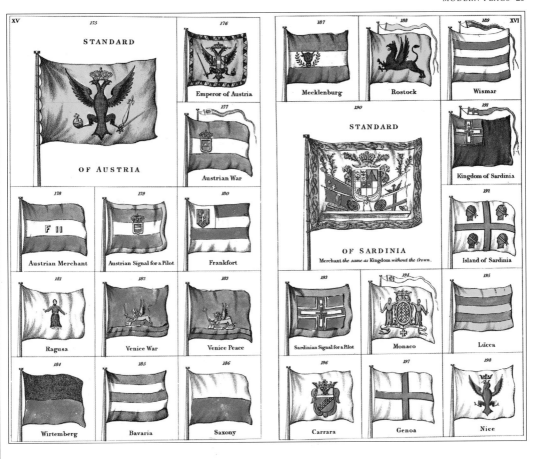

XV	175	176
STANDARD		Emperor of Austria
		177
OF AUSTRIA		Austrian War
178	179	180
Austrian Merchant	Austrian Signal for a Pilot	Frankfort
181	182	183
Ragusa	Venice War	Venice Peace
184	185	186
Wirtemberg	Bavaria	Saxony

187	188	189 XVI
Mecklenburg	Rostock	Wismar
	190	191
	STANDARD	Kingdom of Sardinia
		192
	OF SARDINIA	Island of Sardinia
	Merchant *the same as Kingdom without the Crown.*	
193	194	195
Sardinian Signal for a Pilot	Monaco	Lucca
196	197	198
Carrara	Genoa	Nice

AMERICAN PRESIDENT. 3

UNITED STATES OF AMERICA STANDARD & PENDANT. 1

AMERICAN JACK. 4

AMERICAN ADMIRAL. 5

AMERICAN REVENUE. 7

AMERICAN COMMODORE'S PENDANT. 6

COLTON'S FLAGS OF ALL NATIONS
PUBLISHED BY J H. COLTON. 172, WILLIAM STREET, NEW YORK.

U.S. QUARANTINE. 8

U.S. SIGNAL FOR PILOT. 9

MEXICAN. 10

CENTRAL AMERICA. 11

GUATEMALA. 12

Turkey Ensign & Merchant 49	*Roumania Royal Standard* 50	*Roumania Merchant* 51
Servia Royal Standard 52	*Servia Merchant* 53	*Montenegro Princes Standard* 54
Bulgaria Merchant 55	*Greece Royal Standard* 56	*Greece Merchant* 57
Persia Royal Standard 58	*Persia Merchant* 59	*Siam Royal Standard* 60

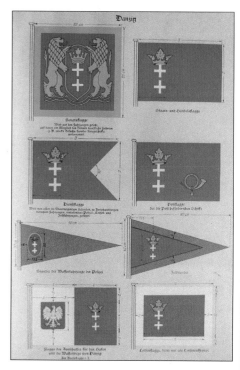

▲ *ABOVE Plate 58 from the album,* Flags of Maritime Nations, *Washington, 1899.*

▲ *ABOVE RIGHT Flags of the Free City of Danzig prepared for the* Flaggenbuch, *1939, but later removed.*

▶ *RIGHT Pictures of some of the 130 military colours and standards preserved in the* Heeresmuseum *(in Vienna) including this colour of the Cisalpine Republic cavalry provided by Abadie Papier-Geselschaft A.G.*

▶ *FAR RIGHT National flag of Yemen (1927–1962) on a card published in 1936 by Sultan Zigarettenfabrik Aurelia in Dresden.*

Bulgaria Cigarettes (*Flaggen der Welt*) and Massary Cigarettes (*Wer nent die Länder, kennt die Fahnen?*). Particularly valuable are the card sets edited by O. Neubecker, the foremost German flag authority, *Länder, Wappen und Nationalfarben* and *Flaggen der Welt*. The set produced by Sultan cigarettes from Dresden to celebrate Germany's hosting of the 1936 Olympic Games in Berlin contains flawless information, and is also a real gem in the art of printing; it was produced in consultation with Karl Fachinger, the forerunner of vexillology. The pictures and information contained in two albums of cigarette cards, edited by O. Neubecker and published in 1950 under the title *Die Welt im bunten Flaggenbild*, are so accurate that these books deserve to be among the leading sources of vexillological knowledge.

▶ *RIGHT (top row) The Flag of the governor general of India (19th century–1950) and the flag of the governor-general of Canada (1921–1957) are a small part of the flag collection produced by the Massary Zigarettenfabrik in Berlin. (bottom row) Lübeck. Flags of the government vessels at sea (1921–1935). Produced by the Massary Zigaretten-fabrik in Berlin.*

▼ *BELOW (left to right) Flag of Cambodia under French protectorate; Presidential standard of Brazil (1907–1968); Presidential Standard of China (1928–1949, and since 1949 Taiwan). Such beautiful and error-free renderings were possible owing to the collaboration with Ottfried Neubecker, the foremost German heraldist and vexillologist.*

In the 20th century several dozen general books on flags have been published, a few of which have made major contributions to vexillology (see Bibliography). These are *Die Flagge* by Vice-Admiral R. Siegel, 1912; a special edition of the National Geographic Magazine, *Flags of the World*, 1917; *Fahnen und Flaggen* by O. Neubecker, 1939; *The Flag Book* by Preben Kannik (in Danish 1956; in English 1957), with several subsequent editions prepared by Christian Fogd Pedersen, the foremost Scandinavian vexillologue; and the comprehensive *Flags Through the Ages and Across the World* by Whitney Smith, 1975.

In 1962 Whitney Smith established the Flag Research Center in Massachusetts, USA, which was the first professional vexillological institute in the world. He coined the word "vexillology", which is now a generally accepted term and used in many languages. Since October 1961 he has published *The Flag Bulletin*, the most authoritative journal on vexillology. Together with O. Neubecker, Louis Mühlemann and Klaes Sierksma, Smith organized the first international vexillological congress in 1965 and established the International Federation of Vexillological Associations (FIAV). The current membership of FIAV comprises 51 vexillological associations and institutions from 30 countries in all six continents. Most publish newsletters, of which the most important are

the Swiss *Vexilla Helvetica*, the Italian *Vexilla Italica*, the Belgian *Vexilla Belgica*, the Czech *Vexilologie*, the Spanish *Banderas*, the South African *SAVA Newsletter*, the American *Raven*, the German *Der Flaggenkurier* and the Ukrainian *Znak*. *The Flag Bulletin* and the publications of these vexillological associations have contributed to the tremendous recent increase in vexillological knowledge.

Kambodja
(französisches
Protektorat)
Nationalflagge

Brasilien
Präsidentenflagge

China
Flagge
des Präsidenten

All About Flags

A flag may be defined as a piece of pliable material, attached at one end so as to move freely in the wind, serving as a sign or a decoration. This word is now common to the nations of north-western Europe (Danish and Norse Flag, *Swedish* Flagg, *German* Flagge, *Dutch* Vlag*), but it does not appear to have come into use in this particular meaning until the 16th century, and the etymology of it is obscure. Perhaps the most satisfactory of the derivations hitherto put forward is that of Professor Skeat, who derives it from the Middle English* flakken *to fly, one of a number of similar onomatopoeic words suggestive of the sound of something flapping in the wind. Its first appearance with a meaning coming within the above definition is a specific term denoting a rectangular piece of material attached by one vertical edge, flown at the masthead of a ship, as a symbol of nationality or leadership. Before the 17th century there was no generic term in the English language that covered the various forms – banners, ensigns, streamers, pendants, etc. – that are now generally included under the term "flag".*

W.G. PERRIN, *BRITISH FLAGS*, CAMBRIDGE 1922

Precise terminology is needed to describe the various characteristics of a flag: its shape, proportions, design and colours. There are many different types of flag, made of different materials and with various accessories. Even hoisting a flag can be done in various ways. In what follows it is assumed that the flag is hoisted on a vertical staff and is flying to the right of the staff. This is termed the obverse, the main side of the flag. In most cases the reverse is a mirror image of the obverse but some flags – mainly military colours – have different obverse and reverse and are really two flags sewn back to back.

The usage of flags has changed radically over the centuries, but some flag customs and etiquette, for example flying a flag at half-mast, have become part of everyday consciousness. Understanding the symbolic language of national flags is particularly important in diplomatic contexts, and on many occasions in recent history serious conflicts have arisen through ignorance or misunderstanding.

◄ **LEFT** *A huge Tunisian flag is displayed in Marseilles, France, during the 1998 World Cup.*

FLAG DESIGN

The first characteristic of a flag is its shape. Most ensigns and national flags are rectangular. Some ensigns are swallow-tailed or double swallow-tailed, two national flags are square and one consists of two triangles. Most yacht flags are triangular or swallow-tailed, and the flags used by the army and navy are much more diversified.

The second characteristic of a flag is its proportions, i.e. the ratio of the width to the length. The width is measured along the hoist,

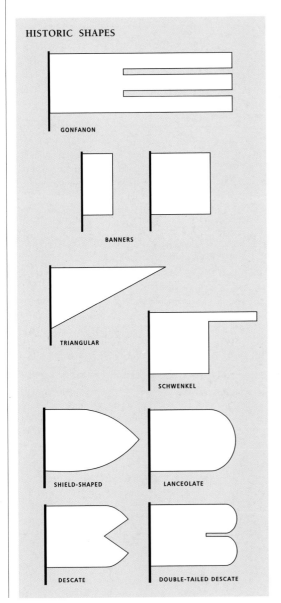

HISTORIC SHAPES

GONFANON

BANNERS

TRIANGULAR

SCHWENKEL

SHIELD-SHAPED

LANCEOLATE

DESCATE

DOUBLE-TAILED DESCATE

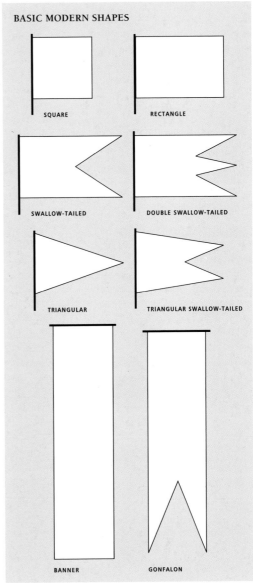

BASIC MODERN SHAPES

SQUARE

RECTANGLE

SWALLOW-TAILED

DOUBLE SWALLOW-TAILED

TRIANGULAR

TRIANGULAR SWALLOW-TAILED

BANNER

GONFALON

so it is the vertical measurement of a flag that is displayed horizontally and a horizontal measurement of a flag that is designed to hang vertically. The length is measured from the hoist to the fly end of a flag, and in triangular and swallow-tailed flags it is measured from the hoist to the apex of a triangle. For the sake of uniformity, organizers of international conferences and sports events usually adopt the same proportions for flags that are displayed together, although this can lead to distortion of the elements of the design. The correct way to present national flags on such occasions, and in flag charts and book illustrations, is to make all the hoists the same width and to retain the official proportions. In this arrangement, only the length of the flags will vary.

The third characteristic of a flag is its design. The terms for the basic parts of a flag are the "hoist" (first half), the "fly" (second half), "top"

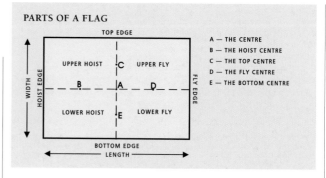

PARTS OF A FLAG

A — THE CENTRE
B — THE HOIST CENTRE
C — THE TOP CENTRE
D — THE FLY CENTRE
E — THE BOTTOM CENTRE

(upper half) and "bottom" (lower half). In addition, there are terms for all the edges and particular points on the "field" (the whole area of the flag). In Europe many flags are historic armorial banners and therefore need to be described in heraldic terms; other flags display the coat of arms on a single-colour field. However, most flags have modern designs based on simple divisions of the field and/or display "simple charges" (simple figures).

Division of the field by horizontal or vertical lines results in horizontal or vertical stripes; dividing the field diagonally creates "bends". If these are of equal width, only their number is given in the flag's description. But if a design consists of stripes or bends of unequal size, the proportionate width must be quoted. For example, the description of the flag of Thailand is five horizontal stripes, 1:1:2:1:1, which means that the middle stripe is twice as wide as each of the outer stripes.

To divide the field into four parts a cross, or "saltire", is used. When the field is divided quarterly, the parts are called "quarters" and their colours are given in the following order: upper hoist, upper fly, lower hoist and lower fly. The colours of the triangles resulting from a division by saltire are given clockwise, beginning with the triangle based on the hoist.

The pieces of a chequered field are called "checks". The description of the field is given as follows: "checky a x b", where "a" is the number of checks in a horizontal line and "b" is their number in a vertical line. The field can also be divided with "gyrons"; there are normally eight or twelve. Their colours are given in a clockwise direction, beginning with the one

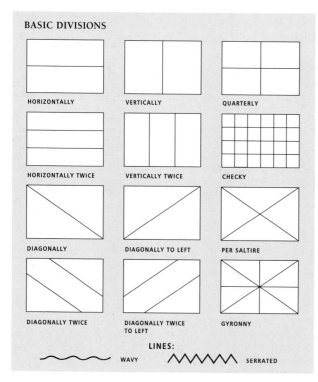

BASIC DIVISIONS

HORIZONTALLY

VERTICALLY

QUARTERLY

HORIZONTALLY TWICE

VERTICALLY TWICE

CHECKY

DIAGONALLY

DIAGONALLY TO LEFT

PER SALTIRE

DIAGONALLY TWICE

DIAGONALLY TWICE TO LEFT

GYRONNY

LINES:

WAVY   SERRATED

BASIC CHARGES

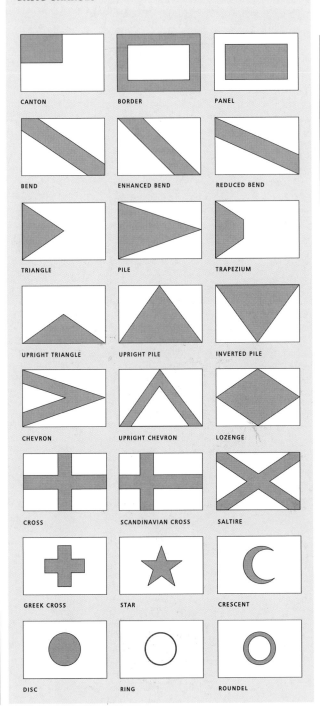

whose longer edge coincides with the horizontal line dividing the hoist in half.

In most flag designs the division lines are straight, but in the design of some national, provincial and civic flags wavy and serrated lines are used. In heraldry there are more than a dozen other decorative lines of partition, which can be seen on armorial banners.

Most modern flags display charges, the most popular being cantons (squares or oblongs), stars, bends (diagonal stripes), crosses, triangles and piles (wedges). Charges such as a cross or bend are sometimes "fimbriated", i.e. edged with narrow stripes. Other charges such as a canton, pile or lozenge often carry another charge such as stars, a badge or other device. In medieval times the most widespread charges were crosses, lions, eagles and fleurs-de-lis, and today the most popular charge is a star. Before the American Revolution the stars that occasionally appeared on flags were heraldic stars with six or eight points. Since 1777, five-pointed stars have been used almost exclusively, and they currently appear on more than 50 national flags.

When a charge appears in a horizontal mirror position it is described as being "reversed". A charge pointing to the top of the flag is "upright" and one pointing to the bottom is "inverted". The width or diameter of charges is always quoted as a proportion of the width of the flag. The exceptions are a normal canton, a normal triangle and a pile. A normal canton covers the entire area of the upper hoist; if its dimensions are different, its proportion of the width of the flag is given. The apex of a normal triangle reaches the centre of the field; if the triangle reaches another point, it is specifically described by quoting the height of the triangle as a proportion of the width of the flag.

The next, very important, characteristic of a flag is its colour. Single colours or colour combinations are the main way a flag conveys its symbolic meaning. They may imply a political or religious ideology, symbolize national traditions or geographical features or, as in many European flags, display livery colours, i.e. heraldic tinctures that do not convey any symbolic meaning. There are seven heraldic tinctures, two "metals" and five "colours". The metals are gold (or) and silver (argent), represented on flags by yellow and white. The colours are red (gules), blue (azure), green (vert), black (sable) and purple (purpure). In Britain the livery colours are usually the first "metal" and the first "colour" mentioned in the "blazon" (a herald's description of a coat of arms), but in continental Europe the livery colours may be all the tinctures (three or four) of a coat of arms.

To simplify the description of livery colours, the International Federation of Vexillological Associations has adopted the following code:

R = red, O = orange, Y = yellow, V = green, B = blue, P = purple, N = black, W = white, Au = gold, Ag = silver, M = brown, G = grey.

There are also symbols for lighter and darker shades of colours:

– light, – – very light, + dark, ++ very dark

This code helps to give a rough idea about flag colours, but it is insufficient to describe specific shades such as United Nations blue, Kenya red, Qatar maroon or olive green.

Other basic rules of flag description are able

▼ BELOW LEFT Flag of the German fleet admiral with construction details. Print of the German Admiralty, 1939.
▼ BELOW Flag specification for the state flag of Germany (1935–1945) produced by the Flag Design Center.

to describe accurately only the simpler flags. To know the exact design and colouring of a particular flag, the reliable source of information is either the official government specification or a specification prepared by one of a few professional vexillologists. Such a specification should contain a large colour illustration of the flag together with enlarged details, accompanied by a description of the type of flag, dates of usage, proportions and exact colours given in the Pantone Matching System or CMYK (cyan, magenta, yellow, black), as used by printers and modern computer systems. Two examples are given here, the specification of the German fleet admiral made in the 1930s by the navy department in Berlin, and one of hundreds of flag specifications prepared by the Flag Design Center.

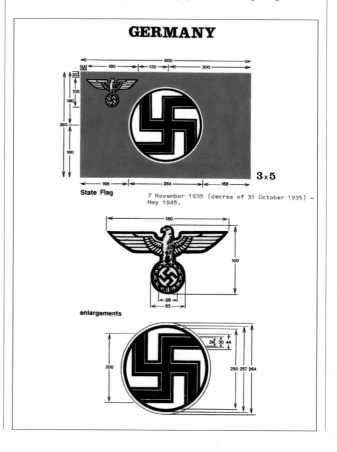

GERMANY

State Flag

7 November 1935 (decree of 31 October 1935) – May 1945.

3 x 5

enlargements

A good flag design should be simple, yet distinctive and meaningful. As a medium of communication a flag must be easily recognizable. The divisions should be chosen not only for aesthetic value but also to enhance the flag's symbolic meaning. The emblems need to be large and as simple as possible, and should be placed in the most important parts of the field, such as the canton or centre of the flag. Light colours should be placed next to darker ones; no more than three colours should be used. Flags are employed as alternatives to written messages so should not bear any lettering or numbers. The reason, as in heraldry, is a practical one: colours and symbols are easier to "read" when a flag is seen from a distance or fluttering. It is also not a good idea to add a hatchment of arms or an armorial shield because the details would not be clear. The only effective way to make a coat of arms into a flag is as an armorial banner.

FLAG DESIGN TERMINOLOGY

Armorial banner A flag whose field consists of the field and charges of a coat of arms. In Great Britain the banner is square or rectangular (proportions 1:2), in Europe it is almost exclusively square

Badge A heraldic emblem, different from the coat of arms (it does not employ a shield)

Bicolour A flag with the field divided horizontally (horizontal bicolour), vertically (vertical bicolour) or diagonally (diagonal bicolour) into two equal parts in two different colours

Border A wide band surrounding a field of different colour

Breadth see *Width*

Canton The area of the upper hoist corner of a flag; also a square or rectangular field covering that area

Charge Any object placed on the field of a flag. The most common are charges that are based on a simple division of the field with straight lines. Frequently used charges are the star, cross, crescent, disc, fleur-de-lis and sun. Unlike the badge, the charge is not used separately

Checky A field bearing squares of alternating colours

Counterchanged Having two colours alternating on each side of a line drawn through a flag or arms

Crest An armorial figure attached to the helmet above the shield of a coat of arms. Sometimes used alone as a badge

Cross A charge in the form of a cross concentric with the field, its arms extending to the edges of the flag. See also *Greek Cross, Scandinavian Cross*

Deface To add a badge or crest to a flag

Disc A circular device of a single colour used as a charge

Ensign-banner A rectangular flag with a field and fringe of livery colours of a coat of arms, charged with the full achievement of the arms

Field The whole area of a flag

Fimbriation A very narrow border of a simple geometric charge, usually in a contrast colour

Flammule A flame–shaped edge to a flag, often used in the past in the Far East

Fly The second half of the flag, the opposite end to the staff

Greek Cross A charge in the form of a cross with arms of equal length

Gyronny Divided into eight or twelve triangles whose apexes meet at the centre of the field

Hoist The half of a flag nearest the staff

Length The dimension of a flag measured from the heading or sleeve to the end of the fly; the opposite of *Width*

Livery colours The principal colours of a coat of arms. On a flag usually the first metal (gold or silver, i.e. yellow or white) is positioned above the first colour (red, blue, green, black or purple)

Obverse The more important, front side of a flag. It is the side to the observer's right from the staff; the opposite of *reverse*

Proportions The ratio of the width to the length of a flag. The proportions of a square flag are 1:1, a flag twice as long as it is wide is 1:2. The proportions of charges are always given in relation to the width of the flag

Quarterly Divided in four equal parts in a crosswise fashion

Reverse The less important side of a flag. It is the side to the observer's left from the staff; the opposite of *obverse*

Roundel A circular emblem of nationality employed on military aircraft and air force flags, usually consisting of concentric rings of national colours

Saltire A diagonal cross whose arms extend to the edges of a flag. Known also as a St Andrew's Cross

Scandinavian Cross A Latin cross positioned on the field of a flag horizontally, with the vertical arms in the hoist portion of the flag

Serrated A jagged division line or edge

Swallow-tailed A flag with a triangular section cut out from the fly end

Tricolour A flag whose field is divided horizontally (called a horizontal tricolour), vertically (vertical tricolour) or diagonally (diagonal tricolour) into three parts in three different colours

Triple swallow-tailed A flag with two symmetrical triangular sections cut out from the fly end

Union mark A symbol expressing the political unification of two territories, used in the canton of other flags. The most widespread is the British Union Jack

Width The measurement of a flag along its hoist; the opposite of *length*. In Commonwealth countries the British term "breadth" is used

TYPES OF FLAGS

"Flag" is an all-embracing general term used for a piece of fabric or other flexible material of distinctive design and coloration as a symbol of the identity of a nation, territory, office, corporation, organization, and so on. There are many types of flag, with different functions and usage as well as design and shape.

FLAG FUNCTION, USAGE AND SHAPE

The types of flags according to function are:
air force flag, armed forces flags, civil air flag, civil ensign, civil flag, colour, command pennant, commission pennant, courtesy flag, distinguishing flag, fanion, guidon, house flag, national ensign, national flag, naval reserve ensign, parley flag, pennon, pilot flag, rank flag, service ensign, signal flag, state ensign, state flag, war ensign;

The types of flags according to usage are:
banner, bannerol, car flag, courtesy flag, drum-banner, indoor flag, jack, lance pennon, outdoor flag, parade flag, parley flag, pipe-banner, table flag, trumpet-banner;

The types of flags according to shape are:
broad pennant, burgee, gonfalon, gonfanon, pennant, schwenkel, standard.

FLAG TYPES TERMINOLOGY

Air force flag A special flag for use at a military airport

Armed forces flags Special flags for each part of the armed forces (army, navy, air force, marines). They are used to mark military garrisons and quarters, and during parades and ceremonies of a particular armed force

Banner (i) General term referring to a square or rectangular flag fastened to a staff or attached to a crossbar, having an armorial or other elaborate design and made of costly material, often hand-painted and/or embroidered. Unless the word is used figuratively, it is necessary to use a more specific term such as armorial banner, royal banner, civic banner, church banner, corporate banner, ensign banner, drum-banner, pipe-banner, trumpet-banner etc;

(ii) Any flag designed to hang vertically from a crossbar, with the design arranged accordingly. It is also called a hanging flag

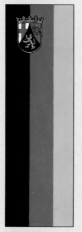

BANNER OF RHINELAND-PALATINE IN GERMANY

Bannerol A small square flag charged with a single quartering of a deceased person and carried at his or her funeral; now obsolete

Battle honour A mark added to a colour or to a flag of a branch of the armed forces to show its military service

Broad pennant A tapering descate or swallow-tailed flag, mostly used by navies as the flag of the head of state. In British and American naval and yachting usage, it is the rank flag of a commodore

Burgee A small distinguishing flag of a club or individual yachtsman, usually either triangular or tapering swallow-tailed. Flown from the main mast, or from the bows in the case of a powerboat

BROAD PENNANT OF THE EMPEROR OF GERMANY

Car flag Any flag flown from a car. Usually the flag of a head of state or government official, i.e. a rank flag or distinguishing flag. In most cases, it is displayed from a staff mounted on the right front fender. In the past it was on a staff clamped to a radiator cap

Civil air flag A flag for use at civil airports and landing fields

Civil ensign A flag designating national identity, flown on commercial or pleasure vessels. Formerly called a merchant flag

Civil flag A flag designating national identity, flown by private citizens on land

Club pennant A triangular flag to be hung vertically, usually charged with the emblem and livery colours of a sporting club

Cockade A rosette originally worn in a hat as a military badge, usually in livery or national colours. Since the 18th century also worn by civilians as an expression of revolutionary or patriotic feelings. In many European countries the first regulations pertaining to national colours related to the cockade, and later the colours of the cockade translated directly into a bicolour or tricolour flag

Colour Flag of a military unit (regiment, battalion or company). It usually has different designs on the obverse and reverse, and is fringed and attached to the staff

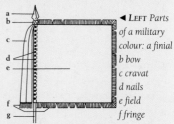

◄ LEFT *Parts of a military colour: a finial*
b bow
c cravat
d nails
e field
f fringe

a
b
c
d
e
f
g

Command pennant A flag identifying the commander of a particular navy formation (flotilla, squadron, group etc) or an individual ship. Usually triangular or tapering swallow-tailed

Commission pennant A very long, narrow flag (of proportions 1:15–1:50 or more), flown on a warship to indicate its commissioned status. If the ship's commander is of the rank of commodore or higher, the commission pennant is replaced by a rank flag. The term *Masthead pennant* is synonymous

COMMISSION PENNANT OF SAUDI ARABIA

Courtesy flag The civil ensign of a country being visited by a merchant vessel or yacht of a different nationality. Usually flown from the foremast or yardarm. It is hoisted on entering a foreign port

Desk flag See *Table flag*

DESK OR TABLE
FLAG, SLOVAKIA

Distinguishing flag A flag identifying a branch of government, military or naval service, or an official. In the latter case it denotes his or her office, authority, rank or command, and indicates his or her presence in a vessel, vehicle or place

Drum-banner A small flag decorating a parade drum. Used by a military, civic or other brass band parading in uniform or historic costume

Eagle (i) A vexilloid with a representation of an eagle on the top of the staff;
(ii) The name of the French colour during the Napoleonic era

Ensign (i) A flag used to indicate the nationality of civil, government and naval vessels. Flown by ships at or near the stern. The term should always be preceded by an explanatory name (war ensign, civil ensign etc);
(ii) In the United States, the lowest commissioned officer in the navy;
(iii) In the 17th and 18th centuries, the usual term for a military colour and the colour-bearer

False colours An ensign worn by a ship not entitled to it

Fan A semi-circular patriotic decoration made of national flags or fabric in livery colours

Fanion (i) A small bicolour used for marking a position in surveying;
(ii) A small pennon in the regimental colours that is used on military vehicles for marker purposes

Flag This term most frequently refers to the rectangular flag used mainly on land by nations, government institutions, agencies and officials, provinces, cities, commercial firms, corporations, organizations, and so on

Flag of convenience The civil ensign of a country with low taxation and without stringent maritime regulations. The term applies to a ship whose owner is not a citizen of that country, but who registers the vessel there to avoid high taxes and in order to hire cheap labour

Gonfalon A long flag with a square or triangular tail, displayed from a crossbar. It originated in medieval Italy (a gonfaloniero was the person who carried such a flag), and is still used there by cities and communes. In other European countries it is used mainly by parishes and various religious associations

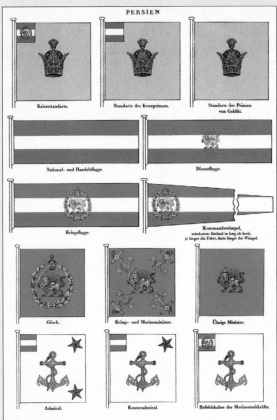

◄ *Left
Distinguish-
ing flags of
Persia
1933–1958:
(top row)
imperial
standard,
crown
prince's
standard,
prince's
standard;
(2nd and
3rd flag in
the 4th row)
ministers of
defence or
navy, other
ministers;
(5th row)
admiral,
rear admiral,
Commander
of the navy.*

Gonfanon Large lance flag with a square or rectangular field, and two to five squared long tails. The term derives from the Norse *gunn-fane*, which means a "war flag". In pre-heraldic and medieval times it was the flag of a ruler for carrying on horseback

Government flag see *State flag*

Guidon A small military flag, usually swallow-tailed or with a fly descate or cloven-descate, serving as a guide to troops. In Great Britain it was originally charged with the Union Flag in the hoist, and the badge and livery colours in the fly. Later guidons were charged with the arms

Hanging flag see *Banner*

Homeward-bound pennant United

finial

cord

tassel

fringe

pole

base

INDOOR FLAG

States term for the *paying-off pennant*

House flag The flag of a commercial firm flown at sea, and from its headquarters or branches on land

Indoor flag A flag made expressly for use in offices. It is made of more expensive fabric and the charge is often embroidered. It also differs from an outdoor flag by having a fringe, and it has a sleeve instead of the heading

Jack A small flag flown from a special jack-staff set in the bow of a warship. Usually hoisted when a warship is in harbour or lying in the roadstead. It may be a diminutive of the national flag, or of historic or other special design

LANCE PENNON
(JORDANIAN)

Jolly Roger Popular term for a black flag with a design in white referring to death. Modern flags show a skull and crossbones. The term was coined in the early 18th century for a flag used by pirates

Lance pennon A small flag, usually triangular or swallow-tailed, attached to the end of a lance

Masthead pennant see *Commission pennant*

Merchant flag see *Civil ensign*

Mourning ribbon Long black ribbon tied in a bow and attached to the staff just above the flag as a sign of mourning. An alternative to half–masting the flag

National flag (i) A flag of a nation-state, or formerly independent state, or of a non-independent national group that has its own government;
(ii) In the case of an independent state, a flag and ensign used by the government authorities, general public and the navy

Naval ensign see *War ensign*

Naval reserve ensign A flag used as a civil ensign on merchant vessels commanded by retired naval officers

OCCASIONAL FLAG – FLAG OF THE BICENTENNIAL
OF THE AMERICAN REVOLUTION (1976)

Occasional flag A flag made for a particular occasion, such as an anniversary, holiday or international congress

Outdoor flag A flag made of stronger fabric with enforced edges and corners,

suitable for hoisting on flagstaffs and able to endure strong winds and inclement weather for a long period

Parade flag A flag to be carried outdoors by a marcher, usually made in the same way as an indoor flag

Parley flag A plain white flag displayed by combatants to request a ceasefire and to indicate the desire to negotiate terms of surrender

Paying-off pennant A commission pennant of a vessel returning home after a long period of service. It has up to 75 m (82 yd) of extra material added to the length

Pendant see *Pennant*

Pennant This is a general term for flags that are tapering, triangular or swallow-tailed in shape, originally flown from a crossbar and in modern times also flown from a vertical staff. Pennants differ from flags mainly in shape, size and manner of display. They originated at sea and some are used in this way (*Broad pennant, Commission pennant, Burgee*). There are, however, many more types of pennants for use on land, mainly as award and souvenir flags of corporate bodies and of sports, fraternal and other organizations

Pennon In medieval times a small personal flag of the arms-bearer below the rank of knight-banneret, intended for use on a lance borne by a mounted warrior. A pennon bore the arms in such a way that they were upright when the lance was in a horizontal position. In Britain since Tudor times pennons have consisted of the livery colours charged with a badge

Pilot flag A flag flown by a vessel requiring or carrying a pilot. Some countries have a special flag for this purpose, but in many others the "G" of the International Code of Signals is used

grommet

appliquéd
eagle

heading

▶ RIGHT
OUTDOOR
FLAG: *flag of
the flag
design center*

hem

sewn
chevrons

hem

Pinsil Scottish triangular flag of proportions 4:9 with a fringe of the livery colours, charged with the crest and a strap badge in the hoist, and a plant badge in the fly. Used as a rallying point by a clan captain in the absence of the clan chief

Pipe-banner A small banner attached to the drone pipes of bagpipes. Military pipe-banners are two-sided, the obverse being charged with the regimental badge and the reverse with the company commander's arms

Quarantine flag A yellow flag flown by a ship that has not yet received medical clearance on arrival. It is the request for a certificate of good health

Rank flag A distinguishing flag indicating the rank of the officer of the navy (commodore to fleet admiral), army or air force (generals)

Regimental colour see *Colour*

Schwenkel A rectangular or triangular tail extending from the upper fly corner of a flag, or a strip along the top edge of a flag, with a dependent tail. Common in medieval

FLAG OF ZÜRICH WITH SCHWENKEL, 15TH CENTURY

Europe, now obsolete. The term is also means a whole flag with a schwenkel

Service ensign An ensign designated to identify a vessel, providing a particular service for customs, mail, fishery inspection, lighthouse service, environmental protection, and so on

Signal flag A flag used to transmit messages, especially at sea. The most widely used are the flags of the International Code of Signals

TRADITIONAL DESIGN OF AN ENGLISH HERALDIC STANDARD

Standard (i) A vexilloid used by the army; (ii) A long, tapering descate flag of heraldic design. Size varied according to the person's rank i.e. the length ranged from 7.3 m (8 yd) for the King to 3.5 m (4 yd) for a knight; (iii) A rectangular flag of heraldic design which is not an armorial banner; (iv) A flag of a head of state

State ensign A flag designating national identity, flown on non-military vessels in government service. Also called a *Government ensign*

State flag A flag designating national identity, used by government authorities and institutions on land. Also called a *Government flag*

Streamer (i) A long ribbon attached to the staff, which is used mainly in the form of battle honours; (ii) A long, narrow pennant used until the 17th century as a decoration on vessels

Table flag A small flag hanging vertically from a crossbar or attached to the staff with a stand. Used during international conferences and document signing ceremonies, or on a desk

Trumpet banner A small flag to decorate a ceremonial trumpet, usually a proper armorial banner. Used by a military, civic or other brass band parading in uniform or historic costume

Vane (i) A small metal flag set to swivel on a rod, mainly to indicate wind-direction. Usually attached to a steeple or roof; (ii) A short pennant used in the 17th and 18th centuries by merchant and naval vessels at each mast where no proper pennant was flying

Vexilloid This serves the same purpose as a flag but differs from it in appearance. It consists of a wooden or metal staff topped by an emblem made of animal bones, feathers, hide, wood or metal

Vexillum A square piece of cloth fastened to a crossbar, the standard of the Roman cavalry

War ensign The naval flag of a nation, also called a naval ensign. Carried by warships at or near the stern

TRUMPET BANNER WITH THE ARMS OF FLORENCE CARRIED BY TRUMPETERS IN HISTORIC COSTUMES IN A PARADE PRECEDING AN HISTORICAL SOCCER GAME

RANK FLAGS OF THE CHINESE AIR FORCE, PLATE FROM THE FLAGGENBUCH, BERLIN 1939

MATERIALS AND TECHNIQUES

The earliest flags were usually made of wool or silk. By the 13th century, the banners of rulers and the military were made of silk taffeta, and after the 15th century of silk damask. From the early Middle Ages these silk fabrics were decorated with colourful designs created using appliqué, gold leaf, chain stitch or flat stitch, or a combination of these techniques. From the 14th to the 16th centuries the ornamentation became more elaborate, featuring emblems of painted leather, delicate embroidery and pearls. From the end of the 16th century through to the 19th century most flags were painted and/or embroidered. The seams of ceremonial banners were often trimmed with silver or gold cord; the cantons or fields were adorned with relief embroidery and decorated with pearls and small gold spangles. The finest examples of craftsmanship are the so-called Julius banners, the war flags presented by Pope Julius II to the Swiss in 1512 as a token of appreciation for the Protectors of the Liberty of the Church.

▲ *ABOVE Relief embroidery has been used on the canton of the Julius banner of Basel (1512).*

◄ *LEFT Large parts of the Madonna with Child, as well as the canton and letters on the border, are painted with gold leaf on the Julius banner of Schwyz (1512).*

◄ LEFT An example of a
printed flag is the civic flag
of the city of Lubin in Poland.

More general purpose flags, used by the army
on land and by merchant or war vessels at sea,
were made of cheaper fabrics, mostly rough or
fine linen. Sendal was another popular fabric.
From the 17th to the 19th centuries most
ensigns were made of bunting and the emblems
were painted or appliquéd on to it.

Only in recent years have fabrics been
developed that can fulfil the numerous
requirements of outdoor flags. The fabric has to
give the flag a lustrous appearance at the same
time as superb wearing strength, and it must
also be washable, fire-resistant, mildew-resistant
and mothproof. The flag should be light and
able to fly well, even in rain, and both the fabric
and the durable, fast colours must be able to
resist high winds, intense sun, dirt and air
pollution. Ideal fabrics for this have proved to be
heavyweight, two-ply polyester or fabrics made
of 25 per cent wool and 75 per cent nylon.

The designs on flags for outdoor use are
normally sewn together; simple charges are
appliquéd on, intricate ones are dyed and sewn.
When many flags of the same design are
required, they are dyed in large silkscreen
workshops equipped with rows of tables 30–
50 m (33–55 yd) in length. The chemical dyes,
identical to those used in textile mills, are
applied one colour at a time and penetrate the
fibres so well that it is almost impossible to tell
which side of the fabric is the reverse. Some flag
emblems are larger than the silkscreen tables, so
they have to be hand-painted using special
paint. To assemble the flags, pieces of fabric in
different colours are joined together with double

seams using colour-matched thread. The top
and bottom hems are made with two rows of
stitching, while the fly-end hem has four rows
of lock stitching with back-stitch reinforcement.
Sometimes there are also several diagonal rows
of stitching in the fly corners. The hoist is
usually inserted and sewn into a heavy white
canvas heading, either with grommets or with
the rope sewn in. In Japan, instead of the
heading, triangular pieces of canvas are used to
reinforce the hoist corners.

The fabrics used for colours and for indoor
and parade flags need to be particularly lustrous,
with a surface suitable for embroidery.
Embroidery is ideal for intricate multicoloured

▼ BELOW Hand-painted
seal of Idaho for a flag of
6 m (6½ yd) hoist.

▼ *Below Detail of*
modern embroidery with
silver metal thread.

designs, and in recent years more and more flag manufacturers are using computer–aided embroidery machines. In the United States the stars of the national flag are embroidered on huge machines that are capable of producing hundreds of star fields simultaneously.

Large flag manufacturers have well-organized production lines, which begin at the art department where paper patterns of flag designs are prepared and stored. In a sewn flag, the relevant pattern is sent to the cutting department, which provides the sewing department with pieces of fabric in the exact sizes and colours needed. Once the pieces of fabric have been stitched together, the emblems are applied on top. Simple pre-cut emblems such as stars, fleurs-de-lis, crescents and crosses are pasted on and large emblems are then reinforced by stitching around the edges. In the finishing department the heading and grommets are added to outdoor flags, and indoor and parade flags are fitted with tabs and fringes.

FLAG MATERIALS TERMINOLOGY

Bunting A traditional all-wool fabric used for making flags from the 17th century to the present day

Calico A plain-woven cotton fabric of Indian origin. Used in the 17th and 18th centuries in Europe for some flags

Cotton A fabric made from the seed fibres of a variety of cotton plants native to most sub-tropical countries. Flag manufacturers use mercerized cotton because of its greater strength and lustre, and modern finishing processes make it resistant to stains, water and mildew. Widely used to make relatively inexpensive outdoor flags

Damask A patterned material, originally made of silk, which originated in the Middle East and was introduced to Europe by the Crusaders in the 11th century. Single damask has one set of warp and weft threads, and can be woven in one or two colours; double damask has a greater number of weft threads

Linen A cloth woven from flax, a plant of the family *Linaceae*. Flax is the oldest textile fibre, used in Anatolia for making clothes in the early Neolithic period, around 8000 BC

Nylon A synthetic plastic material manufactured since the late 1930s as a fibre from long-chain polyamides. Resistant to wear, heat and chemicals. Nylon taffeta is used to manufacture indoor and parade flags and heavyweight nylon is used for outdoor flags

Polyester A material manufactured from Terylene (Dacron) fibres, for which the basis is a long-chain polyester made from organic chemicals (ethylene glycol and terephthalic acid). Very durable, elastic, non-combustible and resistant to chemicals and micro-organisms, but prolonged exposure to even minimal sunlight affects colours

Rayon An artificial silk material, woven from fibres produced from the plant substance cellulose since the end of the

19th century. Used mainly to manufacture smaller dyed flags, 10 x 15 cm to 60 x 90 cm (4 x 6 in to 24 x 36 in). Heavy Bemberg rayon is used for the most luxurious indoor and parade flags

Sendal A fabric with a linen warp and silk weft. Used in northern Europe since the 13th century. It is suitable for painted heraldic banners

Silk A lightweight fabric woven from the filament of cocoons produced by the caterpillars of a few moth species belonging to the genus *Bombyx*. Relatively strong with a smooth, lustrous surface. Silkweaving originated in China in 2600 BC, and was known in Egypt from at least 1000 BC, and since the 12th century in Italy

Taffeta A plain-weave fabric, made of silk or nylon fibres, in which the warp and weft threads are evenly interlaced. Fine with a lustrous surface. Used mainly for indoor and parade flags, and colours

FLAG PARTS AND ACCESSORIES

Most of the accessories on flags for outdoor use constitute part of the design; the two that do not are the canvas heading and the hoist rope or grommets.

Indoor flags have various devices to attach the flag to the staff. These differ from country to country. The most popular device is a sleeve, which in Europe is fastened to the staff with special decorative nails. These nails bear engraved emblems with the names of the institutions or individuals who founded the flag or colour. In the United States of America the sleeve has leather tabs at each end, which attach to screwheads protruding from the staff. In Japan, instead of a sleeve, there are two or three leather triangles with eyelets that enable the flag to be fastened to the staff with decorative tasselled cords. Indoor flags will often also feature a fringe, a decorative tasselled cord and a cravat or the ribbons of an order.

◀ LEFT *Japanese flag for indoor or ceremonial use.*

▼ BELOW LEFT *Heading with a hoist rope, ring and clip. Jack of Saudi Arabia (since 1981).*
▼ BELOW RIGHT *Heading with a hoist rope and becket. Polish jack (1919–1945 and 1959–1993).*

FLAG ACCESSORIES TERMINOLOGY

Cord A decorative, flexible string or rope made from several twisted strands. When attached to a ferrule, it has tassels and is tied in the middle. Used also to finish the edges of a flag. Usually of gold or silver thread, or in national livery colours

Cravat A wide ribbon attached to a staff below the finial, used as a distinction or as a mark of honour with a military colour or flag. Usually in national livery colours and richly decorated

Ferrule A metal ring at the top end of the staff, just below the finial

Finial An ornament on the top of the staff. Usually made of metal in the form of a spearhead, armorial crest or other three-dimensional figure

Fringe A decoration made of twisted thread or metal (gold or silver). Usually attached to the edges of the flag on the three free sides. Appropriate for indoor flags, parade flags and car flags

Grommet A metal eyelet reinforcing a hole near both ends of the heading, through

FINIAL OF THE FRENCH COLOUR OF THE 2ND REPUBLIC (1848–1851)

which clips are attached to a halyard pass

Heading A piece of canvas into which the hoist edge of a flag is sewn. To facilitate hoisting, it may have a rope sewn in or grommets fastened near the upper and lower edge

Sleeve A tube of material along the hoist of a flag through which the staff is passed. Used mainly for a colour or an indoor or parade flag

Staff A cylindrical piece of wood to which the flag is fastened. The staff of a colour is usually made of two pieces connected with a metal tube. See also *Finial; Crossbar, Flagpole, Gaff (Hardware Glossary)*

Tab A small piece of leather sewn inside the sleeve near both ends. When fastened to a screwhead protruding from the staff, it prevents the flag from slipping on the staff

Tassel A tuft of loosely hanging twisted threads or metal hanging from a cord attached to the staff. Used with a colour, or other ceremonial or decorative flag. Without a cord, tassels are also used at the points of a triangular or tailed flag hung vertically

FLAG HARDWARE

It would not be possible to display a flag without a few pieces of specially designed hardware. Beckets and toggles, rings and snaps, grommets and Inglefield clips all allow a flag to be fastened to the rope. Flagpoles make it possible to fly a flag at the desired height whilst flag belts enable someone to carry a heavy parade flag or colour more easily.

There are several ways of fastening a flag to a flagpole. In Europe a rope is sewn into the heading and attached to the halyard with a becket and toggle. Some flags, especially those for use at sea, have looped clips and Inglefield clips instead of beckets and toggles. In the United States brass grommets are inserted on each end of the heading, and the halyard is furnished with clips that attach to the grommets. In Japan the hoist edges are reinforced with triangles of heavy canvas with ribbons, which attach the flag to clips on the halyard.

A flagpole consists of a pole made of glass fibre, aluminium, steel or wood, with a truck on the top. Above the truck is a cap in the form of a disc, ball, eagle or other figure. The bottom part of the flagpole is embedded in a ground socket in a concrete foundation, or permanently welded to a base made of heavy cast aluminium. The halyard passes through a pulley in the truck and is secured to a cleat on the lower part of the flagpole. To prevent malicious damage or theft of flags, modern flagpoles are fitted with an internal halyard system and an access door with a lock. Older flagpoles can be modified with the addition of halyard covers and cleat-cover lock boxes. In cities, outrigger staffs or vertical flagpoles are usually set into a wall. They are constructed in a similar way to flagpoles, but the lower part is mounted in a metal base fastened with anchor bolts through the wall. Much smaller and lighter outrigger staffs are used by private home-owners who are well served by buying an inexpensive kit containing a sectional aluminium staff about 2 m (6 ft) long and a steel mounting bracket with screws.

FLAG HARDWARE TERMINOLOGY

Becket A loop at the end of a hoist rope that fastens to a toggle at the end of the halyard, making it easier to bend on a flag

Case A narrow sack to protect a parade flag in inclement weather, or to store it when not in use

Cleat A metal device with two arms, attached to the lower part of a flagstaff, to which the halyards are made fast

Crossbar A rod bearing a flag (usually a pennant, banner or gonfalon), attached directly or by a rope to a staff. The crossbar usually passes through the sleeve. Parts of the sleeve can be cut out to reveal parts of the crossbar

Flagpole A pole made of wood, metal or glass fibre on which a flag may be hoisted. It may be upright or projecting at an angle from a wall. Sometimes an upright flagpole is fitted with a yardarm or gaff to increase the number of flags that may be hoisted.

CLEAT

This practice is found mainly at naval establishments ashore

Flagstaff see *Flagpole*

Frame A wood or metal device designed to hold the top edge of a flag

Gaff A spar from which a flag is hoisted. It is set diagonally on the aft side of a mast. A flag is attached to a halyard passing through the outer end of the gaff. An ensign is flown from the gaff of the mizzen mast, or of the main mast in a two-masted ship

Halyard The rope to which a flag is bent in order to be hoisted

Inglefield clips Interlocking metal clips used to attach a flag securely to the halyard. Their quick-release mechanism makes it possible to bend on a flag easily

Mast A long, upright post of timber or metal set up on a ship or on a building

Staff see *Flagpole*

Tangle rod A metal device attached to a staff projecting at an angle from a wall, which clasps a flag and prevents it from wrapping around the staff

Toggle A device at the end of a rope sewn into the heading, consisting of an oval-shaped wooden or plastic crosspiece that fastens to a becket at the end of the halyard, making it easier to bend on a flag

TOGGLE

Truck A circular metal cap fixed on the head of a flagpole below the finial. It contains a pulley over which the halyard passes

Yardarm A bar attached horizontally to a mast of a ship or to a flagpole on shore to increase the number of flags that may be hoisted, attached to separate halyards

USAGE AND CUSTOM: ON LAND

From time immemorial flags and banners were used to distinguish bodies of troops and to serve as rallying points when they needed to regroup or retreat. In the Middle Ages the number of banners carried into battle was imposing. There were royal banners, banners of provinces, cities and guilds, and banners of knights who were able to raise their own troops. At Buironfosse, where in 1339 the French and English Armies did not dare to stage battle, the French forces displayed 220 banners and 560 pennons, while the English had 74 banners and 230 pennons. In the battle of Tannenberg in 1410, the 56 banners unfurled by the Teutonic knights and the 91 banners by the Polish–Lithuanian forces were mainly the emblems of cities and provinces. Banners like these continued to be used on the battlefield until the 16th century, when European countries began to build standing armies based on permanent groupings of troops in legions and regiments.

After this date banners began to lose their heraldic character and by the beginning of the 17th century most of them displayed instead painted representations of patron saints or allegorical figures. Gradually all countries began to follow the example set by the French in 1597 and developed consistent designs for their infantry colours and cavalry standards. Military colours served their purpose on the battlefield until the end of the 19th century, when modern warfare made the function of colours in battle obsolete. (Several instances of troops displaying their colours were still reported even in World War II.) Today military colours are displayed only during military or state ceremonies.

In the Middle Ages banners were not only used in battle, however. In peacetime they were proudly displayed on the towers of castles and city halls, carried in triumphal marches and processions, and exhibited during all manner of festivities. The whole life of a banner was closely connected with the local church; every battle banner was consecrated in the church, was kept there in peacetime and was deposited there when it could no longer serve its purpose. Most

of the banners used on the battlefield in the Middle Ages served later to identify states, provinces, cities and guilds, and to this day many cities in Central Europe and Italy use the same flags as in medieval times.

Until the 19th century, the use of flags on land was limited and only a few countries had a national flag. The radical changes in the world that led to the revolutions in Europe of 1848 gave birth to the idea of the nation-state and from then on, in many sovereign countries, the civil ensign became the national flag.

In the same way that the coat of arms had been the sign identified with the ruler and the state, so the national flag was from the beginning a symbol with which people could identify. The concept of a national flag as a symbol of the people rather than the state became prevalent, and in many cases the flag was introduced by leaders of independence movements, revolutionaries or students and was only later officially adopted by government. The case of the British Union Jack, which to this day has never officially been declared to be the national flag, is proof that for the people of a

▲ *ABOVE Armorial banners of Bavaria, Brunswick and Saxony carried in the triumphal procession of the Emperor of Germany Maximilian I at the beginning of the 16th century.*

YOU answered the call to the colors,
YOU proved you were loyal and true;
And we-who can't go-will let others know
The debt that we all owe to you!

◄ *LEFT* British recruitment poster, World War I.
► *RIGHT* American patriotic postcard, World War I.

▲ *ABOVE* British match label.

country legislative action is less important than their feelings. Almost everywhere in the world the national flag is not just a piece of bunting but something so close to people's hearts that they will risk their lives for it. Under foreign occupation, to display the national flag has often been an offence punishable by death, yet there have always been people defiantly hoisting their flag as a strong message that says, "This is our country, we are here to stay and we shall overcome!"

Awareness that the flag is a powerful symbol has induced totalitarian and oppressive regimes to de-legalize the flags of their opponents and to persecute those who defy the ban. In Spain, for example, it was illegal under Franco's regime to display the Basque flag. In answer to this, the Basque separatists hoisted a booby-

trapped flag that would blow up when the police tried to remove it. Israeli authorities have for decades harshly persecuted Palestinians caught with the flag of Palestine, and in the Soviet Union people could be sent to a concentration camp for publicly displaying the national flag of Lithuania, Armenia or any other nation that had been forcibly incorporated into the Soviet Union.

To sustain patriotic feelings during the Civil War in the United States, both sides published postcards of the national and Confederate flags, featuring allegorical figures of Liberty. In most of the countries involved in World War I, patriotic cards and posters displayed the national flag and the flags of the Allies. The message was clear: we fight for our country and have foreign friends on our side.

◄ *LEFT* Flag mutilated during a street demonstration.
► *RIGHT* Flag burning in Warsaw, 1998. Photo courtesy of Miroslaw Stelmach.

▲ *ABOVE LEFT Swiss cantonal flags decorate streets of all their cities, as shown here in St Gallen.*

▲ *ABOVE RIGHT National flags at the UN headquarters in New York.*

▶ *RIGHT Apollo 12 astronaut with United States flag on the moon, 28 November 1969. Photo courtesy of NASA.*

▼ *BELOW LEFT The national flag of Switzerland at the head of an unusual parade.*

▼ *BELOW RIGHT National flags displayed in the lobby of the State Department in Washington DC, 1986.*

A common form of protest against the actions of a foreign country is to publicly burn its national flag. Left-wing students in France burnt the German flag as a protest against the arrest of Red Brigade terrorists. In many countries in the West, refugees from countries subjugated by the Soviet Union have burnt the Soviet flag, and under the regime of Ayatollah

Khomeini the Iranians burnt United States flags. Workers belonging to the Polish "Solidarity" trade unions burnt the European Union flag out of fear that they would lose their jobs if Poland joined the EEC.

A traditional custom involving the national flag is to symbolically plant it in places that are discovered or conquered. The British have taken the Union Jack to all parts of the world. Roald Amundsen in 1911 planted the Norwegian flag at the South Pole, and in 1953 Edmund Hillary and Sherpa Tenzing Norgay placed the flags of New Zealand and Nepal on top of Mount Everest. The United States flag was carried to the North Pole in 1909 by Robert E. Peary, and in 1969 Neil Armstrong and Edwin E. Aldrin took it to the moon.

The political changes and development of international contacts in the 20th century have had a great impact on the development of all kinds of flags. In 1900 there were 49 sovereign countries and by 1998 their number had grown to more than 200. Many of these new countries adopted not only a national flag but also

numerous government services flags, as well as ensigns and other flags for use at sea. Tens of thousands of new flags have been adopted by political parties, trade unions, firms and corporations, youth movements, universities, schools, and yacht and sporting clubs. Occasional flags are designed for anniversaries such as the bicentennials of the American and French Revolutions, and for Olympic Games and international congresses. In some countries there are also flags for special occasions such as Christmas, Easter, Hallowe'en, birthdays or the birth of a baby.

In most countries the daily display of flags is limited to the flags of the head of state, national and state flags, flags of government agencies and officers, flags of certain companies and the flags of political parties, but in some countries flags are almost everywhere. Probably the most flag-filled nation is Switzerland. There, at least three flags (national, that of the canton and that of the commune or town) are displayed together and the larger streets in the cities are decorated with the national flag and the flags of all the cantons. National, provincial and civic flags, mostly in banner form, are permanently displayed in Germany. In the United States and Scandinavian countries the national flag is displayed not only by the authorities and public bodies, but also by a large part of the population in front of private houses. Throughout the world national flags are displayed on state holidays, and it is inconceivable to have street parades or demonstrations without a large number of flags. Hundreds of national or club flags are waved in stadiums and sports arenas by ardent fans, and in the 1990s the custom of painting the colours and design of the national flag on to the body developed.

The steadily increasing use of flags has been augmented by countless international meetings, conferences and sporting events. The national

▲ *ABOVE Three flags from a match label set: Ethiopia (1941–1975); United States (1959); Laos (1952–1975).*

◀ *LEFT This poster, produced in 1991 by Konstantin Geraymovich, was an expression of indignation of the Russian artist at the Soviet military intervention in the capital of Lithuania. The other two dates are those of Soviet invasions of Hungary (1956) and Czechoslovakia (1968).*

▶ *RIGHT Flags used to great effect on a poster promoting the Marshall Plan, produced in 1950.*

▶ *RIGHT Crowds of supporters in Stockholm, Sweden, show allegiance to their national soccer team, 1994.*
▶ *FAR RIGHT American soccer fans at the 1996 Olympics paint their faces with the stars and stripes.*

flags of member-countries are permanently displayed at the headquarters of international organizations throughout the world, for example the United Nations in New York and the Commonwealth Institute in London.

The national flag as the visual symbol of a nation is so deeply engrained in modern consciousness that the media often show a flag as a symbol of a nation rather than just its name. Advertisers use pictures of national flags to suggest the international scope of their business, and large hotels eager to attract international clientele often display many different national flags. Most countries issue postage stamps to honour and promote their national flags. One of the first sets of stamps to illustrate flags in

colour was the famous American set of thirteen flags for the "Over-run Countries", issued in 1943–4. The largest series of 160 national flags was published by the United Nations in 1980–89. Sets of matchbox labels with national flags have been issued in Australia, Germany, Hungary, Spain and the former Yugoslavia. Flags also appear on lapel pins, ties and belt buckles, and on souvenir articles such as keyrings, T-shirts, mugs, umbrellas and playing cards.

▼ *BELOW LEFT Commercial firms use flags in advertising to highlight the international scope of their business. This advertisement was for Stanwell of Denmark.*
▼ *BELOW RIGHT Hotel sticker promoting the Albergo delle Nazioni in Florence, Italy.*

USAGE AND CUSTOM: AT SEA

The first flags identifying nationality were used at sea. The oldest international legal obligation on record for ships to display flags as identification was agreed by King Edward I of England and Guy, Count of Flanders, in 1297. It explicitly compelled merchant ships to "carry in their ensigns or flags the arms of their own ports certifying their belonging to the said ports". From the beginning of the 13th century England claimed sovereignty over the seas and demanded that all ships belonging to other countries should salute the English ships by lowering their topsails, and later also by striking the flag. Captains who refused to do so were regarded as enemies and their ships and cargo forfeited. Foreign ships submitted because England insisted only on a salute and levied no duties on ships passing through the English Channel. The practice became obsolete in 1805, but the custom of saluting a foreign vessel remains to this day. Merchant ships salute each other by dipping the ensign as an act of courtesy; warships do not dip to each other, but if a merchant vessel dips to them they reply.

For a long time the national ensigns of the main maritime powers served as passports for merchant ships sailing to Turkey, North Africa, China and India. Under a treaty made by King Henry VI of France and Sultan Ahmed of the Turkish Empire, from 1604 to 1675 ships of all nations could visit the Turkish ports and trade there only "under the authorization and security of the Banner of France". The situation changed in 1675 when a British–Turkish capitulation treaty reserved the right to free trade in Turkey for the "English nation and the English Merchants and all other nations or Merchants who are or shall come under the banner and protection of England". Similar provisions concerning the protection of ships and citizens and/or free trade were included in treaties made between France and the Turkish vassal states in North Africa: Morocco (1682), Tripoli (1685) and Tunis (1685). Another example is Austria's peace treaties with Morocco and Turkey (1783–5). One of the purposes of these and subsequent treaties was to protect commercial shipping from pirates.

As well as the national ensign there were, and still are, many other flags for use on ships. The oldest is the jack, flown from the bow. Currently private ships display the civil ensign or service ensign on the stern, the house flag on the foremast and (in Britain) the jack on the bow. On sailing ships the civil ensign is often displayed from a halyard attached to the mizzen mast. Yachts fly the civil ensign on the stern and the club burgee or private flag on the mast. On war ships the war ensign is flown on the stern and the jack on the bow; on the main mast either the commission pennant or a command flag, with the rank flag below, is flown.

▼ BELOW *Flags on a warship.*

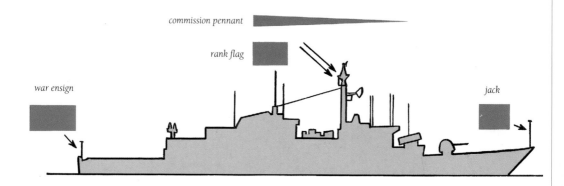

commission pennant

rank flag

war ensign

jack

FLAG ETIQUETTE

There are no international regulations governing flag etiquette but the rules adopted by many countries have so much in common that it is possible to formulate general guidelines. They are slightly different for a flag displayed inside a country and for one at an international forum. The general rule in both cases is that all flags hoisted as a group should be the same width and should be hoisted on separate flagpoles, or separate halyards in the case of a flagpole with a yardarm. The practice of hoisting two or more flags on the same halyard is not correct.

In most countries the following rules are observed for hoisting flags inside the country:

✦ The flag should be displayed in the open from sunrise to sunset, but it should not be displayed on days when the weather is inclement. It may be displayed at night providing that it is well illuminated.

✦ The flag should be hoisted briskly and lowered ceremoniously.

✦ The flag should always be used in a dignified manner. It should never touch the ground, the floor or water. It should never be carried flat or horizontally, but always aloft and free. It should never be used as a table or seat cover, or as drapery of any sort. It should never be used as a receptacle for receiving, holding, carrying or delivering anything.

✦ The national flag should not be displayed in a position inferior to any other flag. The national flag takes precedence over all other flags. When flown with the flags of other sovereign nations, all flags should be flown on separate flagpoles of the same size. The flags should be of the same size or the same width, and should be flown at the same height. The other national flags should be displayed in alphabetical order according to the official language of the country.

✦ When there are two flags displayed, the national flag should be on the left of the observer, facing the staff. The same rule should be observed when the national flag is crossed with another flag; its staff should be

in front of the staff of another flag; see diagram overleaf.

✦ In a line of three flags, the national flag should be positioned in the centre; see diagram overleaf.

✦ In a line of four flags, the national flag should be the first to appear on the observer's left; see diagram overleaf.

✦ In a line of five or more flags, two national flags should be used, one at each end of the line; see diagram overleaf.

✦ In a semi-circle, the national flag should be in the centre; see diagram overleaf.

✦ In an enclosed circle, the national flag should be positioned and centred immediately opposite the main entrance to a building or arena; see diagram overleaf.

✦ The order of flags hoisted together depends on the place of each particular flag in the following hierarchy: (a) national flag, (b) regional or provincial flag, (c) county, parish or commune flag, (d) civic flag, (e) service flag (e.g. police, fire brigade), (f) other flags (university, school, commercial firm, sports club etc).

✦ When the national flag is carried in a procession it should always be aloft and free. In a single line the national flag must always lead. If carried in line abreast with one other flag, it should be on the right-hand end of the line facing the direction of movement; if carried with two or more other flags, it should either be in the centre, or two national flags should be displayed, one at each end of the line.

▲ *ABOVE A huge flag carried flat looks good from above, but since its design is not visible to the spectators standing on the ground it is not correct flag etiquette. In this example, the event is a 4th July parade in Georgia, USA.*

ETIQUETTE

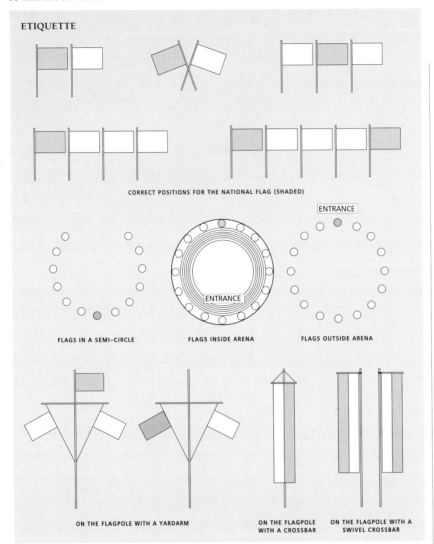

CORRECT POSITIONS FOR THE NATIONAL FLAG (SHADED)

FLAGS IN A SEMI–CIRCLE   FLAGS INSIDE ARENA   FLAGS OUTSIDE ARENA

ENTRANCE

ENTRANCE

ON THE FLAGPOLE WITH A YARDARM   ON THE FLAGPOLE WITH A CROSSBAR   ON THE FLAGPOLE WITH A SWIVEL CROSSBAR

◆ The correct position of the national flag displayed on a flagpole fitted with a yardarm is illustrated above.

◆ When a flag is displayed over the middle of a street, it should be suspended vertically, with its top edge to the north in an east–west street or to the east in a north–south street.

◆ When a flag is displayed vertically on a flagpole with a crossbar, the upper edge of the flag is to be on the observer's left; see above.

◆ When a flag is displayed vertically on a flagpole with a swivel crossbar, the upper edge of the flag should face the flagpole; see illustration above.

◆ When a flag is displayed from a staff on a speaker's platform, it should be on the speaker's right as he faces the audience.

◆ When used to cover a coffin, a flag should be placed so that the hoist is at the head and the top edge is over the left shoulder.

◆ As a sign of mourning the flags on flagpoles are half-masted. A black ribbon is attached to flags hoisted on short outrigger staffs, and a black cravat to military parade flags.

FLAG ETIQUETTE TERMINOLOGY

Bend on a flag To fasten a flag to halyards in order to hoist it

Break out a flag To unfurl a flag that has been rolled and tied in such a way that a sharp tug on the halyard will cause it to open out

Consecration The dedication ceremony of a colour or other flag

Desecration Disrespectful treatment of a flag such as burning it in public, defacing it with inappropriate inscriptions or emblems, mutilating it, trampling it or throwing it on the floor or ground. Punishable in most countries of the world

Dip a flag The custom of lowering a flag briefly and temporarily in salute. A sign of respect used to honour the national anthem, an important person or another vessel

Drape a flag The custom of attaching a black cravat to a staff as a sign of mourning

Dress ship To decorate a vessel with flags for a holiday or special occasion. Until the 20th century all flags in the ship's store were raised on every available halyard but now only signal flags are displayed

Flag officer A naval officer entitled to use a rank flag, usually above the rank of captain

Fold a flag A ceremony performed after a flag is taken down from a flagpole or removed from a coffin it has covered. The flag is folded lengthwise three times in such a way that the upper hoist part is on the outside. A series of triangular folds follows, beginning at the fly, until the flag resembles a cocked hat with only part of the hoist still visible

Half-mast To fly a flag at a point much below its normal position, usually as a sign of mourning. The flag should be first hoisted to the peak for an instant then lowered to the half-mast position. It should be raised again to the peak before it is lowered for the day

Honour a flag Whenever a military unit or civil organization is awarded, the order ribbons are ceremoniously attached to the staff of the colour or banner. The head of state or his deputy personally presents the award at a ceremony held in the presence of the military unit or a representative of the organization

Lay up colours To deposit old colours ceremoniously in a church or museum

Pall flag A flag laid over a coffin, hearse or tomb. This is used mainly at government and military funerals. It is removed from the coffin before it is lowered into the grave

Salute the flag Flags are saluted when being hoisted, lowered or passed in a parade review. Civilians stand at attention, men remove their headgear and military personnel place the right hand to the head in a prescribed salute

◀ **LEFT**
Pall flag – Mother Theresa lying in state with the Indian national flag laid over her body, 1997.

✦ When a flag is no longer in a suitable condition to be used it should be destroyed in a dignified way by burning it privately. At the headquarters of international organizations and at international conferences or sports events, national flags should be arranged in alphabetical order, either in the official language of the host country or in English. National flags hoisted together should be the same width. When the flagpoles form an enclosed circle the order of flags should be clockwise, with the first flag positioned opposite the main entrance.

Flags are designed in such a way that they should be displayed in a horizontal position. There are, however, at least two circumstances when flags are displayed vertically: on a table (see *Types of Flags: Table flag*), and when they are positioned against a wall. In other circumstances vertical is an unsatisfactory way to display flags because coats of arms or emblems may lose their upright position. Indeed, at least four countries, namely Brazil, Pakistan, Saudi Arabia and Sri Lanka, explicitly forbid vertical display of their national flags. However, Liechtenstein, Slovakia and Slovenia have special designs for displaying their national flags in a vertical position, and Germany and Austria both have a custom of turning coats of arms upright in state flags that are hanging vertically. The general rule to be observed when a flag is displayed vertically is that the upper edge of the flag should be to the observer's left (the observer will see the reverse of the flag). The only exceptions are the flags of Liechtenstein, Slovakia and Slovenia, which should be displayed in accordance with their official designs for vertical flags.

FLAG CONFLICTS

The knowledge of flags and flag etiquette is
a very important part of diplomatic protocol,
unfortunately not always observed correctly.
For example, the Iranian delegation to a
European country almost abandoned talks
because the hosts placed on their table the flag
of Iran used by the overthrown Shah regime.
An incorrect vertical display of some flags can
cause serious consternation because the Polish
flag becomes the flag of Monaco or Indonesia,
the Dutch flag becomes that of Yugoslavia, the
Russian flag changes into the Serbian flag and
the civil flag of Ethiopia becomes that of Bolivia.

One of the first recorded incidents happened
in September 1916 when King Vajiravudh
(Rama VI) of Siam was visiting areas devastated
by floods. All the towns and villages he visited
were decorated with the national flag, red with
a white elephant, but one was flying upside
down. The sight of the elephant lying on its
back shocked the King to such an extent that he
decided to adopt a new flag with a simple design
of red and white stripes that was incapable of
being flown upside down.

Serious and long-lasting conflicts have been
provoked by changing the national flag. The
longest was the *Flaggenstreit* (flag conflict) in
Germany after World War I. The struggle was
between those who wanted to restore the

◀ LEFT *The national
flag of Siam (Thailand)
(until 1916).*

◀ LEFT *The national
flag and civil ensign of
Siam (Thailand)
(1916–1917).*

tricolour of 1848 and those who wanted to keep
the flag designed by Bismarck in 1867, so it was
a conflict between the adherents of two
ideologies. The black, red and yellow were
perceived as the colours of the democratic
republic, and of unity, law and freedom, whereas
the black–white–red tricolour, combining the
colours of Prussia (black and white) and
Brandenburg (red and white), was a reminder
of the glorious days of the empire dominated by
the militant Prussia. The situation was so tense
that the republican government decided on a
compromise. The flag of 1848 was restored as

◀ BELOW (*left to right*)
*German national flag
and civil ensign
(1848–1866); German
national flag and civil
ensign (1867–1919);
German civil ensign
(1919–1933);
German civil ensign
(1933–1945).*

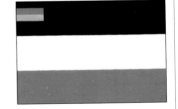

the national flag, but all flags for use at sea (civil
ensign, state ensign, war ensign, jack) remained
black–white–red, with the addition of the
national colours in the canton. When Adolf
Hitler came to power in 1933 the German flags
were changed again. The black–white–red
tricolour was reinstated as the national flag but
it could be displayed only together with the

Hakenkreuzflagge of the Nazi Party. Two years later the *Hakenkreuzflagge* became the national flag and civil ensign, and the base for all other ensigns and flags of the Third Reich.

Similar, but less intense, conflicts occurred between supporters of the Union Jack and the proponents of a new national flag in South Africa in the 1920s, and in Canada in the 1960s. Currently there is conflict in Russia between the pro-democratic forces and the communists who want to restore the Soviet flag. In Belarus patriots are demonstrating under the

with the Olympic rings in white. Then, after Taiwan was denied its seat in the United Nations, the International Olympic Committee denied it the right to use its national flag at the Olympics and demanded that a special flag be designed for the Chinese–Taiwan Olympic team; it was carried for the first time at the 1984 Olympic Games. The flag is white with the national emblem and Olympic rings within a stylised five-petalled flower shape. For political reasons, the national flag of South Africa was also banned and the South African team was

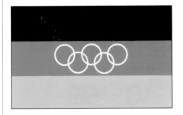

▲ *Above left* All-German Olympic flag (1959–1968).

▲ *Above centre* The Taiwan Olympic flag (since 1984).

▲ *Above right* The flag of the South African team carried at the Summer Olympic games in Barcelona, Spain (1992).

▼ *Below* The national flag of Macedonia (1992–1995).

historic flag against the president, who has decreed a flag similar to that used when Belarus was a Soviet republic.

In the 1990s flag conflicts were clearly visible during street demonstrations in Russia and Germany. In Russia the democrats march under the national flag, the communists under the Soviet flags and the Soviet war ensign, the monarchists under the black–gold–white tricolour or the national flag with the imperial eagle added, and the militant nationalists under the current war ensign. In Germany the militant neo-Nazis carry the imperial war ensign or flags of the *Freie Arbeitspartei*.

On the international scene, there have been several incidents at the Olympic Games. The first involved teams from both West and East Germany who were compelled to use the All-German Olympic flag (*Gesamtdeutsche Olympiaflagge*), the German flag defaced

compelled to use a special flag at the Olympic Games of 1992. At the same Olympics the teams from Bosnia and Herzegovina, Serbia and member-countries of the Commonwealth of Independent Countries were disqualified from holding any flags.

The latest flag conflict began in 1991 when Macedonia broke its ties with Yugoslavia and proclaimed an independent republic. As one of Greece's provinces is also named Macedonia, Greece began to contest the new country's right to this name. The Greek protests intensified in 1992 when Macedonia adopted a flag with the Star of Vergina, associated with King Philip II of Macedon and his son, Alexander III the Great (356–323 BC). Because a similar flag is used in Greek Macedonia, the Greek Prime Minister denounced the flag of Macedonia as a clear provocation. Because of the objections raised by Greece, Macedonia was admitted to the United Nations in April 1993 under the name "The Former Yugoslav Republic of Macedonia" and was denied the right to have its flag flown at the UN headquarters in New York, a move unprecedented in UN history.

Emperors, Sovereigns and Presidents

In the Middle Ages and much later in some countries, the state flag was the personal heraldic standard of the ruler. He was the state, and when his subjects went to battle or sailed the seas they flew his flag.

G.A. HAYES-MCCOY, *A HISTORY OF IRISH FLAGS*, BOSTON, 1979.

In the Middle Ages the ruler was regarded as the embodiment of the state, and for many centuries his banner was synonymous with the national flag. It marked his castle (or his tent in a military camp), was carried into battle and was flown on the masthead of his ships. Before the dawn of heraldry the personal flag of a ruler was plain red, showing that it was the flag of the emperor (*vexillo roseum imperiali*) or of someone with the right to govern in his name. Sometimes the red field of the emperor's flag was charged with a white cross as a sign that he had taken part in a crusade.

Diversification of these flags began in the second half of the 12th century when heraldic devices were introduced, and until the 15th century all of the flags of Europe's rulers were armorial banners. Most sovereigns continued to use armorial banners until the late 19th century, but in the 15th century the monarchs of southern Europe began to use unicolour royal flags, usually a white field carrying the royal coat of arms. At the end of the 17th century Scandinavian monarchs defaced their war ensigns with white panels bearing the whole arms, and a few further modifications have taken place during the last two centuries. These basic designs have served as the models for almost all the royal and presidential banners and flags in use throughout the world even to this day.

◀ **LEFT** *The presidential and national flags decorate the car which carries the president in the motorcade, travelling through Dallas a few moments before John F. Kennedy, 35th President of the United States, was shot.*

MEDIEVAL EUROPE

In the course of the century from 1195 to 1295, most European rulers adopted coats of arms and armorial banners bearing one of the two most important heraldic figures: the lion, the king of the beasts, or the eagle, the king of heaven. There was the imperial black eagle, the three golden lions of England, the red lion of Scotland, the white lion of Bohemia, the black lion of Flanders, the purple lion of Leon, the three blue lions of Denmark, the lion with an axe of Norway and the white eagle of Poland.

In the Mediterranean region the King of Portugal in 1185 adopted a complex coat of arms displaying four blue shields forming a cross on a silver field, each shield charged with five white dots arranged in a saltire (diagonal cross).

◄ *LEFT Royal banners in 1300.*

Holy Roman Empire.

England.

Scotland.

Denmark.

Norway.

Flanders.

Bohemia.

Poland.

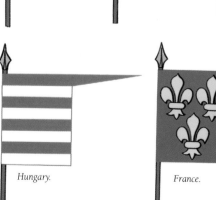

Hungary.

France.

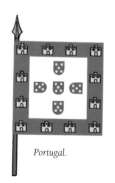

Portugal.

Spain.

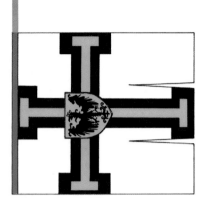

The shields symbolize the five Moorish kings defeated by the Portuguese and the five dots refer to the five wounds of Christ. After the final annexation of Algarve and the wedding of the King to Beatriz of Castile, a red border charged with golden castles was added to the arms. The other three kingdoms on the Iberian Peninsula had quite simple arms. The arms of Castile were the canting arms, a golden castle on red; those of Aragon were four red pallets on red; and those of Navarre were a gold chain arranged per cross, per saltire and in orle (as a border), with an emerald at the centre, all on red. From 1230 to 1479 the Spanish coat of arms was quarterly Castile and León. The arms of Sicily were per saltire Aragon and Hohenstaufen (black eagle on white). The royal coat of arms of France was golden fleurs-de-lis on a blue field; until the end of the 14th century their number was not limited, thereafter it was reduced to three.

Although it was not a kingdom, one of the most important states of the medieval period was the domain of the Teutonic Order. The white banner of the Grand Master of the Order was charged with a yellow and black cross, with the arms of the Holy Roman Empire in the centre.

As we saw in the example of Spain, already by the 13th century a king ruling over more than one domain incorporated their arms in his coat of arms and on his banner. Where there were two territories, this was done by either quartering or impaling the shield. In the case of quartering, the first arms appeared in the first and fourth quarter, and the second arms in the second and third quarter. The arms impaled had the shield divided per pale (vertically), as in the arms of Hungary under the rule of the Anjou dynasty (1387–1437), which displayed the Hungarian arms and the arms of France. In time the number of shield divisions grew to accommodate the arms of the extra territories, but even so at the ruler's funeral the separate banners of all of his domains were carried as well as his state banner.

▲ *ABOVE* (clockwise from top left) *Grand Master of the Teutonic Order; England (1405–1603); Hungary (1387–1437).*

THE MODERN WORLD

An example of a quite complex armorial banner is that of Burgundy, which reunified in the 14th century and for more than 100 years was one of the richest countries of Europe. It extended its possessions northwards to Flanders, Brabant and Holland, but in the 1470s was torn apart by Austria and France. The banner of Burgundy is quarterly the arms of Burgundy Modern (first and fourth quarters), Burgundy Ancient impaling Brabant (second quarter) and Burgundy Ancient impaling Limburg (third quarter), and displays the arms of Flanders on an inescutcheon.

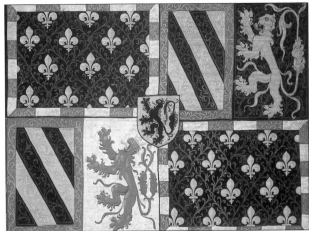

▲ *ABOVE Great Britain (1714–1801).*

The expansion of the domains of other rulers was similarly reflected in their arms and banners. In 1438 Rudolf I of Habsburg was chosen to rule the Holy Roman Empire and Austria was established as his family's principal duchy. The imperial eagle was therefore ensigned in 1493 with the escutcheon of the arms of Austria, and from 1508 to 1519 the arms of Austria were impaled with those of Burgundy. Later the crowned eagle with a sword and a sceptre in its claws appeared on the imperial banner without the inescutcheon. In 1479 the kings of Spain augmented the arms of León and Castile with

the arms of Aragon and Sicily; the arms of Granada were added in 1492, and the arms of Austria, Burgundy Modern, Burgundy Ancient, Brabant, Flanders and Tyrol in 1504. Since 1603 the British royal banner has displayed the arms of England together with those of Scotland and the Irish harp, and since 1714 also the arms of Hanover.

At the end of the 15th century the diversification of the personal flags of European rulers began. The armorial banner still usually

▲ *ABOVE Banner of Burgundy.*

▼ *BELOW Banner of the Duke of Brunswick-Lüneburg (1914–1918).*

◀ *Far left Banner of the king of Saxony (1815–1918).*
◀ *Left Banner of the grand duke of Mecklenburg (1900–1918).*
◀ *Below left Banner of the king of Bavaria (1806–1835).*

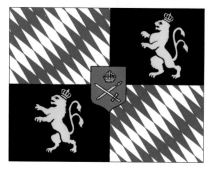

rulers for use at sea. The fields of these flags were white, the only exceptions being the yellow field of the imperial flags of Austria and Russia. Some later royal flags displayed the whole state arms on a red field.

In the 18th century Prussia emerged as one of the most powerful countries in Europe. Its arms had evolved from those of East Prussia, which was created by the secularization of the powerful

prevailed on land, but the Catholic monarchs of Spain introduced a white flag with the arms in the centre, designed for use at sea. In a few countries this kind of flag became the alternative personal flag of the ruler on land and thus the second model of the personal flag for heads of state came into being.

In the late 17th and 18th centuries the second model was adopted by most European

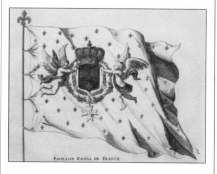

◀ *Left France, royal flag and ensign, (17th to 18th century).*

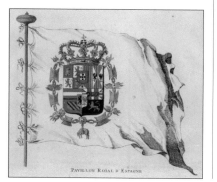

PAVILLON ROIAL D'ESPAGNE

PAVILLON ROIAL DE PORTUGAL

◀ *Far left Spain, royal flag (17th to 18th century).*
◀ *Left Portugal, royal flag (17th to 18th century).*

▶ **RIGHT** *Austria
(German emperor),
standard of the
Emperor.*
▶ **FAR RIGHT** *Tuscany,
royal flag (17th to
18th century).*

▶ **FAR RIGHT** *Russia,
standard of the emperor
(18th century).*
▼ **BELOW** *Spanish royal
standard (1833–1868
and 1875–1931).*

Teutonic Order. In 1525 the Grand Master of the Teutonic Order had sworn allegiance to King Sigismund the Old of Poland and had received from him a white banner defaced with the new arms of East Prussia: a black eagle with the royal crown on its neck, and the royal cipher "S" on its breast. In 1569 the cipher was replaced by the "SA" of the Polish King Sigismund August, and later it combined the letters of the Polish kings and the Prussian princes (VG for Vladislaus-Georgius and JCF for Johannes Casimirus-Frederick). In 1618 East Prussia came under the direct control of the electors of Brandenburg and the eagle was ensigned with their crown. When the kingdom of Prussia was proclaimed in 1713 the crown was replaced with the royal one and the cipher changed to "FR" (*Fredericus Rex*).

The other country to attain the position of a world power at this time was Russia, which at the beginning of the 18th century was modernized by Peter the Great. He introduced the yellow imperial banner with a representation of the state arms in the centre. The arms had been adopted by Ivan III after his marriage to Sophia Paleologue, a niece of the last Byzantine emperor, and were those of Byzantium – a golden double-headed eagle on a red field. In the 16th century this was defaced with the arms of Moscow (St George slaying the dragon) and at the end of the 17th century the colour of the eagle was changed to black and the field to gold.

In some countries until the end of the 18th century the ruler had at least two different flags and in many countries there was no special flag

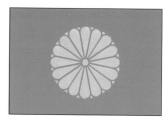

▲ *ABOVE LEFT Royal flag of the Netherlands (1815–1840).*

▲ *ABOVE CENTRE Royal flag of Afghanistan (1930–1973).*

▲ *ABOVE RIGHT Imperial flag of Japan since the second half of the 19th century.*

for the head of state. But in the 19th century the rulers and presidents of all countries began to adopt their flags.

The first presidential flag in the world followed the second model. It was a blue flag with the state arms of the United States in the centre, used on naval ships since the first half of the 19th century and made official in 1882. As commander-in-chief of the army, the President of the United States used a different flag on land. This was also blue with many white stars within its angles and a large crimson

▲ *ABOVE Royal flag of Poland (1605). Personal flag of King Sigismund III.*

▶ *FAR RIGHT ABOVE Flag of the Duke of Anhalt (1815–1918).*

▶ *FAR RIGHT BELOW Presidential flag of Germany (1919–1921).*

star in the centre, heavily outlined in white and defaced with the state coat of arms.

A variation of the second model was the field striped in the livery colours and/or swallow-tailed. Such, for example, were the Polish royal flags of the three kings from the Vasa dynasty (1587–1668).

The third model appeared next. The arms are displayed in the centre of a national flag or war ensign. The first of such flags was the war ensign

introduced in 1690 by Denmark. This had a white square placed in the centre, charged at first with the royal cipher and later with the whole achievement of the royal arms. This model became standard in Scandinavia and was later copied by many other countries.

The third model was adopted by Napoleon I, who in 1804 placed the state arms in gold in the centre of the French *Tricolore*, on which golden bees were scattered. This flag was again in use from 1852 to 1870, and since 1871 the French presidents have placed their ciphers in the centre. The first to add an additional device (the cross of Lorraine) was Charles de Gaulle. From 1974 to 1995 the French presidential flag was charged with the presidential emblem instead of a cipher.

FRENCH PRESIDENTIAL FLAGS

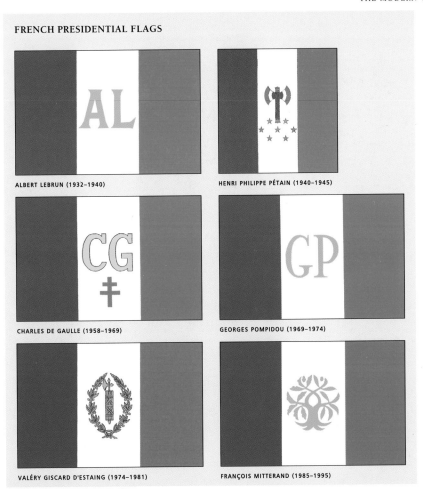

ALBERT LEBRUN (1932–1940)

HENRI PHILIPPE PÉTAIN (1940–1945)

CHARLES DE GAULLE (1958–1969)

GEORGES POMPIDOU (1969–1974)

VALÉRY GISCARD D'ESTAING (1974–1981)

FRANÇOIS MITTERAND (1985–1995)

The first major modification of the second model of the flag of a head of state was accomplished in 1828 when Austria changed the design of its imperial banner. A border in livery colours composed of white, red, yellow and black triangles was added to the yellow square field and the state arms were placed in the centre. This design was copied by Brunswick (1831–84), Bavaria and several other countries after World War I so it may be considered to be the fourth model.

Elaborate personal flags were introduced in 1844 in Prussia for the king, the queen and the crown prince and, although slightly modified in 1858 and 1889, they survived until 1918. Three elements of the design – the cross, the arms encircled with the collar of an order and the emblems in the corners – influenced not only the imperial flags of Germany but also the flags of other rulers. A very similar flag with a cross and three crowns in each corner was adopted by the grand duke of Oldeburg. The flag of the grand duke of Baden had a cross but the emblems in the corners were omitted. The royal flag of Italy, adopted in 1880, followed the Prussian design to some extent. The arms were placed in the centre of a square field and encircled with the collar of the Order of the Annunciation, and in each corner appeared a representation of the royal crown. Thus the fifth model of a royal or presidential flag was established.

FLAGS OF RULERS AND PRESIDENTS FOLLOWING THE AUSTRIAN DESIGN

EMPEROR OF AUSTRIA (1828–1894)

EMPEROR OF AUSTRIA – HUNGARY (1894–1915)

KING OF BULGARIA (1908–1918)

KING OF BULGARIA (1918–1947)

PRESIDENT OF CZECHOSLOVAKIA (1920–1939 AND 1945–1960)

PRESIDENT OF POLAND (1928–1945)

CHIEF OF THE HUNGARIAN STATE (1938–1945)

KING OF ROMANIA (1938–1947)

PRESIDENT OF SLOVAKIA (1939–1945)

CHIEF OF STATE OF CROATIA (1941–1945)

▶ **RIGHT** *King of Prussia's standard (1889–1918). Drawing by Hugo S. Ströhl.*
▶ **FAR RIGHT** *Crown prince of Prussia's standard (1889–1918).*
▶ **BELOW RIGHT** *Empress of Prussia's standard (1889–1918).*

▼ **BELOW** *German imperial flags: (first row) 1871–1890: emperor's standard, empress' standard, crown prince's standard; (second row) 1890–1918: emperor's standard, empress' standard, crown prince's standard.*

▲ *Above* Flag of the
king of Italy
(1880–1946).
▶ *Right* Flag of the
German chief of state
(Adolf Hitler)
(1935–1945).

▲ *Top* Flag of the king of
Württemberg (1884–1918).
▲ *Above* Egypt, royal naval
flag (1923–1952).

◀ *Left* Presidential flag of the
United States (1888–1945).

► *RIGHT Philippines presidential flag (1946).*

► *FAR RIGHT Standard of the Bey of Tunis (19th century to 1957), hand-painted by the Hydrographic and Oceanographic Service of the French Navy.*

When in 1916 the President of the United States decided to have just one flag for use both on land and at sea, he added a white star to each corner of his naval flag. This inspired several countries in Latin America and the Philippines to adopt similar flags. The American presidential flag was modified again in 1945, the four stars in the corners being replaced by a ring of 48 white stars (one for each state) encircling the coat of arms. The number of stars was increased to 49 in 1959 (for Alaska), and to 50 in 1960

Tunis combined emblems from the Turkish military flags with stripes in colours characteristic of the flags of North Africa. The King of Siam chose a blue field with a red border, charged with a combination of the attributes of his royal and military authority and the coat of arms.

In some countries, including Prussia and Germany, there were separate flags for the ruler's wife and for the crown prince. Some monarchies also had flags for the queen mother and other

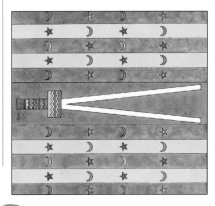

members of the royal family. In the last quarter of the 19th century, for example, Russia had five flags and five broad pennants for the members of the imperial family: empress, crown prince, crown princess, grand duke, grand duchess.

▼ *BELOW Thai royal flag.*

▲ *ABOVE Flag of the king of Annam, hand-painted by the Hydrographic and Oceanographic Service of the French Navy.*

(for Hawaii). The only country that has followed suit is the Philippines.

The models established in Europe for the flags of heads of state were widely copied in the Americas and partly in Africa and Asia. Some rulers, however, adopted flags of a quite different design. The King of Annam followed the pattern of the Chinese flags, while the Bey of

CURRENT PRESIDENTIAL AND ROYAL FLAGS

Contemporary presidential and royal flags are presented in this section in chronological order according to the appearance of each model of flag. The oldest model, the armorial banner, has been used as a personal flag without interruption only by the rulers of Great Britain. Since 1837 the British royal banner has been quarterly England (first and fourth quarters), Scotland (second quarter) and Ireland (third quarter). There are separate armorial banners for the Duke of Edinburgh, the Queen Mother, the Prince of Wales, Princess Margaret and the other members of the Royal Family. The last of these, identical to the royal banner with a border of ermine, made history when it covered the coffin of Princess Diana.

Queen Elizabeth II also has special royal banners when she visits her ex-dominions such as Canada, Australia, New Zealand and Jamaica, or other monarchies of which she is the head of state. If she is visiting a country for which no special banner has been designed, she uses her personal flag which is a blue fringed field with the initial "E" in gold and ensigned with the royal crown, all within a chaplet of golden roses. This flag was used for the first time during the Queen's visit to India in 1961.

Remarkably, armorial banners are used as the flags of heads of state not only in European countries with a long heraldic tradition, such as Norway and Ireland, but in countries where this

tradition is quite recent or non-existent. The oldest example is the royal banner of Tonga, introduced in 1862; another is the royal banner of Thailand, adopted in 1917, which displays the mythical Garuda, the bird of the god Vishnu. The banners of the presidents of Gabon and Guyana are fairly recent; the first was designed by Louis Mühlemann, the famous Swiss heraldist and vexillologist, the second by the College of Arms in London.

The largest group of current royal and presidential flags has a unicolour field charged with the arms or emblem, and in a few cases

▲ **ABOVE** *Royal banner of Great Britain (since 1837).*

◄ **LEFT** *Royal flag of Tonga (since 1862).*

◄ **LEFT** *Royal flag of Norway (since 1905).*

◄ **FAR LEFT** *The personal flag of Queen Elizabeth II.*

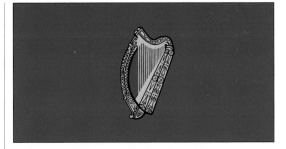 

displaying another device such as the party emblem (Kenya) or an inscription (Bangladesh, Kazakhstan, Malawi). The colour of the field is usually one of the colours of the national flag. Several presidential flags displaying the arms in the centre of a unicoloured field have a border of one to three colours. In the Czech Republic the border is patterned on the Austrian version.

There are several ways to deface a national flag with the arms or a presidential emblem.

They are usually positioned in the centre of the flag but sometimes appear in the upper hoist (Egypt, Finland, Morocco, Turkey), centre hoist (Eritrea, Namibia), top centre (Kuwait, Swaziland) or lower hoist (Saudi Arabia). In a few cases the emblem replaces the one on the national flag (Eritrea, Maldives, Pakistan).

The fifth, and last, model survived mainly in countries that copied the American flag. For example, the presidential flag of Cuba has

been modified to display six stars instead of four, and in the Peruvian flag the stars have been replaced by yellow suns.

These five models inspired the designs of almost all the flags adopted before World War II. Another model was added when the French colonies gained independence. This is the simplest model, a square and fringed variant of the national flag, used in some former French colonies south of the Sahara, and in Tunisia and Syria.

Several flags of heads of state defy classification. Their designs combine features of the first and fourth models (Slovakia), the second, fourth and fifth (Sri Lanka) or the third

and fourth (Liechtenstein). The presidential flag of India looks heraldic but instead of heraldic figures it displays the whole state arms, an elephant, scales and a vase of lotus flowers. The royal flag of the Netherlands is the only flag to have a cross as an additional charge. Around the arms is a ribbon with the insignia of the most distinguished Dutch military decoration, the Order of William.

▲ **ABOVE** (left to right) *Presidential flag of Israel (since 1948); presidential flag of Germany (since 1950); presidential flag of Italy (since 2000); presidential flag of Slovenia (since 1995).*
◄ **LEFT** *Presidential flag of the Czech Republic (since 1993).*

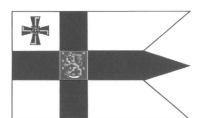

◄ **FAR LEFT TOP** *Presidential flag of Iceland (since 1944).*
◄ **FAR LEFT CENTRE** *Presidential flag of Finland (since 1978).*
◄ **FAR LEFT BOTTOM** *Royal flag of Denmark (since 1972).*
◄ **LEFT** *Presidential flag of Russia (since 1994).*

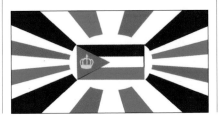

◄ **LEFT** *Presidential flag of the United States (since 1960).*

► **RIGHT** *Royal flag of the Netherlands (since 1908).*

◄ **LEFT** *Presidential flag of Lithuania (since 1993).*

▼ **BELOW LEFT TOP** *Presidential flag of South Korea (since 1967).*

▼ **BELOW LEFT CENTRE** *Presidential flag of India (since 1950).*

▼ **BELOW LEFT BOTTOM** *Royal flag of Jordan (since 1928).*

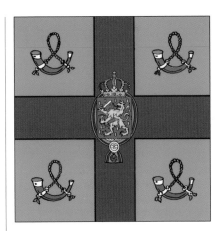

Many countries do not have a special flag for the head of state, including the sixteen monarchies under Queen Elizabeth II of Great Britain. Some one-party countries do not have presidential flags for political reasons and a few simply do not see the need for a special flag.

THE BASIC MODELS OF CURRENT HEAD OF STATE FLAGS

An armorial banner is used in:
GREAT BRITAIN, GUYANA, IRELAND, NORWAY, THAILAND, TONGA.

A unicolour flag defaced with the arms or an emblem is used in:
BANGLADESH, BOTSWANA, BRAZIL, BRUNEI, CAMBODIA, DOMINICA, FIJI, GAMBIA, GREECE, INDONESIA, JAPAN, KAZAKHSTAN, KENYA, KOREA, LITHUANIA, LUXEMBOURG, MALAWI, MALAYSIA, MAURITIUS, MONACO, MOROCCO, MOZAMBIQUE, PALAU, PHILIPPINES, PORTUGAL, SINGAPORE, SPAIN, THAILAND, TRINIDAD AND TOBAGO, UNITED STATES, ZAMBIA.

A national flag or ensign defaced with the arms or an emblem is used in:
AUSTRIA, BELARUS, BULGARIA, CHILE, COLOMBIA, DENMARK, EGYPT, ERITREA, ESTONIA, FINLAND, FRANCE, GABON, GUINEA, ICELAND, KUWAIT, LESOTHO, MADAGASCAR, MALDIVES, MOROCCO, NIGERIA, PAKISTAN, RUSSIA, SAUDI ARABIA, SENEGAL, SEYCHELLES, SUDAN, SURINAM, SWAZILAND, SWEDEN, TOGO, TUNISIA, TURKEY.

A flag with a border and defaced with the arms or emblem is used in:
CZECH REPUBLIC, GERMANY, ISRAEL, ITALY, NEPAL, ROMANIA, SLOVAKIA, SLOVENIA, TAIWAN, TANZANIA, UKRAINE, VANUATU.

A flag defaced with the state or royal arms and with an emblem repeated in all four corners or sides is used in:
ARGENTINA, BELGIUM, CUBA, LIBERIA, MALTA, THE NETHERLANDS, PARAGUAY, PERU, URUGUAY, VENEZUELA.

The heads of state of the following countries have flags that do not conform to any of the models described: CROATIA, DOMINICAN REPUBLIC, INDIA, JORDAN, LIECHTENSTEIN, NAMIBIA, NEPAL, OMAN, SLOVAKIA, SRI LANKA, TURKMENISTAN, UGANDA.

Government Flags

As well as a national flag, over 20 nations also have a state flag for use by government authorities. In five Scandinavian countries the state flag is a swallow-tailed or triple swallow-tailed version of the national flag. The state flags of other countries are their national flags but with the addition of the state arms in the centre.

The United States has one flag for all purposes, but the federal government and military authorities use it only in the official proportions of 10:19, making it the de facto state flag. The same flag in different proportions (2:3, 3:5 and 5:8) is the national flag for other uses, including use by the general public. There are no international regulations pertaining to the use of foreign flags in a country hosting an international conference or officials from a foreign country. Normally state flags should

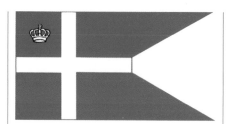

◀ *LEFT Denmark, state ensign (since 1907).*

◀ *LEFT Iceland, state flag and ensign (since 1918).*

be used but there are exceptions to this rule. At the United Nations headquarters in New York, although some countries (Austria, Denmark, Finland, Germany, Iceland, Monaco, Norway and Sweden) have both state and national flags, they choose to be represented by their national flag.

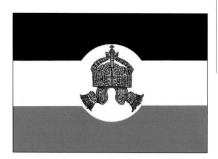

◀ *FAR LEFT TOP Germany, state flag (1893–1918).*
◀ *FAR LEFT BOTTOM Germany, state ensign (1893–1918).*
◀ *BELOW Mecklenburg, state flag (1900–1918).*

GOVERNMENT DEPARTMENTS AND AGENCIES

The United States is the only country with special flags for all its government departments, and some government agencies. They are displayed at, or on, the buildings of the departments and in the offices of high-ranking officials. The oldest is the flag of the National Aeronautics and Space Administration (NASA), introduced in 1960. Other countries have only a few departmental flags: Russia instituted a flag for its Finance Ministry in 1902, and Denmark adopted a flag for its Naval Ministry in 1916.

Many countries have flags for members of the government. The idea of distinguishing important members of the imperial or royal household with flags probably originated in highly hierarchical societies such as China, Russia and Prussia. From China the custom spread to several countries in South-east Asia such as Kelantan, one of the member-states of Malaysia. In the 1930s Kelantan had seven flags for the members of the royal family and the titled members of the royal dynasty, nine for members of the government and eight for the chiefs of districts.

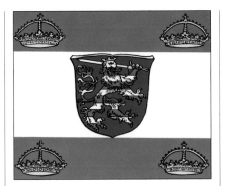

◀ *LEFT Hesse, state flag (1902–1918).*

◀ *LEFT US Department of Treasury (since 1963).*

◀ *BELOW Flags of Kelantan.*

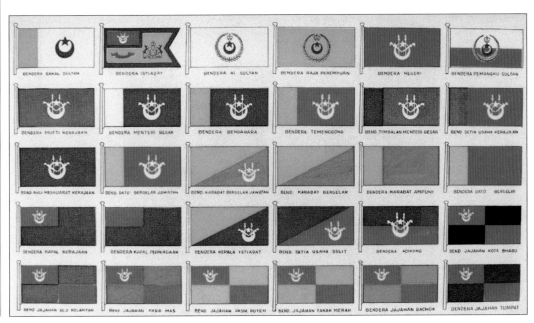

BENDERA BAKAL SULTAN	BENDERA ISTIADAT	BENDERA AL SULTAN	BENDERA RAJA PEREMPUAN	BENDERA NEGERI	BENDERA PEMANGKU SULTAN
BENDERA MUFTI KERAJAAN	BENDERA MENTERI BESAR	BENDERA BENDAHARA	BENDERA TEMENGGONG	BEND. TIMBALAN MENTERI BESAR	BEND SETIA USAHA KERAJAAN
BEND AHLI MESHUARAT KERAJAAN	BEND. DATO' BERGELAR JAWATAN	BEND. KARABAT BERGELAR JAWATAN	BEND. KARABAT BERGELAR	BENDERA KARABAT AMPUNI	BENDERA DATO BERGELAR
BENDERA KAPAL KERAJAAN	BENDERA KAPAL PERNIAGAAN	BENDERA KEPALA ISTIADAT	BEND. SETIA USAHA SULIT	BENDERA ADIKONG	BEND JAJAHAN KOTA BHARU
BEND JAJAHAN ULU KELANTAN	BEND JAJAHAN PASIR MAS	BEND JAJAHAN PASIR PUTEH	BEND. JAJAHAN TANAH MERAH	BENDERA JAJAHAN BACHOK	BENDERA JAJAHAN TUMPAT

  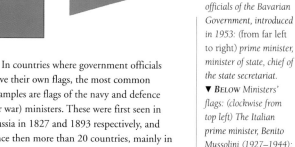

In monarchies, and also in some countries with a republican government, there were (and in a few instances still are) flags for the prime minister. In the past the prime ministers of Italy, Greece and South Africa had their own distinctive flags. Countries that still have a flag for the prime minister include Portugal, Spain, Japan, the Maldives, Thailand, the Bahamas, Barbados, Jamaica, Surinam, and Trinidad and Tobago. In most of Germany there are different flags for the members of the local government (prime minister, ministers, state secretaries, senators and council members).

In countries where government officials have their own flags, the most common examples are flags of the navy and defence (or war) ministers. These were first seen in Russia in 1827 and 1893 respectively, and since then more than 20 countries, mainly in Europe and the Americas, have adopted separate flags for their ministers. Portugal, the United States and Chile have separate flags for their defence minister and their navy minister. Spain, Austria, Thailand, Chile and Ecuador have a separate flag that can be used by other cabinet ministers.

◀ *LEFT Car flags of the officials of the Bavarian Government, introduced in 1953: (from far left to right) prime minister, minister of state, chief of the state secretariat.*

▼ *BELOW Ministers' flags: (clockwise from top left) The Italian prime minister, Benito Mussolini (1927–1944); prime minister of the Bahamas (since 1973); Russian navy minister (1827–1918); German defence minister (1935–1945); Spanish navy minister.*

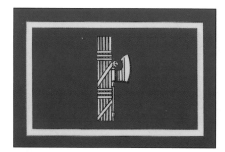 

► **RIGHT** Ministers in the United States: Secretary of State, under Secretary of State; secretary of war, assistant secretary of war; secretary of treasury, under secretary of treasury; assistant secretary of treasury, attorney general.

▼ **BELOW** Current flags of Ministers of defence: (from top) Great Britain, France, Japan, Italy, Slovenia, Colombia.

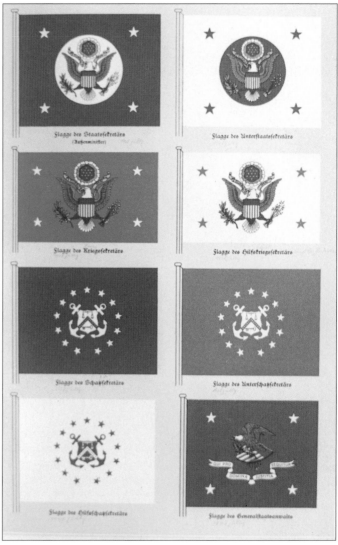

◀ ▼ *LEFT AND BELOW*
*Current distinguishing
flags in the United
States:* (left to right
from top left)
*Secretary of defense,
deputy Secretary of
defense, Under
Secretaries of defense,
assistant Secretaries of
defense, secretary of
the army, secretary
of the navy, secretary of
the air force.*

The most complete set of flags for government officials, as well as departments, is in the United States, where in all departments there are separate flags for the secretary, under-secretary and assistant secretary. The heads of

The Danish flag is the war ensign with a white crown in the canton; the government vessels of Fiji display the national flag with the field changed to dark blue. The field of the government vessels' flags in India and Sri Lanka

many government agencies and services also have their own distinguishing flags. The first to possess his own flag was the secretary of the navy in 1866, followed by the secretary of war in 1897.

In many countries government-owned vessels and vessels that provide services for the government do not fly the civil ensign. In New Zealand and Peru they hoist the national flag but in Argentina, the Dominican Republic, Ecuador, Haiti and Venezuela they hoist the state flag. Denmark, Belgium and some Commonwealth countries have special flags for government service vessels.

is also dark blue, with the national flag in the canton and an emblem in the fly which consists of a golden anchor and two crossed golden anchors, respectively. A few countries also have ensigns for vessels providing specialized services such as fishery control or lighthouse services.

▼ *BELOW Flags of
government service
vessels:* (left to right)
The Bahamas, India.

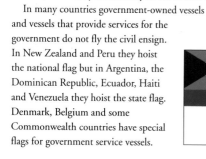

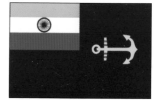

GOVERNORS AND ENVOYS

The colonies of European powers were at first administrated by the trade companies such as the East India Company, but in the 19th century this role was taken over by governors who acted as the representatives of the crown or government. Their flags followed the pattern of the national flag (Germany, the Netherlands, Spain, Belgium); displayed the national flag in the canton (France); or were charged with the state arms (Italy, Portugal).

Since 1891 the Italians had had a flag for their governors and in the 1930s they adopted a different one for the viceroy of Ethiopia which was white with a blue border, the state arms in the centre and yellow fasces in the corners. Portugal had three flags for its governors, all of which displayed the same emblem of the state arms on the cross of the Order of Christ. The flag of the Portuguese governor-

Governor of Belgian Congo.

general is illustrated; the flag of the governor had two vertical green stripes instead of horizontal ones; the flag of the governor of a district had one horizontal stripe.

Great Britain introduced two different flags for the representatives of the king or queen in its dominions and colonies. The flag of the governor-general of a dominion is dark blue, with the royal crest in the centre and the name of the dominion in a scroll beneath. A governor or lieutenant-governor uses the Union flag with a badge on a white disc surrounded by a garland of laurel superimposed on the centre of the flag. The last flag remains unchanged to this day but some of the governor-generals' flags have been diversified by the addition of local emblems such as a maple leaf (Canada), a whale's tooth (Fiji) and a two-headed frigate bird (Solomon Islands). In Canada the lieutenant-governors of the provinces have flags, of which only the flag of the lieutenant-governor of Nova Scotia follows the British pattern, with a garland of

Governor of German colonies.

Governor-general of Dutch colonies.

Governor of the Italian colonies.

Governor-general of Portuguese colonies.

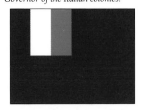

Governor of French West Africa.

Governor of Surinam.

Governor-general of Australia (1902–1936).

Governor-general of Pakistan.

Governor-general of South East Asia.

Governor-general of the West Indies.

Governor-general of the Union of South Africa.

Governor-general of the Federation of Rhodesia and Nyasaland.

▲ **ABOVE** *Historic flags of governors.*

Governor-general of Gibraltar.

Administrator of the French Southern and Antarctic Territory.

▲ **ABOVE** *Current flags of governors.*

maple instead of laurel. The flags of other lieutenant-governors (except that of Quebec) have the same design as that of the lieutenant-governor of British Colombia.

A few countries have special flags for their diplomatic representatives. The first were introduced in Russia in 1833 for the ambassador or envoy extraordinary, consul-general, consul and chargé d'affaires or resident. The flag of the ambassador was in the form of the Russian jack, with the small imperial arms in the white canton. The national flag with the war ensign in the canton, served as the flag of the consul-general, and the flag of the consul was a swallow-tailed version of the consul-general flag. The flag of the chargé d'affaires or resident was white, with the war ensign in the canton. The

designs of these flags were changed in 1870, and again in 1896. Not many countries followed suit but among them were China, Italy and Thailand, which adopted their diplomatic flags at the end of the 19th century. In the 20th century the United States introduced a flag for consuls and flags for envoys were also introduced by Iran (the ambassador's flag and the flag of the envoy extraordinary), Egypt, Spain, Colombia and Mexico (the flag of the Diplomatic Corps and the Consular Corps).

Great Britain has two flags for its diplomats. The flag of an ambassador is the Union flag with the royal arms on a disc encircled by a garland of laurel superimposed in the centre. The consul's flag is identical except that it displays the royal crown instead of the arms.

POST, CUSTOMS AND COASTGUARD FLAGS

The first flag for customs vessels was introduced by Denmark in 1778. It was a specially marked Danish war ensign and was flown by vessels when hailing other ships in the course of duty. In 1793 Denmark adopted a similar flag for mail-carrying ships. At the end of the 18th century two other countries, Spain in 1793 and the United States in 1799, adopted flags for their customs vessels. It was prescribed that the American Revenue ensign, as it was called, would be used by cutters and boats employed in the service of the Revenue and would be "always displayed over the custom-houses of the United States, and over the buildings appertaining to the Treasury Department of the United States". The ensign, which underwent some minor alterations, is still in use today at sea.

Flags for both post and customs services were introduced by Great Britain in the early 19th century; by Russia in 1849 (post) and 1858 (customs); Prussia in 1863; and Norway in 1898. In this century both post and customs flags were adopted by the other Scandinavian countries, as well as by Thailand and Mexico. Currently customs flags are also used in Spain, Russia, Turkey, Brazil, China and Tonga.

France, the United States, Poland and a few other countries use a distinctive post flag. In some countries there are two post flags of different designs; one is flown from the post office's buildings, the other is flown from mail-carrying vessels.

In most countries the responsibility to guard territorial waters and fight against smugglers belongs to the navy and, indeed, it is the only task of the naval forces of most countries in the Caribbean, Africa and Oceania. In some countries, however, guarding the coastline is the

▼ *BELOW Current customs flags: (left to right) Denmark, Great Britain, Russia, Turkey, China, United States, Spain, Ukraine.*

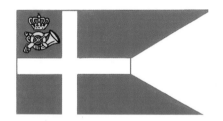

◄ **LEFT** *Post flags: (top row) Norway (since 1898); France (since 1933). (second row) Denmark (since 1939); Free City of Danzig (1922–1939). (third row, far left only) Germany (1950–1995).*

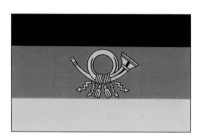

◄▼ **LEFT AND BELOW** *Current coastguard flags: (clockwise from left) United States, Russia, Great Britain.*

duty of a special force, the coastguard, which is not actually a part of the navy. The United States Coastguard has the longest-standing traditions. Their ensign was based on the revenue ensign flown on ships of the Revenue Cutter Service. The name "coastguard" was first used in 1915 when the Revenue Cutter Service merged with the Life-saving Service. The current United States Coastguard ensign was introduced in 1966 and a similar one with six vertical stripes was soon adopted by Haiti. Other countries that currently use a distinctive coastguard flag include Great Britain, Poland, Russia and Yugoslavia.

POLICE FLAGS

Only a few countries have police flags displayed at police stations or elsewhere outdoors. Generally they are of two types: a ceremonial flag made of expensive fabric with embroidered police badges, designed for the interior of the building, or a flag that resembles a military colour. In some countries there is also a distinguishing flag for police commandants, used both as a decoration of office and as a car flag.

The same devices appear regularly on police flags. A flaming grenade is an emblem that Napoleon I granted to his élite troops as a battle honour and it is now used as a police emblem in France, Belgium, the Netherlands and Italy. Another device is a silver (white) star with five to nine points made of different-length rays which is found on police emblems on all continents but mainly in Great Britain and Commonwealth countries, the United States and Germany. Police flags are flown on police stations in Great Britain, Turkey, Finland, Israel and Japan.

In France there is no police flag. The organization of the police resembles that of the military so there are regimental and battalion

▼ **BELOW** *Police flags: (clockwise from top left) Finland, Turkey, Bermuda (central emblem), Brabant, Gendarmerie mobile standard (France).*

standards, in the same design as military colours. The units of the Gendarmerie Mobile and Gendarmerie Départementale have standards with their names in semi-circles above and below a flaming grenade, and the reverse bears a shield with the regional arms or the arms of the legion. Belgium also does not have a police flag but it has a flag for the commandant of gendarmerie, the commandants of the six regions, the commandants of the Mobile Legion and the Royal School of Gendarmerie. These are used in offices and as a car flags.

The Royal Canadian Mounted Police (RCMP) adopted its flag in 1991, together with flags for its divisions in all provinces and territories. All of them have a red field with a blue canton bordered with yellow and defaced with the badge of the RCMP. The flags of the divisions have an emblem in the lower hoist displaying the most characteristic figure from the arms of the province or territory.

In some countries there is a specialized harbour police. Its vessels fly distinctive ensigns, which generally consist of the national or war ensign charged with the police badge.

Military Signs

The flag epitomizes for an army the high principles for which it strives in battle … It keeps men's motives lofty even in mortal combat, making them forgetful of personal gain and of personal revenge, but eager for personal sacrifice in the cause of country they serve.

GILBERT GROSVENOR, *SPECIAL EDITION OF THE NATIONAL GEOGRAPHIC MAGAZINE "FLAGS OF THE WORLD"*, WASHINGTON, 1917.

We shall probably never know when and where vexilloids were first used in battle, but it is safe to guess that large groups of early warriors had signs to rally around and to follow. The oldest surviving vexilloids, from Egypt, follow definite patterns, suggesting that they had evolved from earlier models.

From earliest times a vexilloid or flag carried in battle had a semi-sacred quality. In the Middle Ages and subsequent centuries a new flag was consecrated before a battle and blessed by priests, and after the campaign it was kept in a local church. Mercenaries, and later the soldiers of standing armies, took a holy oath to defend their "colour" to the death. At the time of the crusades, banners with a cross prevailed, but soon armorial banners and pennons, standards and guidons were introduced. Many troops used banners with religious motifs, such as painted figures of the Virgin Mary and Child or various saints.

By the 16th century the banners carried by infantry had reached enormous dimensions, and in the cavalry a large swallow-tailed pennon was the most common form of flag. In the first half of the 17th century regiments began to wear uniforms, and the flags of both infantry and cavalry were therefore in the same colours. Military banners in France, Spain and England acquired marks of national identification: a white cross, the cross of Burgundy and the cross of St George, respectively.

Regulations adopted in the 18th century prescribed both the design and the number of colours in a regiment, and from then on the colour consisted of a staff with a finial and a flag. These three parts were inseparable and had to be treated as a simple unit; sometimes saving just the colour's finial from a battlefield saved the honour of the unit. Standardization gradually occurred in most countries, and more colours acquired national characters. The armed forces of many countries also adopted a wide range of other flags to distinguish the branches of the armed forces and the ranks of their commanders.

◀ *LEFT Banner of the Republic of Venice (15th century).*

BATTLE BANNERS

In the Middle Ages five types of flag were used on a battlefield. Three of them (banner, pennon and pencel) bore the owners' arms, the other two (standard and guidon) were in the livery colours with badges. Most important was the banner representing the troops of the king, prince, duke, earl, baron or bishop, and the banners of the military orders. Royal banners are described in the chapter *Emperors, Sovereigns and Presidents*, but the flag of the Teutonic Order and some territorial flags are illustrated here. The pennon was the personal flag of a knight bachelor responsible for smaller formations of men. The pencel, or *pennoncelle*, was the personal flag of a knight, carried on a lance. The standard and the guidon were used by the infantry and cavalry, respectively, to identify bodies of troops within an army.

▼ *BELOW Territorial flags in the 14th century:* (from left to right) *Teutonic Order; Silesia; Pomerania; Bishopric of Warmia.*

The 16th century witnessed an entirely new way of conducting warfare. In some countries, mainly the German states, mercenaries replaced troops in a province or country. The ruler contracted an experienced soldier to raise and lead a regiment of infantry and provided arms and flags for each company, with up to ten flags for the whole regiment. The design of these banners was usually based on multiple divisions of the field (horizontal, vertical, diagonal and combinations of these) and simple charges such as bend, cross or saltire and narrow wavy triangles. The banners were called *Landknechtsfahnen*, after the German word *Landknecht* (foot-soldier). The banners of these regiments became more elaborate in the 17th century, and regiments fighting on the Protestant side often displayed flags that insulted the

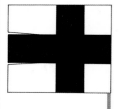   

In contrast with the earlier simplicity, the armorial banners of the 15th century were made of costly materials decorated with rich embroidery. Heraldic figures became very ornate and battle banners with religious motifs gradually became more numerous, the most popular being the Virgin Mary and Child or Christ on the Cross. Spain, Austria and Bavaria used a border on their colours, which was not seen on the colours of Protestant countries. The custom of using religious motifs on military flags survived into the 20th century. The Virgin Mary appeared on Austrian colours until 1938; Christ's Passion was depicted on many Russian colours in the 19th century; St Andrew and his cross appeared on the Serbian colours carried in World War I and St George slaying the dragon was painted on the colours of the Greek Army.

▼ *BELOW* (top) *Bavarian infantry (17th century);* (bottom) *Polish cavalry (17th century).*

Catholic Church and the clergy, or scenes from fables such as a bear with lambs or a fox with hens. Both sides began to use propaganda slogans and allegorical emblems such as the Roman goddesses Fortuna and Justice, an arm in armour emerging from a cloud, or a lion trampling a fallen warrior.

At the beginning of the 17th century the standing armies established permanent units divided into a regular number of companies, with a clear division between infantry and cavalry. Banners reached enormous sizes, exceeding the men's height. During the Thirty Years War (1618–1648) the company under the command of the colonel adopted a different-coloured flag to the other companies in the regiment. In most countries white was chosen for the field of the colonel's flag.

STANDARDIZATION OF COLOURS

Regimentation and standardization began early in the 17th century. The infantry regiments were divided into three wings, each with a distinctive flag. They began to display the colours of the uniforms, the wings being distinguished only by different heraldic badges or symbols. In some countries the colours bore national symbols such as the cross of St George or the cross of Burgundy, in which case they revealed country, regiment and battalion at a glance. A century later the number of wings was reduced to two and so there were only two colours. The first was generally called the "king's or sovereign's colour" and was a symbol of allegiance and service to monarch and country. It was borne by the first battalion, originally the colonel's battalion, and was therefore referred to as the "colonel's colour". The second was known as the "battalion colour" ("regimental colour" in Great Britain and the United States) and represented the honour and traditions of the regiment and the soldier's duty to the regiment.

The first national symbol to appear on military flags was the red cross of Burgundy, introduced in 1516 as the main device of the flags of the Spanish infantry. Under a decree of 1707, each battalion had three colours, and the 1st Battalion carried the colonel's colour, white, with the cross of Burgundy and badges between

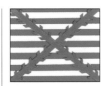

▲ ABOVE *(from top) Spanish colours: Regt. infantry banner (1550); colonel's infantry (1707); regt. infantry (1775); colonel's infantry (1802).*

▲ ◀ ABOVE AND LEFT *French colours: (above) Regiment of Picardy (1597); (left) infantry colour (1812).*

its arms. The regimental colours had fields in the regiment's facing colours or in the principal colour of the coat of arms from the place where the regiment was formed; a badge and the name of the unit were in the centre. In the late 16th century the fields of some flags became multicoloured, borders were added, and some fields and borders displayed very intricate designs. A decree of 1728 introduced a new model of the colonel's colour and provided each battalion with two colours: the 1st Battalion having the colonel's colour and one battalion colour, both white. The battalion colour had the cross of Burgundy with a badge at each end, while the colonel's colour displayed the royal arms with the Order of the Golden Fleece and the provincial arms in each corner. On the reverse the arms were placed on the cross of Burgundy with the provincial arms at each end, and were supported by two red lions. In 1808 the number of colours was reduced to one per battalion: the 1st Battalion used the king's colour in the same design as the previous colonel's colour, and the battalion colour remained unchanged.

The next to standardize their battle flags were the French in 1597. The flags were square, with a width exceeding 180 cm (6 ft). They were divided by a white cross and the four parts of the field displayed the regimental colours. The first four permanent regiments were assigned the following colours: red (Picardy), green (Champagne), gold (Navarre) and black (Piedmont). The colours of the other regiments had fields in two or three colours. Borders and simple devices (squares, fleurs-de-lis, crowns) or mottoes were added, but the basic design survived until 1794. In 1804 Napoleon I introduced the famous "eagles", named after the finial in the form of an eagle of ancient Rome. The plinth on which the eagle stood bore metal numerals indicating the regiment to which the colour belonged. The design was changed in 1812, and again in 1815. The French pattern of colours was adopted by Italy, and in the 20th century by many countries in Europe and elsewhere.

▲ *ABOVE Prussian colours (from left to right) Infantry colour (1701–1729); infantry colour (late 18th century).*

The first colours of the Prussian infantry, introduced in 1701, had a central oval emblem containing the Prussian eagle encircled by a wreath and ensigned with the royal crown, with the royal ciphers in the corners. There were two flags for each battalion. The first flag of the 1st Battalion was called the *Leibfahne*, the second the *Regimentsfahne*. The 2nd battalion had two *Regimentsfahnen* in the same design but with the colours interchanged. The *Leibfahne* had the centre in the regiment's colour and the field in the same colour as the centre of the *Regimentsfahne*. In 1729 a cross was added to the field, which was either wavy or straight. The Prussian design was followed by Baden, Brunswick and Hesse during the Napoleonic Wars, and by Saxony (1735–1810), Russia (1800–57), Bavaria (1841–1918) and Poland (1919).

The first standardization of Russian military flags was carried out in 1712, when the infantry and dragoon regiments obtained flags in the same design. Usually the fields were unicolours, some with simple divisions or charges such as a cross or saltire. The regimental emblem appeared in the upper hoist, with the heraldic charge of the province or town after which the regiment was named. In 1727 the colonel's

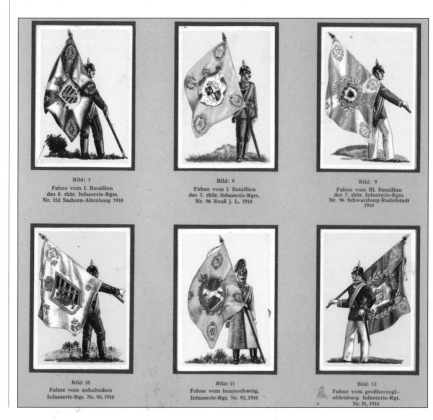

▶ *RIGHT German colours in 1910. Plate from the Fahnen und Standartenträger.*

Bild: 7
Fahne vom I. Bataillon des 8. thür. Infanterie-Rgts. Nr. 153 Sachsen-Altenburg 1910

Bild: 8
Fahne vom I. Bataillon des 7. thür. Infanterie-Rgts. Nr. 96 Reuß j. L. 1910

Bild: 9
Fahne vom III. Bataillon des 7. thür. Infanterie-Rgts. Nr. 96 Schwarzburg-Rudolstadt 1910

Bild: 10
Fahne vom anhaltischen Infanterie-Rgt. Nr. 93, 1910

Bild: 11
Fahne vom braunschweig. Infanterie-Rgt. Nr. 92, 1910

Bild: 12
Fahne vom großherzogl.-oldenburg. Infanterie-Rgt. Nr. 91, 1910

colour in both the infantry and cavalry attained national character. It was white, with a large representation of the imperial arms, and the company and squadron flags had fields in the regiment's facing colour, with a border of triangles. The emblem was the crowned imperial cipher encircled by a wreath, underneath which was a scroll with the regiment's name. Each infantry regiment received a colonel's colour and six company colours, and each dragoon regiment received a colonel's colour and eight squadron guidons. Under Catherine the Great the design of the Russian colours gradually changed until in 1800 it was nearly identical to that of Prussia. Further minimal changes took place in 1803 and 1813. After 1813 the colours of the line infantry were green with white corners; the colours of the guard infantry had the same design, but with yellow fields and corners in different colours.

The first detailed regulations governing the design of British colours were issued in 1747 and reduced the number of flags to two per battalion of the line infantry. The first was the King's colour, i.e. the Union flag with the regimental badge in the centre. Badges recalling service overseas were the green dragon (China), the sphinx (Egypt), the tiger (Bengal) and the elephant (India), and each badge was encircled by a wreath of roses (England) and thistles (Scotland). The other flag was the regimental colour, usually in the regimental facing colour with a small Union flag in the canton and the same badges as on the king's colour. In 1801 the Irish cross of St Patrick was added to the Union flag and the shamrock to the wreath.

The common element of the colours of Swiss regiments in foreign services were the "flammes", long wavy triangles radiating in all directions from the centre to the edges of the field. They were mostly in the livery colours of the regimental owners or commanders. This design was created at the end of the 17th century as the ordnance flag of regiments in service to the king of France and it was later introduced by other Swiss troops in service in the Netherlands, Spain, Venice, England and Naples.

In 1796 the United States Army introduced colours for the infantry. The national colour was blue with a representation of the national arms (in many artistic variations) in gold, and a golden scroll with the name of the regiment; the regimental colours were white or yellow. Very similar colours were used by the cavalry until 1895. In 1841 the infantry were given entirely different colours resembling the national flag.

▲ *ABOVE Austrian colours: (left) Regimental colour (1806–1815); (right) infantry colour (1915–1918).*

◀ *FAR LEFT Battalion colour of the Cisalpine Republic.*
◀ *LEFT Polish legion in Lombardy. Colour of the 1st Battalion of Riflemen.*

appeared in the centre of the company's colour and in the upper hoist of the king's colour. In the kingdom of Hanover, where the same custom applied, the provincial arms were placed in the corners of the military colours. Similarily, the colours of the Spanish infantry bore the provincial arms in all four corners, and the arms of the province encircled by a wreath was the central device for the Finnish colours during World War II.

▲ *ABOVE AND LEFT* (clockwise from far left) *Colours of Swiss troops in foreign services: Spain, France, Great Britain, Holy See.*

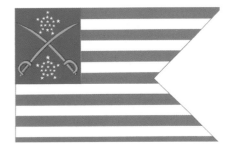

The arrangement of the stars on the new colours varied considerably, as did their colour (white, yellow or gold) and number of points. During the Civil War the Southern armies' battle flag and colours were based on the national flag's design, with inscriptions identifying the regiment and places of victorious battles.

As well as the national symbol, many of the colours used by different armies also carry symbols of the province of the regiment's origin. In Sweden, where regiments were named after provinces, the arms of the province

▲ *ABOVE Colours of the United States: (left to right) Infantry colour (1841 model); artillery regimental colour (Civil War period); first cavalry division (Civil War period).*

▲ *LEFT Battle flag of the Confederacy States of America (1861–1865).*

BATTLE HONOURS

In ancient Rome the military standards, or vexilloids, of the bravest troops were augmented with battle honours, in the form of crowns, wreaths, medals or rings attached to the staff. In modern times there have been several methods of distinguishing a military colour with battle honours: an inscription sewn or painted on the field; a ring attached to the staff; a streamer with metal plates or with embroidered or painted inscriptions; or the order, or other decoration, pinned to the flag or the cravat.

In modern times, the custom first developed in the Prussian Army at the beginning of the 18th century. The awards took the form of a ribbon with a small metal plate, tied to the top of the staff. In 1785 three regiments of the Army of Hanover received the first honours in the form of golden embroidered inscriptions.

In the French Army the first battle honours were added to the colours in 1791. After 1808 the honours were restricted to major victories where Napoleon commanded in person: Ulm, Austerlitz, Jena, Eylau, Friedland, Eckmühl, Essling and Wagram, Marengo and Moscowa (Moscow). In Britain the practice of naming the places of great victories on the colours themselves was sanctioned in 1811. After 1844 the addition of battle honours was allowed only for the regimental colour. The most often awarded honours were for the Battle of Waterloo and the Peninsula war.

In the United States Army awards were inscribed on flags long before the first regulation

allowed this in 1862. During the Civil War the first battle honour appeared in the form of streamers with inscriptions. This practice was supported by many, both military and civilians, who believed that nothing should be allowed to mar the stripes of the national flag. This sentiment grew and in 1890 the United States Army decided to use awards in the form of silver rings or bands only, and in 1920 they were replaced with streamers. The Marine Corps followed suit in 1939, the Air Force in 1956, the Coastguard in 1968 and the Navy in 1971. Today the honours earned by a unit are displayed as streamers attached to the staff of the unit's battle and organizational colour. There are fewer than ten award streamers (commendations and presidential citations) but over 100 campaign streamers.

◄ LEFT Battle awards in the form of streamers: (left) the 3rd Infantry Regiment of Württemberg; (right) the 1st Regiment of Saxon Grenadiers (c.1900).

▼ BELOW Current colours: (from left to right) Germany, Poland, Portugal.

FLAGS OF ARMED FORCES

Many flags have been designed since World War II for use at ceremonies and parades as well as inside offices or headquarters buildings. At least three countries have a special flag for their armed forces as a whole. The flag of the British Joint Services, introduced in 1964, is composed of three vertical stripes of dark blue (the Royal Navy), red (the Army) and light blue (the Royal Air Force). In the centre is a black emblem: a foul anchor for the Navy, two swords for the Army and an eagle for the Air Force. A similar emblem designed for the Canadian armed forces in 1968 is blue on the white field of the Canadian forces ensign, which also serves as the naval jack. China has a flag for use by its Army, Navy and Air Force. It resembles the national flag but instead

▲ *Above left* Canadian forces ensign.
▲ *Above right* Chinese armed forces flag.
▲ *Right* Poland: (from top to bottom) Branches of the armed forces since 1993: Army, Navy, Air Force.

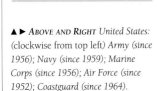

▲▶ *Above and Right* United States: (clockwise from top left) Army (since 1956); Navy (since 1959); Marine Corps (since 1956); Air Force (since 1952); Coastguard (since 1964).

of stars has stylized characters for "8" and "1" to commemorate the date of the foundation of the People's Liberation Army, 1 August 1928.

A few countries have flags for each branch of the armed forces. The United States and South Korea also have a flag for their Marine Corps, and the United States has a fifth flag for its Coastguard. In 1962 the United States Army field flag was introduced. It is the same design as the army flag with an ultramarine blue field, the army emblem (without the Roman numerals) in white and a white scroll inscribed in scarlet. Others authorized to use this flag include separate brigades such as divisions, numbered commands,

▲ *ABOVE Israel:* (from left to right) *Army, Navy, Air Force.*

general officer commands, headquarters of the United States Army garrisons, missions, recruiting main stations and the regional headquarters of the Reserve Officers' Training Corps.

A set of flags for the Polish armed forces was introduced in 1993; their main characteristic was uniform shape and colour. The fields are defaced with representations of the metal cap badges of each branch of the armed forces. The flags of the three branches of the armed forces in Israel have either the national flag in the canton or the flag design on the field. They also have distinctive finials in the same shape as the emblem on the particular flag.

The first army flag was probably the Chinese one, introduced in 1911. Great Britain also chose red for the background of its army flag, adopted in 1938, with the royal crest on two crossed swords. A similar flag was adopted for the Army of Independent India. The army flags of Colombia and Indonesia have a unicoloured field defaced with the army emblem, and the army flags of Japan and Taiwan are variations of the national flag. In other countries the army uses the national flag with an emblem in the centre (Thailand) or in the upper hoist (such as the two crossed sabres of Egypt or the army emblem of Kuwait).

▶ ▼ *RIGHT AND BELOW Army flags:* (from left to right) *China (1911–1928), Great Britain, India, Jordan, Japan, Taiwan, South Korea.*

AIR FORCE FLAGS

Air force flags are flown on land at airfields and where units are stationed. They are also hoisted on a small staff over an aircraft when VIPs are embarking or disembarking.

The first flag for use by the aeronautic division of the army was introduced in Russia at the end of the 19th century. It was similar to many flags used by the navy, a white field with the jack in the canton but with the centre of the fly defaced with the aeronautical emblem in red. The British Air Force flag, introduced in 1918, was patterned on the navy ensigns but with light blue for the field. This colour and the design of the British Air Force flag have been adopted by many countries.

Many countries adopted air force flags with the light blue field but without the canton. Zambia has a roundel in the centre, while Japan, South Korea, Taiwan, Indonesia,

▼ *BELOW Air force flags: (from left to right) United Kingdom, Colombia, India, Sri Lanka, Malaysia, Belgium, Taiwan, Poland.*

the Philippines and Colombia have the air force emblem in the centre. Belgium positioned the air force emblem in the upper hoist and the roundel in the centre, and Kuwait positioned the emblem in the centre and the roundel in the upper hoist. The air force flag of the Netherlands is blue with an orange pile charged with a flying eagle under a crown. The design of the Israeli Air Force's flag resembles the national flag but the shield of David is solid. The flag of the Australian Air Force is a light blue version of the national flag, with the roundel in the lower hoist.

The fields of the air force flags of Spain, Poland and Thailand consist of the national flag. The air force emblem appears in the centre of the top stripe (Spain) or in the centre (Thailand). The Spanish flag also displays the state arms in the centre.

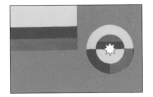

AIR FORCE FLAGS OF THE BRITISH MODEL

The air force flags of the following countries have a light blue field, a canton with the national flag and the air force roundel in the fly:
CANADA, COLOMBIA, EGYPT, GHANA, GREAT BRITAIN, INDIA, JORDAN, KENYA, MALAYSIA, MYANMAR, NEW ZEALAND, OMAN, PAKISTAN, SAUDI ARABIA, SINGAPORE, SRI LANKA, SUDAN.

DISTINGUISHING FLAGS

In most republican countries the head of state is also the commander-in-chief of the armed forces, so there are no special flags for the commander-in-chief. In monarchies such flags are also very rare, although Sweden has such a flag. In some countries there are separate flags for the commanders-in-chief of the army and navy.

Distinguishing flags of chiefs of staff are more common. In Great Britain and Italy the chiefs of the defence staffs have flags, as do the chiefs of

the general staff or the chiefs of the staff of the army and/or the air force in many other countries.

The largest set of these flags is in the United States, where the armed forces use many distinguishing flags. For example, the Army's own flags are adjutant general, chief of the army reserve, judge advocate general, chief of chaplains, chief of the national guard bureau, chief of engineers, surgeon general and inspector general.

▲ ◀ ▼ *ABOVE, LEFT AND BELOW Flags of chiefs of staff: Great Britain, chief of defence staff; France, chief of general staff; Italy, chief of defence staff.*

◀ *FAR LEFT The flag of the commander-in-chief of the armed forces, Sweden.*

▼ *BELOW Flags of the chiefs of staffs in the United States: (left) Joint chiefs of staff chairman; (right) joint chiefs of staff vice-chairman.*

The rank flags of the United States Army correspond with those of the Navy, but the Army uses red for the field colour.

There are also rank flags for the National Guard, blue with the crest of the individual State Army National Guard. The lieutenant-general's flag has three white stars, one on each side of the crest and one above the crest. Two other flags have the crest in the centre of the field: the flag of the major general has one star on each side of the crest; the brigadier general's flag has one star above the crest.

▲ ▶*ABOVE AND RIGHT Rank flags in the United States Army: (clockwise from far left) General of the army, general, lieutenant general, major general, brigadier general.*

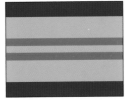
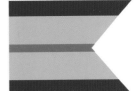

▲ *ABOVE Rank flags in the British Royal Air Force: (from left to right) Marshal, air marshal, air vice-marshal, air commodore.*

▶ *RIGHT Flag of the lieutenant general of the National Guard in New Mexico.*

Naval Ensigns and Flags

At sea, flags became a necessity from the first time a ship ventured out of its home waters. Wherever men have sailed on the oceans their flags have indicated their nationality and allegiance and the ship without a flag has justly been recognized in international law as a pirate.

WHITNEY SMITH, *THE FLAGBOOK OF THE UNITED STATES*, NEW YORK, 1970

The main flag on a ship of war is the war ensign, which identifies its nationality; the jack has a similar function to this. Rank flags and commission pennants indicate the rank of the ship's commander.

For centuries most flags were designed for use at sea rather than on land. The first markings of ownership and nationality were emblems (and later coats of arms) painted on a ship's sails; shields attached along the gunwales served a similar function. When flags were gradually introduced in the 12th and the 13th centuries they became an indispensable means of

identifying the nationality and function of a ship, and the rank of its commander.

Until the 13th century naval activity was local and temporary. All ships were armed to some degree but there was no distinction between merchant and naval ships. To denote nationality, most ships flew the flag of their home port. The first national flags used by ships seem to have been the English cross of St George and the Danish *dannebrog* in northern Europe; the Genoese cross of St George and the Venetian lion of St Mark in the Mediterranean region.

▼ **BELOW** (from left to right) *English red ensign (1653–1801); English white ensign (1653–1702); English blue ensign (1653– 1801); English white ensign (1702–1801); Denmark (since 1625).*

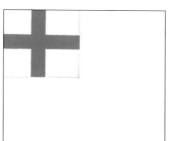

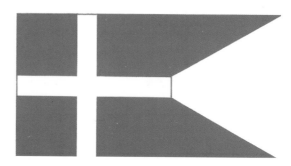

WAR ENSIGNS THROUGH HISTORY

The first navy, equipped with well-armed fighting ships, was organized in England in the first half of the 16th century. Under Elizabeth I (1558–1603) it developed into a major defence force and later played a decisive role in the extension of the British Empire. In Elizabethan times each English ship of war

▼ *BELOW* (from left to right) *Sweden (1663–1815 and since 1906); Sweden (1844–1905); Sweden (1815–1844).*

The design of the British ensigns with the Union Jack in the canton had a great impact on the war ensigns of many other European countries. France adopted a similar ensign in 1790, adding a canton displaying the jack in republican colours to the white field of the ensign used in times of monarchy. The next

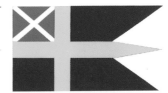

flew a different striped ensign, but the device common to all of them was the cross of St George in the canton. The stripes, mostly horizontal, varied in number (from five to eleven) and colouring (red, white; green, white; red, white, blue; red, green, red, blue, and so on). In 1625 the British Navy was divided into three squadrons, each of which was given an ensign in a different colour. Red was assigned to the centre, commanded by the admiral of the fleet; blue to the van, commanded by the vice-admiral, and white to the rear, commanded by the rear-admiral. This division was abolished in 1864, leaving only the white war ensign. The blue ensign became the ensign of the Royal Naval Reserve and could also be used by the officers of the Reserve when they commanded a private vessel. Currently, the criteria for warrants to wear the blue ensign, laid down in the Queen's Regulations of 1983, are:

> *The officer commanding a ship other than a fishing vessel must be an officer on the Retired or Emergency Lists of the Royal Navy or a Commonwealth Navy, or an officer on the Active or Retired Lists of any branch of the Reserves of such navies. If the rank held on one of these Lists by the officer commanding the ship is below that of Commander, at least one other officer in the ship's company must be an officer on one of the Lists mentioned.*

▶ *RIGHT Sardinia (1815–1848).*

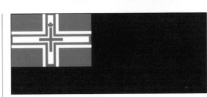

▶ *RIGHT France (1790–1794).*

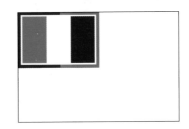

▶ *RIGHT Confederate States of America (1863–1865).*

countries to follow suit were Sweden and Sardinia in 1815, and in 1844 the Swedish jack was changed to display the colours of the flags of Sweden and Norway. The jack, in a square form, was used in the canton of the white war ensign of the Confederate States of America.

Prussia (1819–1850).

Germany (1867–1892).

Germany (1892–1903).

Germany (1903–1919).

Spain (1785–1931).

Austria (1787–1915).

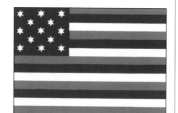

Russia (c.1700–1918 and since 1992).

Soviet Union (1924–1935).

War ensign of the ship Serapis (1779).

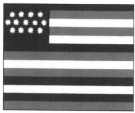

Ensign from the Lotter flag chart (1793).

War ensign from the Scotti flag chart (1796).

Ensign from a Swedish flag chart (1805).

In the 18th and 19th centuries another popular model for a war ensign was the Dutch ensign, with horizontal stripes. In 1701 Prussia introduced a plain white ensign charged with the small arms and the Iron cross. The Spanish ensign, adapted in 1785, displayed livery colours defaced with the state arms. The stripes of the Austrian war ensign, adopted in 1787, were of the same width, charged with the crowned shield of the historic arms.

The united Germany settled on a design combining a Scandinavian cross with a jack in the canton and a small state arms displayed on a white disc in the centre of the cross. There were minor subsequent changes to this design.

The American war ensign was presumably intended to be identical to the national flag but most of the actual ensigns show the stripes in three colours, which conform to the descriptions given by American diplomats in response to questions from European governments. Replying to the kingdom of Naples, Benjamin Franklin and John Adams wrote, "the flag of the United States of America consists of thirteen stripes, alternately red, white and blue". American ensigns with stripes in these three colours are depicted in many British, German, French, Italian and Swedish almanacs, and in flag charts dating from the late 18th and early 19th centuries. It seems that ensigns with three colours of stripes and those with red and white stripes were in use simultaneously. Paintings of ships in John Paul Jones's squadron by a Dutch artist show the ensign of *Serapis* with blue, red and white stripes and the ensign of *Alliance* with red and white stripes.

One of the oldest war ensigns still in existence today is the Russian one, adopted in about 1700 by Peter the Great for his navy, which displays a blue St Andrew's cross on a white field. As in Great Britain, this ensign was assigned to the centre, commanded by the admiral of the fleet; blue and red ensigns with a blue saltire in a white canton were assigned to the van and the rear respectively. Since 1865 the sole war ensign has been the white one.

WORLD WAR II

Among the major nations taking part in World War II only Italy, Japan, the United States, Great Britain and France used the same war ensign that they had used during World War I, which had ended some 21 years earlier. Similarly, most of the ensigns used in World War II are now obsolete; the war ensigns of Japan, Great Britain and France are the only exceptions. Indeed, France's ensign has remained the same since 1853, Great Britain's since 1864 and Japan's since 1889. The war ensign of Poland has now

Germany (1937–1945).

Japan (since 1889).

Croatia (1941–1944).

Italy (1848–1945).

The Norwegian Hirdmarinen.

Romania (1921–1948).

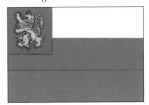

Bulgaria (1928–1947).

only slightly different arms to the World War II version, and the ensign of the United States now has two more stars in the canton. The war ensign of China did not change, but it is now used by Taiwan.

Two war ensigns were also used on land. The war ensign of Nazi Germany was also the flag of the armed forces, and the ensign of the United States was traditionally both the national flag and the ensign.

The Norwegian Hirdmarinen, illustrated here, which was formed by the Quisling regime in 1942 was intended mainly to train recruits for the German Navy.

▲ *ABOVE War ensigns of the Axis countries.*

▼ *BELOW War ensigns of the Allied countries.*

Poland (1928–1945).

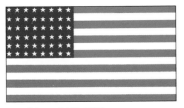

United States (1912–1959).

United Kingdom (since 1864).

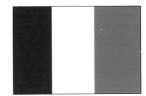

Egypt (1923–1958).

France (since 1853).

Soviet Union (1935–1992).

CURRENT WAR ENSIGNS

Most of the countries that became independent after World War II adopted national flags for general use on land and at sea, i.e. the national flag also served as the war ensign. Almost all of the countries that have adopted distinctive war ensigns were part of the British Empire and most of them followed the example of the British white ensign. The war ensigns of the Bahamas, Ghana, India, Jamaica, Nigeria and the Solomon Islands are white with the red cross of St George and a national flag in the canton. The war ensigns of Bangladesh, Kenya, Malaysia and Singapore are white with the national flag in the canton and in some a badge in the fly, while the ensigns of Australia, Fiji and New Zealand are variations of the national flag and have a white field. Two other war ensigns,

those of Tonga and Ukraine, are clearly based on the British white ensign.

Fewer than 40 countries of the world have war ensigns that differ from their national flags, and in several other cases the war ensign has the same design as the national flag but in different proportions. The ensigns of Grenada, Guyana, Pakistan, and Trinidad and Tobago have overall proportions 1:2 and each stripe of the French has a different width (90, 99 and 111 units when the width of the ensign is 200 units).

The ensigns of the Scandinavian countries, Germany, Poland and Estonia are swallow-tailed and triple swallow-tailed, following the custom that evolved centuries ago in the Baltic Sea region. The Finnish ensign was adopted in 1918 and the current pattern was introduced in 1978,

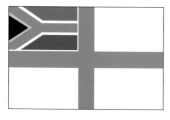

◀ *Far left* Republic of South Africa (since 1994).
◀ *Left* Tonga (since 1985).

◀ *Far left* Ukraine (since 1997).
◀ *Left* Australia (since 1967).

◀ *Far left* New Zealand (since 1968).
◀ *Left* Malaysia (since 1968).

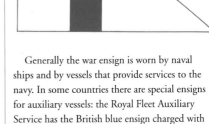

▶ *Right Germany (since 1956).*
▶ *Far right Finland (since 1978).*

when the shape of the arms and the shade of blue were changed slightly.

The war ensigns of other countries are either variations of the national flag (Thailand, Egypt, Saudi Arabia and Bulgaria) or have totally different designs in national colours (Israel, South Korea and Belgium).

Generally the war ensign is worn by naval ships and by vessels that provide services to the navy. In some countries there are special ensigns for auxiliary vessels: the Royal Fleet Auxiliary Service has the British blue ensign charged with a yellow anchor, and the Russian auxiliaries fly a dark blue flag with the war ensign in the canton.

▶ *Right Thailand (since 1917).*
▶ *Far right Israel (since 1948).*

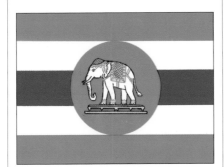

▶ *Right South Korea (since 1949).*
▶ *Far right Belgium (since 1950).*

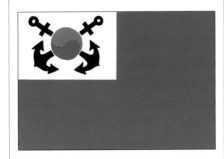

▶ *Right Pakistan (since 1956).*
▶ *Far right Egypt (since 1973).*

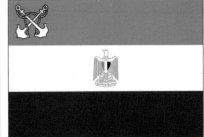

THE JACK

The second flag denoting the nationality of a naval vessel is a flag hoisted from the jackstaff, the top mast on the bow. The jack is usually square and is flown exclusively by ships in harbour or when the ship lies in the roadstead.

Most of the early jacks were identical with the flag used at sea by merchant and naval ships. The first English flag, white with the red cross of St George, was used as the jack of ships of war until 1606 and as the jack of merchant ships until the middle of the 19th century. Like the ensign, it influenced the design of jacks in other European countries and in America. The first to borrow the English design, in reversed colours, was Peter the Great, Tsar of Russia, followed by the Baltic States, which began to organize their navies after World War I. The British jack with a cross and saltire inspired the Dutch to divide the field gyronny in their national colours.

Several jacks are based on armorial banners. Spain has such a long tradition of using armorial banners at sea that it is not surprising that its

◀ *Left Great Britain (1606–1801).*

current jack displays the arms of Castile, León, Aragon and Navarre. The first Italian jack displayed the cross of Savoy; the present one, adopted in 1954, displays the Venetian lion of St Mark and the crosses of the ancient maritime republics Genoa, Amalfi and Pisa. The Croatian jack of 1941–1945 was an armorial banner, charged with the badge of the ruling Ustasha.

Other jacks bear the state arms or emblem as the charge. The shield of the Portuguese arms is

Russia (c.1700–1920 and since 1992). *Bulgaria.*

Latvia.

Estonia.

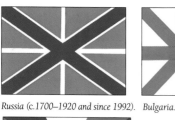

The Netherlands (since end of the 17th century).

Paraguay (since 1934).

Germany (1867–1919).

Soviet Union (1924–1932).

Sweden-Norway (1844–1905).

Norway (since 1905).

Confederate States of America (1863–65).

▶ *RIGHT (clockwise from left to right): Germany (1921–1933); Thailand (since 1917); Soviet Union (1932–1992).*

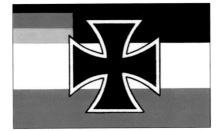

Italy (since 1954).

Finland (since 1978).

placed on an armillary sphere (a navigational instrument in the Age of Discovery). State arms have also appeared on the jacks of Finland, Romania, Persia (Iran) and Peru. A few jacks have white stars on a dark blue field; the Chilean jack has one star, while the jacks of Brazil and the United States display as many stars as they have states (currently 27 and 50 respectively). The second jack of the Soviet Union displayed the main communist emblems from the arms and national flag, the red star and the hammer and sickle.

The last group of jacks are the national flag defaced with an emblem. The German jack, for example, was defaced with the Iron cross and the jack of Thailand with the navy's emblem. In many countries the war ensign takes the place of a distinctive jack (Denmark, Sweden, France, Germany and South Korea), in others it is the same as the national flag (Turkey, Bangladesh,

Japan, Australia, New Zealand, Mexico, Dominican Republic, Colombia and Ecuador) or a square version of the national flag (Belgium). The jack often has the design of the canton of the national flag (Great Britain, Greece, Taiwan, Chile and the United States). In some countries in Latin America it has the design of a historic revolutionary flag (Cuba, Mexico and Uruguay).

Portugal (since 1910).

Taiwan (since 1949), (China 1912–1949).

Italy (1879–1946).

Argentina (since the end of the 19th century).

Spain (since 1945).

United States (since 1960).

Philippines (since 1955).

Current jack of Indonesia.

RANK FLAGS

In a few countries there are distinguishing flags for the commander-in-chief of the navy and the chief of staff of the navy. The predecessors of these flags were admiralty flags, adopted in the early 18th century by the Boards of the Admiralty in Great Britain and Russia. The admiralty managed naval affairs and also functioned as an operational authority, and its prerogatives were transferred in time to the navy or defence department.

In Norway, Finland and Ukraine the commanders-in-chief of the navy use war ensigns with emblems in the canton: a white saltire, a blue anchor over crossed yellow cannons and three stars respectively. The flag of the commander of the Russian Navy is the war ensign with the state arms on a disc surrounded by a garland of laurel. The flags of the chiefs of naval staff in France and Thailand are the national flag with an emblem in the centre.

Distinguishing flags are quite recent but the system of identifying the rank of ships' commanders is more than 400 years old. The English Navy was divided in 1545 into the van, the centre and the wing. The lord admiral (commander of the centre) flew the royal banner at the main and the flag of St George at the fore; the admiral of the van squadron flew the flag of St George at the main and fore; and the admiral of the wing squadron flew the flag of St George at the mizzen and bonaventure mizzen. The fleet sent to attack Cadiz in 1596 was divided into

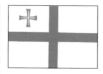

▲ **ABOVE** *Flags of the commander-in-chief of the navy: (top) Portugal, (bottom) Ukraine.*

◀ **TOP LEFT** *British Admiralty.*

◀ **LEFT** *Russian Admiralty.*

▲ **ABOVE** *Flags of the chiefs of staffs of the navy: (top) France, (middle) Italy, (bottom) Russia.*

four squadrons, each with three flag officers. The admiral's command flag was flown at the main, a vice-admiral's at the fore and a rear-admiral's at the mizzen. This system of identifying ranks was retained after the restoration of the monarchy, when there were only three squadrons – red, blue and white. The admiral of the fleet, commanding the red squadron, flew the Union flag at the main, unless he was the lord high admiral and was entitled to fly the royal standard. The vice-admiral and rear-admiral of the red squadron flew plain red flags on the fore and mizzen respectively; the admirals, vice-admirals and rear-admirals of the blue and white squadrons flew plain blue or white flags at the main, fore and mizzen respectively. This system was copied by fleets in other European countries and survived to the 19th century, when it became impractical because of changes in ships' architecture. Command flags of different designs for each flag officer were introduced at this point instead.

Throughout history there have been four basic methods of distinguishing rank among flag officers: (i) the same flag at different mastheads; (ii) the same design in different colours; (iii) the same basic design charged with additional devices for the lower ranks, and (iv) the same basic design charged with additional devices, the number of which increases with the rank. All four methods were employed in the United States Navy from 1817 to 1876. The order of colours denoting seniority was established in 1817. It was used in the Navy until 1870 and is still valid for distinguishing the flags of secretaries, deputy secretaries and under-secretaries in government departments.

Today the first two methods of distinguishing rank are obsolete. The only exceptions to this are the rank flags in the Yugoslav and French navies, which follow the second method. In France an admiral uses the national flag with four blue stars in the centre, and a vice-admiral displays three white stars in the upper hoist of the national flag. A rear-admiral uses the national flag, but with an additional white horizontal stripe of the same width as the vertical one and two white stars in the upper hoist. The third method is used only in the navies of Germany, Great Britain, Greece, Japan and Portugal; all other countries use the fourth method. Five-pointed stars are mostly used but other devices include circles (as in the case of Great Britain, Germany, Portugal, Spain and Colombia); six-pointed stars (the Netherlands); horizontal stripes (Japan and Taiwan), and suns (Peru). The field of a rank flag is generally unicoloured, mostly blue, and occasionally the field is charged with a cross (Great Britain, Germany, Portugal and Colombia) or other device (Japan). In some countries the field has the design of the war ensign (Denmark, Norway and Sweden), the national flag (the Netherlands, Spain, Romania and Mexico) or has adopted the design of its canton (Greece).

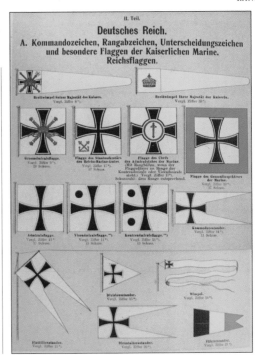

◀ **LEFT**
Distinguishing and rank flags in the German Navy. Plate from the Flaggenbuch, *1905. The rank flags are still in use.*

▼ **BELOW**
Rank and other naval flags as presented in the National Geographic *in 1917.*

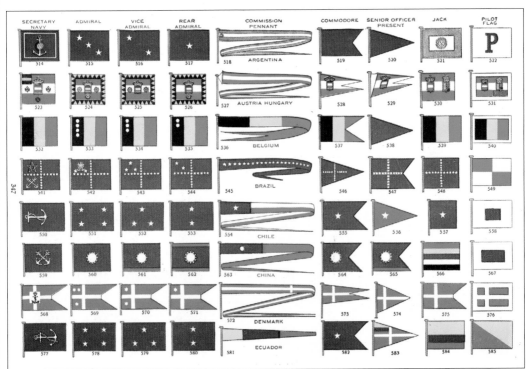

CURRENT RANK FLAGS

GREAT BRITAIN

ADMIRAL

VICE-ADMIRAL

REAR-ADMIRAL

GERMANY

ADMIRAL

VICE-ADMIRAL

REAR-ADMIRAL

SPAIN

ADMIRAL

VICE-ADMIRAL

REAR-ADMIRAL

UNITED STATES

ADMIRAL OF THE FLEET

ADMIRAL

VICE-ADMIRAL

REAR-ADMIRAL

TURKEY

ADMIRAL OF THE FLEET

ADMIRAL

VICE-ADMIRAL

REAR-ADMIRAL

ITALY

ADMIRAL COMMANDER IN
CENTRAL MEDITERRANEAN

SQUADRON ADMIRAL

DIVISION ADMIRAL

REAR-ADMIRAL

PAKISTAN

ADMIRAL OF THE FLEET

ADMIRAL

VICE-ADMIRAL

REAR-ADMIRAL

COMMISSION PENNANTS

In the 13th century it was the custom to attach long streamers to the mastheads of ships purely for decoration, and four centuries later it became a duty of all men-of-war to fly a masthead pennant to distinguish them from merchant ships. Until the late 19th century each English or Russian warship used a pennant of its squadronal colour, either red, white or blue. Today there is only one commission pennant for all naval vessels, which should fly continuously day and night during the period the ship is in commission. If the ship is commanded by a flag officer, the appropriate rank flag replaces the commission pennant. The commission pennant is the longest, but narrowest, flag on a ship. Its width is 6–20 cm (2½–8 in) and its length 15–50 times greater. The largest pennant used during World War II by German warships was 20 cm (8 in) wide and 16 m (17½ yd) long. Most commission pennants copy the design of the national flag or display the national flag in the hoist. Some arrange the national colours differently or display in the hoist only the main design element from the national flag or war ensign.

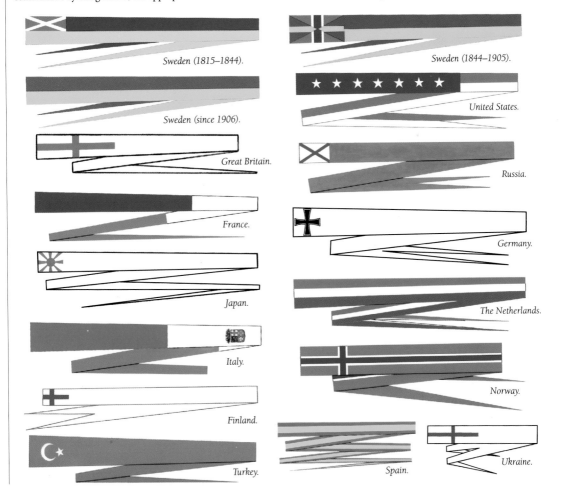

Sweden (1815–1844).

Sweden (1844–1905).

Sweden (since 1906).

United States.

Great Britain.

Russia.

France.

Germany.

Japan.

The Netherlands.

Italy.

Norway.

Finland.

Turkey.

Spain.

Ukraine.

Flag Families

*Flags are a universal characteristic of human civilization. With the exception of the
most primitive societies and nomadic peoples, it appears that every culture has
invented for itself flags of one kind or another – with a remarkable similarity of
form observable throughout the world. The functions of flags are nearly identical
in all societies, and parallels in flag usages may be observed in diverse regions and eras.*

*So strong is the tradition of flags, we may not be far from the truth in surmising that
there is a law – not of nature, but of human society – which impels man to make
and use flags. There is perhaps no more striking demonstration of this than the fact
that, despite the absence of any international regulation or treaty requiring of a
national flag, without exception every country has adopted at least one.*

WHITNEY SMITH, *FLAGS THROUGH THE AGES AND ACROSS THE WORLD*, 1975.

In the Middle Ages flags on land denoted
mainly rulers and the military, but at sea they
were used to denote nationality. With the
growth of international trade in the 17th and
18th centuries, more countries began to adopt
merchant ensigns and these became well known
not only in their home ports but also inland.
Thus in most countries with access to the sea
the merchant ensign, or a flag similar to it,
eventually became the national flag.

Looking at the various flags hoisted at the
UN headquarters in New York, at the NATO
headquarters in Brussels or at stadiums during
international sporting events, we may wonder
why the flags of nations in different parts of the
world have such similar designs. In most cases
the similarity is deliberate. It may be an
expression of common history, traditions or
interests, or it may be a statement that a country
modelling its flag on that of another country
sees that country as a religious or political
role model.

The similarity of flags is as old as the use of
flags themselves, but flag use did not develop
on a large scale until the 19th century and
continued during the 20th. Out of some 195
independent countries only 12 have flags whose
designs were adopted before 1800. Seven of

these (Denmark, Great Britain, the Netherlands,
Russia, the United States, France and Turkey)
have influenced the designs and colours of over
130 national flags and ensigns, which are
grouped into ten large and three smaller "flag
families". Some flags may belong to more than
one flag family, for example flags displaying
the pan-Arab colours and the Muslim crescent,
or those displaying the French colours and
the cross.

▼ *BELOW Flags at the
Rockefeller Center in
New York, 1968, show
the similarities between
many flags.*

THE CHRISTIAN CROSS

The cross is an ancient magical sign and decorative motif known in many parts of the world, such as Mesopotamia, China, Scandinavia and Greece, but today it is universally recognized as the symbol of Christianity. In the first centuries after the death of Christ the main Christian symbol was a fish, often with the Greek word ΙΧΘΥΣ (fish). This can be made into an acrostic: I (I) = Ieus, X (Ch) = Christos, Ξ (Th) = Theou, Y (U) = Uios, Σ (S) = Soter, meaning "Jesus Christ God's Son Saviour". In the 3rd century Christian communities began to use cross-like emblems, such as an anchor with a crosspiece or a human figure with outstretched arms. A breakthrough came in 326 when St Helena, mother of Emperor Constantine, was said to have discovered the cross on which Christ was crucified. This stimulated an increase in the devotion of the faithful and led to the cross being gradually introduced as a symbol of martyrdom, resurrection, redemption and salvation.

From the 9th century to the end of the 12th century a metal cross on the top of a mast was the only device marking

▼ **BELOW** (from left to right) Portugal (1140–1185); Jerusalem; Genoa; Constantinople (14th century); Barcelona (14th century); Sardinia (14th century); Savoy (14th century).

merchant ships in northern Europe. Later the cross became the most common charge of the merchant ensigns of cities and countries in both Northern and southern Europe, for example Cologne, Riga, Elbing, Danzig, Königsberg, Geneva and Marseilles.

The oldest flags with a cross are those of Portugal and the kingdom of Jerusalem. From 1140 to 1185 the Portuguese flag was white with a blue cross on a white field, and from 1185 to 1250 it was white with a cross made of five blue shields; this latter arrangement remains to this day in the centre of the coat of arms of Portugal. The flag of the kingdom of Jerusalem under King Amalrich (1162–1173) displayed five golden yellow crosses on a white field.

Other flags and ensigns dating from the 13th and 14th centuries are charged with a simple

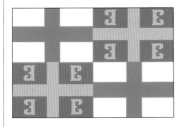

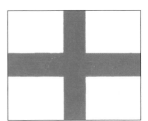

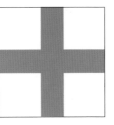

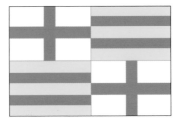

THE CROSS

The current national flags of the following countries and territories belong to this family:
ÅLAND ISLANDS, DENMARK, DOMINICA, DOMINICAN REPUBLIC, FAROES, FINLAND, GUERNSEY, ICELAND, JERSEY, MADEIRA, MARTINIQUE, NORWAY, SHETLAND, SWEDEN, SWITZERLAND, TONGA, WALLIS AND FUTUNA ISLANDS.

cross including the Teutonic Order, England, France, Denmark, Savoy and Malta, and the flags of Barcelona and Constantinople, which display additional devices. The flag of Barcelona has two quarters with the cross and two

displaying the armorial banner of Catalonia. The flag of Constantinople has four letters "B" between the arms of the cross, which are believed to stand for the Greek motto *Basileis Basileon Basileion Basileisi* ("King of Kings ruling

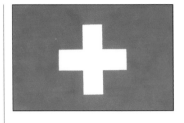

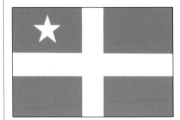

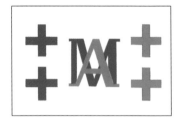

▲ *ABOVE* (left to right
from top left)
*Switzerland, civil
ensign (since 1941);
Livorno; Malta (civil
ensign since 1965);
Samoa (1873–1885);
Rimatara (c.1856–
1891); Tongatapu
(c.1858–1862).*

◄ *OPPOSITE*
(left to right from top
left) *France civil ensign
(1661–1790); Provence;
Calai;, Picardy;
Marseilles; Oldenburg
(1774–1935); Greece,
national flag (1822–
1970); Samos (1832–
1913); Crete (1898–
1913); Sweden, civil
ensign (1815–1844);
Sweden, civil ensign
(1844–1905); Norway,
civil ensign (1814–
1818); Finland, civil
ensign (since 1918);
East Karelia (1920–
1922); Ingermanland.*

over Kings"). It inspired the flags adopted in
subsequent centuries by at least two other
countries in the Mediterranean: in the Sardinian
flag there are Moorish heads between the arms of
the cross, and in the Savoy flag the letters
"FERT" stand for *Fortitudo Ejus Rhodum Tenuit*
(His Courage Saved Rhodes).

In the 17th and 18th centuries the cross was
the main charge of the civil ensign of France,
and of several French provinces (Provence and
Picardy) and ports (Marseilles and Calais). The
official French civil ensign was blue with a white
cross, with the royal arms overall, but it was not
popular and most French merchant vessels used
either provincial or port ensigns or the banned
white ensign. Such widespread use of the cross
in the Mediterranean also influenced the flags
of nations created in the 19th and 20th
centuries such as Greece, Samos and Crete.

Until the end of the 14th century the centre
of the cross corresponded with the centre of the
field. Denmark was the first to position the cross
in such a way that the parts of the field between
the arms of the cross formed squares in the hoist
and rectangles in the fly. This example was
followed by Sweden (1569), Norway (1821),
Iceland (1915), Finland (1918), the Faroes
(1919), East Karelia (1920), and Ingermanland
and the Åland Islands (1921). Thus a large sub-
family, called the Scandinavian cross, came into
being. Modern flags with the Scandinavian
Cross are illustrated in *Flags of Europe*.

As well as simple symmetrical or Latin
crosses, there were some more elaborate versions
of the Christian cross. One of the first, a red
Maltese cross on a white field, is known from
the war ensign of the Cavalieri di Santo Stefano
Order, founded in 1561. A modification of this
cross appeared in the 17th and 18th centuries
on the merchant ensign of Livorno.

Four very old crosses have only appeared on
civil ensigns and flags during the last 100 years.
In Switzerland a white cross on a red field had
already appeared in the 13th century on the flag
of Schwyz and on red schwenkels added to the
flags of other cantons. However, it did not
become the national symbol until 1889
(national flag) or for use at sea until 1941 (civil
ensign). The 900-year-old white Maltese cross
of the Order of the Knights of St John of
Jerusalem appears on the red field of the civil
ensign of Malta. Finally the cross of the
Portuguese Order of Christ, founded in the
early 14th century, became the central emblem
on the flag of Madeira in 1978.

In various forms, the Christian cross also
appears on the flags and ensigns of nations in
other parts of the world. It is a charge of the
flags of Dominica and the Dominican Republic,
and it was placed in the canton of the Liberian
flag of 1827–47. In Oceania it was the charge of
the civil ensigns of Samoa, Rimatara and
Tongatapu, and it is still used by Tonga and by
Wallis and Futuna.

THE MUSLIM CRESCENT

The crescent is one of the oldest symbols known to humanity. Together with the sun, it appeared on Akkadian seals as early as 2300 BC and from at least the second millennium BC it was the symbol of the Mesopotamian moon gods Nanna in Sumer and Sin in Babylonia, Sin being the "Lamp of Heaven and Earth". The crescent was well known in the Middle East and was transplanted by the Phoenicians in the 8th century as far as Carthage (now in Tunisia). In the 12th century it was adopted by the Turks and since then the crescent, often accompanied by a star and mentioned in the 53rd *surah* (chapter) of the Koran, has been the main symbol of Islam.

THE FLAG FAMILY
The current national flags of the following countries and territories belong to this family:
ALGERIA, ANJOUAN, AZAD KASHMIR, AZERBAIJAN, BRUNEI, COMOROS, MALAYSIA, MALDIVES, MAURITANIA, NORTHERN CYPRUS, PAKISTAN, SINGAPORE, TUNISIA, TURKEY, TURKMENISTAN, UZBEKISTAN, WESTERN SAHARA.

The oldest representations of flags with the crescent are on 14th-century navigational charts, or *portolanos*, and the manuscript of a Franciscan friar. There are discrepancies between these sources as far as the colours of fields or

◀ *LEFT* (left to right from top left) *Gabes; Tlemcen; Tunis; Turkey (16th–18th century); Turkey (1793–1844); Egypt (1914–1922).*

crescents are concerned. However, an account of flags from the Middle East and North Africa by the author of *Libro de Conoscimento* confirms the widespread use of the crescent on flags in that region. These include: the flags of the kings of Damascus and Lucha (yellow with a white crescent); Cairo (white with a blue crescent); Mahdia in Tunisia (white with a purple crescent); Tunis (white with a black crescent); and Buda (white with a red crescent). Some of the 14th- and 15th-century *portolanos* show the flag of Tunis as red with one or two crescents, which is presented on several *portolanos* as the flag of the Ottoman Empire. From the 16th to the 18th centuries this flag is usually shown with three white crescents; in 1793 the number of crescents was reduced to one and an eight-pointed white star was added.

After the rule of the Ottoman Empire ended, Turkey was the only Muslim state regarded as a world power. Its flag was known from West Africa to the Far East, and helped to popularize the crescent and star among the Muslim populations of many countries of Asia and Africa. Muhammad Ali, who became Pasha of Egypt in 1805, introduced the first national flag of Egypt, red with three white crescents, each accompanied by a white star. This flag, in turn,

▶ *RIGHT* (from left to right) *Egypt (1923–1958); Rif Republic (1921–1926); Hatay (1938–1939); Cyrenaica (1947–1950); Tripolitania (1951) and Libya (1951–1969); South Arabia (1959–1967).*

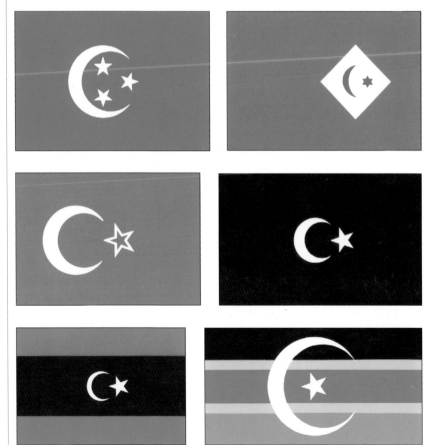

▲ *ABOVE* (left to right from top left) *Azerbaijan (1917– 1920); Kokand (1917); Dagestan (1918–1921); Turkestan (1918–1924); North Caucasia (1919– 1920); Bokhara (1920– 1921); Khoresm (1920– 1922); Maldives (1934); East Turkestan (1943– 1949); Comoros (1975– 1978); Singapore civil ensign (since 1966).*

influenced the design of the first flag of independent Egypt, which was green with a white crescent and three white stars to symbolize the peaceful co-existence of Muslims, Christians and Jews. During the past two centuries the crescent and star featured on the flags of other Arab countries in North Africa and the Middle East. These include Tunisia (*c.*1835), the Rif Republic (1921–1926), Hatay (1938–1939), Cyrenaica (1947–1950), Tripolitania (1951), Libya (1951–1969), South Arabia (1959), Mauritania (1959), Algeria (1962) and Western Sahara (1976). Other regions heavily

influenced by the Turks were the Caucasus and Central Asia. Several countries which achieved independence during World War I adopted flags with the crescent and star, or the crescent alone: Azerbaijan (1917), Kokand (1917), Dagestan (1918), North Caucasia (1919), Khoresm (1920), Bokhara (1920), Turkestan (1922), Uzbekistan (1991) and Turkmenistan (1992). Several countries in Central and South-east Asia also adopted flags with the crescent and star: the Maldives (1934), East Turkestan (1943), Pakistan (1947), the Federation of Malaya (1950), Singapore (1959) and Comoros (1963).

THE UNION JACK

Until the early 17th century and since the 13th century the English flag and jack, used by both merchant and navy ships, had been white with the red cross of St George. The Scottish flag was blue with the white cross of St Andrew. Then, on 12 April 1606 King James I of England and Scotland issued a proclamation:

> *That from henceforth all our Subjects of this Isle and Kingdome of Great Britaine, and the members thereof, shall beare in their Maintoppe the Red Crosse, commonly called S. Georges Crosse, and the White Crosse, commonly called S. Andrewes Crosse, joyned together, according to a forme made by our Heralds...*

This was the birth certificate of what soon became the best-known flag in the world.

Until 1634 the flag was used by both merchant and navy ships, thereafter its use was restricted to the king's own ships or ships in the king's immediate service; English merchant ships reverted to flying the St George's cross and Scottish ships the St Andrew's cross. At the same time the merchant ensign, red with the St George's cross in the canton, came into use and was later legalized in a proclamation of 1674. This proclamation retained the "Flag and Jack White, with a Red Cross (commonly called Saint George's Cross)", and repeatedly warned that use of the Union Jack was illegal. Nevertheless, many merchant captains

GENEALOGY OF THE UNION JACK

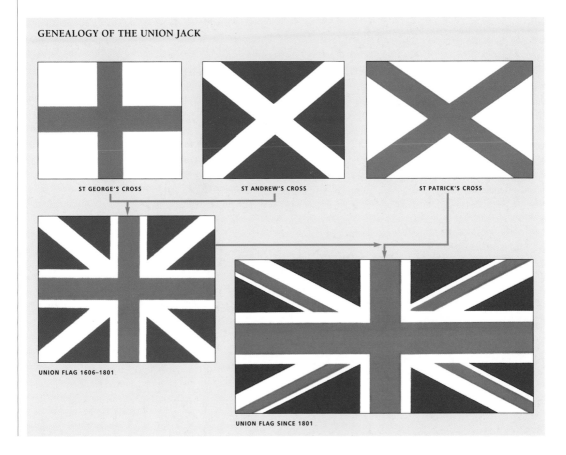

ST GEORGE'S CROSS

ST ANDREW'S CROSS

ST PATRICK'S CROSS

UNION FLAG 1606–1801

UNION FLAG SINCE 1801

◀ FAR LEFT AND LEFT
Red ensign (since 1801);
blue ensign (since 1801).

continued to use the "King's jack" in order to gain advantages such as better protection, exemption from port duties in France as well as exemption from the requirement to use a pilot in Holland.

When the United Kingdom of Great Britain and Ireland came into existence on 1 January 1801, a red saltire called the cross of St Patrick was chosen to represent Ireland. It originated in the coat of arms of the Anglo-Irish family of Fitzgerald and was the main emblem of the Order of St Patrick, adopted in 1783. The idea of counterchanging the white and red saltires assured almost equal status for both of them, and was excellent from an artistic point of view. The new Union flag replaced that of 1606 in the cantons of the merchant ensign, and the red, white and blue ensigns used by the three squadrons of the Navy. On 9 July 1864 an Admiralty order abolished the division of the Navy into squadrons and assigned the white ensign exclusively to the Royal Naval Service, while the red ensign became "the national

colours for all British ships". It was decided that the blue ensign would

be carried by all vessels employed in the service of any public office; by vessels employed under the Transport Department, and the Civil Departments of the Navy (with the Seal or Badge of the office to which they belong at the present), and, under our permission, by ships commanded by Officers of the Royal Naval Reserve Force...

The use of the blue ensign was extended by the Colonial Defence Act of 1865, which allowed "all vessels belonging to, or permanently in, the service of the Colonies" to use this ensign, "with the Seal or Badge of the Colony in the Fly thereof". This Act made possible the enormous future growth in the number of flags with the Union Jack in the canton. More than 100 colonial ensigns have been in use during the last century and some of them, such as those of Australia, New Zealand, Fiji and Tuvalu, became

▼ BELOW (from left to right) Saint Lucia (19th century–1938); Barbados (19th century–1966); British Honduras (19th century–1981); Turks and Caicos Islands (end of the 19th century– 1968); New Zealand (1900–1902); Australia (1903–1908).

▼ *Below* (from left to right) *Grenada (1903–1967); Nyasaland (1914–1953); Tanganyika (1919–1964); Gilbert and Ellice Islands (1937–1979); Burma (1939–1941); Sarawak (1947–1963); Federation of Rhodesia and Nyasaland (1954–1963); Guyana (1954–1966); Solomon Islands (1956–1977); Seychelles (1961–1976); the Bahamas (1964–1973); Dominica (1965–1978).*

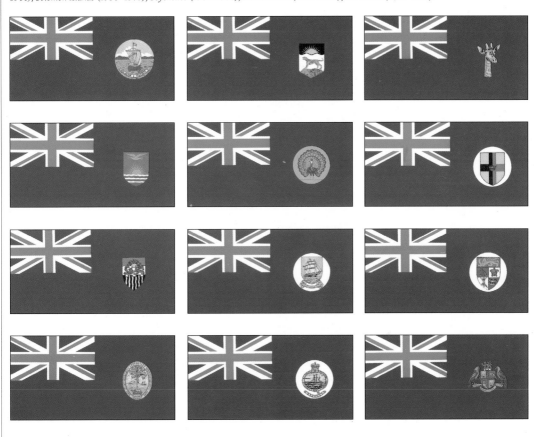

▼ *Below* (from left to right) *Canada (1922–1957), Canada (1957–1965), Union of South Africa (1912–1928).*

after some alteration the national flags of independent countries.

Formally the civil ensign of a British colony was always, and still is, an undefaced red ensign. Only a few dominions and one colony obtained the right to use the British red ensign defaced with a badge. The privilege was first granted to Canada (1892), then to New Zealand (1899), Australia (1903), South Africa (1910), Bermuda

(1915), the Isle of Man (1971), Guernsey (1985), the Cayman Islands (1988) and Gibraltar (1996). The charges on the last two flags mentioned are of ancient origin. The golden cross on the civil ensign of Guernsey was the main charge of William the Conqueror's gonfanon, accorded to him by the Pope before he embarked on the campaign that ended in victory at the battle of Hastings in 1066. The ensign of Gibraltar

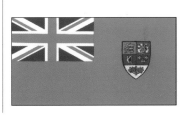

displays the arms granted by King Ferdinand and Queen Isabella of Spain on 10 July 1502. Several former British colonies were so accustomed to the red ensign that after gaining independence they introduced a civil ensign in the form of a red flag with the national flag in the canton. As well as the examples illustrated here,

the civil ensigns of Sri Lanka, Bangladesh and the Solomon Islands also have this design.

The British innovation of putting the national flag in the canton of a flag or ensign greatly influenced the merchant ensigns of many countries that did not have formal ties with the British Empire. The example of the striped Elizabethan

▶ *OPPOSITE Badges of the British Colonies from* Flags of Maritime Nations, *1914.*

◀▼ *LEFT AND BELOW* (left to right from top left) *Hanover (1801–1866); Helgoland (1814–1890); Australia, civil ensign (since 1908); New Zealand, civil ensign (since 1903); Singapore, state ensign (since 1966); Isle of Man, civil ensign (since 1971); Bahamas, civil ensign (since 1973); Guernsey, civil ensign (since 1985); Gibraltar, civil ensign (since 1996).*

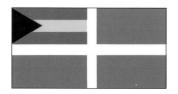

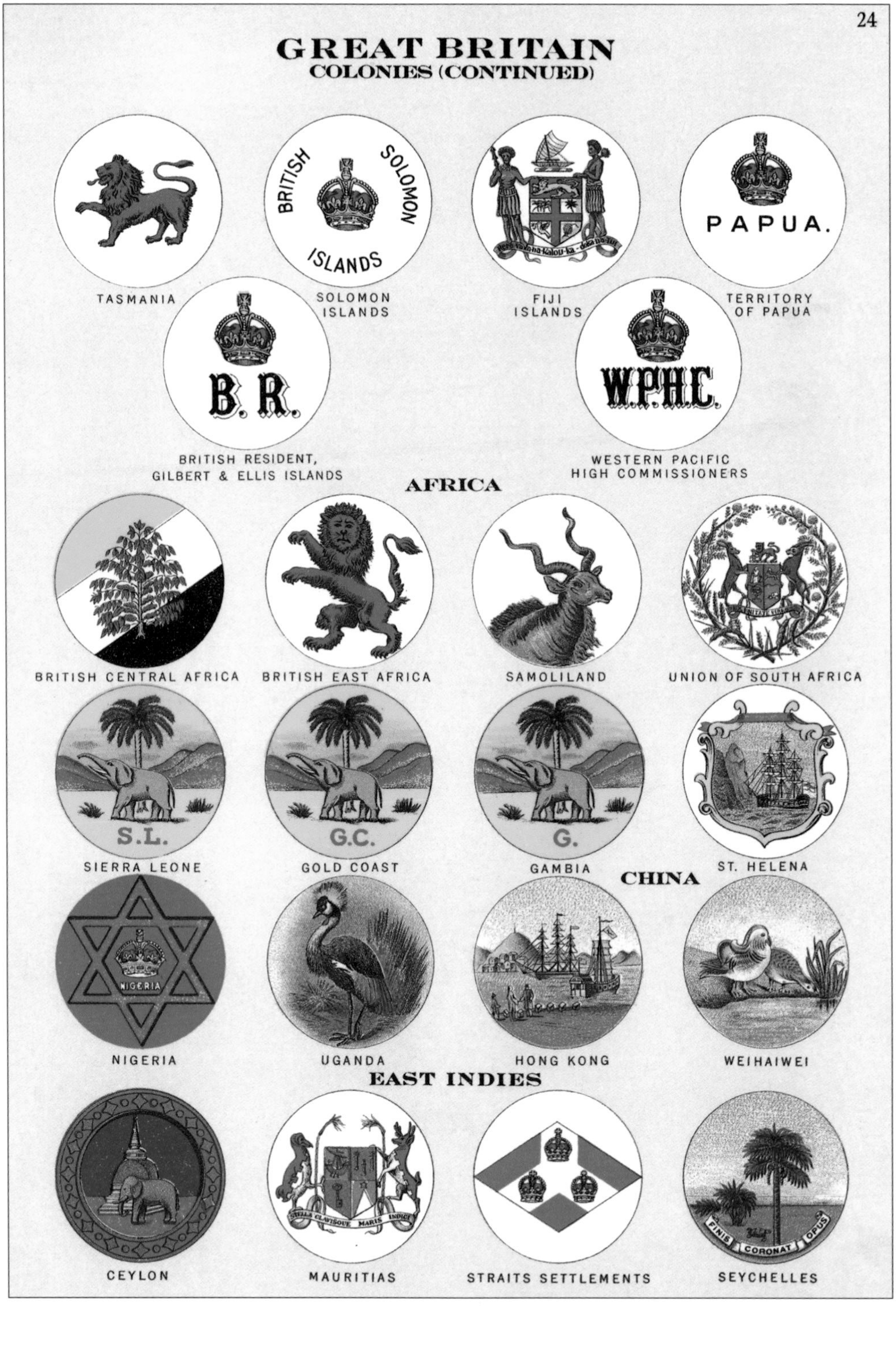
24
GREAT BRITAIN
COLONIES (CONTINUED)
BRITISH SOLOMON ISLANDS
PAPUA.
TASMANIA
SOLOMON ISLANDS
FIJI ISLANDS
TERRITORY OF PAPUA
B. R.
W.P.H.C.
BRITISH RESIDENT, GILBERT & ELLIS ISLANDS
WESTERN PACIFIC HIGH COMMISSIONERS
AFRICA
BRITISH CENTRAL AFRICA
BRITISH EAST AFRICA
SAMOLILAND
UNION OF SOUTH AFRICA
S.L.
G.C.
G.
SIERRA LEONE
GOLD COAST
GAMBIA
ST. HELENA
CHINA
NIGERIA
NIGERIA
UGANDA
HONG KONG
WEIHAIWEI
EAST INDIES
FINIS CORONAT OPUS
CEYLON
MAURITIAS
STRAITS SETTLEMENTS
SEYCHELLES

ensigns induced the Portuguese to adopt a similar ensign in 1640. The blue and red ensigns served as models for the civil ensigns or national flags of Hanover (1801–1866), Sardinia (1821–1848), Greece (1822–1828), China (1928–1949), Taiwan (since 1949), Spanish Morocco (1937–1956), Samoa (1948–1949), the Khmer Republic (1970–1975), and flags of the French colonies (see *The French Tricolore*).

The flag of the United States, a discussion of which follows, was one of the first flags to be modelled on the British ensign.

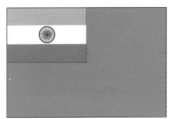

▲ ◄ *Above and Left* (left to right from top left) *Burma (1948–1974); Ceylon (1954–1972); India, civil ensign (since 1950); Pakistan, civil ensign (since 1958); Ghana, civil ensign (since 1961); Greece, civil ensign (1822–1828); Taiwan, civil ensign (since 1949); Spanish Morocco (1937–1956).*

THE FLAG FAMILY

The current national flags of the following countries and territories belong to this family:

ANGUILLA, AUSTRALIA, BERMUDA, BRITISH ANTARCTIC TERRITORY, BRITISH INDIAN OCEAN TERRITORY, BRITISH VIRGIN ISLANDS, CAYMAN ISLANDS, COOK ISLANDS, FALKLANDS, FIJI, HEBRIDES, MONTSERRAT, MYANMAR, NEW ZEALAND, NIUE, PITCAIRN, ST HELENA, SAMOA, SOUTH GEORGIA AND SOUTH SANDWICH ISLANDS, TAIWAN, TONGA, TURKS AND CAICOS ISLANDS, TUVALU.

THE STARS AND STRIPES

From the end of the 15th century North America was colonized by British settlers and the best-known flag was the British red ensign, which in America was used also on land. It was only natural that it should influence the design of the United States flag, often called the Stars and Stripes or Star-spangled Banner.

The first American flag was the merchant ensign, introduced in 1775. It consisted solely of 13 red and white stripes, very similar to the flag of the Revolutionary Society of the Sons of Liberty. The flag hoisted on 2 January 1776 by the Continental Army also had 13 red and white stripes, with the Union Jack in the canton. Called the Grand Union flag or the Continental Colors, it was identical to the flag of the British East India Company although this was probably just coincidence. The Union Jack in the canton symbolized continuing loyalty to Britain, but the stripes were probably taken from the merchant ensign rather than from the flag of the East India Company and symbolized the rebellion of the 13 colonies against British rule.

Some circumstances indicate that the Union Jack had already been replaced by the star-filled canton in 1776, and that the Continental Congress's Resolution of 14 June 1777 only confirmed the design already in use. Substantiating this theory is the terse wording of the Resolution:

Resolved, That the Flag of the United States be 13 stripes alternate red and white, that the Union be 13 stars white in a blue field representing a new constellation.

There is no mention of the size of the Union (the canton) or the shape or configuration of the stars. In fact, from that date there were two different designs for the canton of the American national flag. The so-called Betsy Ross design has the stars arranged in a circle, while Francis Hopkinson's design shows the stars arranged in parallel staggered rows. In both cases the stars were five-pointed, which was a revolutionary innovation in flag design.

▶ *RIGHT Grand Union flag.*

▶ *RIGHT Betsy Ross design.*

▶ *RIGHT Francis Hopkinson's design.*

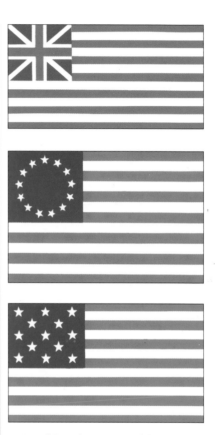

One of the earliest accounts of the symbolism of the flag is by Alfred B. Street, who in October 1777 witnessed the flag at the surrender of the British General Burgoyne at Saratoga:

The stars were disposed in a circle, symbolizing the perpetuity of the Union; the ring, like the circling serpent of the Egyptians, signifying eternity. The thirteen stripes showed with the stars the number of the United Colonies, and denoted the subordination of the States to the Union, as well as equality among themselves.

The growth of the Union posed the question of how the new states should be represented in the flag. After the admission of Vermont (1791) and Kentucky (1792) to the Union, the flag

◄ **LEFT** (from left to right) *Stars forming rings; stars forming ovals; stars forming a star; an early civil ensign.*

► **RIGHT** (left to right from top left) *Hawaii (1815–1825); Uruguay (1828–1830); Texas (1836–1845); Confederate States of America (1861–1863); Vermont (1837–1923); Louisiana (1861–1962); Orange Free State (1857–1902); Liberia (1827–1847); El Salvador (1865–1912); Brazil (1889); North Caucasia (1918–1919); Malaya (1950–1963).*

created on 13 January 1794 displayed fifteen stars and 15 stripes. Between 1796 and 1817 five more states joined the Union but the flag was not modified until 4 April 1818, when the Flag Act raised the number of stars to 20 and reverted the number of stripes to the original 13. Section 2 of the act established the principle for future modifications:

And be it further enacted, that on the admission of every new State into the Union, one star be added to the union of the flag; such addition shall take effect on the fourth of July next succeeding such admission.

Since then the number of stars in the canton of the national flag has been increased 24 times, the latest being on 4 July 1960. From 1818 to this day the number of stars represents the

number of states in the Union, while the 13 stripes symbolize the 13 colonies that achieved independence and formed the United States of America.

For more than 130 years there was no official regulation of the arrangement of the stars in the canton of the national flag. At any given time the flags displayed dozens of designs, the most popular were concentric rings, ovals, diamonds and large stars made of smaller stars. Then, in 1818, President Monroe stipulated that the stars should be arranged in parallel rows. This arrangement was followed by the navy and was officially adopted for all flags in 1912.

▼ **BELOW** *Flag with 48 stars (1912–1959).*

THE FLAG FAMILY

The current national flags of the following countries and territories belong to this family:
ABKHAZIA, CHILE, CUBA, GREECE, LIBERIA, MALAYSIA, PUERTO RICO, TOGO, UNITED STATES, URUGUAY.

The first country to adopt a similar flag to the American one was Hawaii. In an astute political move, the Hawaiian king combined in his country's flag the symbols of the two most influential powers in the Pacific, that is the British Union Jack with the tricolour stripes of the American ensign. Other countries adopted flags inspired by the American design to manifest their adherence to republican ideals of liberty and democracy. These countries included Chile (1817), Uruguay (1828), Texas (1836), Vermont (1837), Cuba (1850), the Confederate States of America (1861), Louisiana (1861) and Puerto Rico (1891). Alternatively, some countries used the stars and/or stripes to represent the number of their subdivisions: Greece (1822); Liberia (1827); El Salvador (1865); Brazil (1889) and seven of its states (Amazonas, Bahia, Goiás, Maranhão, Piauí, São Paulo, Sergipe); as well as North Caucasia (1918); the Federation of Malaya (1950), Togo (1960) and Abkhasia (1992).

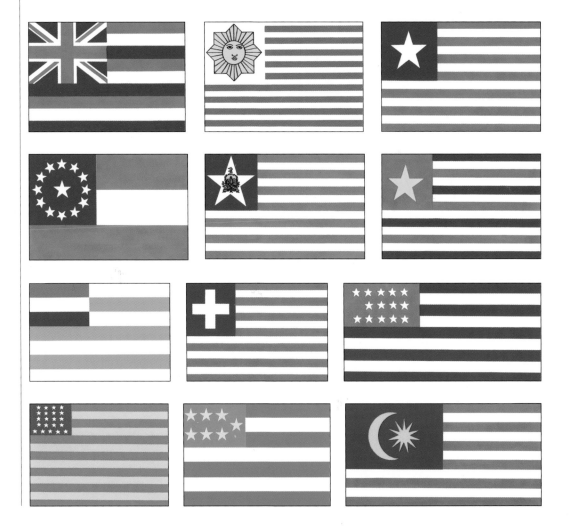

THE DUTCH AND PAN-SLAV COLOURS

Orange, white and blue were the livery colours of William I, Prince of Orange (1533–1584). Armbands in these colours were worn by his soldiers at the siege of Leiden in 1574, and in the 1580s they were used on the horizontal tricolour of the ensign and the flag used on land. Thus was created the first modern flag, displaying simple stripes instead of heraldic devices.

During the 17th century the orange was gradually replaced by red. This may have been because red is more visible at sea, or the reason may have been political: a manifestation of the Dutch estates-general's wish to exclude the House of Orange. The original tricolour survived until at least 1795, when the orange was officially replaced by red.

In the 18th century the Dutch ensign was one of a few that were well known in many parts of the world, especially South-east Asia, North America and South Africa. In South Africa seven political entities adopted flags based on the Dutch design: Natalia (1839), Transvaal (1857), Orange Free State (1857), Lyndenburg Republic (1857), Goshen Republic (1882), New Republic (1884) and the Union of South Africa (1928). In the Americas the original Dutch colours appear on the flag of New York, which is widely used in the city, while the modern colours (using

red instead of orange) appear on the flag of the Netherlands Antilles.

The Dutch flag had an even greater impact on the flags of Slav nations in central and southern Europe. It was a model for the merchant flag of Russia, personally designed in 1699 by Tsar Peter the Great (1672–1725). Eager to modernize his country, he travelled incognito to western Europe in 1697 to gather first-hand information on advanced technology, especially in shipbuilding. He worked for four months as a shipwright in the shipyard of the Dutch East India Company in Zaandam, and

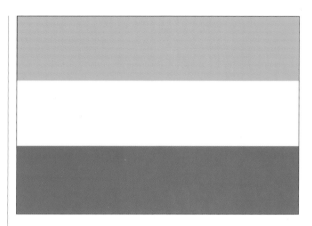

▲ *ABOVE Flag of the Netherlands (late 16th century–1795).*

▼ *BELOW (from left to right) Natal (1839–1843); Transvaal (1857–1877); Goshen Republic (1882–1885); New Republic (1884–1888); South Africa (1928–1994); Netherlands Antilles (1959–1985).*

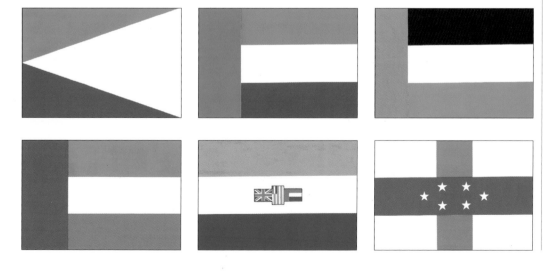

THE FLAG FAMILY

The current national flags of the following countries belong to this family: BULGARIA, CROATIA, CZECH REPUBLIC, THE NETHERLANDS, THE NETHERLANDS ANTILLES, RUSSIA, SLOVAKIA, SLOVENIA, YUGOSLAVIA.

spent some time in the British Navy shipyard at Deptford. On his return to Russia he introduced an elaborate system of naval flags, based on Dutch and British flags and ensigns. The merchant flag, which became the national flag of Russia, was a horizontal tricolour of white-blue-red.

This flag, in turn, inspired other Slav countries to adopt horizontal tricolours displaying the same colours in different arrangements. Nations living under foreign (but not Russian) domination also followed suit. In 1835 the Serbs were the first to adopt a red-blue-white tricolour for their ships on inland waters. In 1848, during the first pan-Slav Congress in Prague, these were proclaimed the pan-Slav colours and were adopted of horizontal tricolours by several Slav provinces of Austria. The Slovaks and Slovenes placed the colours in the same order as Russia, the Serbs adopted a blue-red-white tricolour and the Croats

positioned the colours as in the Dutch flag. The flag adopted by Bulgaria in 1878 was the same as that of Russia, the only difference being the substitution of green for the red. In 1880 Montenegro adopted a merchant ensign, a tricolour similar to that of Serbia with a white cross in the centre of the red stripe. A year later the cross had been removed and a crown with the royal cipher "H.I", for Nikola I, placed in the centre. The Kingdom of Serbs, Croats and Slovenes, established in 1918, adopted a national flag and ensign in the form of a horizontal blue-white-red tricolour, which remained unchanged when the name of the country was changed to Yugoslavia.

A somewhat different flag belonging to this flag family is that of Czechoslovakia (currently the Czech Republic), adopted in 1920.

There are other flags that do not belong to this family, but are worth mentioning because their design (horizontal tricolour) is copied from that of the Russian flag. These are the flags and ensigns of nations that were once part of the Russian Empire and gained independence either temporarily or permanently: Belarus (1918–1919 and 1991–1995), some Cossack states, Lithuania, Estonia, Azerbaijan, Armenia, Uzbekistan and Tajikistan.

▼ BELOW (from left to right) *Russia (c.1700–1858, 1883–1918, since 1991); Bulgaria (since 1878); Slovakia (1848); Montenegro (1881–1918); Serbia (1882–1918); Croatia (1941–1945).*

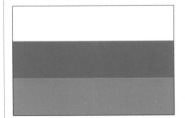

THE FRENCH *TRICOLORE*

The colours red, blue and white have been successively used on French flags from the time of Charlemagne. Red was the imperial flag from the 9th century; blue was the field of the armorial banner of France from the 13th century to 1589, and of the merchant ensign from 1661 to 1790; and white was the French flag and ensign from 1589 to 1790. Nevertheless, it is surprisingly only a coincidence that these three colours appear together on the French national flag; they are, in fact, the colours of the coat of arms of the city of Paris, combined with the white of the Bourbons.

On 13 July 1789, on the eve of the French Revolution, the Paris militia were given blue and red cockades. Four days later in the City Hall the Marquis de Lafayette presented a similar cockade to King Louis XVI, who attached it to the royal white one. The leaders of the Revolution approved the Marquis' proposal to adopt the cockade in the "colours of liberty". The new cockade was received enthusiastically by the people and in the following days the streets of Paris were full of ribbons and flags in the "colours of liberty" in various arrangements.

In spite of this fervour, the official flag and ensign remained unchanged. The addition of a tricolour streamer to the war ensign in 1790 did not satisfy the rebellious sailors, who demanded the introduction of a new one displaying the colours that were already perceived as the national ones. The ensign that was subsequently adopted on 24 October 1790 was white with the canton composed of a red-white-blue vertical tricolour and a white border separating it from the outer border, which was half-red and half-blue. The vertical arrangement of three colours was revolutionary, both geometrically and politically. The order of colours was changed to the present one on 15 February 1794.

A few decades after the French Revolution the colours of the *Tricolore*, as the flag is called, were perceived in Europe and elsewhere as the

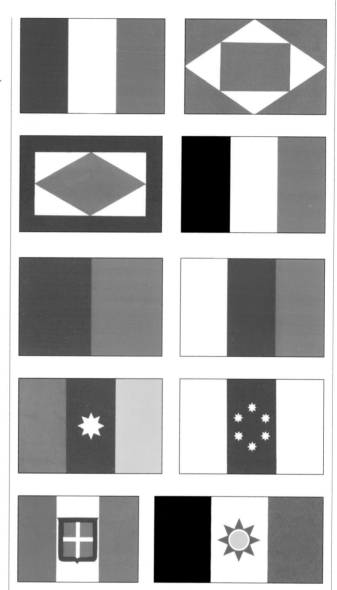

▲ *ABOVE* (left to right from top left) France (1794–1815 and since 1830); Italian Republic (1802–1805); Lucca (1803–1805); Rome Republic; Haiti (1804–1805); Mexico (1815–1821); Colombia, civil ensign (1834–1861); Ecuador, civil ensign (1845–1860); Italy, national flag and ensign (1848–1946); Iraq (1959–1963).

colours of the republican movement. They were adopted by Lucca (1803), Uruguay (1825–1828), the Dominican Republic (1844), Costa Rica (1848) and the Polish insurgents of 1863. Even more influential was the *Tricolore* design introduced by Napoleon in some Italian states. This later inspired revolutionaries and leaders of independence movements in many parts of the world to adopt flags with a vertical arrangement of colours. The first was the French colony of Saint Domingue where the revolutionaries had already in 1803 adopted a blue-red flag: the French flag without the white which they perceived as a symbol of their oppressors. On 1 January 1804 this became the first national flag of independent Haiti. Flags with three vertical stripes were adopted by revolutionary movements or governments in Mexico (1815), Belgium (1831), Colombia (1834), Ecuador (1845), Ireland (1848), Italy (1848) and Iraq (1958), and the King of Romania (1867).

A large group of flags with the French *Tricolore* in the canton are those of the French colonies created in the 19th and 20th centuries. When Saarland was part of the French occupation zone in Germany after World War II, the French authorities introduced a flag displaying the French colours.

The next large addition to the family of vertical tricolours came in the second half of the 20th century, when many former French colonies in Africa adopted flags following the *Tricolore* design.

THE FLAG FAMILY

The current national flags of the following countries belong to this family: ANDORRA, BELGIUM, CAMEROON, CHAD, FRANCE, GUINEA, IRELAND, ITALY, IVORY COAST, MALI, MEXICO, MOLDOVA, PERU, ROMANIA, RWANDA, SENEGAL, WALLIS AND FUTUNA.

FLAGS OF THE FRENCH COLONIES

TAHITI 1845–1880

RAIATEA 1880–1897

RIMATARA 1891–1900

LUANG PRABANG 1893–1947

LEBANON 1920–1943

LATAKIA 1922–1936

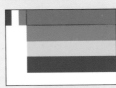

JABAL AD DURUZ 1922–1936

FRENCH MOROCCO 1923–1956

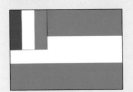

SYRIA 1925–1932

ANNAM 1930–1940

TOGO 1956–1960

GABON 1959–1960

THE LIVERY COLOURS

The simplest national flags, introduced by several European countries during the last two centuries, are those composed of livery colours arranged in two or three horizontal stripes. In most cases the upper stripe is in the colour of a heraldic charge, while the lower stripe displays the colour of the shield, although the reverse order of colours was customary in Austria. When translating coats of arms into flags, gold becomes yellow and silver becomes white. The only exception to this rule is the German flag, called *Schwarz-Rot-Gold* (black-red-gold), which has a golden yellow stripe instead of yellow.

From 1785 to 1931, and since 1936, the colours of the Spanish ensigns have been yellow and red, the armorial colours of Castile, Aragón, Catalonia and Navarre. The Spanish republican

▼ *Below top row* (from left) *Spain, civil ensign (1785–1928); Spain, civil ensign (1931 –1939); Portugal (1821 –1910).* **2ND ROW** *Würt- temberg (1816–1935); Brunswick (1748– 1814); Saxony (1815– 1935);*

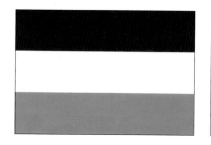

colours (1931–1939) were red, yellow and purple (the colour of the lion in the arms of León). The flag of Portugal from 1821 to 1910 displayed livery colours dating from the 12th century. National flags in livery colours were most widespread in central Europe, especially in the German states and parts of Austria-Hungary. The colours of the proper arms of Austria (a white fess on red field) were

▲ *Above and left* (from left to right) *Saxony-Weimar- Eisenach (1815–1920); Mecklenburg (1863– 1935); Prussia, civil ensign (1823–1863); Germany 1867–1919.*

▶ *RIGHT* (from left to right) *Austria, national flag (1804–1918); Galicia and Lodomeria (1849–1890); Austria-Hungary, civil ensign (1869–1918); Romania (1861–1867); Russia, national flag (1858–1883); San Marino, national flag (since 1862).*

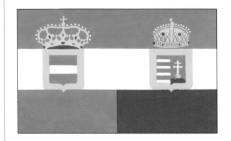

▶ *FAR RIGHT* *National flag of Bohemia (1914–1918); Czechoslovakia (1918–1920) and Poland (since 1919).*

employed on the civil ensign of 1869-1918 and thereafter on the national flag. The national flag of Austria, used from 1804 to 1918, displayed the colours of the imperial arms (a black double-headed eagle on a golden field). A few other examples are the flags or ensigns of Brunswick, Saxony, Saxony-Weimar-Eisenach, Württemberg, Prussia, Mecklenburg, Germany, Galicia and Lodomeria, Hungary and Austria-Hungary. The first flag of Romania displayed the livery colours of Valachia and Moldavia. For a short period the Russian national flag displayed the colours of the imperial arms (black double-headed eagle on a golden field) and white from the charge of the arms of Moscow. Other flags with livery colours are those of San Marino, Luxembourg, Monaco, the Vatican, Poland and Ukraine.

THE FLAG FAMILY

The national flags of the following countries belong to this family:

AUSTRIA, GERMANY, HUNGARY, LUXEMBOURG, MONACO, POLAND, SAN MARINO, SPAIN, UKRAINE, VATICAN.

THE PAN-ARAB COLOURS

The early Arab flags were of one colour, often charged with religious inscriptions. Biographers of the Prophet Muhammad ascribe to him two flags, one black and one white; his followers are said to have fought under the white flag for seven years and with this flag they entered Mecca. White was also the colour of the Muslim dynasty of the Umayyads, the immediate successors of the Prophet and an influential family of the Quraish tribe to which he belonged. Under a white flag the Umayyads ruled the Muslim Empire from AD 661 to 750, and were Muslim rulers of Spain from AD 756 to 1031. Black, the second colour used by Muhammad, was the colour of the Abbasid dynasty that overthrew the Umayyads and ruled the Muslim Empire from AD 750 to 1258.

Green, perceived as the colour of Islam, was the traditional colour of the Fatimid dynasty of caliphs, which ruled in North Africa from AD 909 to 1171. The Fatimids were leaders of the Ismaili sect and claimed descent from Fatima, the daughter of the Prophet Muhammad. Red is the colour of the Hashemites, descendants of Hashim, the great-grandfather of the Prophet Muhammad, and for centuries the hereditary amirs of Mecca. The founder of the modern Hashemite dynasty was Husayn ibn Ali, the amir of Mecca, King of Hejaz (1916–1924) and father of the kings of Iraq and Jordan.

In 1911 a group of young Arabs met in the Literary Club in Istanbul to choose a design for a modern Arab flag, and decided it should be composed of these four colours – white, black, green and red. The symbolism was explained by the poet Safi al-Din al-Hili:

White are our deeds, black are our battles,
Green are our fields, red are our knives.

In 1914 the central committee of the Young Arab Society in Beirut declared that the flag of the future independent Arab state should display the colours of the Umayyads (white), Abbasids (black) and Fatimids (green). However, the Arab Revolt began in Hejaz on 10 June 1916 under a

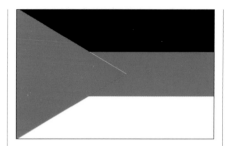

◀ *LEFT Hijaz (1917–1920).*

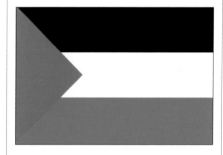

◀ *LEFT Hijaz (1920–1926) and Iraq (1921–1924).*

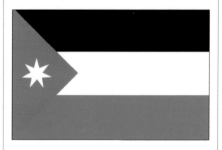

◀ *LEFT Syria (1920).*

plain red flag, traditional for that area. Several months later Sharif Hussein, leader of the revolt, accepted suggestions to adopt the colours white, black and green, and added red, a symbol of his family. The flag was hoisted on 30 May 1917,

THE FLAG FAMILY
The current national flags of the following countries and territories belong to this family:
EGYPT, IRAQ, JORDAN, KUWAIT, PALESTINE, SOMALILAND, SUDAN, SYRIA, UNITED ARAB EMIRATES, WESTERN SAHARA, YEMEN.

a day that might be considered the birthday of the pan-Arab colours.

The flag family started to grow when this modern Arab flag was adopted by Syria in March 1920 and by Iraq in 1921. By adding a white star (Syria) or two stars (Iraq) to the flag, both countries manifested that they were the first and second state to emanate from the "mother-state". The designs of these flags were later modified, but the four pan-Arab colours were retained and were adopted by Transjordan (1921), Palestine (1922), Kuwait (1961), the United Arab Emirates (1971), Western Sahara (1976) and Somaliland (1996).

After the revolution of 1952 in Egypt, the young officers who abolished the monarchy introduced the Arab Liberation Flag, a horizontal red-white-black tricolour, which symbolized the period of oppression (black) overcome through bloody struggle (red) to be replaced by a bright future (white). This flag was the inspiration for the flags of several Arab nations which chose the republican political system, so it could be considered to be the first of the second generation of pan-Arab colours. With the addition of two green stars (for Egypt and Syria), in 1958 it became the national flag of the United Arab Republic. Later similar flags, with or without stars, were adopted by Yemen (1962), Syria and Iraq (1963), South Yemen (1967), Libya (1969) and Sudan (1970).

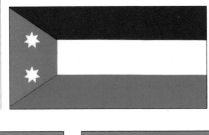

▲ *Above* (left to right from top left) *Iraq (1924–1959); Syria (1932–1958 and 1961–1963); United Arab Republic (1958–1961) and Egypt (1961–1972); Iraq (1963–1991) and Syria (1963–1971); Yemen (1962–1990); Libya (1969–1972); South Yemen (1967–1990).*

THE PAN-AFRICAN COLOURS

Two factors have influenced the choice of colours for the flags of independent countries south of the Sahara. The first, and main, source of inspiration was the green, yellow and red flag of Ethiopia, the oldest independent state in Africa. The second was the red, black and green flag designed in 1917 by Marcus Garvey, the organizer of the first important black unification movement in the United States. He created the flag for the United Negro Improvement Association, but wanted it to become the national flag of a new unified black state he dreamt of creating. In 1957, Ghana became the

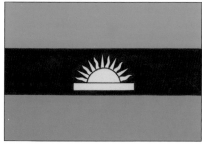

► *RIGHT* (from top to bottom) *Mali Federation (1959–1961); Biafra (1967–1970); Cape Verde (1975–1992).*

◄ *FAR LEFT The national flag of Ethiopia.*

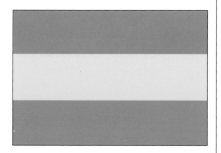

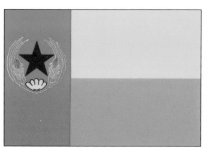

◄ *FAR LEFT Marcus Garvey's flag.*

THE FLAG FAMILY

The current national flags of the following countries belong to this family:

ANGOLA, BENIN, BURKINA FASO, CAMEROON, CENTRAL AFRICAN REPUBLIC, CONGO, ETHIOPIA, GHANA, GUINEA, GUINEA-BISSAU, KENYA, MALAWI, MALI, MOZAMBIQUE, RWANDA, SÃO TOMÉ AND PRÍNCIPE, SENEGAL, SOUTH AFRICA, TOGO, UGANDA, ZAMBIA, ZIMBABWE.

first independent country in western Africa to adopt a flag in these colours. Its flag, in the Ethiopian colours with a black star, was inspired by the flag of the Black Star Line shipping company established by Garvey in Accra.

The Ethiopian colours and pan-Africanism ideas heralded by President Kwame Nkrumah influenced many other African leaders. Indeed, President Sékou Touré of Guinea's extensive description of the symbolic meaning of the red, yellow and green in 1958 helped to consolidate the conviction that these three colours may also be regarded as pan-African.

Ghana's example was followed by other African countries which adopted flags displaying the same colours: the Mali Federation (1959-1961), Rwanda (1961), Zambia (1964), Guinea Bissau (1973), São Tomé and Príncipe (1975), Cape Verde (1975-1992), Zimbabwe (1980), Mozambique (1983) and South Africa (1994).

The first country in Africa to adopt Garvey's colours as its main flag colours was Kenya in 1963, which was closely followed by Malawi in 1964 and Biafra in 1967. In all three flags the black stands for the people, the red symbolizes the blood shed in the struggle for independence, and the green represents the land with its fertile fields and forests.

The Ethiopian colours in various arrangements were adopted by Benin, Burkina Faso, Cameroon, Congo (Brazzaville) and Togo. Some other countries (Angola, Central African Republic, Namibia, Seychelles, Tanzania and Uganda) display on their flags three of the four pan-African colours.

Most of the flags displaying the pan-African colours are still in use (see *Flags of Africa*).

▶ *RIGHT* (left to right) *South Kasai (1960–1962); Cameroon (1961–1975).*

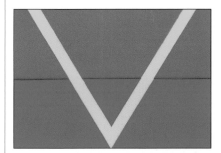

▶ *RIGHT Zanzibar (1963–1964).*

▶ *RIGHT* (left to right) *Burundi (1962–1966); Zaire (1971–1997).*

THE RED BANNER

A red flag has been used as a flag of defiance since the beginning of the 17th century, but its real role as a revolutionary flag began in 1830 in France, and during the Revolution of 1848 the mob in Paris even wanted it to be the national flag. It was again used by the Paris Commune of 1870, and soon after became the flag associated with the socialist movement. It then appeared during the Russian Revolutions of 1905 and 1917, and in 1918, with the addition of golden initials, was adopted by the Russian Republic. Similar flags were adopted by a few independent or semi-independent Bolshevik republics such as Belarus, Ukraine and the Far Eastern Republic, formed in the early years of the Civil War. In 1924 a red flag featuring a red star, a golden hammer and a sickle became the national flag of the Soviet Union. Soon the red star and the hammer and sickle (the crossed tools of workers and peasants) were regarded as the

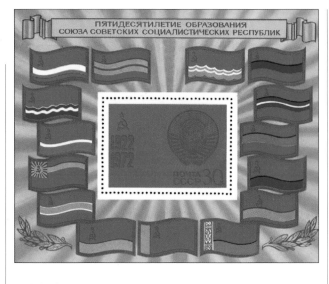

symbols of communism, appearing also on the flags of the Soviet republics.

Before World War II only two other communist countries had adopted national flags based on that of the Soviet Union: Mongolia

▲ ABOVE Flags of the Soviet Republics as depicted on a Soviet souvenir sheet: (clockwise from top centre) Estonian SSR; Armenian SSR; Kirghiz SSR; Moldavian SSR; Azerbaijan SSR; Kazakh SSS; Belarus SSR; Russian SFS; Ukrainian SSR; Uzbek SSR; Georgian SSR; Lithuanian SSR; Latvian SSR; Tajik SSR; Turkmen SSR.

◄ FAR LEFT (from top to bottom) Soviet Russia (1918–1937); Soviet Union (1924–1955); Soviet Union (1955–1991).
◄ LEFT (top to bottom) Soviet Byelorussia (1920–1924); Far Eastern Republic (1920–1922); Mongolia (1924–1940).

▶ *RIGHT TOP* Yugoslavia
(1946–1992).
▶ *RIGHT BOTTOM*
Hungary (1949–1956).

▼ *BELOW* (from left to
right) Bulgaria (1948–
1967); East Germany,
civil ensign (1959–
1973); Afghanistan
(1980–1987).

(1924–40) and Tannu-Tuva (1926–1930). After
the war the Soviet Union installed communist
regimes in central and eastern Europe but their
national flags were retained, although East
Germany, Yugoslavia, Bulgaria, and Hungary
modified theirs by adding a state emblem.

In Asia, several communist countries adopted
red flags with yellow emblems. The first was the

national flag and ensign of Vietnam (1945–
1955), followed by the flags of China (1949),
Cambodia (1976–1989) and Afghanistan
(1978–1980). In 1980 the traditional colours of
the Afghan flag were restored, with the addition
of the state emblem and a red star.

In Africa, only the Congo with its capital in
Brazzaville (1969–1991) copied the Soviet Red
Flag; Angola (1975), Benin (1975–1990),
Zimbabwe (1980), Mozambique (1983) and
Burkina Faso (1984) adopted a red or yellow
communist star. The hammer and sickle became
a hammer and hoe in the flag of the Congo,
and a cog wheel and machete in that of Angola.

▲ ▶ *ABOVE AND*
RIGHT (clockwise
from above) Vietnam
(1945–1955);
Cambodia (1979–
1989); Cambodia
(1976–1979).

▼ *BELOW* (from left
to right) Afghanistan
(1978–1980); Congo
(Brazzaville)
(1969–1991); Benin
(1975–1990).

SMALLER FLAG FAMILIES

Two smaller families of regional character came into being in the first quarter of the 19th century during the struggle for the liberation of Latin America from Spanish rule.

The famous Venezuelan revolutionary, Francisco de Miranda (c.1750–1816), personally designed a horizontal tricolour that symbolized golden America (yellow) separated by the Atlantic Ocean (blue) from bloody Spain (red). It was hoisted for the first time on 4 August 1806 on Colombian soil and, despite the defeat of the revolutionary forces, was not forgotten. So, when Venezuela formally declared independence, a flag in these colours with the yellow the same width as both of the two other stripes became the national flag on 5 June 1811. Miranda's forces were defeated again in 1812 but finally became victorious in 1821. The Venezuelans joined with the victorious Creoles of neighbouring Colombia and Ecuador to form the Republic of Gran Colombia under the same flag. When this fell apart in 1830, Venezuela retained the flag, which with minor modifications is still in use. For a few decades Ecuador and Colombia used flags of different designs but they restored Miranda's tricolour in 1860 and 1861 respectively.

The second of the Latin American flag families encompasses the flags of Argentina and the five states of Central America: El Salvador, Honduras, Nicaragua, Guatemala and Costa Rica. In May 1810 blue and white colours were adopted by revolutionaries in Buenos Aires and a blue-white-blue flag was hoisted by General Belgrano in Rosario on 27 February 1812, and formally adopted by the Argentine government on 25 July 1816. The flag became known in Central America when Louis Aury led a maritime expedition there in 1816 and six years later Manuel José Arce, commander-general of the province of San Salvador, decided to adopt the "Argentinian colours of Belgrano" as the national flag of San Salvador. It was consecrated on 20 February 1822 and a year later served as a model for the flag of the newly created United Provinces of Central America. The centre of the national ensign was charged with the motto *Dios, Unión, Libertad* ("God, Union, Liberty") in golden letters, and the emblem of the United Provinces was placed in the centre of the state flag. Both flags were decreed on 21 August 1823. The main feature of the emblem was a triangle with five volcanoes between the waters of two oceans. The triangle

▼ *BELOW* (from left to right) *Ecuador, civil flag and ensign (since 1860); Colombia, national flag, and government flag and ensign (since 1861); Venezuela, civil ensign (since 1930); Argentina, national flag and civil ensign (1812–1818); United Provinces of Central America, state flag (1823–1838; El Salvador, civil ensign (1838–1865 and since 1912).*

is a Masonic symbol of equality and its three angles represent the three branches of the government: legislative, executive and judicial. The five volcanoes stand for the five states of the Provinces, situated between the Atlantic and the Pacific. After the dissolution of the United Provinces of Central America in 1838, the five countries used various flags. The first to restore the blue-white-blue flag was Nicaragua in 1854, followed by El Salvador in 1865. Costa Rica added a wide red stripe (1848), Honduras added five blue stars (1866) and, finally, in 1871, Guatemala arranged the colours in vertical stripes.

The last family of flags contains three recent flags based on the United Nations flag. The first to adopt such a flag was Eritrea in 1952, using a design that was a compromise between emblems favoured by the Muslims and Coptic Christians. The blue background was chosen as a complement to the flag of the United Nations and was charged with a green wreath composed of two olive branches, with a third olive branch positioned vertically.

The Trust Territory of the Pacific Islands was administered by the United States under a 1947 trusteeship agreement with the Security Council of the United Nations. In July 1965 the High Commissioner revised the Code of the Trust Territory to allow all vessels registered and licensed there to fly the flag of the Territory. The flag was adopted by the Congress of Micronesia at its first session in July 1965, and became official on 19 August. It was a natural choice to adopt the United Nations blue for the field as it also symbolized the Pacific Ocean. The six white stars represented the six districts of the Trust Territory which were Mariana Islands, Marshall Islands, Ponape, Truck, Yap and Palau. In 1978 voters in the Marshall Islands and Palau rejected the proposed constitution for the Federated States of Micronesia. Since then the flag of Micronesia, introduced on 30 November 1978, has displayed four stars only.

The newest addition to the United Nations family of flags was the flag of Cambodia, used from 1991 to 1993. It was designed at the peace conference in Paris on 23 October 1991 as a transitional flag for the reconstruction of the country after many years of civil war and foreign intervention, so it did not display traditional Cambodian emblems or colours. Its colour was the United Nations blue and the only charge was a map of Cambodia with the country's name.

▼ *BELOW* (from left to right) *Guatemala (1851–1858); Guatemala, civil ensign (since 1871); Costa Rica, state flag (1906–1934); Eritrea (1952–1959 and on liberated territory until 1993); Pacific Islands (1965–1978) Cambodia (1991–1993).*

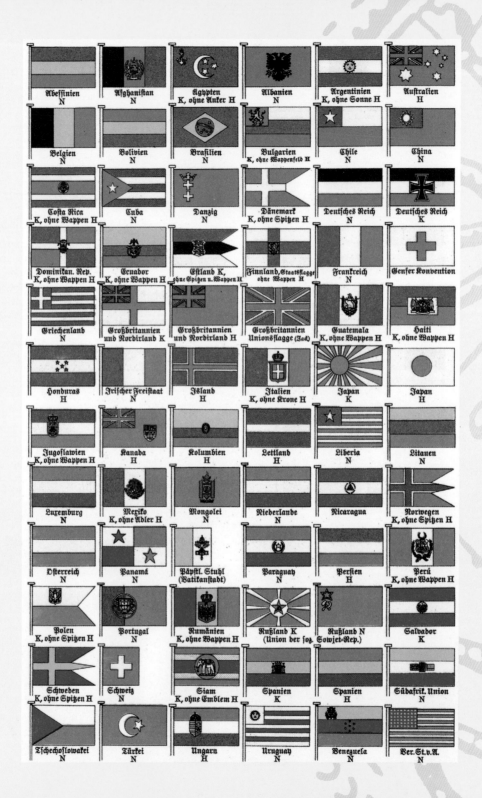

Abeffinien N	**Afghaniftan** N	**Ägypten** K, ohne Anker H	**Albanien** N	**Argentinien** K, ohne Sonne H	**Auftralien** H
Belgien N	**Bolivien** N	**Brafilien** N	**Bulgarien** K, ohne Wappenfeld H	**Chile** N	**China** N
Cofta Rica K, ohne Wappen H	**Cuba** N	**Danzig** N	**Dänemark** K, ohne Spitzen H	**Deutfches Reich** N	**Deutfches Reich** K
Dominikan. Rep. K, ohne Wappen H	**Ecuador** K, ohne Wappen H	**Eftland K,** ohne Spitzen u. Wappen H	**Finnland, Staatsflagge** ohne Wappen H	**Frankreich** N	**Genfer Konvention**
Griechenland N	**Großbritannien und Nordirland K**	**Großbritannien und Nordirland H**	**Großbritannien Unionsflagge (Jad)**	**Guatemala** K, ohne Wappen H	**Haiti** K, ohne Wappen H
Honduras H	**Frifcher Freiftaat** H	**Isfland** H	**Italien** K, ohne Krone H	**Japan** K	**Japan** N
Jugoflawien K, ohne Wappen H	**Kanada** H	**Kolumbien** H	**Lettland** H	**Liberia** N	**Litauen** N
Luxemburg N	**Mexiko** K, ohne Adler H	**Mongolei** H	**Niederlande** N	**Nicaragua** N	**Norwegen** K, ohne Spitzen H
Öfterreich N	**Panamá** N	**Päpftl. Stuhl (Vatikanftadt)**	**Paraguay** N	**Perfien** H	**Perú** K, ohne Wappen H
Polen K, ohne Spitzen H	**Portugal** N	**Rumänien** K, ohne Wappen H	**Rußland K (Union der foz. Sowjet-Rep.)**	**Rußland N**	**Salvador** K
Schweden K, ohne Spitzen H	**Schweiz** N	**Siam** K, ohne Emblem H	**Spanien** K	**Spanien** H	**Südafrik. Union**
Tfchechoflowakei N	**Türkei** N	**Ungarn** N	**Uruguay** N	**Venezuela** N	**Ber. St.v.A.** N

THE WORLD
OF FLAGS

This comprehensive survey of modern flags is designed to be clear
and informative. The national flags of countries of the world are grouped
under each continent, with a map of the continent at the beginning to give
their location. Included here are also flags of de facto independent states,
autonomous or semi-autonomous territories, and flags of subdivisions of
federations and confederations. To complete the survey of flags of the world,
there are descriptions of regional and local municipal flags used extensively
in some countries, and the flags of people and causes. In the 19th and 20th
centuries yacht and private flags became very popular and today there are
numerous flags for business, commerce and personal or
organisational use, including the high-profile flags of sporting events
such as the Olympic Games.

◄ *In 1935 one page was enough to show all the national flags of countries around*
the world. Today there are four times the number of independent countries.
Courtesy of F.A. Brockhaus Gmb H.

Flags of Europe

In the pages that follow, the current national flags of the countries of Europe, from Iceland and the Faeroes Islands to Russia and Chechnya, and their territories, states and provinces are illustrated and described.

For ease of reference, the countries of Europe have been grouped into geographical areas. We begin with the countries of northern Europe before moving on through central and western Europe and down to south-west Europe, and south and south-east Europe. Finally we look at the flags of the Eastern European countries. There are some geographical anomalies, for example, all Russia's flags are illustrated together in this section. The flags of Turkey, Cyprus and Northern Cyprus are all illustrated here.

For each entry, the country or territory's name is given in its most easily recognized form and then in all its official languages. This is followed by a description of its political status and geographic position. The basic data for each flag contains the status of the flag, date of adoption, proportions, and the symbolic meaning.

NORTHERN EUROPE

ICELAND

Republic of Iceland,
Icelandic **Lýdveldid Ísland**.
Republic comprising an island in the N Atlantic.

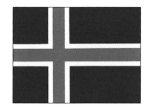

CIVIL FLAG AND ENSIGN

In use since 1913, officially approved 19 June 1915 for use on land and territorial waters, after 1 December 1918 also at sea. Proportions 18:25. State flag and ensign are swallow-tailed.

The design of the flag is based on that of Norway, with the colours reversed. Blue and white are the traditional national colours of Iceland and red symbolizes links with Norway, where most of their ancestors originated. The Scandinavian cross shows that Iceland belongs to the family of Scandinavian countries (see *Flag Families*).

Other symbolic meanings refer to the natural features of Iceland. Blue is the colour of the Atlantic Ocean, white represents the snow and ice covering the island for most of the year, and red the volcanoes on the island.

FAEROES ISLANDS

Faeroese **Fóroyar**, Danish **Færøerne**.
Island group in N Atlantic, outlying part of Denmark with full self-government.

NATIONAL FLAG AND CIVIL ENSIGN

Introduced in 1919, recognized by the local parliament in 1931 and officially approved by the King of Denmark 25 July 1948. The shade of blue was changed to lighter blue 5 June 1959. Proportions 8:11.

The flag was designed by two Faeroese students in Copenhagen, using Norwegian and Icelandic colours with the Scandinavian cross. Red and blue are also traditional Faeroese colours and the white represents the foam of the sea and the clear, bright sky of the Faeroes Islands.

Until 1940 the Faeroese flag was used only on land but in April 1940, after the Germans occupied Denmark, Faeroese ships began to use it at sea. The first to recognize the Faeroese flag were the British authorities; it was officially announced in a BBC broadcast on 25 April 1940 by Winston Churchill, at that time First Lord of the Admiralty, and ever since 25 April has been celebrated as Faeroese Flag Day.

NORWAY

Kingdom of Norway,
Norwegian **Kongeriket Norge**.
Constitutional monarchy in NW Europe.

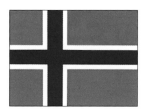

CIVIL FLAG AND ENSIGN

Adopted 17 July 1821 as a civil ensign only in N Atlantic, since 1838 usage unrestricted. Proportions 8:11. Since 1905 state and war flag and ensign have been triple swallow-tailed.

From 1748 to 1814 Norwegian ships flew the Danish *Dannebrog*. In 1814, when Norway was united with Sweden, the Norwegians obtained the right to carry the *Dannebrog* with the canton charged with the Norwegian golden lion, crowned and

holding an axe. Nevertheless, the struggle for a purely Norwegian flag continued and in 1821 the parliament adopted a new design, the *Dannebrog* with a dark blue cross positioned within the white one. The combination of red, white and blue followed the French revolutionary *Tricolore* as well as the flags of the United States and the United Kingdom, and was at that time regarded as a symbol of freedom. The cross was a common symbol of the national flags of Denmark and Sweden.

DENMARK

Kingdom of Denmark,
Danish **Kongeriget Danmark**.
Constitutional monarchy in NW Europe.

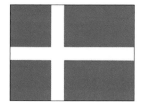

CIVIL FLAG AND ENSIGN

In use since the 13th century, officially confirmed in 1625. Proportions 28:37. State flag and war ensign are swallow-tailed.

The Danish flag, called the *Dannebrog*, is probably the oldest national flag in the world. According to legend, its history begins when the Danish crusaders, led by King Valdemar II the Victorious, were conducting a crusade against the pagan Estonians. The struggle had been going on for some time when the Estonians called all their warriors to arms on St Viti Day, 15 June 1219. The Danes were thrown into confusion by the fierce and unexpected attack, but suddenly a sign from heaven, a great blood red flag with a white cross floated down from the sky. The retreating Danish soldiers caught the flag, counter-attacked with the cry of "Forward to victory under the sign of the Cross", and eventually won the battle.

There is no definite proof that the *Dannebrog* was used at such an early date; the first picture of it appeared in *Wapenboek Gelre* in the second half of the 14th century. However, the *Dannebrog* may originally (in the 12th century) have been a crusade banner or even an ensign. The most probable theory is that the *Dannebrog* evolved in the same way as the flags for the border territories of the Holy Roman Empire (Hanseatic cities or cities in northern Italy), most of which displayed a white cross on red or red on white.

SWEDEN

Kingdom of Sweden,
Swedish **Konungariket Sverige**.
Constitutional monarchy in NW Europe.

CIVIL FLAG AND ENSIGN

Introduced in the 16th century, usage regulated on 6 November 1663, the most recent regulations of colours and proportions laid down in the Flag Act of 1982. Proportions 5:8.

In the royal warrant of 1569, King John III decreed that the golden cross should always be borne on Swedish battle banners. The oldest recorded pictures of the blue flag with a yellow cross date from the end of the 16th century, while reliable evidence that it was also the ensign of Swedish vessels dates from the 1620s. According to the oldest existing flag warrant from 1663, a triple-tailed flag was to be used by all except merchant ships, whose ensign was rectangular. Nowadays, use of the triple-tailed flag is reserved for the royal family and armed forces. The design of the flag was influenced by the Danish *Dannebrog*; its colours were from the coat of arms.

The main shield of the Great Arms of Sweden is divided quarterly and charged with the three crowns of Sweden (in the first and fourth quarters) and the lion of the Folkung dynasty (in the second and third quarters). This arrangement, with a golden cross separating four blue fields, was introduced by King Karl VIII Knutsson in 1448, and set the pattern for the flag.

There are very close ties between Sweden and Denmark, so it cannot be a coincidence that the Swedes added the cross to the arms, as the Danes did in the 14th century, and adopted a flag of the same pattern as the Danish *Dannebrog*.

ÅLAND ISLANDS

Finnish **Ahvenanmaa**, Swedish **Åland**.
Autonomous province of Finland comprising an archipelago in the Baltic Sea.

NATIONAL FLAG

Officially adopted 7 April 1954 for use on land only. Proportions 17:26.

The adoption of the Swedish flag charged with an additional red cross reflects the fact that the population of the islands is predominantly of Swedish origin. The colours are those of the arms of the Åland Islands (golden stag in blue field) and the arms of Finland (golden lion in red field).

FINLAND

Republic of Finland,
Finnish **Suomen Tasavalta,**
Swedish **Republiken Finland**.
Republic in N Europe.

STATE FLAG AND ENSIGN

Adopted 29 May 1918, the most recent regulations came into force 1 June 1978. Proportions 11:18. Civil flag and ensign are without the arms, war ensign is triple swallow-tailed with the arms.

Finland was a part of Sweden from the 12th century until 1809 and, after gaining independence, adopted a national flag patterned on the Swedish one. Similar flags were introduced by Finnish yacht clubs more than half a century earlier, when Finland was under Russian rule. The first yacht club, the *Nyländska Jaktkluben*, was established in 1861 in Helsinki and adopted a white flag with a blue cross, with the arms of the county of Nyland in the canton. The other yacht clubs followed suit, adopting the same design with different arms in the canton. The first to propose the blue and white as national colours of Finland was a poet called Zachris Topelius in 1862. In 1863 the newspaper *Helsingfors Dagblad* suggested that the national flags should be white with a blue cross.

The blue represents the thousands of lakes in Finland and its clear sky; the white stands for the snow that covers the country in the long winters.

ESTONIA

Republic of Estonia, Estonian **Eesti Vabariik**.
Republic in N Europe.

NATIONAL FLAG, CIVIL AND STATE ENSIGN

Approved 4 July 1920, re-adopted 8 May 1990.
Proportions 7:11.

The blue-black-white horizontal tricolour was adopted on 29 September 1881 by the Vironia, the Estonian students' association, and was displayed in great numbers at national song festivals in both 1894 and 1896. During the revolutions in 1905 and 1917 it was used by the populace as a national flag, and when independence was proclaimed on 24 February 1918 it became the Estonian civil flag.

In Estonian folk songs the colours of the flag symbolize the sky (blue), the soil (black) and the aspiration to freedom and hope for the future (white). Another interpretation is blue for mutual confidence and fidelity; black for the supposed ancestors of the Estonians, the black-cloaked people mentioned in Herodotus' *Histories*; and white for the snow that covers the country for half the year.

LATVIA

Republic of Latvia.
Latvian **Latvijas Republika**.
Republic in N Europe.

NATIONAL FLAG, CIVIL AND STATE ENSIGN

Approved 15 June 1921, re-adopted
15 February 1990. Proportions 1:2.

In 1279, long before it became the national flag of Latvia, the red-white-red banner was used by the home guard of Cesis. It was revived in 1870 by a group of Latvian university students in Estonia and used in 1873 at a national song festival in Riga. During World War I these colours became popular and were used by Latvian units of the Russian army, by boy scouts and by civil organizations. In 1917 prominent Latvian artists agreed that the shade of red should be crimson and that the width of the white stripe should be one-fifth of the flag's width. Use of the flag was forbidden under the Soviet occupation, which started on 17 June 1940. On 29 September 1988 its use as a civil flag was legalized and in 1990 it again became the national flag.

LITHUANIA

Republic of Lithuania,
Lithuanian **Lietuvos Respublika**.
Republic in N Europe.

NATIONAL FLAG, CIVIL AND STATE ENSIGN

Hoisted 11 November 1918, re-adopted
20 March 1989. Proportions 1:2.

Since the end of the 14th century the historic flag of Lithuania was red with a white knight and, in 1918, this became the state flag. The Lithuanian Council appointed a special commission to design a national flag and on 19 April 1918 it approved a horizontal tricolour using the colours most popular in traditional Lithuanian cloth.

The yellow is the colour of the sun, symbolizing light, prosperity, nobility, honesty and spiritual greatness. The green is the colour of vegetation, symbolizing the beauty of nature, life, hope, freedom and joy. The red is the colour of the land and of blood, symbolizing love, daring, courage and blood shed for the Fatherland.

THE *VYTIS*

The Lithuanian arms were adopted in the late 14th century. They are called *vytis* in Lithuanian which means "dispatch rider" or "knight". However, since the verb *vyti* means "to pursue, to follow hastily in order to overtake", the name of the arms in English can be translated as "the pursuit".

The Lithuanian arms or "pursuit" depict an armoured medieval knight riding hard on a galloping horse with a sword above his head.

Until the end of the 18th century "the pursuit" appeared on a red field on all Lithuania's battle and state banners. Then,

when Lithuania regained its independence in 1918, the *vytis* or "pursuit" became the main figure on the obverse of both the state and the presidential flag.

The arms were restored again in 1991 and appeared on the presidential standard and military colours.

CENTRAL EUROPE

POLAND

Republic of Poland,

Polish **Rzeczpospolita Polska**.

Republic in central Europe.

CIVIL ENSIGN, STATE FLAG OF LIMITED USE

In use since 1916, approved 1 August 1919.
Proportions 5:8. Civil flag is without arms.

This is the only state flag in the world that
is not used by all of the government
authorities. According to the law, it may be
used only by Polish representations abroad,
civil airports and airfields, harbour
authorities and civil aircraft abroad.

The Polish arms are over 700 years old
and show a white eagle on a red shield.
Officially approved in 1831 as the colours
of the national cockade, they became
popular during World War I.

SLOVAKIA

Slovak Republic,

Slovak **Slovenská Republika**.

Republic in Central Europe.

NATIONAL FLAG

Adopted 1 September 1992. Proportions 2:3.

The first Slovak flag, a horizontal tricolour
of white-blue-red, appeared in 1848. The
colours are those of the arms (white
patriarchal cross, blue triple mountain,

red shield). The same flag was adopted on
23 June 1939 as the national flag of
independent Slovakia and remained in
use until 1945. It again became official on
1 March 1990 and was used in Slovakia,
which at that time was part of
Czechoslovakia. The present flag was
described in the constitution of
1 September 1992, four months before
Slovakia became an independent republic.

CZECH REPUBLIC

Czech **Česká Republika**.

Republic in central Europe.

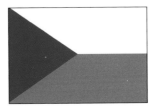

NATIONAL FLAG

Adopted 20 March 1920 as the flag of
Czechoslovakia, proclaimed the flag of the Czech
Republic 17 December 1992. Proportions 2:3.

White and red are the traditional colours of
Bohemia; they stem from the arms (which
feature a white lion on a red field), which
date back to 1192. The first Czech white
and red bicolour flag appeared during
World War I and in 1918 became the first
national flag of Czechoslovakia. As it
displayed only the colours of Bohemia, the
blue from the arms of Moravia and Slovakia
was added in 1920.

HUNGARY

Republic of Hungary, Hungarian **Magyar
Köztársaság**. Republic in Central Europe.

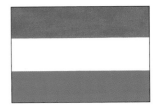

NATIONAL AND STATE FLAG

Adopted in 1848, re-introduced 1 October 1957.
Proportions 2:3.

The first recorded instance of the Hungarian
national colours (red, white, green) dates
from a drum cover of the mid-16th century.
From the beginning of the 17th century they
were used in the seal cord, and later were an
important part of the decorations used at
coronations. In the 1830s patriotic elements
started to use flags with these colours, and
during the revolution of 1848 the Hungarian
tricolour was proclaimed as the national
flag. The colours are those of the Hungarian
arms (red shield, white stripes and
patriarchal cross, green triple mountain).

AUSTRIA

Republic of Austria,

German **Republik Österreich**.

Federal republic in central Europe.

STATE FLAG

Adopted 1 May 1945. Civil flag and ensign
are without arms.

From at least 1230 the Austrian arms
consisted of a red shield with a wide

horizontal white bar. The red-white-red stripes first appeared on the state and war ensign, introduced on 1 January 1787. The red-white-red horizontal bicolour with no charge was adopted in 1918 as the national flag and in 1921 as the civil ensign. After the German occupation of 1938–1945, the flag was re-introduced in 1945.

AUSTRIAN STATES

Austria is divided into nine states (Bundesländer) which have their own flags.

BURGENLAND

STATE FLAG

Adopted 25 June 1971. Proportions 2:3.

The arms in the centre of the horizontal bicolour of livery colours were introduced in 1922. They combine the arms of two families, the counts of Güssing-Bernstein and the counts of Mattersdorf-Forchtenstein, who had extensive estates in Burgenland before they died out in the 15th century.

CARINTHIA

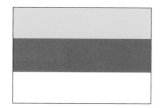

STATE FLAG

Officially adopted 18 June 1946. Proportions 2:3.

This flag has been in use since the 19th century. The colours stem from the arms, which date back to the 13th century.

They were officially adopted in 1930 as the arms of the province.

LOWER AUSTRIA

STATE FLAG

Officially adopted 9 August 1954. Proportions 2:3.

The flag was introduced in the 19th century. The colours are those of the arms (five golden eagles on a blue field), adopted in 1359.

SALZBURG

STATE FLAG

Officially adopted 16 February 1921. Proportions 2:3.

The red-white bicolour has been in use since the 19th century. The colours derive from the second field of the provincial arms and bear the colours of Austria.

STYRIA

STATE FLAG

Officially adopted in 1960. Proportions 2:3.

In the 19th century the flag of Styria was a green-white bicolour; the colours then were reversed in 1960. They are the colours of the arms, which date back to the 13th century and display a silver panther on a green field.

TYROL

STATE FLAG

Officially adopted 10 March 1949. Proportions 2:3.

A red eagle on a silver (white) field has been the arms of Tyrol since the 13th century. A crown was added in 1416, and a green wreath in 1567. The present form of the arms was introduced in 1946.

UPPER AUSTRIA

STATE FLAG

Officially adopted 25 April 1949. Proportions 2:3.

The arms date back to the 14th century and were confirmed in 1930. The colours of the flag stem from the second field of the arms (white and red pallets).

VIENNA

STATE FLAG

Approved in 1946. Proportions 2:3.

The red-white flag has been in use since the first half of the 19th century. The colours are those of the arms (white cross on red field).

VORARLBERG

STATE FLAG

Approved in 1946. Proportions 2:3.

Introduced in the 19th century, the flag's colours are those of the provincial arms, based on the arms of the dukes of Montford, which date back to the end of the 12th century (red gonfanon on silver field).

LIECHTENSTEIN

Principality of Liechtenstein,
German **Fürstentum Liechtenstein**.
Constitutional monarchy in W Central Europe.

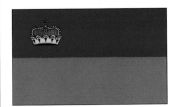

NATIONAL FLAG

Adopted 24 June 1937, the crown modified 18 September 1982. Proportions 3:5.

The national colours of Liechtenstein probably derive from the blue and red livery used in the 18th century by the servants of Prince Joseph Wenzel of Liechtenstein. The horizontal bicolour was confirmed as the national flag in the constitution signed on 5 October 1921. In 1937 the prince's crown was introduced to distinguish it from the civil flag of Haiti.

SWITZERLAND

Swiss Confederation,
German **Schweizerische Eidgenossenschaft,**
French **Confédération Suisse,**
Italian **Confederazione Svizzera,**
Romansch **Confederaziun Svizra**.
Federal republic in W Central Europe.

NATIONAL FLAG

Officially adopted 12 December 1889.
Proportions 1:1. Proportions of civil ensign 2:3.

In 1339 every soldier and officer of the troops leaving for the battle of Laupen was marked with the sign of the Holy Cross. The white cross on a red field has been a common Swiss emblem ever since. From the end of the 15th century a red banner charged with a white cross has been the accepted flag of the Confederation. The current flag was introduced in 1848 as the military colours, and its exact proportions were established in a military regulation of 1852. It became the national flag in 1889.

SWISS CANTONS

The official flags of all Swiss cantons are square armorial banners (*Kantonsfahnen*). Other types of Swiss flags are: (i) a long, vertical, swallow-tailed banner with a square armorial flag in the hoist and vertical stripes in livery colours (*Wappenflagge*); (ii) a long, vertical, rectangular banner of the same design as above, hanging from a traverse projecting at a right angle from a mast (*Knatterfahne*); (iii) a long, vertical, swallow-tailed banner in livery colours (*zweizipflige Farbenfahne*); (iv) a rectangular flag of proportions 2:3 in livery colours (*querrechteckige Farbenfahne*).

AARGAU

CANTONAL FLAG

Adopted in 1803, present form since 1930.

The white waves symbolize the River Aare, and the stars stand for the districts of Baden, Freien Ämter and Fricktal. The livery colours are black and blue.

APPENZELL INNER-RHODES

CANTONAL FLAG

In use since the beginning of the 15th century.

The bear was taken from the arms of the Abbey of Sankt Gallen. The livery colours are white and black.

APPENZELL OUTER-RHODES

CANTONAL FLAG

Adopted in 1597.

When the canton separated from Appenzell, the bear was retained and the letters "VR" (the initial letters for Ussroden – Outer-Rhodes) were added. The livery colours are white and black.

BASEL-LAND

CANTONAL FLAG

Introduced in 1834, the present form established 1 April 1947.

The arms are based on the civic arms of Liestal. The livery colours are white and red.

BASEL-STADT

CANTONAL FLAG

In use since at least the 15th century.

The oldest known representation of the bishop's crozier is on a coin minted in the 11th century; the current shape of the crozier has been in use since the 13th century. The livery colours are white and black.

BERN

CANTONAL FLAG

In use since at least the 14th century.

These are canting arms, i.e. they contain an allusion to the name of the canton (the German word for "bear" is *Bär*). The oldest representation of the bear is on a coin minted in 1224. The livery colours are red and black.

FRIBOURG

CANTONAL FLAG

In use since the beginning of the 15th century.

The arms, based on the banner, were adopted in 1477. The livery colours are black and white.

GENEVA

CANTONAL FLAG

In use since the 15th century.

The black eagle is the emblem of the Holy Roman Empire and the key is a symbol of St Peter. The oldest representations of the arms are in two books published in 1451. The livery colours are yellow and red.

GLARUS

CANTONAL FLAG

In use since the 14th century. The present form adopted 25 June 1959.

The patron saint of the canton is St Fridolin, an Irish missionary who settled there in 500. The livery colours are black, white and red. The black and white together are the same width as a red stripe.

GRAUBÜNDEN

CANTONAL FLAG

Adopted 8 November 1932.

The arms display the symbols of the three parts of the canton, which united in the 15th century: *Grauer Bund* (black and white), *Zehgerichtenbund* (cross) and *Gotteshausbund* (ibex). The livery colours are black, white and blue.

JURA

CANTONAL FLAG

Adopted in 1951, approved in 1976, official since 1978.

The crozier recalls that Jura was part of Basel-Land. The stripes represent seven districts interested in being part of a new canton. In the end only three formed Jura. The livery colours are white and red.

LUCERNE

CANTONAL FLAG

In use since the 13th century.

The canton's colours are older than the arms (adopted in 1386). In the arms the colours are arranged vertically: blue, white. The livery colours are white and blue.

NEUCHÂTEL

CANTONAL FLAG

Adopted 11 April 1848.

The green represents liberty, the white and red are traditional Swiss colours. The livery colours are green, white and red.

NIDWALDEN

CANTONAL FLAG

In use since the beginning of the 15th century.

The key is the emblem of St Peter. The livery colours are red and white.

OBWALDEN

CANTONAL FLAG

Adopted 12 August 1816.

Since the 13th century the canton's arms and banner have been a red-white bicolour. The key of St Peter appeared for the first time on the seal in the 13th century. The livery colours are red and white.

SAINT GALL

CANTONAL FLAG

Adopted 4 April 1803.

The fasces is a symbol of sovereignty and unity; the eight rods (five are visible) represent the eight districts of the canton. The livery colours are green and white.

SCHAFFHAUSEN

CANTONAL FLAG

In use since the 14th century.

The ram (*Schafsbock* in German) alludes to the name of both the city and the canton. Since the 15th century the canton's colours have been green and black.

SCHWYZ

CANTONAL FLAG

In use since the 15th century.

Since the end of the 13th century the banner has been plain red. The oldest recorded picture of a banner with a white cross in the canton dates from 1470. The livery colour is red. The white cross appears on the *zweizipflige Farbenfahne*.

SOLOTHURN

CANTONAL FLAG

In use since the 14th century.

The livery colours are red and white.

THURGAU

CANTONAL FLAG

Adopted 13 April 1803.

The lions are from the arms of the counts of Kyburg. Green represents freedom. The livery colours are green and white.

TICINO

CANTONAL FLAG

Adopted 23 May 1803.

The colours (vertical in the arms, horizontal on the banner) were established in 1930. The livery colours are red and blue.

URI

CANTONAL FLAG

In use since the 14th century.

From the 13th to the 15th century the aurochs's head was without the nose-ring. The emblem (*Uroch* in Old German) alludes to the name of the canton. The livery colours are yellow and black.

VALAIS

CANTONAL FLAG

In use since the 16th century, present form adopted 12 May 1815.

The stars represent the 13 districts of the canton. The livery colours are white and red.

VAUD

CANTONAL FLAG

Decreed 16 April 1803.

The motto is "Freedom and Fatherland" and the green is a symbol of freedom. The livery colours are white and green.

ZUG

CANTONAL FLAG

In use since the mid-14th century.

The arms and banner were originally identical to those of Austria (red field with white band) and were changed when Zug joined the Confederation in 1352. The livery colours are white, blue and white.

ZÜRICH

CANTONAL FLAG

In use since the 13th century.

The oldest known representation of the arms dates from 1389. The livery colours are blue and white.

GERMANY

Federal Republic of Germany, German **Bundesrepublik Deutschland**.
Federal republic in Central Europe.

STATE FLAG

Introduced 23 March 1848, re-introduced in
1919 and again 23 May 1949. Civil flag and
ensign are without arms.

The German national colours are those of
the arms, which are the same as the arms
of the Holy Roman Empire: black for the
eagle, red for its beak and claws, and yellow
for the golden shield. They featured in the
uniform worn by the Lützow Free Corps
(black greatcoats, red facings and hems,
golden buttons) during the war of
liberation in 1813–1815, when the trend
towards the unification of Germany was
growing. The horizontal tricolour of black-
red-gold became the national flag of the
German Federation in 1848 and was
replaced in 1867 with a tricolour of black-
white-red, which was in use until 1919 and
again in 1933–1935.

GERMAN STATES

From 1949 to 1990 West Germany
comprised 11 states (Bundesländer). Since
re-unification with East Germany there are
now 16 states.

BADEN-WÜRTTEMBERG

STATE FLAG

Adopted 29 September 1954. Proportions 3:5.

Black and yellow have been the colours of
the arms of the duchy of Swabia since the
end of the 12th century. They display three
black lions on a golden shield.

BAVARIA

STATE AND CIVIL FLAG

Adopted 2 December 1946. Proportions 3:5.

The Bavarian flag is a horizontal bicolour in
the livery colours. The arms of Bavaria,
which date back to the beginning of the
13th century, have white and blue lozenges.

BERLIN

STATE FLAG

Adopted 13 May 1954. Proportions 3:5.

The bear first appeared on the second
city seal in 1280. A red-white-red flag
with a black bear was introduced in 1913,
and the current design of the bear was
established in 1954.

CIVIL FLAG

BRANDENBURG

STATE AND CIVIL FLAG

Adopted 30 January 1991. Proportions 3:5.

The arms date back to 1330. The flag is in
the livery colours.

BREMEN

STATE AND CIVIL FLAG

*In use without arms since 1691, approved
21 November 1947. Proportions 2:3.*

The originally plain red flag was charged in
the second half of the 14th century with a
white key, the symbol of St Peter, the
patron saint of the city. The current forms
of the great and small arms, and two state
flags, were enacted in 1891.

HAMBURG

STATE FLAG

*Civil flag adopted 14 May 1751,
state flag introduced 8 October 1897,
confirmed 6 June 1952. Proportions 2:3.*

CIVIL FLAG

The castle represents Hammaburg Castle, built by Emperor Charles the Great in AD 808, and the arms date back to 1254. The three towers stand for the Trinity, the cross is a symbol of Christ, and the stars symbolize God the Father and the Holy Spirit. Red flags with the castle were already in use in the first half of the 14th century.

HESSE

STATE AND CIVIL FLAG

Both flags adopted 22 November 1949. Proportions 3:5.

The colours of the flag are taken from the lion in the arms. These stem from the arms of the landgraves (ruling counts) of Thuringia, who from 1130 to 1247 were also landgraves of Hesse.

LOWER SAXONY

CIVIL FLAG

Adopted 13 April 1951. State flag is swallow-tailed. Proportions 2:3.

The flag is in the German national colours and is charged with the arms of the state. The horse (*Niedersachsenross*) has been the symbol of Lower Saxony since the 14th century.

MECKLENBURG-WEST POMERANIA

CIVIL FLAG

Adopted 29 January 1991. Proportions ±3:5.

The flag is a combination of the colours of Pomerania (blue, white), Hansa (white, red) and former flags of Mecklenburg – the national flag (blue, yellow, red) and the civil ensign (blue, white, red).

NORTH RHINE-WESTPHALIA

STATE FLAG

Adopted 10 March 1953. Civil flag is without arms. Proportions 3:5.

The colours of the flag are taken from the arms, which combine the symbols of three parts of the state which are Rhineland (river), Westphalia (horse) and Lippe (rose).

RHINELAND-PALATINATE

STATE AND CIVIL FLAG

Adopted 10 May 1948. Proportions 2:3.

The flag is in the colours of Germany and the state arms. The arms combine the arms of Trier (cross), Koblenz (wheel) and Palatinate (lion), all dating back to the 13th century.

SAARLAND

STATE AND CIVIL FLAG

Adopted 9 July 1956, introduced 1 January 1957. Proportions ±3:5.

This is the national flag of Germany with the state arms. The arms are quarterly: (i) countship of Saarbücken, (ii) Trier, (iii) Lorraine, (iv) Palatinate.

SAXONY

STATE FLAG

Adopted 16 June 1815. Civil flag is without arms. Proportions 3:5.

The civil flag, used 1815–1935 and 1947–1952, was re-adopted in 1991. The arms are those of the duchy of Saxony and date back to the 13th century.

SAXONY-ANHALT

STATE FLAG

Civil flag (without arms) adopted 29 January 1991. State flag described in the constitution of 1992. Proportions 3:5.

The black and yellow bicolour was the flag of the Prussian province of Saxony from 1884–1935 and 1945–1952. The order of the colours has been reversed to differentiate the flag from that of Baden-Württemberg. The arms used are a combination of the arms of Saxony (black and yellow bands, green crown of rue), Anhalt (black bear on red wall) and Prussia (black eagle).

SCHLESWIG-HOLSTEIN

STATE FLAG

Adopted 18 January 1957. Civil flag is without the arms. Proportions 3:5.

The blue-white-red horizontal tricolour became the civil flag for use on land in 1842. This flag was used until 1854, and again in 1864–1935. The colours were taken from the arms, which depict the blue lions of Schleswig and the white nettle leaf of Holstein.

THURINGIA

STATE FLAG

Adopted 10 January 1991. Civil flag is without the arms. Proportions 1:2.

The flag shows the colours of the Thuringian white and red lion, dating from the 12th century. The white stars were added to the arms to commemorate the seven small states that formed the province of Thuringia in 1920.

WESTERN EUROPE

LUXEMBOURG

Grand Duchy of Luxembourg, French **Grand-Duché de Luxembourg**, Letzeburgesch **Groussherzogtum Lëtzebuerg**, German **Grossherzogtum Luxemburg**. Constitutional monarchy in W Europe.

NATIONAL FLAG

Introduced in the present form 12 June 1845, adopted 16 August 1972. Proportions 3:5.

It is only coincidence that this flag is so similar to that of the Netherlands. The colours of the national flag of Luxembourg are those of the arms (red lion, white and blue stripes). Note the lighter shade of blue. An armorial banner has been in use since 1853 as the flag of the Army, and since 1972 as the flag of inland shipping and civil aviation.

FRANCE

Republic of France, French **République Française**. Republic in W Europe.

NATIONAL FLAG

Introduced 20 May 1794, uninterrupted use since 5 March 1848. Proportions 2:3. Civil and war ensign have stripes of different width.

The colours of the French national flag, known as the *Tricolore*, were introduced during the French Revolution when the King added the royal white cockade of the House of Bourbon to the revolutionary cockade of blue and red (the livery colours of Paris).

BELGIUM

Kingdom of Belgium, Flemish **Koninkrijk België**, Walloon **Royaume de Belgique**. Federal constitutional monarchy in W Europe.

NATIONAL FLAG

Introduced August 1830, officially adopted 23 January 1831. Proportions 13:15, proportions of civil ensign 2:3.

The flag, inspired by the French *Tricolore*, displays the colours of the arms of the duchy of Brabant, which date back to the 12th century. The war of independence started in Brabant and found its greatest support there, so its arms became the arms of Belgium (golden lion with red claws and tongue on black field).

BELGIAN REGIONS

In 1993 Belgium became a federal state comprising three nearly autonomous regions: Flanders (Flemish-speaking), Wallonia (French-speaking), and Brussels (bilingual). Each has its own parliament, regional council and government.

BRUSSELS

REGIONAL FLAG

Adopted on 22 June 1991. Proportions ±2:3.

The blue is that of the flag of the European Union. The iris is a well-known flower of

the fields along the river Senne which flows through Brussels.

FLANDERS

REGIONAL FLAG

Introduced 11 July 1985. Proportions 2:3.

This is an armorial flag, the basic design of which dates from the 12th century.

WALLONIA

REGIONAL FLAG

Introduced in 1913. Proportions 2:3.

The cock is a traditional Gallic emblem and recalls Wallonia's linguistic and cultural ties with France.

THE NETHERLANDS

Kingdom of the Netherlands, Dutch **Koninkrijk der Nederlanden**. Semi-federal constitutional monarchy in W Europe.

NATIONAL FLAG AND ENSIGN

Officially introduced 14 February 1796, confirmed 19 February 1937. Proportions 2:3.

The first flag of the Netherlands, introduced in 1574 during the struggle for independence, was a horizontal tricolour of orange-white-blue. Orange was the colour of William I, Prince of Orange, who led the rebellion against Spanish rule and eventually in 1581 established an independent country. During the 17th century red gradually replaced the orange, and in 1796 the red-white-blue was officially confirmed.

Nevertheless, orange is still the Dutch national colour and when the flag is displayed during state holidays or by diplomatic missions abroad it is accompanied by a long orange streamer fastened just above the flag.

THE NETHERLANDS PROVINCES

While all Dutch port cities had their own flags already in the 17th century, the provincial flags came into being during the last 50 years. Nevertheless, they display livery colours or arms that are several centuries old.

DRENTHE

PROVINCIAL FLAG

Adopted 19 February 1947. Proportions 9:13.

White and red are the colours of the bishopric of Utrecht, to which the province once belonged. The black castle is the castle of Coevorden, where in 1227 the rebellion against the bishopric started. The stars represent the former six *fehmic* courts.

FLEVOLAND

PROVINCIAL FLAG

Adopted 9 January 1986. Proportions 2:3.

The flag recalls how the new province was reclaimed from the waters of the IJsselmeer. The dark yellow central stripe, wavy then straight, symbolizes the transformation of the sea into land. Its colour is that of rape, planted in the new polders to stabilize the land; the blue represents water, the green the land. The fleur-de-lis honours C. Lely, who designed the original polders.

FRIESLAND

PROVINCIAL FLAG

Adopted 9 July 1957. Proportions 9:13.

The design is based on the arms from the 15th century. The stripes and waterlily leaves represent the districts of Friesland.

GELDERLAND

PROVINCIAL FLAG

Adopted 13 April 1953. Proportions 9:13.

The colours are those of the provincial arms, combining the arms of the old dukedoms of Gelre (golden lion in blue field) and Gulik (black lion in golden field).

GRONINGEN

PROVINCIAL FLAG

Adopted 17 February 1950. Proportions 2:3.

Green and white are Groningen's colours; red, white and blue are Ommerland's.

LIMBURG

PROVINCIAL FLAG

Adopted 28 July 1953. Proportions 2:3.

The blue stripe stands for the river Meuse and the lion comes from the arms of the duchy of Limburg. Yellow and red are the colours of the arms of Valkenburg, Gulik, Horn and Gelre.

NORTH BRABANT

PROVINCIAL FLAG

Adopted 21 January 1959. Proportions 2:3.

This is the flag of the duchy of Brabant and dates back to the 17th century.

NORTH HOLLAND

PROVINCIAL FLAG

Adopted 22 October 1958. Proportions 2:3.

The colours stem from the arms of Holland (red lion in golden field) and West Friesland (golden lions in blue field).

OVERIJSSEL

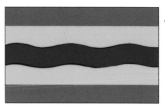

PROVINCIAL FLAG

Adopted 21 July 1948. Proportions 10:17.

The wavy blue stripe symbolizes the river IJssel. The colours are those of the arms (red lion in golden field charged with a blue fesse wavy). They also recall the historic association of the province with Holland.

SOUTH HOLLAND

PROVINCIAL FLAG

Adopted 1 January 1986. Proportions 2:3.

This is the armorial banner of the former countship of Holland.

UTRECHT

PROVINCIAL FLAG

Adopted 15 January 1952. Proportions 2:3.

White and red are the colours of the city of Utrecht. The white cross in a red field is the arms of the bishopric of Utrecht and dates back to the 16th century.

ZEELAND

PROVINCIAL FLAG

Adopted 14 January 1949. Proportions 2:3.

The wavy blue and white stripes symbolize the stripes of sea and land in the coastal area. The arms in the centre date back to the 16th century.

IRELAND

Republic of Ireland,
Irish **Poblacht Na h'Éireann**.
Republic comprising most of the territory of the island of Ireland, NW Europe.

NATIONAL FLAG AND ENSIGN

In use since 1916, recognized in 1922, formally confirmed 29 December 1937. Proportions 1:2.

The flag is based on the French *Tricolore* and displays colours that were used in reverse order during the revolutionary year of 1848. The green represents the Catholics, the orange the Protestants (originally supporters of William of Orange) and the white stands for peace between both parts of the population.

ISLE OF MAN

Isle of Man, Manx **Ellan Vannin**.
Dependency of the British crown in the Irish Sea, NW Europe.

NATIONAL FLAG

TRISKELION

The *triskelion* (from the Greek for "three-legged") is one of the oldest symbols known to mankind. The earliest representations of it were found in prehistoric rock carvings in northern Italy. It also appears on Greek vases and coins from the 6th and 8th centuries BC, and was revered by Norse and Sicilian peoples. The Sicilian version has a represent-ation of the head of Medusa in the centre.

The Manx people believe that the *triskelion* came from Scandinavia. According to Norse mythology, the *triskelion* was a symbol of the movement of the sun through the heavens.

Introduced in 1929, present design adopted 9 July 1968. Proportions 1:2.

The distinctive "Three Legs of Man" have been the emblem of the island since at least the 13th century. At the end of the 14th century they were armed and in this form were the main charge of the Manx flags and ensigns.

UNITED KINGDOM

United Kingdom of Great Britain and Northern Ireland.
Constitutional monarchy in NW Europe.

STATE FLAG AND JACK

Adopted 1 January 1801. Proportions 1:2.

The Union flag, also called the Union Jack, is a combination of the crosses of the patron saints of England (St George's cross, red cross on white field), Scotland (St Andrew's cross, white saltire on blue field) and Ireland (St Patrick's cross, red saltire on white field).

UNITED KINGDOM TERRITORIES

Presented here are the flags of the four parts of the United Kingdom (England, Scotland, Wales and Northern Ireland), as well as flags of three areas within Scotland that enjoy a limited autonomy (Orkneys, Shetland and the Hebrides).

ENGLAND

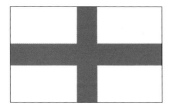

NATIONAL FLAG

In use since the 13th century. Proportions ±2:3.

The red cross of St George on a white field was an emblem of the English Army and (until 1606) an ensign of merchant and naval ships. From 1606 to 1801 it was a jack of merchant ships. According to legend, St George saved a princess from a dragon and with its blood made the sign of the cross on his white shield.

SCOTLAND

NATIONAL FLAG

In use since the 12th century. Proportions ±2:3.

St Andrew, brother of St Peter, was crucified in Patras on an X-shaped cross, and legend says his relics were taken to Scotland and buried there. Since the 11th century St Andrew has been the patron saint of Scotland, and since the 12th century a white saltire of St Andrew has been the Scottish national symbol (since the 15th century on a blue field). On 18 February 2003 the Parliament decided that the shade of blue should be Pantone 300.

ORKNEY ISLANDS

NATIONAL FLAG

Introduced in 1975. Proportions 2:3.

In this banner of arms, granted on 3 March 1975, the boat (a traditional galley) is taken from the arms of the countship of the Orkneys. The arms of Norway (a lion holding an axe) recall that the Orkneys originally belonged to Norway and were one of two provinces entitled to use the royal arms.

SHETLAND ISLANDS

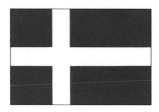

NATIONAL FLAG

In use since 1969. Proportions 2:3.

White and blue are the colours of Scotland. The Scandinavian cross is a reminder that the Shetlands were once settled by the Vikings and indicates that the islands are part of the Nordic countries.

HEBRIDES

NATIONAL FLAG

Granted 9 September 1976. Proportions 1:2.

The British blue ensign is charged with a badge depicting a lymphad (traditional rowing boat) in black. The heraldic boat symbolizes the seafaring traditions and skills of the population.

WALES

NATIONAL FLAG

Approved in 1959. Proportions 2:3.

The red dragon (*Y Ddraig Goch*) dates from the 4th century. In the 7th century it was adopted by Cadwaladr, Prince of Gwynedd, as the charge of his battle standard. White and green were the livery colours of the Welsh Prince Llewellyn, and later of the House of Tudor.

NORTHERN IRELAND

NATIONAL FLAG

Adopted 29 May 1953. Proportions 2:3.

The banner of arms of Northern Ireland was granted by King George V on 2 August 1924. The star representing the six counties is ensigned with the royal crown and charged with the red hand of Ulster. There is a flag of the same design, with a yellow field instead of white.

JERSEY

Bailiwick of Jersey.
Dependency of the British crown in the
English Channel, NW Europe.

NATIONAL FLAG

Granted by royal warrant of 10 December 1980,
introduced 7 April 1981. Proportions unspecified.

For about 200 years the flag of Jersey was
white with a red saltire. The arms, added in
1980, are those granted about 1290 by
Edward I, King of England, to the Bailiff of
Jersey. The shield is ensigned with an
ancient crown, similar to that attributed to
the House of Plantagenet.

GUERNSEY

Bailiwick of Guernsey and Dependencies.
Dependency of the British crown in the
English Channel, NW Europe.

NATIONAL FLAG

Adopted 13 March 1985, officially hoisted
9 May 1985. Proportions 2:3.

The St George's cross symbolizes
constitutional ties with the British crown,
and the yellow cross of William the
Conqueror recalls that Guernsey was once
part of Normandy. William's banner with
this cross appears several times in the
Bayeaux Tapestry, made in the 11th century.

THE DEPENDENCIES OF GUERNSEY

The Bailiwick of Guernsey comprises
Guernsey, Alderney, Great and Little
Sark, Herm, Brechou, Jethou and
Lihou. Some of the dependencies
have their own flags which are white
with the cross of St George and some
additional devices. The flag of Alderney
(proportions 1:2) has a badge of the
island in the centre. The badge is a
British lion with three leaves in his right
paw on a green disc, framed with a
yellow ornamental border. The flag of
Sark (proportions 1:2) displays two
yellow lions in the red canton. The
canton of the flag of Herm (proportions
3:5) is the banner of arms which
features three monks and two dolphins.
The flag of Leonard Joseph Matchan,
the owner of Brechou (proportions 1:2)
is like that of Sark but has his personal
arms in the lower fly.

SOUTH-WEST EUROPE

PORTUGAL

Republic of Portugal,
Portuguese **República Portuguesa**.
Republic in SW Europe.

NATIONAL FLAG AND ENSIGN

Adopted 19 June 1911. Proportions 2:3.

The red stands for revolution, the green for
hope. The armillary sphere (a navigational
instrument of the Age of Discovery)
commemorates Prince Henry the

Navigator, who inspired the sea voyages
that led to the discovery of new lands and
created Portugal's colonial empire.

The central part of the shield shows the
arms of Portugal, adopted by Alfonso
Henriques after the Battle of Ourique in
1139. The five blue shields represent the
defeated Moorish kings of Lisbon, Badajoz,
Beja, Elvas and Évora. The divine assistance
that enabled Henriques to be victorious is
commemorated on each shield by white
dots representing the five wounds of Christ.

The red border which is charged with
seven yellow castles was added to the arms
after the annexation of Algarve and the
wedding of King Alfonso III and Beatriz
of Castile in 1252.

AZORES

Portuguese **Região Autónoma dos Açores**.
Group of islands in N Atlantic, autonomous
region of Portugal.

NATIONAL FLAG

Adopted 10 April 1979. Proportions 2:3.

The colours of the flag are those of the flag
of Portugal from 1830 to 1911; in the
canton is a shield with the arms of Portugal.
The goshawk (*açor* in Portuguese) refers to

the name of the islands. The nine stars represent the islands of Flores, Corvo, Terceira, São Jorge, Pico, Faial, Graciosa, São Miguel and Santa Maria.

MADEIRA

Portuguese **Região Autónoma da Madeira**. Island group in E Atlantic, autonomous region of Portugal.

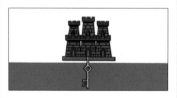

NATIONAL FLAG

Adopted 28 July 1978. Proportions 2:3.

The blue represents the sea, the yellow stands for the land. The cross of the Order of Christ is a reference to Prince Henry the Navigator, who colonized the uninhabited islands.

GIBRALTAR

British dependency in SW Europe.

NATIONAL FLAG

Introduced in 1966. Proportions 1:2.

This banner of arms was granted on 10 July 1502 by King Ferdinand and Queen Isabella of Spain, and was confirmed by the British authorities in June 1936. The castle and the key symbolize the strategic importance of the Gibraltar fortress as the key to the Mediterranean.

SPAIN

Kingdom of Spain, Spanish **Reino de España**. Constitutional monarchy in SW Europe.

STATE FLAG AND ENSIGN

Adopted 28 October 1981. Proportions 2:3.
Civil flag is without arms.

The basic design of the flag (the yellow stripe is twice as wide as each of the red) was introduced on 28 May 1785. With the state arms placed near the hoist, it was until 1931 the war ensign. Without the arms, it was the merchant flag from 1 January 1928 to 27 April 1931. On 29 August 1936 General Franco decreed that it should be the flag and civil ensign of Spain. Since then the state flag is always with the arms, which changed in 1938, 1945, 1977 and 1981.

The colours of the flag are the livery colours of the oldest Spanish kingdoms: the red of León and both colours of Castile, Aragón and Navarre.

SPANISH AUTONOMOUS COMMUNITIES

In 1977–1982 Spain was divided into 17 autonomous communities. They were formed on an ethnic and/or historic basis.

ANDALUSIA

COMMUNITY FLAG

Adopted 30 December 1981. Proportions 2:3.

The colour white represents the homes, the green represents the land.

ARAGÓN

COMMUNITY FLAG

Adopted 14 October 1981. Proportions 2:3.

The armorial banner of Aragón dates from the 14th century. The regional arms display the emblem of the legendary kingdom of Sobrarbe, the white cross of Íñigo Arista, the proper arms of Aragón as used in the 14th century, and the proper arms of Aragón.

ASTURIAS

COMMUNITY FLAG

Adopted 30 December 1981. Proportions 2:3.

The traditional Asturian emblem is the Cross of Victory. From it hang the Greek letters "alpha" and "omega", symbolizing Christ as the Beginning and the End. Blue is the colour of the Virgin Mary.

BALEARES

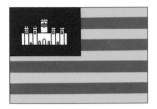

COMMUNITY FLAG

Adopted 25 February 1983. Proportions 2:3.

The flag closely resembles the flag of the kingdom of Mallorca, adopted in 1312. The stripes denote that Baleares has belonged to Aragón since 1228. The castle in the canton is that of Almoraima.

BASQUE COUNTRY

COMMUNITY FLAG

In use since 1894, officially approved 18 December 1979. Proportions 14:25.

The white cross is a symbol of the Catholic faith, the green saltire stands for the holy oak of Guernica and the red field commemorates the blood shed in the struggle for independence. The flag, called *Ikkurina*, was illegal from 1936 to 1977. Persecution for displaying it in public ended on 21 September 1976 and on 19 January 1977 the flag was legalized.

CANARY ISLANDS

COMMUNITY FLAG

Adopted 10 April 1989. Proportions 2:3.

The white represents the snow covering the volcano Pico de Teide on the island of Tenerife, the blue stands for the sea and the yellow for the sun.

CANTABRIA

COMMUNITY FLAG

Adopted 30 December 1981. Proportions 2:3.

White and red are the traditional colours of the region.

CASTILLA-LA MANCHA

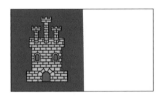

COMMUNITY FLAG

Adopted 30 June 1983.
Proportions 1:2, actual flags differ.

This banner of arms displays the arms of Castile in the hoist and in the fly the colour of the surcoats worn by the crusaders.

CASTILLA-LEÓN

COMMUNITY FLAG

Adopted 25 February 1983. Proportions 76:99.

This regional armorial banner is the same as that used by Spain from 1230 to 1479. It displays canting arms referring to Castile (castle) and León (lion).

CATALONIA

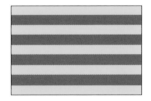

COMMUNITY FLAG

In use since the 13th century, confirmed in 1932.
Proportions 2:3.

The flag displays the stripes of the medieval arms of Catalonia (four red pallets on a golden field), arranged horizontally. Use of this flag was illegal from 1939 to 1975.

EXTREMADURA

COMMUNITY FLAG

Adopted 3 June 1985. Proportions 2:3.

The colours of the flag are those of the two parts of the region, Cáceres (green and white) and Badajoz (white and black).

GALICIA

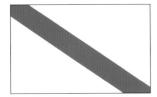

COMMUNITY FLAG

Adopted 5 May 1984. Proportions 2:3.

White and blue are the colours of the Virgin Mary. The design of the flag is based on that of the maritime flag of the city of La Coruña.

LA RIOJA

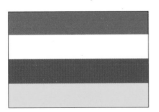

COMMUNITY FLAG

Adopted 31 May 1985. Proportions 2:3.

The colours are taken from the first field of the regional arms. (Above a green mountain on a golden (yellow) field is a red cross between two silver (white) shells.)

MADRID

COMMUNITY FLAG

Adopted 25 February 1983. Proportions 7:11.

Red is the colour of Castile. The stars appear in the arms of the city of Madrid.

MURCIA

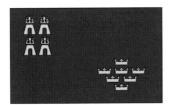

COMMUNITY FLAG

Adopted 9 June 1982. Proportions 2:3.

The castles recall that Murcia once belonged to Castile. The seven crowns stand for the seven provinces of Murcia.

NAVARRE

COMMUNITY FLAG

Adopted 10 August 1982. Proportions 2:3.

The flag displays the shield of the arms of Navarre, which date from the 13th century, ensigned with the royal crown.

VALENCIA

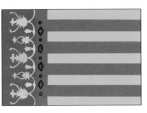

COMMUNITY FLAG

Adopted 1 July 1982. Proportions 2:3.

The flag is almost an exact copy of the flag granted by King James I the Conqueror to the City of Valencia in 1238.

ANDORRA

Principality of Andorra, Catalonian **Principat d'Andorra**, Spanish **Principado de Andorra**, French **Principauté d'Andorre**.

Independent co-principality in the Pyrenees, SW Europe.

NATIONAL FLAG

Adopted in present form in 1993. Proportions 2:3.

The blue-yellow-red tricolour has been in use since the second half of the 19th century. Blue and red are the colours of France, yellow and red are those of Spain, and together they reflect Franco-Spanish protection. The arms combine the arms of the bishopric of Urgel, the counts of Foix, Catalonia and Béarn. The motto is "United strength is stronger".

MONACO

Principality of Monaco, French **Principauté de Monaco**.

Constitutional monarchy under French protectorate, SW Europe.

CIVIL FLAG AND ENSIGN

Adopted 4 April 1881. Proportions 4:5.

The colours are those of the ducal arms of Grimaldi (lozengy (diamond-shaped) white and red). Since the 17th century the flag has been white with the shield of arms.

SOUTH AND SOUTH-EAST EUROPE

ITALY

Republic of Italy, Italian **Repubblica Italiana**.
Republic in S Europe.

CIVIL ENSIGN

Officially adopted 19 June 1946. Proportions 2:3.
The state and civil flag is without arms.

Originally this was the national flag of the
Cisalpine Republic, founded by Napoleon.
The flag's design was influenced by the
French *Tricolore* and was in use from
11 May 1798 to 20 August 1802. It was
reintroduced in 1848 by the King of
Sardinia, who charged the white stripe with
his arms of Savoy and in 1861 this became
the national flag of the united Italy. In
1946 the arms were removed from the flag.

VATICAN

Holy See, Vatican City State, Italian **Santa
Sede, Stato della Città del Vaticano**.
Papal state in S Europe.

STATE FLAG

Officially adopted 7 June 1929. Proportions 1:1.

A flag of this design was introduced as the
merchant flag of the Pontifical State at the
beginning of the 19th century. The colours
are those of the keys of St Peter, which are
the keys to the kingdom of heaven and a
symbol of papal authority. The crossed keys

with the papal tiara have been the emblem
of the papal state since the 14th century.

Although the official proportions are
1:1, the actual flags flown in the Vatican
City are 2:3.

SAN MARINO

Most Serene Republic of San Marino, Italian
Serenissima Repubblica di San Marino.
Republic in central Italian peninsula, S Europe.

STATE FLAG

Adopted 6 April 1862. Proportions 3:4.
Civil flag is without arms.

As an emblem of sovereignty, San Marino
adopted in 1797 a white and blue national
cockade. The colours were taken from the
coat of arms, which displays three white
towers on a blue field. The towers represent
three castles built on three summits of
Mount Titano: Guaita, Cesta and Montale.

The white stands for peace, exemplified by
the white clouds and the snow; the blue is a
symbol of liberty and the sky over San Marino.

MALTA

Republic of Malta,
Maltese **Repubblika Ta'Malta**.
Insular republic in the Mediterranean, S Europe.

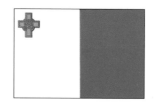

NATIONAL FLAG

Adopted 21 September 1964. Proportions 2:3.

The colours are those of the Knights of St
John of Jerusalem (the white Maltese cross
on a red field), who ruled Malta from 1530
to 1798. In April 1942 King George VI of
the United Kingdom awarded the islanders
the George cross for heroism in World War
II. Since 1964 the George cross bordered in
red has been placed directly on the
white field.

SLOVENIA

Republic of Slovenia, Slovene **Republika
Slovenija**. Republic in S Europe.

NATIONAL FLAG AND ENSIGN

Adopted 24 June 1991. Proportions 1:2.

The national flag, showing the same
arrangement of the pan-Slavic colours as
the flags of Russia or Slovakia, was adopted
by the Slovenian patriots in 1848. In 1991
the newly created arms of Slovenia were
added to the tricolour of white-blue-red.
The main feature of the arms is a stylized
silhouette of Triglav, the highest mountain
in the Slovene Alps. The three yellow stars
on a blue field are from the arms of the
former Duchy of Celje. The wavy lines
symbolize the rivers and the Adriatic Sea.

CROATIA

Republic of Croatia, Croat **Republika
Hrvatska**. Republic in S Europe.

NATIONAL FLAG

Adopted 22 December 1990. Proportions 1:2.

Following the example of other Slavic nations, the Croats in 1848 adopted a red-white-blue horizontal tricolour. When Croatia proclaimed independence in 1941, the arms (checked white and red) were placed in the centre of the tricolour and the badge of Ustasha in the canton. Under communist rule the Croat tricolour was charged with a red star.

The crown surmounting the present state arms is composed of shields with the historic arms of Croatia (golden star above silver crescent), Dubrovnik (two red stripes on a blue field), Dalmatia (three golden lions' heads), Istria (golden goat with red horns and hooves) and Slavonica (golden star above red stripe, fimbriated silver, and charged with black marten).

BOSNIA-HERZEGOVINA

Republic of Bosnia-Herzegovina,
Serbian and Croat **Bosna i Hercegovina**.
Federal republic in S Europe.

NATIONAL FLAG AND ENSIGN

Adopted 4 February 1998. Proportions 1:2.

This flag was one of three proposals presented to parliament by a commission appointed by a special envoy of the United Nations. All three employed the same colours; the blue was to stand for the United Nations but it was changed to a darker blue to correspond with the European Union flag. The blue and the stars represent Europe and the yellow, the colour of the sun, symbolizes hope. The triangle stands for the three ethnic groups: Muslims, Croats and Serbs.

TERRITORIES OF BOSNIA AND HERZEGOVINA

After the civil war, on the basis of the 1996 agreement reached in Dayton (Ohio), Bosnia and Herzegovina was transformed into a federal state with two autonomous provinces.

CROAT-MUSLIM FEDERATION

NATIONAL FLAG

Adopted 6 November 1996. Proportions 2:3.

Red stands for the Croats, green for the Bosnian people and white for purity and peace. The golden fleur-de-lis is from the arms of Tvrtko, who was crowned in 1376 as Stephen I, King of Bosnia, Serbia and the sea-coast. It is a symbol of the Bosnians, while the historic arms of Croatia represent the Croat population. The ten stars symbolize the ten provinces that make up the Federation.

SERBIAN REPUBLIC

NATIONAL FLAG

Adopted in 1992. Proportions unspecified.

The flag is identical to that of Serbia. There are also in use flags with the Serbian historic arms in the centre (in gold instead of the original white), a cross with four flints each resembling the Cyrillic letter "S". They stand for the first letters of the Serbian motto: "Only unity will save the Serbs".

SERBIA

Republic of Serbia,
Serbian **Republika Srbija**
Republic in SE Europe.

STATE FLAG

Adopted 17 August 2004. Proportions 2:3.
Civil flag is without the arms.

This flag, composed of the Serbian tricolour charged with state arms, served as the national flag of the Kingdom of Serbia from 1882 to 1918. The first Serbian horizontal tricolour of pan-Slavic colours, introduced in 1835, was white-blue-red. On 28 January 1838 the present order of colours was adopted. As a part of Yugoslavia under communist regime, Serbia used from 1946 its tricolour with a large red star bordered in yellow, positioned in the centre. In 1992 the star was removed, and as a part of the Federal Republic of Yugoslavia (comprising only of Serbia and Montenegro), and later on as a part of the Republic of Serbia and Montenegro, Serbia used its plain tricolour.

MONTENEGRO

Republic of Montenegro,
Serbian **Republika Crna Gora**,
Republic in SE Europe.

STATE AND NATIONAL FLAG

Adopted 16 September 2004. Proportions 1:2.

The present flag, with the state arms in the centre, recalls the pattern of the state flag of the Kingdom of Montenegro used from 1860 to 1918. The civil flag of that kingdom had an identical arrangement of the three pan-Slavic colours to that of Serbia. In the centre of the blue stripe there were red cyrilic letters H.I. (initials of the king Nicola I) surmounted by a yellow crown. As a part of Yugoslavia under communist regime, Montenegro used from 1946 the tricolour charged with a large red star bordered in yellow. In 1992 the star was removed, and as a part of the Federal Republic of Yugoslavia (comprising only of Serbia and Montenegro), and later as a part of the Republic of Serbia and Montenegro, Montenegro used its plain tricolour of proportions 1:3.

ALBANIA

Republic of Albania,
Albanian **Republika e Shqipërisë**.
Republic in SE Europe.

NATIONAL FLAG

Adopted 28 February 1912, re-established 7 April 1992. Proportions 5:7.

The red banner with the black double-headed eagle was the ensign of George Castriota, known as Skanderbeg, the hero of the uprising against the Turks and founder of the independent state in 1443. He probably chose the eagle on account of a tradition that the Albanians are the descendants of the eagle. They call themselves *Shkypetars* which translates as: "the sons of the eagle".

MACEDONIA

Republic of Macedonia, Macedonian
Republika Makedonija.
Republic in SE Europe.

NATIONAL FLAG

Adopted 5 October 1995. Proportions 1:2.

This is the second national flag of Macedonia since the country proclaimed independence in 1991 (the controversy provoked by the first flag is explained at the end of *All About Flags*). The present flag displays a yellow sun of eight rays instead of the former Star of Vergina with 16 rays.

GREECE

Hellenic Republic,
Greek **Elliniki Dimokratia**.
Republic in SE Europe.

NATIONAL FLAG AND ENSIGN

Adopted 15 March 1822, re-introduced 21 December 1978. Proportions 2:3.

The common device of all the flags used in the war for independence in 1821 was a white cross, the symbol of Christian faith. When in 1822 the Greek government adopted flags for the Army, and merchant and war ensigns, all of them displayed the same Greek cross. The flag of the Navy, and the later flag used on land, was a blue square with a white cross. The war ensign,

in use until 1833, was the same design as the present national flag.

The nine stripes represent the nine syllables of the war cry of independence, *Eleutheria i Thanatos* ("Freedom or Death"). The blue stands for the pure Greek sky, and recalls that God inspired the Greek people to fight for independence in spite of all odds. The white symbolizes the purity and sacred character of the struggle for liberation from Turkish tyranny.

MOUNT ATHOS

Greek **Hagion Oros**.
Self-governing theocratic republic under Greek protectorate, SE Europe.

STATE FLAG

*Date of introduction unknown.
Proportions 2:3.*

The first monastery on Mount Athos, the Great Laura, was founded in AD 963 by St Athanasius the Athonite. In the 11th century several more monasteries were built with the help of the Byzantine Empire, and in 1060 the Byzantine Emperor gave the monastic community its first constitution.

The golden yellow flag is charged with the black Byzantine eagle holding an orb and a sword in its claws. An imperial crown appears above its two heads.

BULGARIA

Republic of Bulgaria,
Bulgarian **Republika Bulgariya**.
Republic in SE Europe.

NATIONAL FLAG AND CIVIL ENSIGN

*Adopted in 1878, re-introduced 22 November
1990. Proportions 3:5.*

Because Russia supported the Bulgarians in their struggle for independence from Turkey, the Constitutional Assembly adopted an almost identical tricolour, although this one had a green stripe in place of the blue one. The colour of the new green stripe symbolizes freedom. The white symbolizes peace and Slavic thought, and the red represents the bravery of the Bulgarian people. Under communist rule (from 1947–1990) the state emblem was displayed on the white stripe near the hoist.

ROMANIA

Romania, Romanian **România**.
Republic in SE Europe.

NATIONAL FLAG, CIVIL AND STATE ENSIGN

*Introduced in 1848, adopted in 1867, re-adopted
27 December 1989. Proportions 2:3.*

Blue, yellow and red are the colours of the arms of the principalities of Walachia (red and yellow) and Moldavia (red and blue). These colours appeared together for the first time in 1848 on a revolutionary vertical tricolour of blue-yellow-red which was based on the French *Tricolore*. Walachia and Moldavia united in 1861 under the name of Romania, and adopted a red-yellow-blue horizontal tricolour. In April 1867 the colours were reversed and arranged vertically. From 1867 to 1989 the state flag was always charged with the actual state arms.

NORTHERN CYPRUS

Turkish Republic of Northern Cyprus,
Turkish **Kibris Cumhuriyeti**.
Republic in NE part of the island of Cyprus,
SE Europe and W Asia.

NATIONAL FLAG

*Adopted 13 March 1984.
Proportions 2:3.*

The national flag of Northern Cyprus retains the white field of the flag of Cyprus. The crescent with the star is the symbol of Islam.

CYPRUS

Greek Republic of Cyprus,
Greek **Kypriaki Dimokratia**.
Republic in NW and S part of the
island of Cyprus, SE Europe and W Asia.

NATIONAL FLAG AND ENSIGN

Adopted 16 August 1960. Proportions 3:5.

The map of the island is dark yellow, symbolizing copper which has been mined here since the 3rd millennium BC. Copper takes its name from the Greek name for the island, *Kupros*, and the crossed olive branches stand for peace between the Greeks and Turks. The white is also a symbol of peace.

TURKEY

Republic of Turkey,
Turkish **Türkiye Cumhuriyeti**.
Republic in SE Europe and W Asia.

NATIONAL FLAG AND ENSIGN

*Adopted in 1793, officially confirmed
5 June 1936. Proportions 2:3.*

Red was the colour of Umar I, the caliph who ruled from AD 634 to 644 and was known as a great consolidator of the Islamic Empire. In the 14th century red became the colour of the Ottoman Empire. The crescent and star is the symbol of Islam.

EASTERN EUROPE

MOLDOVA

Republic of Moldova,
Moldovan **Republica Moldoveneasca**.
Republic in E Central Europe.

NATIONAL FLAG

Adopted 12 May 1990. Proportions 2:3.

In 1940 Bessarabia and Bukowina, a substantial part of historic Moldavia, have torn out of Romania and forcibly incorporated into the Soviet Union under the name of the Moldavian SSR. Striving for independence and eventual reunification with Romania, the Moldavian authorities adopted the flag of Romania and charged it with the state arms (the eagle of Walachia with the shield of Moldavia).

MOLDOVAN TERRITORIES

The Gagauzians and the inhabitants of the territory east of the Dniester river were proclaimed independent republics in 1990 and 1992 respectively. Since 1994, Gagauzia has been an autonomous part of Moldova. The status of the Trans-Dniester Republic is not clear.

GAGAUZIA

NATIONAL FLAG

Adopted 31 October 1995. Proportions 1:2.

Blue is the traditional colour of the Turkic peoples. It symbolizes the sky, hope, kind-heartedness and allegiance to the Fatherland. For the Turkic people the white represents the west and symbolizes where the Gagauzians live; it is also a symbol of friendly co-existence with the Moldavians, Bulgarians, Ukrainians and Russians. The red is a symbol of gallantry and courage in the fight for freedom; it stands for the rebirth of the Gagauzians as a nation and represents their generosity. The three stars represent their past, present and future.

TRANS-DNIESTER REPUBLIC

NATIONAL FLAG

Adopted 3 July 2000. Proportions 1:2.

This former territory of the Moldavian SSR on the east of the river Dniester, inhabited mainly by Russians and Ukrainians, proclaimed independence on 2 September 1991. It retained the flag of the Soviet Moldavia, removed the hammer and sickle, and then in 2000 added them again.

UKRAINE

Ukrainian **Ukraina**.
Republic in E Central Europe.

NATIONAL FLAG AND CIVIL ENSIGN

Adopted 1918, re-adopted 21 January 1992.
Proportions 2:3.

The national colours derive from the arms of the medieval principality of Galicia (golden lion on a blue field). The first Ukrainian flag, adopted by the Supreme Council in 1848, was a yellow-blue horizontal bicolour and this was the first flag of the independent Ukraine, adopted in January 1918. However, in the 19th century most of the flags displayed by the public were bicolours, with the blue at the top, and this order of colours has been official since March 1918. The blue stands for the sky and the yellow for wheat, the main source of the wealth of Ukraine.

AUTONOMOUS TERRITORY

The only autonomous part of Ukraine is Crimea. The peninsula was conquered and settled by Tartars in the 13th century, annexed by Russia in 1783 and transferred in 1954 from the Russian SFSR to the Ukrainian SSR. It proclaimed independence on 5 May 1992 under the name of the Crimean Republic but later agreed to be an autonomous part of the Ukraine.

CRIMEA

NATIONAL FLAG

Adopted 24 September 1992. Proportions 1:2.

The Crimea was transferred in 1954 from the Russian SFSR to the Ukrainian SSR. It proclaimed independence on 5 May 1992 but later agreed to be an autonomous part of Ukraine. The flag displays the Russian colours in a different order. The colours represent the future (blue), the present (white), and the Crimea's heroic and tragic past (red).

BELARUS

Republic of Belarus,
Belorussian **Respublika Belarus**.
Republic in E Central Europe.

NATIONAL FLAG

Introduced 7 June 1995. Proportions 1:2.

When Belarus proclaimed independence in 1991 it readopted the white-red-white tricolour, first introduced in 1918. This was used in great numbers during rallies and demonstrations against the regime of the pro-Russian president. In response a presidential decree was issued introducing the current flag, which is similar to the flag of Soviet Belorussia (1951–1991). A white and red national ornament appears on the vertical stripe at the hoist.

RUSSIA

Russian Federation,
Rusian **Rossiyskaya Federatsiya**.
Federal republic in E Europe and N Asia.

NATIONAL FLAG AND CIVIL ENSIGN

Introduced 1699, re-adopted 22 August 1991.
Proportions 2:3 (decreed 11 December 1993).

The Russian civil ensign was personally designed by Peter the Great, Tsar of Russia, in 1699 and became the national flag of Russia on 7 May 1883. In 1918 it was replaced by a red flag with the golden initials RSFSR in the upper hoist. Since 1990 the white-blue-red tricolour has been used in great numbers by pro-democracy forces.

RUSSIAN REPUBLICS

According to the constitution Russia comprises 21 republics, 49 provinces, six territories, ten administrative areas, two cities with federal status and one auton-omous region. Flags of 20 republics follow. Since Chechnya proclaimed independence, did not sign the Federation Agreement, and was forcibly reincorporated to Russia, it is shown separately.

ADYGEA

NATIONAL FLAG

Adopted in 1830, re-adopted 24 March 1992.
Proportions 1:2.

The green is a symbol of Islam; the 12 stars recall the tribes of Adygeans, united in the 19th century in the struggle for independence. The arrows originally symbolized the brotherhood and bravery of those tribes; today they symbolize the brotherhood and unity of all nationalities in Adygea.

ALANIA

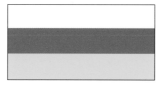

NATIONAL FLAG

Adopted 10 December 1991. Proportions 1:2.

The white and red reflect qualities of the Alanian people – ethical purity and gallantry respectively. The yellow stands for abundance and prosperity.

ALTAY

NATIONAL FLAG

Adopted 2 July 1992. Proportions 1:2.

The white symbolizes faithfulness, as well as mutual understanding between the various nationalities of Altay. The blue stands for the purity of the skies, mountains, rivers and lakes.

BASHKORTOSTAN

NATIONAL FLAG

Adopted 25 February 1992. Proportions 1:2.

The stylized *kurai* flower (*Pleurospermum uralense*) is a symbol of friendship. Its seven petals represent the tribes who laid foundations of unity and consolidation for the Bashkir people. The blue symbolizes the integrity and virtue of the thoughts of the people; the white represents their peacefulnessand readiness to co-operate; the green stands for freedom and eternal life.

BURYATIA

NATIONAL FLAG

Adopted 29 October 1992. Proportions 1:2.

The traditional Buryat *Soyonbo*, consisting of the moon, sun and fire, is a symbol of eternal life. The blue stands for the sky and Lake Baykal, the white symbolizes purity, and the yellow represents freedom and prosperity.

CHUVASHIA

NATIONAL FLAG

Adopted 29 April 1992. Proportions 5:8.

The main charge of the flag is a stylized tree of life, a symbol of rebirth, with the three suns, a traditional emblem popular in Chuvash art. The purple stands for the land, the golden yellow for prosperity.

DAGESTAN

NATIONAL FLAG

Adopted 26 February 1994. Proportions 1:2.

The green is the symbol of Islam, the blue represents the Caspian Sea and the red stands for courage and fidelity.

INGUSHETIA

NATIONAL FLAG

Adopted 15 July 1994. Proportions 1:2.

In the religion and philosophy of the Ingushetians, the solar emblem (in the centre of the flag) represents not only the sun and the universe but also awareness of the oneness of the spirit in the past, present and future.

The red recalls the struggle of the Ingush people for existence and in the defence of their homeland. The white symbolizes the divine purity of the thoughts and views of the nation. The green is the symbol of Islam.

KABARDINO-BALKARIA

NATIONAL FLAG

Adopted 21 July 1994. Proportions 1:2.

The blue stands for the sky, the white represents the snow-topped Caucasus Mountains and the green symbolizes the fields. In the centre is a white silhouette of Mount Elbrus, the highest peak in Europe.

KALMYKIA

NATIONAL FLAG

Adopted 30 July 1993. Proportions 1:2.

The yellow stands for the sun, the people and the religious faith of the nation. The blue represents the sky, eternity and steadiness. The lotus is a symbol of purity, spiritual rebirth and happiness. Its five upper petals represent the continents and the lower four stand for the quarters of the globe. Together they symbolize the will of the Kalmyks to live in friendship and to co-operate with all the nations of the world.

KARACHAYEVO-CHERKESIYA

NATIONAL FLAG

Adopted 3 February 1994. Proportions 1:2.

The blue is the colour of peace, good intentions and serenity. The green represents nature, fertility and wealth; it is the colour of youth, and also of wisdom and restraint. The red is a symbol of warmth and friendship between nations. The sun rising above the mountains represents the hope of the peoples in the Caucasus for a bright future.

KARELIA

NATIONAL FLAG

Adopted 16 February 1993. Proportions 2:3.

Warm feelings, unity and co-operation between the peoples of Karelia are represented by the red stripe. The blue stands for the lakes and the green for the forests.

KHAKASSIA

NATIONAL FLAG

Adopted 25 September 2003. Proportions 1:2.

The use of the Russian colours shows that the republic is part of the Russian Federation. The green, the traditional colour of Siberia, is a symbol of eternal life and rebirth. The emblem is a sign of respect to the ancestors who used the solar symbol; its black colour symbolizes their wisdom.

KOMI

NATIONAL FLAG

Adopted 27 November 1991. Proportions 1:2.

The colours of the flag reflect the geographical location of the republic and its physical features. The blue stands for the sky, the green for the taiga landscape and the white for the snow.

MARI EL

NATIONAL FLAG

Adopted 30 November 2006. Proportions 2:3.

The colours are those of Russia but in different shades. In the centre appears a solar sign, which the traditional national emblem.

MORDOVIA

NATIONAL FLAG

Adopted 30 March 1995. Proportions 1:2.

This republic uses the national colours of Russia in different shades. A local form of the solar emblem is placed in the centre.

SAKHA

NATIONAL FLAG

Adopted 14 December 1992. Proportions 1:2.

The white disc represents the northern sun. The blue, white and green stand for the sky, snow and taiga landscape. The red symbolizes the courage and constancy of the people.

TATARSTAN

NATIONAL FLAG

Adopted 29 November 1991. Proportions 1:2.

The green, the colour of Islam, represents the Tatars; the red stands for the Russians. The white stripe symbolizes peace between the Tatar majority and the Russian minority.

TUVA

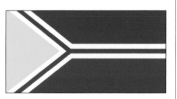

NATIONAL FLAG

Adopted 17 September 1992. Proportions 1:2.

Three days after it was adopted this flag was consecrated by the Dalai Lama, who was

visiting Tuva at the time. The colours stand for prosperity (yellow), courage and strength (blue), and purity (white).

UDMURTIA

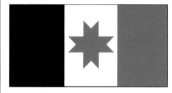

NATIONAL FLAG

Adopted 3 December 1993. Proportions 1:2.

The black is a symbol of the earth and of stability, the white stands for the universe and the purity of moral foundations, and the red represents the sun and life. The solar emblem protects the people against ill fortune.

CHECHNYA

Chechen Republic,
Chechen **Republika Ichkeriya**.
Russian **Chechenskaya Respublika**.
One of the Russian republics in the Caucasus Mountains, E Europe.

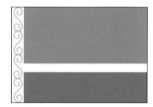

NATIONAL FLAG

Introduced 18 August 2004. Proportions 2:3.

The new flag retains the colours of the former flag in a different arrangement, and has a national ornament at the hoist. When Chechnya was an independent country, the green of the flag symbolized Islam, red symbolized the blood shed in the struggle for independence, and white the road to a bright future.

Flags of Asia

Illustrated here are the current national flags of the countries of Asia, from Georgia and Abkhazia to South Korea and Japan, as well as the flags of their territories, states and provinces.

Because Asia is so vast, we have grouped together its countries into geographical sections. We begin in western Asia, then move on to the Middle East, South-west Asia and then Central Asia. Finally, we look at the flags of the countries of southern and South-east Asia and the Far East. There are some geographical anomalies: the flags of Russia, Turkey, Cyprus and Northern Cyprus can all be found in *Flags of Europe*.

For each entry, the country or territory's name is given in its most easily recognized form and then in all its official languages. This is followed by a description of its political status and geographic position. The basic data for each flag contains the status of the flag, date of adoption, proportions, and the symbolic meaning.

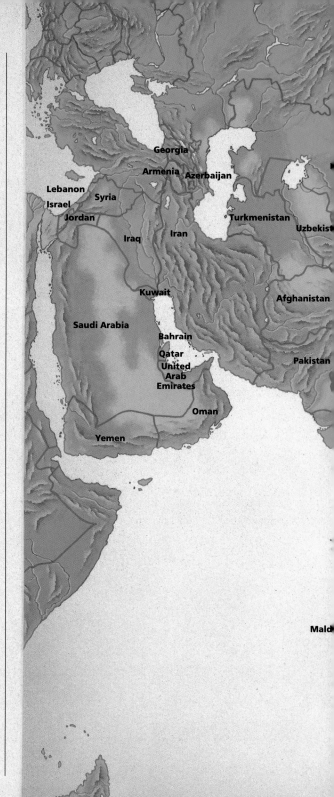

WESTERN ASIA

GEORGIA

Republic of Georgia,
Georgian **Sakartvelos Respublika**.
Republic in W Asia.

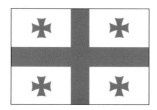

NATIONAL FLAG AND CIVIL ENSIGN

Established on 14 January 2004.
Proportions 100:147.

This was the flag during the reign of Queen Tamar (1184–1213), and is also known from the 14th century *portolanos*.

ABKHAZIA

Republic of Abkhazia,
Abkhaz **Arespublika Apsni**.
De facto independent former autonomous republic in Georgia, W Asia.

NATIONAL FLAG

Adopted 23 July 1992. Proportions 2:3.

This design is based on the flag of North Caucasia, in use 1918–19. The palm of a hand was a symbol of Abkhaz statehood in the 8th–10th centuries and the stars and stripes represent the seven historic districts of Abkhazia. (Seven is a sacred number, often found in Abkhaz mythology, religion and folk art.) The stripes in green and white symbolize the tolerance of the Caucasus people and the peaceful co-existence of Islam (green) and Christianity (white).

AJARIA

Ajarian Autonomous Republic
Georgian **Acharis Avtonomiuri Respublika**.
Autonomous part of Georgia.

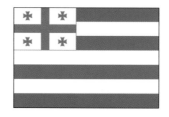

NATIONAL FLAG

Adopted 20 July 2004. Proportions 2:3.

The blue stripes symbolize the sea (Black Sea), the white ones purity. In the canton is the flag of Georgia.

ARMENIA

Republic of Armenia,
Armenian **Haikakan Hanrapetoutioun**.
Republic in W Asia.

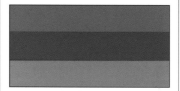

NATIONAL FLAG AND ENSIGN

Introduced 22 April 1918, re-adopted
1 September 1991. Proportions 1:2.

The red recalls the blood shed in the struggle for national existence. The blue stands for the skies, hope and the unchanging character of the land. The orange represents the courage of the people.

NAGORNO-KARABAKH

Armenian **Artsakh**
De facto independent former autonomous republic of Azerbaijan, W Asia.

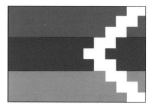

NATIONAL FLAG

Adopted in June 1992. Proportions unspecified.

The flag displays the colours of Armenia but has slightly different symbolic meaning: the blood spilt in the struggle to preserve the nation (red), love of liberty (blue) and bread (orange). The westwards-pointing arrow is a graphic representation of the country's current separation from Armenia proper and its hopes for union with the Fatherland.

AZERBAIJAN

Republic of Azerbaijan,
Azeri **Azarbajchan Respublikasy**.
Republic in W Asia.

NATIONAL FLAG AND ENSIGN

Adopted 5 February 1991. Proportions 1:2.

The main features of the flag are based on the flag introduced in autumn 1917 and used until the occupation of the country by the Red Army in 1920. Blue represents the Turkic world, red; contemporary life and green; the Islamic religion. The crescent and star is the symbol of Islam. The eight points of the star stand for the Turkic peoples.

MIDDLE EAST/SOUTH-WEST ASIA

SYRIA

Republic of Syria,
Arabic **al-Jumhuriya al-Arabiya as-Suriya**.
Republic in W Asia.

NATIONAL FLAG AND ENSIGN

Adopted 30 March 1980. Proportions 2:3.

The present flag is that of the United Arab Republic, used from 1958 to 1961 in both Syria and Egypt. In 1972 Egypt, Syria and Libya formed the Federation of Arab Republics, with a common flag. The policy of reconciliation between Egypt and Israel caused Libya to withdraw from the Federation in 1977, and Syria followed suit in 1980. The Syrian authorities changed the flag because they felt that the Federation flag had been disgraced when it was dipped to the Prime Minister of Israel by an Egyptian guard of honour.

LEBANON

Republic of Lebanon,
Arabic **al-Jumhuriya al-Lubnaniya**.
Republic in W Asia.

NATIONAL FLAG AND ENSIGN

Adopted 7 December 1943. Proportions 2:3.

The red symbolizes sacrifices in the struggle for independence, and the white stands for purity and peace. The cedar is a symbol of

holiness, eternity and peace, and since the 19th century it has been the symbol of the Maronite Christian community in Lebanon.

ISRAEL

State of Israel, Hebrew **Medinat Israel**.
Republic in W Asia.

NATIONAL FLAG

Adopted 28 October 1948. Proportions 8:11.

The flag was designed for the Zionist movement in 1891. The basic design recalls the *tallith*, the Jewish prayer shawl, which is white with blue stripes. The hexagram in the centre is the *Magen David* ("Shield of David"), often erroneously called the Star of David. It became the Jewish symbol in the 17th century and was adopted by the First Zionist Congress in 1897.

PALESTINE

State of Palestine,
Arabic **Daulat Filastin**.
Semi-autonomous state comprising Gaza and part of the West Bank of Jordan in W Asia.

NATIONAL FLAG

Introduced 1922. Proportions 1:22.

The flag is based on a flag used in the Arab revolt of 1917 and displays the pan-Arab colours.

JORDAN

Hashemite Kingdom of Jordan, Arabic **al-Mamlaka al-Urdunniya al-Hashemiya**.
Constitutional monarchy in W Asia.

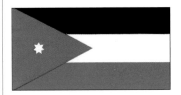

NATIONAL FLAG, CIVIL AND STATE ENSIGN

Introduced in 1921, officially confirmed 16 April 1928. Proportions 1:2.

The flag displays the pan-Arab colours, with the seven points of the star representing the seven verses that make up the *Fatiha* of the Koran: the Fundamental Law of Life, Thought and Aspiration.

SAUDI ARABIA

Kingdom of Saudi Arabia,
Arabic **al-Mamlaka al-Arabiya as-Saudiya**.
Absolute monarchy in SW Asia.

NATIONAL FLAG

Introduced in 1932, present design adopted 15 March 1973. Proportions 2:3.

The flag is very similar to that of the Wahabi sect, in use since 1901. The green is the colour of Islam. The inscription in white *tulth* script reads "There is no God but Allah and Muhammad is the Prophet of Allah", the Muslim Statement of Faith. The sword is a symbol of justice.

YEMEN

Republic of Yemen,
Arabic **al-Jumhuriya al-Yamaniya**.
Republic in SW Asia.

NATIONAL FLAG AND CIVIL ENSIGN

Adopted 22 May 1990. Proportions 2:3.

After the unification of North and South Yemen, the flag retained the common element of stripes in the pan-Arab colours.

OMAN

Sultanate of Oman, Arabic **Saltanat Uman**.
Absolute monarchy in SW Asia.

NATIONAL FLAG AND ENSIGN

Adopted 18 November 1995. Proportions 1:2.

The national emblem of Oman is composed of two crossed swords surmounted by a ceremonial dagger and an ornate belt. The white symbolizes peace and prosperity. The red is the colour of the pre-1970 Omani flag, which was plain red, and recalls the battles against the foreign invaders. The green represents the Jebel Akhdar (the Green Mountains) and stands for fertility.

UNITED ARAB EMIRATES

Arabic **Dawlat Ittihad al-Imarat al-Arabiyah al-Muttahidah**.
Federal monarchy in SW Asia.

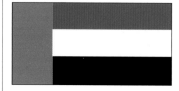

NATIONAL FLAG AND CIVIL ENSIGN

Adopted 2 December 1971, officially hoisted 1 January 1972. Proportions 1:2.

The flag displays the pan-Arab colours. Red is the traditional colour of the emirates and red flags of several tiny Arab states along the southern coast of the Persian Gulf were modified for the first time in 1820 following the General Treaty that was signed by the British and the rulers of eight sheikhdoms. It required that these states "should carry by land and sea a red flag, with or without letters on it, at their option, and this shall be in a border of white". Such were the flags of Sharjah and Ras al Khaimah, while Abu Dhabi, Ajman, Dubai and Umm al Qaiwain used a red flag with a white vertical stripe along the hoist. In 1958 Abu Dhabi exchanged the white stripe for a white canton and in 1961 the flag of Umm al Qaiwain was charged with a white crescent and star. In 1975 the ruler of Sharjah decided to replace his emirate's flag with that of the Union.

ABU DHABI

STATE FLAG

AJMAN, DUBAI

STATE FLAG

AL FUJAIRAH

STATE FLAG

RAS AL KHAIMAH

STATE FLAG

UMM AL QAIWAIN

STATE FLAG

QATAR

State of Qatar, Arabic **Dawlat Qatar**.
Absolute monarchy in SW Asia.

NATIONAL FLAG AND ENSIGN

Adopted in 1948. Proportions 11:28.

The flag used in the 19th century was red with a white vertical stripe along the hoist. In the first half of the 20th century the line separating the two colours became serrated, and the name of the country was often inscribed in white on the red portion of the flag. The local red dyes used in making flags darken when exposed to sun, so the red was officially changed to maroon in 1948.

BAHRAIN

Kingdom of Bahrain, Arabic **Al Mamlaka al-Bahrayn**. Absolute emirate in SW Asia.

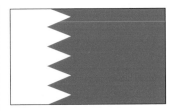

NATIONAL FLAG AND ENSIGN

General pattern since 1933, confirmed (with eight white triangles) in 1972. Present form introduced 14 February 2002.

In the 19th century the flag of Bahrain was red with a white vertical stripe along the hoist. In 1933 the line dividing the colours was serrated to distinguish the flag of Bahrain from those of other Trucial States. The five white triangles symbolize the five principles of Islam.

KUWAIT

State of Kuwait, Arabic **Dawlat al-Kuwait**.
Absolute monarchy in SW Asia.

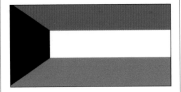

NATIONAL FLAG AND CIVIL ENSIGN

Adopted 7 September 1961. Proportions 1:2.

The flag displays the pan-Arab colours. The black stands for the defeat of the enemy on the battlefield, the red is the blood of the enemy left on the Arab swords. The green represents the fertile land, and the white the pure Arab deeds.

IRAQ

Republic of Iraq,
Arabic **al-Jumhuriya al-Iraqiya**.
Republic in SW Asia.

NATIONAL FLAG AND ENSIGN

Adopted 14 January 1991, the script modified in 2004. Proportions 2:3.

Since 1963 the flag of Iraq has been a red-white-black horizontal tricolour, with three green stars on the white stripe. During the Gulf War, the Revolutionary Command Council chaired by President Saddam Hussein decided to place the words *Allahu Akbar* ("God is Great") between the stars.

IRAN

Islamic Republic of Iran,
Farsi **Jomhori-e-Islami-e-Irân**.
Authoritarian Islamic republic in SW Asia.

NATIONAL FLAG AND ENSIGN

Adopted 29 July 1980. Proportions 4:7.

One of the consequences of the Islamic revolution in Iran was the addition of religious symbols to the Iranian horizontal tricolour. The central emblem is a composite of Arab letters in the form of four crescents and a vertical line in the middle. The five principal parts of the emblem represent the five principles of Islam and together they form the word *Allah*. Other combinations of these elements represent the Book (Koran), the Sword (the symbol of power and solidarity), man's growth, the negation of all idolatrous values, the negation of all powers and super-powers, and the struggle to establish a unified society. The symmetrical form of the emblem signifies balance and equilibrium.

The words *Allahu Akbar* ("God is Great"), written in highly stylized Kufic script, appear 22 times to commemorate Bahman 22, 1357 (11 February 1979), the day of victory for the revolution.

CENTRAL ASIA

TURKMENISTAN

Republic of Turkmenistan,
Turkmen **Türkmenistan**.
Republic in W Central Asia.

NATIONAL FLAG

Adopted 19 February 1992, modified in 1997, in present form established 24 January 2002

The flag of Turkmenistan has the most intricate design of all national flags in the world. It is also one of the most interesting. The green field with the crescent and stars is clearly the symbol of Islam; the crescent and stars represent faith in a bright future, while the white symbolizes serenity and kind-heartedness. The five stars symbolize the five *velayats* (regions): Ahal, Balkan, Dashhowuy, Lebap and Mary. They also stand for the five senses. The five points of each star symbolize the five states of matter: solid, liquid, gaseous, crystalline and plasmatic.

The vertical stripe along the hoist bears five major *guls* of the Turkmenian carpets. Each *gul* is a symmetrical medallion, in some cases divided into four quarters in counterchanging colours. Major *guls* are repeated in rows or in a chequered pattern on the central field of the carpet, and minor *guls* appear on the border. They reflect the national identity of Turkmenistan where carpets were part of traditional nomadic life, used for floors, furniture, and bags, and to decorate camel and horse trappings.

In 1995 the President of Turkmenistan declared a policy of neutrality, which was acknowledged by a unanimous vote of the United Nations General Assembly on 12 December 1995. To immortalize this, crossed olive branches similar to those on the UN flag were placed below the *guls*. The new law stated, "The State Flag of Turkmenistan is a symbol of the unity and independence of the nation and of the neutrality of the state."

UZBEKISTAN

Republic of Uzbekistan,
Uzbek **Uzbekistan Respublikasy**.
Republic in W Central Asia.

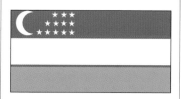

NATIONAL FLAG

Adopted 18 November 1991. Proportions 1:2.

Blue is the colour of the Turkic peoples and also of the banner of Tamerlane, who ruled an Uzbek empire in the 14th century. It is a symbol of eternal skies and of the people as one of the fundamental sources of life. The white signifies peace, the traditional Uzbek wish for a safe journey and striving for purity of thoughts and deeds. The green is the colour of nature, fertility and new life, as well as being the colour of Islam. The red stripes stand for the vital force in all living organisms, which links good and pure ideas with the eternal sky and deeds on earth.

The crescent symbolizes the new republic. The stars stand for the twelve months of the solar Uzbek calendar and are named after the 12 constellations, reflecting the astronomical knowledge of Uzbeks in ancient times.

KAZAKHSTAN

Republic of Kazakhstan,
Kazak **Kazak Respublikasy**.
Republic in W Central Asia.

STATE AND CIVIL FLAG AND ENSIGN

Adopted 4 June 1992. Proportions 1:2.

Blue is the common colour of the Turkic peoples. Here it stands for the endless skies over all people as a symbol of well-being, tranquillity, peace and unity. The sun and a golden eagle represent the love of freedom and the lofty thoughts and ideals of the Kazakhs. Along the hoist is a typical national ornament.

KYRGYZSTAN

Republic of Kyrgyzstan,
Kyrgyz **Kyrgyz Respublikasy**.
Republic in W Central Asia.

NATIONAL FLAG

Adopted 3 March 1992. Proportions 3:5.

The word *kyrgyz* originally meant "red" and red has been the national colour from time immemorial. Red was also the colour of the banner of Manas the Noble, who struggled for unity and formed the Kyrgyz nation. The sun is a symbol of light, eternity and infinite nobility, and the 40 rays stand for the 40 Kyrgyz tribes united by Manas. The sun is charged with a representation of the device covering the roof of a typical *yurt*, the tent used by the Kyrgyz nomads. It symbolizes hearth and home, the unity of time and space, the origin of life and solidarity.

TAJIKISTAN

Republic of Tajikistan,
Tajik **Jumhuri Tojikiston**.
Republic in W Central Asia.

NATIONAL FLAG

Adopted 24 November 1992. Proportions 1:2.

The crown represents the Tajik people. The name is derived from *tajvar*, which means "crowned". In traditional Tajik culture the magic word "seven" is a symbol of perfection, the embodiment of happiness and the provider of virtue. According to Tajik legend, heaven is composed of seven beautiful orchards, separated by seven mountains each with a glowing star on top.

The red is a symbol of the sun and victory; the white stands for purity, cotton and the snow on the mountains, and the green represents the spiritual meaning of Islam and the generosity of nature.

AFGHANISTAN

Islamic Republic of Afghanistan
Dari **Jomhuri-ye Eslami-ye Afghanestan**
State in Central Asia.

NATIONAL FLAG

Introduced in February 2002.
Proportions 1:2.

The present flag resembles the national flag of the Kingdom of Afghanistan, which was in use from 1930 to 1974. Above the mosque appear a *Shahada* and the words *Allahu Akbar* ("God is Great"), below the mosque the date 1380 A.H. (2001 A.D.).

The mosque is flanked by sheaves of wheat symbolizing agriculture and national unity. The colours symbolize the past (black), blood shed for independence (red), and the hope for better future (green).

KASHMIR

Kashmiri Azad Jammu o Kashmir.
Northern, autonomous part of Kashmir within Pakistan, Central Asia.

NATIONAL FLAG

Adopted in 1947. Proportions unspecified.

The flag displays the Pakistani colours, white and green, with the symbols of the Muslim majority (crescent and star) and the Hindu and Sikh minorities (a saffron square). The four white stripes symbolize the four main rivers of Kashmir.

JAMMU AND KASHMIR

Kashmiri Jammu o Kashmir.
Southern part of Kashmir, state of India, Central Asia.

NATIONAL FLAG

Adopted in 1952. Proportions 2:3.

The native plough is a symbol of labour, and the three stripes represent the three provinces of the state.

AFGHANISTAN: FLAGS REFLECT POLITICAL CHANGES

Political change in countries that gained independence in the 20th century are often reflected in changes in the national flag. In Afghanistan, the current flag is the 18th national flag since 1900.

The first three flags (1900–1928) were black with three different state emblems. In July 1928 a horizontal black-red-green tricolour was introduced, and in September of the same year these colours were re-arranged vertically. In January 1929, the black flag was revived but was soon replaced by the vertical tricolour with three different emblems (from October 1930 to 1974).

In 1974 the monarchy was forcibly abolished and the republican regime changed the emblem and restored the horizontal arrangement of the national colours (from April to October 1978 the flag had no emblem). When the communists came to power in October 1978 they adoped a red flag with a new emblem. From 1980–1992, two flags used under the Soviet occupation were horizontal tricolours with an emblem, which until 1987 displayed a red star.

After the liberation of Kabul in 1992 the national flag became a horizontal tricolour of green, white and black with the golden inscription "God is Great" (on the top stripe), and the Muslim Statement of Faith (on the second stripe).

In 1993 the inscriptions were removed, and the state arms in gold was placed in the centre. The Taliban regime introduced in 1997 a white flag charged with a dark green *Shahada* (Muslim Statement of Faith).

SOUTHERN ASIA

PAKISTAN

Islamic Republic of Pakistan,
Urdu **Islami Jamhuriya e Pakistan.**
Republic in S Asia.

NATIONAL FLAG

Adopted 14 August 1947. Proportions 2:3.

The flag of the All-India Moslem League, introduced in 1906, was green with the white crescent and star, the colours symbolizing Islam. A white vertical stripe at the hoist was added to symbolize the non-Muslim minorities after independence. The white and green portions of the flag symbolize peace and prosperity, the crescent progress and the star light and knowledge.

INDIA

Republic of India, Hindi **Bharatiya Ganarajya.**
Federal republic in S Central Asia.

NATIONAL FLAG

Adopted 22 July 1947. Proportions 2:3.

The central figure is a *chakra* (wheel) from the capital of the ancient Asokan column at Sarnath. To a Buddhist the wheel represents the inevitability of existence: *Dharma Chakra* (Wheel of Law). The saffron (orange) symbolizes courage and sacrifice, while the white stands for peace and truth, and the green faith and chivalry.

NEPAL

Kingdom of Nepal, Nepali **Nepal Adhirajya.**
Constitutional monarchy in S Central Asia.

NATIONAL FLAG

Adopted 16 December 1962. Proportions 4:3.

Nepal is the only country in the world to have a flag that is not rectangular or square. The two triangles symbolize the Himalaya Mountains and they also stand for two religions, Hinduism and Buddhism. Crimson is the national colour of Nepal. The moon and sun originally symbolized the families of the king and the prime minister, and the wish that the nation might live as long as these celestial bodies.

BHUTAN

Kingdom of Bhutan, Dzongkha **Druk-yul.**
Constitutional monarchy in S Central Asia.

NATIONAL FLAG

In use since the 19th century. Proportions 2:3.

The present design of the flag was established *c.*1965, when the maroon was replaced by orange and the shape of the dragon was modified. The dragon represents the name of the country (*druk* means "dragon") and its colour stands for purity and loyalty. Its snarling mouth expresses the stern strength of the deities protecting Bhutan, and the jewels clasped in its claws symbolize the wealth and perfection of the country. The yellow stands for the fruitful action of the king in affairs of religion and state; the orange represents religious practice.

BANGLADESH

People's Republic of Bangladesh,
Bengali **Gana Prajatantri Bangladesh.**
Republic in S Asia.

NATIONAL FLAG

Adopted 13 January 1972. Proportions 3:5.

The green represents the greenery of the country, its vitality and youthfulness. The red disc is a symbol of the rising sun of independence after the dark night of a blood-drenched struggle.

SRI LANKA

Democratic Socialist Republic of Sri Lanka,
Sinhala **Sri Lanka prajathanthrika samajawadi janarajaya,**
Tamil **Ilankayc cananayaka sosalisak kutiyarucu.**
Socialist republic consisting of an island in Indian Ocean, S Asia.

NATIONAL FLAG

Adopted 7 September 1978. Proportions 1:2.

In traditional Sanskrit and Pali literature the island is called Sinhaladvipa, the word *sinhala* deriving from the Sinhalese word *sinha* (lion), and since the 15th century a golden lion holding a sword of authority has appeared on the crimson field of the state banner. This flag with a yellow border, a symbol of Buddhism, was adopted as the first flag of independent Ceylon on 4 February 1948. The lion denotes the desire for peace, while the crimson symbolizes national pride. In 1950 the stripes of green (for the Muslims) and saffron (for the Tamils) were added. In 1972 and 1978 the finials in the corners were modified to represent the leaves of the fig tree (*Ficus religiosa*) under which Siddartha Gautama sat when he received enlightenment and became the Buddha. The four leaves stand for love, compassion, sympathy and equanimity, which are virtues extolled by Buddhism.

MALDIVES

Republic of the Maldives,
Divehi **Divehi Rajje ge Jumhuriya**.
Republic comprising 19 clusters of coral islands in Indian Ocean, S Asia.

NATIONAL FLAG AND ENSIGN

Adopted 26 July 1965.
Proportions 2:3.

The crescent is the symbol of Islam. The green stands for peace and prosperity, and the red symbolizes blood shed in the struggle for independence.

BRITISH INDIAN OCEAN TERRITORY

British colony consisting of the Chagos Archipelago in N Indian Ocean.

STATE FLAG AND ENSIGN

Adopted 4 November 1990. Proportions 3:5.
Ensign is in proportions 1:2.

The white and blue wavy stripes represent the Indian Ocean. The palm tree stands for the islands, of which only Diego Garcia is inhabited. The Union flag in the canton and the crown are there to symbolize British sovereignty.

SOUTH-EAST ASIA

MYANMAR

Union of Myanmar, Burmese **Pyidaungsu Myanma Naingngandaw**.
Military republic in SE Asia.

NATIONAL FLAG

Adopted 3 January 1974. Proportions 5:9.

The white represents purity and virtue, the blue symbolizes peace and integrity, and the red signifies courage and decisiveness. The pinion and padi leaves stand for industry and agriculture, and for workers and peasants. The stars represent the 14 constituent member states of the union.

THAILAND

Kingdom of Thailand,
Thai **Muang Thai** or **Pratet Thai**.
Constitutional monarchy in SE Asia.

CIVIL AND STATE FLAG AND ENSIGN

Adopted 28 September 1917. Proportions 2:3.

The flag adopted in 1916 was red with two white stripes, but the central red portion was altered to blue. It was an expression of solidarity with World War I allies (United Kingdom, France, United States and Russia), whose flags used the red, white and blue. The flag is given the name *Trairanga* which means tricolour.

The colours symbolize the blood shed for their country (red), the purity of the people protected by their religion (white) and the monarchy (blue).

CAMBODIA

State of Cambodia,
Khmer **Roat Kampuchea**.
State in Indo-China, SE Asia.

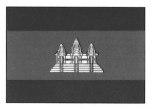

NATIONAL FLAG AND ENSIGN

Adopted 30 June 1993. Proportions 2:3.

The present flag is the seventh since 1948, when the country became independent. All of them except one bore a representation of Angkor Wat, built in the 12th century, which is one of the most impressive temples in the world.

LAOS

Lao People's Democratic Republic, Lao **Sáthálanalat Pasathipatay Pásáson Lao**.
Socialist republic in Indo-China, SE Asia.

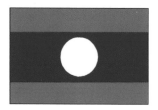

NATIONAL FLAG

Adopted 2 December 1975. Proportions 2:3.

The flag has been used since 1956 by Pathet Lao, the communist guerrilla movement, and became the national flag when it gained control of the country in 1975. The red symbolizes the blood spilt by the Lao people in defence of their Fatherland, the blue stands for the country's wealth, and the white represents the unity of the multi-ethnic society under communist rule.

VIETNAM

Socialist Republic of Vietnam,
Vietnamese **Công Hòa Xã Hôi Chu Nghia Viêt Nam**.
Socialist republic in Indo-China, SE Asia.

NATIONAL FLAG AND ENSIGN

Adopted 30 November 1955. Proportions 2:3.

The red symbolizes the revolution and the blood shed in the struggle for independence. The five-pointed star represents the unity of workers, peasants, intellectuals, young people and soldiers in building socialism.

MACAO

Macao Special Administrative Region of the People's Republic of China.
Former Portuguese colony in SE Asia.

REGIONAL FLAG

Adopted 31 March 1993, will be in use from 20 December 1999. Proportions 2:3.

The five stars, taken from the flag of China, recall that Macao is an inseparable part of China. The stylized lotus flower stands for the people, and its three petals represent the three islands of Macao. The bridge and the waves are emblematic of the natural environment surrounding Macao.

HONG KONG

Hong Kong Special Administrative Region of the People's Republic of China.
Former British crown colony in SE Asia.

REGIONAL FLAG

Officially hoisted 1 July 1997. Proportions 2:3.

The stylized bauhinia (orchid tree) flower represents the people of Hong Kong. The five red stars, taken from the flag of China, state that the Territory is an inseparable part of China.

PHILIPPINES

Republic of the Philippines,
Tagalog **Republika ng Pilipinas**.
Republic consisting of an archipelago in the Pacific Ocean, SE Asia.

NATIONAL FLAG AND ENSIGN

Adopted 19 May 1898. Colours modified 16 September 1997. Proportions 1:2.

The golden sun with eight rays symbolizes liberty and was championed by the first eight provinces to revolt against Spain. The stars represent the three major regions: Luzon, the Visayas and Mindanao. The white triangle stands for purity and peace while the blue and red symbolize patriotism and bravery respectively. The flag is the only one in the world to change the position of its colours: in time of war the upper stripe is red and the lower blue.

MALAYSIA

Federation of Malaysia,
Malay **Persekutuan Tanah Malaysia**.
Federal constitutional monarchy
in SE Asia.

NATIONAL FLAG AND STATE ENSIGN

Adopted 16 September 1963. Proportions 1:2.

The crescent and star is the symbol of Islam, and the 14 points of the star and the 14 stripes represent the 14 members of the Federation of Malaysia. (Singapore left the Federation in 1965 but the flag remains unchanged.) The blue canton symbolizes the unity of the peoples of Malaysia and yellow is the colour of Their Highnesses the rulers.

MALAYSIAN STATES AND TERRITORIES

Malaysia comprises 13 states and three federal territories (Putrajaya, Kuala Lumpur and Labuan). All flags have the proportions 1:2. The crescent and star appear on seven flags and symbolizes Islam, the faith of the majority of the population.

JOHOR

NATIONAL FLAG AND ENSIGN

Adopted in 1870.

The white and blue represent the ruler and the government respectively. The red stands for the warrior caste Hulabalang.

KEDAH

NATIONAL FLAG

Adopted in 1912.

The red is the traditional colour of the state. The *padi* represents the main crop of the state, the crescent stands for Islam and the shield is a symbol of authority.

KELANTAN

NATIONAL FLAG

Adopted in 1924.

The red symbolizes the loyalty of the people who are faithful to the ruler. The spears and daggers represent their strength.

KUALA LUMPUR

FLAG OF THE TERRITORY

Adopted on 15 May 1990.

The blue symbolizes the unity of the population of this federal territory. The colour red stands for courage and vigour, the white for purity, and the yellow for sovereignty and prosperity.

LABUAN

FLAG OF THE TERRITORY

Date of adoption unknown.

The symbolism of the colours is the same as the national flag.

MELAKA

NATIONAL FLAG

Adopted in 1961.

The colours signify that Melaka is a component state of Malaysia.

NEGERI SEMBILAN

NATIONAL FLAG

Adopted in 1895.

The colours represent the authorities: the ruler (yellow), the ruling chiefs of districts (black), and the people (red).

PAHANG

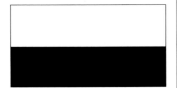

STATE FLAG

Adopted 28 December 1903.

The white stands for the ruler, whose powers depend on the people. Because white can be changed into any other colour, the ruler can be swayed to meet the wishes of the people. The black represents the people, whose rights should not be alienated by the ruler.

PERAK

STATE FLAG

Adopted c.1920.

The colours represent the authorities – the Sultan (white), the Raja Muda (yellow) and the Raja di-Hilir (black).

PERLIS

STATE FLAG

Adopted in 1870.

The yellow stands for the ruler, the blue represents the people. Together the colours symbolize co-operation between the ruler and his subjects.

PINANG

STATE FLAG

Adopted in 1949.

The tree is *pokok pinang*, the betel nut tree (*Areca catechu*) after which the state is named. The blue represents the sea that surrounds the island, the white stands for the state itself in its serenity and the yellow represents prosperity.

PUTRAJAYA

FLAG OF THE TERRITORY

Introduced 1 February 2001.

The territory has been named after the first prime minister of Malaysia, Tunku Abduck Rahman Putra Al-Haj. Putrajaya will be the new capital of Malaysia, and therefore in the centre of the flag appears the state arms. The five krises (Malayan knives) represent the following states; Johor, Kedah, Perlis, Kelantan and Terengganu. The betel nut tree, the bridge and waves symbolize Pinang. Red, black, white and yellow rectangles stand for Pahang, Selangor, Perak and Negeri Sembilan. The tree represents Melaka. In the bottom of the shield there are arms of Sabah and Sarawak, separated by the red hibiscus, the national flower of Malaysia. On the scroll appears the national motto "Unity is Strength". The colours of the flag symbolize unity of the people (blue) and the government (yellow).

SABAH

STATE FLAG

Adopted 16 September 1988.

This is the only flag in the world with displays three different shades of blue: royal (silhouette of Mount Kinabalu), icicle (canton) and zircon (upper stripe). Mt Kinabalu represents the state of Sabah. The zircon blue symbolizes peace and tranquillity, the white purity and justice, the red courage and conviction, the icicle blue unity and prosperity, and the royal blue strength and co-operation.

SARAWAK

STATE FLAG

Adopted 31 August 1988.

The flag displays the colours established in 1870 and used until 1973. At that time the flag was yellow charged with a cross divided vertically into black and red portions. The yellow denotes the supremacy of law and order, and unity and stability in diversity. The black represents the natural resources (petroleum, timber etc), that provide the foundation for the advancement of the people. The red stands for the courage, determination and sacrifices of the people in their tireless pursuit to attain and maintain progress and esteem in the course of creating a model state. The star embodies the aspiration of the people; its nine points represent the nine divisions of the state.

SELANGOR

STATE FLAG

Adopted in 1965.

The yellow and red symbolize flesh and blood respectively, giving life and strength to the state.

TERENGGANU

STATE FLAG

Adopted in 1947.

The flag is a graphic representation of the protection that the sultan (white) spreads around his subjects (black).

BRUNEI

State of Brunei,
Malay **Negara Brunei Darussalam.**
Absolute monarchy in SE Asia.

STATE FLAG, CIVIL AND STATE ENSIGN

Adopted 29 September 1959. Proportions 1:2.

The flag in its present form, except for the crest, has been in use since 1906 when Brunei became a protected state. The colours are those of the flags of the principal signatories to the agreement between Brunei and the United Kingdom: the Sultan (yellow), Pengiran Bendahara (white) and Pengiran Pemancha (black). The crest was added in 1959. The mast and pedestal represent the three levels of government, and the four feathers symbolize justice, tranquillity, peace and prosperity. The hands signify that the government preserves and promotes the welfare of the citizens. The crescent stands for Islam, the state religion. The state motto, written in Arabic script, means "Always render service by God's guidance". The name of the state appears on the ribbon.

SINGAPORE

Republic of Singapore,
Malay **Repablik Singapura,**
Chinese **Xinjiapo Gongheguo,**
Tamil **Sinkappur Kutijarasu.**
Republic comprising mainly Singapore Island in SE Asia.

STATE FLAG

Officially hoisted 3 December 1959.
Proportions 2:3.

The colours represent universal brotherhood (red), and purity and virtue (white). The crescent stands for "a young country on the ascent in its ideals of establishing democratic peace, progress, justice and equality as indicated by the five stars".

INDONESIA

Republic of Indonesia,
Bahasa **Indonesia Republik Indonesia.**
Republic consisting of an archipelago in SE Asia.

NATIONAL FLAG AND ENSIGN

Adopted 17 August 1945. Proportions 2:3.

The flag, officially called *Sang Dwiwarna* (exalted bicolour), symbolizes a living person. The red represents the body and physical life, the white the soul and spiritual life.

EAST TIMOR

Democratic Republic of East Timor,
Portuguese **Republica Democrática de Timor Leste.**
Republic consisting of the east portion of Timor.

STATE AND NATIONAL FLAG

Introduced on 20 May 2002.

This flag (with the star positioned upright) was first hoisted when East Timor proclaimed independence on 28 November 1975, and was banned by the Indonesian occupation that started nine days later. Red symbolizes the blood shed in the long struggle for independence. The black triangle represents colonial oppression, the yellow border stands for a spear of freedom. The white star is a symbol of hope.

FAR EAST

MONGOLIA

State of Mongolia,
Mongolian **Mongol Uls**.
Republic in E Central Asia.

NATIONAL FLAG

Introduced 12 February 1992. Proportions 1:2.

The basic design of the flag dates from 1940. In 1992 the star surmounting the emblem was removed and the design of the *Soyonbo*, an ancient Mongolian symbol, was modified. The blue is the traditional colour of the Mongols and other Turkic peoples and the two red vertical stripes symbolize the double joys of liberty and independence.

The *Soyonbo* is accompanied by several other ancient symbols. The arrowheads, or triangles, pointing downwards mean "Death to the enemy"; two signifying "Death to the enemies of the people". The triangle is a symbol of straightforwardness, honesty and adherence to principles. The two fish in the centre represent men and women. As fish never sleep they are a reminder that

SOYONBO

Marco Polo was the first European to report that Mongolian flags were charged with the sun and moon. In fact, the ancient sign of *Soyonbo* is composed of the sun, moon and fire. Together they represent the wish, "May you live and flourish forever". Fire denotes prosperity, regeneration and ascent, and the three tongues of flame stand for the past, present and future. The sun and moon symbolize the belief that the Mongolians are children of the sun (mother) and moon (father).

the people should always be vigilant for their country. The horizontal bars above and below this image indicate that the highest and the lowest in society should be honest and straightforward in the service of the people. A vertical bar represents a fortress; the two bars illustrate the proverb, "Two friends are stronger than stone".

TIBET

Tibetan **Bod rang-skyong ljongs**,
Chinese **Xi-zang**.
Region of China with limited autonomy,
E Central Asia.

CIVIL FLAG

Adopted in 1912. Proportions unspecified.

The white triangle represents a mountain covered with snow, symbolizing Tibet's location in the Himalaya Mountains. The two lions represent harmony between temporal and spiritual rule. They are holding the wishing gem. This symbolizes the rule of law based on the principle of cause and effect underlying the Ten Golden Precepts and the Sixteen Humane Principles of Buddhism, which are the source of infinite benefit and peace. Above the gem stand the three flaming jewels", representing Buddha (God), Dharma (the Doctrine) and Sangha (the saints, guardians of the Doctrine).

The sun is a symbol of freedom, happiness and prosperity. Its 12 rays represent the 12 descendants of the six aboriginal tribes of Tibet. Their colours are symbolic of the two guardian deities (male and female) protecting the flag. The yellow border of the flag indicates the spread of the golden ideals of Buddhism.

CHINA

People's Republic of China,
Chinese **Zhonghua Renmin Gonghe Guo**.
Socialist republic in E and Central Asia.

NATIONAL FLAG AND ENSIGN

Adopted 1 October 1949. Proportions 2:3.

The red stands for the communist revolution and the large star is a symbol of the communist party. The four smaller stars represent the workers, peasants, bourgeoisie and patriotic capitalists who are united in building communism.

TAIWAN

Republic of China,
Chinese **Chung Hua Min Kuo**.
Republic consisting of an island in
Pacific Ocean, E Asia.

NATIONAL FLAG AND STATE ENSIGN

Adopted 28 October 1928.
Proportions 2:3.

The flag, adopted as the national flag and war ensign of China, was retained by the nationalist forces, which were defeated by the communists and in 1949 found refuge on the island of Taiwan. The 12 rays of the white sun represent the 12 two-hour periods of the day, and together they symbolize the spirit of unceasing progress.

YIN-YANG

The two elements, the feminine yin and the masculine yang, together form a disc, a figure enclosed by a circle, which is a symbol of infinity, perfection and eternity. The red part is the positive element yang, representing the sun, light, day, heaven, movement and activity. The blue part is the negative element yin, symbolizing the moon, darkness, night, earth, immobility and passivity. The yin-yang reflects the immemorial relationship of contradictions and encompasses all opposites such as good and evil, truth and lies, warmth and coldness, life and death. This dualism (yin-yang) in the absolute (the circle) reflects the paradoxes of life and suggests that it is impossible to comprehend fully the complexities of existence and the universe.

The colours stand for the three principles of the people – democracy (blue), the people's livelihood (white) and nationalism (red). The colours also have a dual meaning: blue stands for equality and justice, the white for fraternity and frankness, and the red for liberty and sacrifice.

NORTH KOREA

People's Democratic Republic of Korea, Korean **Chosun Minchu-chui Inmin Konghwa-guk**.
Socialist state in N part of Korean Peninsula, E Asia.

NATIONAL FLAG AND ENSIGN

Adopted 8 September 1948. Proportions 1:2.

The star symbolizes the revolutionary traditions established by President Kim Il Sung. The red represents revolutionary patriotism and the fighting spirit, and the white stands for the Korean nation and its culture. The blue stripes symbolize "the aspiration of the Korean people to unite with the revolutionary people of the whole world and fight for the victory of the idea of independence, friendship and peace".

SOUTH KOREA

Republic of Korea,
Korean **Taehan Min-guk**.
Republic in S part of the Korean Peninsula, E Asia.

NATIONAL FLAG, CIVIL AND STATE ENSIGN

Adopted in 1882, last time modified 21 February 1984. Proportions 2:3.

The white is the Korean national colour, a symbol of purity, peace and justice. The central emblem is a reflection of Chinese cosmogony, in which the opposites of yin and yang unify and co-operate. The yin-yang, a synthesis of the Great Beginning, is called *taeguk* in Korean and from this the flag derives its name *Taeguki*. In the corners are four trigrams, which are also composed of the yin (broken bars) and yang (unbroken bars). Clockwise from the upper hoist, the trigrams symbolize:
(i) heaven, the south and summer,
(ii) the moon, the west, autumn and water,
(iii) the earth, the north and winter, and
(iv) the sun, the east, spring and fire. The black stands for vigilance, perseverance, justice and chastity.

JAPAN

Japanese **Nippon (Nihon)**.
Constitutional monarchy consisting of an island chain in Pacific Ocean, E Asia.

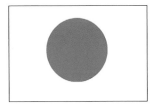

CIVIL AND STATE FLAG AND ENSIGN

Officially adopted 5 August 1854.
Proportions 2:3.

This flag, called *Hinomaru* (disc of the sun) has been in use at least since the 14th century. The red sun recalls the name of Japan (the Land of the Rising Sun) and worship of Amaterasu Omikami (the Sun Goddess), the most venerated goddess in the Shinto religion. The colours also reflect the spirit of Shinto ethics, based on a bright, pure, just and gentle heart. The white stands for purity and integrity, the red for sincerity, brightness and warmth.

SOLAR DISC

The most common feature appearing on flags in the Far East is the disc, which usually represents the sun. The disc appears in many different colours. For example, in Sakha, North Korea and Laos the disc is white; the Mongol banners in the 13th century and the civil ensign of China 1872-1912 feature a yellow disc. In Japan and Bangladesh it is red; in South Korea the disc is red-blue.

The sun is one of humanity's oldest symbols and symbolizes divinity, majesty, life, beauty and goodness. So it is no surprise that the solar disc is often used on flags to represent a ruler.

Flags of Australia and Oceania

The current national flags of the countries of Australasia and Oceania, from Christmas Island and Australia to French Polynesia and the Pitcairn Islands, are illustrated and described in the following pages, together with the flags of their territories, states and provinces.

The countries of this continent, scattered throughout the Pacific Ocean, have been grouped together for ease of reference. We begin in Australia and move swiftly on to the vast Pacific Ocean which is harnessed into the west Pacific, central Pacific, south-west Pacific and finally, the south-east Pacific Ocean.

For each entry, the country or territory's name is given in its most easily recognized form and then in all its official languages. This is followed by a description of its political status and geographic position. The basic data for each flag contains the status of the flag, date of adoption, proportions, and the symbolic meaning.

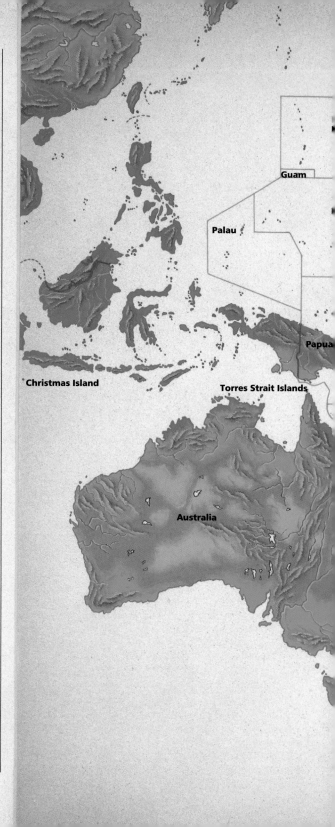

Guam

Palau

Papua

Christmas Island

Torres Strait Islands

Australia

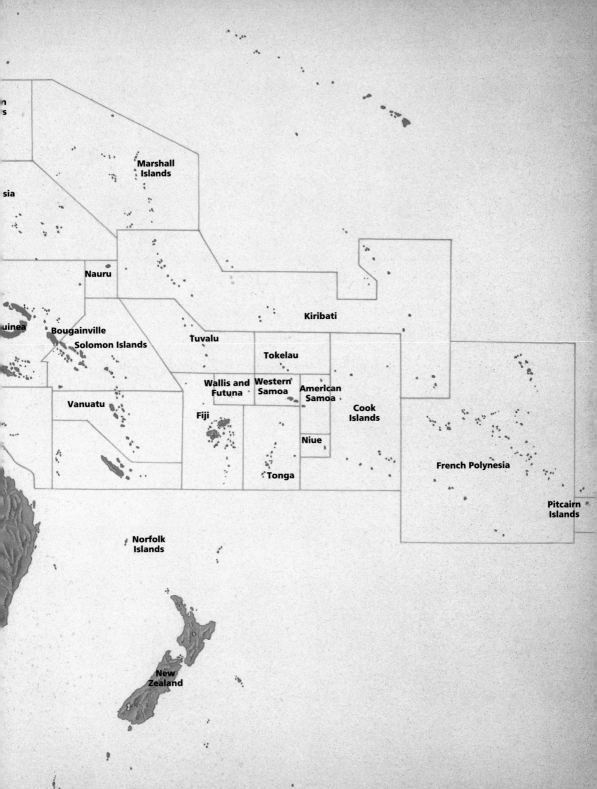

AUSTRALIA

CHRISTMAS ISLAND

Territory of Christmas Island
Autonomous external territory of Australia in
E Indian Ocean.

NATIONAL FLAG

Introduced in 1987. Proportions 1:2.

The yellow and green, the national colours
of Australia, and the stars of the Southern
Cross constellation symbolize the island's
association with Australia. The blue stands
for the Indian Ocean, the green for the
tropical rainforest and the bird is a golden
bosun, unique to the island. A graphic
representation of the island appears on the
yellow disc in the centre of the flag.

TORRES STRAIT ISLANDS

Part of Queensland (Australia)
with limited autonomy.

NATIONAL FLAG AND CIVIL ENSIGN

Introduced in May 1992. Proportions 23:31.

The traditional *dhari* headdress symbolizes
the inhabitants of the islands, which are
represented by the star. The green stands for
the land, the blue for the sea and the black
for the indigenous people.

AUSTRALIA

Commonwealth of Australia.
Federal constitutional monarchy comprising the
continent of Australia.

NATIONAL FLAG

*Introduced in 1901, approved by the
King of Great Britain in 1903. Proportions 1:2.*

The British blue ensign, charged with five
stars forming the Southern Cross and a
sixth to represent the Commonwealth of
Australia, was the design chosen in a
competition in 1901, which attracted
30,000 entries. Subsequently there were
some changes to the stars until their shape,
size and position were precisely specified
on 15 April 1954. The six points of the Star
of the Commonwealth represent the six
states, and the seventh stands for the
Australian Capital Territory, Northern
Territory, and the eight external territories
of the Ashmore and Cartier Islands;
Christmas Island; Cocos (Keeling) Islands;
Coral Sea Islands; Jervis Bay; Norfolk
Island; Australian Antarctic Territory; and
Heard and McDonald Islands.

AUSTRALIAN CAPITAL TERRITORY

FLAG OF THE TERRITORY

Adopted 25 March 1993.

The blue hoist portion of the flag, with the
five stars of the Southern Cross

constellation (as on the national flag),
indicates that this is the federal territory. In
the centre of the yellow portion of the flag
appears a simplified version of the arms of
Canberra, the capital of Australia.

AUSTRALIAN STATES AND TERRITORY

The state flags follow the design of the
British colonial flags, i.e. the blue ensign
in proportions 1:2, charged with a badge.
Almost all of them are older than the
national flag of Australia.

NEW SOUTH WALES

STATE FLAG

Granted 11 July 1876.

The cross of St George is charged with
the English lion and the four stars of the
Southern Cross.

NORTHERN TERRITORY

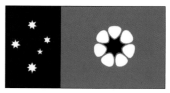

FLAG OF THE TERRITORY

Adopted 1 July 1978.

Black and ochre are the official colours of
the Territory. The stars form the Southern
Cross constellation. The seven petals of
the highly stylized Sturt's desert rose
(*Gossypium sturtianum*) and the seven-
pointed star in its centre represent the
seven states-to-be of Australia.

QUEENSLAND

STATE FLAG

Granted 29 November 1876.

The badge displays a blue Maltese cross surmounted by a royal crown. The shape of the cross resembles the insignia of the military award for valour, known as the Victoria Cross.

SOUTH AUSTRALIA

STATE FLAG

Adopted 13 January 1904.

The golden disc, which symbolizes the rising sun, is charged with a black and white piping shrike (*Gymnorhina tibicen hypoleuca*) perched on the branch of a gum tree. The piping shrike, or white-backed magpie, is the South Australian bird emblem.

TASMANIA

STATE FLAG

Adopted 25 September 1876.

The badge on Tasmania's flag is white with a heraldic lion in red. The same red lion appears in the crest of the Tasmanian coat of arms and the arms of the city of Hobart.

VICTORIA

STATE FLAG

Adopted 30 November 1877.

The flag of Victoria is the only state flag that does not bear a badge. Since 1870 it has been charged with the five stars of the constellation of the Southern Cross. The Tudor crown was added in 1877 and originally signified the state's ties to Queen Victoria and Britain. In 1952 it was replaced by St Edward's crown.

WESTERN AUSTRALIA

STATE FLAG

Adopted in 1953.

As early as 1830, a black swan (*Cygnus atratus*) became the emblem of the colony, which was also known as "the Swan River Colony". Aboriginal legend tells how the ancestors of a section of the Bibbulman tribe of western Australia were originally black swans who changed into men.

The badge, introduced on 27 November 1875, was yellow with the black swan turned out to the fly; in 1953 a mirror image of this was introduced instead.

THE CHANGING STARS

The first recorded attempt to adopt the national flag of Australia occurred in 1824 when Captain John Bingle and Captain John Nicholson charged the British white ensign with four stars. Each of the white eight-pointed stars was placed in the middle of each arm of the St George's cross.

In 1831, Captain J. Nicholson introduced a New South Wales ensign of very similar design. The colour of the cross was changed to dark blue and the fifth star was positioned in the centre of the cross. This flag became very popular in Australia and in the 1880s and 1890s was the chief symbol of the political movement towards the federation of Australian territories.

The first national flag of Australia was hoisted for the first time on 3 September 1901. It was the British blue ensign charged with a large star underneath the canton and five stars forming the constellation of the Southern Cross in the fly. The larger star, called the Commonwealth Star, had six points representing the six states of the new nation. The five stars in the fly had nine, eight, seven, six and five points, reflecting the brightness of the Southern Cross. In 1903, after minor modification, this flag became the current national flag of Australia.

In the last two decades there were several attempts to design and introduce a new national flag without the Union Jack in the canton. It is quite probable that in the near future Australia will have a new flag and it is almost certain that any new design will incorporate the stars of the Southern Cross.

WEST PACIFIC OCEAN

PAPUA NEW GUINEA

**Independent State of
Papua New Guinea**, Pidgin **Papua Niugini**.
Constitutional monarchy in E part of
New Guinea, W Pacific Ocean.

NATIONAL FLAG, STATE AND CIVIL ENSIGN

Approved 11 March 1971. Proportions 3:4.

Young student Susan Hareho Karike,
designer of the flag, chose red and black
because of the widespread use of these
colours in traditional native art. The
Empress of Germany's bird of paradise
(*Paradisaea raggiana augustae-victoriae*) is
peculiar to the island of New Guinea. The
five stars form the constellation of the
Southern Cross, symbolizing the
relationship with Australia and also
referring to a local legend about five sisters.

The flag was only for use on land from
1971 to 16 September 1975, when the
country became independent.

BOUGAINVILLE

Republic of Bougainville.
Secessionist province of Papua New Guinea
in W Pacific Ocean.

NATIONAL FLAG

Introduced 1 September 1975. Proportions 1:2.

When the province of North Solomons
broke ties with Papua New Guinea in
May 1990 and proclaimed independence
under the name of Bougainville, its flag
remained unchanged. The blue background
symbolizes the Pacific Ocean surrounding
Bougainville, which is represented by the
centrally positioned emblem. The black
disc recalls the native Bougainvillean
people. In its centre is an *upe*, the headdress associated with the transition of
young men from adolescence to manhood.
The red stripes on the *upe* generally suggest
leadership. A broad central stripe and two
narrower lateral stripes represent men and
women, since for ceremonial occasions all
men paint the centre of their hair red,
whilst the women decorate the sides of their
hair red and leave the centre black. The disc
is framed by a green ring representing the
island. The white triangles allude to the
carved turtle shells worn by local chiefs and
their queens on ceremonial occasions.

SOLOMON ISLANDS

Constitutional monarchy comprising a group
of islands in SW Pacific Ocean.

NATIONAL FLAG

Adopted 18 November 1977. Proportions 1:2.

The stars originally represented the five
districts of the country, but in 1982 when
the country was divided into seven
provinces, it was decided that the stars
would instead symbolize the five main
groups of islands. The yellow stands for the
sun, the blue for water (the sea, rivers and
the rain) and the green for land, its trees
and food crops.

VANUATU

Republic of Vanuatu,
Bislama **Ripablik blong Vanuatu**.
Republic comprising a group of islands
in SW Pacific Ocean.

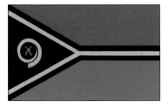

NATIONAL FLAG AND ENSIGN

*Officially hoisted 30 July 1980.
Proportions 11:18.*

The national emblem consists of two
crossed *namele* leaves (*Phoenix sylvestris*)
surrounded by a boar's tusk. The leaves
symbolize peace and their 39 fronds
represent the 39 members of the
Representative Assembly. The boar's tusk is
a symbol of prosperity. The black represents
the people and the rich soil, the yellow
(shaped like the archipelago) symbolizes
peace and the light of Christianity, the
green represents the islands and the red is a
symbol of the unity of the Vanuatu people.

NAURU

Republic of Nauru, Nauruan **Naoero**.
Republic comprising an island in
W Central Pacific Ocean.

NATIONAL FLAG AND ENSIGN

Adopted 31 January 1968. Proportions 1:2.

The blue stands for the Pacific Ocean and
blue skies. The yellow line stands for the
Equator and immediately below it lies

the island, represented by a white star.
Its 12 points symbolize the 12 original
tribes of Nauru.

MICRONESIA

Federated States of Micronesia.
Federal republic comprising most islands of the
Caroline group in N Pacific Ocean.

NATIONAL FLAG AND ENSIGN

Adopted 30 November 1978. Proportions 1:2.

The blue represents the Pacific Ocean. The
stars stand for the groups of islands forming
the Federation.

MICRONESIAN STATES

Since 1947 the Caroline Islands (Chuuk,
Kosrae, Palau, Pohnpei and Yap) have been
administered by the USA as part of the
United Nations Trust Territory of the
Pacific Islands. Palau did not join the
Federated States of Micronesia created
in 1979.

Although some of the four constituent
states have established proportions for their
flags, the flags are manufactured in the
United States in the standard proportions
of 2:3 and 3:5.

CHUUK
*Adopted 7 September 1979, approved
28 January 1980.*

The blue stands for peace. The 38 stars
represent the 38 municipalities and the
coconut tree in the centre is a symbol of
the local agriculture.

KOSRAE
Adopted 30 July 1981.

The blue represents the Pacific Ocean. The
fafa pounding stone symbolizes local
culture, custom, knowledge and prosperity.
The olive branches denote peace and unity
among the state and municipal government
and the people. The four stars stand for the
four main municipalities.

POHNPEI
Adopted in December 1977.

The half coconut shell represents the *sakau*
cup. (*Sakau* is a local drink extracted from
kava roots and hibiscus bark, and used
during traditional ceremonies.) The stars
represent the municipalities. The coconut
branches signify the people's dependence
on coconut resources.

YAP
*Adopted 30 May 1980, officially hoisted
1 March 1981.*

The blue stands for the Pacific Ocean, the
white for peace and brotherhood. The
highly stylized outrigger canoe is a symbol
of the means and ways of accomplishment.
The large circle symbolizes unity, while the
smaller one represents the state and the
people. The star is symbolic of guidance
and the state's goals.

PALAU

Republic of Palau, Palauan **Belau**.
Federal republic comprising a group of islands
in NW Pacific Ocean.

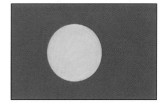

NATIONAL FLAG AND ENSIGN

Adopted 13 June 1980. Proportions 3:5.

The blue stands for the final transition
from foreign domination to independence.
The disc in the centre represents the full
moon, which is the time for fishing, cutting
trees, canoe-carving, planting, harvesting
and celebrating.

▲ *ABOVE State flags on Micronesian postage stamps: (clockwise from top left) Pohnpei; Truk
(Chuuk); Kosra; Yap.*

GUAM

Territory of Guam.
Unincorporated United States territory
comprising the largest of the Mariana Islands
in NW Pacific Ocean.

CIVIL AND STATE FLAG

Approved 9 February 1948. Proportions 22:41.

The basic design of the flag was approved on 4 July 1917, and in 1948 a narrow red border was added. The blue stands for the Pacific Ocean. The seal is in the shape of a sling-shot used by the ancient Chamorros for hunting and warfare. It is a symbol of the protection and endurance of the home government. The seal depicts a typical landscape in Guam, seen from the mouth of the Agana River. The lonely coconut palm tree escaped being uprooted during the destructive typhoon of 1918 and

therefore it symbolizes perseverance, courage, strength and usefulness (coconut is the main crop of the island). In the distance is "Two Lovers' Point" which represents faithfulness to a good cause. According to legend, two lovers preferred to kill themselves by jumping from the Point rather than be forced to marry someone they did not love. The outrigger canoe recalls the fame of the native people, the Chamorros, for their nautical skills. It stands for bravery and skill in making the best of one's environment.

NORTHERN MARIANAS

**Commonwealth of the Northern
Mariana Islands.**
Self-governing incorporated United States
territory in NW Pacific Ocean.

NATIONAL FLAG AND ENSIGN

*Introduced 1 July 1989. Proportions 20:39
(de facto 2:3 or 3:5).*

The first flag, adopted in 1972 and introduced in 1976, was blue with a large white star in the centre, superimposed over a grey *latte* stone in silhouette (*latte* stones, columns of limestone, were used to support traditional houses). In 1989 the emblem was surrounded with a garland of flowers and shells. It underwent some modification in 1991 and 1995.

The blue symbolizes the Pacific Ocean, which surrounds the islands with love and peace, and the star represents the Commonwealth. The *latte* stone symbolizes the culture of the Chamorro people. The circular head wreath made from four flowers (*ylang-ylang, seyur, ang'gha* and *teibwo*) is a symbol of the indigenous Carolinian culture.

CENTRAL PACIFIC OCEAN

KIRIBATI

Republic of Kiribati.
Republic comprising three groups of islands
in E Central Pacific Ocean.

NATIONAL FLAG AND ENSIGN

Officially hoisted 12 July 1979. Proportions 1:2.

This is the heraldic banner of arms of Kiribati. The frigate bird (*Fregata minor*) is a symbol of authority, freedom and traditional dances. The rising sun stands for the Equator, whose length within the borders of Kiribati is more than 4000 km (2500 miles). The white and blue waves symbolize the Pacific Ocean, of which some 5 million sq km (2 million sq miles) belong to Kiribati.

TOKELAU

Overseas territory of New Zealand comprising
a group of islands in Central Pacific Ocean.

NATIONAL FLAG

Adopted in October 1986. Proportions 1:2.

The blue represents the Pacific Ocean. The silhouette of a palm tree represents the local flora and the three stars stand for the atolls of Atafu, Fakaofo and Nukunonu.

AMERICAN SAMOA

Territory of American Samoa.
Self-governing United States overseas territory in Central Pacific Ocean.

CIVIL AND STATE FLAG

Adopted 27 April 1960. Proportions 1:2.

The colours are those of the United States flag, the *Stars and Stripes*. The American bald eagle, a symbol of protection, is holding in its talons a *fue*, or fly switch, the Samoan chief's attribute and a symbol of wisdom, and a *nifo oti*, a Samoan dancing knife. The fact that the eagle holds these symbols of Samoan authority and culture indicates the friendship between Samoan and American people.

SAMOA

Independent State of Samoa,
Samoan **Malotutu'atasi o Samoa i Sisifo**.
Constitutional monarchy in Central Pacific Ocean.

NATIONAL FLAG AND ENSIGN

Adopted 26 April 1949. Proportions 1:2.

On 26 May 1948, before adoption of the current flag, a similar flag with four stars was approved for use on land only. The five stars represent the constellation of the Southern Cross. The colours represent the qualities of freedom (blue), purity (white) and courage (red).

WALLIS AND FUTUNA

French **Territoire des Îles Wallis et Futuna**.
Autonomous French overseas territory in Central Pacific Ocean.

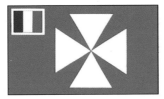

NATIONAL FLAG AND CIVIL ENSIGN

Introduced in 1888.

Originally a red flag with a white cross pattée was used in the 19th century in Uvea. The cross was introduced by the first Marist Brothers, the French missionaries who established the missions. When, in 1886, the Queen of Wallis accepted the French Protectorate it was agreed to charge the canton with the French *Tricolore*.

TUVALU

South West Pacific State of Tuvalu.
Constitutional monarchy comprising an island group in Central Pacific Ocean.

NATIONAL FLAG AND ENSIGN

Officially hoisted 1 October 1978, re-established 11 April 1997. Proportions 1:2.

The British blue ensign, with the field changed to light blue, is charged with nine yellow stars, representing the nine islands of the nation (Nanumea, Niutao, Nanumanga, Nui, Vaitupu, Nukufetau, Funafuti, Nukulaelae and Niulakita). The arrangement of the stars reflects the positions of the islands on the map, oriented to the east (east is at the top of the flag instead of north).

MARSHALL ISLANDS

Republic of the Marshall Islands,
Marshallese **Republic eo an Aelon in Majel**.
Republic consisting of two chains of islands in NW Pacific Ocean.

NATIONAL FLAG AND ENSIGN

Officially hoisted 1 May 1979. Proportions 10:19.

The blue stands for the Pacific Ocean. The star represents the nation, and its 24 points stand for the 24 municipalities. The four longer rays stand for Majuro (the capital), Wotji, Jaluit and Kwajalein. These rays form a cross, the symbol of the Christian faith of the islanders. The position of the star reflects the geographical position of the Marshall Islands a few degrees north of the Equator, which is represented by two stripes. Their shape (widening to the fly) symbolizes the increase in growth and vitality of life. The orange stands for wealth and bravery, the white for brightness.

FIJI

Republic of Fiji.

Republic comprising a group of islands in S Pacific Ocean.

NATIONAL FLAG

Officially hoisted 10 October 1970.
Proportions 1:2.

For the first time in history, the colour of the blue ensign was changed to distinguish this flag from the flags of Australia and New Zealand. The light blue symbolizes the Pacific Ocean. The central device on the shield of arms, granted in 1908, is the cross of St George separating local agricultural products (sugar cane, coconuts and bananas) and a flying dove with a breadfruit

leaf in its beak, the emblem of the Kingdom of Fiji (1871–1874). On the upper part of the shield is a British lion holding a coconut between its paws.

TONGA

Kingdom of Tonga.

Constitutional monarchy in S Pacific Ocean.

NATIONAL FLAG, CIVIL AND STATE ENSIGN

Adopted 4 November 1875. Proportions 1:2.

The flag reflects the deep-rooted Christianity in Tonga. The cross reminds the people that they owe their salvation to the sacrifice made by Jesus on the Cross, the red represents the blood Jesus shed and the white stands for purity.

NIUE

Associated State of New Zealand, an island in S Pacific Ocean.

NATIONAL FLAG

Adopted in 1975. Proportions 1:2.

The larger star stands for Niue, the smaller ones symbolize links with New Zealand. The Union flag recalls the protectorate Great Britain established in 1899 following a request made by the kings and chiefs of Niue. The golden yellow symbolizes "the bright sunshine of Niue and the warm feelings of the Niuean people toward New Zealand and her people".

COOK ISLANDS

Associated State of New Zealand, a group of islands in S Pacific Ocean.

NATIONAL FLAG

Officially hoisted 4 August 1979.
Proportions 1:2.

The British blue ensign stands for links with New Zealand. The 15 stars represent the 15 islands. The stars symbolize heaven, faith in God and the power that has guided the inhabitants of the islands throughout their history. The circle stands for unity and strength.

OCEANIA

For many years Oceanic societies did not use flags and only some of them used vexilloids. This began to change, however, when the Europeans discovered this area of the world, bringing their influences with them. The Spanish first explored the Pacific Ocean in the 16th century, the Dutch in the 17th and the British in the 18th. The French were the first to establish a protectorate in Polynesia, followed by the Germans in Samoa and then the British and the Americans. Most of the French colonies had their own flags and the British had state ensigns and governor's flags. Most American colonies have only adopted their own flags in the last few decades.

Looking at the flags of this area can be a history lesson in itself. Many flags from the colonial period are featured in *Flags through the Ages*. The flag of the governor of the German colonies is shown in context

in *Government Flags: governors and envoys* and closely follows the German national flag of that time. Other flags clearly show their colonial roots in the chapter *Flag Familes*: Rimatara and Tongatapu are part of the family of the *Christian cross;* the Gilbert and Ellice Islands and the Soloman islands are based on the *Union Jack*, and Tahiti, Raiatea and Rimatara show influences from the *French Tricolore*. Many flags from the Pacific Islands have adopted the United Nations blue as this colour also symbolizes the Pacific Ocean.

The royal flag of Tonga is the oldest example of an armorial banner used as the flag of a head of state and dates from 1862; it is still in use today: see the chapter, *Emperors, Sovereigns and Presidents*. Tonga's war ensign is clearly based on the British white ensign: see *Navy Ensigns and Flags*.

SOUTH-WEST PACIFIC OCEAN

NORFOLK ISLANDS

Territory of Norfolk Islands.
External territory of Australia with full internal autonomy, SW Pacific Ocean.

NATIONAL FLAG

Adopted 11 January 1980.
Official proportions 1:2.

The central emblem of the flag is a Norfolk Island pine (*Araucaria heterophylla*). It appeared on the official seal for the first time in 1856.

NEW ZEALAND

Dominion of New Zealand.
Constitutional monarchy consisting of several islands in SW Pacific Ocean.

NATIONAL FLAG AND STATE ENSIGN

Adopted 12 June 1902. Proportions 1:2.

On 23 October 1869 this flag was adopted as the ensign of government vessels, and from 1902 it has also been the civil and state flag. The fly is charged with the four main stars of the Southern Cross constellation.

MAORI FLAGS

The native inhabitants of New Zealand adopted their first flag in 1857 when they chose their *kingi* (king) of *Niu Tireni* (New Zealand). Actually, there were three flags hoisted jointly one above another. The upper and the lower flags were long red rectangles with a white hoist portion charged with the red cross and three white squares with a red cross. In the middle was a red triangular flag with three white squares charged with a red cross.

More Maori flags appeared in the 1860s during the war against the colonists who were taking Maori land. The main feature of these flags was a red cross.

SOUTH-EAST PACIFIC OCEAN

FRENCH POLYNESIA

French **Territoire d'outre-mer de la Polynésie Française.**
Autonomous French overseas territory in SE Pacific Ocean.

NATIONAL FLAG

Adopted 23 November 1984. Proportions 2:3.

The red-white-red horizontal stripes recall the second national flag of the kingdom of Tahiti which was used from 1829 to 1847. The same flag with the addition of a French *Tricolore* became the flag of the protectorate and was used until 1880. After World War II a version without the canton was in popular, but unofficial, use. In 1975, the authorities agreed to allow the flag to be used with a 1:2:1 ratio of stripes.

To distinguish the flag of French Polynesia from that of Tahiti, the emblem was placed in the centre. Its main feature is a *piragua*, which is a status symbol as well as an indispensable boat used for fishing and transportation. Polynesian society is often compared to a *piragua* and the figures in the *piragua* stand for the five parts of French Polynesia: the Windward Islands, the Leeward Islands, the Tuamotu Archipelago, the Austral Islands and the Marquesas Islands. The golden yellow rays symbolize the sun and light, and the blue and white waves represent the riches of the Pacific on which the people have always relied for their livelihood.

PITCAIRN ISLANDS

British colony in SE Pacific Ocean.

STATE FLAG

Adopted 2 April 1984. Proportions 1:2.

The fly of the British blue ensign is charged with the coat of arms, granted on 4 November 1969. The centrepieces are the Bible and the anchor of the ship the *Bounty*. The green triangle represents the rugged cliffs of the island, the blue stands for the sea. The wheelbarrow in the crest stands for the first settlers, while a miro plant represents the wood the islanders use for carving souvenirs for tourists.

Flags of the Americas

The current national flags of the countries of the Americas, from Greenland and Canada to Argentina and the islands of the South Atlantic, are illustrated and described in the following pages, together with their territories, states and provinces.

For ease of reference, the countries of this huge continent have been grouped into geographical areas. We begin in North America and move on through Central America and the West Indies and the Caribbean. Finally, we look at the flags of the countries of South America and the islands of the South Atlantic.

For each entry, the country or territory's name is given in its most easily recognized form and then in all its official languages. This is followed by a description of its political status and geographic position. The basic data for each flag contains the status of the flag, date of adoption, proportions, and the symbolic meaning.

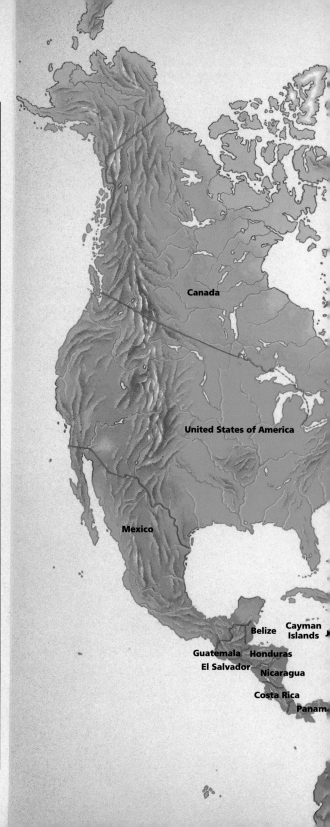

Canada

United States of America

Mexico

Belize

Cayman Islands

Guatemala   Honduras

El Salvador   Nicaragua

Costa Rica

Panam.

NORTH AMERICA

GREENLAND

Dan. **Grønland**,
nat. **Kalaallit Nunaat**.

Island NE of North America, outlying part
of Denmark with full self-government.

NATIONAL FLAG AND CIVIL ENSIGN.

Adopted 6 June 1985. Proportions 2:3.

The colours derive from the flag of
Denmark. The white stands for the ice
covering 83 per cent of the island, and the
red-white disc symbolizes the northern sun
with its lower half sunk in the sea.

CANADA

Federal constitutional monarchy in
N America.

NATIONAL FLAG AND ENSIGN.

*Adopted 15 December 1964, officially hoisted
15 February 1965. Proportions 1:2.*

The maple leaf has been the symbol of
Canada since at least the middle of the
19th century. Red and white were approved
as the official colours of Canada in 1921.

CANADIAN PROVINCES
AND TERRITORIES

When the dominion of Canada was created
in 1867 there were only four provinces
(Ontario, Quebec, Nova Scotia and

New Brunswick). Today Canada comprises
ten provinces and three territories. Their
flags have different official proportions,
but in practice almost all are made and
displayed in the proportion 1:2.

ALBERTA

PROVINCIAL FLAG

*In use since 1967, officially approved
1 June 1968. Proportions 1:2.*

The blue field of the flag is charged with
the shield of arms, granted on 30 May 1907.
The shield displays the cross of St George
and a typical landscape in Alberta.

BRITISH COLUMBIA

PROVINCIAL FLAG

Adopted 20 June 1960. Proportions 3:5.

This banner of arms was granted on
31 March 1906. The Union Jack is a
reminder of British Columbia's origins as a
British colony and stands for its continued
links with the United Kingdom. The crown
represents the sovereign power that links,
in free association, the countries of the
Commonwealth. The sun setting over the
Pacific Ocean, symbolized by the wavy
stripes, reminds us that British Columbia
is the most westerly province of Canada.

MANITOBA

PROVINCIAL FLAG

Adopted 12 May 1966. Proportions 1:2.

The fly of the British red ensign is charged
with the shield of arms, granted on 10 May
1905. The shield displays the cross of
St George and a buffalo standing on a rock.

NEW BRUNSWICK

PROVINCIAL FLAG

Adopted 24 February 1965. Proportions 5:8.

This is the banner of arms, granted on
26 May 1868. The golden lion symbolizes
ties with the United Kingdom. The boat
signifies the importance of shipbuilding
and seafaring to the province.

NEWFOUNDLAND

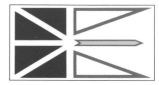

PROVINCIAL FLAG

Adopted 28 May 1980. Proportions 1:2.

The design is based on the British Union
flag. The colours symbolize snow and ice, the
sea, human effort (red) and confidence in the
future (yellow). The red triangles represent
the mainland and island parts of the
province. The yellow arrow stands for hope.

NOVA SCOTIA

PROVINCIAL FLAG

Officially approved 19 January 1929.
Proportions 3:4.

This banner of arms was in use from 1625 to 1868, and was reinstated on 19 January 1929. The field shows the flag of Scotland in reversed colours. The shield displays the Royal Arms of Scotland.

NUNAVUT

FLAG OF THE TERRITORY
Introduced 1 April 1999.

The *inuksuk* in the centre represents the stone monuments that guide the Inuit people on the land and mark sacred and other special places. The star depicted is the North Star.

ONTARIO

PROVINCIAL FLAG

Approved 21 May 1965. Proportions 1:2.

The fly of the British red ensign is charged with the shield of arms, granted on 26 May 1868. The shield displays the cross of St George and three maple leaves.

PRINCE EDWARD ISLAND

PROVINCIAL FLAG

Adopted 24 March 1964. Proportions 2:3.

The banner of arms was granted on 30 May 1905, having been used on the provincial Great Seal since 1769. The lion symbolizes ties with the United Kingdom. The larger tree is the oak of England and the tree saplings represent the three counties of the province.

QUEBEC

PROVINCIAL FLAG

Adopted 21 January 1948. Proportions 2:3.

The white cross is taken from an ancient French military colour. The four fleurs-de-lis are based on the emblem of France under the reign of the Bourbons. The flag is called the *Fleurdelisé*.

SASKATCHEWAN

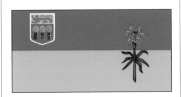

PROVINCIAL FLAG

Adopted 22 September. Proportions 1.2.

The green represents the northern forested areas of the province and the yellow symbolizes the southern grainfield areas. The shield of arms, granted on 25 August 1906, appears in the upper hoist. The fly is charged with the western red lily, which is the floral emblem of the province.

NORTHWEST TERRITORIES

FLAG OF THE TERRITORY

Adopted 1 January 1969. Proportions 1:2.

The blue vertical stripes represent the waters of the Territories and the white for the snow and ice. In the centre is the shield of arms granted on 24 February 1956. The blue wavy stripe is the North-west Passage, the green the forested areas and the red the tundra. The head of an arctic fox represents the local fauna. The yellow rectangles symbolize mineral riches.

YUKON

FLAG OF THE TERRITORY

Adopted 1 December 1967. Proportions 1:2.

The colours stand for the natural features of the province. The cross of St George on the arms stands for the first English explorers, the roundel of *vair* (fur) symbolizes the fur trade, the white and blue wavy lines symbolize the Yukon River, the red triangles represent the mountains. The golden balls symbolize the territory's mineral resources, and the malamute dog, noted for its loyalty, stamina and courage, emphasizes the important role these animals played in the early history of the territory. Below the shield are two crossed branches of fireweed, adopted in 1965 as the emblem of Yukon.

SAINT-PIERRE ET MIQUELON

French **Collectivité territoriale des Îles Saint-Pierre et Miquelon**.
Dependency of France comprising two islands N of North America.

NATIONAL FLAG

This is a heraldic banner of arms. The blue is for the Atlantic Ocean and the ship commemorates French discoverer Jacques Cartier, who came to the islands in 1535. The emblems placed on the vertical stripe at the hoist are a reminder that the colonists came from the Basque Country (*ikkurina*), Brittany (ermine) and Normandy (two lions).

UNITED STATES

United States of America.
Federal republic in Central N America.

NATIONAL FLAG

Adopted 4 July 1960. Proportions 10:19.

The blue canton symbolizes the Union. The 50 stars stand for the 50 states. The 13 stripes represent the 13 colonies which formed the independent nation (New Hampshire, Massachusetts, Rhode Island, Connecticut, Delaware, Maryland, Virginia, North Carolina, South Carolina, Georgia, New York, New Jersey and Pennsylvania). The blue symbolizes loyalty, devotion, friendship, justice and truth; the red stands for courage, zeal and fervency; and the white represents purity and rectitude of conduct.

The *de jure* proportions of the national flag and the state flags are followed only by the government and the armed forces; the flags used by the general public are manufactured in the proportions of 2:3, 3:5 and 5:8.

AMERICAN STATES

The union formed in 1776 by 13 former British independent colonies has grown over the years, and since 1960 comprises 50 states and the federal District of Columbia. Most of the state flags displaying the arms or seal on a blue background are based on state military colours; some of them retain the proportions of these colours (26:33).

ALABAMA

STATE FLAG

Adopted 16 February 1895.
Official proportions 1:1, actual flags 2:3.

The red saltire stands for the most distinctive feature of the Confederate battle flag (a blue saltire with white stars).

ALASKA

STATE FLAG

Adopted 2 May 1927. Proportions 125:177.

This is the winning design in a flag contest. The blue represents the evening sky, the sea and mountain lakes, and the wild flowers that grow in Alaska. The golden yellow symbolizes the wealth that lies hidden in Alaska's hills and streams. The stars form the most conspicuous constellation in the northern sky, *Ursa major* (the Great Bear). The eighth star is Polaris, the North Star, "the ever-constant star for the mariner, explorer, hunter, trapper, prospector, woodsman and surveyor".

ARIZONA

STATE FLAG

Adopted 27 February 1917. Proportions 2:3.

Blue and gold are the colours of Arizona and the flag represents the copper star of Arizona rising from a blue field in front of the setting sun; mining is the most important industry of Arizona and copper is its main product. The red and yellow are the colours of Spain and are a reminder that the first whites to enter Arizona in 1540 were the Spanish *conquistadores*, headed by Coronado.

ARKANSAS

STATE FLAG

Adopted 10 April 1924. Proportions not specified.

The colours of the flag are those of both the United States and the Confederate States of America. The 25 white stars record that Arkansas was the 25th state admitted to the Union. The diamond shape indicates that Arkansas was the only diamond producing state of the Union, and the star above the name of the state commemorates the Confederacy. The other blue stars have a double meaning: they represent Spain, France and the United States, to which Arkansas successively belonged, and note that Arkansas was the third state formed out of the Louisiana Purchase.

CALIFORNIA

STATE FLAG

Adopted 3 February 1911. Proportions 2:3.

The design is based on the flag hoisted in Sonoma on 14 June 1846 when a group of Americans proclaimed an independent California republic. The grizzly bear is a symbol of strength.

COLORADO

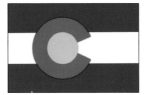

STATE FLAG

Adopted in 1911, officially approved 31 March 1964. Proportions 2:3.

The colours stand for the skies (blue), the gold (yellow), the mountain snows (white) and the soil (red). The capital "C" represents the name of the state.

CONNECTICUT

STATE FLAG

Introduced in 1895, adopted 3 June 1897. Proportions 26:33.

This is the design of the military colours from the Civil War period. The arms were granted on 25 October 1711. The three grapevines symbolize the three original settlements (Hartford, Windsor and Wethersfield), which formed the Colony of Connecticut in 1639. The motto means "He Who Transplanted Still Sustains".

DELAWARE

STATE FLAG

Adopted 24 July 1913. Proportions not specified.

The diamond stands for the state's nickname, the "Diamond State". The arms, adopted in 1777, indicate that the main industry is agriculture. The blue wavy stripe stands for the Delaware River. The ship in the crest recalls the fact that Delaware has access to the sea and to the benefits of commerce. The date recalls the day on which Delaware was the first state to ratify the Federal Constitution.

FLORIDA

STATE FLAG

Adopted 6 November 1900, seal modified in 1966 and 1985.

The red saltire is based on the battle flag of the Confederacy. The seal depicts a typical landscape in Florida, with an American Indian woman representing the original inhabitants of the peninsula.

GEORGIA

STATE FLAG

Adopted 25 April 2003. Proportions 2:3.

The flag design is based on the flag of the Confederate States of America, used from 1861 to 1863. The stars indicate that Georgia was among the first 13 states to ratify the US constitution. Within the ring of stars is the arms of Georgia, and the motto "In God We Trust".

HAWAII

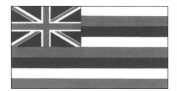

STATE FLAG

Adopted 20 May 1845. Proportions 1:2.

The flag is based on that adopted by the Kingdom of Hawaii in 1816. It combines the symbols of the United Kingdom (the Union Jack) and the United States (stripes of an early 19th-century ensign). The eight stripes represent the eight main islands: Hawaii, Kahoolawe, Kauai, Lanai, Maui, Molokai, Niihau and Oahu.

IDAHO

STATE FLAG

Introduced in 1907, formally adopted 15 March 1927. Proportions 26:33.

The female figure is a symbol of women's suffrage. She also represents liberty and justice, as denoted by the Phrygian cap (a symbol of liberty) and scales. The miner notes Idaho's chief occupation; the tree represents its timber interests; the ploughman and grain represent agriculture, and the cornucopias stand for horticulture. The elk's head refers to state game laws protecting elk and moose.

ILLINOIS

STATE FLAG

Basic design introduced in 1915. Proportions 3:5.

The bald eagle perched on an American shield indicates the allegiance of Illinois to the Union. The water stands for Lake Michigan. The name of the state was added on 1 July 1970.

INDIANA

STATE FLAG

Adopted 31 May 1917. Proportions 26:33.

The torch stands for liberty and enlightenment and the rays symbolize their far-reaching influence. The largest star represents Indiana, the 19th state of the Union. The outer circle of stars represents the original 13 states, and the inner circle of stars stands for the next five states admitted to the Union.

IOWA

STATE FLAG

Adopted 29 March 1921. Proportions 3:4.

The French *Tricolore* signifies ties with France before the Louisiana Purchase. The bald eagle denotes Iowa's allegiance to the Union; it holds in its beak a ribbon with the state motto "Our liberties we prize and our rights we will maintain".

KANSAS

STATE FLAG

Adopted 30 June 1963. Proportions 3:5.

This design, without the word "Kansas", was adopted on 23 March 1927. The sunflower is the state flower, the wreath symbolizes the Louisiana Purchase and the 34 stars record the fact that Kansas was the 34th state admitted to the Union. The state motto "To the stars through difficulties" reflects the political trials of Kansas prior to joining the Union. A man ploughing with horses represents agriculture as the basis of the future prosperity of the state, and the steamboat is a symbol of commerce. The past of Kansas is represented by a settler's cabin, a train of ox wagons going west and a herd of buffalo retreating, pursued by two native Americans on horseback.

KENTUCKY

STATE FLAG

Adopted 26 March 1918. Proportions 10:19.

The seal of the state was adopted in 1792. Above it appears the name of the state and below the seal are two crossed branches of golden rod, the state flower. The two friends embracing exemplify the state motto "United we stand, divided we fall".

LOUISIANA

STATE FLAG

Adopted 1 July 1912. Proportions 2:3.

The emblem is taken from the state seal, adopted in 1902. The pelican is the state emblem of Louisiana and is shown nourishing its young on blood from its own breast, signifying self-sacrifice. The scroll bears the state motto, "Union, Justice and Confidence".

MAINE

STATE FLAG

Adopted 24 February 1909. Proportions 26:33.

The state arms display a white pine (*Pinus strobus*), which stands for the state and its nickname "the Pine Tree State". The moose, native to Maine, is a symbol of large areas of unpolluted forests. The water symbolizes the sea. The farmer resting on a scythe represents the land and agriculture; the sailor resting on an anchor represents the sea, as well as commerce and fisheries. The star and the motto *Dirigo* (I direct) refer to the fact

that the North Star was a guiding star for sailors, trappers and settlers.

MARYLAND

STATE FLAG

Adopted 9 March 1904. Proportions 2:3.

This armorial banner is unique among the flags of the 50 states. It is derived from the arms of two English families, Calvert and Crossland. Sir George Calvert was granted arms in 1622. His sons founded Maryland in 1634 and to create the arms of Maryland they adopted the quarterly arms of Calvert with the arms of Crossland, which belonged to their grandmother's family.

MASSACHUSETTS

STATE FLAG

Adopted 18 March 1908. Proportions 3:5.

A Native American holding a bow and arrow is an old emblem of the colony, dating back to the first half of the 17th century. The star represents the Commonwealth of Massachusetts. The motto was adopted in 1775 by the provincial congress as a message for England, "By the sword we seek peace, but peace only under liberty". The crest (an arm with a sword) was added in 1780.

MICHIGAN

STATE FLAG

Adopted 1 August 1911. Proportions 2:3.

Since 1837 this has been a flag of the Michigan militia. The bald eagle represents the superior authority and jurisdiction of the United States; the elk and moose represent the local fauna. The word *Tuebor* ("I will defend") refers to Michigan's geographic position on the frontier. The sun rising over the lake calls attention to a man standing on a peninsula. His upraised right hand symbolizes peace but his left hand holds a rifle, indicating readiness to defend the state and the nation. On the scroll appears the state motto – "If you seek a pleasant peninsula look about you".

MINNESOTA

STATE FLAG

Adopted 19 March 1957. Proportions 3:5.

The 19 stars are because Minnesota was the 19th state to be admitted to the Union. The motto *L'Etoile du Nord* (the North Star) refers to the fact that Minnesota was once the northernmost state of the Union. The central scene displays a Native American giving way to a white settler.

MISSISSIPPI

STATE FLAG

Adopted 7 February 1894. Proportions 2:3.

The flag displays the national colours. The enlarged canton is charged with the battle flag of the Confederacy. The flag's features were specified on 6 September 1996.

MISSOURI

STATE FLAG

Adopted 23 March 1913. Proportions 7:12.

The 24 stars recall that Missouri was the 24th state to be admitted to the Union. The bears indicate the size and strength of the state. The national arms symbolize the allegiance of Missouri to the union and the crescent stands for a new state, the second to be carved from the Louisiana Purchase.

MONTANA

STATE FLAG

Introduced 1 July 1981.
Proportions 2:3, 3:5 or 5:8.

The basic design of the flag has been unchanged since 1905; the word "Montana" was added in 1981. The seal, dating from 1865, displays the Great Falls of Missouri and the Rocky Mountains. The plough, shovel and pick indicate the state's reliance on agriculture and mining.

NEBRASKA

STATE FLAG

Adopted 2 April 1925. Proportions unspecified.

The main natural features displayed on the seal are the Rocky Mountains and the Missouri River. The smith symbolizes the mechanical arts and agriculture is represented by shocks of grain, growing grain and a settler's cabin. The steamboat and train represent the role of transport.

NEVADA

STATE FLAG

Adopted 8 June 1991.
Proportions 2:3, 3:5 or 5:8.

The star symbolizes the state; its colour stands for silver, the main mineral product of Nevada. The state motto "Battle Born" is a reminder that Nevada was admitted to the Union during the Civil War. The emblem is flanked by two sprays of sagebrush which is the state flower.

NEW HAMPSHIRE

STATE FLAG

Adopted 1 January 1932.
Proportions unspecified.

The sun rises behind a broadside view of the frigate *Raleigh*, which was one of the first 13 vessels ordered for the American navy. It was built at Portsmouth in 1776, the year New Hampshire achieved independence. The nine stars refer to the fact that New Hampshire was the ninth state admitted to the Union.

NEW JERSEY

STATE FLAG

Adopted 26 March 1896.
Proportions unspecified.

Buff is the regimental colour of the New Jersey Continental Line, prescribed by General G. Washington in 1779. Buff became the colour of the field of state regimental colour in 1780. The main device of the arms is three ploughs, as New Jersey was the third state admitted to the Union. The figures of Liberty and Ceres (the goddess of agriculture) support the arms. The horse's head symbolizes vigour.

NEW MEXICO

STATE FLAG

Adopted 11 March 1925. Proportions 2:3.

The colours of the flag are those of Spain. The Zia sun symbol is that of the ancient Zia Pueblo Native Americans.

NEW YORK

STATE FLAG

Adopted 2 April 1901. Proportions 10:19.

The shield displays a landscape with the Hudson River and the rising sun symbolizes a bright future. It is supported by the figures of Liberty and Justice.

NORTH CAROLINA

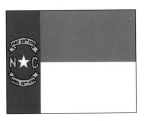

STATE FLAG

Adopted 9 March 1885. Proportions 3:4.

The flag displays the national colours. The star and the letters "NC" symbolize the state. The dates recall two important documents from the era of the Revolution:

the Mecklenburg Declaration of Independence and the Halifax Resolutions.

NORTH DAKOTA

STATE FLAG

Adopted 3 March 1911. Proportions 26:33.

The flag conforms in all respects to the regimental colours carried by the First North Dakota Infantry in the Spanish American War and the Philippine Insurrection, except for the name of the state on the scroll below the eagle.

OHIO

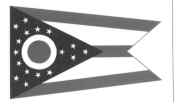

STATE FLAG

Adopted 9 May 1902. Proportions 8:13.

The flag displays the national colours. The white circle suggests the name "Ohio". The 17 stars signify that Ohio was the 17th state to enter the Union. The white circle with the red centre represents a buckeye (*Aesculus glabra*), the state tree, which gave the state its nickname, "the Buckeye State". The shape of the flag represents the hills and valleys of the state. The stripes symbolize the roads and waterways of Ohio.

OKLAHOMA

STATE FLAG

Adopted 9 May 1941. Proportions unspecified.

The blue symbolizes loyalty and devotion, the shield stands for protection, and the crossed olive branch and pipe of peace symbolize the desire for peace.

OREGON

STATE FLAG, OBVERSE

STATE FLAG, REVERSE

*Adopted 26 February 1925.
Proportions 500:833.*

The arms are accompanied by the date of the state's admission to the Union. The 33 stars signify that Oregon was the 33rd state admitted to the Union and the American eagle represents protection. The shield shows the Pacific Ocean in the setting sun with two ships, the British departing and the Americans arriving. The covered wagon represents the settlers, the wheatsheaf and plough are symbols of agriculture, and the pick represents mining.

PENNSYLVANIA

STATE FLAG

Adopted 13 June 1907. Proportions 27:37.

The American eagle denotes allegiance to the Union. The ship, the plough and the three wheatsheaves were taken from the arms of the counties of Philadelphia, Chester and Sussex (which is now part of Delaware) respectively.

RHODE ISLAND

STATE FLAG

Adopted 19 May 1897. Proportions 29:33.

The anchor has the motto "Hope" below it and has appeared on the seals of Rhode Island since 1664. The 13 stars represent the 13 original states.

SOUTH CAROLINA

STATE FLAG

Adopted 28 January 1861.
Proportions unspecified.

The crescent refers to the badge with the inscription "Liberty or Death" worn on the caps of the soldiers of two regiments formed in South Carolina in 1775, who fought during the American Revolution. The palmetto tree is a symbol of victory, adopted in 1776 after the fort at Sullivan's Island, in Charleston harbour, defeated the British fleet. The fort was built out of palmetto tree trunks, which grow abundantly on Sullivan's Island.

SOUTH DAKOTA

STATE FLAG

Adopted 11 March 1963, modified 1 July 1992.
Proportions 3:5.

The sun alludes to the former nickname of the state, "the Sunshine State". Its new nickname, "the Mount Rushmore State", has featured since 1992 around the lower portion of the sun. The seal depicts a typical landscape, in which the ploughman symbolizes agriculture, the steamboat transportation, the smelting furnace the mining industry, the cattle dairy farming, and the trees lumbering.

TENNESSEE

STATE FLAG

Adopted 17 April 1905. Proportions 3:5.

The flag is in the national colours, which symbolize purity (white), lofty aims (blue)

and the fame of Tennessee (red). The three stars represent the three geographical divisions of the state. They also refer to the fact that Tennessee was the third state to join the Union after the original 13. The circle symbolizes unity.

TEXAS

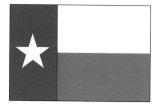

STATE FLAG

Adopted 25 January 1839. Proportions 2:3.

The Lone Star flag was designed for the Republic of Texas, and was retained as the state flag after Texas joined the Union in 1845. The colours represent loyalty (blue), purity (white) and bravery (red).

UTAH

STATE FLAG

Adopted 11 March 1913.
Proportions unspecified.

The beehive represents industry, the main virtue of the first settlers, and the sego lily, the state flower, is a symbol of peace. The American eagle symbolizes protection and the flags denote Utah's support to the nation.

VERMONT

STATE FLAG

Adopted 1 June 1923. Proportions unspecified.

The pine tree is the traditional emblem of New England; the sheaves of wheat and the cow represent agriculture. The two crossed pine branches symbolize the pine sprigs worn at the Battle of Plattsburgh in 1814.

VIRGINIA

STATE FLAG

Adopted 30 April 1861. Proportions unspecified.

Sic Semper Tyrannis ("Thus Ever to Tyrants") is the message of the Virginian seal. Virtus, the symbol of the Commonwealth, is dressed as an Amazon with her foot on Tyranny, represented by the prostrate body of a man holding a broken chain and a scourge in his hands.

WASHINGTON

STATE FLAG

Adopted 7 June 1923.
Proportions 2:3, 3:5 or 5:8.

The green reflects the state's nickname, "the Evergreen State". The present design of the seal, with the vignette of General George Washington, was adopted in 1967. It is an improved version of the seal which was adopted in 1889 when Washington became a state of the Union.

WEST VIRGINIA

STATE FLAG

Adopted 7 March 1929. Proportions 10:19.

The white is for the purity of the state institutions; the blue stands for the Union. The rock is a symbol of stability and continuity, and the date is the day the state was founded. The farmer and miner symbolize the two main industries, and the Phrygian cap (a symbol of liberty) and rifles indicate that the state won its freedom and will defend it by force of arms.

WISCONSIN

STATE FLAG

Introduced 1 June 1981. Proportions 2:3.

The blue flag with the arms was adopted on 29 April 1913. In 1981 the word "Wisconsin" and the date "1848" (admission to the Union) were added. The shield of arms displays symbols of agriculture, mining, manufacture and navigation. The arms and motto of the United States symbolize the allegiance of

the state to the Union, and the badger refers to its nickname, "the Badger State". The main branches of the economy, mining and agriculture, are represented by lead ore and a cornucopia. The sailor and the miner symbolize labour on water and on land.

WYOMING

STATE FLAG

Adopted 31 January 1917. Proportions 7:10.

The red symbolizes the Native Americans and the blood of the pioneers who gave their lives. The white is a symbol of purity and uprightness; the blue is the colour of the skies and distant mountains, and also a symbol of fidelity, justice and virility. The bison represents the local fauna while the seal on it symbolizes the custom of branding livestock. The woman holding a banner with the words "equal rights" symbolizes the political position of women in the state, and the men represent the livestock and mining industries. The lamps signify the light of knowledge.

DISTRICT OF COLUMBIA

FLAG OF THE DISTRICT

Adopted 15 October 1938. Proportions 10:19.

The state flag is the banner of arms of George Washington.

BERMUDA

British colony comprising a group of islands
in the Atlantic Ocean, E of North America.

CIVIL FLAG AND ENSIGN

Introduced in 1915. Proportions 1:2.

Bermuda was the first British colony to fly
the defaced red ensign. The fly is charged
with the arms, granted on 4 October 1910.
The British lion supports a shield
portraying the wreck of the *Sea Venture*,

which in 1609 carried the first settlers and
came to grief on a reef.

MEXICO

United States of Mexico,
Spanish **Estados Unidos Mexicanos**.
Federal republic S of North America.

NATIONAL FLAG AND ENSIGN

Adopted 17 August 1968. Proportions 4:7.

After Mexico achieved independence, it
adopted on 2 November 1821 a flag based
on the French *Tricolore*. The green-white-
red flag was charged with the national
emblem, a modern interpretation of an
ancient Aztec symbol. According to Aztec
legend, an eagle grasping a serpent in its
claws and standing on a flowering nopal
cactus growing from a rock in the middle of
the Tenochtitlan Lake appeared on the site
where the Aztecs decided to build their capital
city in 1325. The emblem has changed its
form several times, the last time in 1968.

Originally the colours symbolized
independence (green), purity of religion
(white) and striving for unity between the
native races and the Spaniards (red). Today
they stand for hope (green), purity (white)
and religion (red).

CENTRAL AMERICA

BELIZE

Constitutional monarchy in Central America.

NATIONAL FLAG AND ENSIGN

Officially hoisted 21 September 1981.
Proportions unspecified.

Blue and red are the colours of the ruling
and opposition parties respectively, and the
50 leaves in the wreath symbolize 1950,
when the independence movement began.
The arms retain the main features of the
arms granted to British Honduras on
28 January 1907: sailors' and woodsmen's
tools and a sailing ship. The tree behind the
shield is a mahogany tree and supporting it
are two men, denoting racial diversity. The
motto means "Flourish in the Shade".

GUATEMALA

Republic of Guatemala,
Spanish **República de Guatemala**.
Republic in Central America.

STATE FLAG AND ENSIGN

Decreed on 26 December 1997.
Proportions 5:8. National flag and ensign
are without arms.

Guatemala, like the other four former
members of the United Provinces of
Central America, has retained the colours
of the Federation's flag. The blue-white-
blue vertical tricolour with the state
emblem was introduced in 1871 and the
form of the emblem was changed in 1968

and again in 1997. The blue stands for
justice and steadfastness, and the white
for purity and uprightness. The main device
of the emblem is a quetzal, the national
bird of Guatemala and a symbol of liberty.
The inscription on the scroll, "Liberty
15 September 1821", is the date when
Central America broke with Spain. The
rifles symbolize the will of the people to
defend freedom, the swords stand for
justice and sovereignty, and the wreath
is a symbol of victory. The latest change
involved the spelling of the date of
independence. Since December 1997
the inscription reads "15 de Septiembre"
instead of "15 de Setiembre".

HONDURAS

Republic of Honduras,
Spanish **República de Honduras**.
Republic in Central America.

NATIONAL FLAG, CIVIL AND STATE ENSIGN

Adopted 16 February 1866. Proportions 1:2.

The flag is based on the flag of the United Provinces of Central America. The five stars refer to the members of the Federation: Costa Rica, El Salvador, Guatemala, Honduras and Nicaragua. The blue stands for the skies and brotherhood; the white for the desire for peace and purity of thoughts.

EL SALVADOR

Republic of El Salvador,
Spanish **República de El Savador.**
Republic in Central America.

STATE FLAG

Adopted 15 September 1912. Proportions 3:5. Civil flag is without arms. Civil ensign, an alternative civil flag and state flag and ensign are without arms, with the inscription "Dios, Union, Libertad" in gold letters on the white stripe.

The flag and the emblem are based on those of the United Provinces of Central America. The Masonic triangle symbolizes equality; its angles represent three branches of government: legislative, executive and judicial. The volcanoes stand for the five nations of Central America flanked by the Pacific and the Atlantic Oceans. Within the triangle are symbols of liberty (a Phrygian cap), the ideals of the people (golden rays) and peace (rainbow). The motto, *"Dios, Union, Libertad"* ("God, Unity, Liberty") reflects faith in God, harmony in the family and the independence of the people. The 14 clusters of leaves represent the number of departments of El Salvador.

NICARAGUA

Republic of Nicaragua,
Spanish **República de Nicaragua**.
Republic in Central America.

STATE FLAG

Adopted 4 September 1908. Proportions 3:5. The alternative civil flag is without emblem.

The flag is based on that of the United Provinces of Central America. The triangle is a symbol of equality. The five volcanoes represent the five nations of Central America flanked by the Atlantic and Pacific Oceans. The Phrygian cap is a symbol of liberty; the rainbow symbolizes peace.

COSTA RICA

Republic of Costa Rica,
Spanish **República de Costa Rica**.
Republic in Central America.

STATE FLAG AND ENSIGN

Adopted 13 June 1964. Proportions 3:5. Civil ensign is without emblem.

In 1848 the present design of the flag with five stripes was adopted. The red was added to obtain the colours of revolutionary France and the national emblem was positioned in the centre. The current design of the flag and the emblem were adopted in 1964. The seven stars represent the seven provinces of Costa Rica and the volcanoes denote the geographical position of Costa Rica between the Pacific and the Atlantic. The sun is a symbol of freedom and the ships symbolize commerce.

PANAMA

Republic of Panama,
Spanish **República de Panama**.
Republic in Central America.

NATIONAL FLAG AND ENSIGN

Introduced 3 November 1903, officially approved 4 June 1904. Proportions 2:3.

The blue and red are the colours of the main political parties (Conservatives and Liberals respectively) and the white denotes peace between them. The blue also symbolizes the Pacific Ocean and the Caribbean, and the red stands for the blood of those who lost their lives for their country. The blue star represents the civic virtues of purity and honesty, and the red star is a symbol of authority and law.

WEST INDIES AND THE CARIBBEAN

THE BAHAMAS

Commonwealth of the Bahamas.
Constitutional monarchy comprising a chain
of islands NW of West Indies.

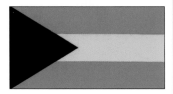

NATIONAL FLAG

Adopted 10 July 1973. Proportions 1:2.

The flag is a graphic representation of the
golden beaches of the Bahama Islands
surrounded by the aquamarine sea. The
black represents the vigour and force of a
united people. The triangle indicates the
enterprise and determination of the
Bahamian people to develop the rich
resources of land and sea.

TURKS AND CAICOS ISLANDS

British crown colony in the N Central West Indies.

STATE FLAG AND ENSIGN

Introduced in 1968. Proportions 1:2.
Civil ensign has a red field.

The fly is charged with the shield of arms,
granted on 26 September 1965. It displays
local flora and fauna: a queen conch shell,
a spiny lobster and a Turk's head cactus.

CUBA

Republic of Cuba,
Spanish **República de Cuba**.
Socialist republic comprising an island in
the W West Indies.

NATIONAL FLAG AND ENSIGN

Introduced in 1850, officially approved
20 May 1902. Proportions 1:2.

The flag was designed by a Cuban poet
Teurbe Tolón in 1849 and was patterned
on the design of the Stars and Stripes. The
star, called *La Estrella Solitaria* ("the Lone
Star"), was selected to light the way towards
freedom and was taken from the flag of
Texas. In time, the Cuban flag itself began
to be known as *La Estrella Solitaria*. The
flag was hoisted for the first time on
19 May 1850 in Ordenas on the north
coast of Cuba where General Francisco
Lopez landed with 600 men and staged
an abortive attempt to free the country
from colonial rule.

The triangle is a Masonic symbol of
liberty, equality and fraternity, and the
three blue stripes stand for the three
sectors into which Cuba was divided by
the Spaniards. The white symbolizes the
pure intentions of the revolutionaries and
for justice; the red is for the blood that was
shed in the struggle for independence.

CAYMAN ISLANDS

British colony in the W West Indies.

STATE FLAG AND ENSIGN

Introduced in 1958, modified in 1999.
Civil ensign has a red field.

The badge displays the whole achievement
of the arms, granted on 14 May 1958. The
three stars represent the three main islands:
Grand Cayman, Cayman Brac and Little
Cayman. The lion denotes loyalty to Great
Britain. A turtle and a pineapple represent
the fauna and flora of the islands.

JAMAICA

Constitutional monarchy comprising an island
in the W West Indies.

NATIONAL FLAG, STATE AND CIVIL ENSIGN

Officially hoisted 6 August 1962.
Proportions 1:2.

The green stands for hope and agriculture,
the black for hardships overcome and to be
faced, and the yellow for natural resources
and the beauty of sunlight.

HAITI

Republic of Haiti, French **République d'Haïti**.
Republic consisting of the W part of Hispaniola
Island in the Central West Indies.

STATE FLAG

*Introduced in 1897, re-introduced
25 February 1986. Proportions 3:5. Civil flag
and ensign are without arms.*

The blue and red are taken from the French
Tricolore and represent the union of blacks
and mulattoes. The arms are composed of a
cabbage palm surmounted by the Phyrgian
cap of liberty and ornamented with
trophies (rifles, flags, hatchets, cannons,
cannonballs, trumpets, anchors etc). The
motto means "Union Makes Strength".

DOMINICAN REPUBLIC

Spanish **República Dominicana**.
Republic consisting of the E part of Hispaniola
Island in the Central West Indies.

STATE FLAG AND ENSIGN, WAR ENSIGN

*Adopted 6 November 1844.
Civil flag and ensign are without arms.
Proportions 5:8.*

In 1839 the Trinitarians struggling for
independence added a white cross to the
flag of Haiti to form their flag. Later the
blue and red were reversed at the fly
portion of the flag. The cross stands for the
Catholic faith, the blue is the colour of
liberty and the red symbolizes blood. The
arms display the national colours and flags,
the Cross and the Bible. The motto above
the shield means "God, Fatherland, Liberty".

PUERTO RICO

Free Associated State of Puerto Rico,
Spanish **El Estado Libre y Asociado de
Puerto Rico**.
Self-governing incorporated territory of the
United States of America, an island in the
Central West Indies.

NATIONAL FLAG

*In use since 22 December 1895, official since
24 July 1952. Proportions 2:3.*

The flag, designed in 1891, is that of Cuba
with reversed colours. The star symbolizes
the Fatherland. The triangle and the colours
represent the republican ideals of liberty,
equality and fraternity.

VIRGIN ISLANDS

Virgin Islands of the United States.
Organized, unincorporated territory of the
United States of America comprising a group
of islands in the E West Indies.

NATIONAL FLAG

Adopted 17 May 1921. Proportions unspecified.

The white is a symbol of purity. The
emblem is a simplified version of the
United States arms and the letters "V"
and "I" stand for the Virgin Islands.

BRITISH VIRGIN ISLANDS

British colony in the E West Indies.

STATE FLAG AND ENSIGN

Proportions 1:2.

The arms, granted on 15 November 1960,
appear in the centre of the British blue ensign.
The central figure is St Ursula, the "wise
virgin" and namesake of the islands. The
eleven lamps represent the 11 virgins
murdered with St Ursula by the Huns.

ANGUILLA

Dependency of the United Kingdom in
the E West Indies.

STATE FLAG AND ENSIGN

Officially hoisted 30 May 1990. Proportions 1:2.

The British blue ensign is defaced with
the shield of arms, which displays three
dolphins, symbolizing unity and strength.
The blue base stands for the Caribbean
Sea surrounding the island.

ST KITTS AND NEVIS

Federation of St Kitts and Nevis.
Federal constitutional monarchy comprising
two islands in the E West Indies.

NATIONAL FLAG AND ENSIGN

Adopted 19 November 1983.
Proportions 2:3.

The two stars stand for hope and liberty,
and the black symbolizes the African
heritage of a major part of the population.
The green represents the fertility of the
land, the yellow the constant sunshine, and
the red symbolizes the struggle to end
slavery and colonialism.

MONTSERRAT

British crown colony consisting of a volcanic
island in the E West Indies.

STATE FLAG AND ENSIGN

Adopted in 1960, modified in 1999.

The British blue ensign is defaced with the
arms, adopted in 1909. The cross stands for
Christianity. The woman with a harp refers
to the Irish immigrants who settled on the
island in 1632.

ANTIGUA AND BARBUDA

State of Antigua and Barbuda.
Constitutional monarchy comprising
three islands in the E West Indies.

NATIONAL FLAG AND ENSIGN

Introduced 27 February 1967. Proportions 2:3.

The sun symbolizes the new era of
independence in the history of the island.
The colours represent its African heritage
(black), hope (blue) and the dynamism of
the people (red). The "V" stands for victory.
The yellow, blue and white indicate the
country's main tourist attractions: the sun,
sea and sandy beaches.

DOMINICA

Commonwealth of Dominica.
Republic comprising an island in the E West Indies.

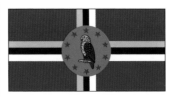

NATIONAL FLAG AND ENSIGN

Adopted 3 November 1990. Proportions 1:2.

The basic design of the flag was introduced
on 3 November 1978. Since then it has
undergone several modifications. The red
circle symbolizes socialism. The sisserou
parrot (*Psittacus imperialis*) is the national
bird, unique to Dominica, and symbolizes
flight towards greater heights and fulfilment
of aspirations. The ten stars represent the
ten parishes of equal status, thus the
equality of the people. The green

symbolizes the lush vegetation; the triple-
coloured cross represents the Trinity of God.
The yellow represents the sunshine, the
main agricultural products (citrus and
bananas) and the Carib people, the first
inhabitants of the island; the black is a
symbol of the rich black soil and African
heritage; the white symbolizes the rivers
and waterfalls, and purity of aspirations.

MARTINIQUE

French **Département de la Martinique.**
French overseas department and administrative
region, an island in the E West Indies.

NATIONAL FLAG

Adopted 4 August 1766. Proportions 2:3.

The flag is the old French merchant ensign
charged with four white serpents.

ST LUCIA

Constitutional monarchy consisting of an island
in the SE West Indies.

NATIONAL FLAG AND ENSIGN

Officially introduced 1 March 1967.
Proportions 1:2.

The triangle represents the twin peaks of
the Pitons, a geological formation of
volcanic origin. The black and white
symbolize the "two races living and working
in unity", the yellow symbolizes the

constant sunshine and the blue stands for the Caribbean and the Atlantic Ocean.

ST VINCENT AND THE GRENADINES

Constitutional monarchy comprising several islands in the SE West Indies.

NATIONAL FLAG AND ENSIGN

Officially hoisted 22 October 1985.
Proportions 2:3.

"The Gems", as the green lozenges and the flag itself are commonly called, is an abbreviation of "the Gems of the Antilles", which is the islands' nickname. They also represent the nature of the country, with numerous islands and peoples. The blue symbolizes the sky and the sea, and the green represents the lush vegetation and the vitality of the people. The yellow stands for the golden sands, the bright spirit of the people and warmth.

BARBADOS

Constitutional monarchy consisting of an island in the SE West Indies.

NATIONAL FLAG AND ENSIGN

Introduced 30 November 1966. Proportions 2:3.

The blue stands for the sea and the sky, and the yellow represents the sandy beaches.

The trident, an attribute of the mythical sea god Neptune, symbolizes some of the traditions of the past but the shaft is broken, indicating the break with the historical and constitutional ties of the past.

GRENADA

State of Grenada.
Constitutional monarchy comprising several islands in the SE West Indies.

CIVIL AND STATE FLAG

Officially hoisted 7 February 1974.
Proportions 3:5. Proportions of the ensign 1:2.

The yellow represents the sun and the friendliness of the people, the green stands for the agriculture and the red is a symbol of harmony, unity and courage. The seven stars represent the island's seven parishes. The nutmeg recalls that this small island is the second-largest producer of nutmeg in the world.

TRINIDAD AND TOBAGO

Republic of Trinidad and Tobago.
Republic of several islands in the S West Indies.

STATE FLAG

Officially hoisted 31 August 1962.
Proportions 3:5. Proportions of the ensign 1:2.

The black represents the dedication of the people, joined together by one strong

bond; it also symbolizes strength, unity, purpose and the wealth of the land. The red stands for the vitality of the people, the warmth and energy of the sun, and the courage and friendliness of the people. The white symbolizes the sea, purity of aspirations and the equality of all men under the sun.

NETHERLANDS ANTILLES

Dutch **De Nederlandse Antillen**.
Autonomous part of the Netherlands consisting of 5 islands in the E and S West Indies.

CIVIL AND STATE FLAG AND ENSIGN

Adopted 1 January 1986. Proportions 2:3.

The colours are based on those of the Netherlands flag. The blue represents the Caribbean and the stars stand for the five constituent parts of the Netherlands Antilles: Curaçao and Bonaire off the coast of Venezuela, St Maarten, St Eustatius and Saba in the Leeward Islands.

BONAIRE

FLAG OF THE ISLAND

Hoisted 15 December 1981. Proportions 2:3.

The star represents the island itself, while its six points recall the six neighbourhoods of Bonaire. The black ring around it, which represents a compass, symbolizes the seamanship of Bonaireans and their purposefulness in orienting themselves between the spirit (which is symbolized by the colour yellow) and the world (symbolized by the colour blue). The red is a symbol of energy, the blood of the people of Bonaire, and their struggle during their daily lives. The yellow stands for brilliant sunshine and the beauty of nature, especially the yellow flowers of brasilia and *Kibrahacha* (axe-breaker) plants. The white symbolizes liberty, tranquillity and peace. The blue is for the sea which provides a basis for their livelihood.

CURAÇAO

FLAG OF THE ISLANDS

Adopted 2 July 1984. Proportions 2:3.

Two stars represent the islands of Curaçao and Klein Curaçao. They are also seen as a symbol of peace and happiness. The five points of each star recall the five continents from which people came and settled the islands. The blue stands for the loyalty of the people; the upper blue symbolizes the sky, the lower stripe the sea. The yellow stripe stands for the tropical sun and reflects the joyful character of the Curaçao population.

SABA

FLAG OF THE ISLAND

Adopted 6 December 1985. Proportions 2:3.

The star represents Saba. Its colour stands for the wealth of natural beauty found on the island and symbolizes hope for the future. The colours symbolize historical and political ties with the Netherlands and the Netherlands Antilles. In addition, the white stands for peace, friendship, purity and serenity; the red for unity, courage and determination. The blue represents the sea which has played a significant role in the survival of the people of Saba. Blue also symbolizes the heavens which remind the people of Saba of God Almighty who created the island.

ST EUSTATIUS

FLAG OF THE ISLAND

Introduced 16 November 2004. Proportions 2:3.

The colours red, white and blue stand for the historical ties with the Netherlands and the fact that St Eustatius belongs to the Netherlands Antilles. In the centre is a silhouette of the island.

ST MAARTEN

FLAG OF THE ISLAND

Adopted 13 June 1985. Proportions 2:3.

The colours are those of the flag of the Netherlands. The arms show an old courthouse, a bouquet of yellow sage (the national flower), and a silhouette of the monument honouring Dutch-French friendship and the unity of both parts of the island. The orange border symbolizes loyalty to the ruling Dutch house of Orange-Nassau. The crest is formed by a yellow disc which represents the sun, and a grey silhouette of a pelican in flight. The motto in Latin, "Semper Progrediens" means "Always Progressing".

ARUBA

Autonomous overseas territory of the Netherlands, an island in the S West Indies.

NATIONAL FLAG AND CIVIL ENSIGN

Officially hoisted 1 January 1986.
Proportions 2:3.

The blue stands for the Caribbean and the skies. The star symbolizes Aruba, with its red soil and white beaches. The four points of the star represent the four major languages (Papiamento, Dutch, Spanish and English) and the four points of the compass, indicating that the inhabitants came from all over the world to live here in unity and strength. The stripes represent the sun and tourism, and the mineral resources of the island.

SOUTH AMERICA

COLOMBIA

Republic of Colombia,
Spanish **República de Colombia**.
Republic in NW South America.

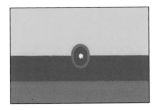

CIVIL ENSIGN SINCE 1890

Adopted 26 November 1861. Proportions 2:3.
National flag and state ensign are
without the emblem.

The colours symbolize sovereignty and justice (yellow); nobility, loyalty and vigilance (blue); and valour, honour, generosity and victory achieved at the cost of bloodshed (red). According to another interpretation, the colours stand for universal liberty (yellow), the equality of all races and social classes before God and the law (blue), and fraternity (red).

VENEZUELA

Bolivarian Republic of Venezuela
Spanish **República Bolivariana de Venezuela**.
Republic in NW South America.

STATE FLAG AND ENSIGN, WAR ENSIGN

Adopted 7 March 2006. Proportions 2:3.
Civil flag and ensign are without arms.

This flag, with yellow, blue and red stripes of equal width, was introduced in 1836 and has since undergone several modifications in the arms and the arrangement of the stars. The eight stars stand for the original

7 provinces (in 1811), and for the historic Province of Guayana. The arms symbolize the unity of 24 provinces (a wheatsheaf with 24 ears), the native people and struggle for independence (flags and weapons), and liberty (a running horse). The cornucopias stand for the country's wealth and prosperity, and the wreath of laurel and palm is a symbol of glory and peace.

ECUADOR

Republic of Ecuador,
Spanish **República del Ecuador**.
Republic in NW South America.

STATE FLAG AND ENSIGN

Adopted 10 January 1861. Proportions 1:2.
Civil flag and ensign are without arms.

The colours of the flag represent the sunshine, grain and wealth (yellow), the sky, sea and rivers (blue), and the patriots and their blood shed in the struggle for freedom and justice (red). Mount Chimborazo and the river symbolize the ties between the interior of the country and the coastal areas; the steamship recalls the first South American steamship, built in 1841 in Guayaquil. The sun is a symbol of liberty and the signs of the zodiac denote the four memorable months (March-June) of the revolution in 1845. The condor is a symbol of strength and valour, and the *fasces* represents the sovereignty of the republic. The flags mounted on lances refer to the duty to defend the Fatherland with arms.

GUYANA

Co-operative Republic of Guyana.
Republic in N South America.

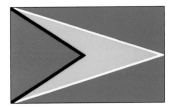

NATIONAL FLAG

Adopted 20 May 1966. Proportions 3:5.
Proportions of national ensign are 1:2.

Whitney Smith, the designer of the flag, chose green for the background because green forests and fields cover more than 90 per cent of Guyana. The red represents zeal and sacrifice, which are part of the nation-building process that the Guyanese are striving towards. The black border indicates the perseverance needed to reach their goal. The "golden arrowhead" represents the golden future the citizens hope will be built upon Guyana's mineral resources. The country's extensive water resources are symbolized by the white border.

SURINAM

Republic of Surinam,
Dutch **Republiek Surinam**.
Republic in N South America.

NATIONAL FLAG AND ENSIGN

Officially hoisted 25 November 1975.
Proportions 2:3.

The golden star is a symbol of the golden future that can be achieved through unity.

The green stands for the fertile land, the white for justice and freedom, and the red for progress in the struggle for a better life.

BRAZIL

Federative Republic of Brazil, Portuguese **República Federativa do Brasil**.
Federal republic in Central South America.

NATIONAL FLAG AND ENSIGN

Adopted 12 May 1992. Proportions 7:10.

The original design, with 21 stars, was adopted on 19 November 1889. The number of stars was increased to 22 in 1960, to 23 in 1968 and to 27 in 1992. The central device represents the sky above Rio de Janeiro at 8.30 a.m. on 15 November 1889, the date of the proclamation of the republic. The 27 stars correspond to the stars of the constellations of the Virgin, Water Snake, Scorpio, Southern Triangle, Octant, Southern Cross, Keel of Argo, Greater Dog and Smaller Dog. Each of 26 stars represents one state of the Federation and the 27th star represents the Federal District. The curved band with the national motto "Order and Progress" stands for the Equator. The green and yellow symbolize the forests and mineral resources respectively.

BRAZILIAN STATES

Since 1889 Brazil has been a federal republic. Currently it comprises 26 states and the federal district where Brasilia, the capital of the country, is located.

ACRE

STATE FLAG

Flag introduced in 1899, officially confirmed 1 March 1963. Proportions 11:20.

Yellow and green are the national colours of Brazil. The red stands for courage.

ALAGOAS

Adopted 23 September 1963. Proportions 4:7.

The colours are taken from the state arms, which display the arms of the cities of Alagoas, Penedo and Porto Calvo. The pictures of a stalk of sugar cane and a

branch of cotton represent the state's two chief agricultural products.

AMAPÁ

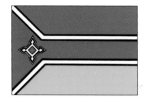

STATE FLAG

Adopted in 1984. Proportions 4:7.

The colours symbolize the sky and law (blue), the green land, faith in the future, freedom and love (green), the natural riches (yellow), purity and tranquillity (white), regard to the past being the source of good (black). The emblem represents the fort of São José de Macapá. The blue star stands for the state.

▲ *ABOVE State flags on Brazilian postage stamps, 1981 (from left to right beginning top right) Alagoas; Bahia; Federal District; Pernambuco; Sergipe.*

AMAZONAS
Flag introduced in 1897, confirmed in 1982.
Proportions 7:10.

The red stripe represents the state and the white stripes stand for the Amazon and Negro Rivers. The larger star symbolizes Manaus, the capital of the state, and the smaller stars symbolize the 24 municipalities existing in 1897.

BAHIA
Flag adopted 26 May 1889. Proportions 7:10.

The red triangle represents the Masonic symbol of the *Inconfidencia Mineira*, the miners' revolt of 1789. Blue, white and red were the colours of the Bahian Revolution of 1798.

CEARÁ
Flag adopted 31 August 1967. Proportions 7:10.

Green and yellow are the national colours

of Brazil. The central portion of the arms displays the bay and lighthouse at Mucuri. The stars represent the municipalities of the state.

ESPIRITO SANTO
Flag officially hoisted 24 April 1947.
Proportions 7:10.

The colours of the flag represent peace (blue), harmony and sweetness (white), and joy (rose). The motto means "Work and Hope".

FEDERAL DISTRICT
Flag officially hoisted 7 September 1969.
Proportions 13:18.

The white stands for purity, and green and yellow are the national colours of Brazil. The four arrows symbolize the balance of centralization and devolution in Brazil.

GOIAS
Flag adopted 30 July 1919. Proportions 7:10.

The stars are those of the Southern Cross constellation. Green and yellow are the national colours of Brazil.

MARANHÃO
Adopted 21 December 1889. Proportions 2:3.

The white star stands for the state. The colours of the stripes represent the three components of the population: the descendants of the Portuguese discoverers and colonizers (white), the native Indians (red) and the African slaves.

MATO GROSSO
Flag adopted in 1890, officially confirmed 11 July 1947. Proportions 7:10.

The flag has the colours of the national flag but in a different arrangement. The star stands for the state.

MATO GROSSO DO SUL
Flag officially hoisted 1 January 1979.
Proportions 7:10.

The state is represented by a golden star shining in the blue sky of hope, symbolizing the wealth of the people's labour. The green stands for the forests and fields. The white band symbolizes the future and friendship among peoples.

MINAS GERAIS
Flag adopted 27 November 1962.
Proportions 7:10.

The triangle recalls the Inconfidencia Mineira, the miners' revolt of 1789.

▲ ABOVE *State flags on Brazilian postage stamps, 1982 (from left to right beginning top right) Minas Gerais; Mato Grosso; Piaui; Maranhão; Santa Catarina.*

PARÁ

STATE FLAG

Flag introduced 17 November 1889.
Proportions 7:10.

The star represents the state and the white symbolizes the river Amazon.

PARAÍBA

Flag introduced 27 October 1965.
Proportions 7:10.

The motto *Nego* ("I deny it") refers to the revolution of 1930, in which the state played a leading part.

PARANÁ

Flag officially adopted 31 March 1947.
Proportions 2:3.

The basic design of the flag was adopted in 1892. The green symbolizes the country's natural wealth, the white stands for its mineral resources. The main device of the emblem is the Southern Cross constellation. The branches of araucaria and maté represent forestry and agriculture.

PERNAMBUCO

Flag officially adopted 23 February 1917.
Proportions 2:3.

The flag was adopted by the republic of Pernambuco in 1817. The star represents the state, the three arches of the rainbow symbolize peace, friendship and union, and the sun signifies that the people of Pernambucos are the children of the sun. The cross refers to the name Santa Cruz (Holy Cross) which was given to Brazil by the European discoverers.

▼ **BELOW** *State flags on Brazilian postage stamps, 1983 (from left to right beginning top right) Amazonas; Goias; Rio de Janeiro; Mato Grosso Do Sul; Paraná.*

PIAUÍ

Flag adopted 24 July 1922.
Proportions 7:10.

The star represents the state. The national colours of Brazil, yellow and green symbolize its allegiance to that country.

RIO DE JANEIRO

Flag introduced in 1947.
Proportions 7:10.

The flag displays the pre-1910 colours of Portugal; the arms were adopted on 29 June 1892. The main feature is an eagle holding in its talons branches of sugar cane and olive.

RIO GRANDE DO NORTE

Flag adopted 3 December 1957.
Proportions 2:3.

The colours of the flag represent the forests and the chalk cliffs. The arms were adopted on 1 July 1909.

RIO GRANDE DO SUL

STATE FLAG

Flag introduced in 1891.
Proportions 7:10.

This design was adopted by the republic of Rio Grande do Sul in 1836. The arms, displaying a Phrygian cap of liberty and suits of armour, were added in 1891.

▼ *BELOW State flags on Brazilian postage stamps* (from left to right beginning top right) *Ceará; Espririto Santo; Paraíba; Rio Grande do Norte; Rondônia.*

An almost identical flag with 21 stripes, designed in 1888, was one of several proposed flags for the Republic of Brazil. It did not become the national flag but was used unofficially as the flag of the state of São Paulo. The number of stripes was reduced in 1932. The white, black and red represent whites, blacks and Native Americans living peacefully together. Blue and white are the historic colours of Portugal, and blue, white and red are the republican colours.

SERGIPE

Flag introduced 1897. Proportions 7:10.

The colours of the flag are those of the national flag of Brazil. The stars are those of the Southern Cross constellation.

TOCANTINS

STATE FLAG

Flag adopted 1 January 1989. Proportions 3:5.

The sun represents the state, which split from Goiás in 1988. The blue symbolizes river Tocantins.

URUGUAY

Oriental Republic of Uruguay,
Spanish **República Oriental del Uruguay**.
Republic in SE South America.

NATIONAL FLAG AND ENSIGN

Adopted 12 July 1830. Proportions 2:3.

RONDÔNIA

Flag adopted 31 December 1981.
Proportions 7:10.

The flag shows the colours of the Brazilian flag, yellow and green. The star stands for the state.

RORAIMA

STATE FLAG

Flag adopted 31 December 1981.
Proportions 7:10.

The flag displays the colours of the national flag of Brazil, yellow and green. The star represents the state and the red line symbolizes the Equator.

SANTA CATARINA

Flag adopted 23 October 1953. Proportions 3:4.

The green lozenge represents the vegetation of the state; the arms were adopted on 15 August 1895. The star symbolizes the state and the Phrygian cap is a symbol of liberty. The eagle represents productivity, the anchor denotes the maritime character of the state and the key indicates that it is the key to southern Brazil. The wreath, made of grain and coffee plants, symbolizes agriculture.

SÃO PAULO

STATE FLAG

Flag adopted 18 November 1932.
Proportions 7:10.

The creators of the flag were inspired by the national colours of Argentina, and by the design of the American Stars and Stripes. It was adopted on 16 December 1828, with nine blue and ten white stripes. In 1830 the number of stripes was reduced to four blue and five white; these nine stripes represent the nine original regions of Uruguay. The sun is a symbol of freedom.

PARAGUAY

Republic of Paraguay,
Spanish **República del Paraguay**.
Republic in S Central South America.

NATIONAL FLAG AND ENSIGN, OBVERSE

EMBLEM IN THE CENTRE OF THE REVERSE OF
THE NATIONAL FLAG AND ENSIGN

Adopted 25 November 1842. Proportions 1:2.

This is the only national flag in the world with a different design on the obverse and reverse. The state seal appears on the obverse and the reverse is charged with the treasury seal. Red, white and blue are the republican colours. They symbolize patriotism, courage, equality and justice (red), steadfastness, unity, peace and the purity of ideas (white), kindliness, love, sharpness, sense of reality, and liberty (blue). The star symbolizes the date of independence, 14 May 1811. The lion guarding the Phrygian cap symbolizes the defence of liberty. The national motto is "Peace and Justice".

BOLIVIA

Republic of Bolivia,
Spanish **República de Bolivia**.
Republic in W Central South America.

STATE FLAG

Adopted 5 November 1851. Proportions 2:3.
Civil flag and ensign are without arms.

The red symbolizes the blood of the national heroes, sacrifice and love. The yellow stands for the mineral resources and for the Incas, who were the first to make use of them. The green is a symbol of eternal hope, evolution and progress.

The arms display symbols of dignity and independence (condor), liberty (sun) and republic (Phrygian cap). The animal kingdom is represented by an alpaca, the mineral kingdom by Mount Potosi and the vegetable kingdom by a breadfruit tree. The wheatsheaf symbolizes agriculture. The ten stars represent the nine departments of Bolivia and the one lost to Chile. The flags and weapons symbolize the will to defend the country.

PERU

Republic of Peru,
Spanish **República del Perú**.
Republic in W South America.

STATE FLAG AND ENSIGN

Adopted 25 February 1825. Proportions 2:3.
The civil flag and ensign do not have arms.

According to legend, General José de San Martin saw a great number of flamingos when he arrived in Peru in 1820. Taking this as a good omen, he decided that white and red should be the colours of the Peruvian Legion that he founded to liberate Peru. The white represents peace, dignity and progress; the red symbolizes war and courage. The arms show symbols of the animal kingdom (*vicuña*), vegetable kingdom (cinchona tree) and mineral kingdom (a cornucopia full of gold and silver coins). The laurel wreath above the shield symbolizes the republic. The palm and laurel wreath around the shield is a symbol of peace and the will to defend the country.

CHILE

Republic of Chile,
Spanish **República de Chile**.
Republic in SW South America.

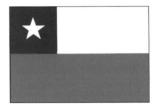

NATIONAL FLAG AND ENSIGN

Adopted 18 October 1817. Proportions 2:3.

The flag was designed by an American, Charles Wood, who fought for Chilean independence as an officer in the army of General José de San Martin. The design is clearly influenced by the Stars and Stripes. The white star is the guiding star on the path of progress and honour. The blue symbolizes the sky; the white symbolizes the snow of the Andes, and the red stands for all the blood shed in the struggle for independence.

ARGENTINA

Republic of Argentina,
Spanish **República Argentina**.
Republic in S South America.

NATIONAL FLAG AND ENSIGN

Adopted 25 February 1818.
Proportions unspecified.

In May 1810 the pro-independence movement initiated the use of the blue and white cockade. It was decreed the national cockade on 18 February 1812, and nine days later a flag in these colours was adopted. The blue and white symbolize the clear skies and snow of the Andes. The sun, added in 1818, is the *Sol de Mayo* ("May Sun"), the national symbol of Argentina. It commemorates the appearance of the sun in cloudy skies on 25 May 1810, when the first mass demonstration in favour of independence took place.

THE SOUTH ATLANTIC

FALKLAND ISLANDS

British crown colony in the S Atlantic.

STATE FLAG AND ENSIGN

Introduced in 1948. Proportions 1:2.

The arms were granted on 29 September 1948. The ram denotes that wool is the principal product of the islands. The ship is the ship *Desire* which was commanded by Captain John Davis when he discovered the Falkland Islands in 1592. The five stars on its sail allude to the Southern Cross constellation.

SOUTH GEORGIA AND SOUTH SANDWICH ISLANDS

British crown colony in the S Atlantic.

STATE FLAG AND ENSIGN

Introduced in 1992. Proportions 1:2.

The arms were granted on 14 February 1992. The colours white, blue and green represent ice, snow and grass respectively. The lion is a symbol of British protection and the torch symbolizes exploration. The stars are from the arms of Captain James Cook, who discovered the islands in 1775.

BRITISH ANTARCTIC TERRITORY

British dependent territory in the S Atlantic.

FLAG AND ENSIGN OF THE RESEARCH STATIONS
AND THEIR VESSELS

Adopted 21 April 1998. Proportions 1:2.

This ensign is flown by Natural Environment Research Council vessels engaged on British Antarctic survey work. The arms were granted to the Falkland Islands' Dependencies on 11 March 1952 and with the crest added in 1963 they were assigned to the new colony. The torch is a symbol of exploration; the white field with wavy blue stripes is the ice-covered land and the Antarctic waters. The shield is supported by the British lion and a penguin which represents the local fauna. The crest shows the research ship "Discovery".

SAINT HELENA

British crown colony in the SE Atlantic.

STATE FLAG AND ENSIGN

Introduced in 1984. Proportions 1:2.

The arms were granted on 30 January 1984. The ship recalls that in 1659 the island became the possession of the British East India Company. The wirebird is endemic to the island.

TRISTAN DA CUNHA

Dependency of Saint Helena in the SE Atlantic.

STATE FLAG AND ENSIGN

Adopted 20 October 2002.
Proportions 1:2.

The arms feature four yellow-nosed albatrosses. Two Tristan da Cunha spiny lobsters serve as supporters, and the crest is composed of the naval crown with a Tristan da Cunha longboat.

Flags of Africa

The current national flags of the countries of Africa, from Morocco and Algeria to Anjouan and Mauritius, and their territories, states and provinces are illustrated and described in the following pages.

For ease of reference, the countries of this continent have been divided into geographical areas. We begin in northern Africa and move on through western, central and eastern Africa. Finally we look at the flags of the countries of southern Africa and the islands of the Indian Ocean.

For each entry, the country or territory's name is given in its most easily recognized form and then in all its official languages. This is followed by a description of its political status and geographic position. The basic data for each flag contains the status of the flag, date of adoption, proportions, and symbolic meaning.

NORTH AFRICA

MOROCCO

Kingdom of Morocco,
Arabic **al-Mamlaka al-Maghrebia**.
Constitutional monarchy in NW Africa.

NATIONAL FLAG, CIVIL AND STATE ENSIGN

Adopted 17 November 1915. Proportions 2:3.

The red is the colour of the sheriffs of Mecca. The pentagram, called the "Seal of Solomon", is an ancient symbol of life and good health.

ALGERIA

Democratic and Popular Republic of Algeria, Arabic **al-Jumhuria al-Jazariya ad-Dimuqratiya ash-Shabiya**.
Republic in N Africa.

NATIONAL FLAG AND ENSIGN

Adopted 3 July 1962. Proportions 2:3.

The colours of the flag symbolize Islam (green), purity (white) and liberty (red). The crescent and star is a symbol of Islam, with the crescent being more closed than in other Muslim countries because the Algerians believe that the long horns of the crescent bring happiness.

TUNISIA

Tunisian Republic,
Arabic **al-Jumhuriya at-Tunisiya**.
Republic in N Africa.

NATIONAL FLAG AND ENSIGN

Introduced c.1835, modified 3 July 1999.

The flag is based on that of Turkey. Until 1850 the star had six points. The star and crescent stand for Islam.

LIBYA

Great Socialist People's Libyan Arab Republic, Arabic **al-Jamahariya al-Arabiya al-Libya al-shabiya al-Ishtirakiya al-Uzma**.
Socialist republic in N Central Africa.

NATIONAL FLAG AND ENSIGN

Introduced in 1977. Proportions 1:2.

This is the only monochromatic national flag in the world. The green is the colour of Islam and is a manifestation of the Green Revolution proclaimed by President Mu'ammar al Qaddafi.

EGYPT

Arab Republic of Egypt,
Arabic **Jumhuriyat Misr al-Arabiya**.
Republic in NE Africa.

CIVIL AND STATE FLAG AND ENSIGN

Officially hoisted 5 October 1984.
Proportions 2:3.

The red-white-black horizontal tricolour was introduced in Egypt after the revolution of 1953. The central white stripe was charged with two green stars from 1958 to 1972, and with the hawk of Quraish from 1972 to 1984. In 1984 it was replaced by the eagle of Saladin, standing on a panel that carries the name of the country. The eagle bears on its breast a shield, sometimes in the national colours.

SOME HISTORIC FLAGS

While formally part of the Ottoman Empire, in the 18th and 19th centuries Algeria, Tunisia and Tripoli (Libya) each had their own civil ensigns. All the ensigns displayed between five and seven horizontal stripes: white-red-green (Algeria), blue-red-green (Tunisia) and red-green-white (Tripoli). While under foreign domination, Algeria (which was under French rule from 1830-1962) and Libya (under Italian rule from 1912-1947) did not have their own flags. After achieving independence, however, they have made changes to their national flags several times.

WESTERN AFRICA

WESTERN SAHARA

Sahara Arab Democratic Republic,
Arabic **al-Jumhuriya as-Sahrawiya ad-Dimukratiya al-Arabiya**.
State in W Africa currently occupied by Morocco.

NATIONAL FLAG

Introduced 27 February 1976. Proportions 1:2.

Western Sahara proclaimed independence and adopted its flag the day after the formal Spanish withdrawal. The design of the flag is based on that of Palestine, with pan-Arab colours and a red crescent and star, the symbol of Islam. The red symbolizes blood shed in the struggle for independence, the black recalls the period of colonialism, the white stands for liberty and the green is a symbol of progress.

MAURITANIA

Islamic Republic of Mauritania, French **République Islamique Arabe et Africaine de Mauritanie**, Arabic **al-Jumhuriya al-Islamiya al-Mauritaniya**.
Islamic republic in W Africa.

NATIONAL FLAG AND ENSIGN

Adopted 1 April 1959. Proportions 2:3.

The green and the crescent and star are both symbols of Islam; the green also represents hope for a bright future. The yellow stands for the Sahara Desert.

MALI

Republic of Mali,
French **République du Mali**.
Republic in W Africa.

NATIONAL FLAG AND ENSIGN

Adopted 1 March 1961. Proportions 2:3.

The flag, based on the French *Tricolore*, displays the pan-African colours. They stand for nature (green), purity and mineral resources (yellow), and for bravery and blood shed in the struggle for independence (red).

SENEGAL

Republic of Senegal,
French **République du Sénégal**.
Republic in W Africa.

NATIONAL FLAG AND ENSIGN

Introduced in 1960. Proportions 2:3.

After the dissolution of the federation with Mali, Senegal retained the colours of the flag and placed a green star in the centre, symbolizing unity and hope. The green is an expression of hope for undisturbed progress, the yellow represents the verdant land and the wealth which will be the fruit of collective labour. The red recalls the martyrs and the common struggle of the African nations for independence; it is also a symbol of life and socialism.

THE GAMBIA

Republic of the Gambia.
Republic in W Africa.

NATIONAL FLAG, CIVIL AND STATE ENSIGN

Introduced 18 February 1965. Proportions 2:3.

The original idea for the flag came from the Gambia, but the design was prepared by the College of Arms in London. The red stands for the sun, the blue represents the river Gambia and the green symbolizes the fertile land and agriculture. The white stripes stand for unity and peace.

GUINEA-BISSAU

Republic of Guinea-Bissau,
Portuguese **República da Guiné-Bissau**.
Republic in W Africa.

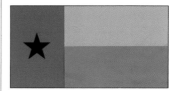

NATIONAL FLAG AND ENSIGN

Introduced 24 September 1973. Proportions 1:2.

In August 1961 the African Party for the Independence of Guinea and Cape Verde adopted a flag in pan-African colours with the party initials (PAIGC) beneath a black star. When independence was proclaimed the flag, without the initials, became the national flag of Guinea-Bissau.

The red stands for the suffering under colonial rule and for the blood shed in the struggle for independence. The yellow symbolizes the fruits of work that contribute to well-being. The green represents the tropical forests of the country and hope for a bright future. The star is a symbol of Africa and its people.

GUINEA

Republic of Guinea,
French **République de Guinée**.
Republic in W Africa.

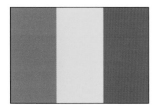

NATIONAL FLAG AND ENSIGN

Adopted 10 November 1958. Proportions 2:3.

The first French colony to achieve independence, Guinea patterned its flag on the French *Tricolore*. Sékou Touré, the first President of Guinea, stated that by choosing the same colours as those of Ghana his country intended to show its dedication to African unity. The colours reflect the national motto "Work, Justice, Solidarity". The red is the colour of blood and reflects the spirit of sacrifice and hard work, and symbolizes the will for progress. The yellow is the colour of the gold of Guinea and of the African sun, which is the source of energy, generosity and equality as it shines on everyone. The green is the colour of the vegetation, agriculture, the productivity of the peasants and the spirit of solidarity in collective enterprises. Thus the three colours of the flag symbolize the three bases of the republic: labour, justice and solidarity.

SIERRA LEONE

Republic of Sierra Leone.
Republic in W Africa.

NATIONAL FLAG

Officially hoisted 27 April 1961. Proportions 2:3.

The green represents the agriculture, natural resources and the mountains. The white stands for unity and justice. The blue is a symbol of hope that the only natural harbour in Freetown will be able to make its contribution to peace throughout the world.

LIBERIA

Republic of Liberia.Republic in W Africa.

NATIONAL FLAG

Adopted 27 August 1847. Proportions 10:19.

The design of the flag copies that of the United States, from where since 1822 freed slaves came to settle in Liberia. The white star represents the shining light of the new republic in the dark continent, represented by a blue square. The 11 stripes symbolize the 11 signatories of the Liberian Declaration of Independence.

IVORY COAST

Republic of Côte d'Ivoire, French
République de la Côte d'Ivoire.
Republic in W Africa.

NATIONAL FLAG AND ENSIGN

Adopted 3 December 1959. Proportions 2:3.

The flag is based on the French *Tricolore*. The orange represents the savannahs of the north and the spirit of national development. The green stands for the forests in the south and for the hope of a better future based on natural resources. The white is the colour of the sky and purity, symbolizing unity between the north and south of the country.

BURKINA FASO

**The People's Democratic Republic of
Burkina Faso**, French **République
Démocratique Populaire de Burkina Faso**.
Socialist republic in W Africa.

NATIONAL FLAG

Adopted 4 August 1984. Proportions 2:3.

The red is a symbol of revolutionary concern to transform the country and the green symbolizes hope and abundance. The star stands for the revolution, leading the nation to a golden future. The yellow represents the undiscovered mineral resources.

GHANA

Republic of Ghana. Republic in W Africa.

NATIONAL FLAG AND STATE ENSIGN

Adopted 6 March 1957. Proportions 2:3.

Ghana was the first country in black Africa to use the Ethiopian colours, which have since been called pan-African. The black star symbolizes the lodestar of African freedom. The red commemorates those who worked for independence, the gold (yellow) represents the wealth of the country (its former name was the Gold Coast) and the green stands for forests and farms.

TOGO

Republic of Togo,
French **République Togolaise**.
Republic in W Africa.

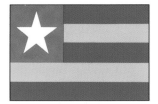

NATIONAL FLAG AND ENSIGN

Adopted 27 April 1960. Proportions 2:3.

The green symbolizes hope and the yellow signifies faith in work as the way to achieve material, moral and spiritual well-being. The red is a symbol of charity, fidelity and love, the virtues that make people love their neighbours and sacrifice their own lives, if necessary, for the triumph of the principles of humanity and the lessening

of human misery. The white is the colour of purity, reminding all citizens to be worthy of their nation's independence.

BENIN

People's Republic of Benin, French
République Populaire du Benin.
Socialist republic in W Africa.

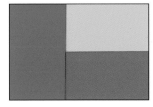

NATIONAL FLAG AND ENSIGN

Adopted 16 November 1959, re-established 1 August 1990. Proportions 2:3.

The green denotes hope for renewal, the red evokes the ancestors' courage and the yellow refers to the country's riches.

CAPE VERDE

Republic of Cape Verde, Portuguese
República de Cabo Verde.
Republic comprising an archipelago in the Atlantic, W Africa.

NATIONAL FLAG AND ENSIGN

Officially hoisted 25 September 1992. Proportions 10:17.

The ring of stars symbolizes the unity of all parts of the country. The ten stars represent the ten main islands of the archipelago: São Tiago, Santo Antão, São Vincente, São Nicolau, Sal, Boa Vista, Fogo, Maio, Brava and Santa Luzia. The colours symbolize the

sky and the sea (blue), peace (white) and the efforts of the people (red).

NIGERIA

Federal Republic of Nigeria.
Federal republic in W Africa.

NATIONAL FLAG

Officially hoisted 1 October 1960. Proportions 1:2.

The green reflects the green land of Nigeria and stands for its agriculture. The white symbolizes peace.

SÃO TOMÉ AND PRÍNCIPE

Democratic Republic of São Tomé and Príncipe, Portuguese **República Democrática de São Tomé and Príncipe**.
Republic consisting of several islands in the Gulf of Guinea.

NATIONAL FLAG AND ENSIGN

Adopted 5 November 1975. Proportions 1:2.

The two stars represent the two main islands of the nation: São Tomé and Príncipe. The red stands for the blood shed in the struggle for independence, the green is the colour of the rich vegetation and the yellow represents cocoa, which is one of the main agricultural products.

CENTRAL AFRICA

NIGER

Republic of Niger,
French **République du Niger**.
Republic in N Central Africa.

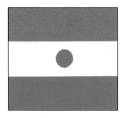

NATIONAL FLAG

Adopted 23 November 1959.
Proportions unspecified.

The orange represents the Sahara Desert, with the white being a symbol of purity and innocence. The orange disc represents the sun and symbolizes the sacrifices made by the people, their firm commitment and their determination to defend human rights and justice. The green, a symbol of hope, represents the fertile and productive zone of Niger.

CHAD

Republic of Chad,
French **République du Tchad**.
Republic in N Central Africa.

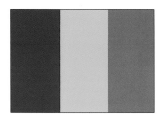

NATIONAL FLAG

Adopted 6 November 1959. Proportions 2:3.

The blue represents the rivers and forests, the yellow symbolizes sand and the desert, and the red is a symbol of sacrifice and the blood of martyrs.

CAMEROON

Republic of Cameroon,
French **République du Cameroun**.
Republic in W Central Africa.

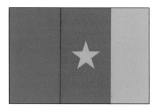

NATIONAL FLAG AND ENSIGN

Adopted 20 May 1975. Proportions 2:3.

The green stands for the luxuriant vegetation of the south, and also represents hope for a rich, prosperous, hard-working and unified Cameroon. The red is a symbol of sovereignty and of unity between the north and the south. The yellow represents the soil of the north, wealth and the sun. The star symbolizes unity.

CENTRAL AFRICAN REPUBLIC

French **République Centrafricaine**.
Republic in W Central Africa.

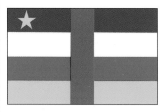

NATIONAL FLAG

Introduced 1 December 1958.
Proportions unspecified.

The flag displays the colours of France (blue-white-red) combined with the pan-African colours (green-yellow-red) to show that Europeans and Africans should have respect and friendship for one another. Their common bond, their red blood, is represented by the vertical red stripe

binding all the stripes together. The star symbolizes independence.

EQUATORIAL GUINEA

Republic of Equatorial Guinea,
Spanish **República de Guinea Ecuatorial**.
Republic in W Central Africa.

NATIONAL FLAG AND ENSIGN

Adopted 12 October 1968, re-adopted
21 August 1979. Proportions unspecified.

The blue represents the sea linking the mainland of the country with Bioko and other islands. The colour green symbolizes its tropical forests and natural riches, the white stands for peace and the red commemorates the blood shed in the struggle for independence. The main device of the arms is the tree under which King Bonkoro signed the treaty with Spain in 1843. The six stars represent the six districts of the state.

GABON

Gabonese Republic,
French **République Gabonaise**.
Republic in W Central Africa.

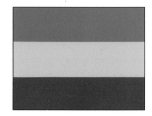

NATIONAL FLAG AND ENSIGN

Adopted 9 August 1960. Proportions 3:4.

The design of the flag was inspired by the geographical position of Gabon. The green (forests) and the blue (Atlantic Ocean) are separated by the yellow stripe, which stands for the Equator and the ever-present sun.

CONGO

Republic of Congo,
French **République du Congo**.
Republic in Central Africa.

NATIONAL FLAG

*Adopted 18 August 1959, re-established
10 June 1991. Proportions 2:3.*

The green stands for nature and peace. The yellow represents the natural wealth and expresses hope for a better future. The red is a symbol of independence and of the dignity of all humanity.

CONGO

Democratic Republic of Congo, French **République Démocratique du Congo**.
Republic in Central Africa.

NATIONAL FLAG AND ENSIGN

Introduced 18 February 2006. Proportions 2:3.

The blue flag with a large yellow star in the centre was the flag of Congo from 1885 to 1960, when the six stars along the hoist were added. The star stands for unity,

blue for the river Congo, yellow for wealth, and red for blood shed in the struggle for independence.

RWANDA

Republic of Rwanda, Kinyarwanda **Republika y'u Rwanda**, French **République Rwandaise**.
Republic in E Central Africa.

NATIONAL FLAG

Adopted 31 December 2001. Proportions 2:3.

The colours of the flag represent happiness and peace (blue), development as a result of work (yellow) and a hope for prosperity based on rational use of the resources.

EASTERN AFRICA

SUDAN

Democratic Republic of Sudan,
Arabic **Jumhuriyat es-Sudan**.
Military republic in NE Africa.

NATIONAL FLAG AND ENSIGN

Officially hoisted 20 May 1970. Proportions 1:2.

The red stands for struggles and for the martyrs in the Sudan and the great Arab land. The white is the colour of peace, optimism, light and love. The black

BURUNDI

Republic of Burundi, Kirundi **Republika y'Uburundi**, French **République du Burundi**.
Republic in E Central Africa.

STATE FLAG

*Adopted 26 December 1968. Proportions 3:5
(established 27 September 1982).*

The colours represent the struggle for independence (red), hope (green) and peace (white). The three stars symbolize the national motto "Unity, Work, Progress".

represents the Sudan and the Mahdija Revolution, during which a black flag was used. The green symbolizes Islamic prosperity and agriculture.

ERITREA

State of Eritrea,
Tigrinya **Hagere Eritrea**.
Republic in NE Africa.

NATIONAL FLAG

Adopted 24 May 1993. Proportions 1:2.

The basic design of the flag is identical to the flag of the Eritrean People's Liberation Front. The olive wreath with an upright branch in the centre recalls the emblem on the first flag of Eritrea (1952).

ETHIOPIA

Federal Democratic Republic of Ethiopia, Amharic **Hebretesebawit Ityopia**. Republic in NE Africa.

STATE FLAG

Adopted 6 February 1996. Proportions 1:2.

The Ethiopian horizontal tricolour dates back to *c.*1895. In 1996 the new national emblem was placed in the centre of the flag. The blue symbolizes peace and the pentagram represents the unity of the nations, nationalities and peoples of Ethiopia.

The original symbolism of the colours denoted the Christian virtues. In the present official symbolism, the green represents fertility, labour and development; the yellow, hope, justice and equality, and the red, sacrifice and heroism in the cause of freedom and equality.

DJIBOUTI

Republic of Djibouti, French **République de Djibouti**, Arabic **Jumhuriya Djibouti**. Republic in NE Africa.

NATIONAL FLAG AND ENSIGN

Officially hoisted 27 June 1977.
Proportions 21:38.

The colours of the flag stand for the sea and sky (blue), the earth (green) and peace (white). Green and blue are also the colours of the two main population groups, the Afars and Issas respectively. The red star recalls the struggle for independence and is a symbol of unity.

SOMALILAND

Republic of Somaliland, Somali **Jamhuriyadda Somaliland**. De facto independent republic in NE Africa.

NATIONAL FLAG AND ENSIGN

Introduced 14 October 1996.
Proportions unspecified.

The flag displays the pan-Arab colours; the star stands for the republic. On the green stripe is *Shahada*, the Muslim Statement of Faith.

SOMALIA

Somali Democratic Republic, Somali **Jamhuriyadda Dimugradiga ee Soomaliya**. Republic in E Africa.

NATIONAL FLAG AND ENSIGN

Officially introduced 12 October 1954.
Proportions unspecified.

The adoption of the blue was influenced by the blue field of the United Nations flag. The five points of the star represent the five countries in which the Somalis live: Somali (Italian colony), British Somali, Ethiopia, Kenya and Djibouti.

KENYA

Republic of Kenya, Kiswahili **Jamhuri ya Kenya**. Republic in E Africa.

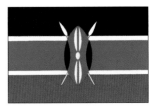

NATIONAL FLAG, CIVIL AND STATE ENSIGN

Officially introduced 12 December 1963.
Proportions 2:3.

The colours symbolize the people (black), the struggle for independence (red) and agriculture (green). The white stripes stand for peace and unity. The Masai shield and spears represent the will to defend freedom.

UGANDA

Republic of Uganda, Kiswahili **Jamhuri ya Uganda**. Republic in E Central Africa.

NATIONAL FLAG

Officially hoisted 9 October 1962.
Proportions unspecified.

The colours of the flag derive from the flag of the Uganda People's Congress, the party

SOUTHERN AFRICA AND INDIAN OCEAN

that won the first elections. They symbolize the people of Africa (black), sunshine (yellow) and brotherhood (red). The crested crane (*Balearica pavonia*) is the symbol of Uganda and has already appeared on the colonial badge in the early 20th century.

TANZANIA

United Republic of Tanzania,
Kiswahili **Jamhuri ya Muungano wa Tanzania**.
Republic in E Africa.

NATIONAL FLAG AND ENSIGN

Adopted 30 June 1964. Proportions 2:3.

The colours of the flag combine those of the flags of Tanganyika (green, yellow, black) and Zanzibar (blue, black, green). They symbolize the people (black), the land (green), the sea (blue) and the mineral wealth (yellow).

ZANZIBAR

Semi-autonomous part of Tanzania.

NATIONAL FLAG

Hoisted 9 January 2005. Proportions 2:3.

This is the flag of independent Zanzibar (January – April 1964), with the flag of Tanzania in the canton. The blue symbolizes the sea (Indian Ocean), black stands for the people, and green represents the land (islands of Zanzibar and Pemba).

MOZAMBIQUE

People's Republic of Mozambique,
Portuguese **República Popular de Moçambique**.
Republic in SE Africa.

NATIONAL FLAG AND ENSIGN

Introduced in April 1983.
Proportions unspecified.

The flag follows the design of the Frelimo Party flag. The star symbolizes the spirit of international solidarity. The book, hoe and gun stand for study, production and defence. The red recalls "the centuries of resistance to colonialism, the armed national liberation struggle, and the defence of sovereignty". The other colours represent the riches of the soil (green), the African continent (black), the mineral riches (yellow), and justice and peace (white).

MALAWI

Republic of Malawi,
Chichewa **Mfuko la Malawi**.
Republic in SE Africa.

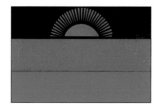

NATIONAL FLAG

Officially hoisted 6 July 1964. Proportions 2:3.

The leading force in the struggle for independence was the Malawi Congress Party. Its flag, a horizontal tricolour of

black-red-green, served as the basis for the national flag. A sun emblem was added to symbolize the dawn of hope and freedom for the whole of Africa. The black stands for the people of Africa, the red symbolizes the blood of the martyrs of African freedom, and the green represents the vegetation of Malawi.

ZAMBIA

Republic of Zambia.
Republic in S Central Africa.

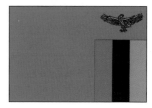

NATIONAL FLAG

Officially hoisted 24 October 1964. Shape of the eagle modified in 1996. Proportions 2:3.

The eagle in flight symbolizes freedom in Zambia and the ability to rise above the country's problems. The red represents the struggle for independence, the black the people of Zambia, the orange its mineral wealth and the green its natural resources.

ANGOLA

Republic of Angola,
Portuguese **República de Angola**.
Republic in SW Africa.

NATIONAL FLAG AND ENSIGN

Introduced 11 November 1975. Proportions 2:3.

The red symbolizes the blood shed in the struggle for independence. The black stands for Africa. The cog-wheel and machete are symbols of the workers and peasants respectively. The star symbolizes international solidarity and progress. The yellow signifies the wealth of the nation.

NAMIBIA

Republic of Namibia.
Republic in SW Africa.

NATIONAL FLAG AND ENSIGN

Adopted 21 March 1990. Proportions 2:3.

The sun symbolizes life and energy. The golden yellow represents the plains and the Namib Desert. The blue represents the sky, the Atlantic Ocean, the marine resources of Namibia, and the importance of rain and water. The red stands for the people, their heroism and their determination to build a future of equal opportunity for all. The green is a symbol of the vegetation and natural resources. The white refers to peace and unity.

BOTSWANA

Republic of Botswana.
Republic in S Central Africa.

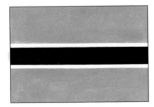

NATIONAL FLAG

Officially hoisted 30 September 1966.
Proportions 2:3.

The blue symbolizes the sky and reliance on water. The black and white represent the majority and minority of the country's population respectively.

ZIMBABWE

Republic of Zimbabwe.
Republic in S Central Africa.

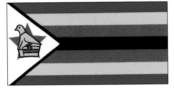

NATIONAL FLAG AND ENSIGN

Officially introduced 18 April 1980.
Proportions 1:2.

The emblem displays a red star, representing socialism, and the Great Zimbabwe Bird, which represents the great past of the country. The colours of the flag symbolize the majority of the population (black), the blood shed in the struggle for independence (red), the mineral wealth (yellow), the agriculture (green) and peace (white).

SOUTH AFRICA

Republic of South Africa,
Afrikaans **Republiek van Suid-Afrika**.
Republic in S Africa.

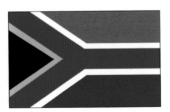

NATIONAL FLAG, CIVIL AND STATE ENSIGN

Officially introduced 27 April 1994.
Proportions 2:3.

The flag combines the colours of the Boer republics (red, white, blue) with the colours of the African National Congress (black,

green, yellow), which came to power in 1994. The ANC is shown as a driving force behind the country's convergence and unification which is symbolized by the "Y" shape.

LESOTHO

Kingdom of Lesotho,
Lesotho **Mmuso wa Lesotho**.
Constitutional monarchy in S Africa.

NATIONAL FLAG

Introduced 4 October 2006.
Proportions 2:3.

The colours symbolize rain (blue), peace (white) and prosperity (green). The black Basotho hat represents the people of Lesotho.

SWAZILAND

Kingdom of Swaziland,
Swazi **Umbuso we Swatini**.
Absolute monarchy in SE Africa.

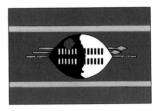

STATE FLAG

Adopted 30 October 1967. Proportions 2:3.

The red symbolizes the battles of the past, the yellow represents the wealth of the country's resources and the blue stands for peace. The black and white Swazi shield is that of the Emasotha Regiment, formed in the late 1920s. Behind the shield appear their assegais and a traditional fighting stick with *tinjobo* tassels, made from widow-bird and loury feathers.

MADAGASCAR

Democratic Republic of Madagascar,
Malagasy **Repoblika Demokratika n`i Madagaskar**.
Republic comprising an island in the Indian Ocean.

NATIONAL FLAG AND ENSIGN

Adopted in October 1958. Proportions 2:3.

The choice of colours for the national flag was influenced by the fact that white and red were the flags of the Hova Empire in the 19th century. The green was added for the peoples living on the coast. The colours symbolize purity (white), sovereignty (red) and hope (green).

COMOROS

Union of the Comoros,
French **L'Union des Comores,**
Arabic **Al Ittihad al-Qomori,**
Comoran **Udzima wa Komori**.
Republic in the Indian Ocean.

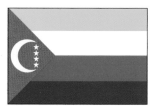

NATIONAL FLAG AND ENSIGN

Adopted early in 2002. Proportions 2:3.

Green and a crescent are symbols of Islam. The four stars and four stripes represent the four islands – Nwali (yellow), Mayotte (white), Nzwami (red) and Gran Comore (blue) despite the fact that Nzwami (Anjouan), Nwali (Mohéli) and Mayotte are de facto separate political entities.

ANJOUAN

State of Anjouan
De facto independent country comprising an island in the Indian Ocean.

NATIONAL FLAG AND ENSIGN

Approved on 25 February 1998. Proportions 2:3.

The red flag with a right hand and a crescent was used by the Sultanate of Anjouan in the 19th century. Red was for centuries the colour of the Arab colonies along the coast of eastern Africa and on the islands in the Indian Ocean, and the crescent is the symbol of Islam.

SEYCHELLES

Republic of Seychelles,
Creole **Repibik Sesel**.
Republic consisting of a group of islands in the Indian Ocean.

NATIONAL FLAG AND ENSIGN

Adopted 8 January 1996. Proportions 1:2.

The flag is a combination of the colours of the two main political parties, the Democratic Party (which is represented by blue and yellow) and the Seychelles People's United Party (represented by red, white and green). The blue symbolizes the sky and the sea; the yellow represents the sun; red stands for the people and their determination to work in unity; white symbolizes social justice and harmony; and green stands for the land.

MAURITIUS

Republic of Mauritius.
Republic comprising an island in the Indian Ocean.

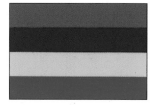

NATIONAL FLAG

Officially hoisted 12 March 1968. Proportions 2:3.

The red stripe represents the struggle for freedom and independence, the blue stripe stands for the colour of the Indian Ocean. The yellow stripe symbolizes the new light of independence, and the green stripe represents agriculture and symbolizes the colour of lush, green Mauritius throughout the year.

Flags of International Organizations

These flags are presented in chronological order, beginning with the flag of the Red Cross, which has existed since 1863. The latest addition to the family of international organizations is the Portuguese-speaking community, whose flag was adopted in 1996.

THE RED CROSS

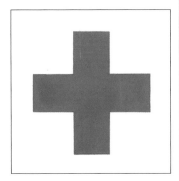

The International Committee of the Red Cross was established in 1863. Its activities follow the Geneva Conventions of 1864, 1907, 1929, 1947 and 1977 on the treatment of prisoners of war and the protection of civilians during hostilities and natural catastrophes.

The flag was proposed by the Red Cross's founder, the Swiss philanthropist Henri Dunant, and was adopted in 1863 as the flag of Switzerland in reversed colours. The flag used in Muslim countries, which was adopted in 1876, displays a red Muslim crescent instead of the cross.

THE COMMONWEALTH

Originally the members of the Commonwealth of Nations were the United Kingdom and its self-governing Dominions. The term "British Commonwealth" began to be used after World War I. In 1949 the name was changed to the Commonwealth and in 1965 the Commonwealth Secretariat in London was established. A total of 54 independent countries from all parts of the world belong to the Commonwealth.

The flag displays the letter "C" (as the first letter of "Commonwealth") which encircles a central globe, denoting the global scope of the organization. The number of lines forming the letter "C" does not correspond to the number of member-states.

LEAGUE OF ARAB STATES

The main aim of the Arab League is to protect the independence and sovereignty of the 22 member-states, and to safeguard their interests. The flag was adopted in 1945, the year the organization was founded. The green and the crescent symbolize Islam and the name of the organization appears in the centre of the emblem. The chain is a symbol of unity and the laurel wreath stands for peace as well as dignity.

UNITED NATIONS

The United Nations was established in 1945 to promote international peace, security and co-operation. It is the largest and the most important international organization, with 185 member-states. Its specialized departments handle international issues including economic, monetary, scientific, educational, social, judicial and health matters.

The flag was adopted on 20 October 1947. The colour blue and the olive branches symbolize peace, and the map of the world represents the organization's global concerns.

PACIFIC COMMUNITY

The Pacific Community has recently replaced the South Pacific Commission established in 1947 by Australia, New Zealand, Great Britain, France, the Netherlands and the US, who administered territories of the South Pacific. The flag was adopted on 6 December 1999. The dark blue field and stars represent the clear night skies of the Pacific. The number of stars indicates the number of member countries and territories. The arch of stars stands for the secretariat tying the members together. The sail symbolizes movement and change. The coconut palm is a symbol of wealth.

ORGANIZATION OF AMERICAN STATES

This name and the charter of the organization were adopted in 1948. The main goal of the member-states of OAS is to uphold sovereignty and to work for peace and prosperity in the region. The flag, adopted in 1965, has been modified several times as the flags of new member-states were added to the emblem; currently the emblem displays the flags of 35 member-states.

NORTH ATLANTIC TREATY ORGANIZATION

NATO was formed in 1949 by the countries of western Europe and North America, originally as a united defence against the threat of Soviet aggression. The flag was adopted in 1954. Its dark blue field represents the Atlantic Ocean, the circle is a symbol of unity and the compass symbolizes the common direction towards peace that has been taken by the 19 member-nations.

ORGANIZATION OF PETROLEUM EXPORTING COUNTRIES

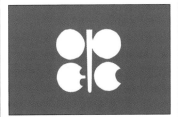

OPEC was set up in 1961 by the main oil-producing countries and currently has 11 members; the flag was adopted in 1970. The emblem is formed from the stylized letters "OPEC".

AFRICAN UNION

Since July 2002 the African Union is the successor of the Organization of African Unity formed in 1963. It uses the flag of the OAU, adopted in 1970. The colours of the flag symbolize the natural environment of Africa (green), its golden future (golden yellow) and a peaceful co-existence (white). The emblem is a golden map of Africa encircled by a golden wreath.

ASSOCIATION OF SOUTH-EAST ASIAN NATIONS

ASEAN was formed in 1967 to promote regional stability and economic co-operation. The flag, adopted in 1997, displays the colours of the flags of the member-states. The blue stands for the sea, the sky and friendship. The emblem is formed of ten *padi* stalks, representing the ten member-states.

CARIBBEAN COMMUNITY AND COMMON MARKET

CARICOM is a regional organization, established in 1973 to promote unity, economic integration and co-operation between the small, insular countries of the Caribbean. It has a total of 14 members. The stripes of the flag represent the sky and the sea, and the yellow disc stands for the sun. The letters are the initials of the community.

ORGANIZATION OF THE ISLAMIC CONFERENCE

The main aim of the organization, founded in 1974, is to promote unity and to prevent foreign interference in the domestic affairs of the 35 member-states. The flag, in pan-Arab colours, was adopted in 1981. The green and the crescent symbolize Islam, and the inscription in the centre reads *Allah u Akbar* ("God is Great").

UNION OF THE ARAB MAGHREB

This was set up in 1989 to co-ordinate the communications and economic policies of its member-countries. The flag was adopted in 1990. The five stars represent the UAM members: Morocco, Mauritania, Algeria, Tunisia and Libya; the colours were taken from the flags of the member-countries.

COMMONWEALTH OF INDEPENDENT STATES

This was formed on the eve of the fall of the Soviet Union in 1991; the 12 member-states are all former Soviet republics. The flag was adopted on 19 January 1996 and the emblem symbolizes aspiration for an equal partnership, unity, peace and stability.

EUROPEAN UNION

The flag, originally adopted on 8 December 1955 by the Council of Europe, was taken over by the European Union on 29 May 1986. The blue symbolizes the sky, the 12 golden stars in a circle represent the union of Europe.

LA FRANCOPHONIE

This organization provides an institutional framework of official and private organizations and associations representing the interests of the French-speaking community, encompassing 47 countries. The emblem conveys the idea of bringing together and denotes the universal character of La Francophonie. The five parts of the ring symbolize the five continents where members of the community live (North America, Europe, Africa, Asia and Oceania).

COMMUNITY OF NATIONS OF THE PORTUGUESE LANGUAGE

The main aim of the CPLP (Comunidade dos Países de Língua Portuguesa) is to promote unity and co-operation. The flag, adopted on 17 July 1996, displays the historic colours of Portugal (blue and white) and a logo symbolizing the close ties among the seven member-states.

Regional and Local Flags

In the Middle Ages many European provinces were independent or semi-independent political entities, some of which have retained their original flags. But in central Europe provincial flags as such began to appear only in the 19th century, and most of them date from the second half of the 20th century. Throughout the world provincial flags fit into a general pattern that is particular to each country or has some features in common with other countries.

Some municipal flags, such as those of Genoa or Elbing, are among the oldest flags in the world but, like provincial flags, most were designed in the 20th century. With both provincial and municipal flags the principal factors influencing design are heraldry and the use of charges, whether these are armorial devices, Japanese *mons* or modern logos.

✳ *ABOVE* FLAG DISPLAY ON A STREET IN LUCERNE. ALL CIVIC AND COMMUNE FLAGS IN SWITZERLAND ARE IN THE FORM OF A SQUARE ARMORIAL BANNER.

REGIONS AND PROVINCES

The first country to provide its provinces with flags (*Landesfarben*) was Prussia. In 1882 the government of Prussia approved the flags of Brandenburg, Hanover, East Prussia, Pomerania, Posen, Rhineland, Silesia, Westphalia, West Prussia and Hohenzollern. The provincial flag of

Saxony was approved in 1884, and that of Hessen-Nassau in 1892. All of these flags displayed horizontal stripes in livery colours, based on the arms approved or granted in 1881. The flag of Posen was changed in 1896 to show Prussian colours rather than Polish, and was changed

Alsace.

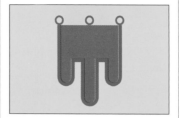

Auvergne.

Franche-Comté.

FLAGS OF PRUSSIAN PROVINCES

BERLIN (1861–1911).

BRANDENBURG (1882–1935).

EAST PRUSSIA (1822–1935).

HANOVER (1882–1935).

HESSEN-NASSAU (1882–1935).

HOHENZOLLERN (1815–1935).

POMERANIA (1882–1935).

POSEN (1882–1896).

RHEINLAND (1882–1935).

SAXONY (1884–1935).

SCHLESWIG-HOLSTEIN (1866–1935).

SILESIA (1882–1935).

WESTPHALIA (1882–1935).

WEST PRUSSIA (1882–1923).

POSEN (1896–1923).

POSEN-WEST PRUSSIA (1923–1935).

UPPER SILESIA (1925–1935).

again in 1923 when Posen was united with West Prussia.

In many other European countries provincial flags are mostly heraldic banners. For example, the flags of the provinces of France and the counties of Norway are all armorial banners. Regional banners have been introduced in France during the last few decades but some, such as the flags of the duchies of Anjou and Maine or the kingdom of Burgundy, were already known in the Middle Ages. In contrast to the French armorial banners, which are quite complex, the flags of the Norwegian counties display single, simple heraldic figures. Many of them were proposed in 1930, but they were only officially adopted between the 1950s and 1989. The flags illustrated here were adopted in 1960 (Troms), 1965 (Nordland) and 1989 (Oppland). For a long time the flags of all nine provinces in Belgium were armorial banners. But now there are ten provinces,

PROVINCES OF NORWAY

Nordland.

Oppland.

Troms.

and some of the existing provinces have adopted new flags. Heraldry has influenced all the Belgian designs but the only armorial banner is the flag of West Flanders. Finland is the only country where the provincial flags, which display the livery colours, consist of very long pennants.

The flags of the Japanese prefectures are modest yet very distinctive: their chief characteristic is their uniformity of style. Nearly all of them display a *mon* or logo in the centre of a unicoloured field, often an

Former flag of the Thai Province of Nonthaburi

PROVINCES OF BELGIUM

Antwerp.

East Flanders.

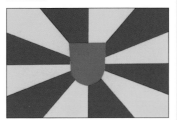

West Flanders.

PENNANTS OF THE PROVINCES OF FINLAND

Uusimaa
Ruotsinkielinen Uusimaa
Varsinais-Suomi/
Ruotsinkielinen Pohjanmaa
Häme
Etelä-Pohjanmaa
Kainuu

Ahvenanmaa
Satakunta
Karjala

Savo
Keski-Pohjanmaa
Varsinais-Suomi

Pohjois-Pohjanmaa

Kymenlaakso
Lappi

Siniristi (koko Suomen
yleisviiri)
Keski-Suomi
Etelä-Karjala

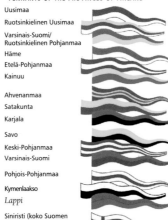

PREFECTURES OF JAPAN

Hokkaido.

Toyama.

Tokio.

unusual colour such as dark brown, rust brown, plum, lavender, violet or turquoise green. These flags were adopted after World War II, mostly in the 1960s. The colourful provincial flags of Papua New Guinea, adopted in 1978–1979, are very different. Although they do not display traditional heraldic figures, their appearance resembles armorial banners. Most of the emblems contain local birds or animals, insignias of authority, leadership and bravery, or artefacts used during ceremonies.

Province of Mindoro Occidental, Philippines

East New Britain.

Madang.

Simbu.

Provincial flags in other countries are either standardized, as in the Philippines and Thailand (changed in 2003), or display common emblems or colours. Provincial flags in Morocco were for several decades

PROVINCES OF MOROCCO

Casablanca.

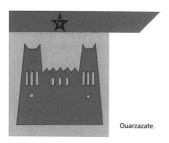

Ouarzazate.

UNITED STATES COUNTIES

Franklin (Illinois).

square armorial banners with a *schwenkel* in the national colours (the arms of the provinces were established in 1968). Provincial flags in Liberia have the national flag in the canton, while those in the Philippines display the seal of the province in the centre of a unicolour white, yellow or red field. The field of almost all the provincial flags in Venezuela is white and all of them are defaced with the coat of arms of the province. The only exception is the flag of Sucre, which is a diagonal bicolour of white and blue with 14 white stars in the lower hoist and the provincial coat of arms in the upper hoist. Until recently flags of all Thai provinces have used the national flag with a circular emblem of the province in the centre. The flags of some Argentinian provinces display the national colours of light blue and white.

The most diversified provincial flags are those of the United States. Most consist of a plain field embossed with the state's seal and the symbol of authority, and in many the field is also charged with inscriptions such as the name of the state and the date of

its foundation or incorporation. There are a multitude of designs based on partitions of the field and displaying various emblems, and some of them are very innovative.

France has recently developed a series of flags that are unsuccessful from a vexillological perspective. The departments and regions, which as we have already seen have beautiful armorial banners, have also adopted white flags charged with logos in shapes and colours that are difficult to recognize from a distance. In most cases the logos are accompanied by long, illegible inscriptions. This, of course, means that it is difficult to recognize and distinguish between the flags when in use.

Nord-Pas-de-Calais. Typical example of new French regional and departmental flags.

Santa Clara (California).

Sussex (New Jersey).

CIVIC FLAGS

In several European countries there is a general design for municipal flags. In Switzerland they are all square armorial banners. In Portugal they are square, gyronny and defaced with the full achievement of the civic arms. In Slovenia all the municipal flags have the proportions 1:3 and display the main heraldic figure from the coat of arms; the field is either plain or partitioned in one of ten different ways; seven have a square field at the hoist.

Slovakia is the only European country where the flags of all 135 cities and towns were established centrally by the Heraldry Commission of the Ministry of Internal Affairs. The flags are swallow-tailed, in proportions 2:3, and display the livery colours. 105 of the flags are composed solely of two to nine horizontal stripes, ten have fields charged with a saltire and ten are quartered. The flags of rural communities are triple swallow-tailed and also display the livery colours.

In Italy and Spain municipal flags are more diverse. Some designs, however, are more frequently used than others and are characteristic of the country, namely a

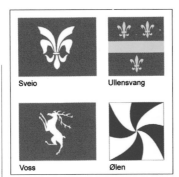

Sveio   Ullensvang

Voss   Ølen

vertical bicolour or a field charged with a cross in Italy and a plain field charged with a coat of arms in Spain. The use of a civic flag in the form of a gonfalon has survived in many Italian cities.

Municipal flags in Germany, Austria, the Czech Republic and Poland have several common characteristics. Most of them are horizontal bicolours or tricolours, they display livery colours and are often defaced with an armorial shield or the full achievement of arms. In West Germany just over 100 cities use the white-red bicolour, whereas the red-white bicolour has been adopted by more than 130 cities. Other bicolours are very popular there: blue-white (almost 90 cities), blue-yellow (65 cities), red-yellow (more than 60 cities) and black-

Lviv.

Kovel.

yellow (more than 50 cities). Much more inventive, distinctive and recognizable flags have been designed in recent years in Poland, the Czech Republic and the eastern part of Germany. The trend is to introduce more ingenious partitions of the field and to display some heraldic devices from the arms instead of the whole coat of arms. Ukrainian cities have begun to acquire municipal flags only in recent years and fewer than a quarter of the 1500 cities have their own flags. They are usually

▲ ABOVE Typical examples of flags of the communes in Hordaland (Norway).

▲ ABOVE RIGHT Two typical Ukrainian municipal flags.

◀ LEFT Ceremonial flag of Rome, at the town hall.

▶ RIGHT Polish municipal flags.

Bari.   Ancona (Italy).

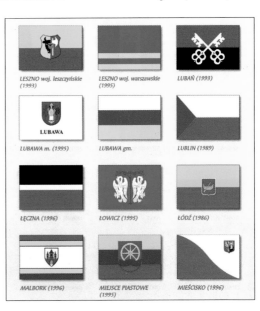

LESZNO woj. leszczyńskie (1993)

LESZNO woj. warszawskie (1995)

LUBAŃ (1993)

LUBAWA m. (1995)

LUBAWA gm.

LUBLIN (1989)

ŁĘCZNA (1996)

ŁOWICZ (1995)

ŁÓDŹ (1986)

MALBORK (1996)

MIEJSCE PIASTOWE (1995)

MIEŚCISKO (1996)

Millville (New Jersey).

Chicago (Illinois).

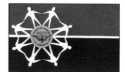

Kettering (Ohio).

Lubbock (Texas).

Memphis (Tennessee).

Milwaukee (Wisconsin).

Pittsburgh (Pennsylvania).

New York.

Amsterdam (Holland).

Barcelona (Spain).

Bergen (Norway).

Warsaw (Poland), Prague (Czech Republic)

City of London (United Kingdom).

Paris (France).

St Petersburg (Russia).

▲ *ABOVE* (top two rows) *United States city flags; (bottom two rows) European city flags.*

square, mostly charged with the civic coat of arms and with a decorative border. Official flags are mounted on staffs with a traverse bar.

Heraldry has very much influenced the municipal flags of Norway, Sweden, Great Britain, Finland, Belgium and the Netherlands. In the Netherlands almost all of more than 800 municipalities have their own flags. Over 20 per cent of them are composed only of several stripes (up to 13), in most cases horizontal, in some vertical or diagonal. The designs of the other flags are distinctive and very recognizable, with extensive use of livery colours and the main armorial figures instead of the full arms. Some of the most beautiful municipal flags have been created in South Africa since the 1960s. There are armorial banners, flags with the armorial shield or full achievement of arms, or flags displaying one or a few heraldic figures from the civic arms. Heraldry has also greatly influenced the design of municipal flags in many countries of the Commonwealth, mainly Canada and Australia. In the countries

of Latin America most municipal flags display the whole achievement of the civic coat of arms.

In the United States the most common design of a municipal flag is a plain field, in most cases blue, defaced with the civic seal. The second characteristic is an extensive use of lettering spelling out the city's name, the date of its foundation or incorporation, its locality in a state or county, and its nickname or motto. Some flags have graphic symbols with a written explanation

Flags of contrade in Siena.

underneath. As one vexillologist remarked, too many American flags are "literally littered by lettering". There is also a multitude of designs based on both traditional and unusual partitions of the field. The emblems are sometimes so intricate that they are imperceptible when the flag is flying; others are simple, modern and very distinctive. Many newer municipal flags as well as some older flags are excellent examples of ingenious flag design.

Some European cities have different flags for each district. The best known are the colourful flags of the *contrade* in Siena, in Italy, which date back to the beginning of the 13th century. Each *contrada* has its own mayor assisted by councillors. There have been 17 *contrade* since the end of the 17th century. Each *contrada* has its own colours, usually forming an intricate pattern, and an emblem that corresponds to the name of the district (for example, eagle, dragon, giraffe, owl, porcupine, unicorn, panther, and so on). These colours and emblems are used on the square flags which resemble armorial banners.

Flags of Peoples and Causes

Since time immemorial people have been eager to show their colours. In fact there was almost no mutiny, rebellion or defiance movement without its distinctive flag. Since the end of the first half of the 19th century, nations subjugated by world powers began to adopt their own flags. At first there were flags of nations living under the Austro-Hungarian, and then under Prussian or Russian rule. This trend continues, and today several dozen nations without statehood use their flags to denote either their identity or an aspiration to have their own state.

The 20th century witnessed the adoption of flags by political parties and fighters for freedom and independence. The flag of a political movement became the national

flag for the first time when the Nazi flag became Germany's national flag. The Nazis were also the first political movement to treat the flag as a political weapon. The use of flags during parades and rallies created an aura of might and invincibility; a tactic that was later copied by the Soviet Union and China.

Many current flags are closely associated with politics and the struggle for independence. Whether the flag belongs to the Albanians in Kosovo or the Palestinians, it manifests their defiance and aspirations.

▲ **ABOVE** *A demonstrator seen through an Albanian flag in Kosovo, March 1998.*
◄ **LEFT** *Palestinian youths armed with a flag and stones approach Israeli soldiers on the West Bank, March 1988.*
► **RIGHT** *Hoisting a giant flag to celebrate the anniversary of the liberation of Ho Chi Minh City, Vietnam.*

NATIONS AND ETHNIC GROUPS

National flags for nations and ethnic or cultural entities without statehood first appeared in North America, where ethnic diversity is greatest. In the United States there are 558 federally recognized Native American nations and tribes. Twenty years ago very few had their own flags but there are currently about 180 tribal flags. Two acts passed by the Federal Government spurred the creation of flags: the United States Self-Determination and Education Assistance Act (1975) and the United States Indian Gaming Regulatory Act (1988) which allowed Native Americans to use gaming and tribal casinos as an economic resource.

The Arapahos in Wyoming adopted a flag during World War II and modified it in 1956. Red stands for the Arapahos, white for long life, black for happiness. Eleven Sioux tribes living in South Dakota have a

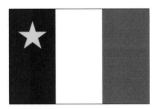

Acadians in Canada.

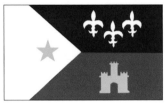

Acadians in Louisiana.

Arapaho.

Crow Tribe.

United Sioux Tribes.

common white flag. The number of tepees represents the number of tribes, and the arrowheads in the central emblem symbolize the four compass directions, the four seasons and the four natural elements. One of the most distinctive flags, designed in 1967, belongs to the Crows who live in Montana. The tepee symbolizes the home and its four poles represent the original treaty area agreed with the United States Government in 1868. They also stand for the four directions and the four seasons, i.e. for the limits or framework within which life takes place. The flag depicted here has the old seal; in the new one the white star and the stars of the Big Dipper (the Plough) constellation are omitted.

The flag of the Acadians who live in Canada, mainly in northern New Brunswick, was adopted in 1884. It is the French Tricolore with a yellow star, symbol of the Virgin Mary, and symbolizes the Acadians' fidelity to their origins and their faith. The flag of the Acadians in Louisiana was adopted in 1965 when they celebrated the 200th anniversary of their arrival there. It symbolizes their French origins (three fleurs-de-lis on blue) and the Spanish rule over Louisiana at the time of their migration (yellow castle on red). The yellow star symbolizes the Virgin Mary as Our

Lady of Assumption, their patroness, and also commemorates the Acadians' participation in the American Revolution.

African-Americans use the flag created in 1917 by the famous black activist Marcus Garvey for a new homeland for American blacks in Africa. Irish-Americans prefer to use a flag specially designed for them rather than the national flag of Ireland. It is based on the flags of the 1798 rebellion and the Irish motto *Erin go bragh*, meaning "Ireland for ever".

Many nations without statehood live in Europe. Some of them use flags that have become the flags of the regions. For their national flags the Basques, Catalonians and Galicians use the flags of autonomous communities in Spain, while the flags of the

Afro-Americans.

Irish-Americans.

Flamands and Wallons have become the flags of regions in Belgium. The Alsatians are descendants of Germanized peoples of Celtic origin, and those who are striving for a greater degree of autonomy use a red-white horizontal bicolour. The Breton flag displays an ermine canton and nine horizontal stripes. The ermine has been the arms of Brittany since the 12th century, the five black stripes represent the dioceses of the French language, and the four white stripes stand for the dioceses of the Breton language. The Cornish flag is black with the white cross of St Piran, patron saint of Cornwall, and dates back to the beginning of the 15th century.

One of the oldest national flags is a white flag with a Moor's head, an armorial banner of Corsica dating back to at least the 14th century. It is still used by those Corsicans who have never reconciled themselves to French rule over their island. The emblem of the Crimean Tatars, *tarak tamga*, appears in the upper hoist of the field of their flag which is light blue, the national colour common to all Turkic peoples. Although the Kashubians have lived for many

Alsatians.

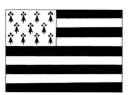

Bretons.

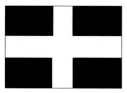

Cornish.

Corsicans.

Crimea Tatars.

Gypsies.

centuries under German rule, they have preserved both their language and the consciousness that they are part of the Polish nation. Their flag displays the colours of the coat of arms of the duchy of Kashubia (black griffin on gold), not as a sign of separatism but to show their identity as an ethnic group with their own language, tradition and culture.

Normandy displays two flags: heraldic and modern. The armorial banner with two golden lions (one above the other) on a red field originated in the 12th century. The Scandinavian cross on the modern flag denotes that they are the descendants of people from Scandinavia (via the Vikings). Gypsies, or Romanies, were originally

Kashubians.

Normans.

nomadic people from India and by the end of the 16th century were living in many European countries. Their flag, not adopted until the 1970s, reflects the fact that the wheel enabled them to move freely on wide green plains under the blue sky. The wheel takes different shapes. One of the newest national flags is that adopted in 1986 by the Samis, or Lapps. For thousands of years these people lived in areas of northern Europe that now belong to Norway, Sweden, Finland and Russia. In 1956 they set up the Nordic Sami Conference, which in 1983 proclaimed the Land of Sami across international borders where they want to preserve their common language, history, traditions, culture and way of life.

Sami.

Scots.

The Scottish blue flag with a white St Andrew's cross is one of the oldest national flags in the world but the Scots prefer to use the Royal Banner of Scotland and some Scots living in the United States recognize the banner with the tressured lion as their national flag. The triskelion, an ancient emblem of Sicily known at least from the 4th century BC, is composed of three bare legs and the face of a Gorgon. It appears on the flag used by the Sicilians since 1990 as their unofficial regional flag. In 1848 the Sorbs adopted a flag in pan-Slavic colours: the blue stands for the sky, the red for love and the white for innocence. The Sorbs are the descendants of the Wends, a Slavic people who in the Middle Ages occupied large areas of the eastern part of Germany. Today they predominantly live in Lusatia.

Sicilians.

Sorbs.

In 1950 the Amboinese proclaimed an abortive independent state, the Republic of South Moluccas. Although it was suppressed by the Indonesian army, their use of the national flag manifested their will to be free. The red is the colour of their traditional dress and a symbol of courage; the blue is the sea and its riches; the white represents the beaches, a symbol of purity; the green represents the fertility of the land.

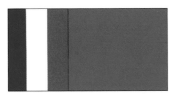

Amboinese

The flag of the Balkars, a Turkic people living in the Caucasus Mountains, was adopted in 1993 and displays the Turkic light blue and a silhouette of Mount Elbrus. The white stands for purity; the upper white stripe symbolizes the heavenly and spiritual attitude of the nation, and the lower stripe stands for their way of life.

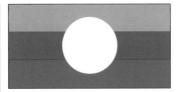

Shans.

Kurds.

Kachins.

Despite the numerous uprisings and promises by world powers that they will have their own state the Kurds, who live mainly in Iran, Iraq and Turkey, are the largest nation in the world still without statehood. Their flag displays the colours of the Iranian flag with a yellow sun in the centre. According to some sources there is also another Kurdish flag: a horizontal tricolour of red, yellow and green. There are several nationalities in Myanmar (formerly Burma) who are struggling to create separate states, among them the Arakans, Kachins, Karens, Mons and Shans. (The Arakans and the Mons in the past formed several kingdoms which existed until the 1700s.) The red and green of the Kachin flag stand for courage and the land respectively, and the crossed native swords represent the love of the homeland and the will to defend it. The flags of at least two liberation movements and parties are used by the people. The ochre in the Shan flag is the colour of the saffron robes of Buddhist monks, testifying that Buddhism

Balkars.

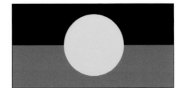

Australian Aborigines.

Kanaks.

is the national religion; the green stands for the land and for agriculture; the red denotes the Shans' bravery, and the white disc of the moon symbolizes their love of peace and their willingness to co-exist peacefully.

The Australian aborigines adopted their flag in 1971 but it was only decreed as their official flag in 1995. The black represents the aborigines, whose ancestors have lived in Australia for more than 40,000 years; the red stands for the earth and for the blood spilled by aboriginal people in defence of their land; and the yellow disc symbolizes the life-giving sun. The flag of the Kanaks, a people native to New Caledonia and striving for independence from France, was introduced in 1984. The colours are significant: the blue symbolizes the sky, perfection and sovereignty; the red stands for blood and the equality of all races; the green represents the land, and the yellow disc symbolizes the sun. The silhouette of an ornamented spire symbolizes tradition.

RELIGIOUS FLAGS

Out of the main religions of the world only one has its own flag, which is used wherever the faithful congregate. It is the Buddhist flag, adopted in 1950 as the internationally recognized flag of all Buddhists of the world. Its five colours represent the five auras that emanated from the Buddha when he was in the Gem Chamber in the fourth week of his enlightenment. According to Buddhist belief, the blue is the colour of the Buddha's hair, the yellow stands for all impure secretions of the human body, the red for blood, the white for bones and for purity of words and deeds, and the orange for those parts of the body that are orange.

Of the many Christian denominations only a few have flags. There is no Catholic flag, but the yellow and white of the Holy See and the white and blue of the Virgin Mary are used to decorate churches at festivals. In the United States a fringed flag

of the Vatican City is used in Catholic churches and a fringed flag of the State of Israel in synagogues; there is also a Christian flag, designed in 1897 for use in Protestant churches. Some Protestant churches do have their own flags: the flag of the Episcopal Church is white with a red cross of St George and a blue canton with nine white crosses in saltire. Since 1938, Church of England churches have displayed a white flag with the red cross of St George and, in the canton, the arms of the see to which the particular church belongs.

In the United States and Great Britain there are church pennants to indicate that a ship's company is engaged in divine service. These date back to the Anglo-Dutch wars and were used to indicate a truce so that services could be performed at sea. In Catholic countries there is a multitude of banners designed to be carried in processions and displayed during

religious holidays. They are mostly pictorial in character, bearing painted or embroidered representations of the Virgin Mary, the Trinity or various saints.

The Muslims have mostly unicoloured flags, usually green, with religious inscriptions and simple emblems such as a crescent or the hand of Fatima. There are reports that in some countries the adherents of the Ismaili sect have a green flag with a red bend. The Sikhs, who live mainly in the Indian state of Punjab have their own flag, although some reports consider this an ethnic rather than a religious flag. It is a triangular saffron (orange) flag with a black traditional Sikh emblem consisting of a ring, two crossed daggers and a spear.

Christian flag.

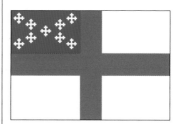

Episcopal church.

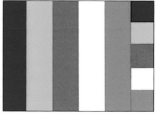

Buddhist flag.

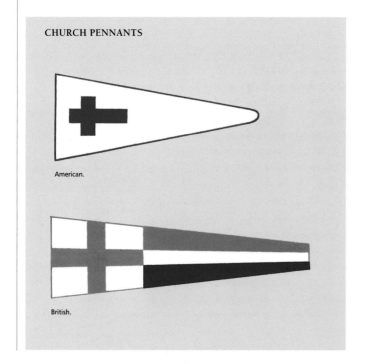

CHURCH PENNANTS

American.

British.

FLAGS OF REVOLT AND DEFIANCE

Throughout the course of history social and political upheavals, rebellions and revolutions have always been carried out under a flag. Some of these flags influenced the design of national flags and a few eventually became national symbols; many more were carried by rebels who did not succeed in their struggle. Their emblems were either symbols familiar to the rebels or new symbols created to convey their ideas. For example, at the end of the 15th century German peasants rebelled under a white pennant with the emblem of a golden peasant shoe, *Bundschuh*, which in contrast with the boots worn by the nobility was a symbol of peasantry. The Bundschuh Rebellion flared up several times until 1525, when it was finally suppressed.

The taxation imposed by the British on the American colonists was met by defiance and led in 1765 to the foundation of the Sons of Liberty, a secret patriotic and radical society that was involved in the Boston Massacre (1770) and the Boston Tea Party (1773). Their flag displayed nine red and white stripes, symbolizing the nine colonies that participated in the Stamp Act Congress of 1765. The stripes in the national flag of the United States may well stem from this defiant flag.

Bundschuh pennant.

Polish peasants with their scythes upright played an important role in the Kosciuszko Insurrection of 1794. In the battles against Russsia they carried a red standard with the motto "Feeding and Defending" above weapons crossed behind a wheatsheaf. In the first half of the 19th century there were numerous kingdoms and principalities in the territory of modern-day Germany. Inspired by the French Revolution of 1830, the students from some of these German states began to agitate for unification. They adopted a flag with three horizontal stripes in the colours of the uniforms of the *Lützow Freikorps* and the inscription *Deutschlands Wiedergeburt* (Rebirth of Germany). Without the inscription, this flag became the national flag of Germany in 1848.

Australia's most famous rebellion was that of the miners of the Ballart goldfields in Victoria in 1854 against the imposition of licence fees. They raised a blue flag with a white cross bearing the five stars of the Southern Cross constellation. A few days later the flag was raised again by a group of diggers at the Eureka Stockade, who took an oath, "We swear by the Southern Cross to stand truly by each other, and to fight to defend our rights and liberties". The stockade was overwhelmed by the police, but the Eureka flag became a symbol of independence and liberty, and inspired the design of the Australian national flag.

The newest addition to the flags of defiance and rebellion was that of the *Solidarnosc* (Solidarity) movement in Poland. In the first days of the famous strike at the Gdansk shipyard a young artist created a logo in which he spelt the name of the movement in such a way that the letters resembled people marching close together under the Polish national flag. Since then a white flag with this logo has been the symbol of opposition against communist rule, and in a free Poland remains the flag of the trades unions. In two known instances people in revolt did not need to adopt a new flag, it was enough to cut out the communist state emblem from the flag to show what they stood for. The first instance was during the Hungarian uprising of 1956, and in 1989 a flag with a hole in it was again carried in street battles in Romanian cities.

Flag of the Sons of Liberty.

Banner of Polish peasants participating in the Insurrection of 1794.

Flag carried by advocates of the unification of Germany in the Hambach Festival of 1832.

Flag of the Eureka Stockade, Australia (1854).

Flag of Solidarnosc (Solidarity) since 1980.

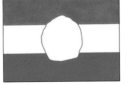

Flag of the Hungarian uprising (October to November 1956).

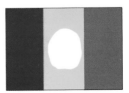

Flag of the Romanian uprising (1989).

Flag of the Federal Republic of Padania, an Italian state that does not officially exist.

FLAGS OF GUERRILLA MOVEMENTS

Vietkong.

Sandinistas.

Eritrean People's Liberation Front.

The Tigre Liberation Front.

The Western Somali Liberation Front.

SWAPO (South West African People's Organization).

MPLA (Movimento Popular da Libertação de Angola).

UNITA (União Nacional para a Independência Total de Angola).

FNLA (Frente Nacional para a Libertação de Angola).

FRELIMO (Frente da Libertação de Moçambique).

RENAMO (Resistencia Nacional Moçambicana).

Kurdistan Workers' Party.

In Italy a peaceful struggle to create a new state of Padania is led by the Northern League, formed in 1984. The Federal Republic of Padania was proclaimed on 15 September 1986 in Venice, but formally does not exist. Nevertheless the flag of Padania with a green "Sun of the Alps" is carried during demonstrations in favour of the new state.

Since the 1960s in various parts of the world, mainly in Africa and Asia, armed insurrections have aimed to achieve independence or to impose a communist regime. The best known are the communist guerrillas of Vietkong in Vietnam and the Sandinistas in Nicaragua. The struggle for independence in Angola was conducted by the MPLA (People's Movement for the Liberation of Angola); the FNLA (National Front of the Liberation of Angola) and the UNITA (National Union for the Total Independence of Angola). In Mozambique the struggle for independence has been conducted by two movements hostile to each other. The stronger one was the FRELIMO (Front for the Liberation of Mozambique) and its flag, adopted in 1962, displayed the pan-African colours. The other was the RENAMO (Mozambican National Resistance), which rejected both communist and fascist ideologies. The colours of their flag, adopted in 1977, symbolized the nation (blue) and the struggle for independence (red). The field was charged with RENAMO's seal. The Kurdistan Workers' Party is the main political and military force of Kurds fighting for their own state.

For more than a decade its flag has been seen in many cities of Europe during demonstrations for a free Kurdistan.

Two famous rebel flags are still in use. The "Jolly Roger" pirate flag is usually black with images such as a skull and crossbones, or skeletons with a scythe or hourglass. Some people claim that "Jolly Roger" is a corruption of the French *jolie rouge* and in fact the flags of pirates from the Barbary states were red. The jack of the Confederate Navy, used from 1863 to 1865, is also known as the rebel flag. It is still revered by some people and groups as a symbol of southern states' rights.

The Jolly Roger.

The rebel flag.

FLAGS IN POLITICS

Since late medieval times certain colours have had particular meanings. In Europe white was connected with purity and nobility. Red was originally the colour of empire and royalty but later became the colour of defiance, mutiny and revolution. The combination of red and black is used mainly by anarchosyndicalists. White was adopted by Francis I of France (reigned 1515–1547) and became increasingly popular as the colour of royalty, perceived as such since the 18th century, and today it is the main colour of royalist movements. Black is used on African flags to represent the country and the people. The colour can also have a dual symbolism, being the colour of mourning as well as defiance of law and order. Black flags were used by

Monarchists.

Anarchists.

Socialists.

Anarchosyndicalists.

FLAGS OF NATIONALIST MOVEMENTS

NSDAP 1920–1945. Nationalsozialistische Deutsche Arbeitspartei.

Sudeten German Party.

Arrow Cross.

Fronte della Gioventú.

Afrikaner Resistance Movement.

Yedinstvo, Russian National Unity.

Flemish National Union.

Hlinka Guard.

Rikshird.

Freie Arbeitspartei.

Afrikaans Student Federation.

National Bolshevik Party, Russia.

mutineers and pirates, and today they are the flags of anarchists and are often seen at protests. Many anarchists place a large white letter "A" in a ring on the black flag. Red flags were displayed as a sign of defiance as early as the 17th century. Sailors demanding better pay and working conditions hoisted them during mutinies at Portsmouth, England, in 1797 and at St Petersburg, Russia, in 1905. The same flag was used by the revolutionaries in France in 1830, 1848 and 1870, and since the Paris Commune (1871) it has been regarded as a socialist symbol, adopted in the 1920s by the communists in Russia. At the other end of the spectrum, it was also adopted by the Nazis in Germany.

The flag of the NSDAP (*Nationalsozialistische Deutsche Arbeitspartei*) was designed personally by Adolf Hitler, who combined the socialist red with two other colours of pre-war Germany. A white disc charged with a black swastika became the symbol used by foreign Nazis. The flag used by the Imperial Fascist League in Britain from 1933 to 1940 had the white disc and swastika in the centre of the Union Jack. The *Parti National Social Chrétien*, founded in Montreal, from 1933 to 1938 had a blue flag charged with a red swastika on the white disc. The flag of the NSDAP also served as a model for emblems adopted by nationalist movements in several countries, during Hitler's lifetime and afterwards. The flags shown opposite were used by the Flemish National Union in the Netherlands, the Sudeten German Party in Czechoslovakia, the Hlinka Guard in

FLAGS OF COMMUNIST PARTIES

Ethiopian Workers' Party.

People's Democratic Party of Afghanistan (1980–1992).

Revolutionary Party of Benin.

FRELIMO (since 1983).

Slovakia, the Arrow Cross in Hungary and the Rikshird in Norway; those currently in use belong to the Freie Arbeitspartei in Germany, two organizations in South Africa and two in Russia. One of the emblems, a black Celtic cross on a white disc, became the international symbol of young nationalists in several European countries. It is placed in the centre of a red field, as in the flag of the Italian *Fronte della Gioventú*.

The Soviet Union was a one-party state so the communists had no need to adopt a special flag. The red flag with a star and crossed hammer and sickle served all purposes and became a model for the flags of communist parties in many countries. Shown here are the flags of the Ethiopian

Workers' Party, FRELIMO (Mozambique) the Revolutionary Party of Benin, and the People's Democratic Party of Afghanistan in which the Soviet sickle has been replaced by a hoe. The fascist movements in Italy and Spain adopted emblems recalling the great past of their countries: the ancient Roman fasces and the yoke and arrows of the Catholic monarchs, respectively.

Many non-socialist political parties have flags displaying the national colours and often charged with the party initials. In Europe and the Middle East party flags display abstract emblems; in Africa and Asia they are charged with simple devices, mainly stylized animals such as an elephant or cockerel to symbolize strength, courage and perseverance.

Featured here is the flag of the National League for Democracy of Aung San Suu Kyi, who leads the struggle for democracy in Myanmar and was awarded the Nobel Peace Prize, one out of the hundreds of flags used by political parties in Asia. The flag combines elements of the flag of the Anti-Fascist Resistance Movement (red flag with a white star) with a peacock, the traditional Burmese emblem.

Socialist party of Belgium

National League for Democracy (Myanmar)

House and Private Flags

Most of these flags were introduced in the 19th century; indeed, many of them were introduced in the last half century. The most numerous are yacht and private flags, but there is a steadily growing number of house flags for shipping and trade companies, and all kinds of commercial firms. Tens of thousands of schools, universities, associations and clubs also have their own flags.

▼ **BELOW** *Flags of shipping companies of North and South America in 1933. Plate from* Lloyd Reederei-Flaggen der Welt-Handelsflotte, *Bremen.*

COMMERCE AND BUSINESS

In the Middle Ages guilds and livery companies had their own banners, used during festivities and in battle. Some of the emblems they adopted, particularly in European countries, represented their trade or occupation: a pretzel represented the bakers; scissors, the tailors; a candle, the candle-makers; a key or keys, the locksmiths; an anchor, the boatmen; and a boot or shoe, the shoemakers.

The first commercial flags were those of the English trading companies, used at the end of the 16th century. The most famous and long-lasting was the East India Company (established 1600), followed by its great rival the Dutch East India Company (established 1602). There was also the Dutch West India Company from 1621 to 1794, which established several

Smith's guild, Strasbourg (15th century).

Smith's guild, Basel (15th century).

colonies in the West Indies and Guiana. To distinguish them, their ensigns used national emblems, the English cross of St George and the Dutch horizontal tricolour. The Dutch ensigns differed only in their initials: "VOC" for the *Vereenigde Oostindische Compagnie* and "GWC" for the *Geoctroyeerde West Indische Compagnie*. A "C" above the

"VOC" stood for Capetown. The flags of the six chambers of the Dutch East India Company displayed stripes in different colours, with the initials "VOC" and an additional letter above it: "A" stood for Amsterdam; "D" for Delft; "E" for Enkhuizen; "H" for Hoorn; "M" for Middleburg, and "R" for Rotterdam. The Danish East India Company and the

Ensign of the British East India Company (c.1616–1707).

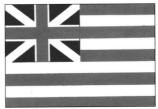

Ensign of the British East India Company (1707–1801).

Ensign of the British East India Company (1801–1873).

Ensign of the Dutch East India Company.

Ensign of the Dutch West India Company.

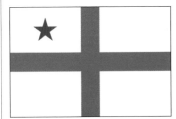

Italiana Trasporti Maritimi.

Black Star Line.

BP tanker company.

HSBC, previously the Midland Bank, house flag.

P&O house flag.

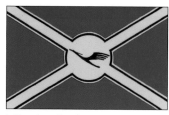

Lufthansa house flag.

Spanish Philippine Company had their own flags based on the national flag. The modern house flags of trade and shipping companies originated at the end of the 18th century. These do not use national flags as a pattern, but sometimes adopt the national colours of their home countries. A rare exception was the flag of the Hudson's Bay Company, which from the 1820s used the British red ensign with the white letters "HBC" in the fly. Since the 19th century each shipping company has had its own house flag, which identifies the company to which a ship belongs. This flag or its emblem is also usually painted on the ship's funnel. The most common characteristics of house flags are simple partitions of the field, and extensive use of initials and simple emblems. One of the simplest yet most distinctive designs for a house flag is that of P&O (Peninsular and Oriental Steam Navigation Company), which became its logo and is used on its land vehicles.

The house flags of the shipping companies inspired other commercial firms to adopt their own flags. Among the numerous airline flags, the most distinctive and attractive are (or were) those of Lufthansa, Air France, Sabena, BEA, Swissair and Qantas. Even better known are the flags of oil companies such as Shell, BP, Mobil, Texaco and Statoil, which are displayed at every filling station. Other examples of corporation flags are those of hotel chains (Hilton, Marriott, Sheraton and Holiday Inn), fast food franchises (McDonald's,

Denny's and Burger King) and car manufacturers (Volkswagen, Mercedes, Volvo, Chrysler, Ford and GM). Some corporations conduct business under different names and different flags (for example, Exxon in America, Esso in Europe). Others use flags in different colour variation, for example, Volkswagen uses a white flag with its logo in blue and a blue flag with the logo in white.

The best house flags have simple designs and distinctive features, making them easy to recognize. The general characteristic of a corporate flag is a plain-colour field with a simple corporate logo in the centre. If the logo is very simple, large and has a distinctive shape it is easy to identify from a distance, but unfortunately there is a multitude of flags with intricate emblems and a lot of lettering. As most of the fields are white, hundreds of house flags look alike and are unsuitable for outdoor use because they lack the important characteristic of distinctiveness.

Esso.

Getty oil company.

Statoil.

Volkswagen.

Sheraton.

ORGANIZATIONAL AND PRIVATE FLAGS

Salvation Army.

World Scouting.

Federation of European Scouting.

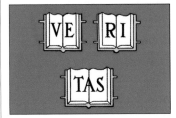

Harvard University.

The Smithsonian Institute.

The College of Europe.

In the early 19th century many European countries set up clubs to promote national consciousness, for example gymnastic clubs in the Slavic countries run by Sokol (Falcon), students' corporations and choral clubs. Each of these clubs adopted its own flag or banner which was designed in the artistic spirit of the time. This trend became much stronger in the 20th century and flags and banners were adopted by youth, social and charitable organizations, scientific associations, clubs, schools, universities and even local fire brigades. Two examples of such flags are those of World Scouting and the Federation of European Scouting (FSE); both flags display the fleur-de-lis which is universally recognized as the scout symbol.

Universities and scientific institutions often adopt armorial banners. Their second choice is a unicoloured field defaced with a coat of arms, armorial shield or emblem. The armorial banners of Harvard University and the Smithsonian Institute show that not all flags in the United States display seals combined with lettering. The flag of the College of Europe bears a simple emblem composed of the letters "B" for Bruges, where the school is located, and "E" for Europe; the colours correspond to those of the flag of the European Union.

National colours are also displayed on the flags of vexillological associations. Just two elements – the national colours and the letter "V" (vexillology) – can create many different and distinctive designs. The

Italians made "V" part of their emblem, while the Bretons combined two "V"s (*Vannielouriezh Vreizh* – Breton Vexillological) in a saltire. In the Polish flag the partition line forms "W" for *weksylologia* (vexillology in Polish). The red saltire in the flag of the Belgian association recalls the cross of Burgundy and the yellow "V" stands for "vexillology". The Swiss vexillologists settled for an entirely different design, which resembles the Swiss military flags.

Flags of organizations are quite recent but personal flags have been in use since the beginning of the heraldic era. For example, in Great Britain the armorial banner of the Spencer family was established in 1476 and, before her marriage to Prince Charles, Lady

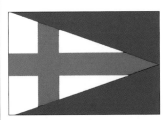

Flag Institute (Great Britain).

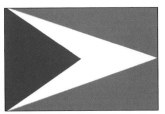

Vexilologicky Klub (Czech Republic).

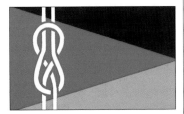

Deutsche Gesellschaft für Flaggenkunde (Germany).

FLAGS OF VEXILLOLOGICAL ASSOCIATIONS

Centro Italiano Studi Vessillologici (Italy).

Societas Vexillologica Belgica (Belgium).

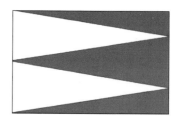

Polskie Towarzystwo Weksylologiczne (Poland).

North American Vexillological Association (USA and Canada).

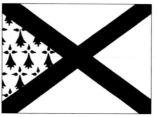

Kevarzhe Vannielouriezh Vreizh (Brittany).

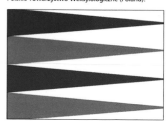

Nederlandse Vereniging voor Vlaggenkunde (the Netherlands).

Sociedad Española de Vexilología (Spain).

Société Suisse de Vexillologie (Switzerland).

Diana Spencer was entitled to use it. The Spencer arms also appeared in the second and third quarters of the banner of Winston Churchill, who inherited them through the dukes of Marlborough. Many modern personal flags have also been designed by famous artists. In some countries there are festivities for hoisting private flags.

Two historic venues in Great Britain permanently display the armorial banners

of the knights of two important orders. The banners of the Knights Grand Cross of the Most Honourable Order of the Bath are in Westminster Abbey in London. These are the Royal Banner, the Banner of the Prince of Wales, Great Master of the Order, and the banners of 33 knights. The armorial banners of the Knights of the Order of the Garter are displayed in the Choir of St George's Chapel in Windsor Castle.

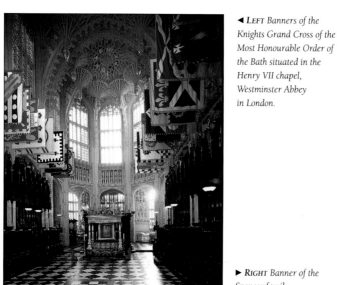

◄ *LEFT Banners of the Knights Grand Cross of the Most Honourable Order of the Bath situated in the Henry VII chapel, Westminster Abbey in London.*

► *RIGHT Banner of the Spencer family.*

FLAGS IN SPORT

One of the oldest sports is shooting, and in the Middle Ages clubs for crossbowmen had their own flags. This tradition was taken over by rifle clubs, which still exist in many countries of Central Europe. In Great Britain cricket clubs, sailing clubs and rowing clubs have their own flags; the designs are usually based on simple field partitions and some display charges such as crosses, stars, three curved swords, a rampant horse, a rose, anchors or dolphins.

The first and best-known flag used in sport is that of the Olympic Games. It was designed in 1913 and was flown for the first time in public in Paris on the 20th anniversary of the foundation of the International Olympic Committee. The flag was first hoisted at the Olympics in Antwerp in 1920. The white stands for

Flag of Olympic Games.

peace and friendship between the competing nations, and the rings represent the five continents and denote the global character of the Olympic movement. During the opening ceremony a large Olympic flag is raised on a flagpole at the stadium and remains there during the Games. The athletes take the oath holding a corner of the Olympic flag and various forms of the flag are used during the opening and closing ceremonies. At the end of the 1992 Games in Barcelona the athletes held over their heads the largest Olympic flag ever made, 75 m (82 yd) wide and 105 m (115 yd) long.

The most widespread use of flags is by football (soccer) fans. After World War II many football clubs, mainly in communist countries, adopted flags but these were

rarely used and in most cases club regulations did not allow fans to use them. Instead the fans used homemade flags displaying the clubs' colours and even today in most countries flag manufacturers produce such flags, only rarely with the

club emblem. In the United States flag manufacturers produce different flags for the American football teams, with the clubs' colours in common. These flags all serve as a means of identification but in some sports special flags are used for marking and signalling. In many field games small unicoloured flags mark the corners or boundary line of the field and larger flags are used as markers to define the path in skiing events. In soccer the linesmen use two flags (red and yellow, one for each team) to signal to the referee a breach of the rules or that the ball has gone out of play. In car racing a black and white chequered flag is used to signal the end of the race.

Flag of the Redskins, Washington DC.

◀ **LEFT** *Banner of the Bavarian
Rifle Association.*

YACHT FLAGS

The first yacht club, the Water Club of the Harbour of Cork, was formed in 1720 in Ireland. Another two clubs (Starcross Yacht Club and Cumberland Fleet) were established in England in the 1770s, but the custom of flying yacht club burgees on the main masthead was not established until early in the 19th century when several dozen yacht clubs were established in Great Britain, and more than 20 in the United

US yacht ensign.

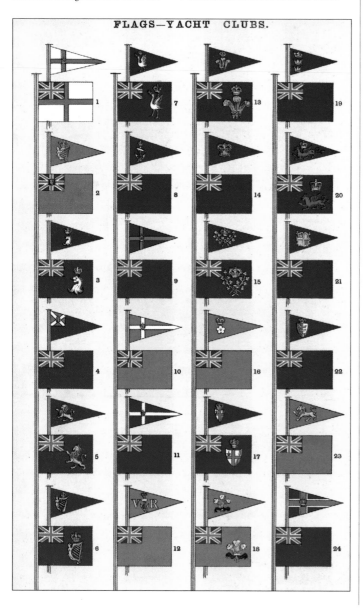

FLAGS—YACHT CLUBS.

States. Clubs were also established in many countries of the British Empire: Gibraltar, 1829; Canada, 1837; Tasmania,1838; Bermuda, 1844; India, 1846; Australia, 1853; South Africa, 1858; New Zealand, 1871; Malta, 1873. In Europe, clubs were established in: Sweden, 1830; France, 1838; Russia, 1846; Belgium and the Netherlands, 1847; Portugal, 1856; Denmark, 1866; Germany, 1868.

Four types of flags are used in yachting: (i) ensign, (ii) club burgee, (iii) flag of a yacht club officer and (iv) private flag. The ensign denotes nationality and in Great Britain most of the yacht clubs have the privilege to use either the British red ensign or the British blue ensign, either plain or defaced with the club emblem. In 1922 this privilege was enjoyed by 52 British yacht clubs and today by almost 100 clubs. The first national yacht ensign was adopted in the United States and was approved by the secretary of the Navy on 7 August 1848. It is the national flag but instead of the union with 50 stars it has a blue canton with a foul anchor encircled by 13 stars. Special yacht ensigns exist also in Belgium (civil ensign with the royal crown in the upper hoist), Spain (national flag with a blue royal crown in the centre), France (civil ensign with a white star in the centre of the blue stripe and a blue star on the white stripe) and Poland (civil ensign with a badge in the upper hoist). The Royal Yacht Club of Norway uses the war ensign with the club badge on a white square in the centre of the cross, and the ensign of the Royal Netherlands Yacht Club is the national flag with the badge in the centre.

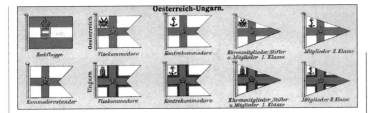

◀ LEFT *Yacht club flags, Austria and Hungary, 1913. (Top row): merchant flag, Austria: vice-commodore; rear commodore; honorary members, founders and 1st class members; 2nd class members. (Bottom row): commodore, Hungary: vice-commodore; rear commodore; honorary members, founders and 1st class members; 2nd class members.*

In some instances a yacht displays the undefaced war ensign. The first such privilege was granted in Great Britain in 1859 to the Royal Yacht Squadron, and in 1863 the Prussian government entitled members of its Royal House to use the war ensign on their yachts and pleasure vessels. Currently some Italian yacht clubs may also use the war ensign.

The club burgee represents the club of which the yacht's owner is a member. It is usually triangular, in a few instances rectangular or triangular swallow-tailed, and the proportions are 2:3. The burgee of

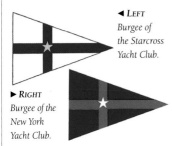

◀ LEFT
Burgee of the Starcross Yacht Club.

▶ RIGHT
Burgee of the New York Yacht Club.

the Starcross Yacht Club was a canting one, a yellow five-pointed star centred on a blue Cross of St George on a white field. Its design influenced the burgees of several clubs in Great Britain and the United States. A cross and saltire are still today the most popular charges but field partitions are rare; the emblems include crowns, stars, heraldic devices, nautical instruments, species of marine life and initials.

In a few countries officers of yacht clubs have flags, such as those used in the 19th century in Austria-Hungary. Today there are usually four flag officers: commodore, vice-commodore, rear commodore and fleet captain. In some clubs there are also flags for commodores and honorary commodores, as well as for the secretary and treasurer. In at least one instance (Great

Lakes Cruising Club of Chicago) there are distinctive flags for a fleet surgeon and a judge advocate. In the United Kingdom and some Commonwealth countries the flags of club officers are swallow-tailed, otherwise their design is generally the same as the club burgee. The flags of the vice-commodore and rear commodore are distinguished from the commodore's flag by one and two balls respectively in the upper hoist. In the United States the officers' flags have the design of the canton of the yacht ensign; the order of colours is the same as in the Navy.

The private flag represents an individual yacht owner and have their own distinctive style. It is rectangular, only rarely triangular or swallow-tailed. Private flags of yachtsmen are registered to avoid complications that might arise if they were used by more than one person.

In recent decades fun flags have appeared on yachts. They are especially popular in the United States, where they are used to advertise social activities on board such as a party, cocktails or beer. Other fun flags signify "Wife on Board", "19th Hole" or "Jolly Roger".

RANK FLAGS OF YACHT CLUBS IN THE UNITED STATES

Commodore.

Vice-commodore.

Rear commodore.

Fleet captain.

FUN FLAGS

Wife aboard.

Cocktail.

THE HISTORY AND APPLICATIONS OF HERALDRY

———

HERALDRY EMERGED AT A TIME WHEN FIGHTING MEN BECAME
UNRECOGNIZABLE – TO BOTH FRIEND AND ENEMY – INSIDE THEIR
SUITS OF ARMOUR. THE SOLUTION TO THE PROBLEM OF IDENTITY
LAY IN THE SHIELD, WHICH COULD BE DECORATED WITH A DESIGN
THAT WAS AS UNIQUE AS A FINGERPRINT AND VISIBLE FROM A
DISTANCE. AS ARMORIAL BEARINGS WERE HANDED DOWN FROM
ONE GENERATION TO THE NEXT, THEY CAME TO INDICATE
DESCENT AS WELL AS IDENTITY. FROM ITS FUNCTIONAL
BEGINNINGS, HERALDRY GREW INTO A SCIENCE OF HEREDITY,
WITH A SYSTEM OF LAWS TO REGULATE IT, AND A UNIQUE
LANGUAGE THAT MEANT THE VISUAL CODES COULD BE RECORDED
AND COMMUNICATED ACCURATELY.

◄ *A jousting scene from a medieval tournament*
shows how heraldry grew from the use of a simple
device on a shield to a means of decorating
clothing and horse trappings

THE ORIGINS AND DEVELOPMENT OF HERALDRY

Many theories have been put forward to account for the evolution and perfection of heraldry. Its birth coincided with changes in the nature of European society itself, which was becoming more sophisticated, with more and more estates passing from one generation to the next.

Throughout Europe, the general trend to migration that had characterized the Dark Ages had come to a halt. Family roots were now firmly bedded in, with the village settlement in place and, at its centre, the first two "estates": the priest, who prayed for all, and the knight or lord who fought for all. By the 13th century, the notion of gentility was firmly established among the lordly classes, who sought connections with similarly genteel families through marriage. The idea of a stable, ancient and exclusive bloodline was accentuated, and the development of the shield of arms created an ideal symbol to confirm the hereditary nature of that descent.

◀ *A medieval stained glass window showing the king of France bearing a shield of arms.*

THE BIRTH OF HERALDRY

The Bayeux Tapestry, created to record the victory of William I, Duke of Normandy, at the Battle of Hastings in 1066, provides a vivid and detailed picture of 11th-century warfare. Scenes of the battle show that emblems were displayed on the shields of the Norman knights, but they are not considered to be heraldic devices, as the same knights bear different symbols in other episodes of the work.

Conventional heraldic thought puts the beginnings of heraldry a full century later, though it has been suggested that heraldic devices were actually in use on the battlefield of Hastings – not on the Norman shields, but on the standards and pennons borne by senior commanders of the Flemish contingent in Duke William's army – and even that heraldry originated among the heirs of the Emperor Charlemagne, who died in 814, two and a half centuries before the Battle of Hastings. Thirty years after Duke William's victory at Hastings,

▼ *The fanciful creatures on the shields of the knights on the Bayeux Tapestry, are perhaps a presage of the birth of heraldry.*

the Byzantine Princess Anna Comnena (1083–c1148) was casting her curious and careful eye over the shields of the Frankish knights who were passing through Byzantium on their way to join in the First Crusade. In the *Alexiad*, her journal of those far-off times, the princess mentions with much admiration that the shields of the Frankish knights were "extremely smooth and gleaming with a brilliant boss of molten brass", yet the account is most interesting for what it makes no mention of – any suggestion of personal devices or patterns such as those we describe by the term "heraldry".

EARLY HERALDIC CHARGES

In England the birth of heraldry is closely associated with the long but troubled reign of Henry I (1068–1135), known for the feuding within the royal family as its members struggled for power. An illustration in a late 12th-century manuscript of John of Worcester's Chronicle illustrates the nature of the age. As Henry lies in troubled sleep, in his nightmare he is surrounded by jostling knights, intent, it would seem, on

▲ *These Arabic roundels, from the time of the Crusades, show a marked similarity to the early heraldry of Christian Europe.*

▲ *Personal seals often show rider and horse bearing heraldic garments, as in this fragment of the seal of the Count of St Pol, 1162.*

doing the king mischief. As well as their upraised swords, the knights bear the kite-shaped shields of their age, charged with bends, chevrons and other geometric patterns associated with early heraldry.

By the second half of the 12th century, the male members of the nobility of Europe were starting to place upon their shields certain devices, or "charges", which had become associated with their families. Symbols such as chevrons and lions appeared on their seals and military accoutrements. Some surviving seals from this period bear pictures of mounted knights carrying shields of arms, while on others the shield itself is the principal device. At the same time, the marrying of shield and symbol was starting to become hereditary. It is this splendid coupling that we recognize as heraldry.

▲ *Henry I of England having a nightmare involving knights whose shields suggest patterns soon to be adopted on heraldic shields.*

WILLIAM LONGESPÉE'S SHIELD

In 1127–8, Henry I knighted his son-in-law, Geoffrey Plantagenet, Count of Anjou, and (according to John of Marmoutier, who also wrote a chronicle of the king's reign in about 1170) on that occasion the king invested Count Geoffrey with a blue shield decorated with fanciful golden lions. Certainly such a shield is shown on Geoffrey's splendid enamel tomb-plate – taken from his burial place in Le Mans and now in the Musée de Tessé, Le Mans – but the plate and the account both date from up to 30 years after the investiture.

▼ *The effigy of William Longespée. The design of his shield of arms is almost certainly identical to that of his grandfather's.*

It is certain, however, that Geoffrey's illegitimate grandson, William Longespée ("Longsword"), Earl of Salisbury and half-brother to Kings Richard I ("Coeur de Lion") and John, is depicted on his tomb in Salisbury Cathedral bearing a shield that is similar, if not identical, to that of his grandfather. Geoffrey, Count of Anjou died in 1151; William Longespée in 1226: the two depictions of their shields are usually cited as the first real evidence in colour of one shield of arms descending to another person in a hereditary manner.

ROLLS OF ARMS

Whatever the reasons for heraldry's origins – the ancient symbols borne on seals and flags, the feudal system of 12th-century Europe, the tournament, advances in armour – by the beginning of the 13th century this use of symbols had been transformed into a science of heredity, and

▲ *The tomb-plate of Geoffrey of Anjou, bearing a similar shield to the one later used by his grandson, William Longespée.*

the heralds, who were to give that science its name, had started to keep records of the shields of all that enjoyed its use. These were the splendid documents known as "rolls of arms", which were often illuminated, and which carefully recorded the retinue of some great lord, identifying the arms of all his vassals.

Many medieval rolls of arms, whether illustrated or not, list the shields of arms of men taking part in a particular event, such as a battle or tournament. Others link together groupings of knights in particular areas. Such documents provide the historian with information about the make-up of society at a period when much of Europe was forming itself into a network of nation states. One splendid surviving example is the armorial of about 1370 compiled by Claes Heinen who, as Gelre Herald, was an officer-of-arms to the Duke of Gelderland (which is now part of the Netherlands). In it, the large arms of feudal overlords are shown with the smaller arms of their vassals grouped around them. The information seems surprisingly accurate for its time, and was perhaps obtained from contacts with fellow heralds of different nations.

HERALDRY IN MEDIEVAL SOCIETY

The rise of the tournament and the refinement of the armourer's craft, which allowed the well-dressed fighting man to have his face protected behind a great iron helmet, are the two main reasons given for the explosion of armorial devices between 1150 and 1250; these twin developments also gave medieval knights ideal outlets for their peacock-like pride and natural pomposity.

The evolution of the tournament as the principal showcase for knightly prowess – apart, that is, from periods of actual warfare – assisted, even if it did not directly influence, the nature of heraldic display. This close relationship can be seen in the fact that the crest worn on top of the helmet, the second most important accoutrement in the heraldic "achievement" (the complete display of armorial bearings), was in certain countries afforded only to those of tournament rank – that is, the richest and most influential of the knightly class.

▼ *The confusion of a medieval melée depicted in a scene from the treatise by King René of Anjou (1409–80).*

THE FEUDAL SYSTEM

Feudalism, from the medieval Latin word *feodum* (meaning knight's fee), as it developed in early medieval France, was not new but had evolved to cope with the troubles of the age. Since the 9th century, western Europe had been increasingly threatened by the Vikings from the north and the Muslims, Slavs and Magyars from the east. The skilled horseman, or knight, became the essential element of the western European defensive – and offensive – structure, and kings were more or less dependent on knights to provide the armoured formation needed for battle.

In return for their service to the king, the greater lords received grants of land. The lords would, in turn, parcel up their estates into smaller areas of land, each considered enough to support a knight. In his turn, the knight pledged loyalty to his lord and swore to fight for him, and consequently the monarch, whenever required. Each lord held his lands in "fief" from his overlord, and each vassal made an act of homage to his overlord, and took an oath to the effect that his possession of his estate was conditional on the service he rendered.

▲ *A stained glass window from Chartres Cathedral, France, shows the king with his shield of arms setting out to war.*

MEDIEVAL WARFARE

When an army took to the field, the chances of any actual fighting were quite small. Towns might be besieged and villages pillaged, but for much of the time the rival forces saw little of each other. Manpower was essential to the smooth

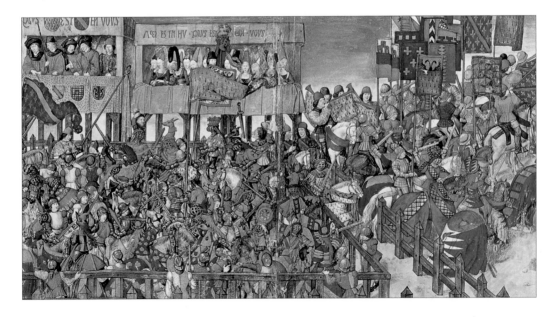

▲ *An illustration from* The Genealogical History from Bruce to Edward I. *The shield in the centre shows an escarbuncle, a design that probably began as a shield boss.*

◄ *Duke William (middle) lifts his helmet at the Battle of Hastings to show his face.*

running of the nation and if a treaty could be brought to fruition so much the better. Great battles such as Crécy (1346), Agincourt (1415) and Towton (1461) were the exception rather than the rule. Towton, where as many as 30,000 died, took place during the Wars of the Roses, but the actual campaigning that took place during the entire period of conflict, from the first battle of St Albans in 1461 to the death of Richard III at Bosworth in 1485, amounted to only a few weeks.

When it did happen, medieval fighting was a gruesome and bloody affair, with weapons designed for hand-to-hand combat. The longsword could sever entire limbs, and the warhammer could inflict crushing and fatal blows to the head. These were the weapons of the knight and would have been too expensive for the ordinary foot soldier, who relied on weapons made by the local blacksmith, such as poleaxes, and billhooks. But these could pull a fully armed knight off his horse, or disembowel the horse to bring the knight down.

While armour gave the knight some protection, it had its disadvantages. An hour's fast fighting would be taxing for any man, but for a heavily armoured knight it could be lethal in itself. It should also be remembered that often more men died of disease while on the march between engagements than were killed in battle.

IDENTIFICATION IN BATTLE

With knights encased in armour, it is clear that armorial devices would have been exceptionally useful, both to their allies and their enemies. A scene in the Bayeux Tapestry records a moment when Duke William was forced to throw back his helmet, exposing his face for instant recognition, even though in 1066 the helmet worn by the European knight still allowed much of the wearer's face to be seen. In the mid-12th century the Anglo-Norman poet Robert Wace wrote that at Hastings the Normans "had made cognizances so that one Norman would recognize another", and the Norman French terms connoissances and recognitiones, both of which were used in the 12th century to describe armorial devices, testify to their roles as emblems of recognition. Yet there is an important fact to be remembered when reading Wace's comment – by his day, a century after Hastings, the well-dressed warrior had started to wear the great helm, which covered all of the face except for the eyes, making identification even more difficult than it would have been at the time of the Norman conquest of England.

The Genealogical History from Bruce to Edward I is a surviving manuscript from c1264–1300. It depicts medieval battle between knights who bear shields that are adorned with simple geometric patterns. One particular illustration (seen here) shows both riders and horses wearing "a coat of arms" as well as a knight banneret (top right), an oblong banner that ensured that even though a knight might not be seen, his presence on the field was evident.

▼ *Louis XII leaves for battle in 1502 in full war gear, as is his horse.*

CHIVALRY AND HERALDRY

Heraldry is so closely associated with that extraordinary medieval phenomenon, chivalry, that it is instructive to explore the interplay between the two, one being very much the plaything of the other. Literally, chivalry meant the lore of the horse soldier, or rather the man who could afford the horse, its trappings and the weapons of the mounted warrior, notably the lance: in other words, the knight. At its birth, heraldry was the province of the knights; it was through the loyalty of such men that wars could be fought and won.

THE CHIVALRIC CODE
The armoured knight and his force formed the backbone of the medieval European army. If disciplined, they could turn the tide of battle, but battles were sometimes won without the combat even starting: the sight of the armoured cavalry could be enough to cause their enemies to flee.

Without battles to keep them occupied, men in fighting mood could get bored and become a liability to the ruler, his people and the Church. Something was needed to curb the semi-legalized vandalism of marauding knights and it evolved in the form of the nebulous set of ethics now called the "code of chivalry", which gradually refined into a loose set of rules aimed at civilizing the high-born. It was a theme picked up by writers of the time, including Raymond Lull, Honoré Bonet and Christine de Pisan.

▲ *Medieval illustrations such as this used heraldry to depict the brotherhood of mounted knights in battle.*

Lull (c1232–c1315), an Aragonian of noble blood, was well versed in knightly deeds and wrote of love and the pursuit of it in the style of the troubadours of southern France. Amorous by nature, he often cheated on his wife, until he had a vision of Christ on the cross, which he interpreted to mean he was to change his life. His work thereafter was to convert the heathen to Christianity, through prayer, preaching and writing books, one of the most influential being his *Libre del Ordre de Cavayleria (Book of the Order of Chivalry)*, written in 1275. For centuries this was considered the standard textbook on the subject and was widely translated.

Christine de Pisan (c1364–c1430), a disciple of Honoré Bonet (*fl. c*1380), provided a fascinating insight into the workings of the medieval mind in her book of 1408–9, *Le Livre des Faits d'Armes et de Chevalerie (The Book of Feats of Arms and Chivalry)*, which deals with such varied themes as banning the use of poisoned arrows by Christians, and saving the souls of warriors. She was clearly acquainted with the latest trends in military thinking in the early 15th century, and tackled questions, such as "Should the Emperor make war on the Pope?" and "Can a madman be justly held prisoner?" Her answer – "No" – to the second question displays a level of humanity uncommon in her age.

▼ *Christine de Pisan presenting* The Book of Feats of Arms and Chivalry *to Queen Isabeau of France.*

◀ *Parade shield, Flemish, 15th century. Part of an attempt to tame the warrior by stressing the nature of courtly love, here the gallant knight tells his lady "it is you or death". Note the lance rest top left.*

Drawing on such diverse sources as Roman military strategy and the love songs and martial epics of the German *Minnesinger* and French troubadours, Lull, de Pisan and others attracted the attention of the rulers of Europe, most of whom sought to make their courts centres of learning and chivalric enterprise. They also hoped that through such pursuits as courtly love, tournaments and orders of chivalry, they would pacify their unruly courtiers and weld them into a coherent force that saw loyalty to the overlord as a benefit rather than a hindrance.

In its simplest form the code required that its followers should honour their lord, defend the Church – including, when possible, taking up arms against the infidel – and protect the weak, the poor and all women. In reality, true followers of such noble aims were rare, and even those warriors who were held up by medieval writers and the Church as paragons of chivalry would today be looked upon in a very different light.

It says much of those times that one of the men who most epitomized the code of chivalry was not a Christian knight at all, but the infidel ruler Saladin (1137–93), Sultan of Egypt and Syria, who led the Muslim army against the Crusaders in Palestine. As for that most Christian monarch, Richard Coeur de Lion, his observation of the code was less punctilious: in 1191, over 2,500 prisoners in the captured garrison of Acre were put to the sword, for little reason other than Saladin had not observed the treaty between himself and Richard "to the word".

LOVE AND HERALDRY

Heraldry had a great part to play in chivalric ideals. The winning of a good lady through love and brave quests was a popular theme, and books were liberally scattered with allegorical arms. Often medieval chroniclers used the castle as a symbol of a lady's virtue that was to be stormed and captured by the knight's love and passion.

The most delightful depictions of shields of arms appear in a unique survival from about 1300, the Manesse Codex, now in the University of Heidelberg. This collection of songs is illustrated with no less than 140 miniatures showing knightly troubadours – each identified by his shield – preparing for a tournament, sighing for love or wooing a mistress.

▲ *A scene from the Manesse Codex in which the victor receives his prize (a jewelled chaplet) from the Queen of the Tournament.*

▲ *A depiction in ivory of knights assaulting the castle of love.*

MEDIEVAL MILITARY DRESS

Heraldry grew up during a period of radical changes in the dress of the military man and, as those changes took place, so did the nature of heraldry, or rather its application. In time, heraldry even came to be thought of as another weapon in the warrior's armoury – it could, and did, win or lose battles. So important to each other were the twin subjects of heraldry and armour, that not only did the terms "armory" and "armour" combine, but actual pieces of armour were often represented on shields, in crests and as heraldic badges.

CHAIN MAIL

In the late 12th century, when heraldry started to appear on the battlefield, the high-ranking military man was largely

◀ An illustration of the tomb effigy of William Longespée, showing the knightly gear that would render him anonymous but for his shield and tunic.

encased in chain mail. Mail had been used by the Romans, who called it *macula*, meaning a net or mesh. Each link in medieval chain mail was forged of iron wire, the ends of which were hammered flat and riveted after the ring had been linked through four others. A chain mail shirt that has survived from the 15th century weighs around 9kg (20lb).

The later application of iron and steel plate tended to give better protection against the bruising blows of war hammer and sword, but chain mail was surprisingly good at keeping out ordinary arrows, and at the Battle of Arsouf in 1191, during the Third Crusade, Richard Coeur de Lion's men were said to have survived in spite of arrows sticking out of their mail like so many bird's feathers.

Long after mail had ceased to be the main form of body armour, it was still being used as flexible "in-filling" at points of the body where mobility was needed, such as behind the knees or under the arms, and plate armour could not be worn. Underneath the mail, a quilted undergarment called a "gambeson" was worn, which was padded with wadding: old rags, horsehair or bunches of dried grass – anything that would keep the wearer insulated, both from any extreme weather and the blows of an enemy.

▲ The typical military dress of a medieval crusader c1250. The loose-fitting tunic was an ideal surface for the display of heraldry.

▶ A 15th-century chain mail shirt, a highly effective piece of protection.

PLATE ARMOUR

Gradually the knight laid off his chain mail in favour of iron or steel plate and, as the armourer found ways to provide more complex and composite armour, each piece acquired its own name. The chest and back were protected by the "cuirass". Legs were enclosed in "cuisses", elbows were protected by "couters" or "gard-de-bras" (the badge of Lord Fitzwalter), hands were enclosed in gauntlets or "mains-de-fer", the neck was guarded by an "aventail" (the badge of Lord Montague), and the shoulders sported plates known as "ailettes", bearing the arms of the wearer.

BADGES FROM ARMOUR
These are some of the pieces of armour that were taken up as badges by medieval knights.

▲ A gard-de-bras, worn on the elbow. ▲ A chamfron, worn by a knight's horse.

▲ An aventail, worn at the neck.

▲ The closed helmet. ▲ A crampet, for the end of a scabbard.

Iron and steel were not the only materials used for armour. "Plastics" (a general term for materials that could be moulded into shape) included "cuir-bouilli" (leather boiled in oil), bone and even cow-horn. The last, when heated, could be unravelled into translucent sheets and was sometimes also used as a cheap alternative to window glass, showing the ingenuity of the late medieval artisan. Leg guards, which were known as "greaves", shoulder-guards and even arm-guards could all be made of such materials. By the middle of the 14th century the linen surcoat had been largely superseded by the "jupon", a close-fitting quilted coat, usually decorated with the bearer's arms.

The great armour manufacturing areas of the 15th and 16th centuries were northern Italy – notably Milan – Nuremberg and the Low Countries. Military men living outside these areas who wanted the best had several options open to them. If they were very rich they might employ their own armourer. Failing this, they could purchase armour from travelling salesmen who visited the leading trading centres. The third option was to have a model made of their torso and limbs, in wax or wood, which could be sent to an armourer for measuring and fitting, and records in royal and noble archives bear testimony to this practice. A letter of 16 March 1520,

▼ *A tabarded knight at prayer depicted in glass, England, 1403.*

▲ *By the end of the 15th century, knights were discarding the heraldic surcoat in order to display their armour.*

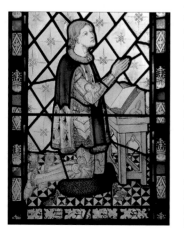

◀ *The arms of Nuremberg used here as an armourer's mark in the 15th century.*

from François I of France, asks that an "arming doublet" (an undergarment) belonging to Henry VIII of England be sent as a size guide for a new cuirass, which François wished to present to the English king.

By the end of the 15th century the well-dressed knight was encased almost entirely in steel plating, the brightness of which gave it the name of "alwyte" (all white). From the details of its lines and flutings, curves and edgings – just as today with the cut of a good suit – those in the know were able to tell where and even by whom the armour had been made. In addition, the manufacturer would have signed the plate with his punched maker's mark, which was sometimes heraldic. By the end of the 15th century the surcoat, tabard, or jupon, had become things of the past, for the armour itself was what was being shown off.

▲ *A depiction of the changes and adaptations in styles of armour and accoutrements from the 12th century to the 15th century.*

FIGHTING IN ARMOUR

Needless to say, armour, whether chain mail or steel plate, was not the most comfortable of coverings. In hot weather the knight could literally cook, while in winter he might freeze. Commanders often had to berate their men during battle for taking off vital pieces of armour, in an attempt to keep cool. Many a medieval treatise on warfare pleaded for caution among the knightly classes. It might be freezing cold, it might be unbearably hot (especially in Palestine), but on no account should you discard your armour: discomfort was far preferable to death.

Some measure of comfort would have been gained by the wearing of a doublet (a long-sleeved tunic reaching to the hips) and long hose, like tights. At points that needed to be flexible but also required protection, mail was attached to the material. The underside of the armour was lined with fine materials. As for the weight of armour, it is a fact that a full harness of plate armour of about 1470 was no heavier – in fact it was sometimes lighter – than the full marching kit of a British infantryman of World War I. Furthermore, a fully armoured knight could mount his steed easily and without the aid of the crane seen in old films.

▶ *A tilt helmet, from the 15th/16th century, also known as the "frog face".*

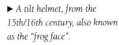

FASHIONS IN HELMETS

The head, being the most vulnerable part of the body to attack, had long been protected in war by some form of metal headgear. By the time the heraldic story started, the most popular form of helmet for the warrior in Britain and other European countries was a pointed conical iron helmet with a nose-guard, similar in form to those shown in the Bayeux Tapestry. This design allowed much of the bearer's face to be seen. Gradually the helmet lost its conical point and a flat plate of iron was riveted across the top of the head. More and more of the face became protected behind iron plating, and this style is known as the "pot helmet".

At this period, around 1200, most of the body was protected by chain mail, which would also have extended over the wearer's neck, hair and the sides of the face. It was made bearable by a cloth lining, which was probably padded. Over the mail head-covering a cloth cap would have been worn, also reinforced by padding. The helmet would have sat upon this "arming cap", which gave some degree of comfort to the wearer as well as acting as a shock absorber for any blows on the helmet. Further comfort was given by air holes cut in the side of the helmet.

Although some armorial devices made an appearance on the helmet as early as 1250, it was almost another century before the

▲ *An English great helm, c1370.*

▲ *A barred tourney helm, 16th century.*

▲ *Walter von Hohenklingen's tomb effigy. In death he chose to be depicted with all the accoutrements of his knightly rank, including tourney helm and shield of arms.*

heraldic crest became popular. The pot helmet gradually evolved into the "great helm", made with a series of hammered plates usually rising to a gradual point.

A second, close-fitting helmet was made to fit under the great helm so that the knight now wore two layers of iron, and this in turn evolved separately, with or without a visor. This streamlined helmet, known as the "bascinet", was so popular with medieval knights that it was worn in various forms from around 1330 to 1550. It covered only the top of the head and the sides of the face, and chain mail was attached to its lower edges by cords. When the great helm, which tended to be relegated to the tournament, was worn over the bascinet each was cushioned from the other by a padded lining.

It was the great helm that became the main platform for the heraldic crest, which was usually made of lightweight materials such as hollow wood, paste board, stiffened cloth or leather stretched over a wooden or wire frame and filled with a combination of materials including tow, sawdust or even sponge. Both the bascinet and the great helm can be seen on the grave slab of Walter von Hohenklingen, in the Swiss National Museum, Zurich.

HORSE ARMOUR AND TRAPPINGS

The knight was a mounted warrior, and his horse was a valuable commodity that also needed its own protection. This led to the steed having its own "chamfron" or head-guard (the badge of the Earl of Shrewsbury) and "peytrel" or chest-plate. The horse could be dressed overall in the fashion of the day with a splendid "trapper" bearing the owner's arms. This was an embroidered cloth that reached down to the fetlocks, leaving only the horse's eyes, ears and nose uncovered. Its cost could be the equivalent of £20,000 ($30,000) today.

By the mid-14th century the combination of the skilled arts of the armourer and the embroiderer meant that Sir Geoffrey Luttrell could enter the lists dressed in a display of heraldic grandeur in which his personal arms appeared on no less than 17 separate displays.

HERALDRY BITES THE BULLET

Many surviving pieces of late harness show a proof mark: a bullet "bruise" in some inconspicuous place, by which the armourer had proved that the plate could withstand the shot of handguns. Firearms, increasingly used towards the end of the 15th century, are not respecters of rank or person, and were fired at a distance, which rendered heraldic identification superfluous. By 1500 the great age of heraldry on the battlefield was over. From then on it was used as an indicator of blood lines, marriage connections and degree (status).

▼ *Sir Geoffrey Luttrell, preparing for tourney, from the Luttrell Psalter, 14th century. Sir Geoffrey's arms appear 17 times.*

THE TOURNAMENT

running battles. The knights and their entourages fought violently with each other through town and village street at great risk of serious injury, not only to themselves but also to innocent locals, who were considered totally expendable.

Tournaments, "those games overseen by the devil", were railed against by religious men from the earliest days. As early as the 9th century, Pope Eugenius anathematized them, and a succession of popes attempted to ban tournaments, even going so far as excommunicating the participants. Their preachings usually had little or no effect. It is easy to see why the popes saw tournaments as the work of Satan, as some of Christendom's finest military leaders fell on the tourney field: men who, if they did have to fight their fellows to the death, the

War, which was never far from men's minds in the heyday of heraldry, needed training for. Archers had their practices at the butts, but military commanders pitted their skills against each other on the tourney field. Martial sports of some kind have surely existed from the earliest days of organized fighting. The Greeks and Romans made full use of military sparring matches and contests of strength and courage and so it was in the medieval period. This rough type of military "play" often so closely resembled real battle conditions that it often resulted in casualties – even deaths. If there was any difference between the tournament melée and the medieval battle, it was the involvement of judges, who attempted to bring some semblance of order to the motley business. Another difference was the weapons, which tended to be slightly less lethal than those used in warfare.

ORGANIZED MAYHEM

It is easy to imagine the medieval tournament as having all the atmosphere of a modern fair and sporting event combined. This may have been true when tournaments became formalized, but in the early days such events were more akin to

▲ *Tournament participants and audience at the lists, from a late 15th-century illustration of Froissart's* Chronicles.

▼ *A 16th-century tournament with broken lances littering the field. By this time the tournaments were more closely regulated.*

clerics felt should have aimed their aggression at the infidels in the Holy Land. Florent, Count of Hainault, and Philip, Count of Boulogne, were both killed on the tourney field in 1223, and as late as 1559 Henri II of France was mortally wounded during a joust, when his visor was pierced by the lance of Gabriele de Montmorency. Henri died in an age when the tournament was supposedly a formal and disciplined affair; certainly by the 16th century it had become somewhat more refined than the tournament that was held in 1240 at Nuys, near Cologne, when it is recorded that 60 knights and squires perished, trampled under horses' hooves, choked by dust in their armour, or simply succumbing to exhaustion.

TOURNAMENT EVENTS

The tournament was a series of contests reflecting the types of warfare enacted by the higher military ranks. The "melée" was the event that most closely aped the style of fighting that the combatants would probably encounter on a real battlefield. It more nearly resembled a mounted rugby scrum than any genteel sparring match. In the battle engagement, any number of mounted men slugged it out with swords, maces and other hand-held weapons.

Jousting was counted the most noble and prestigious sport to be enjoyed on the tourney field. In this, two mounted knights

▲ *A painting of a tournament in Siena in honour of Ferdinand I de' Medici, with the arms of participants and nobility displayed.*

▼ *The perils of jousting are shown clearly in this depiction of the death of King Henri II of France in 1559 at a tournament in honour of Philip II of Spain.*

bearing lances would run against each other in the "lists", an area enclosed by fences. In the early 15th century, to offset the increased danger of longer, heavier lances, a wooden barrier (the "tilt") was introduced to divide the course, with one man on either side of it.

Along the edge of the jousting field lay the spectators' enclosures and the tented encampments of the participants, all ablaze with heraldry. All the participants vied with each other in putting on the greatest display of splendour. They would be announced to the crowds by their heralds shouting out their names and titles, and often their arms would be shown to the crowds by men or boys dressed up as monsters, angels, ancient heroes or giants – surely a possible origin of the heraldic supporters of later days. With a blast of trumpets, the two knights would course towards each other, urging their horses to

▲ *The breaking of lances during the clash of contestants. Note the lance tips or coronels that were used for jousts* à la plaisance.

▼ *The extravagant splendour of the 16th-century tournament, this one held in Rome for the Vatican Court in 1565.*

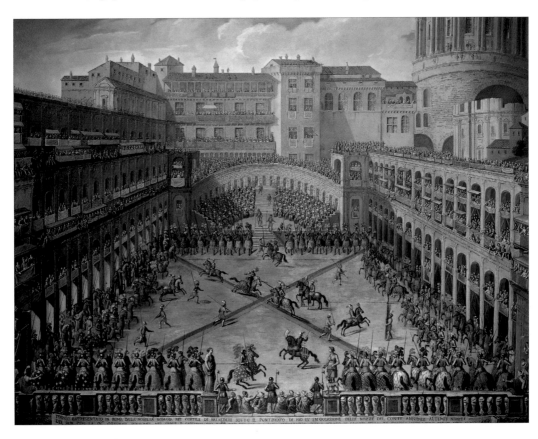

build up the maximum speed possible in the area of the lists, which might be 200m (220 yards) or more. The clash of men and weapons, when it came, could be dramatic and, despite being mounted in a high-backed saddle, a knight could often be catapulted into the air by the force of his opponent's lance.

A joust would usually be *à la plaisance* ("of peace"), using lances with special blunted tips, called coronels. The lances were often made of hollow wood, so that they would shatter on impact. If, however, a grudge match, or joust *à outrance* ("to the end"), had been commanded, all was for real, with sharpened weapons. The competition carried on to the point where one man was either injured or killed.

The matches were closely monitored by the judge, who notched up tallies of broken lances, and at the end of the competition the winner might be awarded a prize. This could be anything from a ring, a gold chain, or a jewel, to a kiss from the "Queen of the Tournament", one of the ladies present who was chosen to reign over the proceedings. The ceremony of prize-giving could be both formal and glorious, with the prize handed over to the Queen of the day by a herald. The winner was ceremoniously brought forward and the prize presented by the Queen, with suitably gracious words of esteem.

▼ *The gorgeous apparel of a tourney knight and his horse was hugely expensive.*

THE COST OF TOURNEYING

The tournaments could make or break competitors. One of the complaints of the popes and other senior prelates against these events – beside the fact that they led to the maiming and death of many fine men – was that the heavy expense of participation led to the ruin of large numbers of poorer knights, who often pawned all their belongings, and even their estates, to finance their entry into the lists. But if a knight was prepared to take the risk, the rewards could set him on the road to greater things. And there was certainly money to be made at the tournament.

One such professional knight was William Marshal (1146–1219), who eventually served as adviser to no less than four English kings and was created Earl of

▲ *The effigy of William Marshal, of whom it was written "Behold all that remains of the best knight that ever lived."*

Pembroke. William was born into a good family, but the Marshal estates were devolved upon his older brothers. He was therefore expected to find his own way in the world, and did so in successful and dramatic fashion.

Apprenticed to William de Tancarville's household in Normandy, William Marshal was a quick learner in the ways of the medieval martial man. When, in a melée at a tournament in Maine, the young William gained the capture of three knights through his own prowess, he saw the way his life was to run. As in a real battle, it was ransom that could make or break a man's

▲ Unsuitable for battle, the full regalia a knight wore for tournaments was for identification and to show his wealth and position.

fortune. With the money and horses William won that day he was able to join the ever-growing number of knights who wandered round Europe from tourney to tourney, making good use of their fighting skills to amass wealth and increase their

own prestige. These roving warriors attracted other such men to their side, and grew into a force of professional military men who came to form the backbone of many of medieval Europe's armies.

In 1167 he teamed up with a Flemish knight, Roger de Gaugi, agreeing to take part in as many tournaments as they could and divide the ransom spoils between them. William continued to take part in tournaments until 1183, and remained undefeated throughout 16 years of competition. Later, on his death bed, he recalled that he had taken over 500 knights prisoner during those years. Such was the life of the tournament roundsman.

THE FIELD OF CLOTH OF GOLD

Tournaments provided the major aristocracy and royalty of Europe with an arena in which they could show off their wealth and largesse. By the 15th century kings were keen to be the patrons of these gaudy and glorious shows. Marriages, coming of age, truces, treaties and alliances: all were seen as possible excuses for a tournament, the medieval equivalent of the ultimate

party. The most incredible spectacle of this kind took place in 1520 and came to be known as the Field of Cloth of Gold.

It was a meeting at Guines in June 1520, between François I of France and Henry VIII of England, arranged to celebrate a peace between the two nations. For once, instead of fighting each other, each monarch attempted to outdo the other with a show of magnificence. Although other events were organized, the tournaments were the main excitements of the week. The participants were housed in two encampments, each with over 1,000 lavishly decorated tents. Between the two camps stood the Tree of Chivalry. This extraordinary structure bore the shields of the two monarchs, bound together by garlands of green silk. The tree's trunk was covered in cloth of gold and at its foot, in complete harmony, stood the heralds of both kingdoms.

▼ A painting showing the famous tournament, The Field of Cloth of Gold, at the moment of the extravagant entry of Henry VIII of England, on 7 June 1520.

THE ROMANTIC REVIVAL

Tournaments became few and far between in the first half of the 17th century, and seem to have died a natural death by the 1650s. There was a brief renaissance in the first half of the 19th century, when members of the European aristocracy, bowled over by the Romantic revival of medievalism, which included the historical romances of Sir Walter Scott, saw themselves as the proud and natural successors to Parsifal, the Swan Knight, and to Arthur and the Knights of the Round Table.

It was in Scott's own Scotland that the last great attempt at re-creating the medieval chivalric ideal was staged, to celebrate the coronation of the young Queen Victoria in 1837. The coronation was a toned-down affair, shorn of many of its more splendid trappings by a thrifty Whig government. This caused particular resentment in one young Scottish aristocrat, Archibald Montgomerie, 13th Earl of Eglinton. His stepfather had been one of those Tory gentlemen who considered themselves deprived of their rightful, if small, parts in the coronation ritual by Whig penny-pinching. As a lover of chivalry, Lord Eglinton decided to right the wrong done to him and his family. He could and would provide the chivalric splendour worthy of his race – he would revive the tournament.

The grand event was held at the Earl's estate at Eglinton, south of Glasgow. Lord Eglinton's enthusiasm fired many other noble souls into wanting to revive their family's fame – that is, until they realized the actual expense involved and the training and degree of expertise required for the event. So out of the original 150 entrants expected, only 13 knights actually turned

▲ One of the contemporary illustrations of the Eglinton Tournament shows the procession of Lord Eglinton and other participants.

out for the tournament. However, this in no way deterred the crowds that came to witness the fun. An estimated 100,000 people turned up but, as is so often the case, the British weather decided to stop play. The rain came down in buckets, turning the lists into a quagmire.

Although ridiculed by many at the time for its fanciful attempts at re-creating a golden age, which in reality never existed, what was truly amazing was that Lord Eglinton's attempts were probably as true to the 15th-century tourney scene as anything attempted since that period itself.

▼ The breaking of lances during the jousting at the Eglinton Tournament.

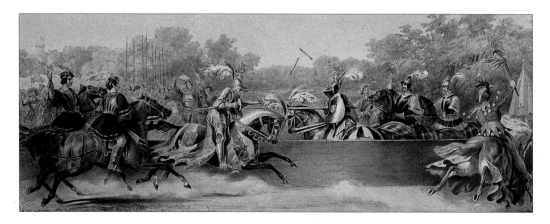

BADGES AND LIVERIES

In medieval Britain, most of the populace would not have known the arms of even the greatest magnate, but they would quite probably have recognized the badge (also known as cognizance) – the distinguishing emblem – of the major nobility, as well as the liveries, or clothing, that were worn by their servants.

BADGES

The badge is a particularly British heraldic tradition but is also known in Italy, where nobility were represented by devices, known as *imprese* or "impresses". The badge became fashionable in England in the late 14th century. The emblem used could be a single charge taken from the

arms of the owner or, as was often the case, it might be an entirely different object chosen at the will of the bearer. As such it was very personal, and in certain great families various members would possess their own badge, quite distinct from those of their relations. Some families made use of many different devices: Richard II of England's favourites were the white hart, and the seed pod of the broom plant, "broom cod" as it was called then. It is thought that a sprig of broom (in Latin *planta genista*) had given the name Plantagenet to his line.

Badges were particularly associated with the struggles for power between two royal houses, which later came to be known as the Wars of the Roses (1455–85). This

◄ *A rare surviving pewter badge from the late 14th to early 15th century of the "broom cod" device of Richard II of England.*

name was coined later from the supposed badges of the rival royal houses of York (the white rose) and Lancaster (the red rose). During this period of civil disorder, the retinues of the major nobility amounted to private armies, whose members would wear their master's badge and colours or "livery" to declare their allegiance. The sight of the badge could instil either comfort or fear in the minds of the peasantry, depending on which device they saw – it might belong to the troops of their own lord, or might be that of some mighty rival. Bands of armed men roving around the country, intent on mischief, were a phenomenon of the age. In this atmosphere,

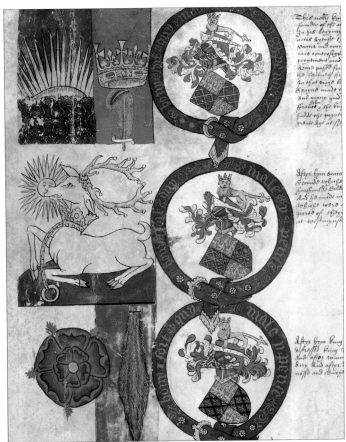

◄ *The badges and personal liveries of (top to bottom) King Edward III, Richard II and Henry IV from Writhe's Garter Book.*

▼ *A carving of the salamander, the badge of François I of France (1515–47).*

▲ *Worked into this chasuble are the combined badges of Henry VIII (the Tudor rose and portcullis), and Catherine of Aragon (the pomegranate), celebrating their marriage.*

▲ *A splendid and rare survival of the silver crescent, badge of the Percy family, Dukes of Northumberland. This example dates from the early 15th century.*

wearing the badge of a particular lord gave some degree of immunity from prosecution in the local court, since the chances were that the magistrate was also in the pay of the same magnate.

THE BATTLE OF BARNET

The white mullet, or star, of the de Veres was partially responsible for one famous defeat during the Wars of the Roses. In 1471, Richard Neville, Earl of Warwick, the former friend and supporter of the Yorkist king Edward IV, was fighting against him, having now sided with his Lancastrian rival, Henry VI. The two armies met at Barnet. The royal troops wore the rising sun of York; Warwick's forces were wearing red tunics upon which was the white ragged staff. (The bear and the ragged staff of Lancaster were, initially,

▶ *The tomb effigy of Sir Richard Herbert, who wears the famous Yorkist collar of suns and roses.*

two separate badges, combined only in later centuries.)

On that day Warwick was joined by the troops of John de Vere, Earl of Oxford. At the height of the battle, which was fought in thick mist, de Vere's forces managed to drive the Yorkists backwards. After this success they attempted to rejoin the main Lancastrian force, and appeared out of the mist at some distance from their colleagues. Warwick's archers, mistaking the

star on Lord Oxford's badge for the Yorkist sunburst, believed they were being attacked by King Edward's men, and let loose a shower of arrows. Oxford's troops believed that their former comrades had turned traitor and what had lately seemed destined to be a Lancastrian victory soon turned into a shambolic defeat for them. Warwick was killed and King Edward was able to march on to Tewkesbury and complete the defeat of King Henry's cause.

LIVERY

Personal liveries could take the form of robes in a lord's colours (these did not necessarily have to be the same colours used in his arms), the wearing of his badge, or badges, and in some cases among the greater nobility, a collar. Such livery collars tended to differ slightly in the metal they were made of, depending on the rank of the wearer. The collar of interlocking "Ss" of the House of Lancaster was used by Henry IV, who granted the right to wear it to individuals as a mark of his favour, and it is still being worn in England to this day, notably by the heralds and kings of arms.

Various monarchs attempted to curb the powers of the rival nobles by passing statutes against the wearing of liveries and the maintenance of private armies. Richard II's statute of 1390 was prompted by these practices, and was aimed at those "…Who wore the badges of lords…so swollen with pride that no fear would deter them from committing extortion in their shires."

Other complainants at the time bemoaned those "Officers of great men that weareth the liveries, the which…robbeth and despoileth the poor", and "hats and liveries…by the granting of which a lord could induce his neighbours to maintain him in all his quarrels, whether reasonable or not." Richard II responded with an ordinance that aimed at inhibiting lords from "giving livery of company to anyone unless he is a family servant living in the household." Exceptions were made for some

▲ *A depiction in stained glass of a banner bearer for the Swiss city and canton of Berne, from the first half of the 16th century.*

▼ *Richard II portrayed in the* Wilton Diptych *of 1395, in which he wears his personal badges – a white hart and broom cods.*

▼ *The collar of an English herald – the Ss are a survival from the livery collar of the House of Lancaster.*

lords, but later monarchs continued to try to curb the power of the nobles by statutes of livery and maintenance.

As late as the reign of Henry VII, the king exercised such statutes (in 1495 and 1504) and could even apply them to his most trusted friends and admirers, as when he visited John de Vere at Castle Hedingham. Henry was led by his host to the castle through two lines of the earl's numerous servants, each wearing coats of their master's livery. The king berated his host for exceeding the limits laid down respecting the number of household retainers, saying "My lord, I have heard much of your hospitality, but I see it is greater than the speech…I may not endure to have my laws broken in my sight. My attorney must speak with you." A hefty fine was soon demanded.

▲ *The* impresa *of the Rusconi family – an ice crampon, a worthy device for a family based in the mountains of north Italy.*

▲ *One of the many badges, combining device and motto, used by the Visconti family, Dukes of Milan, in the 15th century.*

STATUTORY UNIFORMS

As well as the statutory attempts that were made to limit the wearing of liveries, laws were enacted throughout Europe to curb the populace's entitlement to wear certain furs, jewels or styles of dress. In numerous states, specific groups of people were made

▼ *An illustration from one of the books of ready-made* imprese *designs.*

to wear certain items of dress, or to have some sign to indicate their social status.

In 15th-century Germany the women in a layman's family had to wear a yellow veil. European Jews often had to wear a yellow patch – a theme taken up some five centuries later by the Nazis – and prostitutes were distinguished by a number of modes of dress, depending on their age and the country in which they lived. In the time of Charles V of France (1364–80), prostitutes had to wear on their arm a ribbon different to the colour of their dress.

IMPRESE

In northern Italy from the late 14th century onwards it was customary for the greater nobility to maintain *imprese*. These were badges that were usually accompanied by a personal motto or phrase. Families such as the Rusconis of Valtellina had just one *impresa*, an ice crampon. Ruling dynasties made use of many. The theme of the personal *impresa* on the

Italian model was later taken up by the jousting fraternities of France and England, who consulted poets and allegorical story-writers to achieve a suitable combination of badge and motto. Often, such an armorial marriage would exist for just one tournament or pageant, being discarded at will by the bearer. The noble warrior clearly had to have his wits about him if he wanted to achieve on each occasion a new and effective device, but help was at hand by way of books written by designers of these curiosities of conceit. The furnishing of a new *impresa* for every occasion was an expensive business, and it gradually diminished in popularity as the tournament declined in the 17th century.

MODERN BADGES

In England, the badge has been enjoying a comeback since 1906, when heralds started granting them again, together with the standard. It has been suggested that the marrying of badge and standard for modern-day armigers is illogical, because it presumes that they have a following in the medieval manner. On this basis, the standard and its "badge" should be granted only to institutions, such as schools and colleges. Nevertheless, the granting of a badge along with a new coat of arms to an individual had become commonplace at the English College of Arms by the end of the 20th century.

HERALDIC FLAGS

There is surely no more emotive symbol of belonging than a flag or standard. Such objects of attention are as old as history itself. Heraldry has appeared upon flags almost from its very start. There is a suggestion that heraldic designs make an early appearance in the Bayeux Tapestry, on the flags, pennons or guidons of the Flemish contingent in Duke William's army. On the opposing side, the "wyvern" or two-legged dragon of Wessex is held high by King Harold's standard-bearer. The lance pennons of Normans and Flemings at Hastings were obviously made of cloth, but it would seem that the standard of Wessex was carved in wood or metal. Whatever the

▶ *A Renaissance interpretation of Roman standard bearers, which graphically illustrates the rousing effects of flags.*

▼ *Part of the medieval Powell Roll of Arms, c1345, showing designs for the banners of English high-ranking commanders.*

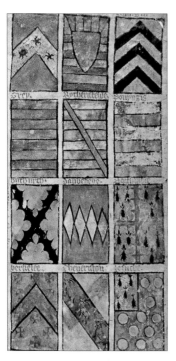

materials, both armies made use of "flags" of some sort on that fateful day, and almost certainly they were meant as objects of veneration, both for individuals and for entire units.

KNIGHTS BANNERET

One type of flag, the banner, gave its name to a class of medieval military men, the knights banneret, or bannerets for short. These high-ranking commanders were able to bring a body of men to a battle under their own banner – a square or oblong flag bearing the knight's own arms. (In the 12th and 13th centuries the banner tended to have a width one-third of its length, whereas in later centuries it became square.) The banner was a most important indicator to the troops of their commander's presence on the field of battle. Held high above the banneret's head, the banner went wherever he did, and the two

▶ *A funeral banner* (Totenfahne) *of the Swiss Counts von Toggenburg c1436.*

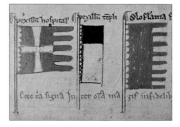

▲ *Banners of the Knights Hospitallers and Templar, and the Oriflamme of France.*

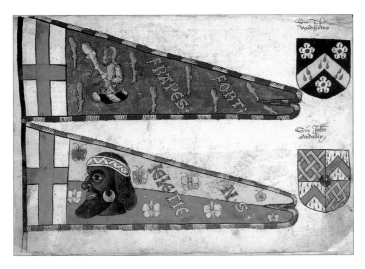

The most famous flag of this type was the Oriflamme of France, which was kept for centuries in the Abbey of Saint Denis (the burial place of the French royal family). Various suggestions have been made as to the exact appearance of the Oriflamme, but it would seem to have been made of red silk with golden trimmings, and hung from a staff of gilded wood or metal: hence its name, which means "golden flame". Some accounts say that the Oriflamme was last seen in use at Agincourt (1415), where its bearer, William Martel, Seigneur de Baqueville, lost his life defending it. Other chroniclers say it remained in the Abbey of Saint Denis until at least the 18th century, when it was described as being in a very unkempt state.

▲ *Standards of English nobility, from the first half of the 16th century – each with the cross of St George in hoist.*

were seldom separated, unless through the death of the banner-bearer.

The banneret could be so created on the battlefield as a reward for his bravery. Prior to that moment, he would probably have been a bachelor or "bas chevalier", a lower knight who bore as his rank a long pennon that had a triangular tail or tails, with his arms in a panel near the pole. Whoever was in overall command that day – a king, prince or other commander – would indicate his appreciation by taking the knight's pennon and cutting away the tails, thus making it into a banner.

The banneret had some special prerogatives. In France, he could place a banner-shaped weathervane above his castle, and could also choose his own *cri-de-guerre* or war cry. In the Low Countries, he had a circlet or coronet of rank in his crest.

PENNONS AND STANDARDS

Two other types of heraldic flag were popular with the knightly class. One was the pennon, a triangular flag that could bear either arms or a badge. The other was the standard, a long tapering flag, larger than the pennon, which could have a split or rounded end. Instead of the bearer's arms, the standard tended to show the badge or device of the bearer. This could appear singly or several times, and was often accompanied by the motto or *cri-de-guerre*. The "hoist" of the standard (the area at the top of the flag near the pole) tended to bear the national device. The main background to the standard was made up of the livery colours of the bearer. While a knight bachelor was entitled to bear a standard but not a banner, a banneret was entitled to both.

THE GONFALONE

Flags are, of course, not the exclusive preserve of the nobility. The military places great importance on regimental colours, and in the Catholic Church the position of gonfalonier, or standard-bearer, of the Church, was one of the most prestigious offices the pope could bestow.

The office of gonfalonier takes its name from another type of flag popular among city states and other nations during the medieval period, the gonfalone. Such flags were often of huge size and bore many tails. They were carried hanging down from a cross beam, rather like the sail of a ship. Before a battle the gonfalone was blessed by the clergy and it was a great disgrace to lose it, for some were considered to have miraculous powers. Because of its size, a gonfalone was often borne on a cart, driven by a member of a particular family for whom the post was hereditary.

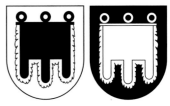

▲ *The characteristic shape of the gonfalone itself became a heraldic charge, perhaps adopted by families whose ancestors had been the hereditary bearers.*

▼ *A carroccio (flag cart) from the arms of the Grulli family, hereditary carroccio drivers to the City of Florence.*

HERALDS
AND THE LAW
OF ARMS

By the 15th century, heralds had become the acknowledged experts in

everything associated with arms, and from that time the study and "noble

science of arms" became known as heraldry. As with all matters of heraldry,

the law of arms has varied widely depending on time and place, and

medieval writers differed in their opinions concerning who should and

should not bear arms. Some contested that only those of noble stock had

such a right, while others suggested that anyone should be able to assume

them. The matter continues to be debated among heraldists, though most

governments now take little interest in it, apart from enshrining somewhere

in law their people's right to adopt arms at will, and for those who have

done so to protect their arms in the same manner as a surname.

◀ *A beautifully restored German* Totenschild,
or death shield, for a member of the Jörg
family of Nördlingen.

MEDIEVAL HERALDS

The term "herald" seems to have its origins in the Old German word *beerwald*, suggesting a caller or proclaimer to the army. Certainly, early references to heralds in French medieval romances seem to suggest they shared a common ancestry with the minstrels and messengers of noble households. Other 12th- and 13th-century writers refer to freelance individuals who followed the newly fashionable sport of tourneying across Europe, employed to cry out the names of knights and recount their lineage and acts of prowess.

Heralds took an interest in matters armorial. At tournaments, and in battle, the heralds needed to recognize and memorize the arms of the participants, and for this purpose they compiled pictorial rolls of armorial bearings. (Rolls of arms were initially actual rolls of parchment or vellum, but the term also came to be used to describe armorial records in book form.) Some rolls, known as "ordinaries", were classified by all the different devices, or charges, that could be placed on a shield.

MEMBERS OF THE HOUSEHOLD

By the end of the 13th century heralds had become attached to noble households, where they were employed as messengers, proclaiming challenges for forthcoming tournaments on their lords' behalf. It would seem that a herald was still allowed

▼ *A 15th-century herald with the banners of the judges overseeing a tournament.*

▲ *The herald of the Duke of Brittany, wearing the ermine tabard of his master, shows the Duke of Bourbon the arms of contenders in the tournament.*

to journey for some length of time away from the household, amassing information on the tourney and all that was associated with chivalry; for if his lord wanted to be seen as a man of quality he was expected to be well acquainted in such matters.

Originally the freelance heralds had taken their titles at will, but as they became accredited to certain noble households they took their official names from their masters' own titles or badges, or from charges that appeared in their arms: Toison d'or ("golden fleece") was the herald of the Burgundian order of that name; Montjoie took his name from the *cri-de-guerre* of the French kings, "Mont joie de Saint Denis"; and the name Blanch Sanglier ("white boar") came from the personal badge of Richard Duke of Gloucester, later Richard III. Heralds themselves do not normally figure on family arms, but the Spanish family of de Armas, which descends from

the herald Juan Negrin, king of arms to the kings of Castile, bears on its shield an arm holding a banner charged with the arms of the kingdoms of Castile and León.

Early references to the herald were often none too complimentary: perhaps they were written by minstrels who saw themselves under threat from these men who

▼ *The arms of the de Armas family, which unusually contains a charge alluding to their ancestor's position as a king of arms.*

vied for their masters' attention. One late 13th-century poet, Henri de Laon, thought that the herald pursued an idle profession, worthy only of greedy men: "What's more, lords would give shelter to up to four of these ne'er-do-wells who tended to talk more than good folk of other callings, yet at the same time do very little."

By the late 14th century the herald had advanced to become a permanent fixture in the households of royalty and the major nobility – to help in organizing tournaments or to act as a personal emissary. While lesser nobles might have only one herald, the households of ruling dukes, princes and kings were more likely to contain a formal heraldic staff headed by a king of arms, the highest ranking officer of arms. "Pursuivants" (literally "followers") were apprentice heralds.

All heralds wore the arms of their master, together with certain other insignia designating their exact rank, and by the 15th century the heralds had assumed a more respectable role than in earlier times.

▼ *An armorial from the 15th century, showing shields of the knights of Normandy.*

▲ *Jean le Fevre, King of Arms to the Order of the Golden Fleece, 1431, wearing the tabard of his master, the Duke of Burgundy.*

HERALDS AT WAR

On the medieval battlefield, where strategy and tactics took second place to precedence among the nobility, the heralds were attached to the retinue of the marshal who led the army, and assisted him in mar-

▲ *A facsimile of a portrait of John Talbot, the Earl of Shrewsbury, wearing his distinctive heraldic tabard.*

shalling the forces on the battlefield, in camp and on the march.

The heralds were given the medieval equivalent of diplomatic immunity, even when journeying in a country at war with their own. They were kept busy on missions of national and royal importance, treating with the opposite side, helping in exchanges of prisoners or the ransom of knights. At such times they would regard each other as members of an international fraternity, often speaking each other's language. This degree of companionship between heralds went so far as keeping council with each other on the field of battle and exchanging tallies of the dead.

An account of a battle between the French and the English in 1453, at Castillon in France, illustrates the nature of medieval warfare and the relationship between herald and master. Among those killed was the English commander John Talbot, Earl of Shrewsbury. So disfigured was the corpse, that Talbot's personal herald could not identify his lord, until, that is, he placed a finger in the bloody maw that was the Earl's mouth, feeling for a gap between his teeth. Upon finding it he took off his tabard, signifying the end of his office, and only then did he sink down and mourn the death of his master.

THE OFFICE OF THE HERALDS

Few countries today still retain any formal heraldic corporate body, but each nation retains its own distinct heraldic styles, laws and customs, reaching back through many centuries. The English College of Arms in London is today the most active, and the longest surviving, heraldic authority, having received its first charter of incorporation in 1484, during the brief reign of Richard III.

THE HOME OF THE COLLEGE OF ARMS

Richard III gave the officers of arms a house called Coldharbour in London, but his successor, Henry VII (1485–1509), promptly gave this building to his mother, Margaret Beaufort. It was not until 1558 that the heralds were once again given a permanent home, this time by Mary Tudor. Although the original building, called Derby House, was destroyed during the Great Fire of London in 1666, the College of Arms has had its home on the same site beside the Thames ever since. Set into the façade of the building are plaques bearing the heraldic devices of the Stanley family, Earls of Derby, who were the original owners of the house destroyed in the Great Fire. The heraldry includes the Stanley badge of an eagle's leg "erased a la quise" (torn away at the thigh).

PRINCIPAL OFFICERS OF ARMS

Since medieval times, officers of arms have been divided into three ranks: kings of arms, heralds and pursuivants. In England, the officer of state responsible for overall control of matters heraldic and ceremonial is the Earl Marshal of England, the Duke of Norfolk, in whose family the office is hereditary.

From at least 1300 (probably earlier) there seems to have been a territorial division of heraldic duties in England. North of the River Trent heraldic matters are controlled by Norroy (or "Northern") King of Arms. South of the Trent, the officer responsible for overseeing grants of arms and other such duties is Clarenceux King of Arms, who most probably takes his title from the private herald of the medieval Dukes of Clarence.

In 1415 William Bruges was the first officer appointed as "Garter King of Arms". Two years later he was given further precedence as the principal king of arms, a fact that was to rankle with the regional kings of arms who wished to lose none of their own powers. Among the duties of Garter is the overseeing of all patents of arms, heraldic matters concerning the Order of the Garter itself (the most senior order of knighthood in Britain, whence comes his title), and the introduction of new peers into the House of Lords.

THE MODERN ENGLISH HERALD

Like their late medieval forebears, heralds today are concerned on a daily basis with the granting of arms, both to individuals and to corporate bodies. They are also often consulted for their expertise in historical matters, from pedigrees to providing background material for television documentaries or films. More formally, they act as assistants and advisors to the Earl Marshal at great state occasions such

► *An English king of arms from early 1805, wearing his crown of office.*

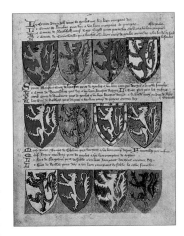

▲ *A page of an ordinary of arms – a list of charges used in heraldry – shows lions rampant and their combinations in family arms.*

as the coronation of the sovereign, or the state opening of Parliament. In addition to the officers employed on a full time, or "ordinary", basis, there are others who, through their own merit, are singled out by the Earl Marshal to be "extraordinary" pursuivants or heralds. They are honorary heralds who exercise ceremonial duties on an occasional basis. The extraordinary officers hold titles taken from the various peerages held by the Earl Marshal.

The English College of Arms is the largest heraldic authority and makes about 200 grants of arms each year. Other nations with heraldic authorities include Scotland, Ireland, South Africa and Canada.

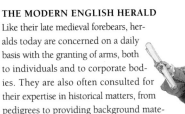

THE ENGLISH HERALDS

Garter King of Arms The principal herald, whose title comes from his duties to the Order of the Garter.

Clarenceux The title probably originated with the herald of the Duke of Clarence, third son of Edward III; responsible for matters south of the River Trent.

Norroy and Ulster "Northern King", responsible for affairs north of the River Trent; his office was twinned with Ulster in 1943.

HERALDS:

All the heralds are named after possessions of the royal family, or, in the case of Somerset, the Beaufort family.

Chester

Lancaster

Richmond

Somerset

Windsor

York

PURSUIVANTS:

Bluemantle Named after the blue field of the arms of France.

Portcullis Named after the badge of the Tudors/Beauforts.

Rouge Croix Named after the red cross of St George.

Rouge Dragon Named after the supporters of the Tudor arms.

EXTRAORDINARIES:

Beaumont Pursuivant

Matravers Pursuivant

Surrey Pursuivant

Howard Pursuivant

Wales Herald Extraordinary

TABARDS AND INSIGNIA

At one time all heralds wore some form of official dress, but in most nations this custom came to an end after World War I. Now, only English and Scottish officers of arms maintain their ceremonial garb. On British state occasions, such as the coronation of a sovereign, the officers of arms will wear their full heraldic regalia of tabard and knee breeches, and carry their wands or staves of office, thereby continuing a tradition unbroken for seven centuries and more.

THE TABARD

In the 13th century, when the herald acted as his master's messenger or "envoy", he would probably have worn the latter's own tabard, or short surcoat, and this would most likely have been a cast-off garment that had lost its first bloom. The tabard of the time would have been constructed from several layers of cloth cut in the form of a thick letter "T". The front and back panels, and both the

► Gentil Oiseau
Pursuivant of the Holy Roman
Empire, c1450, tabard athwart.

▼ Imperial heralds in the
funeral procession of
Spain's Charles V, 1558.

sleeves were embroidered with the arms of the master. A pursuivant was singled out from officers of arms of higher rank by wearing his tabard "athwart": the shorter panels designed to fit over the arms were worn over the chest and back, with the longer panels over the arms. In England this practice was known from the 15th until the late 17th century, and it was customary for the tabard to be arranged in this way by the Earl Marshal when the pursuivant was admitted to the office. If the pursuivant was later promoted to the rank of herald, the tabard was turned around to its more normal position.

On certain occasions, heralds would wear the tabard of a lord other than their own, particularly during funerals of the major nobility, when they would wear tabards bearing the arms of the

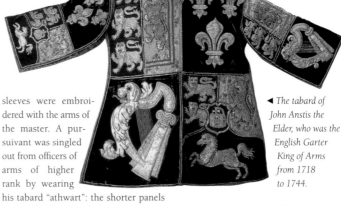

◄ The tabard of
John Anstis the
Elder, who was the
English Garter
King of Arms
from 1718
to 1744.

deceased. They might also have their tabards decorated with shields of other lords, knights and judges present at a tournament. This is splendidly illustrated in one of the great heraldic works of art, Le Livre des Tournois (The Book of Tourneys) by King René of Anjou (1409–80). He founded the Order of the Crescent in 1448 and, in between organizing countless tournaments, wrote the work in 1450 and helped to illustrate its pages.

From the 16th century onwards it would seem that officers of arms of different degrees – king of arms, herald and pursuivant – each wore a tabard made from materials commensurate with their rank; in France, each rank's garments were

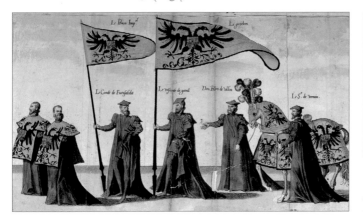

▲ Russian heralds at the forefront of the
procession at the coronation of Nicholas II of
Russia in 1896.

distinguished by name. The practice is still maintained in England and Scotland, where kings of arms wear velvet, heralds have satin, and pursuivants silk damask tabards. Each tabard is heavy and the wearer has to be dressed by experts for ceremonial events.

A story is told of a recent state occasion when it was arranged that the English officers of arms should sit together in a row. As space was limited, they were packed together very tightly, with unfortunate results: the gold wires on the English royal lion and the harp of Ireland became knitted together, and after the ceremony the row of royal officers had to be prized apart.

◄ *King Edward VIII of England and his officers of arms in full regalia, at the State Opening of Parliament in 1936.*

CROWNS AND SCEPTRES

Kings of arms are known to have worn crowns from the 15th century, when they seem to have been set with little shields and lozenges. The English kings of arms today still include in their insignia crowns designed in the early 18th century bearing a standing circle of stylized leaves.

Officers of arms from various nations have long worn badges of office and

carried sceptres or wands, which usually differ in detail according to rank. Garter King of Arms has a badge and sceptre for his office, both of which bear the arms of the Order of the Garter, while the sceptre also bears the royal arms.

In 1906 the English regional kings of arms, heralds and pursuivants were given black batons with gilt ends, each with the badge of their particular office attached at

the head. These were replaced in 1953 with white ones based on earlier models, the heads of which were said to bear blue birds or martlets. The current rods still have a blue bird, which is similar to those birds in the arms of the College of Arms. The form carried by the officers ordinary also has a gold coronet at its head, while that of the officers extraordinary does not.

▼ *The neck badge of an English officer of arms, still in use today.*

▼ *The badge and sceptre of Garter Principal King of Arms.*

▼ *The old-style baton of Clarenceux King of Arms.*

THE RIGHT TO ARMS

Heraldic writers through the ages have concerned themselves over the exact nature of arms – who should bear them, when and why, and whether they indicate noble status. The feudal structure of medieval European society only served to help the heraldic cause – what was good for the local ruler was also good for his vassals. By the 14th century the users of heraldry included not only knights and their overlords, but also their ladies. Other sections of society, such as abbeys and their abbots, and towns and their burghers, were also keen to embrace the noble art.

THE SPREAD OF HERALDRY

The heady combination of colour and symbolism meant that heraldry was soon adopted and adapted to suit the requirements of the nobles of many European nations. On the fringes of Europe, in Russia, Lithuania, Poland and Hungary, the military elite saw the appeal of the new science. In Poland, where the noble tribe, or *ród*, was the essential unit of society, the

▶ *A page of a pedigree, with "tricked" arms of the Lambert family, from the herald's visitation notes of Wiltshire, 1565.*

▼ *A Flemish armorial pedigree, c1590, of the Despres family.*

old tribal symbols were adapted to fit the heraldic shield. Unlike the rest of Europe, one shield of arms was used by the entire tribe, and the distinguishing marks that identify family branches in other countries are virtually unknown in Polish heraldry. The Hungarian nobility went for family arms, and at least a third of these referred to the enduring battle against the Islamic "Turkish menace", which for centuries attempted to make inroads into the eastern borders of Christendom. Disembodied parts of dead Turks featured on many Hungarian shields.

Heraldry's pictorial nature made it an ideal medium for the decoration of houses, castles, cathedrals and town halls, on the grand or miniature scale. It could dignify the heading of an illuminated address, supply the design for a signet ring, or decorate

▲ *A Hungarian grant of arms from the early 16th century showing the age-old fight between the Hungarians and Turks.*

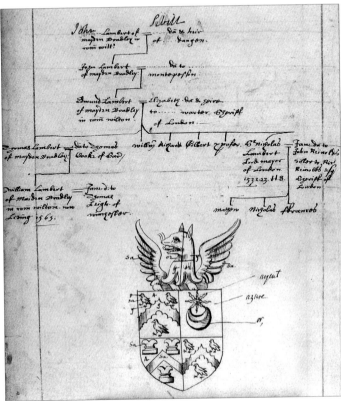

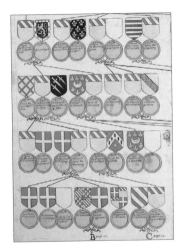

▲ *Christine de Pisan presents her famous and extensive works on chivalry to King Charles VI of France.*

the elaborate wedding arches erected by a loyal populace to welcome a princely bride and groom: all were excellent stages for the display of armorial bearings.

The desire to be identified by arms filtered down through the classes so that many a new-made man, with the power of money behind him, attempted to gain both shield and crest for himself and his heirs, and there were always purveyors of arms who were pleased to oblige with a suitable design: no matter that it was not lawfully gained, it looked good. To counteract the inroads that merchants and other self-made men were making into their prerogatives, the nobility looked to their pedigrees – their authentic arms provided proof of their noble descent and guaranteed their right to acceptance at court and to the ancient orders of chivalry.

THE REGULATION OF HERALDRY

In her book *Le Livre des Faits d'Armes et de Chevalerie*, Christine de Pisan describes a supposed discourse with her spiritual advisor, the Abbé Honoré Bonet, a famed writer on chivalry who had died many years before. Among the questions posed by Christine are, "If a man adopts arms already borne by another, may he retain them?" to which the answer is, "No". Another question is, "If a German knight entering the realm of France finds a Frenchman using the same arms, has the German a just cause for complaint?" Again the answer from Bonet is "No", as they are subjects of different countries and princes.

Which individuals and institutions are, or were, entitled to bear arms? The answer is not simple and depends very much on the age and the nation involved. In some countries, arms have been held only by the nobility. In France during the 17th century, however, even peasants were encouraged to bear a shield of arms, so that they could be taxed for it. In many countries, personal arms can now be adopted at will and may, as in Sweden, be lumped together legally with trademarks and afforded the same protection. Stronger protection tends to be given to civic and military heraldry.

England and Scotland have stringent and longstanding measures in place to protect arms, and during the reign of Henry VIII the English heralds were empowered by royal command to go into the shires and seek out false gentlemen who had assumed arms without due cause. These heraldic progresses were known as "visitations". In the Holy Roman Empire the right to grant arms was at times delegated to the *Hofpfalzgrafen* or "counts of the palace".

THE COURT OF CHIVALRY

In England and Wales the basis of the law of arms is that no one may bear and use them without lawful authority, and that arms are an inalienable right, inherited in accordance with the laws and usages of arms. If, in the view of an officer of arms, these laws are being infringed, the offended party has the right to take the case to the Court of Chivalry, which last sat in 1954 to hear a case brought by the Lord Mayor, aldermen and the citizens of Manchester against the Manchester Palace of Varieties Ltd. The plaintiffs had alleged that the defendants had made illegal use of the arms of the Corporation of Manchester on their company seal. The case was judged in favour of the plaintiffs.

The English Court of Chivalry has its origins in the Courts of the Constable and Marshal, and dates from the first half of the 14th century. As matters armorial were associated with the military class, the chief of the army sits in judgement.

▼ *The Court of Chivalry in session at the College of Arms, London, 1800.*

THE HERALDIC FUNERAL

People of wealth and station in society required a good send-off, commensurate with their rank. The art of "dying well" was much on the minds of the late medieval nobility of Europe, but in the main this meant shows of largesse to the poor and payments for masses to be sung to propel the soul heavenwards. However, just so that God and the angels would know exactly who they were dealing with, the trappings of rank were displayed prominently during the lying-in-state, at the funeral and at the place of burial.

By the 14th century it had become the practice at funerals of royalty and the nobility for a prominent display of heraldry to be included in the pageantry of the event, and these heraldic funerals became increasingly elaborate statements of the deceased's social status and wealth.

THE FUNERAL TRAPPINGS

During the procession the coffin would probably be covered by a pall bearing the arms of the deceased. For members of high nobility and royalty the bier might also be surmounted by a faithful representation of the dead person, dressed in robes of degree

▼ The design of 1619 for the hearse of Anne of Denmark, Queen of James I.

▲ The "State Ship" of Charles V, Holy Roman Emperor, 1558. Part of the spectacle of the royal funeral in Renaissance Europe.

and coronet. On either side of the bier would walk heralds bearing the elements of the deceased's heraldic achievement – his helm and crest, shield of arms, tabard, gauntlets, spurs and sword.

Central to the display in the church was the hearse, a large and often elaborate temporary structure made of wood, metal and cloth, built in the main body of the church. For higher ranks, the hearse was sometimes so elaborate it resembled the chapel in which the deceased would in due course be buried. The hearse had receptacles for burning tapers, in between which would be set the armorial bearings of the deceased, usually made of buckram.

Upon entering the church the coffin would be placed within the rails of the hearse, where the principal mourners would also take their places. The funeral of a high-ranking member of the nobility was attended not only by family members and other mourners, but even by the deceased's warhorse, decked out in the heraldic trappings of its master.

In Italy and Spain, well into the 20th century, the high-born would have lain "in state" at home before the funeral. The body lay either in a coffin or on a bed of state, dressed in court dress, with the bed itself covered with cloth of gold upon which

were embroidered the family arms. For the highest rank, household staff would hold mourning banners bearing arms. The hearse was also decorated by a number of

▼ A show of knightly rank – the tomb of the Black Prince, in Canterbury Cathedral, England, displays his full knightly regalia.

banners, standards, guidons and lesser flags, the exact number of which was regulated by degree. These and the rest of the achievement would in time be hung near to the burial place of the deceased, providing an awesome display of pomp.

THE HERALDS' ROLE

In Britain, the great age of the heraldic funeral was between 1500 and 1700. The marshalling of such events was largely the responsibility of the officers of arms, who jealously guarded their rights because of the fees due to them, which were known as "funeral droits". These were payable from the estate of the deceased and were considerable, the fee itself depending on the deceased's degree and the rank of the herald. The English heralds kept a keen eye on anyone – especially painters and engravers – who might encroach on their offices, and at times the various parties set to brawling with each other over their fees at the very door of the church, as the noble corpse was going to its final rest.

Every facet of the noble funeral was regulated by the heralds, from the number of mourners, their degree and the size of their trains, to the number, shape and size of the flags. The following letter to Garter Dethick, who held office from 1586–1606, gives some idea of the detail involved:

Good Mr Garter, I pray you, as your leisure doth best serve you, set down advisedly and exactly, in every particular itself, the number of mourners due to my calling, being a Viscountess of birth, with the number of waiting-women for myself, and the women mourners, which, with the chief mourner and her that shall bear the trayne, will be in number ten, beside waiting women, pages and gentlemen wishers. Then I pray you the number of chief mourners of Lords, Knights and gentlemen... Good Mr Garter, do it exactly; for I find forewarnings that bid me to provide a pick-axe etc. So with my most friendly commendation to you, I rest,
Your old Mistress and Friend,
Elizabeth Russel, Dowager.

▲ *The coffin of Christine, Duchess of Braunschweig-Bevern; the arms are those of her mother's family, Pfalz-Zweibrucken.*

The reply Mr Garter sent is very lengthy and includes the following details for the funeral procession:

That it include 4 Bannerolls [a type of heraldic banner showing "impalements" for family marriages], the Great Banner borne by a Knight or esquire, a preacher, a Garter King of Arms and 2 heralds. The Lady Chief Mourner was

▲ *The heraldic fittings on the coffin of the widowed Countess of Cholmondsley, 18th century, in Malpas Church, Cheshire, England.*

to have for her gown, mantle, traynes, hood and tippets, 11 yards of black cloth. Garter King of Arms was allowed liveries as a knight, 6 yards of cloth, the heralds 5 yards...

▼ *The heraldic achievements – the shield, sword, helmet, crest and so on – being carried by mourning attendants at the funeral of Charles VI of France, 1422.*

◀ *The monument to Alice, Dowager Countess of Derby, d1636–7, thought to be a representation of a heraldic hearse.*

THE ROTHES FUNERAL

The funeral of John, 1st and only Duke of Rothes, shows just what a heraldic funeral on the grand scale involved. The Duke had died on 27 July 1681, and his funeral took place almost a month later on 23 August. Having held the office of Lord High Chancellor of Scotland, he was afforded a full state funeral. It included every possible type of heraldic funeral trapping, as well as two complete regiments of artillery.

After the troops there followed the two conductors with crêpe in their hats and black staves over their shoulders, then two little "gumpheons" (gonfalones or square flags), one bearing a death's head with the

words *Memento mori* ("Remember you must die"), the other bearing an hourglass with the words *Fugit hora* ("Hours fly"). Then there followed a line of poor men in mourning cloaks that bore the Duke's cipher and coronet. Next came a trumpeter, his banner charged with the ducal achievement, then a cavalier on horseback. Next was a banner of the ducal colours or liveries borne by a gentleman. He was followed by the Duke's servants.

There then followed the Pencil of Honour, a swallow-tailed flag bearing the entire achievement, then one with the paternal arms (Leslie), followed by the Standard of Honour (similar to the pencil but with a square end). The warhorse was led by two "lacquies", who were bareheaded. Two trumpeters followed, then the Bute and Carrick pursuivants of arms in mourning gowns and tabards. Another small group of heraldic flags then followed: the Great Gumpheon, another gumpheon bearing the arms of Abernethy with a "laurel wreath in mourning" and the Little Mourning Standard.

After a group of gentlemen in mourning gowns and hats, there followed another two pursuivants, Kintyre and Dingwall, after which came the spurs, gauntlets, the breastplate, targe (shield), helm and wreath, and sword. Two more retainers then led the deceased's packhorse, after

which walked a goodly procession of officers and counsellors of Edinburgh, members of the judiciary and government and representatives of the peerage, followed by the last of the pursuivants, Unicorn and Ormonde. Two trumpeters then announced eight bearers with banners of kinship. On the paternal side (the right) were those of the Earl of Roxburgh, Hamilton of Evandale, the Earl of Perth and the Earl of Rothes; and on the left the descent through his mother from the Duke of Antragne, the Earl of Tullibardine, the Duke of Lennox and the Earl of Mar.

The mourning horse then followed, bearing a black trapper adorned with panels bearing the ducal arms. The last of the heraldic flags, the Great Mourning Banner, bore the ducal achievement and motto. Two more trumpeters announced six heralds: Islay, with the shield of Leslie; Albany, with that of Abernethy; Marchmont, with the crest, motto and wreath; Rothesay with the helm, coronet and mantling; Snowdon with the sword and Ross with the targe.

The Duke's servants and household officers followed, after which was led the Duke's horse for riding to Parliament covered with a richly embroidered saddle-cloth. Next came a gentleman bearing the Duke's coronet (with cap), followed by two archbishops and then Lord Lyon (the principal Scottish officer of arms) in tabard and

▼ *The funeral of Elizabeth I of England in 1603. The mourners carry banners of the Queen's ancestors.*

The Chariott drawne by foure Horses vpon which charret stood the Coffin couered wth purple Veluett and vpon that the reprefentation, The Canopy borne by S[r] Knights

mourning cloak carrying a diamond-shaped "hatchment" bearing the Duke's entire heraldic achievement.

More trappings of Parliament followed, including the Lord Chancellor's purse. Then followed the most extraordinary sight of the whole incredible spectacle: the coffin of the Duke itself, carried beneath a pall or mortcloth decorated with the arms of the Duke and his relations. These were interspersed with death's heads, ciphers and silver tears. Upon the cloth, which was borne along by close relations, was the Duke's coronet. The coffin was carried beneath a great canopy decorated like the pall, the poles of which were carried by noblemen's sons. Then followed the principal mourners and the mourning coach, the official procession being brought to a close by His Majesty's Guard.

The procession was said to have reached 8km (5 miles) in length. The entire affair cost about £30,000 ($42,000), the equivalent of some £3 ($4.2) million at today's prices, which was supposed to have been paid by the government, although in the end the family was left to pick up most of the enormous bill.

From the end of the 17th century, Protestant Britain saw a "noble rebellion" against the profligate cost of the grand heraldic funeral, which had become prohibitive even for the richest of families. Many of the traditions and the trappings that had been associated with such a funeral, such as armour for example, had themselves become long outdated and scarce, although up to that time there were still specialist manufacturers who carried on producing special "funeral armour".

▲ *The heraldic funeral par excellence – the coffin of the Duke of Rothes with a pall and canopy charged with his arms and teardrops. Note his coronet on the coffin.*

▼ *Just one small section of the Duke's funeral procession including his "cavalier" or champion and various types of mourning flags befitting a duke's degree.*

HATCHMENTS AND TRAPPINGS

From the medieval period until quite recently, the death of a member of the nobility was marked by a series of "memorials". While some were temporary, others were permanent, and were principally aimed at maintaining the status quo – the chief weapon in the armoury of status being heraldry.

TOMBS AND HERALDRY

On early memorials, whether in stone and brass, enamelled or carved, heraldry was limited to the bearer's own personal shield and crest. Soon, however, the place of burial was being used as a platform on which the nobility could show off not only the arms of their own family, but also those to whom they were united through marriage. By the Renaissance the grand monuments of the aristocracy displayed a series of shields for family marriages, often borne by fantastical figures such as angels. The children of the deceased were also often depicted on the tombs, kneeling with shields (for boys) and lozenges (for girls). The canopies and sides of the tombs, the dress of the effigies and even the most intricate of decoration might be used to support a display of heraldry. Death itself could be called upon to support the shield, or sometimes the shield of the deceased might be shown upside-down.

In Italy, gravestones often bear fully coloured arms of the deceased executed in *pietra dura*, an inlaying technique using a variety of coloured stones, but in most countries they tend to be carved in local stone and uncoloured. Whereas in Britain the flat stones set into the floors of many parish churches bear the arms of the deceased only, in Germany and the Low Countries they often bear a series of shields down the sides of the stone, those on the left for the father's side, those on the right for the mother's side.

CABINETS D'ARMES

During the Middle Ages, the trappings of knighthood were carried in the funeral procession and afterwards lay in the church near the grave of the deceased. In the Low Countries a new practice grew up in the 16th century, whereby the actual pieces of armour, sword, gauntlets, helm and tabard were replaced with painted reproductions, usually made of wood. These were grouped in a frame, together with the shields of the paternal and maternal grandparents. The background to the display was painted in mourning black. Such framed displays were called *cabinets d'armes*, or *cabinets d'honor*. It is thought that this practice led to the use of hatchments (a corruption of "achievement"), the

▲ A good example of a cabinet d'armes for a member of the de Schietere family, of Bruges, who died in 1637.

diamond-shaped mourning boards, many of which are still found hanging in parish churches in England today. The hatchment was hung outside the home of the deceased for a period of mourning, perhaps as much as a year and a day, indicating to visitors that a death had occurred in the family. The custom still persists in Britain, albeit rarely.

▲ The hatchment for Prince Leopold, Duke of Albany, youngest son of Queen Victoria.

▲ A splendidly restored Totenschild for Bürgermeister Hans Jörg, portrait included.

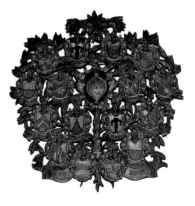

▲ A Swedish heraldic mourning panel for Per Brahe, d1680.

DECIPHERING HATCHMENTS

From the background of the hatchment and the composition of the arms, it is possible to work out the sex and marital status of the deceased. For a single person (bachelor, spinster, widow or widower) the background is all black. Where no marriage has existed, a shield (for a man) or a lozenge (for a woman) bearing the patrimonial arms is shown. In the case of a bachelor the helm and crest also appear. As the diamond-shaped lozenge is thought a somewhat plain shape, it is sometimes accompanied by a decorative blue bow.

Things become more complicated when a marriage has been made. When one of the couple survives, the background of the hatchment is divided vertically black and white, with black – as the colour of mourning – behind the deceased's half of the arms and white behind the survivor's half. When a wife dies before her husband, her hatchment bears a shield with no crest (a bow often being substituted), and the right-hand half of the background is black. If the husband dies first the whole achievement is shown, with black behind the left half. If the hatchment is for a widower, an all-black background is shown with shield, crest and marital coat of arms. If it is for a widow, the marital coat appears on a lozenge. These are the simplest cases, and there are many hatchments whose composition taxes the onlooker and can prove hard to interpret: in the case of a man who has married several times, for instance, the arms of all his wives may appear, with separate backing for each marriage.

Although a family motto often appears on a man's hatchment, it is just as likely to be replaced by a Latin phrase relating to death and resurrection, such as *Resurgam* ("I shall rise again"), *In coelo quis* ("There is rest in heaven") or *Mors janua vitae* ("Death is the doorway to life").

While many English parish churches contain one or two hatchments to a lord of the manor, or previous vicar, some have splendid collections for a whole family: such as that of the Hulse family of Breamore, Hampshire, where the church displays a set of hatchments that date from the early 18th century to the 1990s.

HATCHMENT DESIGNS

Examples of designs on funeral hatchments, which declare the status and position of the deceased person. From top – left to right – these are hatchments for: 1) A married man, 2) a married woman (note the bow on the top), 3) a widowed man, 4) an unmarried man, 5) a widowed woman, 6) an unmarried woman, 7–10) a widowed man who has survived two wives.

THE COAT
OF ARMS

The phrase "coat of arms" is a variant of the more ancient term "coat armour", which describes one of heraldry's principal accoutrements, the surcoat or tabard, which was worn for much of the late medieval period over a warrior's armour. Coat of arms is therefore something of a misnomer, for while it originally meant an actual garment bearing armorial devices, it has now come to represent the entire panoply of the personal achievement of arms, including shield, helm, crest, mantling, motto and supporters – but without any sign of an actual coat. The style of the full achievement of arms has changed over the centuries, developing from simple representations to the florid artistic visions of the Rococo period and the absurdities of the 19th century, when a crest might not connect to its helmet, and mantling looked more like foliage than cloth. An important factor to remember when describing a coat of arms is that the shield is described from the bearer's position behind it. The heraldic right, called dexter, and the heraldic left, called sinister, are the opposite to the normal right and left.

◄ *The arms and proud motto of the Spanish family,*
Manrique de Lara.

THE COMPLETE ACHIEVEMENT

The heraldic achievement is a grand affair consisting of several component parts. The first is the arms themselves on the shield, surmounted by the helmet, the detail of which may change to denote the rank or degree of the armiger. On the helmet usually sits that other important heraldic accoutrement, the crest. Hanging from the top of the helmet is a loose piece of cloth known as the mantling. For the medieval knight this cloth once perhaps served to give some protection to the back of the helmet; in heraldry it is normally depicted in the main metal and colour of the arms.

The mantling is attached to the helmet by means of twists of cord known as the wreath or torse. As with the mantling, the twists tend to be in the principal tinctures of the arms. If a crest coronet or circlet is borne this usually replaces the wreath (as

▶ *A full achievement typical of those granted in modern times by the English College of Arms, in this case to the author.*

▼ *The same achievement as right, but this black and white depiction of it has been hatched – each colour is represented by a system of lines and dots.*

LIVERIES

BADGE BANNER

CREST

MANTLING

CIRCLET (more often a wreath)

HELMET

SHIELD OF ARMS

MOTTO

PAVILION OR MANTLE

CROWN OR CORONET

WREATH

CREST

BADGE BANNER

SUPPORTERS

COMPARTMENT

DECORATIONS

SHIELD OF ARMS

▲ *The more elaborate full achievement of nobility, in this case the emperors of Germany, with crown and supporters.*

in the author's arms shown left) although sometimes the two items do appear one on top of the other. In English heraldry a motto, if borne, appears below the shield; in Scotland, above it. If a badge is also borne by the armiger it might appear alongside the full achievement on a banner of the liveries, as seen here, but this is not common.

This combination – of shield of arms, helm, crest, mantling and wreath – is the achievement of any armiger. For those of

▶ *The arms of Queen Elizabeth II: the shield is surmounted by the gold helmet of a sovereign.*

higher rank the full achievement can be much grander, with the shield supported by men or beasts; if the holder has a title, such as count or duke, the coronet of rank will also appear. In Britain the coronet sits above the shield, between it and the helm. In other nations the coronet might appear on the helm.

If the armiger is a member of an order of knighthood, the circlet or collar of his order may encircle the shield. For titled members of the aristocracy, a robe or mantle might also appear as a backdrop to the arms. Sovereigns tend to replace the mantle with the pavilion – a domed cloth on which sits the crown.

Such an achievement is a complex and expensive composition to show in its entirety, so an armiger is more likely to denote ownership of property, whether on a book cover or a private jet, by using just the crest or the combination or crest and motto. Holders of a peerage might also place their coronet above the crest or simple shield of arms. Once arms have been granted they may be displayed at will.

THE SHIELD

Ever since its inception, heraldry has relied on the shield for the main display of armorial bearings. All other parts of the achievement – such as the crest, mantling, wreath and supporters – depend on the shield, and while there are many cases of a shield of arms being granted by itself, no one can be granted a crest unless the family has at some time previously been granted a shield of arms. Although armorial bearings are often found on different items such as banners and surcoats, it is the shield that is considered the armorial platform without equal.

EARLY SHIELDS

From the very beginnings of organized fighting, the shield was one of the principal means of protection, and was used to stop sword, axe or arrow. Once a weapon passed that first defence, the only things left to protect the soldier were his body armour and his own fighting skills.

The ancient Greeks used round shields, while the Romans preferred large rectangular shields with slightly rounded ends. Each nation's soldiers decorated their shields with various devices: these might be national, regimental or tribal in nature, but were not truly heraldic in that they

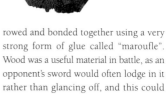

▶ *A rare medieval battle shield, an ideal platform for the heraldry that followed in the 13th and 14th centuries.*

were seldom personal, nor did they have any hereditary significance.

SHIELD CONSTRUCTION

At the start of the heraldic story in the second half of the 12th century, the shield was so long that it could cover almost half the bearer's body, and it was normally curved to fit around the torso. The shields used at the Battle of Hastings were kite-shaped and this style continued into the early 1200s, although by then the top edge of the shield was usually straight. Gradually, as the wearing of plate armour increased, the shield diminished in size until it was about a third of the height of the bearer.

Surviving medieval shields show that they were usually made of wooden sheets glued together in an early form of plywood. Several sheets of coarse-grained wood, such as beech or lime, were fur-

rowed and bonded together using a very strong form of glue called "maroufle". Wood was a useful material in battle, as an opponent's sword would often lodge in it rather than glancing off, and this could give the shield-bearer a split-second advan-

▼ *Round shields favoured by Greek warriors often showed devices that many centuries later appeared in heraldry.*

▼ *The seal of Count Conrad of Oettingen, c1229, shows heraldic charges almost certainly arising from the shield's construction.*

▼ *The English army at Hastings with long kite-shaped shields, the shape adapted to heraldic usage some 100 years later.*

▲ *Examples of heraldic devices that most probably arose from the construction of the medieval shield. Clockwise from top left, the shields are those of Valletort, Navarre, Mandeville and Holstein.*

▲ *The German and Italian knights in this 14th-century battle scene bear the flatiron or heater-shaped shield, which became the most common platform for heraldists.*

tage, which could make the difference between life and death. The shield was covered with leather (from horse, ass or buck), parchment or linen. The leather was first boiled in oil to make cuir-bouilli, another good defensive material. Often the exterior was also coated with gesso, or fine plaster, into which a decorative "diapered" pattern might be worked, resembling the designs woven into damask fabrics. Over the gesso surface the armorial bearings of the wearer were applied. These could either be painted flush with the surface, or moulded into slight relief.

SHIELD FITTINGS

The shield was given extra strength by nailing on metal studs, bands and other reinforcements, and some of these additions probably gave rise to heraldic charges themselves. Within this class of "structural" heraldry are examples such as the arms of the great Anglo-Norman family of Mandeville, whose "escarbuncle" (a wheel-like device in the centre of the shield) probably started off as a metal boss. The arms of Count Conrad II of Oettingen (c1229) show a "saltire" or diagonal cross, which probably originated as metal reinforcing bands, and those of Reginald de Valletourt of Cornwall, from the time of

King John, probably show not only the wooden slattings of the shield but the strengthening edge with its nails. It is also possible that the chain in the arms of Navarre started in similar fashion. Even the nettleleaf of Holstein was probably formed by a serrated metal border.

Various materials, from leather to padded cloth, were used for the inner side of the shield, and to these were fixed straps and padded cushions, the latter to allow extra comfort for the bearer and also to absorb the shock of sword and axe blows. Most medieval shields were also contoured to fit the body. Obviously the shield could not be held at all times; when not actually in use it was strung around the bearer's side by a leather strap known as a "guige".

All of this shows a sensible approach to the business of war as seen from the bearer's point of view. The medieval armourer was highly skilled and his shield, despite its size, was surprisingly light and well constructed, as was late medieval armour in general. The most important collection of surviving medieval shields is now in the University Museum of Marburg in Hesse, Germany. They originally lay in the Elizabethkirche in Marburg, having

been placed there by members of the Teutonic Order, and it is from them that historians have learned much about the construction of the shield.

By the late 13th century the shield's size had diminished considerably, and it had taken the form of the "heater" shield, so-called because it was shaped like the base of a flatiron. The heater shield proved remarkably popular and it is this shape that in the main has served heraldry since the 14th century.

THE TOURNEY SHIELD

From the late 14th century a new form of shield appeared, specifically for use on the tourney field. It was in the shape of a rectangle with curved edges – usually with slightly concave sides and top and with a convex base. While the war shield retained its flatiron shape for centuries, for tournaments the shield became a much more decorated affair, with scalloped edges and flutings. The tourney shield often bore

▲ *Knights taking part in a tournament of the 15th century bear concave shields specially designed for the tilt.*

► *The simple heater shield of the late 13th century.*

▲ *As art forms changed to more elaborate and florid designs so too did the heraldic shield, although in this example the notch at the top for the lance does still survive.*

elaborate devices – sometimes they were partially heraldic, often not – which gave out bold messages of love and bravura, the former for the ladies sitting in the viewing galleries around the arena, the latter for any would-be challenger. For use in jousting, the shield might also have a special notch cut out of the top corner to allow the lance to be "couched", or rested, more easily. By the late 15th century the armourer's expertise had advanced to such a degree that special rivets and bolts were often fitted on the body plates to take lance-rests and extra defences. There was at one time a tourney shield that could actually be fixed to the wearer's breastplate, and the lance rested at its corner.

◄ *This monument to the Earl of Hereford from 1621 shows how the shield itself began to assume a non-martial appearance.*

THE SHIELD IN HERALDRY

Strictly, for the purposes of heraldry, the shield takes one of two forms. The first is the shield proper, which bears the arms of men, and the second is the lozenge, a diamond-shaped device used to display the arms of women. In fact, however, the shape of the heraldic shield varied considerably over the centuries and can reveal much about the period when it was used, and even the country of origin of the bearer. The tourney shield made its appearance in heraldry and, along with the heater shield, was often depicted as being tilted slightly to one side. There is nothing heraldically significant in this: along with all the fancifully shaped shields that appeared on paper and in architecture, it simply reflected the artistic style of the period in which it was used.

▼ *With the Renaissance the mantling and helm became ever more intricate, as in this example from the mid-16th century.*

FASHIONS IN HERALDIC ART

From the 12th to the 16th century, the shapes of heraldic shields followed the fashions of real shields used in battle, but after the Renaissance artistic licence made inroads into all manner of decorations –

including heraldry. Artists and engravers saw the shield, and the armorial accoutrements that surrounded it, as ideal objects for embellishment. The arms were placed in highly ornate frames, held up by cherubs and draped with garlands, until in many cases the actual arms appear as an afterthought in the decorative scheme. But the Renaissance treatment of heraldry was nothing compared with the Rococo style of the 18th century, when shields ceased to be anything of the sort, instead becoming swirling and curving creations resembling the inside of a seashell. The heraldic shield took on forms that a medieval knight would have gaped at – certainly the scroll-like edges and fantastical flutings would have caused more harm than good if he had borne such a shield on the battlefield, as the enemy's lance could have found plenty of handy points to

affix to, rather than being deflected by the clean curves of the medieval shield.

The Rococo style had emerged from a great period of artistic and architectural triumph – the Baroque. No visitor to Rome can fail to be impressed at the sheer size of heraldic decoration lavished on the city by the popes of that period, each one seemingly wanting to outdo his predecessor by placing his own arms over gateways and triumphal arches, and on obelisks. The supreme example of heraldic ostentation must be the design of the church of Sant'Ivo alla Sapienza in Rome. Because Pope Urban VIII (1623–44) was a member of the Barberini family, the architect, Francesco Borromini, is said to have based his plan on the heraldic bees that appeared in the Barberini arms.

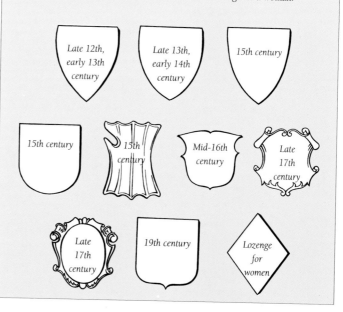

◀ *An 18th-century bookplate showing the elaborate heraldic style of the Rococo period.*

*William Dowdeswell Esq.
of Pull Court,
Worcester Shire.*

COMPLEXITY AND OBFUSCATION

At least the Rococo had some style about it, even if heraldry was corrupted to suit the contorted shapes of that style. What followed in the late 18th and 19th centuries can only be described as the heraldic doldrums. Shields became fat and unattractive, with tiny helmets perched above them bearing outsized crests and even more outsized wreaths, though each dropped well away from the top of the helmet upon which they were meant to sit. Perhaps the shields needed to be fat, given the complexity of designs they had to bear, which sometimes amounted to entire landscapes or complete historical accounts.

▼ *The climax of heraldic design was the fantastical Rococo period, when the arms became simply an excuse for the frame.*

▲ *The distinctive horse-head shield and the teardrop form are both shapes that are particularly favoured in Italy as a background for heraldry.*

SHIELD SHAPES
These illustrations show how the heraldic shield developed from the traditional flatiron shape through the tourney shield with the notch, the complexities of the Renaissance and the Rococo, back to the simple designs of modern heraldry and the lozenge for a woman.

Late 12th, early 13th century

Late 13th, early 14th century

15th century

15th century

15th century

Mid-16th century

Late 17th century

Late 17th century

19th century

Lozenge for women

THE CREST

After the shield, the second most important constituent part of an achievement of arms is the crest. This is the three-dimensional object that adorns the top of the helmet. While many modern writers cite the shield on the tomb plate of Geoffrey, Count of Anjou as the first example of true heraldic arms, they often pass over the little lion that adorns the Count's cap. Possibly this is the forerunner of the heraldic crest, although helmets had long been "crested" with various devices, including the brush-like structures surmounting the helmets of Roman legionaries.

THE HELMET AND DISPLAY

The true "heraldic" crest would seem to have taken shape a century or so after the advent of armorial bearings. Manuscripts from the 13th century sometimes show heraldic charges painted on the sides of knights' helmets, and it has been suggested

▼ The tomb-plate of Geoffrey, Count of Anjou, d1151. His conical cap bears a lion passant – was this in fact an early crest?

that the paint and lacquer used probably acted as an early form of rustproofing. From the early 13th century the top of the helmet was often flattened out and heightened into a fanlike crest. These projections were ideal for the display of painted motifs, usually copied from the bearer's shield.

Even from this early period the crest would appear to have been associated with men of tournament rank – the higher nobility – and in later centuries in certain countries crests were forbidden to all except those entitled to enter the lists. Tournaments were the most costly of sports and the participants were expected to put on a really exciting display of colour and bravado. Some outstanding examples appear on the seals of German knights from the 13th and 14th centuries. They show crests in the manner of wind chimes or revolving plaques edged in peacock feathers, some of which would whistle and rotate as the bearer charged his opponent, like heraldic mobiles. Such a display – like the wings worn by Polish lancers in the 17th and 18th centuries (which also had whistles attached to them) – was probably intended to strike awe and even terror in the opponent, but also satisfied the vanity of the wearer.

In the 14th century a type of crest called the "panache" was popular, especially among English knights. It consisted of

▼ These elaborate crests, taken from the personal seals of German knights in the late 14th century and early 15th century, show

▲ This crest from a helmet, c1350, is a rare survival of the buffalo horns so beloved by German medieval families.

layers of feathers decorating the helmet, which rose to a peak, often following the contours of the bascinet – the domed helmet much in vogue at the time.

GERMAN CRESTS

From the 15th century crests became highly complex, and in Germany the craft of crestmaking was a profession of note.

German helmets were often surmounted by buffalo horns or pairs of wings (frequently decorated with charges

wind chimes and mobiles that would have been suitable for a dramatic grand entrance to the tourney field.

▲ *The arms of the Folkunga dynasty of Sweden; the buffalo horns on the helmet are adorned with little flags.*

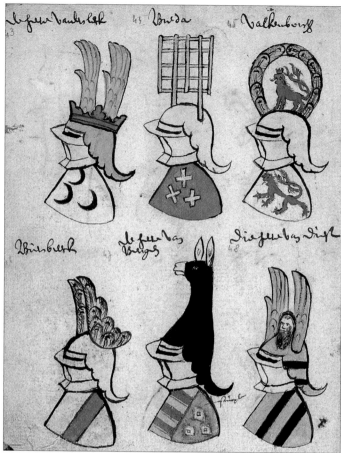

▲ *The Huldenberg Armorial, a Flemish heraldic armorial of the late 15th century, shows the wings and peacock feathers that were popular in North European heraldry.*

taken from the shield of arms). It has been suggested that the curved shapes of such ornaments may have aided in the deflection of sword blows. The edges of these typically Germanic crests were further enhanced with little leaves or bells, but the most popular decoration of all was peacock's feathers, which featured on as many as half of all crests.

The spaces between the wings or horns afforded a platform for even greater elaboration: conical caps, towers and human figures were added to elicit the admiration of the tournament audience, and sometimes the crests of two families were combined to make a "crest of alliance". Often the human figures in medieval German crests were without arms, and their dress, or even their skin, forms the mantling of the helm – the material protecting its back and sides. In old German such limbless figures were called *Menschen-tumpf*, "men's torsos". Unlike German crests, those of the English and French

◀ *Menschentumpf (men's torsos) were popular crests in late medieval German heraldry.*

nobility tended to be separate from the mantling. Instead, the crest appeared to sit within a twisted cord of material known as the wreath or torse.

MULTIPLE CRESTS

In Britain, France, Italy and Spain, crests were seldom as complex as those found in Germany, and in those countries a family seldom used more than one crest, as opposed to German aristocracy and royalty, who often had as many as half a dozen or more crested helms above their shields, each crest tending to represent not so much a family as a fiefdom. In Britain, buffalo horn and peacock's feathers are almost unknown, and the heads of men or demicreatures tend to be unaccompanied, unless by crest coronets. In Spanish

heraldry, crests were so rare that they are almost non-existent (only used by a few ancient noble families). Ostrich plumes are the usual adornment to the Spanish heraldic helmet.

Where an English family has assumed a second surname through marriage to a heraldic heiress, a second crest may be adopted. Occasionally, a second crest may be granted or assumed on some special occasion, usually by "augmentation" – an addition to the arms that in some way reflects the gratitude of the donor, who would usually be royal.

▲ *The arms of the Princes of Lippe, late 19th century. In German lands multiple crests were common within the arms of the higher nobility.*

GRUESOME REMINDERS

One of the most deadly creatures in all heraldry must surely be the viper in the crest (and on the shield of arms) of the Visconti family, the medieval rulers of Milan. The various stories of the viper's origin must have bought many a truculent Italian child to obedience. One tale tells of an enormous serpent that had terrorized the locality and had to be placated by regular offerings of fresh babies; it was finally vanquished by an early Visconti. Another story concerns Ottone Visconti, who is said to have killed a Saracen prince, Voluce, beneath the walls

of Jerusalem during the First Crusade. Ottone took Voluce's own crest – a ferocious dragon or serpent devouring a child – as his own. No family has enjoyed its heraldry as much as the Visconti, and a special place is afforded to the viper, which has been depicted in the fullest possible way through the centuries, and can be seen today throughout the world on the badge of Alfa-Romeo cars.

Human heads of various races recall past conflicts. Of these, the Saracen's head is the most common, reflecting the exploits of the Crusader knights. The Hazelriggs of Noseley in Leicestershire have as their crest a Scot's head, commemorating the family's part in the harrying of Scotland by Edward III (1327–77). Though they are not used as a crest, it is also worth mentioning the

three Englishmen's heads in the arms of the Welsh family of Bulkeley-Williams. Together with many other Welsh families, they claim descent from the 13th-century Welsh chieftain Edynfed Vychan. The heads commemorate an incident during a conflict between the English and the Welsh, when the chieftain surprised a band of soldiers from the household of Ranulph, Earl of Chester. In the action that followed, three of Ranulph's principal commanders were killed. The story goes that the Tudors, another family who claimed descent from Edynfed Vychan, also adopted the three heads as charges, but upon their arrival at the English court thought it prudent to turn the heads into three helmets.

The Hamond-Graeme baronets (extinct) of the Isle of Wight had – in addition to another – a rather gruesome crest: two erect arms issuing from clouds in the act of removing a human skull from a spike; above the skull a marquess's coronet between two palm branches. The whole composition is a prime example of a "paper crest", which could never actually have adorned a medieval helmet.

The story behind the crest refers to a member of the Graeme family, a follower of the Marquess of Montrose, who was

▼ *The infamous and highly ferocious viper of the Viscontis, devouring a child.*

executed in Edinburgh in 1650 after his attempt to avenge the death of Charles I. The Marquess's head was placed on the roof of the Tolbooth, the city prison, but his Graeme relative managed to retrieve it and hide it until it could be afforded a proper burial in the Montrose vault.

MANTLING AND WREATH

The crested helm was an elaborate affair that was further decorated with a large piece of cloth, secured to the top of the helmet by cords or other fastenings. In

▼ *The rather gruesome crest of the Hamond-Graeme family in which a skull is lifted from a spike in remembrance of an ancestor's 17th-century exploit.*

▲ *The early heraldry of the Scandinavian nobility closely followed the styles favoured in Germany, as here in the crests of the families of Thott (left) and Wrangel (right)*

of Sweden. The Wrangel crest shows the type of mantling that is reminiscent of its possible origin – a makeshift sunshade used by the Crusaders.

British heraldry this cloth helmet cover is called the mantling. Usually the mantling is bi-coloured – its upper surface bearing the principal colour in the arms and its underside the principal metal – although three or four colours may be employed, as is the case in Spanish and Portuguese heraldry.

In the earliest depiction of crests the cloth mantling was quite simply portrayed, hanging down as one complete piece of cloth covering much of the side of the helmet. Later, especially during the age of heraldic decadence in the 17th and 18th centuries, the mantling was slashed into many elaborate pieces, often resembling foliage rather than cloth. Families of ancient lineage tended to frown on such effete depiction and kept to the simple style of the 14th and 15th centuries.

◀ *An illustration from the Manesse Codex (c1300) in which a certain Herr Harwart fights a bear. The crest above the bear's head is of the early fan-plate type.*

The attachment of mantling and crest to the helm was often hidden by a wreath or torse of twisted cloth, usually in the same colours as the mantling. In Spanish and Portuguese heraldry, the mantling appears not to be connected to the helmet, but is portrayed rather like a backdrop to it. In the late medieval period it was not unknown for the mantling to serve as a setting for charges taken from the arms or family badge.

Various heraldic experts have suggested that both the mantling and the wreath may have originated during the age of the Crusades. Wearing any form of plate armour in the heat of the Middle Eastern sun cannot have been pleasant, and there are tales of knights actually cooking in their kit. It is possible that some degree of comfort may have been gained from adapting the local headdress and wearing it over the top of the helmet, and certainly the combination of simple mantling and wreath bears a strong similarity to traditional Arab headgear.

THE HELM AND CORONET

As early as the 12th century, the mounted warrior's helmet had become a platform for heraldic colour and charges, which were often painted on its side and may have helped to protect its surface.

▼ *Helmets of degree for French royals and nobles, in the second half of the 18th century.*

However, in terms of armorial bearings it was a long time before the helmet itself became a truly heraldic accessory – before the late 15th century it was included in the coat of arms simply as a support for the crest. The helmets depicted in early heraldic manuscripts and on monumental effigies followed whatever style happened

◀ *The helm show in King René's tournament book – here the crest of a knight who has offended a lady is struck down.*

to be in favour at the time. They were little used to indicate rank, and armorials show all degrees, from knights to monarchs, using the same type of helmet.

HELMETS AND RANK

From around 1500 the bearing of crowns and coronets on the helmets of those of royal rank became common, and at the same time the grilled "pageant helmet" was appearing, which had a number of ornamental bars across the face. During the Renaissance, the depiction of the grills, and even the metals of the helmet, became increasingly embellished according to rank. The helmet was soon to become yet another piece of "paper heraldry", with grandiose patterns, gold and silver edgings and specified numbers of bars depending on the rank of the bearer. The arms of the lesser nobility bore either the closed helm, which had a solid visor and fully covered the face, or the frog-faced tilt helm.

▼ *An Italian ornamental helmet with crest and wreath from around 1450–70, and other later additions.*

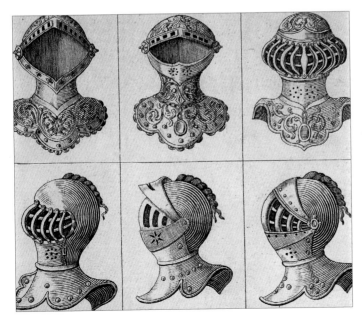

▲ *Heraldic crests were added to whatever style of helmet was popular at the time; here the crest of the Wittelsbach dukes of Bavaria surmounts a sallet helmet.*

▲ *The crowning of Queen Elizabeth II of Great Britain, in 1953, in Westminster Abbey. A coronation is the one occasion when all peers wear their coronets of rank.*

As with most heraldic accoutrements, it was France that led the fashion in the portrayal of helmets. French heralds not only drew up patterns for the helmets of different ranks – from the sovereign (all gold with visor open), down to new nobility (plain steel with three bars) – but also specified the position in which the helmet was to be depicted. Most faced right, or "dexter"; a helmet facing in the opposite direction ("sinister") indicated illegitimacy. Spain and Portugal followed suit with

▲ *A modern heraldic coronet, for a region of the Gabon – l'Ogooué-Ivindo.*

equally elaborate helmets, but in the Holy Roman Empire (centred on the German-speaking regions) no such contrived system of helmets developed. The German titled nobility used the grilled helmet but without any specific numbers of bars, while new nobility (down to the third generation) were supposed to use the closed helm. However, in the late 19th century, German and Scandinavian families of ancient lineage attempted to assert their superiority over the newly ennobled by setting their arms in the style of the 14th and 15th centuries, the helm being the great helm of that period.

The nobility of England knew only two styles of heraldic helmet. The barred helmet, in silver with gold bars, was given to the members of the peerage, or major nobility. Knights, baronets and gentlemen were given the plain steel closed helm, with the visor open for the first two degrees and closed for gentlemen.

CORONETS AND CROWNS

From the 14th century, crowns or jewelled circlets began to appear in the arms of many families, not only those of royal rank. At the same time, however, some documents of the age also show the arms

of rulers bearing crested helms without any distinguishing royal headgear. Crowns and coronets are common in heraldry, either above the shield or helm, or as charges.

Early heraldic coronets tended to be simplified versions of those worn by kings and princes. From a jewelled circlet rose a series of leaf-like embellishments, which in later centuries became formalized as fleurs de lis, strawberry leaves and other standard designs. The styles of coronets of rank among the aristocracy was set in the 16th and 17th centuries, although Europe's nobility had actually been wearing coronets for centuries.

The Renaissance brought with it an ever more formalized system of coronets, with tops constructed of specific numbers of leaves and pearls depending on the bearer's rank. In most cases these are heraldic conventions, and such designs were never actually worn. Southern European states took the heraldry of France as their model, while northern Europe looked to the Holy Roman Empire for styles and patterns.

The only nobility (as opposed to royalty) actually to wear their coronets were, and are, the British, where coronets are worn by peers on only one occasion – the coronation of the sovereign. At the moment of crowning the peers place their crowns on their heads. In recent times heraldic coronets have been designed for civic councils, not only in Europe but as far afield as Gabon in West Africa.

THE SUPPORTERS

Supporters, as their name suggests, are those heraldic accessories that support the shield of arms. They may be human figures, animals or mythical beasts, and very rarely they can also be inanimate objects. Supporters are by no means as common as the other components of a coat of arms, the shield, crest and helmet. They are mainly associated with the highest ranks of nobility and royalty. Various suggestions have been offered to explain the origins of heraldic supporters. One such suggestion

▲ *An angel supporting a shield of arms on a medieval church roof, the possible origin of many a heraldic supporter.*

▼ *Angels supporting the arms of the Empire and Nuremberg, by Albrecht Dürer, 1521.*

concerns the flights of angels that decorate many a medieval church roof. Often the angels hold symbols of saints or representations of the Passion, and some also support the shields of benefactors; perhaps the first supporters were echoing this device. Another explanation for the presence of supporters is as space fillers in the designs of medieval heraldic seals. In this context, supporters were a delightful conceit by which the seal engraver could avoid any large blank areas, which would not imprint well. An example of this is the seal of Gilles de Trazegnies, which shows his shield of arms suspended over the shoulders of a bear by its guige (the strap used to suspend the shield when not needed in battle). This seal has been dated to 1195, one of the earliest instances of a heraldic supporter. Almost half the seals of English

▼ *The wildmen supporters of the Kingdom of Prussia, with traditional oak leaf nether garments and headgear.*

barons found on a letter to the pope dating from 1300–1 have complex designs with Gothic-style archings and piercings. The spaces between these patterns and the shield are filled with dragons, lions or similar charges; often pairs of the creatures appear to be resting on the edge of the shield – very much like the supporters of a century or two later.

Supporters in the form of monsters – usually human figures of ferocious appearance, such as giants or wild men of the woods – could well have their origins in the fantastical displays put on during tournaments and pageants sponsored by noble participants. The knights would have their entrance announced by their servants, who would be dressed up for the occasion in the most fanciful of costumes.

HUMAN FIGURES

Since most members of the nobility of Europe like to trace their ancestry back to a warrior forebear, it is not surprising to find military figures supporting the shields of many titled families. Human supporters have been adapted to suit the period and the profession of the bearer, but possibly the most curious warrior supporters are two Augustinian friars, each bearing a sword, belonging to one of the princes of Monaco. They commemorate the legendary capture of Monaco in 1297 by

▼ *Francisco Grimaldi and his companion, both disguised as Augustinians, supporting the shield of the princes of Monaco.*

Francisco Grimaldi and his companions, who disguised themselves as Augustinians and thereby utterly surprised the garrison.

Soldiers often appear as supporters to commemorate a battle or campaign in which an ancestor proved himself. Such supporters are popular in British and Russian heraldry and Hungarian hussars support the shields of various Hungarian counts. Armoured knights were very popular in the 18th and early 19th centuries.

OTHER SUPPORTERS

In the Holy Roman Empire, some cities with rights of free trade and exemption from certain taxes bore their arms on the imperial *Doppeladler* (double-headed eagle). The families of high-ranking nobles – counts and princes of the Holy Roman Empire – also often bore their arms on the breast of this creature, surely one of the most impressive charges in the entire heraldic menagerie. Few English families were entitled to the use of the imperial eagle, associated as it was with a Catholic monarchy, but the Dukes of Marlborough and Earls Cowper (both princes of the Holy Roman Empire) and the Barons Arundell of Wardour made use of the right, with licence from the British monarch.

The grandest creature of all must be the *Quaternionenadler*, emblem of the Holy Roman Empire between the 15th century and 17th century. Here the double-headed eagle was fully displayed, with each pinion of its wings bearing a group of four shields representing the empire's lands.

▼ *The curious supporters of the counts de Grave – peacocks with human faces.*

Curious marriages of monster and man also arise, surely none more exotic than the human-faced peacock supporters of the de Grave family in France.

Most supporters are borne in pairs, but this is by no means the rule. An early example of a single supporter is the goat-headed eagle of Count Gottfried of Ziegenhain (*Ziege* is the German word for goat) of the late 14th century. A branch of the Scottish family of Campbell has the unique distinction of placing its arms in front of a Scottish heraldic ship, the "lymphad". This was probably adapted from a similar vessel found in the arms of Lorne, which were also quartered by the Campbells.

Rarer than the single supporter are multiple supporters. Of these, the most curious example appears on the arms of the d'Albret family, former Constables of France. For this heraldic balancing act, the supporters are two lions, each wearing a helmet and supporting an eagle. A more modern example of multiple supporters was granted in 1981 to Air Chief Marshal Sir John Davis, Knight Grand Cross of the Order of the Bath. The supporters are two black eagles, but also, under the wing of one, a young eaglet appears, representing

▲ *The double-headed eagle of the Holy Roman Empire, 1587, the wings charged with groupings of shields.*

▶ *The statue of a heraldic salmon supporting the arms of Greystock, made for Thomas, Lord Dacre (1467–1526).*

Sir John's former position as chief officer overseeing training of aircrews.

MODERN TRENDS

In England and Wales, supporters are currently granted only to peers of the realm, Knights of the Garter, Grand Cross, of the Orders of the Bath, St Michael and St George, the British Empire and the Royal Victoria Order. In Scotland supporters are granted to the Knights of the Thistle and holders of old feudal titles.

In recent years the British House of Lords has seen the exodus of most hereditary peers,

▲ *An unusual case of a single supporter, the heraldic ship of the Campbells of Craignish.*

▼ *A heraldic balancing act – the supporters of the d'Albrets.*

▼ *A mother eagle guards its fledgling – the allusive supporters (dexter) of the late Air Chief Marshal, Sir John Davis, GCB.*

who have been replaced by an increasing number of life peers. This wind of change has been reflected in the nature of the heraldic supporters granted to the "lifers", who often eschew traditional creatures such as lions, wyverns, dragons and griffins. In their place stand more personal figures such as family pets, for when life peers die so also do their supporters.

The crime writer, P. D. James, now Baroness James of Holland Park, has two tabby cats to support her lozenge of arms. Baroness Perry of Southwark, another fan of the feline species, also decided on two cats for her supporters – a tabby tom and a Persian female. The latter is depicted standing on a pile of books, as she is not as big as the tabby. Dogs, too, have

▶ *A traditional choice of supporters – a lion and a stag – is depicted in the decadent Rococo style. The animals' general lack of interest means the shield isn't actually supported at all.*

▲ *A British bulldog supporter and an American bald eagle celebrate the marriage of an Englishman – Lord Hanson – to his American wife.*

their day in the modern world of heraldry. Lord Cobbold chose for his supporters two golden labradors based on his pets. As Lord Cobbold is a hereditary peer, unusually his dog supporters descend in the male line so long as the family continues.

▲ *The arms of Baroness Perry showing her domestic cat supporters.*

THE COMPARTMENT

Beneath the shield, placed as if to give supporters a foothold or resting place, is an object known as the compartment. Although instances of animal and human supporters lodged in parks or on mounds are known from the late medieval period, the compartment seems mainly to have been a product of the Renaissance, when heraldic artists expressed the artistic motivation of the age by showing the arms in

▼ *In the arms of the Old Town of Belgrade, the supporters stand on a battlemented compartment.*

elaborate frameworks, with the shield and supporters placed on splendid pedestals decorated with classical motifs, masks, foliate symbols and strapwork. Later artistic periods lent their styles to shield supporters and compartment alike.

By the 19th century the compartment had largely been reduced to a piece of metalwork looking rather like a bracket for an old gas lamp, with the heraldic supporters performing a rather precarious balancing act. Even more common was the use of the paper scroll as a platform, upon which stood horses, griffins, or even elephants.

Royal burghs of Scotland are entitled to stand their heraldic supporters on a special compartment that is formed of turretted and embattled masonry, often with the motto set in a plaque in the compartment, something copied in arms of the Old Town of Belgrade.

In recent years, the Canadian Heraldic Authority has included in many of its grants of arms to civic and regional authorities, compartments that reflect the geography, flora and even fish of the area. The supporters of the City of White Rock, for example, stand on a white rock charged with two forts, while the arms of the

▲ *Kangaroos support the shield of the Australian Northern Territory on a compartment of sand.*

Canadian Heraldic Authority itself rest on a compartment strewn with two maple leaves. The Authority's most curious innovation is its amalgamation of compartment and single supporter by placing a shield on a cathedra, or bishop's chair.

The English heralds have been granting compartments for some years, one of the most unusual being the arms granted to the Northern Territory of Australia in 1978. The grant of arms quotes the compartment as having a "grassy sandy mound", the shield of arms takes the brown colour of the local earth and bears the following charges: "Aboriginal rock paintings including a woman with styled internal anatomy".

▼ *The arms of Canada's cathedral churches shows an interesting combination of the single supporter and the compartment.*

MOTTOES AND INSCRIPTIONS

The coat of arms often includes a word or short sentence known as the motto. The position of the motto is somewhat nebulous compared to that of the shield of arms and crest. In England, where it appears below the shield, it is not even mentioned in a grant of arms and can be changed at will. Most mottoes are of relatively recent origin. In Scotland, however, the motto is considered a hereditary item much in the manner of the arms and crest, and is therefore mentioned in grants and matriculation of arms.

ANCIENT WAR CRIES

The motto probably has its origin in the *cri-de-guerre* or war cry of medieval warlords, used to rally their retinues and imbue in them a sense of loyal pride and bravura. In this league are the mottoes of the great Irish families of Butler and FitzGerald, who respectively rallied to their chiefs under the calls of *Butler a boo*, and *Crom a boo*. "A boo" was the Erse cry to victory, and Croom Castle a principal property of the FitzGeralds.

Scottish mottoes, which appear above the crest, are very much in the manner of the ancient war cry. Among the most famous are *Gang warily* of the earls of Perth,

▼ *The famous war cry of the Dukes of Leinster,* Crom a boo, *was later adopted as the motto on their arms.*

▲ *The simple* Through *motto of the Dukes of Hamilton, depicted above the crest, in typical Scottish fashion.*

and *Through* of Hamilton, and the less familiar but curious *Beware in time* of Lumsden of Innergelly, and *Enough in my hand* of Cunningham of Cunninghamhead, which is borne above the crest of a hand bearing the upper part of an anchor. Other branches of the Cunningham family bear *Over fork over* and their arms are charged with their famous "shakefork". This is said to commemorate one of the family who, while fleeing enemies, disguised himself as a farmworker forking hay. Mesmerized by the closeness of his foes, he nearly gave himself away until a companion whispered in his ear the words that now provide the family motto. Like many similar picturesque tales, they were almost certainly invented to give an ordinary heraldic charge a noble origin.

Among the abundant references to the bloody history of the Scots crown in the heraldry of that nation's noble families, are the crest and motto of Kirkpatrick. The

crest – a hand holding a bloody dagger – and the motto *I mak sikker* ("I make sure"), refer to the supposed outcome of a feud between Robert the Bruce and Red Comyn. Robert the Bruce managed to wound Comyn but the deed was finished by Bruce's follower, Kirkpatrick, who made the fatal thrust with his own dagger.

The motto of the Robertsons of Struan is *Virtutis gloria merces*, "Glory is the reward of valour." Like the crest – a hand grasping a crown – it refers to the capture in 1437 of the murderers of King James I by Robertson, the Chief of Clan Donnachaidh. An unconventional and unexplained feature of the arms is the figure of a naked man, chained and manacled, lying beneath the shield.

A curious happening is responsible for the motto *Prenez harleine tirez fort*, "Take aim and shoot strongly", borne to this day by the ancient family of Giffard of Chillington in Staffordshire, along with the two crests of a panther's head and an archer with a quiver of arrows and a drawn bow. They commemorate an event on the Giffard estate when Sir John Giffard was teaching his young son archery. A panther, a gift to Sir John, had escaped and was about to attack a woman and her baby. Sir John told his son to take aim with his bow and arrow. The lad did so, but with obvious trepidation, so Sir John whispered in his ear the words that became the family's motto. The boy did take aim, fired strongly, and according to legend, managed to kill the panther with a single shot.

▼ *The two crests of a bowman and panther belonging to the Giffards of Chillington.*

▲ *A heraldic statement of the love borne between Sigismondo Malatesta, Lord of Rimini, and his lady, Isotta degli Atti.*

▲ *The proud motto of the Manrique de Lara family of Spain.*

PIETY AND AFFIRMATION

Many mottoes urge both onlooker and bearer to espouse Christian values or even, as in that of the great French family of

▲ *A statement of sovereignty – Vespasius Gonzaga, Duke of Sabbioneta, acclaims the freedom of his little state from the parent duchy of Mantua.*

Montmorency – *Dieu ayde au primer baron chrestien* – to ask God to assist the family. Others affirm the nobility of the line, among them being *Let Curzon hold what Curzon held* of the Curzons of Kedleston in England (whose estate has remained in the family from the Norman Conquest until the present day), and the splendid *Nos non venimos de reyes, que reyes vienen de nos* of the great Castilian family of Manrique de Lara, which asserts "we do not come from kings, kings come from us".

INSCRIPTIONS ON THE SHIELD

Letters and words used as charges on the shield are not uncommon but tend to be frowned upon by many in the heraldic world as inauthentic. Nevertheless, letters and words are often used for the proudest reason, the "SPQR" (*Senatus Populusque Romanus*) of the Roman Empire being the most famous case. During the Renaissance, the rulers of northern Italy often combined their family arms with their ciphers, but the great mercenary general Sigismondo Malatesta went one better. He quartered his arms with his own initials and with those of his lover, Isotta degli Atti.

A lettered shield, worthy of remark, is that in the former arms of the island of Saaremaa in Estonia. In the first half of the

16th century the island's ruler, Bishop Johannes Kievel, was an admirer of Duke Friedrich III of Saxony, protector of Martin Luther. Consequently, he gave to Saaremaa a shield bearing the letters "DWGBE", the initial letters of Duke Friedrich's personal motto *De wort Gottes blist ewig*, "The word of God endureth forever".

▲ *As a statement of loyalty, Bishop Johannes IV Kievel remembers the motto of Duke Friedrich III of Saxony, on the shield of the island of Saaremaa.*

THE LANGUAGE
OF HERALDRY

Many people are baffled by the language used by heraldists in the English-speaking world. In many countries it relies heavily on Norman French, the language of William the Conqueror, which was spoken by the nobility in much of Europe during the period when heraldry was evolving. To take one example, "Vert three estoiles Or" would be the correct way to describe a green shield upon which were three gold stars with wavy rays, yet none of the descriptive words are English. In other nations, such as Germany, heraldic language is much nearer to modern-day usage.

The language of heraldry is known in the English-speaking world as "blazonry", from the old German word *blasen,* meaning to blow a horn. At a tournament, it was the duty of the medieval herald to call out the names, titles, genealogy and arms of the participating knights, accompanied by a flourish of trumpets, and the word thus also came to mean a public proclamation.

◄ *The unusual crest of the Davenport family of Capesthorne, England – showing an anonymous felon on his way to execution.*

COLOURS, METALS AND FUR

Heraldic language – no less vivid than the contrasting colours and bright metals of heraldry itself – paints a word picture of the luxurious accoutrements of medieval nobles. The terms suggest exotic and costly goods imported from the far corners of the known world, such as sable – the sleek, black fur of the marten, brought by merchants from far-off Muscovy – or gules, the rose-red dye produced in Persia and Turkey. The general term used to define all colours and textures on a shield of arms is equally picturesque and evocative: colours, metals and furs are together known as "tinctures", a word that at one time meant a dye or tint.

COLOURS AND METALS

To begin the "blazoning", or description in heraldic terms, of any shield of arms, it is necessary to deal with colour, since the very first word used in the description refers to the colour of the background or "field"

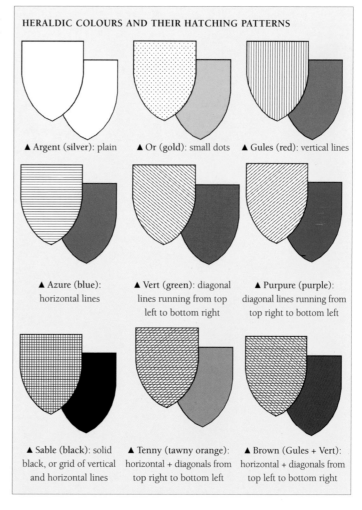

HERALDIC COLOURS AND THEIR HATCHING PATTERNS

▲ Argent (silver): plain

▲ Or (gold): small dots

▲ Gules (red): vertical lines

▲ Azure (blue): horizontal lines

▲ Vert (green): diagonal lines running from top left to bottom right

▲ Purpure (purple): diagonal lines running from top right to bottom left

▲ Sable (black): solid black, or grid of vertical and horizontal lines

▲ Tenny (tawny orange): horizontal + diagonals from top right to bottom left

▲ Brown (Gules + Vert): horizontal + diagonals from top left to bottom right

▲ *Two good examples of the reason behind the rule against colour on colour. From a distance identification would be very difficult.*

of the shield. There are five main colours in heraldry (although this differs slightly from nation to nation): red, blue, black, green and purple. Some mixed colours, known as stains, are also sometimes used. The two metals – gold and silver – are usually depicted as yellow and white. In British heraldry Norman French names are used for colours and metals, though gold and silver are also sometimes used in blazonry instead of "Or" and "Argent".

The colour green has intrigued heraldic writers for centuries. Some suggest that it

was actually unknown in early heraldry, yet one of the earliest compilations of arms, illustrating the *Historia Anglorum* (written between 1250–59 by an English cleric, Matthew Paris) clearly shows the shield of one of chivalry's greatest names, William Marshal, with a field of gold and green.

THE RULE OF TINCTURES

An important heraldic principle governs the use of colours and metals: "Never place a colour on a colour or a metal on a metal". It is a very sensible rule, remembering that the original purpose of heraldry was quick and ready identification on the battlefield. Life could depend on it. A blue charge on a black field, for example, or gold on silver, would be difficult to distinguish in the melée of medieval warfare. However, as long as the charge lies partly on an opposite – such as a red lion on a field of gold and blue – this does not constitute a breaking of the rule.

The rule is not strictly observed in some countries, and Archbishop Bruno Heim in his book *Or and Argent* (1994) gives many examples of gold charges on a white field, the most famous being the arms of Jerusalem. Some heraldic writers have suggested, however, that the gold crosses on this shield were originally red, but that medieval painting methods and materials caused the red to oxidize, causing later heraldists to mistake the original colour.

HERALDIC FURS

▲ Vair   ▲ Countervair   ▲ Potent   ▲ Counterpotent

▲ Ermine   ▲ Ermines   ▲ Erminois   ▲ Pean

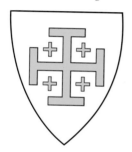

▲ *The arms of Jerusalem, possibly an exception to the rule against metal on metal, allowed because of the holiness of the city.*

FURS

In addition to the colours and metals, heraldry makes use of "furs" – patterns that suggest the costly furs worn by the medieval nobility. The two main furs are "ermine" and "vair", and each has several derivatives. Fur, just like a coloured field, can have any variety of charges placed upon it, and can take the place of either metal or colour.

Ermine is the highly prized winter fur of the common stoat. The animal's coat changes colour from chestnut brown to white except for the tip of its tail, which remains black. In heraldry, ermine is shown as a white field strewn with little black tail-tips, usually accompanied by

three black dots, which represent the fastenings by which the pelts were sewn into a robe. Ermine by itself constitutes the arms of the dukes of Brittany and makes a simple but splendid appearance in *The Book of Tourneys* of King René of Anjou.

Vair is indicated by a white and blue pattern said to represent the pelts of a species of squirrel, the blue-grey fur from its back arranged alternately with the paler fur from its underbelly. Vair was the arms of the Beauchamp family of Somerset, England and is often included in the quarterings of Henry VIII's wife, Jane Seymour.

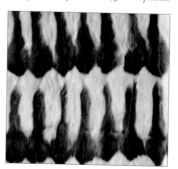

▲ *A real piece of vair, the fur made from the back and fronts of squirrel pelts sewn into a warm and handsome covering, from which the heraldic fur is derived.*

HATCHING AND TRICKING

It is, of course, not always possible to use colour in depictions of arms, and various methods of identifying heraldic colours in black and white have been used. The two most common are known as "hatching" and "tricking". Silvestro de Petra Sancta, a 17th-century Jesuit writer, devised the method of showing colours represented by lines and dots, which was later named hatching, and which has been universally used.

A simple description of a shield of arms can also be made by tricking: this involves a sketch of the arms being annotated with abbreviations for each colour, as in the example below. In this system azure becomes az, gules gu and so on.

▲ *An example of the tricking of a crest, where each colour is denoted by the letters of the heraldic tincture.*

THE DIVISION OF THE FIELD

The entire surface of the heraldic shield is known as the field, and its tincture is always described first in blazonry. It is said that the simplest arms are the best, and indeed there have been cases where an ancient family has borne for its arms a shield of just a single plain colour. The most famous example is probably the noble French family of d'Albret, which bore a shield simply Gules, while the English knight, Sir Thomas Holland (1320–60) abandoned his ancient family arms in favour of a plain shield Sable.

Of course, to allow for the numerous variations needed to ensure that every shield is unique, a more elaborate scheme is usually required. Any number of motifs, known as charges, may be placed on the field, from basic geometric shapes to representations of any object, animate or inanimate. Whether or not charges appear, the field may be divided into sections of different colours.

DESCRIBING THE DIVISIONS

When the shield is divided, or "parted", into various simple divisions or blocks, this is signalled by the words "party per", (divided by) or more simply "per", followed by the particular nature of the division, such as "party per chevron" (divided by a chevron) or "party per pale" (divided in half vertically). The descriptions of the

▼ *The field of the Fisher family of Lancashire is diapered with little fishes.*

▲ *The later version of the d'Albret family arms, the 2nd and 3rd quarters are the original arms – here hatched to represent gules – the 1st and 4th quarters were augmented by the King of France.*

divisions utilize the names given to the corresponding "ordinaries" – the fundamental geometric charges (see opposite). Where the shield is parted in an even number of small divisions the number of divisions is then specified, such as "bendy of six"; "paly of eight"; "barry of ten". Any parted field can bear another charge or charges of either a metal or a colour, without breaking the metal-on-metal, colour-on-colour rule.

In spite of their simplicity, it is quite possible for one of these basic divisions of the shield to comprise a family arms. For at least 650 years, the ancient English family of Waldegrave has used a shield that is simply Per pale Argent and Gules (a shield divided in half, one half silver, one half red). The Scottish dukes of Argyll, Chiefs of the Clan Campbell, bear Gyronny of eight Or and Sable; the Campbells of

London bear Gyronny of eight ermine and Gules, and the Swedish family of Natt och Dag ("night and day") derived its name from its simple shield Per fess Or and Azure (divided in two horizontally, one half blue for night and one half gold for day).

DIAPERING

Where a shield has a large expanse of field, the artist often adds textural interest with a faint overall pattern. This technique is called "diapering", and can lead to the most beautiful of heraldic art forms as long as the pattern is not mistaken for part of the heraldic design.

SHIELD DIVISIONS

The simplest way of creating arms that are distinct from any other, is to divide the surface of the shield into two parts by a line, one part a metal – gold or silver – the other a colour. Further variations can be made by subdividing the shield with more lines, and varying the edges of the lines in many ways. The option of adding furs to the variations makes the possibilities for new but simple geometric designs almost endless.

▲ (Party) per pale   ▲ (Party) per fess   ▲ (Party) per bend

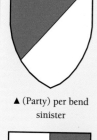  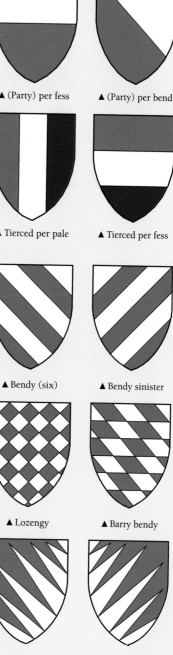

▲ (Party) per bend sinister   ▲ (Party) per chevron   ▲ (Party) per saltire   ▲ Tierced per pale   ▲ Tierced per fess

▲ Quarterly   ▲ Gyronny   ▲ Barry (six)   ▲ Bendy (six)   ▲ Bendy sinister

▲ Paly   ▲ Chevronny   ▲ Chequy   ▲ Lozengy   ▲ Barry bendy

  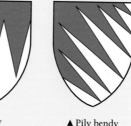 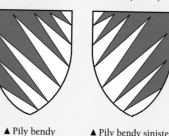

▲ Paly bendy   ▲ Gyronny of twelve   ▲ Pily   ▲ Pily bendy   ▲ Pily bendy sinister

THE HONOURABLE ORDINARIES

The most simple charges, or devices, found on the heraldic shield are geometric patterns called the ordinaries. These charges have long been considered to hold a special place in heraldry, hence the appellation "honourable". The ordinary normally occupies about one-third of the area of the shield, and can be borne alone or in conjunction with other charges. It can also itself bear further charges. In blazonry, the ordinary is always mentioned directly after the field.

Various theories about the origins of the ordinaries have been put forward, including the fanciful suggestion that the chevron, for example, is a charge suitable for the head of a family who gives shelter to other family members. An interesting but unexplained visual clue lies in a Roman mosaic representing the amphitheatre of Lyons in France (and now in the city's museum). The mosaic shows a wooden palisade around the arena that contains many of the ordinaries and subordinaries found in heraldry. Whether there is a link between a Roman geometrical conceit and heraldry, or if it is just a curious coincidence is still debated.

VARIATIONS ON THE ORDINARIES

Some of the ordinaries, such as the bands, can also be borne in smaller forms in pairs or more. These diminutive ordinaries have names that reflect their nature, so that chevrons give rise to chevronels, pales to pallets and two or more bends are described as bendlets. Any ordinary can be "voided" by having its centre removed to reveal the field or another tincture; it can also be "fimbriated", that is, edged with a narrow band of another tincture.

THE CROSS

The heraldic cross is formed by a combination of the "fess" (horizontal band) and the "pale" (vertical band). In its simple form it is set centrally on the shield, with each limb extending to one edge. The cross has bred more variants than any other

THE ORDINARIES
Although various writers quibble about the exact number of ordinaries, the following selection, with their diminutives behind them, is generally considered to be a complete list:

▲ The chief

▲ The pale and pallets

▲ Fess ▲ 2 bars ▲ A barrulet

▲ Bend ▲ 3 bendlets ▲ A riband

▲ Bend sinister ▲ 2 bendlets sinister

▲ Chevron ▲ 3 chevronels

▲ Saltire ▲ A fillet saltire

▲ Pall ▲ A fillet pall

▲ Cross ▲ A fillet cross

▲ Pile ▲ 3 piles in point

charge: some writers say there are over 30 variants, others over 50, while one 19th-century writer listed 450. Apart from the simple cross the most commonly met with are the "cross" patty (or "formy") where the four limbs are wide at their heads but narrow towards the central join, and the Maltese or eight-pointed cross, which is similar to the former except that the heads

of the limbs are notched at their centres. If the bottom limb of the cross narrows to a point it is said to be "fitched". Crosses patty and "crosslet" can often be found with this variant, and are then described as a "cross patty fitchy" or a "cross crosslet fitchy".

▶ A Flemish armorial c1560 showing ordinaries and divisions of the field.

VARIATIONS ON THE CROSS

▲ Cross potent:
T-shaped limbs,
resembling crutches.

▲ Cross patonce:
Concave, tapered
limbs, with each head
divided into three.

▲ Cross fleury or
flory: the accentuated
points end in the form
of a fleur de lis.

▲ Cross crosslet: The
heads of each limb are
themselves crossed.

▲ Cross bottony:
Straight limbs, each
headed with three
roundels or buttons.

▲ Formy (Patty)

▲ Maltese

▲ Moline

▲ Pommée

▲ Fleuretty

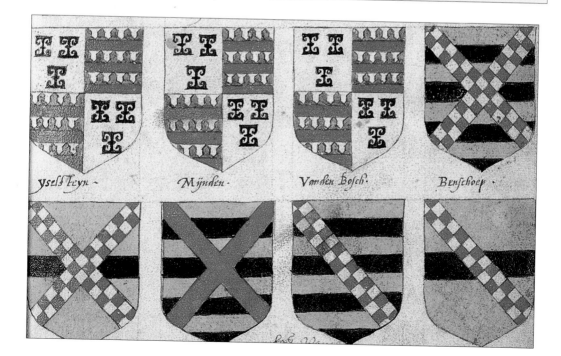

yselsTeyn -   Mijnden ·   Vanden Bosch·   Benschoep ·

THE SUB-ORDINARIES

The lesser geometric charges are known as the "sub-ordinaries"; they can be borne singly or in groups according to their nature. The sub-ordinaries are deemed the less common of the geometric patterns found on shields of arms, but like many of the honourable ordinaries, most of them owe their origins to the construction of the medieval shield.

The most non-controversial sub-ordinaries are the "canton" (and its larger cousin, the "quarter"), the "bordure", the "inescutcheon", the "orle" and the "tressure". The last four are probably reminders of metal reinforcements that were part of the structure of the medieval shield. Other writers have also included further charges in the list of the sub-ordinaries, including the "lozenge" and its derivatives, the "rustre", "mascle", and "fusil", the "gyron", the "pairle", the "billet" and "flanches".

The bordure, or border, is simply that: a border around the edge of the shield. In Scottish heraldry the bordure is often used as a means of identifying junior branches of the family, the bordure bearing charges taken from the arms of the mother (see Difference Marks and Cadency). A similar practice is found in Spanish and Portuguese heraldry, where the bordure may even include small shields of arms of near relatives.

The inescutcheon is a small shield borne as a charge. It may be plain or may bear other charges and may be in any number, not just single. The arms of Burrell, Baron Gwydir, make use of this and another sub-ordinary, blazoned Vert on each of three escutcheons Argent a bordure engrailed Or, while the family of Hay, Earl of Erroll, High Constable of Scotland, are blazoned Argent three escutcheons Gules.

The orle appears as an inner border set between the middle and edge of the shield. French heraldists also call it a faux, or false, escutcheon, or inescutcheon voided.

The tressure is really little more than a narrow orle and often appears in pairs in Scottish heraldry where, garnished with fleurs de lis, it is usually associated with the royal arms of Scotland and other families allied to the Scottish monarchy through marriage.

The canton is a square or rectangle in the dexter chief corner of the shield, smaller than the less-common quarter. The canton often bears other charges and in the heraldry of some nations can be used to denote certain relationships.

Flanches are always borne in pairs, and are formed by arcs on each side of the shield extending from the upper corner to a point slightly to the side of the base.

The lozenge is a diamond-shaped charge that has several variants, the most common being the mascle – a lozenge with its centre removed to show the field. A rustre is a lozenge pierced with a circular opening, and a fusil is an elongated lozenge. A field patterned overall with lozenges is "lozengy"; with squares it is "chequy".

A billet is a small elongated rectangular

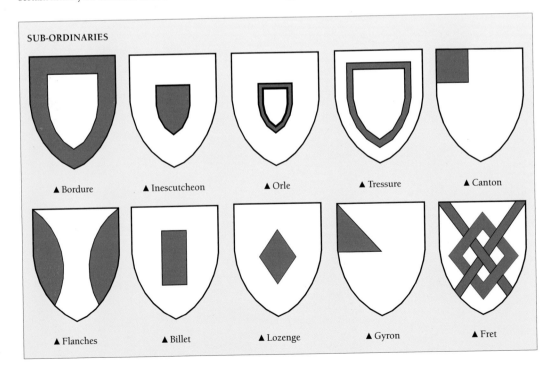

SUB-ORDINARIES

▲ Bordure   ▲ Inescutcheon   ▲ Orle   ▲ Tressure   ▲ Canton

▲ Flanches   ▲ Billet   ▲ Lozenge   ▲ Gyron   ▲ Fret

figure. Numerous billets are often strewn across the field, described as "billety".

The gyron is a triangular charge that seldom appears singly. Usually the shield is divided into a number of gyrons, arranged like the sails of a windmill, and the field is described as "gyronny of [the number of pieces]". The most famous example of a gyronny coat is that of the Scottish family of Campbell, who bear Gyronny of eight Or and Sable. Branches of the family often charge the gyrons with other charges or vary their edges and colours.

The "fret" is formed of interlaced bendlets and bendlets sinister. It can be encountered in the singular but is more often repeated to cover the whole field in an interlacing pattern, which resembles a garden trellis; this is then described as "fretty".

▲ *The nine billets, and fiddle, on the arms of the family of Winter of Bohlanden.*

OVERALL PATTERNS

Generally, if charges are repeated on a shield, their number tends to be less than ten, and is specified in the blazon. Furthermore, they are usually placed within the perimeter of the shield so that they appear in their entirety. Sometimes, however, small charges – which may be of any kind – are strewn in a plentiful degree all over the shield. This effect is described as "semy".

There are special terms for the strewing of certain charges. For example, a shield strewn with billets is billety and one strewn with fleur de lis is semy de lis. Any object, no matter how humble or curious, can be strewn across the shield – such as semy of coffee beans in the arms of the district of Haut Ogooué in Gabon.

ROUNDELS

Plain round charges called "roundels" are depicted in heraldic colours and metals. Whereas in most heraldics the roundel is

▲ *A novel use of semy – the chief in the shield of the Gabonaise region of Haut Ogooué is semy of coffee beans.*

described simply in its true colour, English blazonry has a distinct name for each roundel. The "bezant", or gold roundel, is said to be named after the gold coin of Byzantium, while the "torteau", or red roundel, resembles a tartlet. A blue roundel is a "hurt", which may refer either to a bruise or to a hurtleberry (blueberry). Droplets are a variation of the roundel, and look something like tadpoles. They are known as "gouttés". Once again, in English heraldry Norman French is utilized: red droplets are goutté de sang – drops of blood – gold droplets are goutté d'or. A roundel bearing blue and white wavy bars is often used to denote water: this is termed the "fountain". It is seen in the arms of the Sykes family, since a "syke" is a spring or fountain.

The English family of Stourton makes use of fountains and a bend to tell the story of their ancient estate. Six springs rise at Stourhead, forming the source of the River Stour: three were originally inside the estate boundary, the other three outside. The Stourton arms, Sable a bend Or between six fountains, neatly describes the geography and history of the estate.

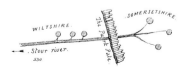

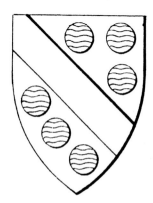

▲ *The six fountains and bend in the arms of the Stourton family reflect the position on the family property of six springs. A sketched map above explains the pattern.*

LINES OF PARTITION

Heraldry is nothing if not inventive and over the centuries its regulators have come up with every possible method to ensure that each shield of arms can be unique. This is especially true of the many ways that a shield can be divided. To increase the number of possible variations, the edges of the divisions and the ordinaries, which are known as "lines of partition", can be drawn in many different styles.

Partition lines make the fullest use of the edges of the ordinaries and they are considered sufficiently distinctive for unrelated families to have a coat of arms that is identical in colour and ordinary, but with different edges. For example, a green cross with straight edges on a white shield may belong to a family unrelated to one whose white shield bears a green cross with wavy edges. In fact, lines are included in the blazon only if they are not straight.

Apart from the styles shown here, in recent years new lines of partition have been evolved by the heraldic artists of Scandinavia, South Africa and Canada.

COUNTERCHANGING

One of the most enjoyable stratagems in blazon is a partitioned shield that is counterchanged. Counterchanging is the

▲ Counterchanging in practice on the shield of a community in Greenland. The shield here is divided per fess.

COMMON LINES OF PARTITION

The following shields show a selection of the many ways in which the heraldic division can be varied.

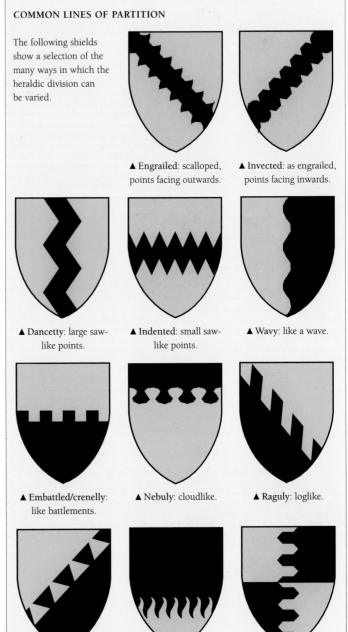

▲ Engrailed: scalloped, points facing outwards.

▲ Invected: as engrailed, points facing inwards.

▲ Dancetty: large saw-like points.

▲ Indented: small saw-like points.

▲ Wavy: like a wave.

▲ Embattled/crenelly: like battlements.

▲ Nebuly: cloudlike.

▲ Raguly: loglike.

▲ Dovetailed

▲ Rayonné: like flames.

▲ Urdy: serrated.

dividing of the shield in such a manner that it is part of a metal and part of a colour, and then by arranging the charges in such a manner that they be reciprocally of the same colour and metal. This sounds a complicated business, but counterchanging can in fact be one of the simplest and most effective ways of varying one very simple shield of arms from another.

The arms of the Anglo-Norman family of d'Abitot provide an example of how counterchanging can produce a striking design. The d'Abitot arms are Per pale Or and Gules three roundels counterchanged. They should be compared with the non-counterchanged alternatives, which are the arms of the Courtenay family (Or three torteaux) and its opposite, the arms of Dynham (Gules three bezants).

These three personal shields show how a certain configuration of charges can be changed through tincture. The families to which each shield belongs most probably bore no relation to each other, although changes of tincture were also sometimes employed for different members of the same family.

In the case of the Courtenay arms we can see how exact blazonry can be, the roundels each given its particular name, ie red roundels torteaux, and in the Dynham arms, gold roundels or bezants. Finally the d'Abitot arms combine these two designs but come up with something entirely different, by counterchanging both the field and the intersecting third roundel, resulting in a very distinctive shield.

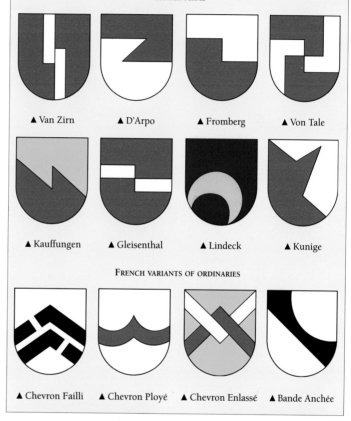

EUROPEAN VARIANTS OF LINES OF PARTITION

Certain charges, divisions of the shield, partition lines and so on, are peculiar to a particular area or nation. In 1886, in his work entitled *Heraldry English and Foreign*, Robert Jenkins gave the following examples of variants and the names of some ordinaries that would seldom, if ever, be met with in English heraldry.

FAMILY ARMS

▲ Van Zirn   ▲ D'Arpo   ▲ Fromberg   ▲ Von Tale

▲ Kauffungen   ▲ Gleisenthal   ▲ Lindeck   ▲ Kunige

FRENCH VARIANTS OF ORDINARIES

▲ Chevron Failli   ▲ Chevron Ployé   ▲ Chevron Enlassé   ▲ Bande Anchée

▲ *The shield of the Courtenay family: Or three torteaux.*

▲ *The Dynham shield – a reversed version of the Courtenay shield: Gules three bezants.*

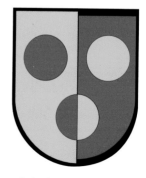

▲ *Finally the shield of the d'Abitots: Per pale Or and Gules three roundels counterchanged.*

BLAZONRY

The term blazonry refers to the special and distinct language that is used in the description of heraldry. Many a casual visitor to the world of heraldry can be baffled and put off by the nature of blazonry, but in fact it is a very user-friendly language, so exact in its phraseology that, once learnt, it enables one heraldist to impart to another an accurate and full description of any coat of arms through a concise verbal picture. Blazonry is a precise language, which it needs to be, for the nature of heraldry itself depends on the uniqueness of each coat of arms.

DESCRIBING A SHIELD

Any charge can be married to any other in any number of ways to make up a shield of arms. Often, the more ancient the arms, the simpler the design. It is in fact possible to have a shield of arms bearing no charges at all. The d'Albret arms were originally simply Gules (a plain red shield) though in 1389 they were "augmented" with the arms of France, becoming Quarterly one and four Azure three fleurs de lis Or two and three Gules (the shield was divided into four, quarters one and four were blue with three gold fleur de lis in each, quarters two and three remained the original red colour).

We have seen some of the fundamental charges employed in heraldry. Let us now see how they are "blazoned". The blazon needs to include all the details of tincture and number that an artist would need in order to reproduce the shield accurately. It always follows a set pattern:

1 The field, including any divisions
2 The ordinary
3 The principal charges on the field, followed by any lesser charges
4 Any charges on the ordinary
5 Any sub-ordinaries
6 Any charges on the sub-ordinaries
A further refinement of the language of blazonry is the means of describing the exact position on the shield any charge might take. The names of these parts and points of the shield are explained in the box.

THE PARTS AND POINTS OF THE SHIELD

For the purposes of accurate description, the heraldic shield is divided into different areas.

The dexter (right-hand) and sinister (left-hand) sides of the shield are always described from the point of view of the bearer of the shield, a throwback to the days when shields were actually carried. So from the reader's viewpoint, right is left and left is right. Most heraldic charges, particularly animate ones, are drawn so they are facing dexter, as it is considered the more "worthy" side. So from the point of the viewer, rather than a bearer, any lions, for example, on the shield, would usually face the left-hand side of the shield.

A B C: chief (top part of the shield), sub-divided into:
    A: dexter chief point
    B: middle chief point
    C: sinister chief point
D: honour point
E: fess or heart point
F: nombril or navel point
G H I: base, sub-divided into:
    G: dexter base point
    H: middle base point
    I: sinister base point

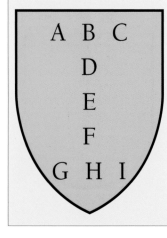

Here are three examples of how blazonry describes a shield. The first example is the arms of the family of Winneberg: Gules a bend Argent indented between six crosses couped Or.

1 The field is described first: Gules – a plain red background.

2 The next most important feature is the ordinary, in this case a bend Argent, noting any partition line, here indented.

3 Any lesser charges follow: between six crosses couped Or.

The arms of the town of Gerville, Seine-Maritime, France, is described as: Argent on a bend Azure between two Phrygian caps Gules three mullets of six points Or.

1 The field is silver, the ordinary: on a bend Azure. ("On" anticipates point 3 below. As the lines of partition are straight they are not mentioned.)

2 The lesser charges on the field: between two Phrygian caps Gules.

3 If any charges are borne on the ordinary, these are mentioned next: three mullets [stars] of six points Or.

The more complex arms of the Johnson family, Suffolk, are described as: Sable on a fess between two double manacles Argent three pheons Gules on a chief Or a demi lion between two lozenges Azure.

1 The field: Sable.

2 The ordinary: on a fess.

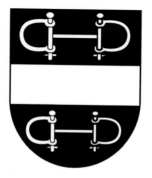

3 The lesser charges on the field: between two double manacles Argent. (As both fess and manacles are silver, the colour is mentioned only once.)

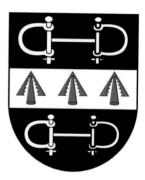

4 The charges, and their colour, on the ordinary are then described: three pheons [arrowheads] Gules.

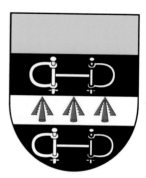

5 If a chief is borne in addition to another ordinary, as here, it is mentioned next: on a chief Or.

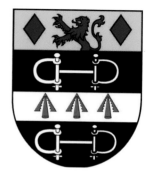

6 Any charges that appear on the chief now follow: a demi lion (the head and top half of a lion) between two lozenges Azure.

HERALDIC BEASTS

Although the earliest heraldry consisted mainly of simple geometric patterns – for easy identification at a distance – beasts, birds and monsters had begun to figure as emblems on shields and flags long before the birth of heraldry itself. We know that in ancient Greece the Athenians took an owl as their city's symbol. In ancient Egypt many of the gods were depicted partly or wholly in the forms of animals that lived alongside human beings, such as the jackal, cobra and hawk. The Bible records the instruction, "Every man of the children of Israel shall pitch by his own standard, with the ensign of their father's house" (Numbers 2:2), and of the 12 tribes of Israel no less than half took an animal as their symbol.

THE LION

Lions were in evidence at the very birth of heraldry – perhaps they were even the very first charge. When knighted in 1127 by his father-in-law, King Henry I of England, Geoffrey, Count of Anjou was given a shield bearing fanciful golden lions. The lion, believed to be the king of beasts, was

▼ *The lion, king of beasts: a page from a Dutch ordinary of 1570 shows family arms charged with the lion rampant.*

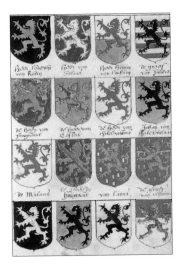

naturally a favourite symbol among the fighting men of medieval Europe, and was one of the more exotic beasts of the medieval heraldic menageries.

All postures or inclinations of an armorial charge are termed "attitudes", and this is especially relevant to creatures. Not surprisingly the lion is afforded the greatest number of attitudes – some writers have given it as many as 60 different positions. Besides its attitude, a lion or any other creature may also be distinguished by attributes. For example, a lion "passant" (attitude) may also be "langued" (tongued) in a tincture other than the normal red, and "armed" with teeth and claws.

Heraldry is an exact science. It needs to be if the individuality of a shield of arms is to be preserved, therefore attributes and attitudes are important. It could be that one family's blue shield bears a gold lion "rampant", another's a gold lion "rampant guardant" (looking at the viewer), while a third has a gold lion "rampant reguardant" (looking backwards): there is enough difference in the position of the head to give three distinct arms. Adding a forked tail ("queue fourchée") to the lions provides three more distinct arms.

OTHER BEASTS

Obviously many an early bearer of a lion chose the creature to reflect his own ferocity and bravery. The same may be said of those who chose bears, wolves and other carnivorous animals. Strength could be suggested by other creatures. The noble Moravian family of Pernstein bore on a white shield a black auroch's head "couped affronty" (with no neck visible, facing the viewer). According to a family legend the founding father of the Pernsteins was a charcoal burner of extraordinary strength called Vénava. He managed to catch a wild auroch and led it to the court of the king at Brno, where he cut off the poor beast's head with a single blow of his axe. The king was so impressed that he gave Vénava great estates and the right to commemorate his feat on his shield of arms.

▲ *This 1823 Bavarian grant of arms, to Baron Peter Kreusser, includes a variety of beasts from the heraldic menagerie.*

LIONS OR LEOPARDS

In 1235 the German emperor Frederick II presented Henry III of England with three leopards as a living shield of arms. Was this a reflection of the English arms at that time? If so, are the creatures in the English arms meant to be leopards? Confusion arises from the interpretation of heraldic terms describing the attitude of the lion. In English heraldry, the creature most often shown rearing up on one hind foot and boxing with its front paws is a lion "rampant", whereas if it is walking sedately across the shield it is a lion passant. In the arms of England the three lions are "passant guardant", walking and looking at the viewer. In French heraldry, the lion is always assumed to be rampant, while the creature that appears passant guardant is always a leopard. Furthermore, in French heraldry a rearing lion, looking at the viewer (in English "rampant guardant"), is called a *lion léopardé*, and a lion passant is a *léopard lionné*!

MOST COMMON ATTITUDES OF THE LION

▲ *Statant*

▲ *Combatant*

▲ *Rampant*

▲ *Rampant guardant*

▲ *Couchant*

▲ *Passant*

▲ *Salient*

▲ *Rampant double-queued*

▲ *Rampant reguardant*

▲ *Rampant queue fourchée*

▲ *Sejant*

▲ *Cowed*

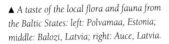

▲ *A taste of the local flora and fauna from the Baltic States: left: Polvamaa, Estonia; middle: Balozi, Latvia; right: Auce, Latvia.*

Like many heraldic stories, it is impossible to know whether the auroch appeared on the Pernstein shield before or after the legend arose, but it is carved on the family's former castle at Pardubice.

While many men of warlike disposition would not have minded being represented by a bull, there must be few that would have chosen to bear its castrated equivalent, the ox. However, if Nicholas Upton, the 15th-century English heraldic writer, is to be believed, he was instrumental in the granting of a shield charged with three oxheads to a gentleman who had had the misfortune to have been maimed in the testicles by the thrust of a spear.

Another creature that Upton might have thought equally suitable for this client

▼ *A marvellous depiction carved in stone of the porcupine badge of King Louis XII of France, 1498–1515, Chateau de Blois.*

would have been the beaver, whose scent glands, located near its rear, were sought after for various medicinal cures. Upton, along with other medieval writers, believed that these glands were in fact the beaver's testicles and that, when it realized that men were after them, it sensibly chose to sacrifice them by castrating itself with its teeth. Beavers, once common in much of Northern Europe, are now found only in the forests of Scandinavia and the Baltic States, and they appear in the arms of the Estonian district of Polvamaa.

Heraldry gives symbolic protection to all creatures, great and small, and whereas warriors might choose martial beasts such as lions, bears and wolves, country communities

▲ *The elephant in the arms of the Counts of Helfenstein, an unusual animal charge, chosen as a delightful pun on the family's name.*

often prefer to commemorate gentler creatures. In Latvia, the rivers and forests yield up their wildlife to local heraldry. The arms of Auce – a black crayfish on a red field – enjoyably break the colour-on-colour rule. In the arms of Balozi a frog sits below a chief charged with water-lily leaves, while squirrels in the arms of Baldone and hedgehogs in those of Vilaka recall the creatures found in many gardens.

◀ *The arms of the Pernstein family of Moravia bear the popular bull's head as both a charge and a crest.*

▲ *Vénava kills his auroch in a relief carving at the family seat, the Castle of Pardubice.*

▲ *The camel on the arms of the city of Petropavlovsk, in the old Russian Empire, at the cross-roads where East met West.*

EXOTIC BEASTS

Of the more unusual animals, elephants were relatively well known to medieval heraldists (Henry III of England was given one for his menagerie by Louis IX of France in 1254). The elephant was used as a symbol of strength and dependability, and as such it was chosen for the arms of the city of Coventry in England. A particularly enjoyable example appears in the Zurich armorial roll (1335–45) for the von

▼ *A tigress looks in the mirror at itself (third quarter) in the arms of the English family of Sibell. While she was beguiled by her own image her cubs were left unprotected.*

Helfenstein family of Swabia, chosen for its punning value with the family name.

Other exotic beasts in the heraldic menagerie include that of the eastern territories and cities of the old Russian Empire (such as Petropavlovsk) who favoured the camel in their civic heraldry, and when Sir Titus Salt, Baronet, of Saltaire, Yorkshire was granted arms, he chose as a crest the alpaca, from whose fine wool he had made his fortune.

ANIMAL PARTS

It is not only whole creatures that are used in heraldry; various parts of their anatomy make their way on to shields. Wolves' teeth famously appear on the Kinsky arms of Bohemia, while others include the bones of fish, and various types of amputations. The bits of animals that are all quite commonly used in heraldry include heads that are either "erased" (torn off at the neck) or "couped" (clean cut), various horns and antlers, and even the paws ("gambs") of bears and lions, which can also be either erased or couped.

DOMESTIC ANIMALS

Cats, dogs and horses are all corralled into heraldry, as are the unfortunate victims of the hunt: boar, deer, hares and rabbits. The stag hunt was for centuries the exclusive

▼ *The wolf's teeth on the shield of the Czech Count Kinsky, seen here on a beautifully crafted embellishment on a wrought-iron gate. The teeth themselves are very stylized.*

sport of the nobility, so it is no wonder that, after lions, deer probably appear most commonly upon shields and are therefore afforded the next largest group of personal attitudes. The English Cottington family enjoy two hinds in their arms "counter-tripping", which have the rather comical appearance of a Push-me-Pull-you.

Greyhounds are popular in Italian heraldry, while in British heraldry the talbot, a large and powerful ancient hunting hound, is often found. However, man's best friend comes no truer than the dog on the crest of a Mr Phillips of Cavendish Square, London, who early in the 19th century was swimming in the sea off Portsmouth when he got into a strong current and was in danger of being drowned. A perceptive Newfoundland hound saw his predicament, leapt into the water and dragged him to safety. When Mr Phillips found that his canine saviour was a stray, he took the brave dog home and gave him every kind attention that he deserved. Furthermore, the Phillips family recorded this happy outcome in a new heraldic crest and motto, the full blazon being: Upon a mount Vert in front of a Newfoundland dog sejant, reguardant proper an escutcheon thereon, in base waves of the sea, and floating therein a naked man, the sinister arm erected all proper. The motto is *Auspice Deo extuli mari*, "God being my leader, I brought him out of the sea".

▼ *Mr Phillips' faithful friend, the dog who saved his life and became his crest.*

HUMAN FIGURES

Human beings – and parts of them – appear often in heraldry, mainly reflecting enemies of the medieval period. The human figure is usually shown fully clothed or, if nearer to nature, is girded around the loins with an extremely uncomfortable "vestment of leaves" described by one English heraldic writer as "vegetable knickers". However, a naked

▲ *The wildmen in the arms of the Wood family, traditionally girded with oak leaves.*

▼ *The all too realistic nature of Hungarian arms borne out here in a grant of 1636.*

man in all his glory appears in the arms of the Scots baronets Dalyell of the Binns and a breast of sorts, distilling milk, appears in the arms of the English family of Dodge.

Hungarian heraldry affords many instances of the human being in action, whether it be of the bloody kind – slitting the throat of an unfortunate deer or shooting a Turkish soldier – or gentler pursuits such as playing the organ, or reaping corn.

KINGS AND QUEENS

Naturally, the appearance of kings and queens in heraldry is counted to be the highest of all honours. In most cases the monarch commemorated tends to be anonymous, but the Castilian family of de Avila has in its arms an imprisoned king in chains, representing King François I of France, taken prisoner by Don Diego de Avila in 1528 during the Battle of Pavia. The Savoyard family of Amoreto also keeps a Moorish king chained to the chevron in its arms.

The Weldons, Baronets of Rahenderry in Ireland, have the bust of the Virgin Queen, Elizabeth I of England, as their crest. Family records say only that it was given as a mark of distinction by the Queen herself for some great service done to her by a Weldon.

▼ *King François I of France stands in chains on the shield of the de Avila family.*

VICTIMS AND VILLAINS

The Spanish family of Miranda commemorates a famous legend on its shield of arms. It bears the busts of five virgins, rescued from rape and murder by Alvar Fernandez de Miranda, while on pilgrimage to Santiago de Compostella. The arms of the city of Lichfield in England record a less favourable fate than that of Alvar's virgins: on old seals of the city council the shield bears "on a landscape proper several martyrs in divers manners massacred."

The English family of Davenport of Capesthorne Hall in Cheshire has what is thought to be a unique crest of a felon's head within the noose from which he is about to be hanged. It refers to the power of life and death, "without delay and without appeal", which the Davenports exercised over vast areas of forest land in north-east England.

HEARTS AND OTHER ORGANS

Human hearts often make their appearance on shields of arms, one forming the central charge in the arms of the Scots family of Douglas. Sir James Douglas was a close companion of King Robert the Bruce of Scotland (1306–29); at the end of his life the king, who had long wished to take part in a Crusade, gained Sir James's promise

▼ *The virgins saved from a "fate worse than death" by a member of the Miranda family.*

▲ *The crest of the Davenport family of Capesthorne – showing an anonymous felon on his way to execution.*

that he would carry the King's embalmed heart to Jerusalem and bury it in the Holy Sephulchre. When the King died in 1329, that is just what Sir James set off to do, but was killed in battle on his journey. Some say he threw King Robert's heart into the fight before following it to certain death. The Douglas family added a red heart to their arms, which was later crowned.

The north Italian family of Colleoni bore three pairs of testicles on their shield. In

▼ *The three pairs of testicles of the Colleoni family, adorning the ceiling of their castle of Malpaga, near Bergamo, north Italy.*

the virile and thoroughly human Middle Ages this was no disgrace, but the dubious gentility of the late 19th century led these vital charges to be described in some ordinaries as three upside-down hearts.

Female genitalia appear on the shield of the medieval Italian family of Conati, but perhaps the most bizarre example of heraldic "vivacity" can be seen on the shield of a Hungarian gentleman, István Várallyay, who in 1599 was granted arms of male sexual organs beneath an arm grasping a mallet. As many Hungarian family arms vividly portray the severed parts of dead Turks, this shield could be taken to represent some particularly unpleasant fate befalling yet another Turkish soldier captured in battle. In truth, however, these particular parts are those of a stallion – Várallyay was a farrier and gelder in the Hungarian army and, being proud of his swiftness and expertise in castrating horses, wished the fact to be recorded in heraldry.

The Indian state of Wankaner has in its arms a representation of the Hindu adoration of the god Shiva, through the veneration of the male phallic symbol of the *lingam*. The arms show Shiva's *trishul*, or trident, wrapped around with snakes, and the round-ended raised stone sculpture that represents the *lingam*, or generative force.

ARMS AND LEGS

Parts of the human body feature regularly in heraldry. The most common are arms or legs. The arms of the Isle of Man are Gules three legs conjoined in fess point in armour proper. They were borne by the ancient kings of Man, and appear as a quartering in the arms of Montagu, Stanley and Murray, all later Lords of Man. The legs probably derive from a Norse symbol for luck introduced by Man's Viking invaders.

A curious human appendage is the wooden leg of the Swede, Per Larsson, who when fighting during the Thirty Years War had his leg amputated. On his eventual ennoblement he took the name Stöltenhielm (*stolt* means "stilt") and a wooden stilt was a main feature in the arms he adopted.

▲ *István Várallyay's shield, with the curious charges that actually celebrate the bearer's profession of farrier and gelder of horses.*

▲ *The arms of the Indian state of Wankaner bring the Hindu worship of Shiva to heraldry.*

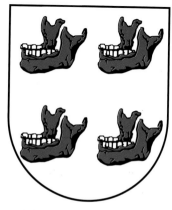

▲ *The highly literal arms of the Portuguese family of Queixada, whose name means simply "jawbone".*

FOWL, FISH AND PLANTS

After animals, the second most popular heraldic charge is birds – most usually the eagle but also less exalted species. Fish of various kinds also sometimes appear, and flowers, trees and even vegetables have also played their part in the heraldic story. Of flowers, the rose and the lily are most commonly met with, and each has a stylized form – the five-petalled heraldic rose and the fleur de lis.

▲ *The stork in its vigilance on the arms of the Hungarian family of Ballint of Técső. If it slept the stone would fall and waken it.*

▼ *The heraldic aviary in the coat of arms of the Barons Arundel shows the imperial eagle behind the shield, the owl as a supporter, and six hirondells (swallows) on the shield.*

HERALDIC BIRDS

If the lion is the king of beasts, the eagle, for medieval heraldic writers, was the queen of birds. From Roman times it was associated with empires, and black eagles were said to be the bravest of all. Both the Byzantine and Holy Roman emperors considered it personal to them.

Many other birds, real, fanciful or fantastic, inhabit the heraldic menagerie, particularly the martlet or *merletten*. The martlet, a swift-like creature, has no feet when depicted in heraldry (and the *merletten* has neither feet nor beak), because it was believed by medieval writers never to land. Such birds were spoken of by Crusaders who had seen them in the Holy Land. The martlet was often given as a heraldic charge to younger sons of the English nobility, as a reminder to "trust to the wings of virtue and merit, and not to their legs, having no land of their own to put their feet on."

The pelican also displays a mixture of fact and fancy. In heraldry it is often depicted using its beak to wound itself in the breast ("vulning"), using the blood it sheds to feed its young. Such a symbol of self-sacrifice is therefore often found in religious arms.

CREATURES OF THE WATER

The dolphin, the most commonly occurring sea creature in heraldry, is classed as a fish by heraldic writers, as is the whale, although both are, of course, mammals. All

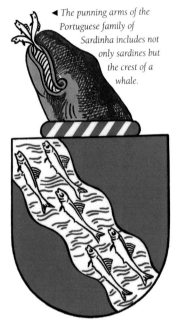

◄ *The punning arms of the Portuguese family of Sardinha includes not only sardines but the crest of a whale.*

kinds of fish have appeared as various heraldic charges, but size and ferocity seems to have been foremost in the minds of the medieval heralds. Not surprisingly, therefore, numerous arms can be found bearing the pike, such as the Portuguese family of Lucio, and the Czech town of Dolni Breszov.

▲ *The ferocious and all too realistic pike devouring a smaller fish in the arms of the Czech town of Dolni Breszov.*

FLOWERS

Heraldic writers have credited the rose with many properties. It is seen as an emblem of secrecy, being good, soft, and sweet-smelling, but surrounded by evil, signified by its thorns. In medieval England the rose was a popular symbol within the royal family, reaching its zenith during the reigns of the Tudor monarchs. The white rose was a favourite badge of the royal house of York. The red rose of the rival house of Lancaster has a less certain provenance, but it is certain that Henry Tudor (later Henry VII) took it to be the Lancastrian symbol when he united it with the white rose after his marriage to Elizabeth of York in 1486.

The double Tudor rose was a favourite device of Henry VII's son, Henry VIII, and on his marriage to Catherine of Aragon he combined it with the Queen's badge, the pomegranate of Granada. An abundance of roses and pomegranates erupted throughout England, until the eventual divorce of the unhappy couple led to the defacing of any such badge in public places and churches. This must have left Herr Arnold

▼ *The fleur de lis of the French kings from their crypt in the abbey of St Denis. The shield is encircled by the Order of the Holy Ghost (St Esprit).*

▲ *Left: the rose and pomegranate charge on the arms of Herr Arnold Bilson – a design he might later have regretted after the divorce of Henry VIII and Catherine of Aragon. Right: The potato flowers of the French town of Ploudaniel.*

Bilson, presumably a German merchant in England, in an awkward situation: he had been granted arms charged with a Tudor rose and pomegranate "dimidiated" (halved).

The fleur de lis, the heraldic lily, was associated with the royal house of France long before the advent of heraldry. It is possible that the fleur de lis is a heraldic representation of the flag iris, though one of the many legends surrounding the symbol is that it evolved not from flowers but from three toads, supposedly the arms of Pharamond, King of the Franks in the first half of the 5th century.

As part of the French royal insignia, the fleur de lis can be traced back to the reign of Robert II, "the Pious" (996–1031), son of Hugh Capet. The royal coat of arms, of a blue shield strewn with golden fleurs de lis (semy de lis), made its first appearance during the reign of Louis VIII (1223–6). It is supposed that the number of lilies was reduced to three during the reign of Charles V (1364–80) in honour of the Holy Trinity, although his successor, Charles VI (1380–1422) is known to have used both semy de lis and three fleurs de lis on different occasions.

In modern heraldry, the semy variant is called "France ancient", the three fleurs de lis "France modern". It is possible that the change was an attempt by the French monarchs to distance their arms from their old enemies the English kings, who, starting with Edward III (1327–77) had asserted their claim to the throne of France by quartering the French arms (France ancient) with the lion of England. If such

a ploy was indeed attempted, it did not work, for Henry V of England (1413–22) changed the French quarters in his arms to France modern.

HERALDIC PLANTS

As for other plant life in heraldry, it can lead from the exotic – as with the palm trees in the arms of Maintirano, Malagasy Republic – to the humble, including the potato flower of Ploudaniel, Finistere, France, and the thorn bush (*Spina*) of the Italian family of Malaspina.

The broom plant, or *planta genista* is the emblem of humility, and became the badge adopted by the royal house of Plantagenet. Wheatsheaves, or "garbs", according to Guillaume, were the symbol of plenty and could signify the "harvest of one's hopes". Fruits also symbolized plenty.

The clover leaf, or "trefoil" frequently appears, not least as the shamrock, the plant symbol of Ireland. If a narrow tapering stem is shown projecting from it (or from any other leaf or flower), it is said to be "slipped". Heraldic variants of the trefoil have different numbers of leaves: the quatrefoil (four leaves), cinquefoil (five leaves) and the octofoil (eight leaves), which in England is the mark given to the ninth son.

▼ *The arms of the Italian Princes di Massa, which includes the thorn tree of the arms of the Malaspina family.*

MONSTERS AND FABULOUS BEASTS

People like to be thrilled by the unknown or strange, so it is not surprising to find in medieval armorials many examples of mythological creatures such as griffins, dragons, centaurs, unicorns and mermaids. Such monsters may have been the product of pure imagination, but it is more likely that they were the result of the need to exaggerate – most medieval heraldists and their patrons having heard at second-, third-, or even fourth-hand of the strange and wonderful creatures discovered in the far-off Indies or Americas.

▶ *The arms granted to Josef Moise in 1867 during the reign of Emperor Franz Josef of Austria includes a fire-breathing panther.*

▼ *The vibrancy and imagination of medieval heraldry is shown here in the wyvern crest of Sir John Grey de Ruthin.*

We have seen how medieval heraldry treated the relatively familiar lion, putting it into positions that would probably cause the real beast to fall over backwards. The panther was depicted equally fantastically, usually spouting flames from nostrils, mouth and even ears. Medieval bestiaries were the fuel for further heraldic fancies. These works, often wonderfully illustrated, told of cockatrices, bonacons and wyverns: fabulous creatures best encountered only in books and manuscripts. So ferocious were they that often they could turn people to stone on sight, or kill with their breath. Most medieval folk believed these creatures really did exist, and for someone who considered even the next village to be foreign territory, monsters provided just one more reason not to venture far from their own doorsteps.

THE DRAGON

Said to be the greatest of all serpents, the dragon had a scaly body and wings (usually depicted as bat-like). Its head was often horned and tufted, its tail thorny and pointed. It is quite possible that it had its origins in the unearthed fossils of prehistoric beasts. The sheer size of the skeletons that would have been found from time to time throughout the known world, would have been enough to overawe the finder, and real dragons are still alive and well on the island of Komodo off Indonesia, tales of which must have passed between traders many centuries ago.

Dragons lived in caves or deep in the earth's core, where fire was their constant companion; no wonder then that dragons themselves could breathe fire. In British heraldry the dragon is shown with four legs, but this is a late development, for

▲ *A centaur with a bow aiming skywards, an apt charge to appear on a badge for a German Army anti-aircraft unit.*

▲ *The wyvern, a heraldic beast used in England who in earlier times may well have been a dragon.*

▲ *The heraldic griffin, often seen as the guardian of treasure.*

▲ *The bonacon here seems gentle, but its unique defensive technique was all too awesome and far from benign.*

before the 15th century it was usually shown as having just two. In English heraldry the two-legged dragon tends to be called a wyvern or a basilisk, though in the rest of Europe the matter is not so distinct.

THE GRIFFIN

The heraldic monster with the forepart of an eagle and the hindquarters of a lion is called a griffin, or gryphon. Although not quite as popular as the dragon in heraldry, it nevertheless captured the imagination of many noble minds, for the griffin was the guardian of gold and hidden treasure, and was therefore a creature to be met on many a medieval quest.

▲ *The unicorn on the arms of the Polish noble tribe of Boncza – one of the few mythical beasts in Polish heraldry.*

In British heraldry a so-called male griffin is shown without wings, its body covered in tufts of formidable spikes, which are usually of a different colour to the rest of its body. Confusingly, the ordinary griffin is also normally depicted as having male sexual organs: just what a female griffin should look like is not made clear by heraldic writers. In English heraldry the griffin when in the rampant position is described as being "segreant".

THE UNICORN

Many a medieval prince kept a so-called unicorn's horn in his collection of curios, though in reality this was likely to be the tusk of a narwhal. The subject of many noble fantasies and legends, the unicorn is considered by many to be the most beautiful creature in the heraldic menagerie. In effect it is part horse, part heraldic antelope, with a large twisting horn or tusk issuing from its forehead. It is also depicted as having a lion's tail and a little tuft of hairs under its chin. So pure a creature is the unicorn that it is often entirely white, apart from its horn, tufts, mane and hooves, which are gold. When regally collared and chained, unicorns are the supporters beloved of the Scots monarchs.

In medieval romances, tales were told of how the usually untameable unicorn would befriend a gentle damsel of noble birth whom it sensed to be a virgin. When the noble creature had found such a lady it would lay its head in her lap and go to sleep. It was only at such a moment that hunters could steal in and capture or kill this wonderful prey.

The purity of both the unicorn and virgin was made much of by medieval writers, who compared the two symbols to Christ and the Virgin Mary. Because of this sacred connection some heraldic authors of the medieval period considered that the unicorn should not be sullied by placing its image on shield or crest. However, by the 16th century it had become a popular charge in heraldry all over Europe, appearing on shields as far apart as Poland, where it is borne by the Herb (clan or tribe) of Boncza, and in Italy by the Bardi family of Florence.

▲ *An exotic flavour is given to the ancient theme of the mermaid in the arms of Mouila in the Gabon, where a sirene was said to haunt the local river luring men to her lair.*

OTHER BEASTS

Like the salamander, depicted as a lizard surrounded by flames, the phoenix often appears in the arms of towns and cities that have been rebuilt after destruction in war. Classical writers asserted that only one phoenix existed at a time, and lived for 500 years. Knowing its end to be near, it made a nest that the sun's rays ignited, frying the poor bird. Out of the embers came its successor.

A creature peculiar to English heraldry is the bonacon. Somewhat like a bull with blunted horns that were turned inwards, the bonacon was said to defend itself by emitting burning excreta which could cover an enormous area.

MARINE MONSTERS

The mermaid was busy luring sailors to various fates, happy or decidedly nasty, from earliest times. Said to be half woman, half fish, she probably arose from sailors' sightings of the dugong or sea-cow.

The sirene seems to be a curious cousin of the mermaid with two tails. A version is found in the arms designed in the late 20th century for the commune of Mouila in the Gabon. Said to appear from time to time to claim a local man for her husband, the sirene displays two splendid scarlet tails. The white sister of Mouila's sirene appears in the arms of several European families, including the Amari of Sicily.

INANIMATE CHARGES

Heraldry has always made full and free use of every kind of object, and coats of arms reflect life's events from the cradle to the grave. The arms of the French town of St Germain-en-Laye include a very grand baby's cradle that also bears the date – 5 September 1638 – on which the future Louis XIV was born. At the other extreme, the last resting place of one of the earliest humans, found during mining activities in northern Rhodesia (now Zimbabwe), is suggested by a skull in the arms of Broken Hill, granted in 1954. A complete skeleton in a somewhat reflective pose in the civic arms of Londonderry, Northern Ireland, recalls the unhappy fate of a local nobleman, Walter de Burgo, who was starved to death in a dungeon on the orders of one of his own family members.

CLOTHING AND ACCESSORIES

All kinds of dress can be met with, from the mundane (the breeches in the arms of the family of Van Abbenbroek from Zeeland) to the curious (a French wife's hood, the heraldic badge of the English 16th-century nobleman Lord Ferrers). As early as the 14th century, fashion was appearing on the nobleman's shield. The lady's sleeve or "maunch", which had a pendulous pocket to house the owner's prayer book or missal, was a popular charge in English and French heraldry throughout the late medieval period.

A medieval lady might well also have treasured a necklace of Baltic amber, such

▲ From the cradle – Louis XIV of France's birth is remembered in the arms of the town of St Germain-en-Laye.

▲ To the grave – a rather bored skeleton of Walter de Burgo in the arms of the city of Londonderry, Northern Ireland.

▲ A pair of sandals is the charge for the Spanish family of Abarca.

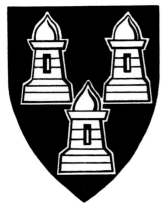

▲ The buildings of the gentry – three of the cotes that they kept their doves in, the punning arms of the English family of Sapcote.

▲ The way we earn our bread – the sewing machine in the arms of Clydebank, Scotland, home of Singer sewing machines.

▲ The inventor, proud of his works – the corrugated boiler flue that made a fortune for Samson Fox of Harrogate.

as the one found in the arms of the Lithuanian coastal resort of Palanga, where lumps of the fossilized resin are often washed up on the beaches.

BUILDINGS AND WORK

Fortresses and bridges appear on shields, as do homes, from the stone building in the arms of the town of Frontenhausen, Bavaria, to the Inuit igloo that forms the crest of the Territory of Nunuvut, Canada. Even the turrets of Indian homes, or *gonkhs*, find their way on to the arms of Halvad Dhrangadhra in Gujarat. A church features in the punning arms of the Asturian family of Iglesia.

The workplace, whether it be the coal mine of the community of Bütten (in the arms of Landkreis Peine, Westphalia) or a

▲ *The food we eat – the sugar loaves of Waghausel, Landkreis Karlsruhe, Germany, appearing here in the trademark of the sugar refinery of that town.*

▲ *The warrior chef. The cheese grater and noodle flattener crest of the Master of the Kitchens to the Holy Roman Emperor.*

sewing machine made in a factory at Burgh of Clydebank, Scotland shows that heraldry can reflect the lifestyle of the worker just as well as that of a medieval knight. Whether the corrugated boiler flue of Samson Fox of Harrogate, England or the section of bracing in the arms of the Bossom baronets (also English) constitute good heraldic charges, is open to dispute.

Both knight and motorway magnate need to eat, and the kitchen has often figured in heraldic imagination, sometimes turning the most mundane objects into comical or bizarre charges. Even the proverbial kitchen sink probably features on a shield somewhere – certainly the table does. Charges taken from the kitchen include the sugar loaf of Waghausel, Landkreis Karlsruhe, Germany; the standing dishes in the punning arms of the English family of Standish; a trivet (Trivet of Cornwall); and a kettle hanger for the town of Zwijndrecht in the Netherlands. So important was the medieval kitchen in the running of a noble or royal household that the Master of the Kitchens to the Holy Roman Emperor was afforded his own very distinctive crest – a cheese grater and a noodle flattener.

TRANSPORT

In the last two centuries the railway has cut its way across the heraldic shields of towns from Swindon in England to Kaisiadorys in Lithuania. The former has a conventional locomotive of the late 19th century (there was much correspondence between the town council and the College of Arms in London over the exact make of the locomotive), while in the arms of the latter, four stylized silver steeds, streaming steam and smoke, pass back and forth across a black shield to represent the two major railways running through the town.

Cars also found their way on to the proud shields of factory towns such as Koprovince in the Czech Republic, the home of the first Czech car, the President, which rolled off the production line in 1897. Air travel was to make its mark on shields from the early 20th century onwards, a startling example being found in the arms of the commune of Sandweiler

▲ *The four rather dashing stylized iron horses of Kaisiadorys, Lithuania.*

▼ *The President car on the arms of Koprovince in the Czech Republic.*

▲ *A jet lands on the runway of the airport at Sandweiler, Luxembourg. Traditional heraldic ordinaries with a modern flavour.*

▲ *The arms of the aviator, Mary, Duchess of Bedford, drawn up and insisted upon by her husband, in spite of the heralds' disapproval.*

in Luxembourg. Sandweiler is home to Luxembourg's international airport, so a passenger jet lands on an intersection of runways in the arms.

One aircraft that had rather a bumpy journey through the heraldic skies, made its maiden flight in the unofficial arms of Mary, wife of the 11th Duke of Bedford. The Duchess was a well-known lady aviator in the 1930s and her husband wished the College of Arms to record the fact in a

grant of arms to his wife, but the heralds would not sanction the design, which the Duke had himself helped to create, including the Duchess's favourite plane, the Spider. This seems not to have bothered His Grace one jot: he claimed that his family, the Russells, had long ago used arms not granted by any herald, and what was done in the past was good enough for his dear wife in her own time.

Even the parachute has been used as a heraldic charge, most notably in the arms of Ste Mère-Eglise in Normandy, commemorating the day in 1944 when the paratroopers of the US Army's 101st Airborne Division landed in and around the town's church – one man even found himself draped across the church tower, an event memorably depicted in the film *The Longest Day*.

SPORTS AND GAMES
Heraldry can also catalogue the lighter side of life, such as the tennis-playing youths in the arms of the Tosetti family of Massiola, northern Italy. In Britain where the weather is not so propitious for outdoor sports, board games find their way on to the heraldic shield, as in the arms of

the Pegrez family with its backgammon boards, and the arms of the Matthias family of Lamphey in Pembrokeshire: Gules on each of three dice in perspective Argent 11 ogresses six in front three on the sinister two on top.

▲ *A tennis match in the arms of the north Italian family of Tosetti, in which, for reasons unknown, the players are not wearing any clothes.*

▼ *Three backgammon boards appear in the arms of the English family of Pegrez.*

◀ *The arms for the French village of Ste Mère Eglise in Normandy, commemorates the landing of American paratroopers at the church, during the liberation of the region from Germany in 1944.*

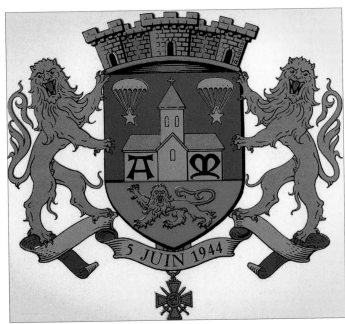

▲ A skiing warrior in the arms of the town of Lillehammer, Norway.

▲ Arms of Sir George Edwards – blue skies and Concordes for a life in aviation.

▲ The town of Spa in Belgium, famous for its waters, has the old spa as its arms.

▲ The local coal mine in the arms of Bülten in Landkreis Peine, Germany.

▲ Oerlese and ...

▲ ... Rietze, towns in Germany that maintain a heraldic link with local farming.

▲ The sails of the ships in the arms of the Scottish Royal Burgh of Elie and Earlsferry are charged with the arms of local lords.

▲ The ship, star and crescent in the arms of the Danish port of Nörresundby were originally on a seal and adapted to a shield.

▲ A detailed depiction of an oared 18th-century sailing ship for the Crimean port of Kostroma.

PUNNING HERALDRY

The richness of heraldic imagery and imagination is nowhere more apparent than in those arms that have been devised as a play on the bearer's name. Punning or, as it is known in Britain, "canting" heraldry, can account for almost half the designs of some nations' heraldry.

Although the great majority of arms dating from the early days of heraldry were of a simple geometric nature, the heraldic imagination at work in the arms of León and Castile (which have always featured a lion and a castle) is a good example of the simplicity of the practice.

A PLAY ON WORDS

The motto of the Scudamores is *Scuto amore divinis* ("The shield of divine love"): the shield bears a gold field with a red cross patty fitchy. The Montagus (or Montacutes) bear three fusils (elongated lozenges) conjoined in fess, the tops of which are supposed to suggest the tops of mountains or *mons acutus*. The prize for the most tortuous wordplay must probably go to the arms of the powerful Mortimer family, whose arms include blue and gold bars with a white escutcheon over all. The blue represents the skies of

▶ *The simplicity of punning or canting – the quartered arms of Castile and León, Toledo Cathedral, 16th century.*

▲ *The three bear's paws of Trebarefoote.*

▲ *The three hands of Tremayne.*

▲ *The Scudamore shield of divine love.*

▲ *The family arms of Rotenhuet (red hat) of Silesia.*

▲ *The arms of the Rosensparre (rose chevron) family of Denmark.*

▲ *The family arms of Swinhufvud (swine head) of Sweden.*

the Holy Land, the gold its sands, while the escutcheon is said to represent the Dead Sea or *mortuo maris*.

In Cornwall, the local placenames offer plenty of opportunities for good puns on the number three through their common prefix "Tre". Trebarefoote has Sable a chevron between three bear's gambs (feet) erect and erased Or, and Tremayne has Gules three dexter arms conjoined at the shoulders and flexed in triangle Or, fists clenched Argent.

One of the most delightful examples has survived through the skill and imagination of the late medieval English stonemason who, asked to fashion the crest of a member of the Mordaunt family for a tomb in Northamptonshire, produced a grinning Moor showing all his teeth – literally "Moor's dents". A modern-day equivalent is the former Aeroplane and Armaments

▲ *The bustard stands in his coombe.*

▼ *The Moor shows off his splendid set of teeth in the Mordaunt crest.*

Experimental Establishment based at Boscombe Down in England. The English heralds came up with the local bird, a bustard, standing in a coombe (valley) on a down. That left the "Bos" which was provided by pinning the poor bustard's wing with the boss from a horse's bridle.

A EUROPEAN TRADITION

Medieval wordplay ranges from the commonplace to the curious. The Zurich armorial roll, held in the Swiss National Museum, supplies many splendid examples of punning German arms from the early 14th century. The Rand family arms are Sable a turnip Proper leaved Vert (*Rande* is German for "turnip"). The von Helfensteins of Swabia have Gules on a quadruple mount Or, an elephant statant Argent and as the Old German word for "beggar" is *betler*, the Betler family arms are Argent a beggar habited in Sable, his

shoes Or, on his shoulder a knapsack of the field, suspended by a cord Gules, a pilgrim's staff in his sinister hand, and in his dexter a begging bowl, both of the last.

Scandinavian heraldry has a long history of punning, and has made excellent use of the device. The medieval period produced the simple arms of the Swedish noble families of Sparre – Azure a chevron Or (*sparre* is a roof span, or chevron) – and Swinhufvud: Azure a boar's head couped Or (*swinhuf* meaning swine's head).

Probably the most innovative of modern punning heraldry emerged in Finland in the latter half of the 20th century. A good example is the arms of the municipality of Aanekoski, which translates from the local dialect as "sounding river" (*ääni* means "voice" and *koski*, "rapids"): Sable on a bend wavy Argent three horns stringed Gules.

▲ *The sounding rapids of Aanekoski, Finland.*

MESSAGES AND
DECLARATIONS

It might seem that once the design of a shield had been settled it would never change. On the medieval battlefield or tourney ground this would have been true, but heraldry is a great adaptor and certain traits have crept in over the centuries that would not have been used by a 13th-century knight. Above all, heraldry was the plaything of the European aristocracy, and arms could be a useful way of accentuating their owner's place in that closely knit class. Coronets of rank started to appear in the 15th century, and special marks of favour granted by a grateful monarch could be thrust in the faces of rivals by displaying them in a coat of arms. Relationships to other families through marriage could be indicated by placing the two sets of arms together. In England if a wife had no brothers she was deemed a heraldic heiress, her children having equal right to have her father's and mother's arms on heraldic quarters, and as other generations married heiresses, so the original arms could be pushed into one corner of the shield by other symbols.

◀ *The arms of the Princes Bagration of Russia, with
the princely mantle and crown.*

AUGMENTATION OF ARMS

Rulers have always availed themselves of orders and decorations to reward those who have served their country, but there is another way for a grateful ruler to thank the patriot or the peacemaker – by the augmentation of armorial bearings. Augmentations are additions to arms that in some way reflect the gratitude of the donor. They are added either by "honour"– when the grantee has performed deeds of merit – or by "grace", whereby the sovereign grants part of his or her arms to a relative. It cannot be said that Henry VIII did much for his wives, but he did give augmentations of grace to the families of three of them.

The augmentation is often a charge from the donor's own arms, or a new coat in the form of a quartering. In the latter case (in British heraldry) the new quarter of augmentation takes first place, with the old arms moving into the second quarter. Crests and supporters may also be given as augmentation. In Britain, an augmentation takes the form of a new grant from either the College of Arms (England and Wales) or Lord Lyon (Scotland), which tends to include a special citation mentioning the reason for the augmentation.

▼ Colonel Carlos' royal companion in the branches of an oak tree is commemorated in the family arms.

▲ Dr Lake bravely rides on in the crest of augmentation, while his 16 wounds are on the 1st quarter to the family arms.

AUGMENTATIONS OF CHARLES II

The reason for the granting of augmentations of honour is neatly summed up in the words of the English King Charles II who, after the Civil War, issued a warrant to Sir Edward Walker, Garter King of Arms, to grant "unto any person of eminent quality, fidelity and extraordinary merit that shall desire it, such augmentation of any of our Royal Badges to be added unto his Armes, as you shall judge most proper to testify the same".

Among the augmentations that Sir Edward granted, several referred to Charles II's escape after the defeat of the Royalist forces at Worcester in 1651, in which he was aided by loyal friends. Early in his escape, the King and his companion Colonel Careless evaded their pursuers by hiding in an oak tree at Boscobel House. This episode was remembered in augmentations to Colonel William Carlos (as his name was now) and the Penderel brothers, tenants of Boscobel. Both families received a full grant of arms which included an oak tree surmounted of a fess charged with three crowns.

Among other extraordinary episodes of the King's flight was riding pillion on the bay horse of Mistress Jane Lane, disguised

as a tenant's son. Not only were the Lanes granted a canton of the royal arms of England, they were also later granted a crest of augmentation: Out of a wreath Or and Azure a demi horse Strawberrie colour, bridled Sable, bitted and garnished Or, supporting an imperial crown Gold.

During the English Civil War an augmentation was granted to Dr Edward Lake for his valour at the Battle of Edgehill in 1642 when he was wounded no less than 16 times, one of which rendered his left arm useless. He was then said to have taken his horse's reins in his teeth, an action that is recorded in the crest of augmentation. All 16 wounds are also remembered in the coat of augmentation, which took the first quarter of his arms. This shows a dexter arm in armour grasping a sword, from which flies a flag of St George. The cross is charged with a lion

▲ The arms of Abensberg, Bavaria, (left), later augmented with swords (right) for the town's help in the Napoleonic wars.

▼ Drake's ship does its balancing act upon the globe of his extravagant arms.

▲ *The arms of concession to Christopher Columbus; the original family arms are in the base of the shield.*

passant guardant from the royal arms, and in each quarter of the flag are four red escutcheons, one for each wound.

VOYAGES OF EXPLORATION

The late medieval period saw the monarchs of Europe vie with each other in gaining for themselves the wealth of the wider world. They were aided by professional sailors who put their lives and ships at risk in return for a small part of the riches and prestige they might present to their sovereign, but all too often these great voyagers received shabby compensation for their efforts. They could, however, receive heraldic recognition. The shield borne by the descendants of Christopher Columbus contains four separate quarters as augmentations, the original family arms being relegated, almost as an afterthought, to a point in the base of the shield. A crest of the royal orb, a rare distinction in Spanish heraldry, was also given together with the motto:

A *Castillion y Leon, nuevo munda, dio Colon*, "To Castile and León, the new world was given by Colón".

Another explorer, Vasco da Gama, of Portugal, received the ancient shield of arms of Portugal as an augmentation: Argent five escutcheons in cross Azure each charged with five plates. He was also given the crest of a demi man dressed "a l'Indienne" holding a shield of the augmented arms and a branch of cinnamon, all evoking his epic voyage to India and the Spice Islands.

The English adventurer, Sir Francis Drake, was said to have been using the arms of another Devon family of the same name, whose head complained to Elizabeth I, calling the famous explorer an upstart. The Queen retorted that she would give Sir Francis arms which would far outshine those of his namesake. Those arms, Sable a fess wavy between two estoiles irradiated Argent, neatly sum up his voyages between the North and South Poles. The crest is a case of paper heraldry and could never be used on any helmet. Various depictions show a ship on top of a globe being guided by a hand from clouds, holding a golden cord; above the clouds a scroll with the motto *Auxilio divino* ("By divine aid"). The blazon of the crest also includes "in the ship a dragon Gules regarding the hand".

FRENCH AUGMENTATIONS

The French monarchs were not usually forthcoming with granting any augmentations, but they could not avoid acknowledging the part played by Joan of Arc in the eventual eviction of the English. In 1429, Charles VII granted to Joan's family a simple but splendid shield

▲ *Vasco da Gama's voyages to the Spice Islands are remembered in his crest of concession (augmentation).*

▲ *A diplomatic alliance remembered heraldically – the viper of the Viscontis is augmented by the fleur de lis of France.*

of a blue field charged with an erect sword supporting the French crown and two fleurs de lis in fess. These arms recall an account by the chronicler, Holinshed, that Joan wielded a sword "With five floure delices graven on both sides", and although there is no evidence to suggest Joan used the arms, they were used by the descendants of her brothers, upon whom Charles VII conferred the name Du Lys.

Both the Viscontis of Milan and the Medicis of Florence could be said to have been awarded augmentations "of grace" by French monarchs. In 1395 Charles VI

▼ *The arms of Joan of Arc's brothers' descendants, her sword upholding the crown.*

▲ *Heraldry in 3D: the arms of the Medicis with the topmost roundel charged with the fleur de lis of France.*

conceded by special diploma to Gian Galeazzo Visconti the right to quarter the arms of France (ancient) within a double border the external Gules the internal Argent. The Medici arms are thought to include a pun on their name, the red roundels in the shield possibly being pills (*palle*) handed out by doctors (*medici*). In 1465 Louis XI granted the Medicis the right to replace the top roundel with a blue one charged with three gold fleurs de lis.

RALLYING TO ARMS

The arms of many Polish families evolved on the battlefield, and they offer some unusual examples of augmentation. In 1386 the neighbouring states of Poland and Lithuania were joined through the marriage of the daughter of the last Polish king of the Piast dynasty to Grand Duke Jagiello of Lithuania. The Polish arms (a white eagle on a red field) were afterwards quartered with Lithuania's charging knight.

Under the Jagiellon dynasty, if a man was raised to nobility through valour, it became the custom to give him a shield charged with an arm in armour holding a sword. This coat was known as the "Pogonia". Later Polish kings – notably those of the Vasa dynasty – would grant foreigners, such as ambassadors, who had offered good service to the state, part of the Polish eagle as an augmentation. (Venetian ambassadors to London also managed to obtain augmentations to their arms, and several examples are extant which bear in their design the lion passant guardant Or of the English sovereign.)

The arms of Moravia, Azure an eagle displayed chequy Argent and Gules, have long been considered one of the most beautiful in medieval heraldry. When the Moravians came to the aid of the Holy Roman Emperor Frederick III (1440–93) he granted them the right to change the white chequers of the eagle to gold. In 1848, the year of revolution, Moravians supporting the Czech independence movement pledged support to the ancient eagle with white and red chequers, while German-speaking Moravians used the augmented gold and red chequered bird as their symbol.

Many Russian noble arms include the ciphers of sovereigns and charges taken from the arms of the Romanov emperors, but surely the most augmented arms of all must be those of Count Alexander Suvorov-Rymniksky, commander of the Russian Armies, whose brilliant strategies helped to bring about the eventual defeat of Napoleon. As commander-in-chief of the Russo-Austrian Army during the Second Coalition, he drove the French out of northern Italy in 1799 and was created Prince Italiysky. He had also previously defeated a Turkish force on the banks of the River Rymnik in Turkey in 1789. The augmentations to his arms included a "rendering of the map of Italy", an escutcheon bearing the name of Emperor Paul I, and two lightning bolts issuing from thunderclouds striking a crescent reversed above a river in bend inscribed *R Rymnik*. His services to the Russian nation were commemorated not only by an imperial decoration, but also by the Soviet Union.

▲ *The proud eagle of Moravia sports its distinctive golden chequers.*

The German emperors made full and free use of the Prussian eagle (often as supporters) in augmentations to those who had assisted in their rise to imperial power in the 19th century. Alexander von Schleinitz, Prussian Foreign Minister, received supporters to his arms of two Prussian eagles charged on the breast with the arms of Hohenzollern. Otto, Prince Bismarck, who brought about German unification, was granted a Prussian (black) and a Brandenburg (red) eagle as supporters: they supported two armorial bearings, those of Alsace and Lorraine, the territories regained from France in 1870–1.

LATER AUGMENTATIONS

In the late 18th and early 19th centuries heraldry in most countries was in a state of decay, or rather decadence. The augmentations granted to the military and naval heros of Britain were typical of the period, with battle scenes, bombardments, storming of forts and "casts of thousands",

or medals with inscriptions and too detailed to be legible. The arms of Rear Admiral Sir Charles Brisbane included a chief "thereon on waves of the sea a ship of war under sail between two forts, the guns firing and on the battlements the

Dutch flag all proper". Colonel James Stevenson-Barnes had a canton charged with his gold cross and the Portuguese Order of the Tower and Sword; his arms also included a chief bearing a curtain of fortification and the name *St Sebastian*.

Medals and decorations remained in vogue as augmentations to arms well into the 20th century. On 2 May 1918 the Finnish city of Vaasa was informed that: "To commemorate the time when Vaasa as the temporary capital was the heart of the liberation of Finland [from Russia], the Senate have decided to give the City the right to add the Cross of Liberty to its coat of arms." Another Finnish city, Mikkeli, housed the headquarters of Marshal Mannerheim's army, and on 21 December 1944 the medal of the Cross of Liberty was suspended from its shield. This was the second augmentation given to Mikkeli, in 1942 it was granted a pair of crossed marshal's batons.

▼ *One of three shield designs supplied by the heraldic artist to the Vaasa authorities for consideration. Here the augmentation is simply placed on the heraldic charge.*

▼ *Another suggestion put before the committee made the augmentation of the cross more prominent.*

▼ *In this suggestion the charge becomes secondary as the augmentation takes pride of place with the star of the order.*

ABATEMENTS AND DEGRADATIONS

Augmentations were marks of honour, given in the main to the strong and heroic, those who had rendered great service to their sovereign and their nation. But military men can also go astray. They may contravene the code of chivalry, or even betray their own country. What then should become of such traitors, debauchees, boasters and other miscreants? For the treacherous knight, his class had a most terrible ceremony – "the degradation from knighthood".

KNIGHTS AND KNAVES

John Selden, in his work *Titles of Honour* (1614), describes the case of Sir Andrew de Harclay, Earl of Carlisle, who in the 16th year of the reign of Edward II (1307–27) was condemned as a traitor,

▲ *The reversed royal arms of Portugal on the shield of Castello-Rodrigo, a rare case of an abatement put into practice.*

having secretly treated with the Scots against the King's favourite, Hugh Le Despenser. Edward was told of Harclay's doings and ordered the Earl's immediate apprehension. Harclay was seized at Carlisle and brought against a court of his peers. The Earl was found guilty, and sentence was pronounced against him that the sword (which he had received from the King "to defend his Lord" and with which he had been made Earl) should be taken from him, and his gilt spurs hacked from his heels by a "knave", after which the Earl's sword was to be broken over his head. The Earl was divested of his tabard, his hood, his coat and his "girdle". When this was done Sir Anthony Lucy (one of the judges) said to the Earl "Andrew, now art thou no knight but thou art a knave."

Selden also quotes the case of Sir Ralfe Grey, a Knight of the Bath who was

◄ *The defaced arms of Henry Courtenay, Marquess of Exeter, attainted and executed in 1539 after falling foul of King Henry VIII.*

▼ *The arms of Plommenfelt, a Swedish nobleman. His arms were erased after he was declared "dead" in punishment for slandering the Swedish king.*

degraded from knighthood. The Constable of England, being empowered to sit in judgement, said to the accused, "The King has ordained that thou should have had thy spurs stricken off by the hard heels, by the hand of the Master Cooke… and here thou mayest see, the Kings of Armes, and Heralds and thine own proper coat of armes which they should teare off thy bodie, and so shouldst thou as well be degraded of the Worship, Noblenesse and Armes, as of thy Order of Knighthood."

The Constable had with him another coat of arms, reversed (upside-down) as a sign of dishonour, which should have been worn by Sir Ralfe on his way to the place of execution, but it seems that he was spared this further token of degradation as the King remembered the good service done by the former knight's grandfather to the King's "Most Noble Predecessors".

In the case of knights of certain orders, the Garter included, further punishment could be expected. In addition to the measures taken during the service of degradation, their trappings of knighthood – targe, helm and crest – were to be torn down from their place in the chapel of the order, and literally kicked out into a nearby ditch; the knight's shield was also broken in pieces. In the Catholic Church a similar ceremony of defrocking was ordained as the most serious penalty reserved for clergy who had broken ecclesiastical laws.

CIVIC BETRAYALS

The 17th-century heraldist John Guillim cited the case of Sir Aimery of Pavia, a Lombard, an unworthy Captain of Calais in the time of Edward III (1327–77), who sold the town to the enemy for 20,000 crowns. Guillim described Sir Aimery's arms as "Light blue, four mullets yellow, two in fess, as many in the chief, reversed (upside-down)".

In Portugal, the town of Castello-Rodrigo was made to bear a shield charged with the arms of Portugal reversed, because the townsfolk had closed the gates on a rival claimant to the Portuguese throne who subsequently proved victorious. This is one of the very few cases of an abatement put into practice.

MARKS OF ABATEMENT

Various English books on heraldry include certain marks of dishonour that have been termed "abatements". They employ charges and stains – the lesser and rare colours tenny (tawny or orange) and sanguine (blood red) – borne together in a fashion otherwise uncommon in heraldry. The sixth edition of John Guillim's monumental work *A Display of Heraldry* (1724), "improved" by Sir George Mackenzie, listed the abatements. They are illustrated below. Most of these abatements were probably the doodlings of some herald in the Tudor period. The English herald J. P. Brooke-Little, in his foreword to his revision of Boutell's *Heraldry* (1970), asserted that "there is no such thing as a mark of dishonour in English heraldry." Nor does such a system exist anywhere else.

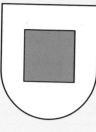

▲ A delf tenny: he who revokes his own challenge.

▲ Argent a point dexter parted tenny: a boaster of martial acts.

▲ Or a point in point sanguine: effeminacy.

▲ Or a point champaine tenny: one who kills a prisoner after surrender.

▲ Argent a gore sinister tenny: a coward to his enemy.

▲ Or a plain point sanguine: a liar.

◀ A combination of two marks of abatement: Argent a gusset sinister sanguine: he who is "devoted too much to the smock", or womanizing, and Argent a gusset dexter sanguine: a man too fond of drink. If guilty of both, the man should bear both gussets, as here.

▲ The shield reversed: a traitor, also denotes death.

FANTASTICAL ARMS

Heraldry has long been seen as an accoutrement of the high-born, both present and past. From the 15th to the 17th centuries, heraldic writers increasingly sought to bestow arms on those of high rank in history and legend. Rulers, saints, biblical characters and legendary figures both good and bad, were assumed to have borne arms, as their like did in more recent times. No matter that documentary evidence was at the least scant, the heraldic writers felt that it was their duty to invent retrospective arms for those who were thought to be worthy of them.

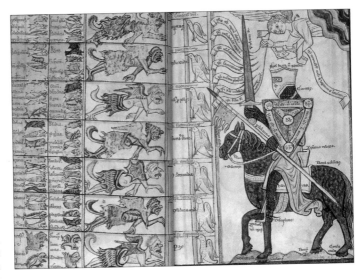

HOLY ARMS

The holy Trinity – God the Father, Son and Holy Ghost – was represented in the "Arms of the Faith", the three joined in one upon the shield. The symbols of the Passion can often be found on a series of shields displayed in parish churches throughout Europe. The three kings, or wise men, who

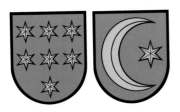

▲ ▼ *Attributed arms for the three wise men: Casper, top left, Balthasar, top right, and Melchior, bottom.*

visited the Christ child also had arms attributed to them by medieval heraldists. As for Satan, the Prince of Darkness, he also held a rank of sorts and was therefore afforded arms in medieval manuscripts: a shield with frogs and a fess accompanied him as he dragged the souls of fallen knights from the field down into hell.

In India, the arms of various Hindu gods, in particular Hanuman the monkey god, appear in the arms of several states.

▼ *The charge attributed to Hector, champion of Troy, and one of the Nine Worthies thought to deserve posthumous arms.*

▲ *A Christian knight, his shield charged with the attributed arms of the holy Trinity, rides out to fight vice and heresy, shown here in the form of devils, in a 13th-century illuminated manuscript.*

THE NINE WORTHIES

Many allegorical tales of the medieval period concerned the Nine Worthies of the World, a group composed of those who were believed to have been the greatest warriors of history. Their characters were especially appealing to the writers of the early Renaissance, who attempted to recreate their heroic feats.

Three of the Worthies were outstanding commanders of the classical world: Hector of Troy, Julius Caesar and Alexander the Great; three were biblical heroes of the Old Testament, Joshua, Judas Maccabeus and David; and three were European Christian warriors, King Arthur of the Britons, King Charlemagne of France, and Godfrey de Bouillon, the leader of the First Crusade. The Worthies of this splendid band were notable rulers and generals, men to be feared and followed, and would therefore surely all have merited arms. Consequently, armorial bearings were devised for all nine. The arms given to the Worthies by heraldic

▲ *Four Saxon kings who lived long before heraldry was established, are depicted with attributed arms in the quarters of the stained glass shield at Capesthorne Hall, Cheshire, England.*

▼ *The arms of the princes Bagration of Russia, whose ancestral claims are declared with King David's harp, and the sling he used to slay Goliath.*

◀ *A spirited depiction in Celtic style of arms attributed to King Arthur by the Cornish artist Dennis Ivall.*

writers of the 16th and 17th centuries reflected the attributes and character generally attributed to each man. Ferocity, bravura, steadfastness and mercy naturally featured strongly. Many of their arms therefore bear lions in various attitudes, and creatures such as wyverns, dragons and double-headed eagles. The Jewish heroes bore symbols usually associated with the Tribes of Israel.

OTHER ATTRIBUTED ARMS

Some families still extant today make use of arms attributed to supposed early ancestors of theirs. The English family of Temple quarters in its arms Or an eagle displayed Sable attributed to Leofric, Earl of Mercia, who was the husband of the more famous Lady Godiva. However, this claim to fame in family history is mundane compared to that of the Russian Princes Bagration, who claim descent from King David of the Jews,

and bear in their arms his harp, and the sling and stone with which he slew Goliath. Other Russian princely families bear in their arms the figure of the Archangel Gabriel, from whom they claim descent.

Men such as King David, Julius Caesar or Leofric, Earl of Mercia, all obviously lived long before heraldry was invented. The shields they were given posthumously are therefore called "attributed arms". Some of the most famous arms are those attributed to King Arthur and his Knights of the Round Table, and these have been extensively used in artistic depictions of the Arthurian legends from medieval times up to the pre-Raphaelites.

King Arthur has at least three separate shields of arms attributed to him, including Azure three crowns in pale Or, and Vert a cross Argent in the first quarter a figure of the Virgin holding the Christ Child Or. Arthur's first knight and champion, Sir Lancelot du Lac was given Argent three bendlets Gules, and Sir Perceval bore a shield Purpure semy of plain crosslets Or.

ALLIANCES

The joy of heraldry is that it can, by colours and symbols, make an instant visual statement in the most splendid manner, and over the centuries its supporters adapted it to suit their own needs. By the late 15th century, its purpose on the battlefield was in the main lost (due to the discourteous nature of gunfire and to the pride of the wearer in his splendid new "alwyte" armour), but heraldry found other uses. As far back as the 13th century, arms were being married to others to symbolize family ties through marriage, and that was not all they could express. Individuals of knightly rank could, and indeed did, make use of their arms to express ties of friendship and devotion, passion or duty.

EXPRESSIONS OF UNITY

In times gone by, kings would set their arms alongside those of other rulers to assert that they were part of an international élite without equal, and according to medieval thought it was a position they maintained when they were elevated to heaven, where a special "celestial palace" was reserved for the souls of deceased royalty. At the other end of the heraldic hierarchy, the local landowner could also choose to decorate his castle or manor house with the arms of his equals in the locality. A charming example can still be seen at the former home of the Fairfax family at Gilling Castle in Yorkshire, England. The castle's Great Chamber was decorated in the Elizabethan period with a frieze of painted trees, from which hang the shields of all the landowning families that governed the local administrative districts, or "wapentakes".

▲ *As these crusading knights gather for their voyage to the holy land their arms are proudly displayed on shields and banners.*

▶ *The unity of marriage: again heraldry is utilized in a 15th-century manuscript which shows Isabeau of Bavaria arriving in Paris for her marriage to Charles VI of France, with their impaled arms much in evidence.*

▲ *Another use of heraldry was to extol the merits of feudalism. In the Armorial General, 14th century, the arms of the King of England are followed by those of his vassals.*

Elsewhere the comradeship in arms of various knights was recorded less formally. Graffiti is by no means a product of the modern age: witness the crudely etched shields, crests and signatures scratched into the stone and plaster of the Sanctuary of the Nativity in Bethlehem some seven centuries ago by Crusaders, who were probably part of a contingent of knights from Flanders.

▲ *Alliances of brotherhood were an important function of heraldry in the 13th century, a fact borne witness to by the graffiti such as this crest left behind by crusading knights in the Church of the Nativity in Bethlehem.*

▶ *Three versions of the Brackenhaupt (hound's head) crest. 1 Crest of Lentold von Regensburg. 2 The differenced crest of Oettingen. 3 The crest later adopted by Hohenzollern of Brandenberg.*

CREST PARTNERSHIP

On 10 April 1317 Burgrave Friedrich IV of Nuremberg, a member of the Hohenzollern family, purchased a new crest for his arms from Lentold von Regensburg. Burgrave Friedrich paid 36 marks for the privilege, an enormous sum in those days. The crest in question was a golden *Brackenhaupt*, a hound's head with red ears. At the same time, Lentold von Regensburg reserved the right of certain of his relations to use the same crest during their lifetime. In September of the same year, the Burgrave exacted from Lentold another document in which the latter confirmed that, "I give full power and right to the Burgrave to use the crest as if I were present myself, in case others should contest his right to use it."

Prior to the purchase, the Burgrave had entered into a *Helmgerossenschaft* (crest partnership) with the Counts of Oettingen, the crest in this case being a *Schirmbrett* (wooden panel) ornamented with peacock feathers, typical of German crests of the period. This crest partnership had existed between the two families principally because of a marriage alliance, but had lapsed by the time that the Burgrave purchased the second crest from Lentold von Regensburg. However, the Oettingens attempted to cling to their interest in a possible succession to the estates of the Burgrave and promptly adopted the *Brackenhaupt*, much to the annoyance of the Hohenzollerns.

A lengthy heraldic dispute now ensued, which was resolved in 1381 when a panel of noble and royal arbitrators decided that the Oettingens could continue to use the gold hound's head, but would have to

difference its red ears with a white saltire from the Oettingen shield of arms. Furthermore, it was decreed by the heraldic judges, the "saltire must be at least a finger's breadth and this clearly visible". The Oettingens have honoured this ruling to the present day.

GIFTS OF FRIENDSHIP

On some occasions, German knights purchased the arms of others. In 1368 Hans Traganer, sold his arms and crest to Pilgrim von Wolfsthal, vowing that he and his offspring, would from that moment forever cease to use their arms.

Arms and crests were not only sold but also handed over as gifts. In 1286, Duke Otto of Austria bestowed upon Count William of Julich his crest – a crown with peacock feathers – as a mark of friendship. In 1350, at the Holy Sepulchre in Jerusalem, Matthew de Roya bestowed upon the knight Hartmann von Cronenberg, his crest of a boar's head.

▼ *Alliances through marriage are recorded through a heraldic pedigree of the English family of Hesketh, 1594.*

THE ARMS OF WOMEN

From the evidence of seals, it would seem that between the 13th and 15th centuries it became customary for European noble-women to use the arms of their fathers and husbands on shields alone, without a crest. The seals themselves were often of an oval shape, similar to those of ecclesiastical institutions and clerics. As with the seals of armigerous men, those of armigerous women also often show the bearer herself, sometimes holding a shield in each hand. Some medieval monuments also show women bearing shields.

STATUS IN THE FAMILY

Although heraldry by its nature related to the individual, it quickly became the ideal medium to denote noble alliances, none more so than marriage. By the 15th century a complex system of marks and marrying of arms could show the viewer the exact status of the per-

son or persons whose arms they were studying. Sons, daughters, wives and widows were all able to denote their place in the family unit. Furthermore, the family could show its alliance with other families of noble status through the heraldic pedigree. In Britain, this was particularly true during the Tudor and Stuart periods, when the old nobility was increasingly on the defensive against merchants and other "newly made men" who were keen to acquire the trappings of gentility, including of course, family arms.

The clues to marital alliances, so important to the nobility of Europe, and the symbols of marital status and placing in the family unit, are complex and evolved over centuries. These are ongoing, with new rulings being enacted in recent years by the heraldic authorities of Canada and England on the rights of daughters and married women.

▲ *Joan, Countess of Surry's seal, c1347, perhaps the origin of the lozenge shape that was later chosen to display a woman's arms.*

THE LOZENGE

A shield, being an article of warfare, was traditionally associated with men, and as such it was not considered appropriate for women. From the late medieval period, a diamond-shaped device – the lozenge – came into use for the armigerous lady

▼ *In the formative period of heraldry, 1150–1300, it is not uncommon to find women depicted with shields of their family arms, as here on this Welsh lady's tomb in the Priory Church, Abergavenny.*

◄ *The armorial garments of this medieval English lady were probably never worn but used simply as an illustrative device to proclaim her noble status on funerary memorials and manuscripts.*

▼ *Three generations of English women. From left: a widow with impaled arms, not an heiress, her daughter, a widow heiress, her granddaughter, a spinster, quartering her father and mother's arms.*

▲ *A depiction of the arms of Queen Juliana of the Netherlands before her succession as HRH Princess of Oranje-Nassau, Duchess of Mecklenberg.*

although, like so much in heraldry, just when the diamond was first used in this way is not clear. A remarkable English seal has survived from around 1347 for Joan, daughter of Henrie Count de Barre, widow of John de Warrenne, Earl of Surrey. Included in the seal's complex design are five tiny lozenges, the central lozenge bears the arms of Warenne, the lozenges in the flanks, of de Barre, and those above and below the arms of England – Countess Joan's mother was Eleanor, daughter of King Edward I of England. The seal is also diapered with castles and lions rampant for the countess's grandmother, Eleanor of Castile, first wife of King Henry.

By the 15th century the diamond or lozenge had become the normal platform for the display of the single woman's arms in Britain, France and the Low Countries, and so it continues to this day, the somewhat harsh shape being softened at times into the oval. However, whereas the oval has sometimes been used by men, the lozenge seems an entirely female device.

The unmarried woman simply uses her father's arms on the lozenge or oval, sometimes accompanied by a blue bow and ribbon, a symbol of maidenhood. (A heraldic writer in the 1800s suggested that unmarried spinsters in danger of remaining so should unite in an "order of the lozenge" and advertize for partners.)

While a bachelor is entitled to the family arms on a shield surmounted by helm, crest and motto, in most heraldic traditions a woman, married or not, cannot bear a crest. In Germany an unmarried daughter can bear the shield of her father's arms surmounted by a wreath or torse. In Scotland, a woman who is a clan chief is entitled to bear the crest above a lozenge or oval.

▼ *The lozenge is rather a hard shape and attempts were made to "feminize" it, as in this 18th-century display of the arms of the Duchess of Kendal, mistress of King George I of England.*

IMPALEMENT AND MARRIAGE

When marriage was depicted on seals and monuments in the early days of heraldry, it tended to be by way of complete shields of arms for the families of both the husband and the wife, shown separately. In the late 13th century a process started by which two separate arms were placed side by side on a shield. At first, in order to fit both arms on to a single shield, each was simply chopped in half, or "dimidiated", in a somewhat unfortunate way. This curious marriage of two separate arms did not persist for long, and by the end of the 14th century the practice of showing the full set of charges for both coats on one shield had become the norm. In heraldic terms, the wife is called "femme" and her husband "baron", which in this context does not indicate rank.

DIMIDIATION

An example of the earlier practice of dimidiation can be seen in the arms used by Margaret of France after her marriage in 1299 to Edward I of England. Before marriage, the Queen as a daughter of France would simply have borne the ancient arms of France. Queen Margaret's seal shows her shield divided in half vertically, with the lion of England for her husband on the dexter half, and the lilies of France on the sinister side. As both charges are cut in half by the dividing line,

▲ *Dimidiation threw up some curious creatures, such as in the arms of the English port of Great Yarmouth. Here the royal lions of England have their hind parts replaced with herrings.*

the front half of the English lion is married to the fleur de lis of France.

Not only marital coats suffered from dimidiation. The arms of some cities and towns (the English Cinq Ports being the most famous examples) also showed heraldic alliances in such a fashion, and dimidiation could result in some fascinating combinations. It is slightly modified in the arms of the Czech town of Zlonice. Here the sinister half of a black eagle is

▲ *In much of Europe, when two arms are shown for husband and wife, the charges are turned to face each other; in heraldic terminology they are "respectant".*

dimidiated with a coat per fess but, while most of the eagle is sliced through, its head is left intact and allowed to enter the dexter half of the shield.

IMPALEMENT

The word "impalement" sounds like some medieval form of torture (just as the "bend sinister" of the bastard seems to imply some hideous heraldic secret), but the term is simply used to denote a side-by-side alliance of two coats on a shield. It was the practice for which dimidiation paved the way, the difference being that impalement shows the charges of the two coats in their entirety. The only exception is made for some bordures or charges said to be "in orle", or following the edge of the shield. These are still cut off by the vertical division of the two coats. The placing of two or more separate coats of arms on a single shield is called "marshalling".

Marital impalement is particularly observed in British heraldry, yet even here there are differences in practice. In England it is used when the wife has brothers who will carry on her own family arms, so that she is not classed as a heraldic heiress. In such a case the children born to the marriage inherit only the arms of the father. In Scotland, however, impalement is used in both cases, whether

▲ *The dimidiated arms of Margaret of France after her marriage to King Edward I of England in 1299.*

◄ *In the arms of the town of Zlonice in the Czech Republic, the eagle's head transcends the impalement line.*

▲ *This hatchment for a Dutch widow has her arms upon an oval-shaped shield as opposed to a lozenge.*

▲ *In the impaled arms of a French princess. The lozenge is within the cordelière.*

▼ *The arms of a Dutch widow impaled with those of her husband and surrounded by shields recording marital alliances.*

▲ *A page from a Flemish pedigree and armorial of 1590, with the husband's achievement (centre) turned towards his wife's lozenge.*

the wife is a heraldic heiress or not. In France and the Low Countries no distinction is made.

In much of Europe a marital coat is denoted not so much by impalement as by two separate shields set "accolee", or side by side. Often these are tilted to touch each other at one corner, and the charges of each shield are turned towards each other, instead of facing to the left as is the more normal position. Should a bend be included in the design of the husband's arms this too is turned, giving it the appearance of a bend sinister. In Germany the shields of both husband and wife are surmounted by helm and crest; a display of two complete achievements is there known as an *Allianzwappen* or *Ehewappen*.

WIVES AND WIDOWS

In a recent ruling, the English kings of arms ordained that a married woman may bear her paternal arms, even if her hus-band is not armigerous, on a shield or banner differenced by a small escutcheon of a contrasting tincture in the corner or elsewhere on the shield, in a manner most suitable to the design.

Furthermore, the ruling states that even if the wife comes from an armigerous family she may bear her husband's arms alone, the shield charged with a small lozenge. Widows revert to the lozenge but with the impaled arms of husband and wife. In Europe it has often been the practice for the widow's lozenge to be placed within a "cordelière" (knotted cord). In England a divorced woman may revert to a lozenge of her family's arms, her divorced status shown by the differencing of a small mascle in some suitable place on the lozenge.

HEIRESSES AND SIMPLE QUARTERING

From the late medieval period onwards, pedigrees and other family papers and memorials show the contents of shields being marshalled in an ever more complex way, through a heraldic stratagem known as "quartering". This was a method used throughout European heraldry, principally to display alliances made through marriage, and it indicates how estates or

▼ *Many a church interior shows the pomp and piety of the local nobility through memorials that are bright with heraldry. This English couple have their family arms above their heads while the husband's family, the Newdegates, celebrate a previous marriage with quartered shields at the head and base of the memorial.*

fiefdoms were established and built up through such alliances.

As with other aspects of heraldry, quartering differed in various minor ways between nations, and it is important to remember this when viewing a quartered shield. Mistakes can be made when reading the messages that are declared, unless the rules of the nation in which the arms evolved are also taken into account.

ESCUTCHEON OF PRETENCE

In England, a heraldic quartering occurs after a marriage with a heraldic heiress – a woman who has no brothers, so that her family lacks a direct male heir. In such a case, the husband, instead of placing his wife's arms beside his on the marital shield (as an impalement), places them upon a small shield in the centre of his own arms. This small shield is called an "escutcheon of pretence", the husband in this case "pretending" to be the male head of his wife's family. Any children born to such a marriage are entitled to bear not only their father's arms, but also those of their mother (on a shield for a son, or a lozenge for a daughter), as quartering.

HOW QUARTERING WORKS

In the simplest case, where just one heraldic heiress has married into the family, the shield or lozenge is divided in four quarters. The patrimonial arms appear in the top left and bottom right hand quarters (numbered 1 and 4) and the arms of the heiress are placed in the top right and bottom left hand quarters (2 and 3).

The next heraldic heiress who marries into the family again takes her family arms to her husband, who places them in the centre of the already quartered arms, as another escutcheon of pretence. In the next generation, these arms appear as a new third quarter (bottom left) of the quartered arms. The shield should always have an equal number of quarterings (although this was not so in past times), and until a third heiress enters the scheme, the patrimonial arms are repeated in the fourth quarter

▲ *In England the widow who is also a heraldic heiress reverts to the lozenge of her husband's arms with an escutcheon of pretence – here we see the arms of Nelson with a quartered escutcheon.*

(bottom right).This is all well and good until a fourth heiress is married.

Supposedly there can only be four quarters which have all now been used up, but heraldry can be pragmatic and the term "quarter" is used for any number of separate arms on one shield. It is possible for a newly armigerous man, without any quarterings to his family arms, to marry the heiress of an ancient family with many quarterings. The children of such a marriage will bear not only their father's arms, but also all the quarters of their mother's arms. Therefore in just two generations a shield can go from simple to complex.

NATIONAL VARIATIONS

Elsewhere, the adding of quarterings and the nature of what in England would be thought of as an escutcheon of pretence, have their own system and meaning. In Scotland the escutcheon is reserved for an important fiefdom, usually one associated with a title held by the holder of a peerage, while in Germany the escutcheon is normally reserved for the family arms and the quarterings are kept for the arms associated with various fiefdoms and families that brought territory to the estate now held by the family.

In Britain more than one crest can be borne by a family, usually when two or more surnames are used in a hyphenated form. Noble German families usually place a crested helm above the shield for each quartering, and some families of courtly or princely rank may display as many as 20 crests above the shield. In Scandinavia as

▼ *The escutcheon of pretence for an heiress is clearly displayed in the centre of her husband's shield.*

a family was advanced to a higher degree the arms tended to be augmented with the addition of quarterings – the escutcheon being kept for the original family arms.

In England and Wales, marriage to a non-armigerous wife was simply indicated by a blank impalement or escutcheon. It seems an absurdity, but some authorities thought it necessary to show the exact heraldic status of the husband. The pedigree books of the House of Lords for peers of the realm record many such heraldic curiosities. No similar practices seem to be employed outside England and Wales.

◀ *The arms of the Counts von Creutz in the House of Nobility, Helsinki. The background quarters were added as the family passed up the ranks of the nobility.*

▲ *In Germany and Austria the escutcheon is usually reserved for the original arms.*

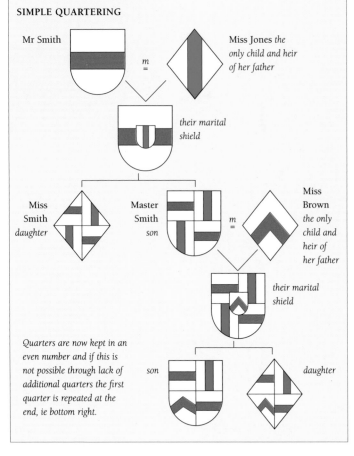

SIMPLE QUARTERING

Mr Smith   *m =*   Miss Jones *the only child and heir of her father*

their marital shield

Miss Smith *daughter*   Master Smith *son*   *m =*   Miss Brown *the only child and heir of her father*

their marital shield

Quarters are now kept in an even number and if this is not possible through lack of additional quarters the first quarter is repeated at the end, ie bottom right.

son   *daughter*

COMPLEX QUARTERINGS

In Britain, families of ancient lineage may have shields bearing many heraldic quarterings, sometimes running into hundreds. Heraldists divide into two schools of thought about multiple quarterings. There are those who despise such a shield, believing it to be a vulgar show of pretension. Others see it as a welcome chance for a piece of heraldic detective work – working back through the various quarterings with the help of pedigrees. A many-quartered shield can lead the viewer into all kinds of adventures when trying to decipher it: they may make their own family connection, or turn up stories of murder, mayhem, heroes and heroines. It can be fun to make a map locating all the families illustrated on just one shield, though in some cases the map will have to be very large.

REPEATED QUARTERS

Should an heiress whose family has amassed its own heraldic quarterings marry into the family, these are in turn placed in their own chronological order. The English scheme provides the viewer with no clue as to which heiress brought in which quarters, but Scottish heraldry provides the clue by keeping such a set of quarters together in an impartable group or "grand quarter".

In Britain, should an armiger have no sons but several daughters, each is classed as a co-heiress, and all are equally entitled to transmit their father's arms to any children they may have in marriage. Looking closely at the grand quarterings of the Dukes of Buckingham and Chandos, it is possible to see that some individual quarters are actually identical with others dotted around the shield, because they represent marriages to the descendants of co-heiresses, and since at any time the English aristocracy represents less than one per cent of the nation's population, marriage within that group is bound to throw up such heraldic curiosities.

The great Anglo-Norman family of de Clare terminated with the three daughters and co-heiresses of Gilbert de Clare, Earl

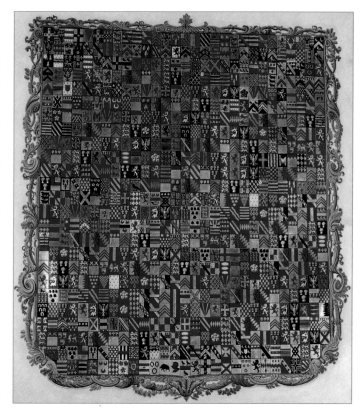

of Hereford and Gloucester (their brother, Gilbert, having been killed in 1313). These grand ladies were able to transmit the arms of de Clare, Or three chevronels Gules, to their children, who also married into great families. It was therefore possible for a family such as the Grenvilles to marry into other families of rank and antiquity, each of whom represented an heiress of the de Clares.

PEDIGREES

In continental Europe it was at certain times necessary for noble families to prove their ancestry by showing descent from 16 great-great-grandparents, all of whom were expected to be armigerous. Such an armorial pedigree is called "Proof of Seize-quartiers". Not only was such a proof desirable for those wishing to attend a

▲ *Possibly the most impressive collection of quartering ever used for an English family, these are the 719 quarters of the Dukes of Buckingham and Chandos.*

royal court or trying to enter one of the various orders of chivalry, but also for those attempting to become officers in certain military regiments.

A lesser pedigree was also often used in continental Europe for memorials, gravestones and the like. In such cases, the shield of the deceased would be placed in the centre of the memorial, and down either side would be shown all the shields of arms of the parents, grandparents and sometimes great-grandparents, both on the male and female side. These heraldic pedigrees in stone can still be seen in many European churches.

COMPLEX QUARTERING

This chart gives an example of how quarters accumulate over the generations, as heiresses marry into the family, and yet more quarters are added to the shield.

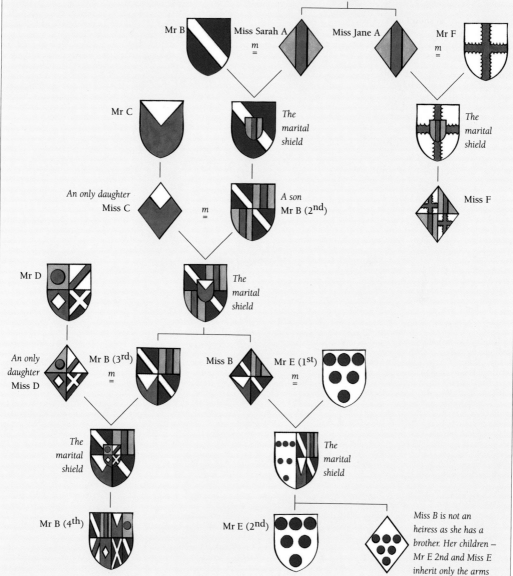

Mr A

Mr A *has no sons, his 2 daughters are termed co-heiresses and can equally impart their family arms to their children as a quartering.*

Mr B   Miss Sarah A
m
=

Miss Jane A   Mr F
m
=

Mr C

The marital shield

The marital shield

An only daughter Miss C
m
=

A son Mr B (2nd)

Miss F

Mr D

The marital shield

An only daughter Miss D

Mr B (3rd)
m
=

Miss B   Mr E (1st)
m
=

The marital shield

The marital shield

Mr B (4th)

Mr E (2nd)

Miss B is not an heiress as she has a brother. Her children – Mr E 2nd and Miss E inherit only the arms of their father

DIFFERENCE MARKS AND CADENCY

It is said that the raison d'être of heraldry is its ability to celebrate the individual's identity in visual terms, so that the coat of arms can be thought of as the pictorial signature of the bearer. Just how individual the arms are, in fact, depends on the nationality of the user. For instance, in Poland an identical coat of arms may be borne by many different families with no blood relationship because it is used by a whole tribe, or ród. In some countries, personal shields are distinguished only between branches of royal houses. In Scotland families update their heraldry through a process of rematriculating their arms through the court of Lord Lyon. The distinguishing features used for this are known as "cadency" or "difference marks".

▼ *English cadency marks, as set out in the 6th edition of John Guillim's* A Display of Heraldry *(1724).*

SONS AND DAUGHTERS

Much of heraldry can be accused of sexism, as daughters are not considered as important as their brothers. In England, until recently, they were afforded little notice at all unless they were classed as heraldic heiresses. Even then, should there be several daughters and no sons, the daughters had no marks of difference or cadency between them, each bearing an identical lozenge of their father's arms. On the Iberian peninsula the situation seems to be much more sensible, and the female side of a family is considered every bit as important as that of the male. In Portugal anyone is entitled to choose their surname and arms from whichever side of the family they wish, and a system of difference marks denotes from which side of the family the arms are derived and whether they come from parents or grandparents.

The newest national heraldic authority,

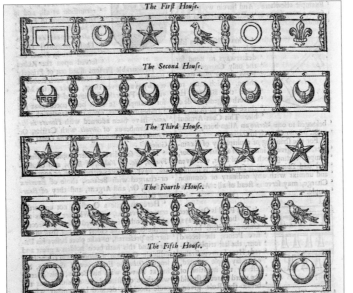

The First House.

The Second House.

The Third House.

The Fourth House.

The Fifth House.

The Sixth House.

CANADIAN CADENCY MARKS

These are the new marks of cadency given by Canada to each daughter of an armigerous family.

First, second and third daughters.

Fourth, fifth and sixth daughters.

Seventh, eighth and ninth daughters.

that of Canada, has also given difference marks to each daughter in the same way that sons have their coats differenced.

MARKS OF CADENCY

While difference marks may be applied to a variety of family and heraldic relationships, cadency tends to be used to indicate sons. It is very much the preserve of English heraldry, in which a set of small marks are placed upon the shield for male children up to the ninth son. The heraldic writer Beryl Platt sees their origin in the symbols adopted by the heirs of Charlemagne. She belives that the Count of Boulogne, whose family used these marks, had set great store by the dialogues of the Emperor Charlemagne with his confessor Alcuin, and would have found references there to heavenly and natural symbols as inspirational devices. In Boulogne the sun stood for the Count, the crescent for his second son, the star for his third son, and the bird for his fourth son. The cadency marks of later children could also have been taken from Charlemagne's dialogues. The most important and fre-

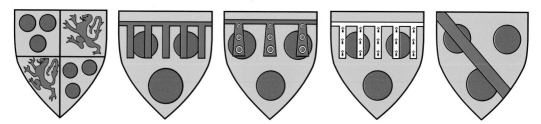

▲ *Medieval difference marks for members of the Courteney family of Devon, England.*

quently used mark is the "label". It is an addition to arms not only in English heraldry, but also in Scotland, France, Spain, Portugal, Belgium and Italy. In England it has long been used as the mark of the eldest son, and a plain white label is given to the heir apparent of the sovereign.

The origin of the label might be found in the sculpted shield of a 13th-century English knight, probably Sir Alexander Giffard, in Boyton, Wiltshire. The shield bears the ancient arms of Giffard – Gules three lions passant Argent. Over the whole shield there is the label, most probably representing a cord stretched over the charges on the shield. From the cord were attached several ribbons, and at this early stage their number seems not to have been of any significance (Sir Alexander's shield shows five ribbons). By the late 15th century, how-

ever, three ribbons or "points" seem to have been fixed as the number for an eldest son. Such is the finesse of the stone carvers' work at Boyton, the contrasting crudeness of the label shows clearly its deliberately temporary nature. It would seem that the eldest son was expected to remove the label when he became head of the house.

Other sons, from the second to the ninth, all have their own cadency marks, but there is no rule about the use of such marks (which are usually placed in the centre chief point). It is possible for sons of sons of sons to place their own cadency mark on a cadency mark, and so on, but this may become an absurdity as the mark becomes so small as to be useless. Furthermore, should any quarterings be added by a family branch (through marriage to a heraldic heiress) this would in itself be considered sufficient difference as to negate any need for a cadency mark.

Adopted children may use the arms of their adoptive parents (after a royal licence has been granted to do so), charged with two interlaced links of a chain. In certain cases, an English family may assume the arms of another through royal licence, usually because of a so-called "name and arms clause" in the will of the last of a line. Often this was done when the father of an heiress wished to see his family arms and name continue, as on the shield of Vere Fane-Bennett Stanford of Preston, England. His wife's arms appear twice, once on an escutcheon and also as the first quarter of the main shield, differenced by a cross crosslet, as there was no descent by blood.

Recently English married women have been allowed to bear (if they should wish to) their own family arms alone on a shield, as opposed to their marital arms. This is made clear by the inclusion of a small blank escutcheon on the main shield, as seen on the arms of Margaret Thatcher.

▼ *The shield of Sir Alexander Giffard of Boyton, showing how the first labels might have been temporarily constructed.*

▼ *A blank escutcheon in the arms of Baroness Thatcher denotes that these are her own arms, rather than her husband's.*

▼ *The arms of Vere Fane-Bennett Stanford, who assumed the arms of his wife's family, differenced by cross crosslet.*

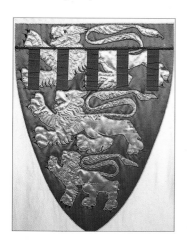

ILLEGITIMACY

We have seen how certain marks have become associated with children born to armigerous parents, albeit those quite obviously married. What, then, is the position of those children born out of wedlock – the illegitimate? The matter is ambiguous at best. Nowadays, in many countries, the illegitimate child is entitled to most, if not all, of the legal rights of a legitimate child, but in previous ages he or she was considered to be without parentage, without name and unable to inherit titles and estates. Although on these terms such children may seem not to have occupied a very enviable position, in truth, in many noble houses, more affection was given to them by their father than his legitimate issue, who, having an automatic right to succession, might be more prepared to rebel against parental control.

THE BATON AND BEND SINISTER

In 1463 the chief herald of the Duke of Burgundy wrote, "a bastard may carry the arms of his father with a baton sinister", thereby making mention of just one of the many heraldic marks used to differ the arms of the illegitimate over the centuries. No hard and fast rule existed in most nations as to what marks the illegitimate should bear, so long as they were sufficiently distinct from the normal cadency

▲ Even the heraldic badge could be used to show illegitimacy. Here the Beaufort portcullis is so differenced for Sir Charles Somerset KG.

▲ The arms of John Beaufort, son of John of Gaunt, before his legitimization, confusingly the bend is in the normal position.

marks of legitimate sons. The bend sinister was a popular mark to denote illegitimacy. By the 17th century this had often shrunk to a baton sinister. (The modern meaning of the word "sinister" has given such a mark an unfortunate reputation, whereas of course, it really refers only to the direction of the bend – top right to bottom left from the bearer's point of view.)

In England the baton sinister became associated with royal bastards, who were often given such a mark charged in some personal way. One illegitimate son of William IV (1830–7), the "Sailor King", had his baton sinister charged with golden anchors, while others might have their batons charged with a royal badge such as the white rose.

THE BORDURE

In 1397 the children born to John of Gaunt and his mistress, Katherine Swynford (whom he married in that year) were declared legitimate by an act unique in English history. Soon afterwards the children, the Beauforts, were permitted to bear the quartered arms of France and England within a bordure compony (a border divided into segments) of John of Gaunt's own livery, white and blue.

Curiously, the bordure compony placed around the arms of the Beauforts after their legitimization came to be used as a mark to denote bastardy, the baton sinister being used more often for royal illegitimates. In Scottish heraldry, the bordure compony is the only recognized mark of illegitimacy. Members of the Stewart family, however, bore arms differenced not only by two bordures compony, but by a bendlet sinister compony as well. Something of a milestone was reached in 1780 when the heralds granted the arms (as a quartering) of the arms of Sacheverell within a bordure wavy to a descendant, John Zachary, the

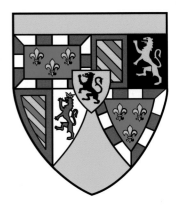

▲ ▼ Two 15th-century examples of arms for two illegitimate sons of the dukes of Burgundy. Their fathers' quarters are shown on voided shields.

▲ *An unusual combination – the bordure added to the Beaufort arms after their legitimization and the bend sinister of illegitimacy on the one shield – for Sir Charles Somerset KG (d1526) natural son of Henry Beaufort, 3rd duke of Somerset.*

bordure wavy in this case being used to denote illegitimate descent. From that time onward the bordure wavy has been mainly used for the English illegitimate offspring, and their descendants.

In Scotland the crest is not differenced but in England it is, and illegitimate descent can be denoted either by pallets wavy, saltires wavy or bendlets sinister.

▲ *The Sacheverell arms granted to John Zachary, 1780, the first time that a bordure wavy was used to denote illegitimacy.*

▼ ▶ *The arms that were granted in 1806 to Maria and William Legh, two of the seven illegitimate children of Colonel Thomas Legh, of Lyme.*

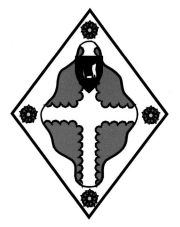

HERALDIC INHERITANCE

In England it is necessary for the father to acknowledge paternity if the illegitimate child wishes to claim heraldic descent. A royal licence can then be issued granting use of the father's arms, duly differenced by certain marks (usually the bordure wavy) denoting illegitimacy. But the process is lengthy and requires the sovereign's authorization. The heralds may therefore suggest that instead of this traditional procedure the illegitimate child petitions for new arms that are based on the arms of the father.

It is generally held that illegitimate children cannot inherit any quarterings that were previously built up by their father's family, yet there is much evidence to show that they often have. A further curiosity in English heraldry is that a female bastard is treated as the heraldic heiress and can transmit her father's arms, with a suitable mark of difference, to her children. As for modern and more enlightened times we may look to the heraldry of the Republic of Ireland, where illegitimacy has no place.

◀ *The arms of Sir Richard de Clarendon, illegitimate son of Edward the Prince of Wales, utilizing the feathers from his father's shield for peace.*

HOW A MEDIEVAL FAMILY USED ITS ARMS

Si monumentum requiris, circumspice ("If you would see his monument, look around"): these words, carved above the north door of St Paul's Cathedral in the City of London, refer to the cathedral's designer, Sir Christopher Wren. Yet the very same words could have been used by many men centuries before Sir Christopher's age, who, through heraldry on castle and in church, sought to ensure their family's and their own immortality.

One medieval family of the West of England, the Hungerfords of Farleigh Castle, afford an example of the none too subtle way in which the nobility of Europe sought to stamp its authority over vast tracts of land and all that lived upon it. In stone, stained glass, parchment and needlepoint, the Hungerfords and many of their kind used heraldry to make a statement: "I am my arms. Hurt them and you hurt me – at your great peril be it."

▼ *On the ruins of Farleigh Hungerford Castle, the family arms above the main gate still proclaim the Hungerfords' lordship.*

ASSERTION OF IDENTITY

The Hungerfords were not remarkable in any way, but were typical of their times: sometimes cultured, sometimes violent, self-made, monied, landed, immensely proud, medieval in thought and deed. The family enjoyed its heyday in the late 14th and early 15th centuries, just at the time when the rival royal houses of York and Lancaster were flexing their muscles. It also happened to be the peak of that English heraldic phenomenon, the badge or cognizance; and the Hungerfords made the fullest possible use of their own device – a sickle or, its variation, three interlaced sickles – in many different ways.

Heraldry played a large part in the noble family's daily life. The Hungerfords stamped their arms on seals, barns, outbuildings and chantries, and set their sickles on seats, ceilings and church towers. Walter, 1st Baron Hungerford, a friend and adviser to the Lancastrian kings, had his arms set, as was his right as a Knight of the Garter, within the Chapel of St George in Windsor Castle itself. At court

▲ *A roof boss in St Thomas' Church in Salisbury denoting the trappings of patronage. It was the Hungerford family's large donations that helped to pay for the church's restoration in the early 1600s.*

he would probably have donned his great collar of "Ss", the livery collar of the dynasty he served so faithfully.

THE ACQUISITION OF ARMS

Although not perhaps remarkable in their class and time, the Hungerfords are intriguing in their use of arms, possibly taking as their own the arms of the Heytesbury family (Per pale indented Gules and Vert a chevron Or), whose

▼ *The quartered arms of Heytesbury and FitzJohn (Hungerford) appear in an elaborate medieval tiled floor from their former property at Heytesbury.*

▲ *The much-used sheaf and sickle crest of the Hungerfords is carved in stone on the roof of St Thomas' Church, Salisbury.*

▼ *The Hungerfords made full use of heraldic seals. The top seal, of Sir Robert Hungerford before 1449, differences not only the arms but the banners, crest and badge of his father, Lord Walter, while the bottom one also includes the supporters.*

heiress had married a Hungerford. They also seem to have done the same with the arms of another family, FitzJohn of Cherhill (Sable two bars Argent in chief three plates), which later became the acknowledged arms of Hungerford.

The Hungerford crest of a "garb" (a wheatsheaf) between two sickles may also have been adopted from that of another family, Peverell; such arms of alliance were not unusual at the time. The Hungerfords had most probably originated as lower gentry and were non-armigerous, becoming so through marriage with the heiresses of more well-to-do families. Even the nature of the garb in the Hungerford arms has an element of mystery about it – is it in fact a sheaf of wheat or pepper, a play on the name Peverell? The Hungerfords delighted in the use of their sickles, often charging their memorials and property with interlacings of sickle, a design well suited to many household ornaments and items of furniture.

In the will of Lord Walter Hungerford, Knight of the Garter (proved at Croydon, 21 August 1447), his son Robert was left

▲ *Along with other families of their time, the Hungerfords took the arms of more influential families for their own. In time the bars and roundels of the FitzJohns became the accepted arms of Hungerford. They also changed their crest from the talbot's head to the garb of the Peverells.*

"2 altar cloths of red crimson velvet, with diverse compresses de sykeles curiously embroidered…my great alms dish of silver having on each side a lion supporting my coat of arms; and a pair of silver dishes bearing knots of sickles". Sir Robert Hungerford was, according to his father's will, to bequeath these items to his heir.

The Hungerfords, proud and privileged as they undoubtedly were, lived in a troubled age. In the records of the time we can read of a rising in 1400 against King Henry IV, during which the rebels took several of the King's "lieges" (lords) prisoner. They compelled Lord Walter, "the King's Knight, to go with them and robbed him of the King's Livery called 'Colere' [the collar of Ss] which he was wearing, worth £20", an enormous sum in those distant days.

▲ *Like his father, Robert, 2nd Baron Hungerford was a staunch supporter of the House of Lancaster, and proudly wore the collar of Ss of that house.*

Times were to get better for Lord Walter, for in December 1418 he was rewarded with the Lordship of Homet in Normandy in return for an annual fee of a lance to which was attached a fox's brush (tail), one of the heraldic badges of Henry IV. However, a large part of the Hungerford revenues which arose from the acquisition of spoils in the French wars were used to bail out Lord Walter's grandson, Sir Robert, who was taken prisoner at the Battle of Castillon in 1453, a battle which brought the Hundred Years' War to a close with defeat for the English. One of the members of the deputation sent over to France to treat with Sir Robert's captors was Chester Herald – fulfilling one of the many duties undertaken by the heralds of the time.

HERALDRY AND ETERNITY

The Hundred Years' War, the Black Death and death in childbirth were among many perils the Hungerfords had to face, just as they reached the peak of their power in the English West Country. Beyond death, there was Purgatory, that period in which souls were lodged in Heaven's waiting room, waiting for their family to purchase a promotion heavenwards through prayer and

good deeds. Here too, heraldry had its part to play. The Hungerfords, in common with many of their peers, endowed "chantries", chapels where the priests were employed solely to sing or chant daily masses for the noble benefactors. The wills of the latter make frequent mention of the trappings of their chantries and the priests that served

them. Presumably it was hoped that, if God in his Kingdom was looking down, he would notice the arms and badges of the noble family concerned and be grateful for the display. That, at any rate, must have been the thinking of Lord Walter, when he gave to the Abbey Church of Bath a cope of red velvet patterned with waves, and two other copes of gold damask velvet, that was "worked with myne armes for better memory".

The theme was taken up in the will of Lord Walter's daughter-in-law, the formidable Margaret Botreaux, Lady Hungerford. In the document she bequeaths to the Priory of Launceston (in Cornwall) a pair of vestments of red and green (the Hungerford livery colours) with the arms of Hungerford and Botreaux on the cross, and a further new pair of vestments to be worked with the arms of Hungerford, Beaumont and Botreaux. At

▼ *The finesse of the medieval craftsman is apparent in this complex seal design of Margaret Botreaux, widow of Robert, 2nd Baron Hungerford.*

▲ *Heraldry could be used in the most mundane ways. Here it embellishes the lock plate of the family vault at Farleigh Hungerford.*

▲ *Ever the self-publicists, the Hungerford family placed its heraldry on all kinds of property. This interlaced sickle badge was uncovered recently above a false ceiling in a farmhouse, some five centuries after its crude manufacture.*

▼ *Keeping the money in the family, a Hungerford marries his cousin. The crescent, centre left, denotes the younger branch on these impaled arms.*

Salisbury Cathedral, the wonderful altar cloths that the Lady Margaret gave included several bearing Lord Hungerford's crest and arms. Even the chantry chapels themselves, as in the case of the Hungerford Chapel in Wellow church, near Bath, might be brightly painted in the family livery colours.

On Salisbury Plain, over the borders of Wiltshire into Somerset and Gloucester and far and wide in the West Country, the Hungerford name spread itself. Whenever they acquired land, and wherever they had their souls prayed for, they stamped their authority through heraldry. Even on their last journey, entombed in their coffins, the Hungerfords could still afford a final nod to their arms, as the lock panel on their own family vault at Farleigh Castle was charged with the Hungerford shield. So famous were they in the West Country that other noble families in the area were keen to show an attachment to them through arms. In the 18th century, long after the Hungerfords had left the Plain, the Pleydell-Bouveries chose to use Lord Walter's chantry chapel in Salisbury Cathedral for their own pew, decorating it with over 50 shields of arms recording the Hungerford marriages and their descent from that family.

▲ *The priest of the Hungerford family, at Wellow church, Somerset, was surrounded by the heraldry of those he was expected to pray for, from the family arms to their red and gold liveries used as ceiling patterns.*

▼ *In common with others in that exalted band, the Knights of the Garter, Walter, 1st Lord Hungerford's arms appear on his stall plate in St George's Chapel, Windsor.*

PATENTS OF ARMS

From the late medieval period, those who were granted arms usually received them by way of a document, written on parchment, vellum or paper. The earliest form of patent was quite simple, a single sheet with the seal authorizing the grant suspended from it by a cord. The arms of the recipient were portrayed in colour, either in the margin or in the centre of the document. A legally worded text, in Latin or the language of the issuing authority, described the arms and to whom the grant was made.

Patents of arms gradually became more elaborate, and their decoration might include the armorial bearings of the sovereign or heraldic authority. In English patents, the leading capital letter might enclose a portrait of the king of arms who had signed and sealed the document. The borders and headings of the patents

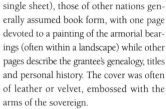

▲ *A detail from the Deissel grant shows the fine workmanship of the trained miniaturists responsible for much of the heraldic art of 17th-century Austria.*

▼ *A grant of arms for Jacob Johann Deissel, an Austrian doctor, who was ennobled in 1663 by Emperor Leopold I. It is a typical example of 17th-century arms produced for the scientific, military and government personnel who served the imperial household. The grant was presented in a unique iron case and a wooden sealbox.*

became heavily embellished with scrolls and strapwork, interspersed with birds, flowers, beasts and allegorical devices. Sometimes the actual coat of arms appears almost as an afterthought.

While English and Scottish grants have kept much to their original format (on a

single sheet), those of other nations generally assumed book form, with one page devoted to a painting of the armorial bearings (often within a landscape) while other pages describe the grantee's genealogy, titles and personal history. The cover was often of leather or velvet, embossed with the arms of the sovereign.

Today, those national heraldic authorities that still exist keep in the main to the traditions set down centuries ago in their particular country. When drawing up patents of arms, therefore, the book form of the patent still exists in Spain while the single sheet form is still framed in England, Scotland, Canada, and the Netherlands. Ireland has more recently taken up the book form of the patent.

The selection of patents and grants shown on these pages date from the 17th to the late 19th century, and are from a collection in the possession of the celebrated Dutch heraldic artist and engraver, Daniel de Bruin. The collection offers a remarkable glimpse into the artistic traditions of several major European heraldic authorities. It also offers an insight into how heraldry continued to reflect the political affiliations of the individual states, the rewards given by rulers to their loyal subjects and servants, and the continuity of a heraldic tradition. The grants also show the charm and expertise of the artist's work in attempting to make a standard document personal.

Sadly, the wonderful tradition of the illuminated patents came to an end with the fall of the monarchies after World War I, but by that time most such documents had evolved to a standard printed form where only the armorial bearings were

▶ *An Austrian patent of nobility of 1819, presented to Karl von Rodiezky Freiherr von Weizelbrag, a military officer who fought against Napoleon. The imperial arms are flanked by those of the provinces in which Rodiezky served. The style of the grant, with its spirit of conservatism, is typical of those produced in early 19th-century Austria.*

▲ A grant of 1795 to the Georgievies brothers by Emperor Francis I, King of Hungary. The arms of the provinces decorate the canopy.

▶ A grant of 1767 by Empress Maria Theresa of Austria to a Dutch banker, C. A. Verlugge. The imperial arms are flanked by the arms of Hungary and Bohemia.

where only the armorial bearings were painted and the letters handmade. Yet, in recent years the College of Arms in London has returned to the more ancient form of having elaborate illuminated

▼ The cover of a grant of arms by Emperor Franz Josef of Austria, c1867, employs the imperial eagle. The wax seal is protected by a metal seal cover.

borders included in the patent or grant. This form of illustration has led to a flowering of artistic talent and style, which echoes that of the late medieval period through to the 18th century. Provided the client can afford the required fee, a patent's border may bear a collection of flowers and foliage, individual badges and charges taken from the arms of the grantee, fanciful creatures, or birds and animals found in the grantee's home or locality.

This wide choice of pictorial elements in the grant happily continues the tradition illustrated by the 1663 grant to the Austrian doctor Jacob Deissel, in which the local flora of his land is depicted and his profession symbolized; while in the grant of 1795 to the Hungarian Georgievies brothers, the left hand corner shows a local scene that probably includes a picture of the brothers' family mansion.

▶ A 1745 patent of Maximilian III, Elector of Bavaria, to Philipp Paret. The pages of the book patent record the brave conduct of the ennobled Paret during his time as an officer in the imperial Wallonian Dragoon Regiment.

TANDEM BONA CAUSA TRIUMPHAT.

TIBI FIDELIS

ROYAL HERALDRY AND NOBILITY

The heraldic achievement presents a picture of the family history and alliances that have placed a monarch on the throne or a duke and duchess in their castle. Royal and noble families have always been keen to display this effective indicator of their lineage and title, and occasions of state ceremonial provide welcome opportunities for the full splendours of heraldry to be seen and enjoyed. Much of the pomp of such occasions derives from the strict observance of distinctions of rank; as heraldry has developed its refinements have included numerous details that define positions in a social hierarchy, whether of royalty, nobility, military order or the church.

◄ *The arms of a British peer, Lord Howe, with the supporters, coronet of degree and helm allowed by his rank — that of baron.*

ROYAL HERALDRY

For centuries royalty has been seen as the fount of all noble titles and grants of arms, so it is not surprising to find that monarchs availed themselves of heraldry. Yet crowns, sceptres, orbs and other royal trappings were latecomers to the world of heraldic accoutrements. Until the late 15th century, there was seldom anything to differentiate the heraldic achievement of a king from that of a knight. However, on seals of the late 13th and early 14th centuries, crowns were sometimes depicted over the shields of royal individuals.

CROWNS

Heraldic crowns were imitations of actual headgear worn by monarchs. By the late 16th century royal crowns were often depicted with crimson or purple caps within them, and were embellished with raised "arches", decorated with gems and pearls, rising from the circlet and crossing over the head. In some royal families the number of arches was reduced for lesser members. While the English sovereign's crown has two intersecting arches, for

example, the coronet of the Prince of Wales has only one. Other members of the royal family have coronets without any arches.

▼ *The coronation of the English King Henry IV in Westminster Abbey, 1399. The royal arms are held by officials before the dais.*

▲ *The arms of Anne, Princess Royal of Great Britain. The supporters and lozenge are both charged with a personal label (labels are used by both male and female members of the British royal family). The coronet is that of a son or daughter of the sovereign other than the heir apparent.*

▲ ▼ *Subtle differences of rank can be shown by coronets surmounting the royal arms. Above is the coronet for a Swedish royal prince, below, that of the heir to the throne.*

▲ *The arms for the Counts of Rosenborg, the title given to Danish royal princes who married morganatically – marrying outside royal rank.*

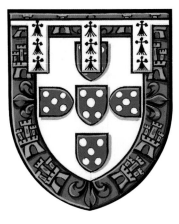

▲ *The Portuguese Duke of Coimbra (d1449) bears a label taken from the arms of his maternal family, the Dukes of Lancaster.*

▲ *The white label of the royal line of Orléans on the arms of France was further differenced by crescents for the Counts of Angoulême, a junior branch.*

The crown of the dauphins of France, after 1662, had arches formed of dolphins, taken from the charges in their arms.

Elsewhere there was less differentiation between family members. In Austria, for example, the emperor bore a curiously shaped crown with high arches enclosing jewelled "horns", but the crown prince and all the other archdukes bore identical crowns of more conventional appearance.

Today, some republics still retain the trappings associated with former royal powers. In Hungary, the 1,000-year-old

▼ *The personal arms of King Matthew Corvinus of Hungary (1458–90) are placed over quarters for Hungary ancient, Hungary modern, Dalmatia and Bohemia, and surmounted by St Stephen's crown.*

▲ *The label of Prince William of Great Britain. The escallop is taken from the arms of the Spencers, his mother's family.*

crown of St Stephen, considered one of the finest examples of the medieval goldsmith's craft, is such a symbol. The crown's history is remarkable: having many times been hidden, stolen, lost and found, after World War II it was spirited out of Hungary to America, where it was kept safe from the Hungarian communist authorities. It was returned in 1978 and is now in the National Museum in Budapest.

The absence of a crown can be just as telling. The Swiss, proud of their freedom from any royal authority, often placed the peasant's hat of William Tell over a shield bearing the arms of the various cantons.

Although the crown is the most obvious sign of royal rank, the arms of the sovereign are often accompanied by a pavilion or robe of estate strewn with crowns or charges taken from the royal arms, and the shield is surrounded by the orders of chivalry specific to the monarchy. The pavilion is a domed tent surmounted

by the crown, with its sides drawn back to display the royal arms placed within it. Though it is common to the arms of most sovereigns, it has never found favour in British royal arms.

ROYAL DIFFERENCE MARKS

In Britain particularly, marks were added to the shields of sons and other relatives to distinguish them from the head of the family. The descendants of British kings also bore such marks, which were known as "brizures", which mainly consisted of labels, bordures and bends. For centuries the heir apparent to the sovereign has borne a three-pointed label. The earliest example seems to have been Azure, and the number of points could vary, but during the lifetime of Edward the Black Prince (1330–76), it became normalized as three points Argent. The Black Prince was created Prince of Wales in 1343, and the same label is still borne to this day by the heir apparent to the sovereign.

Other children of a British sovereign use labels bearing small charges that are mainly taken from royal badges, such as roses or crosses of St George. For some centuries the grandchildren of the sovereign have borne five-pointed labels, but the most recent label to be assigned to a royal grandson – that of Prince William, eldest son of

▲ *The foundation document for Henry VII's Chapel in Westminster Abbey, London. The royal arms are supported by the red dragon of Cadwallader, a badge of the Tudors.*

▼ *The arms of the Emperors of Austria and their major dominions – the arms of the Kingdom of Hungary bear the crown of King Stephen, with its bent cross.*

the Prince of Wales – has only three points. The central point is charged with an escallop taken from the arms of his mother's family, the Spencers, whose arms include three escallops Argent.

The French royal family was divided into numerous branches, each of which differenced the royal arms with their own particular brizures. These included the white label used by the House of Orleans and the red bend of the Bourbons. When the lesser branches of these lines in time put out their own branches, each differed the brizure of their branch with smaller charges. The Counts of Angoulême, for example, charged the white label of the House of Orleans with red crescents.

In Russia, members of the Romanov dynasty tended to difference their arms by means of supporters to show their proximity to the throne.

▶ *The arms of the monarchs of Europe in the late 18th century. This plate, taken from a French work on heraldry, places the Catholic kingdoms first, and the Protestant states lower down the page.*

ROYAL QUARTERINGS

As with most ancient families, the arms of the ruling dynasties of Europe often started with the simplest designs. The Hohenzollerns started with a shield quartered in white and black; their neighbours the Habsburgs had a red lion rampant on a gold field. At the height of their powers, when the Hohenzollerns were Emperors of Germany and the Habsburgs were Holy Roman Emperors, both were able to sport shields of many quarterings: each quarter represented a lordship, county, principality or kingdom over whose fortunes the emperor held sway. Yet at the heart of each grand design could still be found the red lion of the Habsburgs and the simple quarters of the Hohenzollerns.

Some monarchs, such as those of France, made relatively little use of quarterings in their arms. The fleurs de lis of France are thought by some to be symbols of the Virgin Mary, by others to be three toads. The creatures of the English kings, which have at times been thought of as

DANGEROUS DIFFERENCES

It seems incredible that the display of arms alone would be enough to topple men of power and influence. Yet during the reign of Henry VIII this was the fate of Henry Howard, Earl of Surrey and his near relation Edward Stafford, Duke of Buckingham. Henry had a paranoid suspicion of anyone with a claim to his throne, and while both men had the right to bear differenced versions of the royal arms, they were rash in their ostentatious use of royal heraldry. It was even suggested that the Earl of Surrey had removed the difference marks from his arms, asserting his claim to be more royal than the King. Whether guilty or not, the two aristocrats were executed.

either lions or leopards, were of equally ancient and mysterious origin. The English monarchs quartered the French royal arms with their own to back up their claim to the throne of France, even placing the French arms in the most prominent quarters (1 and 4), and the fleurs de lis remained in the British royal arms as late as the 19th century. British monarchs kept their arms simple by displaying only quarters representing their kingdoms: England, Scotland, Ireland and France. But when the British throne passed to the House of

Guelph (Hanover) in 1714 the royal shields became more complex, including quarters for Brunswick, Lüneberg and Hanover. Over the last three was a small escutcheon charged with the crown of Charlemagne, indicating the office of Archtreasurer of the Holy Roman Empire, held by the British monarch as Duke of Brunswick and Lüneberg.

Members of the Swedish royal family include as quarterings the arms of the province from which they take their ducal title, for example Varmland or Uppland.

THE BRITISH NOBILITY

Evolved over a millennium, the British nobility has developed a multitude of mannerisms, styles of address, dress, insignia and duties so complex and contrived that few outside its ranks understand them. While noble families no longer wield the power and wealth they once commanded, even a Labour government continues to see a need for lords and ladies of sorts: although it removed most of the hereditary holders of peerages from the House of Lords in 1998, it offered some ordinary citizens the chance to become "people's peers", and deck themselves out in scarlet and ermine.

Naturally, members of the nobility do not go around from day to day wearing their robes and coronets. In fact most of them will now have little chance of wearing their robes officially ever again, unless it is for the coronation of a sovereign. However, at least one of their number was, until quite recently, given to having his daughter dress up in his coronation robes and thrill impressionable visitors by processing down corridors when his ancestral home was open to the public.

PEERS AND PEERESSES

The word "peer" is derived from the Latin *pares*, meaning "equal" and it refers to the collective nature of the upper aristocracy. This is because despite their different ranks – from duke to baron – all holders of peerage titles were until recently entitled to a seat and vote in the House of Lords, one of the two chambers of the British Parliament. Only a few of these hereditary peers are still chosen to sit and vote in the upper House. Since the passing of the House of Lords Act, 1998, the majority of those entitled to such a seat and vote are holders of a life peerage, and their titles become extinct upon their death.

RANKS AND TITLES

The British peerage is divided into five ranks. In order of seniority, these are duke, marquess (or marquis), earl, viscount, and baron. Life peers rank as barons, and are entitled to wear the robes and coronet of that rank. Many people assume that a British lord has to live on, or own, the estate from which he derives his title: that the Duke of Somerset must own that county, or that the Earl of Plymouth lives in that city. This is certainly not the case, though in the medieval period such men may well have derived their titles from the land they governed on behalf of the king.

Of the five ranks, the highest, duke, derives its name from the Latin *dux*, or war leader. Dukedoms have always been bestowed sparingly and there have been

◀ Until the 18th century, the funerals of the nobility were occasions for a prominent display of heraldry. The funeral trappings included the hatchment, a diamond-shaped board bearing the arms of the deceased. This impressive hatchment is that of John, 1st Duke of Atholl, d1722.

to a nobleman of high repute. In the Holy Roman Empire, a count of the marches, or *Markgraf*, was responsible for guarding the easternmost borders.

The middle rank, that of earl, is the oldest of the five. It derives from the *earldorma*, the Anglo-Saxon official appointed to administer a shire on behalf of the monarch. The equivalent rank in the French nobility was the *comte* (or count), and in Germany, *Graf*. The administrative duties of the earl or count meant that he was a busy man and would often have needed a deputy or "vice-count" to assist him. From this subordinate office the rank of viscount arose.

The lowest rank of the peerage, that of baron, was introduced by William I from France into England. By the 13th century the barons were "summoned by writ" to take their place in the King's Council, or Parliament. The Scottish equivalent of this rank is a "lord of Parliament", or simply a "lord". In Scotland the title of "baron" is feudal by nature, and occasionally it may be purchased; it does not now give the bearer a seat in the House of Lords but does have certain heraldic insignia.

periods since 1448, when the first non-royal dukedom was conferred, during which no holder of the rank was living. In Britain, where the rank of prince is not used outside the royal family, all male children of the sovereign are styled prince, and their daughters, princesses. It has also long been the case that the younger sons of the sovereign are each given a dukedom, those of York, Kent and Gloucester being reserved for the royal family.

David Lloyd George, British Prime Minister from 1916–22, complained that a fully equipped duke was as costly to maintain as two dreadnoughts, and less easy to scrap. Those who upheld the peerage system countered by saying that a British duke "in full sail" was twice as effective as any battleship and much more difficult to sink.

The rank below duke is marquess. It derives its name from a guardian of the marches, or borders – a sensitive and strategic office entrusted by the sovereign

▲ *The Parliament of Edward I (1272–1307) in session: the parliamentary robes worn by the lords sitting opposite the bishops are very similar to those of today's peers.*

▼ *At his 1991 introduction to the House of Lords, Lord Runcie (centre) is flanked by Garter King of Arms and Black Rod (left), and two peers of the same rank (right).*

FORMS OF NOBLE ADDRESS AND COURTESY TITLES

The wife of a duke is a duchess. The wife of a marquess is a marchioness; that of an earl, a countess; that of a viscount, a viscountess; and that of a baron, a baroness. All holders of a peerage, up to and including marquesses, are addressed in speech as "My Lord" or "Your Ladyship", and their wives as "My Lady". A duke and duchess are both addressed as "Your Grace".

In the British peerage, only the head of a family bears the title (as opposed to the practice of some other nations, where many members share the rank). However, the eldest son of a duke, marquess or earl may, during his father's lifetime, use one of his father's lesser titles (often accrued before the senior title). Such a title is known as a "courtesy title" because of its acknowledgement by the royal court, though it has no legal standing. Should the "courtesy lord" have children of his own, his eldest son may use another of his grandfather's lesser titles. For example, the Duke of Leinster's eldest son is known as the Marquess of Kildare, and in turn his eldest son is styled the Earl of Offaly; the

▼ *The Earl and Countess Mountbatten of Burma in their coronation robes, at the coronation of Elizabeth II in 1953.*

eldest son of the Marquess of Zetland is styled the Earl of Ronaldshay, and his eldest son is Lord Dundas.

A younger son of a duke or marquess is given the style of Lord, followed by his name: for example, "Lord Charles Brown". A daughter is styled "Lady Jane Brown". The younger son of an earl, or any son of a viscount or a baron, is styled "the Honourable Charles Brown". A daughter is "the Honourable Jane Brown", or "the Honourable Mrs Brown" if married. In conversation or informal correspondence, "Hons" are addressed as Mr, Miss or Mrs.

The eldest son of a peer is permitted to use his father's supporters – differenced by a label and with the consent of Garter King of Arms – only if he is summoned to Parliament in the lifetime of his father. However, there are many examples to be found of eldest sons bearing their father's supporters and even coronets of rank, despite never having received such a summons. All this is very confusing, not only to foreigners trying to understand the most complex honours system in the world, but also to the British themselves. Such arcane intricacies were dismissed by Oscar Wilde in a letter to Robert Ross:

> …I have written to him [Lord Alfred Douglas] to tell him that… for him to try and pose as your social superior because he is the third son of a Scotch marquis and you the third son of a commoner, is offensively stupid. There is no difference between gentlemen. Questions of title are matters of heraldry – no more.

Peerages normally pass through the male line by direct descent, or sideways through brothers and their issue. Certain titles (usually ancient baronies or earldoms) can pass through the female line, and should the holder of such a title be a woman she is said to be a peeress "in her own right".

RIGHTS AND PRIVILEGES

The privileges of a British peer have been eroded by time, especially since 1998, when most of the "hereditaries" lost their right to sit in the House of Lords. They

▲*The Earl Marshal of England, His Grace the Duke of Norfolk in 1998. He wears his parliamentary robes and holds his gold baton of office.*

used, for example, to be entitled to trial by their peers, presided over by the Lord High Steward. The last case of this kind was that of Lord Clifford, who was accused of manslaughter in 1935. Peers are still able to claim the right of direct access to the sovereign, but the present Queen has probably not been much bothered by any lords or ladies seeking her advice.

Before the 1998 House of Lords Act, there were over 850 hereditary peers who were entitled to a seat and a vote in the House of Lords. Although those times have gone, for many the House of Lords is still the most exclusive of all London's clubs. In past centuries that sense of belonging was sometimes marked in pompous ways by the peers themselves. In the 16th century for example, Elizabeth I's Lord Chancellor, Sir Christopher Hatton, erected replicas of the arms of every one of his fellow peers at his home at Holdenby, Northamptonshire, while Lord Burghley decorated his mansion with a map showing the arms of every major landowner in the country.

ROBES AND CORONETS

There are two types of peers' robes: those worn for Parliament and those worn at a coronation. Parliamentary robes, known since the late medieval period, are worn when the peer is introduced into the House of Lords and during the state opening of Parliament. They are made of fine scarlet cloth trimmed with white fur. Each peer's rank can be deduced by the number of rows, or "guards", of fur borne on the front. The robe of a duke is "powdered", or decorated, with four guards of ermine, spaced equally, with gold lace above each row. The robe of a marquess has four rows on the right and three on the left, each with gold lace. An earl's robe has three rows of ermine and gold lace. The robes of a viscount and a baron are identical, each having two guards of plain white fur and gold lace.

Peers' robes are made by Messrs Ede and Ravenscroft, the court tailors, in London. Few people today – even peers of the realm – can afford real ermine, and rabbit fur or "coney" tends to be used instead, dyed to imitate the black spots of ermine. If the peer should take pity on the rabbit or ermine, he or she may prefer to have synthetic fur. A baron's parliamentary robe at the time of writing would cost the new peer £2,000 (US$3,000), although one enterprising peeress ran hers up on her own sewing machine, using fabric purchased in the local market. For gold lace she used gold foil patterned with the

▼ *The arms of Lord Mowbray, Segrave and Stourton. As a baron, his coronet of rank bears six balls on the rim, of which four are visible. It appears surmounting his arms without helm or crest.*

▲ *Peers' robes charge the arms of the London firm of Ede and Ravenscroft Ltd, which has made robes for the British peerage for centuries.*

points of a comb. Coronation robes are much more costly and are, of course, seldom seen, unless they happen to be placed on public display in the peer's country house. The official description states that these robes or mantles:

> …are created out of crimson velvet, edged with miniver [white fur], the cape furred with miniver pure, and powdered with bars or guards of ermine according to their degree:
> Barons: 2 guards
> Viscounts: 2 guards and a half
> Earls: 3 guards
> Marquesses: 3 guards and a half
> Dukes: 4 guards
> The said mantles or robes to be worn over full Court dress, or regimentals.

If a duke were to ask the court tailors to make him a set of coronation robes today, he would probably have to pay more than £10,000 (US$15,000).

The wives of peers, and peeresses in their own right, wear coronation robes or mantles powdered with guards in number according to their (or their husband's) degree. The robe or mantle also has a train, which varies in length from one yard for a baroness, to two yards for a duchess.

While in other nations coronets of rank are simply heraldic ornaments, the unique distinction of the British peerage is that they do get to wear actual coronets according to their degree, albeit only on one rare occasion – at the exact moment the monarch is crowned. Coronets of rank are officially described as follows:

> The coronets to be silver gilt; the caps of crimson velvet turned up with ermine, with a gold tassel on the top; and no jewels or precious stones are to

be set or used in the coronets, or coun-
terfeit pearls instead of silver balls.

• The coronet of a Baron to have, on
the circle or rim, 6 silver balls at equal
distance.

• The coronet of a Viscount to have,
on the circle, 16 silver balls.

• The coronet of an Earl to have, on
the circle, 8 silver balls raised upon
points, with gold strawberry leaves
between the points.

• The coronet of a Marquess to have,
on the circle, 4 gold strawberry leaves
and 4 silver balls alternately, with latter
a little raised on points above the rim.

• The coronet of a Duke to have, on
the circle, 8 gold strawberry leaves.

The coronets worn by the peers' wives are
smaller variants of those of their husbands.

Although no precious stones or pearls
are now permitted to adorn peers' coronets, those borne by medieval earls would
almost certainly have been heavily jewelled. Most aspects of coronet design were
set in the 17th century; before that time,
barons did not wear coronets at all but
were permitted to wear only a cap of scarlet and ermine.

▼ *The arms of Francis Russell, 2nd Earl
of Bedford c1580. Little except the helmet
of degree has changed since then in the
composition of a peer's arms.*

▲ *The full splendour of the arms of a
modern British peer, Baron (Lord) Howe,
with supporters, coronet of degree and helm.*

THE HERALDRY OF PEERS

Peers of the realm enjoy the right of supporters and a depiction of the coronet of
their degree. The latter is placed directly
above the shield and not upon the helmet,
which is placed above it with the crest. The
helmet of a peer is silver, garnished with
gold, and set in profile showing five bars.
However, it is not necessary for the helmet
itself actually to appear in the achievement,
which is often simplified to include only
the coronet – with or without its cap – and
the crest. The peer may also place a robe
of estate in the armorial achievement, but
this is seldom done. A Scottish peer bears
crimson mantling lined with ermine.

Should a married woman be a peeress
in her own right, the situation becomes
more complicated. The complete marital
achievement uses two sets of arms, with
the husband's on the dexter side and the
wife's on the sinister side. Traditionally,

peeresses in their own right have been, by
their nature, heraldic heiresses. The peeress's husband therefore martials his arms
in the normal fashion, with an escutcheon

▼ *The marital achievement of a peeress in
her own right, married to a commoner, her
arms appear on the right, her husband's
shield with her escutcheon on the left.*

of pretence of his father-in-law's arms in the centre of his shield. The escutcheon is "ensigned", or surmounted, with the correct coronet of rank for his wife. Should the husband himself be a peer, he uses the complete achievement of his degree, with supporters, coronet and so on. If he is a gentleman he simply uses the arms of that degree. In both cases, to the sinister of the husband's achievement is that of the peeress on a lozenge borne by supporters and ensigned with her coronet. If the peeress is Scottish, she can also bear in her achievement the crest of her family.

In recent years many women have been made life peers. They are thus peeresses in their own right but – provided they have brothers to carry on their family arms – not heraldic heiresses. If such a peeress is married, her husband impales his and his wife's arms on the shield, with his wife's complete achievement alongside.

When the husband of a peeress in her own right dies, she shows her situation by bearing two lozenges, the one to the dexter with the marital coat, the sinister remaining as before. The widow of a peer who is not a peeress in her own right uses the dexter achievement only – the marital arms martialled on a lozenge – but this is still "protected" by the supporters and coronet of her husband's peerage. The wife of a lord, knight or baronet enjoys her husband's title, being "Lady So and So", yet if plain Mr Jones marries a peeress in her own right, he remains plain Mr Jones.

THE BARONETAGE

There is one other rank in the British nobility that is hereditary yet does not entitle the bearer to a seat or vote in the House of Lords. This rank, which manages to confuse many, is that of baronet. In effect, the holder of a baronetcy is treated as a hereditary knight. He is therefore known as, say, Sir John Smith, and can place "Bt" after his name. Coming somewhere in precedence between knights and peers, the baronetage was considered by some to be particularly associated with "new money". It is said that Queen Victoria found it a useful way of ennobling members of the working class. At one point in the 19th

century, so many wealthy brewers were members of the baronetage that it was nicknamed "the beerage".

The baronetage had its origins with James I (1603–25), who created the degree of baronet as a way of raising funds. The title was granted on payment of a fee of £1,095 – the sum required to maintain 30 infantrymen in Ulster for three years – and the first 100 letters patent were ready in 1611. A similar idea was promulgated for Scotsmen prepared to finance the settlement of Nova Scotia. The Baronets of Nova Scotia bear the arms of a British knight (with helm affronty with visor open), augmented with the arms of Nova Scotia. This can be borne on a canton or inescutcheon, or as a badge suspended below the shield by a tawny ribbon. Baronets of Ulster – and more lately of the United Kingdom – bear in similar fashion the red hand of Ulster on a white field.

TITLES FOR SALE

The selling of baronetcies raises the question of whether it is possible to buy other titles. At certain periods the sale of knighthoods and peerages was all but blatant. It seems that anyone who could afford it could advance themselves to the ranks of knights and lords if they wished. Certain courtiers, often favourites of the sovereign, saw it almost as their duty to obtain – at a price – titles for their friends or family. Sir Robert Peel was driven to write: "The voracity of these things quite surprises me. I wonder people do not begin to feel the distinction of an unadorned name."

By Victoria's reign the business had been somewhat tightened up, but there was one more scandal over the sale of titles in the 1920s, when the Liberal Party, then in power under Lloyd George as Prime Minister, saw the sale of titles as a possible means of augmenting party funds. It was claimed that costs would vary from £10,000 for a knighthood to £100,000 for a peerage, and the go-between chosen to sound out likely clients was the "peerage broker" J. Maundy Gregory. The furore created by this shady dealing in titles for political ends ultimately assisted in Lloyd George's fall from office and the passing of

the Prevention of Abuses Act (1925). This made it an offence to accept "any gift, money or valuable consideration as an inducement or reward for procuring…the grant of a dignity or title of honour".

There are few chances of seeing peers in their finery, except from the House of Lords visitors gallery when a new peer is introduced. On such an occasion, the new peer is dressed in parliamentary robes and accompanied by two fellow peers of the same rank. Garter King of Arms leads them into the chamber in full ceremonial uniform, complete with tights, tabard and chain. The centuries-old ceremony involves much bowing and doffing of hats.

▼ *The shield of a baronet of the United Kingdom is charged with an escutcheon bearing the red hand of Ulster, and the helm is that of a knight (with its visor open).*

THE ORDER OF THE GARTER

The rise in chivalry brought with it messages of loyalty, heroism, glory and brotherly love. It was seized upon by the princes of Europe, who saw it as the ideal stratagem with which to bond men of rank and military expertise, creating elite brotherhoods – the chivalric orders – that would serve them in both war and peace. One of these was the English Order of the Garter. Medieval and romantic writers, inspired by the ethos of chivalry, drew on the stories of King Arthur and the Round Table, the English connections of which served Edward III's political ambitions when he instituted the Order of the Garter. The year has been disputed but is believed to be 1348, although it has also been suggested that the Order was founded some four years earlier, when the King set up a round table for knights who had taken part in a great tournament at Windsor.

INSIGNIA OF THE ORDER

The original members of the Order were the King and the Prince of Wales (Edward the Black Prince), together with 24 companions, who each took a blue garter as their device. It has been suggested that the

garter was intended to represent a sword belt, but the more romantic story concerns an incident at a ball held in Calais, when a garter fell from the leg of Joan, Countess of Salisbury. Seeing the smirks of the courtiers and the Countess's discomfort, King Edward picked up her garter and uttered the words, "Honi soi, qui mal y pense" ("Evil be on him who thinks it").

It may be no coincidence that the colours of the Garter – blue and gold – were also those of the French arms, when at the time of its foundation Edward III was making a claim to the French throne. Although the earliest depictions of the Garter robes show them to have been murrey (maroon) strewn with garters, by the 15th century they were blue and bore a single garter on the left shoulder. Members of the order have also always worn an actual garter on the left leg below the knee.

Gradually the insignia were increased. Henry VII (1485–1509) introduced the splendid collar, consisting of gold knots alternating with red roses encircled by garters. From this is suspended the George, a mounted figure of St George slaying a green dragon. The star of the Order was

▼ *A splendid design of 1589 showing the arms of the knights of the Garter from 1486–1589, enclosed on the Tudor Rose.*

▼ *The Garter has been used to encircle not only the arms of the knights but also the prelates and chancellors of the Order.*

instituted by King Charles I in 1629. It bears the red cross of St George, encircled by the garter and surrounded by silver radiating beams.

THE INSIGNIA IN HERALDRY

Since the Tudor period it has been the norm for a Garter knight to place his arms within the garter. It is also permissible to place the arms within the collar of the Order, although this is seldom done today, possibly because the collar is such a complex item to paint accurately. Other British orders of chivalry follow this pattern, and

▲ *Roger Mortimer, Earl of March (d1398) in robes of the Garter. The portrait is taken from a 15th-century document.*

their members place their arms within a circlet bearing the motto. Knights Grand Cross may place their arms within the collar of their order. Knights (and baronets) show their degree by placing above their shield a steel helmet with a plain visor, fully open.

When a knight of a chivalric order displays a marital achievement of arms, two shields (or ovals) are depicted side by side. That on the dexter has the knight's arms alone within the circlet or collar of his order, that to the sinister has the full marital achievement of husband and wife (impaled or with escutcheon of pretence) within a wreath. The helmet of degree sits

at the junction between the two shields. The two coats show that the knighthood was conferred on the man and not his wife, but she through courtesy enjoys her husband's title and is addressed as "Lady" (followed by her husband's surname).

In Britain, when a woman is awarded with the equivalent of a knighthood, she is called a dame (Dame Grand Cross or Dame Commander), and may place her lozenge within the circlet of the order.

DISPLAYS OF ARMS

During his lifetime, the banner and crested helmet of each Garter knight is hung above his stall in St George's Chapel in Windsor Castle. At the back of each stall is an enamelled metal plaque bearing the knight's arms, and while the banner and crest are taken down on his death, his stall plate

remains, so that the earliest of these date from the late medieval period.

The shields of the Garter knights hang in St George's Hall, also in Windsor castle, and many were destroyed during a fire in 1992. The replacement shields met with disapproval among heraldists, as the work was given to a sign painter (who afterwards said that he never wanted to see another shield in his life). The shields of those appointed since 1999 have been created by a full-time heraldic artist.

The other British orders of chivalry also have chapels attached to them. The Chapel of King Henry VII in Westminster Abbey, London, is home to the Order of the Bath, and contains the stall plates of such famous members as Lord Nelson, the Duke of Wellington and Lord Kitchener of Khartoum. The Order of St Michael and St George has a chapel in St Paul's Cathedral. St Paul's also houses the Chapel of the Order of the British Empire in its crypt, although there are no stall plates there and the banners all relate to the Royal Family. The Royal Victorian Order has its home in the Queen's Chapel of the Savoy. Its stall plates include that of Sir John Miller, showing Sir John himself – not once but twice – as supporters to his own shield.

▼ *The late Major General Sir Hugh Sykes, Knight Grand Cross of the Most Exalted Order of the Star of India, encircled his arms with the collar of that Order.*

THE ORDER OF THE GOLDEN FLEECE

The earliest orders of chivalry in Europe were religious, formed with the intent of creating bands of military men to fight in the Holy Land. As the structure of society in western Europe changed during the 14th century, with the dominance of the Church giving way to royal power, a number of temporal orders of chivalry were founded to strengthen and glorify the position of kings. Perhaps the most glorious of these royal knighthoods belonged to the Duchy of Burgundy, whose dukes were as powerful and wealthy as any king of Christendom.

Seeing the prestige of Edward III's Order of the Garter, Philip the Good, Duke of Burgundy (1419–67) decided to create a similar institution to bond together the highest nobles of his own realm. He gave each male member of his house, and his most trusted counsellors and friends, a bejewelled golden chain, the forerunner of the collar of the Golden Fleece. The Order of the Golden Fleece (La Toison d'Or) was founded in 1430 in celebration of Philip's marriage to Isabella of Portugal. As with the Garter knights, Duke Philip exacted a vow from the Knights of the Golden Fleece to defend the Church and his ducal house from all malignant foes.

CHAPTER MEETINGS

In common with other orders of chivalry, the knights were to meet in a chapter, which was to be held every few years in one of the great cities of Burgundy. The first chapter was held in 1431 at Lille (now in northern France) and 25 knights were installed on that occasion. As with the

▲ *The 15th-century Burgundian court was "the richest in Christendom". Here, Charles the Bold, Duke of Burgundy (1466–77) presides over his council. The border around the scene bears the arms of all his territories.*

Garter, stalls in the chapel of the Order were decorated with the armorial achievements of the knights. However, in the case of the Golden Fleece, where chapter meetings were held in various Burgundian cities, sets of arms dating from separate meetings can be found in churches across northern France and Belgium. The chapter meetings often coincided with other lavish spectacles laid on by the Dukes of Burgundy. These events were the envy of the princes of Europe, few of whom were able to equal Burgundian opulence.

At a meeting of the chapter the Duke of Burgundy sat as Grand Master. On either side of him, the knights would take their places, each wearing the collar of the

◀ *The arms of the Dukes of Burgundy on the tomb of Charles the Bold in Bruges. The quarters are 1st and 4th Burgundy modern, 2nd Burgundy ancient with Brabant, 3rd Burgundy ancient with Limburg. The escutcheon bears the arms of Flanders.*

Order. The chapter meetings were administered by officers, each with a specific duty. The Chancellor of the Order, normally a high-ranking prelate, was responsible for the great seal. He organized the meetings and reported to the Grand Master on any wrongdoings of the knights. He also spoke the funeral oration after the death of a knight. The Treasurer looked after the statute books and the collars of the Order, each of which was numbered and returned on the death of a knight. The Secretary wrote down the minutes and recorded the martial deeds of the knights.

As with most orders of chivalry, the Golden Fleece had its own herald called, appropriately, Toison d'Or King of Arms. This officer wore a badge of office, a

▲ *The stall plate of Philip II of Spain, Sovereign of the Order of the Golden Fleece, placed in St Baaf's Cathedral, Ghent for the 23rd chapter meeting of the Order in 1559.*

version of the collar of the Order known as the "potence", decorated with the arms of all the knights at a particular chapter meeting. The herald was responsible for much of the ceremonial associated with the Order and for making sure that the knights' heraldry was correctly marshalled.

INSIGNIA OF THE ORDER

The shield of arms of each knight of the Golden Fleece is enclosed within the collar of the Order, each link of which depicts the device or badge of the Dukes of Burgundy – a steel within a flint emitting showers of sparks. Suspended from the central flint in the collar is a representation of the golden fleece, and a line from Philip's speech: "I will disperse my enemies and strike before they are ready." One of the theories mooted for the choice of the golden fleece as the Order's device is an allusion to the wool trade, source of Burgundy's great wealth; another is that it referred to the Argonauts, whose quest for the golden fleece embodied the qualities that Philip sought in his own knights.

The potence of the King of Arms and the robes of a knight of the Order are displayed in the Kunsthistorisches Museum in Vienna, and many other museums have fabulous examples of the insignia.

DIVISION OF THE ORDER

The male line of the house of Burgundy came to an end in the 15th century, when all the fortunes of that extraordinary land fell to the great heiress, Mary of Burgundy, the sister of Charles the Bold. Mary married the Habsburg Archduke Maximilian, who became Holy Roman Emperor in 1493. Mary and Maximilian's grandson, Charles, eventually succeeded to the throne of Spain in 1516.

When the Habsburg bloodline became extinct in Spain, the Austrian Emperor, Charles VI (1711–40), claimed sovereignty of the Golden Fleece from the Bourbon monarchs of Spain, and in 1713 re-instituted the Order in Vienna. From that time the Golden Fleece continued separately in each of the two countries. The Austrian branch admitted only Catholics, but the Spanish branch became a civil order in the 19th century, and current members include Queen Elizabeth II of Britain.

Despite the fall of so many European monarchies in the first half of the 20th century, several of the great temporal orders of chivalry survive, among them the Order of the Garter and the Order of the Thistle. Two Scandinavian orders, the Danish Order of the Elephant (1462), and the Swedish Order of the Seraphim (1748), maintain splendid displays of heraldry relating to current and former knights of the orders.

▼ *The collar of the Golden Fleece, shown in its full form in a Flemish armorial of the late 16th century.*

HERALDRY IN THE CHURCH

Heraldry was adopted by the Church not very long after its birth on the battlefield. It hardly needed to be shown what to do with arms, since its hierarchy tended to be drawn from the nobility, the class that had already adopted heraldry. Although princes of the Church were supposed not to take part in war, two of the most militant men on the battlefield of Hastings in 1066 were Odo, Bishop of Bayeux, who was the half-brother of William of Normandy, and Geoffrey, Bishop of Coutances. These fighting prelates used their weapons in as terrible a fashion as any other Norman warrior.

Ecclesiastical users of heraldry developed their own methods of displaying their arms, tending to place them on the oval seals they had used since long before heraldry appeared. Whereas the military man displayed himself on his seal in a warlike manner, a proud prelate would show him or herself – abbesses often made use of armorial seals – in the act of blessing, accompanied by a shield of his or her personal arms. The seal of an abbey, cathedral or other institution often bore its patron saint together with the arms of the institution (if used) as well as those attributed to the saint. This is still the case for many dioceses and monastic institutions. During the

▲ *The arms of cardinals portrayed in a 15th-century window of Toledo Cathedral, Spain, are surmounted by their red hats.*

period when heraldry was being used in its true form by medieval knights in warfare, western Europe knew only one Church. The heraldry of the Catholic Church has since provided the model for other Christian denominations, including the Protestant clergy, although they tend to use simplified forms.

PAPAL ARMS

The Pope places his family arms on a shield ensigned by the papal tiara. Behind the shield are placed the keys of St Peter: a gold key points to the dexter, symbolizing papal power extending up to heaven, and a silver key points to the sinister, symbolizing power over the faithful on earth. The keys are often joined together by a red cord. During the period between the death of a pope and the election of his successor (known as the interregnum or sede vacate), the keys pass to the cardinal-camerlengo (the papal treasurer), who bears them in saltire beneath another emblem peculiar

to the Catholic Church, the pavilion known as the "ombrellino", which is, in fact, an umbrella. Both keys and pavilion are usually placed above the shield of the camerlengo, indicating that it is his duty to watch over the rights of the holy see until the election of the new pope.

THE CARDINAL'S HAT

Since the 13th century, the rank of cardinal has been distinguished by the wearing of a red hat, adorned with cords intended to be tied under the chin. It was long the custom for a cardinal's hat to be hung above his tomb, and you can often still see these dusty insignia hanging in cathedrals in Catholic countries. The red hat found its way into heraldry, where it ensigned the cardinal's arms. The cords hung down on either side of the shield and were often

▲ *The arms of Pope John Paul II, as used for papal notepaper, display the symbols of the papacy: the crossed keys and tiara.*

▲ *The oval seal design typical for a religious institution or individual here shows the punning arms of Milton Abbey, Dorset, England: a mill on a tun (barrel).*

ornamented with tassels. Their number was not fixed at first, but under Pope Pius VI (1775–99) it became the custom to set 15 tassels on either side.

▼ *Great events in the Church calendar could be recorded through heraldry. This page from the Chronicle of the Council of Constance (1414–18) shows the arms of the great clerics who sat for the election of Pope Martin V (elected November 1417).*

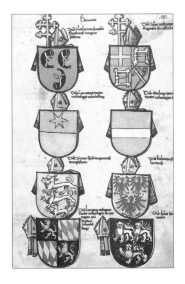

ARCHBISHOPS AND BISHOPS

Resident archbishops may make use of the "pallium". Originally a toga-like vestment, this shrank to a Y-shaped band worn over the shoulders. It is often used as a charge in the arms of archiepiscopal dioceses.

Archbishops can also make use of a double transfixed cross behind their shield, while bishops place a simple cross behind theirs. High prelates of the Protestant Church may choose a shield of arms ensigned with a precious (jewelled) mitre. Sometimes a crozier and cross is placed in saltire behind the shield.

In northern Europe, and especially in Britain, it is quite common for archbishops, bishops and abbots to marshal their personal arms with those of their diocese or abbey. In British dioceses, the shield is impaled (as in a marriage): the dexter half bears the arms of the see and the sinister half the arms of the bishop. As Protestant clergy are allowed to marry, the hatchment of a bishop or archbishop often shows two shields of arms, that on the dexter with the arms as just described, that on the sinister bearing the personal arms further impaled with those of the wife's family.

ECCLESIASTICAL PRINCES

For centuries, archbishops, bishops, abbots and even abbesses were able to rule over certain territories in the Holy Roman Empire. These mighty princes of the Church often used achievements of arms every bit as grand as any other ruler. Some did not even bother to show any mark of ecclesiastical dignity, preferring to use mantles, princely hats or coronets of rank. More often they combined both ecclesiastical and lay insignia, and adorned their palaces and churches with some of the grandest achievements of arms ever seen.

Their arms often include not only the symbols of their pastoral duties, such as the crozier and cross, but a sword. This seems a most unlikely object to find in the arms of a churchman, or even a churchwoman, but it signifies that they literally had power of life or death over their subjects. A sword can even be seen in the arms of Abbess Elizabeth Antonia of Saxe-Meiningen (1713–66). Though Abbess

▲ *The modern achievement, including a mitre and robe, of an archpriest of the Ukrainian Orthodox Church in Canada, the Very Revd Waldemar Kuchta.*

Elizabeth's jurisdiction was confined to the cathedral and convent of Gandersheim in Lower Saxony, and her subjects numbered fewer than twenty, she asserted her independence from the Dukes of Brunswick by placing the imperial eagle behind a cartouche of the abbey's arms. These were divided Per pale Sable and Or, the imperial colours commemorating the early abbesses of Gandersheim, who were imperial princesses.

In Britain the sword-in-arms of prelates was virtually unknown, except in the arms of the Bishops of Durham. Durham Cathedral appears in many ways to be more castle than church, and a real castle stands right behind the great church. The prince-bishops of Durham were given palatinate status by the medieval English kings, making them virtually sovereign rulers in their diocese, because they were expected to maintain their own standing army and keep vigil against the invading Scots. The prince-bishops maintained the unique distinction of placing their mitre within a ducal (or heraldic) coronet. Earlier bishops also included in their mitre an ostrich plume, thus combining a bishop's hat with a warrior's crest. Their seals showed them as knights, charging into battle, with swords held aloft.

RELIGIOUS ORDERS OF CHIVALRY

Medieval Europe was dominated by two powers, the knights and the Church. While the Church often railed against the excesses of troublesome knights, who were not averse to sacking the odd abbey, it was into the local church that the knights' bodies were eventually carried. These violent characters were the same men whose memorials often appeared in due course in the stained glass windows of the church.

THE FIRST CRUSADE

Pope Urban II (reigned 1088–99), saw a way to channel the violence of the military. Rather than beseeching men to stop fighting, he encouraged them to take their aggression out on the principal bugbear of the Christian world – the Muslims. His rough and ready evangelism appealed to the fighting men of Europe: they saw the possibility of achieving not only eternal glory, but also earthly riches.

Urban used the symbolism of the crucifix during his rallies of 1095, announcing that it should be the token of their cause. The message immediately took effect, as men tore up strips of coloured cloth and stitched crosses on their tunics. Despite many setbacks, the First Crusade (1096–99)

▲ *A seal showing two impoverished Templar knights frugally doubling up on one horse.*

achieved its aim: Jerusalem was captured and its inhabitants – men, women and children – were murdered in an orgy of brutality.

While the prospect of riches was an obvious draw, there were some of high rank who espoused the noblest aims of chivalry. For several years prior to Jerusalem's capture, a group of knights had acted as protectors to pilgrims to the city. At the time of the First Crusade they lived near the Temple of Solomon in Jerusalem. In 1119 Hughes de Payns and Geoffrey de St Omer incorporated the group into a religious order, the Poor Knights of the Temple of Solomon, usually known as the Knights Templar. So poor did the early Templars claim to be that their seals often depicted two men riding a single horse. The

idea of priest-knights soon caught on and led to a flowering of other military orders of chivalry. Among them were the Knights of the Order of St Lazarus of Jerusalem, who maintained leper hospitals, and the Knights of the Hospital Order of St John of Jerusalem (the Knights Hospitallers), formed to aid sick and weary pilgrims. Some of the great dormitories they built still survive. The Hospitallers and the Templars acquired great wealth and built vast castles. There was little love lost between these two powerful orders, and when not fighting the "infidel", they were apt to fight each other.

INSIGNIA OF THE ORDERS

Each religious order of chivalry settled on a cross of a particular form and colour, and some of these symbols are still familiar today, none more so than the white eight-pointed cross of the Hospitallers, now called the Sovereign and Military Order of St John of Jerusalem, and known as the Order of Malta. The British branch of the Order became the Most Venerable Order of St John, whose members are famed for their voluntary relief work as the St John's Ambulance Brigade.

The Prince Grand Master of the Order of Malta quarters his family arms with those of the Order, and his shield is placed on an eight-pointed white cross surrounded by a rosary. The whole is placed on a black princely mantle and ensigned by a princely crown of degree. Other high-ranking prelates (notably Bailiffs Grand Cross) are entitled to bear a chief of the Order – Gules a cross Argent – and have a banner of the Order carried in procession.

▼ *Arms of the Hoch- und Deutschmeister (Grand and Teutonic Master) of the Teutonic Order.*

▼ *Left to right: The arms of the Order of the Knights Templar, the Order of St Lazarus, and the Sovereign and Military Order of St John of Jerusalem (the Order of Malta).*

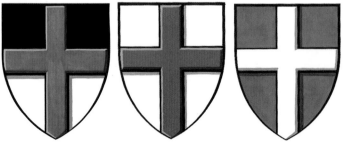

▲ *Arms of the 78th and current Grand Master of the Sovereign Military Order of Malta, Fra Andrew Bertie. From medieval times the grand masters have quartered the arms of the Order with those of their family.*

Protestant chapters of the Order were formed in the late 16th and 17th centuries. Their heraldry conforms in the main to the Sovereign and Military Order of St John of Jerusalem, except that various national symbols are added to the decorations, arms and banners.

Of the other religious military orders, the most famous were the Teutonic Order of Germany and the Orders of Santiago and Calatrava, both of Spain. The crosses of each order have often found their way into the heraldry of their members. The Teutonic Knights, who maintained their fighting traditions by opposing pagan tribes along the eastern Baltic, displayed a black crutched cross (cross potent) which told of their origins caring for sick and wounded knights and pilgrims who came from their homelands.

Until the 14th century, there was at least one nation – Lithuania – which the Teutonic Order could still attempt to convert through the sword, but in 1386 Grand Duke Jagiello of Lithuania converted to Christianity (having married Jadwiga, heiress to the Polish throne). However, the Order continued to invade his borders and tried his patience so much that in 1410 he exacted a terrible revenge. At the Battle of Grunwald, hundreds of the Teutonic Knights were killed. Some, it is claimed were roasted in their armour on spits by the victorious Poles.

It is sometimes supposed that in the arms of Jerusalem the gold crosses borne on a white field were originally red. This version is used by the Order of the Holy Sepulchre, which originated when knighthoods were conferred on Crusaders visiting the Church of the Holy Sepulchre in Jerusalem. It is said that the knights of the Order were dubbed with the sword of Godfrey de Bouillon, a leader of the First Crusade. Its members may place their shields on the main cross potent and include the four small crosses couped around the edge or, like the members of the Order of Malta, they can place the cross alongside their achievement of arms, as best befits the design. The highest ranking members can quarter the crosses with their personal arms.

The Knights of St John left their mark through their heraldry wherever they went, especially on Malta, where the arms of the Grand Master can be seen on many buildings. In the former Conventual Church of the Order, now the Pro-Cathedral of St John in Valetta, a collection of 400 tesselated floor plaques in multi-coloured stone indicates by their arms the burial places of many members of the Order of Malta.

▲ *A medieval miniature shows the Knights of St John receiving orders from their Grand Master, Pierre d'Abusson (whose arms appear on the building top right), during the Siege of Rhodes by Muhammad II in 1486.*

▼ *One of the finest displays of heraldry in the world is to be found on the floor of St John's Pro-Cathedral in Valetta, Malta, where the arms of many officers of the Order of St John are executed in marble.*

CIVIC AND
STATE HERALDRY

Most people feel the need to belong, whether it be to a football team, a
town or a nation. Identification with such an entity engenders a sense of
security and strength, and from that strength comes pride. The emblems
adopted by the sovereigns of Europe in the late Middle Ages soon became
identified not so much with the rulers themselves but with their entire
realms. The English were united behind the strength of the royal leopards,
the French were protected beneath their golden lilies. As the nation state
became a reality during the medieval period, the major cities and city states
of Europe also grew in wealth and power, believing themselves as rich and
mighty as any ruler or dynasty.

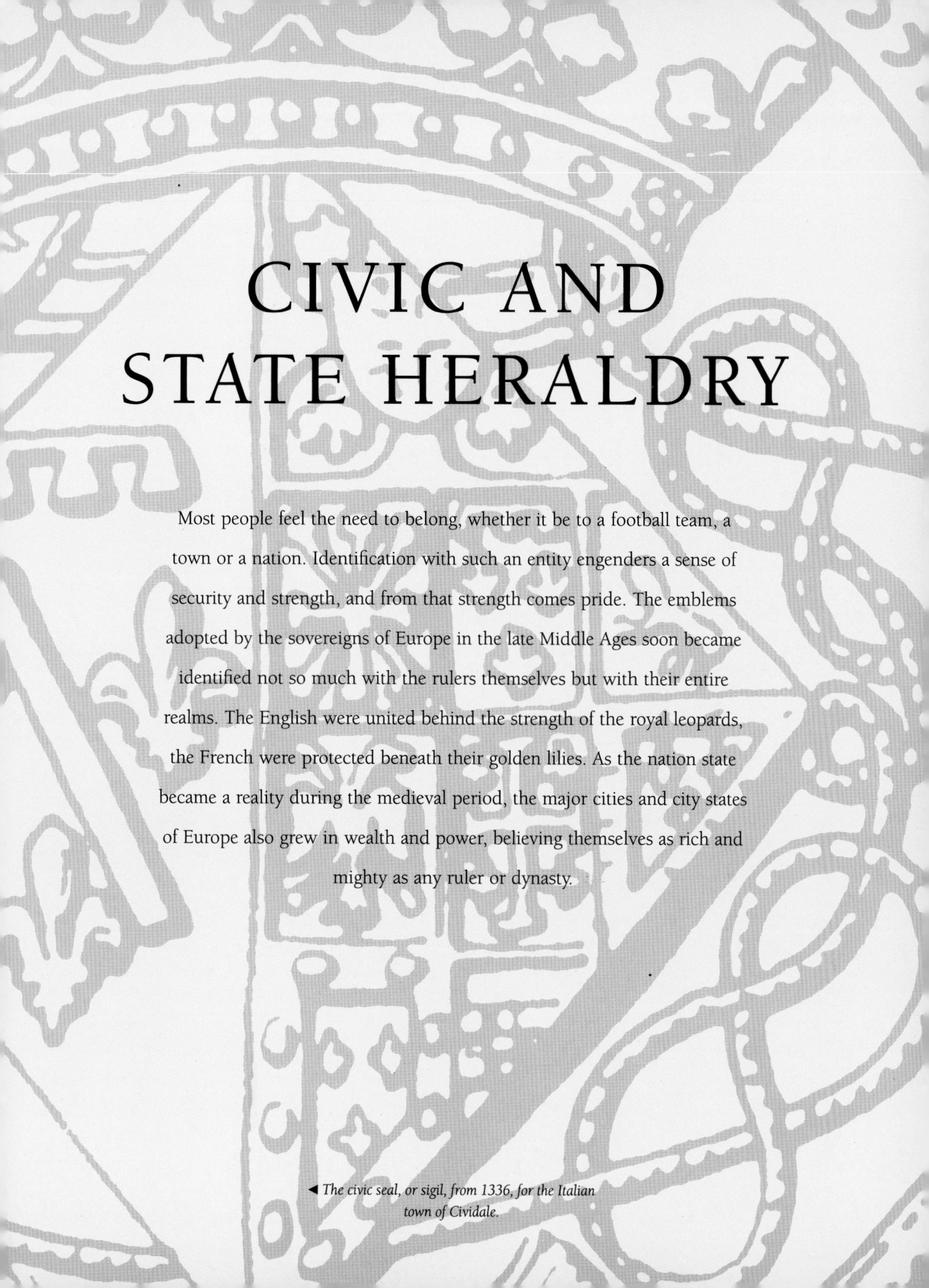

◄ *The civic seal, or sigil, from 1336, for the Italian*
town of Cividale.

CIVIC AND NATIONAL ARMS

Like the Church, whose religious and chivalric orders had embraced heraldry on a corporate basis, the towns and cities of Europe united their people behind devices that often reflected the protective nature of civic government. Their shields bore stylized views of municipal fortifications, with battlemented walls and turrets, or a gateway with its portcullis and other defences, asserting the defensive power and strength of the corporation.

Many early civic arms incorporate older devices found on the council's official seals. These often depicted not only the fortifications of the place, but also its patron saint, an important figure in the town or city's history. Not every town felt the need to put its protection in the hands of its patron saint alone. Where a municipality was under the influence of a local magnate or prince, who might or might not have a residence in the town, the arms of the ruler often filled the space within the gateway on the municipal shield. A combination of the arms or figures of the saint and the ruler was also common.

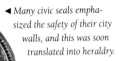

◀ Many civic seals emphasized the safety of their city walls, and this was soon translated into heraldry.

CIVIC ARMS AND EMBLEMS

As with personal arms, in the early stages of heraldry civic arms were usually adopted at will. It was only in the 15th and 16th centuries that towns started to be granted arms in a formal way, by letters patent issued on behalf of the sovereign. Provinces and counties tended to be known by the arms of their rulers, or used arms based upon theirs. Many are still in use, although major land reforms and boundary changes throughout Europe in the 19th century resulted in widespread reform of regional district heraldry.

In Britain any corporate body, from a city to a company, is entitled to apply for arms, but many towns, district councils and county councils that are not armigerous are adopting logos rather than arms, to represent themselves as dynamic and forward-looking. Perhaps this is because many of the arms granted in the 20th century were not the most imaginative of

designs, with over 70 per cent having as a principal charge a blue and white wavy line to represent some local water feature. The use of supporters is reserved for civic authorities viewed by the heralds as having some special eminence or distinction.

In Britain there is technically no such thing as "county" or "city" arms, as the arms are considered to belong to the body corporate: that is, the council or corporation in whose name they are granted. In Scottish heraldry, corporations are given a special type of helmet, called a "sallet", to differentiate them from personal arms.

NATIONAL ARMS

The need for a device representing national unity has been recognized for centuries, by both republics and monarchies. Some of the earliest republican arms must be those of the Swiss cantons. Instituted during the late medieval period, they were borne on the banners under which the famous Swiss troops marched. Swiss-trained bands were prized by other states for their prowess and discipline. Among the most famous of the cantonal arms were the white cross on red of Schwyz, the black ox head of Uri and the black bear of Appenzell.

When they were not fighting for other nations, Swiss troops kept in training by fighting those of the neighbouring cantons. One of the many disputes that arose between the cantons of Appenzell and Uri occurred when the people of Appenzell derided those of Uri by claiming – through the use of their arms – that they were as thick-headed as an ox. The inhabitants of Uri got their own back by taunting the Appenzellers, flourishing the latter's arms with the black bear missing its genitals. This was too much for the Appenzellers, who attacked Uri to avenge the insult.

WORLDWIDE HERALDRY

From the late medieval period onwards, heraldic writers gave arms to nations and rulers who had never actually encountered heraldry. To the writers this was no matter. Such was the nature of sovereignty that all

▼ The arms of two Czech towns, Prague New Town (left) and Tábor (right) show how the motifs of civic seals were translated on to heraldic shields. Both include emblems of the kings, emperors and dynasties under which the towns prospered.

monarchs, whether Christian or heathen, alive or dead – and their realms – were of noble status and deserving of heraldry. Thus the Shah of Persia was given a shield charged with a sun in splendour surrounded by stars, and the Sultan of Turkey was granted the Ottoman crescent, with the shield ensigned by a turban.

In time, as Europeans settled in all continents as a result of trade or conquest, heraldry was adopted by their rulers. Today, some eight centuries after the birth of heraldry in Europe, many nations and their rulers have achievements of arms. They range from the kings of Jordan to the republics of Indonesia and Bolivia. As far south as Antarctica itself, heraldry has made its mark. The English heralds designed arms for the Falkland Island Dependencies on 11 March 1952, and in 1963 the crest of the Antarctic research ship *Discovery* was added to the arms.

▲ *Arms of the major European monarchies at the beginning of the 20th century (left to right, top to bottom): Prussia, Austria, Hungary, Bavaria, Russia, Germany, Britain, Saxony, Italy, Spain, Württemberg. At the end of World War II all but two were extinct.*

▼ *The boroughs (contrades) of Siena in Italy attempt to outdo each other in magnificence at the opening procession of the festival of the Palio. This early 17th-century painting portrays the prosperity, independence and pride of the city-state.*

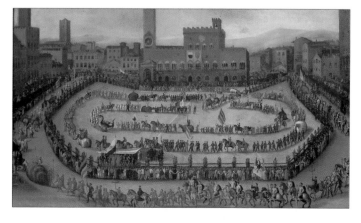

THE GARTER SERVICE

There are two annual events at which the full panoply of British state ceremonial can be observed by the public, and each has its own unique display of heraldry. The first is the service of the Order of the Garter in St George's Chapel, Windsor, which takes place on a Monday in mid-June, with a spectacular procession.

INVESTITURE

The investiture of new Knights of the Garter is held on the morning of the service in the Throne Room at Windsor. Two officers of the Order – Garter King of Arms and the Gentleman Usher of the Black Rod – bring in the knight or lady elect. He or she is brought, between two knight sponsors, to the sovereign, who personally invests him or her with all the insignia of the Order. For men, a garter is tied around the left leg and is held there by Garter King of Arms while the following admonition is read out, recalling a time when members of the Order formed the backbone of the monarch's military command structure:

To the honour of God Omnipotent and in Memorial of the Blessed Martyr, St George, tie about thy leg, for thy renown, this most Noble Garter. Wear it as a symbol of the Most Illustrious Order, never to be forgotten or laid aside, that thereby thou mayest be admonished to be courageous, and having undertaken a just war, with which thou shalt be engaged, thou mayest stand firm, valiantly fight courageously and successfully conquer.

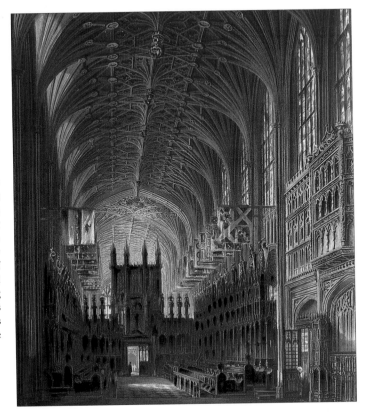

THE PROCESSION

After the investiture follows lunch, after which the Garter Knights assemble in their robes in St George's Hall, the largest room in the castle, before processing to their service. They walk from the royal apartments to St George's Chapel, which lies at the foot of the hill inside the castle's outer

▲ *St George's Chapel, Windsor Castle, seen in an engraving of 1810. The stalls of the Knights of the Garter are dominated by their armorial banners, helms and crests.*

▼ *An etching by Marcus Gheeraerts the Elder, showing the procession of the Knights of the Garter in 1576.*

bailey. The first part of the procession is headed by the Constable and Governor of Windsor Castle, whose uniform includes insignia unique to his office, including a depiction of the castle's Royal Tower.

The Military Knights of Windsor follow, in their scarlet uniforms. They are the successors of the 26 impoverished ex-soldiers originally appointed as "bedesmen", people who were employed to pray for the souls of the Garter Knights. According to the letters patent instituted by Edward III in 1348, and subsequent statutes, each bedesman was to wear a red cloak with a small shield bearing the cross of St George. The cross still forms part of the insignia of the Military Knights, who also wear a silver cut Garter star and crown.

The Military Knights are followed by the officers of arms in their tabards and Tudor

MILITARY AND NAVAL KNIGHTS OF WINDSOR

All retired military officers, the Military Knights live in lodgings allocated to them in the 16th century: a row of houses built against the inner side of the castle wall opposite St George's Chapel. Apart from attending the Garter ceremony, they continue to fulfil the duties imposed on them in 1348 by attending chapel every Sunday to pray for the sovereign and the Knights of the Garter. Once known as Poor Knights, their name was changed in the 19th century, after rude and satirical verses about their alleged infirmity had been broadcast about the town of Windsor.

Between 1795 and 1892 there were also Naval Knights of Windsor. However, such was the nature of the old sea-dogs that there was much discord, not only amongst themselves, but also with the Military Knights. Far from leading a "virtuous, studious and devout life", they were wont to frequent taverns and bawdy houses in Windsor and were known to belabour each other with their crutches and wooden legs.

bonnets, bearing a crowned Tudor rose, worn especially for the occasion. Behind the heralds come the Garter Knights in full robes, bonnets with ostrich plumes and the collars of the Order. Next are the Princes of the Blood and finally the officers of the Order leading the sovereign's procession. As with all the officers of the British orders of chivalry, each man has insignia of office, the most famous being the black rod borne by the Gentleman Usher of the Black Rod. The Garter officers wear cloaks bearing a shield with the cross of St George.

Next come the sovereign and consort, with the trains of their mantles held up by pages in the royal livery. On the sovereign's mantle is a large representation of the Garter star instead of the normal badge of the Order. The sovereign's party is followed by the Yeoman of the Guard. As the entire procession weaves its way to St George's Chapel, the festival atmosphere is maintained by military bands and the processional route is lined by troopers of the Household Cavalry. The pouches they wear on their cross belts bear the royal arms and their helmets continue the theme of the day by sporting the star of the Garter within a wreath.

The procession is met at the chapel by the clergy, and yet again the pageantry and pomp associated with royalty is manifest. The various members of the sovereign's ecclesiastical household are entitled to wear scarlet cassocks. Royal chaplains are

▲ *The standard of the Yeomen of the Guard, as approved by King George VI on 27 June 1938. It includes the badge of the House of Windsor (bottom right), newly created to appear on this standard.*

identified by a badge consisting of a silver-gilt wreath, crown and the sovereign's cypher; priests-in-ordinary wear a similar badge in silver. The steps to the chapel are lined by the officers of arms, and at the moment of the sovereign's entrance a fanfare sounds. If a new knight has been invested in the morning he will be led to his stall by Garter King of Arms. The Chancellor of the Order then calls out the knight's name, and there follows a service, after which the royal party and the rest of the participants return to the castle.

▼ *The Military Knights of Windsor leaving St George's Chapel after the Garter Service.*

THE STATE OPENING OF PARLIAMENT

The ceremonial meeting of the British sovereign with parliament has its origins over 1,000 years ago, when the king consulted with his peers – other aristocrats in many ways as powerful and wealthy as he. In time the sovereign became more remote from his subjects, until events such as the signing of Magna Carta, the Civil War and the Revolution of 1688 brought the monarchy back into line.

Before the ceremony can proceed, a detachment of the Yeomen of the Guard, in their Tudor uniforms, search the cellars of the Palace of Westminster. They are looking for would-be terrorists following the example of Guy Fawkes who, on 5 November 1605, attempted to overthrow James I and his government by exploding barrels of gunpowder hidden in the cellar.

THE ROYAL PROCESSION

The sovereign is preceded by the royal regalia, which are allocated a coach of their own. In addition to the Imperial Crown, these include the Cap of Maintenance symbolizing the monarch's religious orthodoxy,

▼ The arrival of Queen Victoria at the House of Lords to open her first Parliament. The scene includes the Lord Chancellor, with his purse, and Garter King of Arms.

and the Sword of State which indicates his or her duty to defend justice. The sovereign follows in the Irish State Coach, escorted by the Household Cavalry.

At the moment the sovereign enters the Houses of Parliament the royal standard is raised on the Victoria Tower. The sovereign is greeted by the Earl Marshal of England, the Duke of Norfolk (or his deputy), who carries a gold baton tipped with ebony. Also present is the hereditary Keeper of the Palace of Westminster, the Lord Great Chamberlain. He wears a uniform of scarlet and gold, with blue collar and cuffs. Suspended from a hip pocket is his gold key of the Palace of Westminster, and in his right hand he bears his wand of office. Also in attendance are the Officers of Arms in their tabards. The sovereign is escorted up the royal staircase to the Robing Room. The staircase itself is a heraldic feast, its walls covered with the arms of sovereigns and their cohorts going back to the birth of heraldry.

In the Robing Room the sovereign is vested with the Imperial State Crown and dons the crimson Robe of State, whose train is carried by four pages dressed in the royal liveries, before the procession moves off. Amongst the many details to be noticed are the sticks carried by Gold Stick

▲ At the state opening of Parliament in 1958, Queen Elizabeth II processes to the Lords Chamber, preceded by the Lord Great Chamberlain. The Yeomen of the Guard line the processional route.

in Waiting and Silver Stick in Waiting, two senior officers in the Household Cavalry. Their office dates from Tudor times, when the sovereign was constantly protected by two chosen guards, who even slept outside the bedroom door. Charles II commemorated their devotion to duty by presenting sticks bearing either a gold or silver head inscribed with his cypher. The cypher of the current sovereign also appears in the badge of office of the Mistress of the Robes, the senior lady of the royal household.

The scene is further enhanced by the Yeomen of the Guard and the Honourable Corps of Gentlemen at Arms, who have their origin in the Band of Gentlemen Pensioners, a personal guard drawn from the king's confidants. The Gentlemen at Arms carry poleaxes with blades engraved with the royal arms. Their uniform has a scarlet coat with gold epaulettes and belt, blue trousers and brass helmet topped by white feathers. The helmet plate bears gilt royal arms quarterings within the Garter, mounted on a silver cut star. Their badge of a portcullis appears on their uniform and on their standard, devised by the

▲ *The Standard of the Honourable Corps of Gentlemen at Arms, with battle honours and the portcullis badge of Henry VIII, in whose reign the bodyguard was formed.*

English College of Arms in 1936. While it is based on the tapered shape of a cavalry ▸ standard, that of the Yeomen of the Guard is almost square. It bears the badges of the various dynasties it has served, from the crowned hawthorn bush of Henry VII to the badge of the House of Windsor, a representation of the Round Tower of Windsor Castle.

▼ *The Palace of Westminster is a haven of heraldry. Here, an artist restores the painted arms of the Chiefs of the General Staff on the Peers' Staircase.*

On the way to the House of Lords the royal procession passes by numerous armorial achievements, reflecting not only the history of the Houses of Parliament, but the leadership of the nation. At the top of the Peers' Staircase are the arms of Chiefs of the Imperial and General Staff, and at the bottom the arms of former Speakers of the House of Commons (since 1700) who have become peers.

In the Lords Chamber, the windows are set with the arms of peers and below them appear the arms of the Lord Chancellors. Much of the detail of the chamber is heraldic, from the ceiling bosses to the posts that support the curtain running around the gallery. Like much of the Palace of Westminster, the room dates from after the fire of 1834.

THE GRACIOUS SPEECH

The chamber's grandest feature, the throne, stands on a golden platform set with royal emblems. The royal party take their places and in front of them sit the peers. The Lords Spiritual (the bishops) are in their ecclesiastical robes, the Law Lords in robes and wigs, and the Lords Temporal (life peers and representative hereditary peers) in their parliamentary robes.

The Lord Chancellor approaches the sovereign holding his own insignia of office, the Lord Chancellor's Purse, embroidered with the royal arms within a border of cherub's heads. The purse formerly contained the matrix of the Great Seal of the Realm, but today it holds the text of the speech which the sovereign will read to the assembled Lords and Commons.

The sovereign is not allowed to enter the Commons, so they are commanded to attend by the Gentleman Usher of the Black Rod, who wears his chain of office and carries the Black Rod itself. The Speaker leads the Commons to the Lords, and when all are assembled in the Lords Chamber, the sovereign begins the Gracious Speech, which sets out government policy for the coming year.

THE YEOMEN OF THE GUARD

Enhancing the pageantry of the state opening of Parliament are the Tudor uniforms of the Queen's Bodyguard of the Yeomen of the Guard. They wear the plant badges of the United Kingdom on the breast of their tunics: the combined rose, thistle and shamrock, on a background of scarlet and gold, the royal livery colours. Not to be confused with the Yeomen Warders who guard the Tower of London and wear a similar uniform but without the cross belt, the Queen's Bodyguard of the Yeoman of the Guard is the oldest royal bodyguard in existence, having served for more than 500 years. They can be observed not only at the state opening of Parliament but also at the annual Garter service in Windsor.

MILITARY HERALDRY

The military forces of the world have long been custodians of heraldic tradition. Amalgamations and changes of rulers, governments and commanding officers, have kept the heraldic designer busy devising new badges, standards or uniforms. While the medieval knight's horse bore a "trapper" or saddle-cloth resplendent with the arms of its rider, its modern equivalent – the tank – is likely to bear the heraldic liveries of a regiment.

The history of military heraldry is of course as old as heraldry itself. The military are upholders of tradition, and can give the heraldist a splendid insight into national heraldry and history. Although centuries have passed since military men wore full plate armour in battle, reminders of that remote age remain. British army officers of senior rank still wear "gorget patches" on their collars that once supported the steel gorget, or throat guard, of the medieval knight. In certain armies, some officers (normally guard commanders) still sport the gorget itself, which may bear the arms of the monarch or state.

PERSONAL LIVERIES

For centuries the military forces of Europe were recruited according to the feudal system. Lords agreed to support their leader during war through "liveries and maintenance", in return for estates with which they met the great expense of maintaining private armies. The wearing of a lord's heraldic colours and badges (liveries) was a striking aspect of the medieval scene, especially during the period of inter-dynastic strife in England now known as the Wars of the Roses (1455–85).

As late as the 19th century, certain European armies still included regiments paid for and equipped by "colonel proprietors": rich men or women, normally of high rank, who saw such private troops as liveried retainers. They naturally expected the troops to wear their heraldic colours, albeit as "facing colours" on the cuffs and collars of their uniforms. There was much jostling between the nobility to outdo not

▲ *The arm badge of the Royal Svea Lifeguards of the Swedish Army, showing the regimental arms.*

only the enemy, but also their fellow colonels, in the most recherché styles. The tradition of the colonel proprietor survives today in a muted form, in the honorary commanders of certain regiments. Even in republican France, some regiments bear the arms of former commanders from the days of the *ancien régime*.

European monarchs have long had a habit of swapping splendid uniforms with each other, making their cousins honorary colonels of regiments. By this means, almost a century after the "collapse of the eagles", these symbols of the Prussian and Austrian monarchies are still borne by British soldiers. The double-headed eagle of the Habsburgs (with their arms on its breast) is worn by the 1st The Queen's Dragoon Guards on their cap badge.

▲ *Military badges. Left, a pocket badge for the Swedish district staff of Norlands. Right, a Danish army heraldic collar badge.*

FLAGS AND STANDARDS

The medieval tradition of a military unit going into battle under the standard of its commander is now obsolete (although Lord Lovat's piper famously led the Lovat Highlanders in the attack on D-Day in 1944, bearing His Lordship's pipe banner). However, as late as World War II, British tanks sported pennons of their regiment when going into battle.

Like all military insignia, unit flags differ from nation to nation. Some armies, notably those of republics, utilize the national flag with the addition of unit title

▼ *The shape of the standard favoured by medieval noblemen is still maintained in the flags of certain British Army units, especially artillery units.*

▲ *The simplicity of Norwegian military heraldry is exemplified in the badge of the Norwegian Army 6th Division (left) and a cap cockade (right) for the Norwegian King's Guard during the reign of Olav V.*

and battle honours. Others, as in the Swedish and Finnish armies, use the regimental badge and colours.

In the British Army, the small medieval badge-bearing flag – known as the "guidon" – has its modern equivalent in the company colours of the regiments of Foot Guards and the pennons of the regiments of the Royal Artillery. In each case the flag is long, narrowing at its end into one or two tails. Royal Artillery pennons are crossed by diagonal bands bearing the regimental motto, with the regiment's badges set in the segments between the bands, similar to the standard of a medieval English nobleman. Each company of Foot Guards has its own heraldic emblem, most of which are taken from well-known royal badges or "cognizances".

NATIONAL ARMY INSIGNIA

King Gustavus I of Sweden (1523–60) is widely credited with the formation of the first truly national army, based on a system by which each prince maintained an infantry and a cavalry regiment. By the early 19th century its units were bearing provincial arms on their helmet plates and other insignia. From the late 1970s, Swedish army units were also given formal achievements of arms, with the shield of the province surmounted by a royal crown.

Many European armies retain their national colours in the form of a metal cockade, maintaining a tradition dating back three centuries or more, of troops wearing a cloth cockade in the livery colours of their commander on their headgear. The armies of Denmark, Finland,

Norway and Sweden are all known by their cockades, splendid variants of which are worn by the troops of the guards regiments in Oslo and Copenhagen. The full military cockade worn by these troops usually comes in two parts or "buttons": the top button bears the national colours and the lower bears the national arms.

The arms of countries, provinces or districts provide the theme for many regimental badges, whether in uncoloured metal – as in the collar and shoulder insignia of the Finnish, Danish and Swedish armies – or in full colour, as on the shoulder patches also worn in the latter two forces. The Danish armed forces also wear striking heraldic collar badges, including a medieval knight on his charger and a plumed war helmet.

The insignia adoped by the Norwegian Army follow the tenets set by the leading heraldist Hallvard Trætteberg, using a shield with just two tinctures and in most cases only one charge (single or multiple), such as the crossed retorts of the NBC (nuclear, biological and chemical) Unit, or the wolf's head of Brigade North. One exception was the badge of the Royal Guard (HM Kongens Garde) during the reign of King Olav V. It bore the king's monogram (V) between two knives (swords), and was known as "the dinner service" by members of the unit.

REGULATORY SCHEMES

The two World Wars saw what amounted to a free-for-all in unofficial insignia, as soldiers sought to inject some humour, often of a bawdy and derogatory kind, into the mud and chaos of modern warfare and to enliven their drab uniforms.

Eventually, various nations came up with regulatory schemes. One of the most interesting suggestions, in 1937, was for units of the French Army to bear shields taken from the arms of the places in which they were located. However, the French government disliked the designs that we produced, in which time-honoured, pre-revolutionary symbols relating to royal and imperial power were prominent, and the scheme was shelved. Since World War II, the French Army has sought to regulate all

military insignia so that they follow certain heraldic tenets. Ideas for a unit badge normally start with the unit itself, and the suggested design is sent to the Service Historique de l'Armée de Terre in the Château of Vincennes (which maintains a collection of 15,000 unit badges), to ensure that it conforms to the ideals of clarity and sobriety cherished by the service. The insignia will often be allowed to include the arms of the local town or province. If acceptable, it is passed to the French defence ministry to be formally approved, and is given an authorized number. For a badge worn by a fighting unit the number is prefixed by the letter G (for *guerre*); for a "brevet", or specialist badge,

▼ *The pocket badge of the French 1st Parachute Hussar Regiment bears the arms of its founder, Count Ladislaus Bercheny.*

▼ *The pocket badge of the French Army's 1st Transport Regiment bears the arms of the city of Paris, where it is based.*

▲ *The heraldic beret flash and crest (now superseded) of a unit in the 172nd Infantry Brigade (Alaska) in the United States Army.*

the prefix is GS. There is even a specialist badge for a French Army war artist, which bears a shield and helm as its design.

The United States Army has its own Institute of Heraldry, which lays down specific patterns for military insignia. Each unit or battalion at regimental level is entitled to a coat of arms that is formally granted by the Institute. The grant shows the achievement of arms in full colour with its formal blazon, and also explains the symbolism behind the design.

Each colour-bearing unit in the army is entitled to its own crest as well as shield, but for new units without battle honours the crest is omitted, with the idea that, at a later date, some event in its war service will give rise to a suitable crest. The shield

should be the standard shape, as on official drawings, and the design upon it true heraldry, of a simple uncluttered nature. Embattled lines of partition are reserved for organizations that have captured a fortified objective. For National Guard units the crest is normally that of the state to which the unit belongs, and units in the Army Reserve are entitled to bear the crest of a "minuteman proper" (one of the militiamen of the fledgling Republic, so named because they undertook to be ready for action at a minute's notice).

The unit badge is normally described as a "crest", although this refers to the complete design. Worn by enlisted men on side caps and shoulder straps, it is officially known as "distinctive insignia", or DI. Each regiment or comparable unit in the US Army has its own branch colour, upon which is embroidered the arms of the United States, with the national shield and crest replaced by those of the unit.

It is stipulated that the unit motto should not include "anything of a sordid, malign or malevolent character, implying animosity or partiality towards nations or groups of nations, or which stresses the destructive nature of warfare", although many unofficial unit badges of the Vietnam era certainly did not follow this advice – "Peace", "Hell" and "Bomb Hanoi" were popular themes, as well as "Kill".

Much official American military heraldry is of excellent quality and combines the best of ancient and modern heraldic

styles. For instance, the arms of the 152nd Field Artillery Battalion are blazoned: Gules, on a canton of the same, fimbriated Or a projectile (artillery shell) bendwise, scintillant of the last. In addition to the heraldic tinctures, corps colours may also be used, as in the arms of the 201st Engineer Battalion: Per bend wavy Buff and Azure [the colours of the Quartermaster Corps] a fleur de lis Argent.

The fleur de lis is found in the arms of those units deployed in France in either or both of the two World Wars. The Institute of Heraldry designates other charges for particular campaigns, such as tomahawks for the Indian Wars or a cactus for Mexican campaigns. As an armorial charge indicative of a certain campaign, the fleur de lis can also be found in the arms of regiments of the Italian Army, which have distinctive pocket badges. The trident from the arms of the Ukraine and the lion of Abyssinia are among other charges used.

FULL ACHIEVEMENTS OF ARMS

Spanish Army units have their own achievements of arms, although only the shield tends to be used for uniforms while the full achievement is kept for more formal occasions. The insignia are regulated by the Spanish Army's Institute of History and Military Culture.

Each major unit of the Spanish Army has its own arms, a full achievement accompanied by the following exterior ornaments: the branch insignia placed in

▼ *The full armorial achievement for the 20th Anti-aircraft Regiment of the Spanish Army.*

▼ *In the arms of Bravo Group, KFOR, of the Portuguese Army, a "plate engrailed" makes an excellent parachute canopy.*

▼ *The Portuguese Army Archives Department is represented by a magpie and a shield division suggesting bookshelves.*

saltire behind the shield (such as the crossed batons of a *capitan general*, for the army headquarters). Above the shield is placed a royal crown. Any decorations worn by the unit are placed below the shield, but if the unit has the distinction of the *laureada*, the highest decoration it can win, this appears as a laurel wreath ornamented with sword blades encircling the shield. The achievement is complete when accompanied by scrolls bearing the regimental title, its nickname (if it has one), the *cri-de-guerre* (if borne) and the regimental battle honours.

The resulting arms are some of the most splendid heraldic compositions in modern military use. They show a fascinating diversity of themes, with each *tercio*, or unit, of the Spanish Foreign Legion bearing the arms of a famous warrior, such as Don Juan of Austria or the Gran Capitan Don Gonzalo Fernandez de Cordoba. The Special Operations Groups each have an animal in their arms associated with ferocity, or some means of attack: for example, SOG Valencia has a black bat, taken from the arms of Valencia but also indicating the unit's speciality – night attacks.

Other units take part or all of the arms of their home base or area of recruitment. The 50th Motorized Infantry Regiment "Canarias" includes, as well as charges taken from the arms of its base Gran Canaria, a dragon pierced by lances representing "the expulsion from the island of the English pirate, Admiral Francis Drake".

Finally, a happy combination of ancient and modern symbolism makes up the arms of Regional Engineer Unit 21. Its shield bears a bulldozer in front of a cross composed of a road intersection, while the border features the traditional punning charge of the ancient kingdom of Granada, the pomegranate.

Portuguese military units are also granted full achievements of arms, and many of their designs are simple but striking, such as a parachute canopy, which is heraldically interpreted as a "plate engrailed". The device used for the shield of the Portuguese Army's General Archives Department – books arranged on shelves shown as Paly per fess counterchanged –

is accompanied by that legendary collector, the magpie, as a crest.

In the German Army, the Bundeswehr, some freedom is allowed in insignia design. Formality is observed in the design of the arm badges of major units – divisions, brigades, corps and schools – which often bear the arms of the province in which the unit serves, but the pocket badges of smaller units are left to the commander. If he has little interest in heraldry, the designs, though always on a shield, can be complex and distinctly non-heraldic.

The matter has, however, been corrected in many cases by the "education" of unit commanders by one man with an extensive knowlege of heraldic design – Lt Col Herbert Lippert. His designs range from Teutonic Knights (from Marburg, the unit's home town) firing into the air with a bow for Air Defence Battalion 340, to a double-headed griffin (the vigilant custodian of treasure) for Direction and Replacement Battalion 855. He has made extraordinary use of counterchanging, with four semi wolves courant, for Field Replacement Battalion 24 (stationed in the town of Wolfhagen).

COMMEMORATIVE BADGES

In areas of eastern Europe that formally came under the influence of Imperial Russia, there has been a continued tradition of military insignia, much of it heraldic. The designs have a common origin in the splendid breast badges worn from the latter half of the 19th century until 1917 by units of the Imperial Russian

▲ *On a badge worn by Russian airborne troops, a parachute appears on the breast of the double-headed eagle, a legacy of the tsarist era.*

Army. It was the tradition in that army for a commemorative badge to be awarded to individuals, not so much for regimental identification but on meeting certain requirements, such as length of service. These regimental commemorative badges, made from enamelled metal, often bore imperial symbols, cyphers of the Russian sovereign and the imperial eagle, accompanied by the arms of the province or city from which the regiment recruited.

As for today's Russian Army, once again the double eagle appears on much of its insignia, both official and non-official. However, the peaked caps of the military now bear two badges – the lower one has the red star with the hammer and sickle, and the upper badge bears the double-headed eagle charged on the breast with St George and the dragon.

Between 1918 and 1939 Poland was once again a free and independent nation. The Polish Army reorganized and made use of commemorative breast badges in a similar fashion to the Imperial Russian Army. These often contained the monograms of former monarchs or *hetmen* (traditional commanders), and the arms of the town, city or province from which the regiment took its title.

◄ *A fascinating example of counterchanging in the badge of the German Army's Field Replacement Battalion 24.*

NAVAL HERALDRY

As with the armies of the world, the other fighting services have adapted their national heraldry to suit the ways in which it could be displayed on their equipment and uniforms. Warships traditionally bore the arms of the sovereign splendidly carved on their sterns. Figureheads were usually associated with the vessel's name, but could also be fashioned to hold a cartouche of arms.

The sterns of the great warships built between the 16th and 18th centuries were platforms for some of the grandest displays of heraldry ever seen. A spectacular example can be seen on the stern of the 17th-century Swedish flagship, the *Vasa*, raised from Stockholm harbour in 1961, which bears the complete achievement of arms of the sovereign, Gustavus Adolphus, for whom it was constructed. A model of a 17th-century Danish warship, in the Naval Museum in Copenhagen, shows that the ship itself bore not only cartouches of arms for all the Danish territories but also those of the Duchy of Brunswick-Lüneburg for Sofie Amalie, the Queen of Frederick III (1648–70).

ROYAL NAVY INSIGNIA

Many modern navies model their insignia on those of the British Royal Navy. As with army regiments, naval badges often started life unofficially, devised by ship's companies and their captains, and might be displayed on anything from a gun tampion to the ship's stationery. Though the Navy tried to impose some order, the Badge Committee set up in 1914 soon lapsed.

In 1916 Major Charles Ffoulkes RM, founder of the Imperial War Museum in London, was asked by the shipbuilders, Swan Hunter, to design badges for 20 ships they were building for the Royal Navy. Ffoulkes subsequently offered his

▲ *Ships were considered apt platforms for heraldry, and some figureheads, such as this one on HMS* Victory *at Portsmouth, England, bore the royal arms.*

services free to the Admiralty, and the Ships Names and Badges Committee was set up on 10 December 1918.

Between 1918 and 1937 Ffoulkes designed 550 ships' badges for the Royal Navy, and many contained heraldic charges associated with the ship's name and taken from

◀ *For centuries the seals of admirals bore their arms on the sails of ships of the period. This fine example is the seal of Richard Duke of Gloucester (later King Richard III of England), Admiral of England, c1480.*

▶ *A model of the 17th-century Danish naval vessel,* Sofie Amalie, *named after the Queen of Frederick III of Denmark. The white horse of Hanover is surrounded by shields of arms of the kingdom of Denmark and the Dukes of Brunswick-Lüneburg.*

▲ *Pictures from earlier centuries suggest that flags flown from ships could be vast, like this royal standard flying from a French warship of the 18th century.*

personal or civic arms. The first was for HMS *Warwick* and bore the bear and ragged staff device of the Earls of Warwick. The badge of the cruiser HMS *Effingham* had a demi lion pierced through the mouth, taken from the "Flodden augmentation" of the Howard family, of which the Earls of Effingham were a branch. Other

badges incorporated puns, such as a flying dove in front of a shakefork (a heraldic charge in the shape of a letter Y) for HMS *Dovey*. The symbol was placed within a frame of plaited rope, with a plaque above bearing the ship's name, surmounted by an imperial crown. The frame differed in shape for each type of vessel: battleships took a circular frame; cruisers, a pentagon; destroyers, a shield; auxiliaries, sloops, aircraft carriers and shore establishments, a diamond. During World War II the shapes were revised, and now all ships and Fleet Air Arm Squadrons take circular badges; shore establishments have diamonds and Royal Fleet Auxiliaries, pentagons.

The Royal Netherlands Navy follows the theme closely. Its badges are round, surrounded by a plaited rope tied at the base in a reef knot. The shield is surmounted by a naval crown, of the kind placed on memorials to Dutch naval heroes. Any motto is placed beneath the shield. Behind are placed crossed anchors, a device of the Dutch Admiralty since the 17th century. The anchor device is popular across the world: the Royal Danish Navy and the Royal Norwegian Navy favour a single anchor in pale behind a shield of arms, with a royal crown surmounting the shield.

One of the more bizarre RNN designs, for the gunboat *Flores*, was designed a year

▲ *The badge of the former Royal Netherlands Ship,* Flores, *depicts the tree of skulls from the island whose name it shares.*

after the boat's decommissioning in honour of its service during World War II. The charge is a stylized version of the extraordinary *scheldenboom*, or "tree of skulls", traditionally erected on the island of Flores and hung with the skulls of the islanders' vanquished enemies.

HERALDIC SHIPS' BADGES

Dutch naval badges are often fully heraldic in that they bear the arms of naval heroes such as Tromp or de Ruyter, or of towns, provinces or cities. United States Navy

▲ *Some Royal Netherlands Navy ships, such as the frigate* Bloys van Treslong, *have badges charged with naval heroes' arms.*

badges also often bear the arms of naval heroes, presidents, or other famous people. They may show the full arms or a made-up device taken from the arms of an eminent person. The badge for USS *Winston S. Churchill* (the first US Navy ship to be named after a British politician) contains a fleur de lis, cross of St George and lion passant guardant – all charges referring to Churchill's personal arms, and those of England. The ships of the Federal German Navy have maintained their own tradition of bearing the arms of cities, provinces and famous commanders on their prow, initially on the warships of World War II such as the *Graf Spee*, *Bismarck* and their class.

In recent years the Russian Navy has replaced the Soviet naval ensign bearing the hammer and sickle with one of the oldest war ensigns still in existence, the cross of St Andrew (blue on white), first adopted in about 1700 by Peter the Great. Peter also adopted for his own navy a reversed variant of the British jack, which he knew from his time spent with the Royal Navy.

An extraordinary manifestation of the tumultuous changes that have taken place in Russia may be seen on the conning towers of the nuclear submarines of the Russian Navy. These now bear the double-headed imperial eagle, with St George and the dragon on its breast.

▼ *The badges designed for ships of the British Royal Navy still follow the pattern set in the first half of the 20th century.*

▼ *The USS* Winston S. Churchill's *badge, named after Britain's wartime leader, bears charges from the Churchill family arms.*

AIR FORCE INSIGNIA

During World War I, fuselage art on aircraft showed a flair for design influenced by the most modern art of the age. Sometimes the individual unit markings designed by the pilots themselves extended along the entire length of the aircraft. French crews devised some of the most innovative air force "heraldry", and squadrons of today's Armée de l'Air bear many of the unofficial badges adopted then, amongst them the Sioux Indian chief's head chosen by the Lafayette squadron.

While the French still allow a free hand in the design of unit insignia, other air forces, such as those in Britain and the United States, maintain a much stricter control and have official authorities to design and monitor the use of formal badges. In the US Air Force, squadrons must have a pictorial device displayed on a disc, while the emblem of a flag-bearing unit (with a headquarters component) should be armorial, with the device on a shield. Unit insignia must be prepared in two versions: full colour, and subdued (olive green and black) for use in combat. Despite such strictures, towards the end of the Vietnam War there was a proliferation of non-authorized insignia, such as the badge chosen by a USAF base hospital in Korea specializing in the treatment of venereal diseases, which depicted a VD germ in a white coat bearing a syringe.

Just as close co-operation with the Royal Navy set the pattern for the insignia of various other navies, the same was the case with the allied air forces during World War II. The insignia of the Royal Flying Corps – the forerunner of the Royal Air Force – began unofficially, but an Inspector of Royal Air Force

▼ *Aircraft of the United States Air Force tend to bear the badges of wing, squadron and command.*

▲ *Two examples of pocket insignia of French Air Force airbase units: that of BA106 (top) bears the arms of Bordeaux, that of BA118 (bottom), Mont-de-Marsan.*

▲ *The badge of 22 Squadron, Royal Air Force, with its pi symbol for "22 over 7".*

Badges was appointed in 1936, and the connection with traditional heraldry was acknowledged by the selection of an officer of arms to fill the Inspector's post, as is the case today.

Every RAF badge consists of a circular frame in the form of a laurel wreath, in which the title of the unit appears, ensigned by the royal crown and bearing a motto on a scroll beneath the badge. The central plaque often contains a heraldic allusion to the unit's history and location. One of the simplest and most original charges is the *pi* symbol in the badge of 22 Squadron. In 1916 the squadron was based for a time with No 7 Wing and when the wind lay in a certain direction its aircraft had to take off over the roof of No 7 Wing's headquarters – hence 22 over 7, or the *pi* symbol.

Commonwealth air forces maintained the RAF pattern, though the laurel wreath was usually replaced by plants of national origin, such as the maple leaf for Canada, fern for New Zealand or lotus for India. Other nations have also followed this scheme. The wreath of unit badges in the Royal Netherlands Air Force is constructed

out of orange leaves and fruit – the badge of the House of Orange. The Royal Danish Air Force has a coat of arms for each unit, and replaces the wreath with a wing.

Some RAF units, notably schools and colleges, have a full achievement of arms. The crest of the Central Flying School is a pelican vulning itself (feeding its young with its own blood). The arms of the former Royal Aircraft Establishment

▼ *The arms of a Royal Danish Air Force Squadron painted on an aircraft fuselage.*

symbolized its research into early flight with a pterodactyl, while the Empire Test Pilot School, at Boscombe Down in Wiltshire, had a crest of an eagle rising from an astral coronet, fondly known by the students as the "chicken in a basket". (The College of Arms grants this coronet to institutions associated with aviation, as well as senior ranks of the RAF.) Although the ETPS has been absorbed into the Defence Evaluation and Research Agency, the crest is still retained in outline on the tailfins of the school's training aircraft.

▲ *The air forces of the world tend to adopt a flamboyance not met with in navies and armies. Here a Tornado fighter bomber of the German Air Force, elaborately painted for an air show, still bears the cross of the Teutonic Knights, dating back to the time of the Crusades.*

▼ *The Empire Test Pilot School at Boscombe Down in Wiltshire, England, uses the crest from the unit's arms on its aircrafts' fuselage or tail. It shows an eagle rising from an astral coronet.*

THE POLICE AND SECRET SERVICES

So many police forces have direct or indirect connections with their nation's military forces that it is not surprising to see a marked resemblance between their insignia. However, the United Kingdom appears to be unique in that its heraldic authorities have on several occasions granted full heraldic achievements to police authorities.

POLICE INSIGNIA

The uniform worn by British police forces was standardized in 1934, although many new items of clothing have been added since then. Nearly all bear the insignia of the particular force. Many use armorial bearings or the county arms, and tend to feature the royal cypher within a circlet and star. The most prominent armorial achievement of any British police force must be that of the Metropolitan Police in Greater London, whose portcullis is distinctively featured on its police cars. The arms also include a double tressure flory counter-flory taken from the Scottish royal arms, symbolizing the Met's world-famous headquarters, Scotland Yard.

Like several other police forces that possess arms, the Metropolitan Police does not actually use them on its cap and collar

▼ *This badge follows the pattern set by the Canadian Heraldic Authority for Canada's police badges. The municipal arms and provincial flower are standard elements.*

badges. The Wiltshire Constabulary was granted full armorial bearings in 1989, but does not use them in any form on its insignia and vehicles, although it has gone to the trouble of having a splendid heraldic standard manufactured, which is borne at formal parades. Its design includes the crest of a bustard, the county bird, holding a truncheon. The arms of various other British regional forces feature cap bands, police dogs and even the pavements pounded by policemen "on the beat".

The French and German provincial police bear their provincial or department arms on arm and helmet badges, as do many other regional and municipal police forces worldwide, from New South Wales to Maryland. In France the three fleurs de lis of the Bourbon dynasty, symbols proscribed by the revolutionaries of the First Republic, now serve the police in the Paris (Ile de France) region. In recent years the Canadian Heraldic Authority has granted formal heraldic badges for Canadian municipal police services. All the designs conform to a standard pattern, which includes a shield of arms in its centre.

The police are not the only public service to make use of armorial bearings, whether their own or those of their locality. British ambulance and fire services often sport arms in their insignia, on both uniforms and vehicles. In 1995 the South Wales Fire Service was granted full armorial bearings, which are used on the service's fire engines. The design of the shield is an adaptation of the three chevrons in the arms of the de Clares, the

▲ *The design for the cap badge of the South Wales Fire Service, appropriately charged with its heraldic badge.*

ruling family in the area during the Middle Ages. In the Fire Service design, the chevrons are differenced by being "rayonny" (in flames); above and below the chevrons are "gutty de larmes" (drops of water), and the crest is a lion bearing another heraldic charge, a "water bouget" (leather water bottle) with which to extinguish the flames.

SECURITY SERVICES

The world's so-called secret services are not so secret as to want to remain heraldically invisible. Even the USA's clandestine Phoenix Programme (set up to assassinate Viet Cong collaborators) adopted that mythical bird as its device. The Phoenix

▼ *When on formal parade, the Wiltshire Constabulary fly their standard which includes the crest of the bustard with a truncheon.*

▲ *The patrol cars of Scotland's Lothian and Border Police sport the force's full arms, including the sallet helmet given by the Scottish heralds to corporate organizations.*

Programme was said to be the Central Intelligence Agency's action army during the Vietnam War, and while the phoenix insignia was unofficial, the CIA itself has had armorial bearings since 1950. The shield, Argent a compass rose of sixteen points Gules, and the crest, Or a wreath

▲ *The warning eye of the American bald eagle keeps watch over the shield of the CIA.*

Argent and Gules an American bald eagle's head erased, are officially interpreted as follows: "The American Eagle is the national bird and is a symbol of strength and alertness. The radiating spokes of the compass rose depict the coverage of intelligence data from all areas of the world to a central point." The CIA arms are displayed in many forms, both in the organization's headquarters building and on its medals: the Distinguished Intelligence Medal places the arms on the breast of the national eagle, as befits US governmental institutions.

The old and much respected foe of the CIA, the Soviet Union's Komitet Gosudarstvennoi Bezopasnosti, or KGB, also maintained its own insignia. Its mission as the sword and shield of the state was to protect the hammer and sickle of communism, and it even had its own branch colour, royal blue, the sight of which on its arms, shield and cap bands was enough to put fear in all but the bravest hearts. Its present-day successor, the Federal Security Service, has managed to keep the sword and shield in its insignia, while replacing the hammer and sickle with the old tsarist symbol of the double-headed eagle displayed.

The KGB's most loyal friend, the East German Staatssicherheitsdienst – better known as the Stasi – used the GDR's state arms on its flag and breast badge in a typically militant socialist fashion. This was cynically known amongst Soviet conscripts as "hurrah art".

In Britain the Secret Intelligence Service (MI6), has not bothered to obtain a heraldic device of its own, but has permission to use the royal arms. However, its colleagues in the Security Service (MI5) do use their own heraldic badge designed by the College of Arms. It features a winged sea-lion, reflecting the Service's association with the armed services, and portcullises, symbolic of Parliament, which allude to its function of upholding Parliamentary democracy. The portcullises are interspersed with the rose of secrecy and green cinquefoils, whose five petals refer to MI5,

▲ *The badge of the British Security Service, otherwise known as MI5.*

◀ *The breast badge of the Russian Federal Security Service, successor to the KGB. The design keeps the shield and sword used by the KGB, but replaces the hammer and sickle with the imperial double-headed eagle.*

and whose colour has been associated with intelligence at least since World War I. The Security Service's motto is *Regnum defende*, "Defence of the realm".

▲ *The dreaded East German Security Ministry, better known as the Stasi, included in its insignia the state arms with hammer and compasses.*

INSIGNIA OF OFFICE

Since the late medieval period it has been common for a man or woman of high rank who holds an official position, usually at court, to wear or carry some form of insignia as an emblem of his or her high office. The earliest form of insignia seems to have been a wand or staff, which may have had its origin in ordinary staves such as those carried by shepherds, and examples can be found in the scenes of daily life painted on the walls of Egyptian tombs. Paintings dating from the Old Kingdom (c2700–c2150 bc) depict bailiffs or tax collectors using a form of truncheon when attempting to exact payment from recalcitrant farmers. Wooden batons have also been found in the tombs of Egyptian temple officials, bearing inscriptions asking for long life, prosperity and good health.

OFFICIAL INSIGNIA IN ARMS

Some of the earliest heraldic insignia of office are depicted on the seals of medieval admirals. These use the motif of a sailing

▼ *Under the Bourbons, French court officials placed their insignia, including bottles, horns and wolves' heads, beside their shields.*

ship, with the arms of the officer placed on the ship's sails, flags and streamers. By the 17th century admirals tended to show their office by placing anchors behind their shields of arms. In France, where many insignia of office originated, even rank was indicated by them: admirals of France had a pair of anchors in saltire, the cross bars strewn with fleurs de lis, vice-admirals had one plain anchor in pale behind the shield, and admirals of the galleys placed a grappling anchor behind their shield.

There is no hard and fast rule regarding the bearing of insignia of office. Some appear only as heraldic accoutrements, while others are actual objects, borne on ceremonial occasions. The French court of the 17th and 18th centuries made use of a splendid array of heraldic insignia, ranging from the

▲ *The arms of justice of the hereditary Constables of Navarre are proudly borne at either side of the shield of the Dukes of Alba.*

crowned batons semy de lis of the Master of the Royal Household, to the extraordinary wolves' heads placed on either side of the shield of the Grand Louvetier (Grand Wolf Huntsman).

THE CONSTABLE

As the highest-ranking officer in the medieval army, one of the constable's duties was the overseeing of martial law, including the passing of the death penalty. In time, the shields of the high constables were placed between two "arms of justice" – arms in armour issuing from clouds holding their sword of office. On taking his office, the Constable of France was presented with the sword itself, in a sheath of royal blue, semy de lis. One of the greatest Constables of France was Bertrand du Guesclin, who held the office from 1370–80. When he knew that he was dying, he sent the great sword back to

Grand Bouteiller Echanson
André de Brignole
Supprimée.

Grand Pannetier
Jean Paul Timoléon de Cossé
Duc de Brissac.

Grand Veneur
Louis Jean Marie de Bourbon
Duc de Penthièvre.

Grand Fauconnier
Louis Cesar de la Baume le Blanc
Duc de la Vallière.

Grand Louvetier
le Marquis de Flamarens
le Comte de Flamarens en Survivance.

Grand Maréchal de Logis
Louis Michel Chamillart
Comte de la Suze.

▲ *A painting of the thanksgiving service for George V and Queen Mary, 1935. The Lord Chamberlain leads the Court with his staff of office, and the route is lined by the Yeomen of the Guard in their Tudor tunics.*

Charles V, saying: "Take it and return it into the King's keeping, and do you tell him that I have never betrayed him or it." This the King knew, and remembering du Guesclin's loyalty gave him the rare honour for a commoner of burial in the Abbey of Saint Denis, the traditional resting place for French royalty.

In recent years the constableships of two nations, Navarre and Scotland, have been in the hands of noblewomen. In the former case, the Duchess of Alba (who is the most titled lady in the world) places her shield between the arms of justice, the clouds bearing the arms of Navarre. Her shield quarters the royal arms of the British House of Stuart in a bordure compony (a border divided into segments) signifying illegitimacy, since the Dukes of Alba are descended from a natural son of James II.

THE MARSHAL

In practice, many of the duties of the medieval constable devolved on his deputy, the marshal, who carried a black gold-tipped baton as the insignia of his office. In France, by the reign of Philip IV (1285–1314), the marshal sat in judgement on certain cases at a great marble

table in the Palais de Justice in Paris, administering a blow, or *bastonarde*, to the guilty with his baton.

By the 18th century, the baton seems to have passed wholly into heraldic usage in France, for when Marechal de Duras (1715–89) attempted to try the anti-revolutionary lawyer and historian Simon-Nicolas-Henri Linguet, he threatened to use the baton to condemn him, whereupon Linguet retorted, "Monsieur le Marechal, you would not know how to use it." The marshal did not share the constable's right to the arms of justice in his heraldic achievement: instead he placed crossed batons behind his shield, a practice taken up by marshals throughout much of Europe, including the Earl Marshal of England.

The Riksmarskalsk (Marshal of the Court) of Sweden still has a staff with a maroon shaft decorated with gold crowns, which appears in the armorial achievements of recent holders of the office.

In England, where the hereditary title is held by the Dukes of Norfolk, the Earl Marshal was for centuries unable to exercise his office personally because he was a Catholic, and it was common for his duties to be administered by a deputy, who placed one baton in bend behind his shield. Such a device can often be found in the margins of patents of arms (mainly from the Georgian period). The hereditary constableship, long held by the family of

Stafford, Dukes of Buckingham, was abolished by Henry VIII after the attainder of the third Duke on grounds of treason in 1521. The office is revived temporarily for the coronation of the sovereign, its ceremonial duties being undertaken on other occasions by the Earl Marshal. Conversely, in Scotland, the hereditary post of Earl Marshal, long held in the family of Keith, was lost through attainder. The hereditary constableship of Scotland is alive and well, and is held by the Hays, Earls of Erroll.

▼ *The plaque of a Knight of the Swedish Order of the Seraphim. Behind the shield are the batons of the Marshal to the Royal House and of the Chancellor of the Order.*

THE CHAMBERLAIN

At the Danish court, the Chamberlain has a staff decorated with golden leaves and bears on his court uniform the insignia common to all chamberlains, a gold key – a reminder of the time when such officers were trusted by sovereigns with the keys to their private apartments. Such keys usually have the sovereign's cypher in the bow (the ring at the top of the key). Chamberlains of the British royal household wear the key on Garter blue ribbon.

In heraldry, most chamberlains place crossed keys behind their shield, but in England a Lord Great Chamberlain places the white wands of a high court official in saltire behind the shield, while the key is placed in fess below it. (The title of Lord Great Chamberlain is hereditary but it is not a full-time post, whereas the office of Lord Chamberlain is not hereditary but the holder is involved in the day-to-day running of the royal household.)

THE STAFF OF OFFICE

A wand or staff of office was common to most court officials, and apart from marking their status, it was a useful tool for fending off the common people. Usually

▶ *Proud of his status at court as well as in the Church, Cardinal Wolsey is portrayed here holding the baton of the Lord Chancellor of England.*

▼ *Originally the key to a sovereign's personal apartments, the chamberlain's key – the highest sign of trust – has been worn on his court uniform since the Middle Ages.*

made of wood, or perhaps of ivory, it could be a short baton or as tall as the man who bore it. It was ceremonially presented to the official by his master or mistress when he took up his office, and – equally ceremonially – was broken in pieces when he relinquished the office, or on the death of those whom the officer had served.

Today, the staves of office of the British royal household are little changed from those their predecessors used centuries ago, except for one innovation: a silver ferrule halfway up the shaft, bearing the title of office, has a screw thread that allows the staff to be "broken" ceremonially when the officer relinquishes his post. The two halves are then handed back and can be screwed back together to give the ex-officer a memento of his former position.

The breaking of staves was a popular allegorical theme in former centuries. Elizabeth I of England, during one of her royal progresses around her realm, was "accosted" by a savage man covered in moss and ivy, bearing an oaken staff in his

▼ *The staff of an officer of the royal household is fitted with a screw, allowing it to be re-assembled after its ceremonial "breaking" when the officer retires from his post.*

hand. After regaling the Queen with words in praise of his patron – her favourite, Robert Dudley – the "savage" broke his staff in half, "like a dismissed Chamberlain", and threw away the pieces, unfortunately hitting the Queen's horse on the head with one of them. The ceremonial breaking of the wand of office is made much of in an account of the funeral in 1574 of Edmund, Earl of Derby: "The Steward, Treasurer, and Comptroller, when the body was buried, kneeling on their knees, with weeping tears, brake their staves and rods over their heads, and threw the shivers of the same into the grave."

OFFICIAL BADGES

While much European court ceremonial disappeared, along with the courts themselves, after the end of World War I, little changed in the British royal household. The splendid uniforms of the officers of state were retained, and upon them the jewelled badges and the great golden keys.

Among the most fascinating of the badges is that of the Marshal of the

▼ *The badge of a former Master of Ceremonies to the English court bears the olive branch of peace on the front and the sword of war on the reverse. Nowadays, such a badge is worn by the Marshal of the Diplomatic Corps at the Court of St James.*

Diplomatic Corps, with its oval pendant. On one side it bears a hand grasping an olive branch, and on the other a hand grasping a sword. The story goes that in times of peace the olive branch was turned to the viewer, but when war was declared with another nation, its ambassador would receive an ominous visit from the Marshal – or rather his predecessor the Master of Ceremonies – who by this time would have swivelled his badge around to the martial side. Today, this badge may be glimpsed through the carriage windows when the Marshal of the Diplomatic Corps accompanies a new ambassador on his way to present his credentials to the Queen.

Another badge with a picturesque history is that worn by members of the Corps of Queen's Messengers. These gentlemen attend to the diplomatic mail that passes between British embassies and the Foreign Office, and the nature of their duties has given rise to many tales of bravura and adventure. Their neck badge is an oval bearing the sovereign's cypher within the Garter. Below it runs a little silver greyhound: did this originate from one of the heraldic supporters of the House of Tudor,

▼ *A delicate silver greyhound, perhaps one of the most romantic of all insignia, hangs from the badge of a member of the Corps of Queen's Messengers.*

or did it start life as one of the stands of a silver bowl used by Charles II in exile in the Netherlands? The tale is told that, as he gave his orders to his secret messengers, one asked, "How shall we be known?" King Charles snapped the little greyhounds off the bowl, giving one to each messenger and saying, "This will be your badge."

Neither the badge of the Marshal of the Diplomatic Corps, nor that of the Queen's Messengers, is used in an armorial achievement. In Scotland, however, castle governors, the Lord High Constable and many other high officials are still granted armorial insignia.

The need to be recognized and honoured lies deep within the psyche, a fact remembered by such modern institutions as the burger-bar giant McDonald's, which awards stars to its workforce to be worn as evidence of "rank". Each star has a different design – starting with crossed mop and brush and passing on through burger bun and chip fryer to smiley face (for good customer relations) – and with it comes an increment in pay. In all, five stars can be awarded, making the bearer the equivalent in military rank of a field marshal.

▼ *Doormen in the Palace of Westminster wear the badges of royal messengers. The figure of Mercury below this badge denotes a door keeper of the House of Commons.*

HERALDRY IN UNIVERSITIES AND SCHOOLS

Although they came later to the heraldic scene than towns or ecclesiastical bodies, universities and other major teaching establishments throughout Europe did take up heraldic devices. Often these tended to be limited to seals, but where arms were granted to or assumed by universities and schools, it was common to adopt the heraldic device of the establishment's founder and link it to a symbol of learning.

COLLEGE FOUNDERS

While most universities have arms or a seal common to the entire establishment, the colleges of the major English universities have individual arms which often have ancient origins, again usually with some obvious reference to the founder.

Amongst the most interesting arms are those of Clare College and Pembroke College, both in Cambridge. In the case of Clare College the arms of the husband and wife have been reversed, as Elizabeth, daughter of Gilbert de Clare, 3rd Earl of Gloucester, was considered far more important in estates and degree than her first husband, William de Burgh, Earl of

▲ *Margaret Beaufort's arms grace the entrance to Christ's College, Cambridge.*

Ulster. Her family arms therefore took the heraldically more important side (dexter of the marital shield). Elizabeth outlived three husbands, a fact remembered by the tears of mourning placed on a black border around the arms.

Pembroke College was founded in 1347 by Marie, daughter of Guy de Chastillon, Comte de St Pol, and wife of Aylmer de Valence, 2nd Earl of Pembroke. The

college arms have preserved the practice of dimidiation: the coats of de Valence and de Chastillon are cut down the middle and the dexter half of Valence is wedded to the sinister half of de Chastillon.

The grandest displays of heraldry in Cambridge must surely be the arms of Margaret Beaufort (1443–1509), mother of Henry VII. This proud and pious lady founded two colleges: Christ's and St John's. Both sport the Beaufort arms, complete with their yale supporters. The ground beneath the yales' hooves is scattered with Margaret's cognizance, the daisy flower or marguerite.

Oxford University is not to be outdone in heraldic honours by its younger rival. Among the shields that speak of extraordinary times in English history are the arms of that pompous prince of the Church, Cardinal Thomas Wolsey, Archbishop of York and Lord Chancellor, who founded Christ Church College. Included in the Cardinal's arms are many allusions to the institutions and individuals to which he owed his fortunes. His birthplace, Ipswich, is represented somewhat grandly by the arms of families that

◀ ▶ *The cloisters of the University of Padua are richly decorated with the arms of noble students of previous centuries, which have long outlived their bearers.*

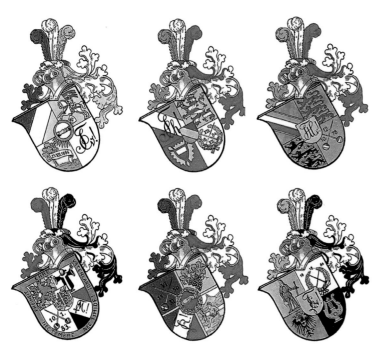

▲ The arms of student fraternities from the University of Heidelberg often bear duelling swords (epées), which can be seen crossed in three of these shields.

▲ The arms of Stephen Coombs, of the Katarinaskolan in Uppsala, Sweden, include the school arms (lower right) and those of his old college, Balliol, Oxford (top right).

at one time held the Earldom of Suffolk: de la Pole (leopards' faces Azure) and Ufford (a cross engrailed). The lion passant guardant on the cross represents Pope Leo X, from whom Wolsey received his cardinal's hat. The rose stands for Wolsey's position as a royal minister and the Cornish choughs are a reference to his namesake, Thomas à Becket.

Each college displays its arms to full effect in many different places, from the façade of the building to the silver on the table. More often than not they will be encountered along with those of benefactors, ancient and modern. In Oxford, the arms of all the colleges can be seen on the doors of the Bodleian Library.

STUDENTS' ARMS
Some European universities made much of the arms of students, since many came from noble families. The finest display of students' arms appears in the precincts of

the University of Padua, in northern Italy. Although it dates mainly from the 19th century, many shields still decorate the university's ancient courtyards and testify to the prestige it enjoyed all over Europe.

A unique feature of German heraldry is the arms of student fraternities displayed in the universities. These fraternities were famous for their duelling societies, and scars on the faces of young noblemen were considered a sign of honour. Each fraternity's members tended to come from the same region, so their arms included not only duelling swords, but also charges taken from the arms of their homeland. The centre of the arms often bore an inescutcheon upon which was placed a motto, or monogram, such as VCF for "Vivat, Crescat, Floreat" (Live, Flourish, Flower).

SCHOOLS
Though school arms are common in Britain, they are unusual elsewhere in Europe. The tradition does exist in Sweden, where schools display heraldic flags of their municipality. In 1993, the Katarinaskolan (St Katherine's School) at Uppsala assumed arms that were registered

in the Skandinavisk Vapenrulla (the Scandinavian Roll of Arms). They were the suggestion of Stephen Coombs, the Chairman of the Board of the School's Educational Foundation, and take as their badge a Catherine wheel surmounted by a cross formy. The wheel with its spikes refers to the martyrdom of St Katherine, but is also identified with Little Karin who, according to a Swedish folk song, was laid in a barrel with spikes.

▲ Religion was central to the medieval scholar's life and often a school or college looked to a particular saint for patronage. The arms of Eton College, for example, are charged with the lilies of the Virgin Mary.

MEDICAL HERALDRY

Most corporate heraldry contains a number of common symbols or charges that are particularly related to the profession or institution concerned. These charges can get very repetitive, but they do provide a clue to identity. They are a phenomenon chiefly related to British and Commonwealth heraldry, and are not often found elsewhere. The charges that frequently appear in arms related to medicine are good examples of this kind of usage.

Some medical arms, such as those of St Bartholomew's Hospital in London, have no such charges. William Wakering, Master of the Hospital from 1423–62, used the armorial bearings Per pale Argent and Sable a chevron counterchanged. These arms were not granted to Wakering or his family but because he was Master for such a long time they became associated with the hospital and are recorded as such in a 16th-century roll of arms.

SNAKES AND OTHER BEASTS

A good example of a "themed" charge is the snake, which almost invariably has a connection with medicine and is frequently used by medical institutions as well as in the personal arms of medical practitioners. For centuries the snake was thought to possess wisdom and mysterious healing powers. Temples used by ancient healers included pits of harmless snakes, thought to have healing properties.

▲ *Lord Leycester's Hospital in Warwick, England, maintains a fine display of heraldry, including the bear and ragged staff of the Earls of Warwick and the shield of the Dudley family above it.*

As snakes periodically shed their skin, appearing to be reborn, they were seen as vehicles of immortality.

Snakes were also associated with Aesculapius, the Greek and Roman god of medicine. A legend told that as he was examining a patient, a serpent crept in, climbed his staff and imbued him with wisdom. In heraldry, the snake is usually depicted twined about a rod, known as the staff of Aesculapius. Snakes can also be found in other attitudes, such as knotted, or devouring their own tails, and may be

entwined about other charges. A particular species may be blazoned occasionally, such as the red-bellied black snake of the Royal Brisbane Hospital, or the Children's python (*Liasis childreni*) in the arms of the Australian Royal Children's Hospital Board.

Two mythical creatures more or less exclusive to medical heraldry are the caladrius and the opinicus. The caladrius, a bird found in ancient bestiaries, was credited with therapeutic powers. It was pure white, and the lower part of its leg was reputed to "purge" diseases of the eye. The opinicus had lion's legs, dragon's wings, pointed ears, a long bill and a camel's tail. It was granted as a crest to the Barber Surgeons of London in 1561.

INANIMATE CHARGES

Surgical instruments have been used as heraldic charges from early times. Perhaps the best known is the fleam, a form of lancet used for blood-letting. In heraldry it resembles an elaborate figure seven. It was used in the arms of the Company of Barbers of London in 1451. A spatula was included in the badge of the Fellowship of Surgeons of London in 1492, and both instruments were incorporated in the arms of the Worshipful Company of Barber Surgeons of London in 1569.

In its arms granted in 1672, the Royal College of Surgeons of Edinburgh has a bordure charged with seven surgical instruments which, though not specified individually, are described as "several instruments indicative of the art". Scalpels, ophthalmoscopes, inhalers, dental and mammary probes and syringes have all been used as charges.

The shield of the Royal College of Pathologists (1971) is Argent a bar wavy Gules between in chief two torteaux and in base a benzene ring Sable. The use of straightforward charges illustrates the four disciplines of pathology: the red wavy line suggests histopathology, one torteau represents a red cell for haematology, and the second stands for biology. Microbiology is represented by the benzene ring.

▼ *The gates of Bristol General Hospital, bearing fine representations of the city arms.*

▲ *In the arms of the British Association of Urological Surgeons, the compartment is appropriately strewn with sweet peas.*

▲ *In the arms of The Faculty of Accident and Emergency Medicine, a wounded supporter sports a multitude of injuries.*

Plants naturally have a place in medical heraldry by virtue of their curative properties. The foxglove, opium poppy and cocaine plant are all associated with anaesthetics or painkillers. The mandrake is found in the crest of the Association of Anaesthetists of Great Britain and Ireland (1945). A poisonous plant of southern Europe, it was used in the Middle Ages as a sedative and painkiller. Its knobbly, forked roots were thought to resemble the human figure, and when pulled from the ground it supposedly emitted a piercing shriek that sent people mad. The pome-

▼ *The Urological Society of Australia's charge of a view up the neck of the bladder when peered at through a cystoscope.*

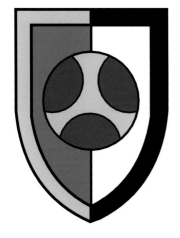

granate is usually depicted in heraldry as split, showing its many seeds, and is used to represent fertility. It was used in the arms of the Royal College of Physicians by Garter Barker in 1546. In more modern times, a British institution serving urologists has been granted arms in which the compartment is strewn with sweet peas.

SUPPORTERS

The supporters of medical arms include mythical beasts, real animals and birds, and real people as well as gods and goddesses. The latter, in addition to Aesculapius, include his daughter Hygeia, goddess of health. She is shown holding a bowl with a snake entwined about her arm drinking from the bowl. Machaon and Podalrius, sons of Aesculapius, are also often used. They were said to have been Greek surgeons at the Siege of Troy, where Machaon removed an arrow from the wounded Menelaus. Machaon is usually seen holding a broken arrow in his hand. Egyptian deities are represented in British arms by the goddess Isis, who appears in the arms of the National Institute of Medical Herbalists, and by Imhotep, the god of medicine, seen in the arms of the Institute of Health Service Management.

The patron saints of surgeons, Cosimo and Damian, support the arms of the Fellowship of Surgeons, and St Barbara, the patron saint of the injured, supports the shield of the Institute of Accident

Surgery. Hippocrates, founder of medical ethics, appears in several achievements.

More recent medical figures include William Harvey (1578–1657), who discovered the circulation of the blood and supports the arms of the British Medical Association, and Dr Benjamin Golding, founder of Charing Cross Hospital in 1818. British anaesthetists, Dr John Snow (1813–58) and Dr Joseph Clover (1825–82) support the shield of the Royal College of Anaesthetists. The sinister supporter of the Arms of the Royal College of Paediatrics and Child Health is Thomas Phaire, author of the first book on paediatrics written in English in 1553.

Anonymous figures include nurses in uniform and – for the Royal Victoria Eye & Ear Hospital, Australia – a surgeon gowned and ready for the operating theatre. A boy and a girl support the shield of the Australian Royal Children's Hospital.

The horn of the unicorn was believed to possess healing as well as aphrodisiac properties when ground down, and when hollowed out and used as a cup it was thought to combat poisonous substances. The horn of the rhinoceros was thought to possess similar properties, and both are displayed as the crest and supporters of the Society of Apothecaries.

▼ *The shield of a 19th-century English doctor, Thomas Smith, combines the hand feeling a pulse of the College of Physicians, with the rod and serpent of Aesculapius.*

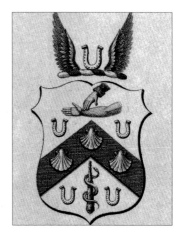

GUILDS AND LIVERY COMPANIES

In the late medieval period the growing wealth and power of the mercantile classes, and the guilds and fraternities to which they belonged, allowed them to make inroads into the preserves of the aristocracy. Naturally, the latter were none too happy about this chipping away of their prerogatives by the self-made men who had their power bases in the cities of Europe. However, various laws that attempted to safeguard the dress and other attributes of the nobility were of little use: the money of the merchants could not be ignored by lords or even kings.

Merchants and craftsmen organized themselves into guilds that safeguarded their trades, which were in some ways the forerunners of modern trades unions. A member who had served as an apprentice in his craft, and who had paid his dues and been initiated into the rites and mysteries

of the guild, could expect a degree of protection against the hardships of medieval life. On his death he would know that the other guild members would give him a splendid funeral, complete with heraldry.

The wealth of the guilds, and of the individuals who made up their numbers, was vast. Merchants were often richer and lived in greater splendour than any petty European prince. It is not surprising that among the earliest English patents of arms are those of several guilds. The very same arms – such as those of the Mercers, Vintners, and all the other trades that helped to make the living in London among the richest in the medieval world – may still be seen in the annual Lord Mayor's Procession through the city. Each guild, or livery company, makes its presence known through its own particular arms and colours, or liveries.

THE GREAT TWELVE

The order of precedence of the London livery companies (of which there are now over 100) was established in 1515. The most senior companies are known as the Great Twelve, and are:

1 Mercers
2 Grocers
3 Drapers
4 Fishmongers
5 Goldsmiths
6/7 Merchant Taylors
7/6 Skinners
8 Haberdashers
9 Salters
10 Ironmongers
11 Vintners
12 Clothworkers

The Merchant Taylors and the Skinners disputed the sixth and seventh positions in the list, and as a result they change places every year at Easter (hence the expression "at sixes and sevens").

▲ Heraldry has come a long way from the medieval battlefield to the Nottinghamshire coalfield of Manton Colliery.

◄ The traditional procession in Siena, Italy, of the city's guilds, where the participants dress in medieval costume.

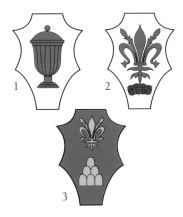

▲ *The officers and magistrates of the city state of Florence enjoyed their own arms of office, including: 1 Masters of the Salt, 2 members of the Mercantile Tribunal, 3 officers of the* monte comune *(the public debt).*

CRAFT SYMBOLS

All over Europe the pride men took in their professions and civic status was made manifest in symbol and colour. If he had not yet become armigerous, the merchant could content himself by showing off his individual mark, possibly placed on a shield. Many churches and houses from England to Switzerland were decorated

▼ *In 1715 Thomas Doggett, a staunch Hanoverian, instituted a rowing race on the River Thames. Six royal watermen still compete for the coat and badge, shown here, which bears the white horse of Hanover.*

with such marks, often in the form of initials and crosses. In England, merchants of the wool trade, or "staple", used such devices not only on their homes but also to mark their wool bales.

The arms of the guilds often included some obvious symbol of their craft, such as a pretzel for the bakers and an ox and axe for the butchers. The guild's patron saint was also often included, although after the Reformation in England several livery companies adopted new arms more attuned to the times, and any symbols overtly associated with Catholicism were judiciously shelved.

From such fraternities, other organizations emerged, such as the freemasons, in whose ceremonial heraldry plays its part.

▲ *A medieval grant of arms to the Tallow Chandlers of London, 1463. The power of the city guilds was made manifest through the splendour of their arms.*

Their insignia apes that of a royal household, with keys and staves of office like any court chamberlain. The "jewels" of lodge officers often include not only the arms of the town or region from which the lodge members come, but also the arms of influential local families, who may have provided past masters of the lodge.

▼ *In procession in Bruges, Belgium, the guilds still make a fine showing of their arms, most of which include motifs alluding to their particular trades.*

GLOBAL
HERALDRY

Although heraldry uses an international language, achievements of arms
have always been devised and regulated by national authorities. The royal
heralds, around whom the various heraldic institutions grew up, were in
the service of individual monarchs, and over the centuries many nations
developed their own distinct heraldic styles. From its beginnings in
northern Europe, heraldry spread all over the world during the eras of
global exploration and conquest. While some countries no longer maintain
their own heraldic authorities, the tradition is thriving in many parts of the
world, and new ideas and artistic innovations continue to
invigorate the heraldic realm.

◀ *The arms of the Jewish congregation of Shaar
Hashomayim in Canada, with the crest borne on a
helmet in the style of the Maccabeans.*

SCOTLAND

No country has a more diverse and fascinating application of heraldry than Scotland. It is one of the few nations with a true heraldic institution that can boast a continuous history going back centuries. Although smaller than the English College of Arms, the Court of Lord Lyon is every bit as adventurous and innovative when it comes to heraldic interpretation and application.

THE COURT OF LORD LYON

In Scotland the chief herald is Lord Lyon King of Arms. In the old kingdom of Scotland, Lord Lyon was a Privy Councillor and minister of the crown. The nature of kinship, which permeated Scottish society at all levels, gave rise to a regiment of men known as "sennachie", or bards, who called out the pedigrees and histories of the chiefs of clans and "septs" (other families loyal to a clan) at formal gatherings. Lord Lyon was Chief Sennachie of the royal line, and it was his duty to recite the king's pedigree during a coronation.

The new Lord Lyon, appointed in 2001, is considered to be more attuned to the legal side of his duties than to the heraldic side. This reflects the fact that he is concerned with many matters attached to Scottish clanship, and may often be

▼ Scottish Officers of Arms make a proclamation in Edinburgh.

involved in the judging of genealogies. The sacrosanct nature of heraldry in Scotland means that Lord Lyon's roar can be very loud. In recent years Sir Malcolm Innes, when Lyon, pursued anyone who presumed to bear arms not officially registered, from ice cream vendors and football teams to the owner of Harrods. In January 2000, Mohamed Al Fayed was ordered to remove the arms of the Chief of Clan Ross, which he had erected on his Scottish castle, Balnagowan, the ancestral home of the Ross family.

That case pales into insignificance compared with a 1958 grant of arms to the English town of Berwick-on-Tweed, which until 1482 was part of Scotland. The town council petitioned the English heralds for a coat of arms, but seemed to dislike the design. The townspeople then petitioned Lord Lyon, since in Scotland ancient arms are a form of heritable property, and it was held that Berwick had established an ancient right to arms in Scotland.

The heraldic author Lt Col Robert Gayre stated that Scotland could look upon Berwick as occupied territory, wrested from its own country and held as a base for further pretentious aggression against Scotland. The arms Lord Lyon matriculated included not only the bear and wych-elm, but also chained bears for supporters and the coronet and compartment applicable to a Scottish royal burgh. Eventually, the

▲ The arms of Berwick-upon-Tweed as matriculated with the Scottish heraldic authorities in 1958.

controversy died down and Berwick received a patent from the College of Arms in 1977: this time they ensured that the bear and wych-elm had prime position.

With the exception of Lord Lyon and Lyon Clerk, the Scottish heralds are paid only nominal fees and pursue full-time careers elsewhere, often in spheres appropriate to their heraldic duties, such as in law firms and museums or as artists. There are three heralds in ordinary: Marchmont, Rothesay and Dingwall, and four pursuivants in ordinary: Dingwall, Kintyre, Carrick and Unicorn. There are also two pursuivants extraordinary: Falkland and March. In addition, some Scottish peers of ancient title are entitled to their own private officer of arms: the herald of the Earls of Erroll, Hereditary High Constables of Scotland, is called Slains Pursuivant and bears a tabard of his master's arms, Argent three escutcheons Gules.

The Scottish officers of arms can be seen wearing their tabards and badges of office on such occasions as the installation of the Governor of Edinburgh Castle, when the standard of the Governor is unfurled above the Castle gates. The standard bears both the arms of his office and his personal arms. Also on view are the six Scottish State Trumpeters, with the royal arms of Scotland embroidered on their trumpet banners. The State Trumpeters also attend Lord Lyon at the reading of royal proclamations at the Mercat Cross in Edinburgh.

THE ARMS OF SCOTLAND

The red lion rampant within a double tressure flory counter-flory, was first used on a seal of Alexander III of Scotland in 1251, although the red lion was probably previously used by William I, "The Lion" (1165–1214), and a border of fleurs de lis was used in the arms of his son, Alexander II (1214–49). When James VI of Scotland acceded to the English throne in 1603 after the Act of Union (as James I), the ramping lion of the Scots was placed in the second quarter of the royal arms. When the British sovereign visits Scotland the quarters are reversed, Scotland taking the first quarter.

The British royal family is, in effect, the chief clan of Scotland and uses certain heraldic insignia as with any other clan. Royal Stewart tartan and its variants are worn, and the royal crest for Scotland may at times be observed. The sovereign's eldest son has his own heraldic banner for use in Scotland, where he is Duke of Rothesay, Earl of Carrick, Baron Renfrew, Lord of the Isles, Great Steward of Scotland. He uses a plain label in conjunction with his Scottish arms.

THE ORDER OF THE THISTLE

Scotland's own order of chivalry is the Most Ancient and Most Noble Order of the Thistle, founded in 1540, and its Knights in their dark green mantles take their places in the stalls of the Chapel of the Order, attached to St Giles Cathedral in Edinburgh. The Chapel, inaugurated in 1911, is full of heraldic symbolism, and attached to the stall backs are the stall plates of the Thistle Knights, while their banners are grouped around the pillars in the body of the Cathedral.

THE ROYAL COMPANY OF ARCHERS

In Scotland the sovereign's bodyguard is formed by the Royal Company of Archers. Originating as a private archery club in 1676, it received a royal charter from Queen Anne, for which the "reddendo", or service in return, was to present the sovereign, when

▲ *The jacket of an archer in the Royal Company of Archers, topped with the bonnet of an officer, with two feathers.*

▼ *The hat of the High Constable of Holyroodhouse, with black cock's feathers and the silver stag and cross of Holyrood.*

> ### BLAZON OF THE ROYAL ARMS
> As Queen of the Scots, Elizabeth II bears Quarterly 1 and 4 Or a lion rampant Gules armed Or and langued Azure, within a double tressure flory counter-flory of the second [Scotland]; 2 Gules three lions passant guardant Or [England]; 3 Azure a harp Or stringed Argent [Ireland]. Encircling the shield is the collar of the Most Ancient and Most Noble Order of the Thistle. The crest is an imperial crown proper surmounted by a lion sejant affronty Gules imperially crowned holding in his dexter paw a bared sword and in his sinister a sceptre, both proper. On a compartment vert with thistles proper are the supporters: dexter a unicorn Argent armed tufted and langued Or imperially crowned proper and gorged with an open crown chain reflexed over the back Or and supporting a banner of St Andrew; sinister a lion rampant guardant Or imperially crowned proper supporting a banner of St George. On a scroll above is the motto *In defens*; and in the compartment the motto of the Order of the Thistle, *Nemo me impune lacessit.*
>
>

▶ *The baton of office of the Hereditary Master of the Household in Scotland, a position held by the Dukes of Argyll, has at its head the lion that surmounts the crest of the Scottish royal arms.*

requested, with a pair of barbed arrows (an archer's "pair" numbering three). The Company's field uniform is dark green with crimson piping for men, gold for officers, and its insignia includes the reddendo of arrows and the star of the Order of the Thistle. The officers also have collar badges. Their bonnets are decorated with eagles' feathers: one for men, two for officers and three for the Captain General. The Secretary outclasses them all, by wearing a Malayan condor's feather.

THE SCOTTISH CLAN SYSTEM

The clan – the word stems from the Gaelic for "children" – is an enlarged family unit. It ensures that all within its ranks are equal. The common kinship of the clan, whether real or nominal, knits together every Highland community. While official records refer to the Earl of Argyll, the Lord of the Isles or Lord Lovat (as they would be known in Edinburgh), in their own lands these lords are simply called the MacCailean mor (son of great Colin), the MacDonnal (son of Donald), or the MacShimidh (son of Simon).

Although predominantly a Highland phenomenon, the clan system was also found in the Lowlands, amongst great names such as the Douglases. The terrible feuding between Highland and Lowland clans reached the highest levels of Scots society and had many victims within the royal house itself, as kings were often merely the pawns of other great families. It is a theme often reflected in heraldry. Even a playing card, the nine of diamonds, is called the "curse of Scotland" because nine lozenges appear in the arms of John Dalrymple, 1st Earl of Stair, who instigated

▼ *At a gathering of Clan Donald at their ancestral seat, banners of the chief and chieftains are much in evidence.*

the massacre of the Macdonalds at Glencoe in 1692. The hammer in the arms of Naesmyth and the oak tree and frame saw in the crest of Hamilton both refer to incidents during which family members had to disguise themselves as workers to avoid discovery by enemies pursuing them during Scotland's more turbulent moments.

CLAN INSIGNIA

Personal heraldry in Scotland is closely linked with the clan system, and stringent rules protect armigers and their heraldic status. The full panoply of clan insignia can be seen at annual clan gatherings, at events such as the Highland Games. Apart from wearing the clan tartan, of which there may be several versions, clan members wear on their bonnets a silver badge (or for women, a brooch) of the chief's crest within a strap and buckle, which also bears the chief's motto, slogan or war cry.

The crest on the badge is not that of the wearer but the property of the clan chief. Armigers may display their own crest within a plain circlet bearing motto or slogan, and place this behind the badge on a silver feather. The head of a large clan branch, officially recognized as such by the Lord Lyon, may bear crest, circlet and motto with two feathers. A clan chief

▲ *The arms of the late Sir Fitzroy Maclean include a feudal baron's cap and insignia of the hereditary Keeper of Dunconnel.*

places three feathers behind the badge, and a peer may add the appropriate coronet of rank. Even members of the royal family keep to this tradition, wearing the Scottish royal crest on Balmoral bonnets.

HERALDIC FLAGS

At a clan gathering a selection of heraldic flags will be on display, representing the clan chief, chieftains (the heads of family branches) and other senior figures. Such flags are closely regulated by Lord Lyon and come under his legal jurisdiction through an Act of Parliament of 1672. All are recorded on the matriculations of arms of those entitled to such honours.

The most important flag to look out for is the standard, which is granted only to those who have a "following", such as a clan chief. One of the most splendid heraldic accoutrements in use today, the Scottish standard has an unbroken history from the feudal standard of the late Middle Ages. It is viewed as a headquarters flag

and does not necessarily mean that the chief is present: this is indicated by the square personal banner displaying his own arms. Ancient Scottish standards normally had the saltire on the hoist (the section of the flag nearest the pole), but modern standards more often bear the owner's personal arms in this area. The remainder is divided into two tracts of the livery colours for chiefs of clans or families, three tracts for very major branches – chieftains – and four for others. The standard is very long, ranging from 7 metres (8 yards) for the sovereign to 3.5 metres (4 yards) for knights and barons. It is tapered and split into two rounded ends (for peers and barons), or unsplit with a rounded end for non-baronial chiefs. It usually bears the owner's crest and heraldic badges, which include the clan's plant badge separated by transverse bands bearing the owner's motto or slogan. If the owner is a peer or feudal baron, the flagpole may be ensigned by a coronet or chapeau of degree.

The guidon is similar to a small standard, one third shorter than the standard assigned to feudal barons. It is assigned to

▼ *The Braw Lads Gathering, Galashiels – one of several "ridings" in Scotland where heraldry is much in evidence.*

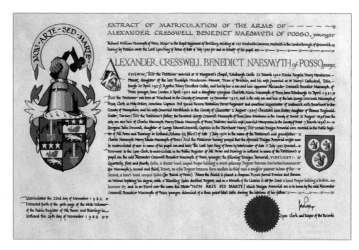

EXTRACT OF MATRICULATION OF THE ARMS OF ~ ~ ~ ~ ~
ALEXANDER CRESSWELL BENEDICT NAESMYTH OF POSSO, younger

▲ *A matriculation of arms for Alexander Naesmyth of Posso, from the Court of Lord Lyon. This includes the feudal chapeau for an heir of a barony not in possession.*

lairds (the rough equivalent of English lords of the manor) who have a following.

The fourth type of flag to look out for is the "pinsel". This triangular flag denotes a person who represents the chief in his or her absence. On the chief's main livery colour is his or her crest within a strap of the second livery colour and a buckle (gold for full chiefs) bearing the motto. Outside the strap and buckle, a gold circlet is inscribed with the chief's or baron's title. On top is the coronet of rank or baronial cap. The flag also bears the plant badge and a scroll inscribed with the motto.

FEUDAL BARONIES

The clan chief or chieftain may also be a feudal baron. Lands that have been vested by charter from the Crown (or, rarely, by other high nobles) give the possessor special rights, including certain forms of public justice not normally found on ordinary estates. The holders of such feudal baronies are termed barons or baronesses. (The Scottish equivalent of an English baron is a lord of Parliament.) Before 1587, feudal barons were also entitled to sit in the Scottish Parliament, so the holders of Scottish feudal baronies enjoy certain heraldic honours akin to those of the peerage. These include a chapeau or cap of maintenance, which is placed directly above the shield between it and the helm. The colour of the chapeau shows the particular form of barony:

1 Chapeau Gules, furred ermine: baron of the kingdom of Scotland still in possession of the barony.

2 Chapeau Azure, furred ermine: the heir to such a barony, not in possession.

3 Chapeau Gules, furred ermines (contre-ermine): a baron of Argyll and the Isles, or one of the older earldoms still in possession.

4 Chapeau Azure, furred ermines: the heir to such a barony, not in possession.

Scottish barons place behind their shield a feudal-baronial mantle, Gules, doubled of silk Argent, fur-edged of miniver and collar ermine, and fastened on the right shoulder by five spherical buttons Or.

The heirs of barons possessed of a barony before 1587 are entitled to clan heraldic supporters (this may also be the case for barons before 1627, but the point is not fully resolved). Feudal barons may also display a baronial helmet, "of steel with a grille of one or three grilles garnished with gold". A barony implicitly has a baron court, of which the presiding judge is baron-baillie and the executive officer is the baron-serjeant. Each has his own insignia and is entitled to heraldic mention of these when matriculating arms.

WALES

Over the centuries British monarchs have maintained in their shields heraldic references to the major nations over which they ruled: the "leopards" of England, the ramping lion of the Scots and the harp of Ireland. Yet one nation, Wales, has seldom figured within their achievements. There never was a king of all Wales, the country was split for centuries into kingdoms, principalities and lordships, and the Welsh had their own names for each degree. Under the English crown Wales has always been called a principality.

Not surprisingly, the Welsh themselves have often seen this as an example of the desultory way in which the government in London regards them. It is telling that the name "Wales" comes from an Anglo-Saxon term for "stranger". The strangers in this case were the Celtic inhabitants of the British Isles who took refuge from the Anglo Saxons in the hinterland of Wales.

After 1066, the Welsh gained new neighbours, the Normans, who in time made inroads into Wales itself. The Norman and Plantagenet kings often gave the borderlands to their most trusted nobles, who marked out for themselves semi-independent territories. One of the most imperious of those Anglo-Norman dynasties was the family of de Clare, Earls of Pembroke and Gloucester. They were early enthusiasts of heraldry, and it was through the de Clares and other Norman magnates that it spread to Wales.

Although it was not as widespread and popular among the English nobility, heraldry was certainly being used by the middle of the 13th century. In Gwynned, for instance, two sons of Llewelyn the Great used arms quartered with four counterchanged lions passant, gold and red being the favourite colours.

THE IMPORTANCE OF LINEAGE

Anyone in medieval Wales, of whatever status, was expected to be able to recite his or her own lineage for five generations. Surnames were not used, except among the English settlers. A man was Evan, son

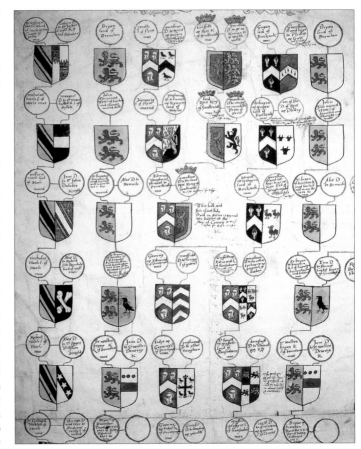

▲ The Welsh interest in genealogy is demonstrated by this pedigree of 1593 for Anne Harle, showing descent from Edward Vaughan, Lord Steward of all Wales.

▶ This 19th-century bookplate for a Welsh family includes many of the arms attributed to the princes and noble tribes.

of Howel, son of Llewelyn, and so on. The close-knit nature of Welsh society meant that no further recognition was needed, and the local bards could always be called upon to recite a full lineage.

The all-powerful figure in Welsh lineage was the antecedent known as the noble progenitor. Most of these dated from the

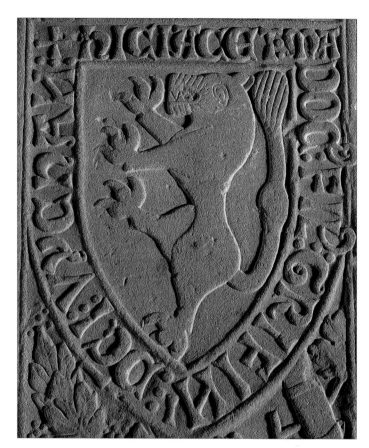

▲ *Heraldry was introduced into Wales by the late 13th century and its style was often adapted to suit Celtic taste, as here on the gravestone of Madog ap Gruffudd, Vale Crucis Abbey, Clwyd.*

▼ *One of Ada Lansdown-Williams' modern painted tiles displaying her lineage in her house near St Davids.*

in general, it seemed that they would have been of armigerous status whenever they lived, and that their descendants were automatically entitled to the arms – whether real or attributed – of their noble progenitor. Such arms were invented, often using symbols taken from the potent store of bardic poetry and story-telling.

Many Welsh families still proclaim their descent from one or more of those warrior lords. One such ruler was Hywel Dda (Hywel the Good), "The Law Giver", whose 10th-century realm covered much of South Wales. Among many sensible and pragmatic laws he made was this: "It is required of those of noble descent, that their lineage be proclaimed to all in prominent places about their dwellings."

An extraordinary interpretation of this command was made around 1909 by Mrs Ada Lansdown-Williams, who used heraldry to display not only her own lineage but that of her husband, in her manor house on the Welsh coast. The house, now a hotel, contains a display of painted tiles illustrating a lineage going back to the times of the Law Giver himself. She seems to have completed her heraldic scheme in time for the 1,000th anniversary of Hywel Dda's accession. It is a glorious reminder of the staying-power of Celtic lore.

Dark Ages, when the power vacuum left after the collapse of Roman power was filled by the rule of tribal leaders, strong men whose character bound the people together in desperate times. Some were real men, others semi-legendary. It has been suggested that King Arthur himself was an amalgam of several rulers. To the Welsh people of the late medieval period, men like Cilmin Troed-ddu (Cilmin of the Black Foot) of Caernarvonshire, or Hedd Molwynog of Denbighshire, were most certainly real people and a proud ancestry to be preserved and honoured.

As heraldry filtered into Wales through warfare, trade and even inter-marriage, arms were assumed by some Welsh magnates, such as Gruffyd ap Llewelyn (the Great). More often, they were attributed to chieftains who had ruled in pre-heraldic times. To the bards, and to Welsh society

THE DRAGON OF WALES
Linked with King Arthur, the red dragon was also said to have been the emblem of Cadwalader, a Welsh prince of the 7th century. The Tudor dynasty used Cadwalader's dragon in their armorial bearings, notably as a supporter, and to this day the badge of the Prince of Wales is a red dragon.

WELSH TRIBAL ARMS

In 1485 a Welshman, Henry Tudor, Earl of Richmond, succeeded by right of battle to the English throne. The Welsh nobles who followed in his wake often sought to register not only their pedigrees but their arms with the English heralds. The continuity of the oral tradition meant that a Welsh pedigree was likely to be more genuine than many of the illuminated family trees drawn up for English earls and barons. The English heralds were quick to recognize the authenticity of Welsh gentility, and maintained close relations with the bards.

The arms of the Welsh royal and noble tribes are for the most part extremely simple, with lions the favourite charges. The same arms were often borne by many families, each claiming descent from a common ancestor. It is tempting to see parallels between the Welsh noble tribe and the Polish *ród*, and it is true that several Welsh families may be grouped under one heraldic emblem. However, in Wales the arms definitely descend from just one person to his descendants alone. Whereas in Polish heraldry a shield hardly ever bears more than one distinct coat, Welsh family arms often show several quarterings, some of which (through marriage with other close-linked families) may be repeated.

For a nation rich in legend it is not surprising to find charges with stories to tell in Welsh arms. Several legends surround

the arms of Moreiddig Warwyn of Breconshire, who lived in the 12th century. The name Warwyn means "Fair Neck" and may reflect an unusual birthmark on his neck. One tale tells how his mother, while pregnant, was sleeping in her garden and awoke to find an adder sliding over her. Her fright manifested itself through her son's birthmark, hence the snake wrapped around the boy's neck which appears in his arms and those of the families claiming descent from him, notably the Vaughans of Golden Grove and Tretower.

Another famous tale concerns the arms of Cadifor ap Dinawal, Lord of Castell Hywel in South Glamorganshire. In 1165 the Lord Rhys, ruler of Deheubarth, attacked Cardigan Castle, held by one of the great Anglo-Norman families, the de Clares. Scaling ladders were put up against the castle walls and the first over the battlements was Cadifor. The Lord Rhys rewarded Cadifor with grants of land and his own daughter in marriage. The arms of Cadifor's descendants include the three ladders and a castle on a chief, with a spearhead "imbrued" (blooded).

Despite the intermittent feuding between the Welsh and English throughout much of the medieval period, families

◀ The lesser arms of Charles, Prince of Wales. The escutcheon is charged with the arms of the last native Prince, Llewelyn the Great.

from either side took root on the "foreign" side of the border. In time this led to English families dropping their surnames and adopting the practice of reciting their lineage. The Williams family of Abercamlais, Penpont and Aberavon in Breconshire is one such. Their arms (Argent a chevron Gules between three bulls' heads couped Sable) are the same as those of Bullen or Bollon, for the Williams claim descent from Lawrence or Thomas de Boulogne, one of the Anglo-Norman knights in the van of Bernard de Newmarch during the conquest of Breconshire. Sir Thomas Boulogne, or Bullen, was rewarded with lands in the Upper Usk Valley and his descendants live there still (one descendant of the English branch of the family was said to be Anne Boleyn, mother of Elizabeth I). In time, the name Boulogne was dropped and the son of Lawrence, following the Welsh custom, was called John ap Lawrence. Three generations later a son called William was born and his name, once again following the English custom, was adopted as a surname.

THE PRINCE OF WALES

After centuries of strife, Llewelyn the Great succeeded in unifying Wales, and was recognized as Prince of Wales by the English monarch, Henry III (1216–72). Llewelyn's grandson used his grandfather's title but was a thorn in the side of Edward I (1272–1307) and was defeated in 1282. Edward created his son, the future Edward II, the first English Prince of Wales.

The famous badge of three ostrich feathers, thought of as that of the Princes of Wales, dates from the lifetime of Edward the Black Prince, who was created Prince of Wales by his father Edward III in 1343. It is not actually the badge of the Prince of Wales but is in fact that of the heir to the English throne.

▼ The later arms of the Tudors, with three helmets replacing Englishmen's heads: not a good design to flaunt at the English court.

▼ From Welsh gentry to English earl: Edmund Tudor was made Earl of Richmond by his half-brother King Henry VI.

The following shields are a selection of the arms that appear frequently in Welsh genealogies. Some were actually used, but many were attributed later by the bards.

▲ Arms of Ynyr, King of Gwent.

▲ Arms of Rees ap Tewdwr, King of Deheubarth, used by Earls of Shrewsbury.

▲ Arms of the founder of the 15th Noble Tribe, Edynwain ap Bradwen.

▲ Arms of Cadifor ap Dinawal, reflecting his attack on Cardigan Castle.

▲ Arms of Jystyn ap Gwyrgant, King of Morgannwg.

▲ Arms of Elystan Glodrudd, King between the Wye and the Severn (old Radnorshire).

▲ Arms of Cilmin Troed-ddu ("of the Black Foot"), founder of the 4th Noble Tribe.

▲ Arms of Moreiddig Warwyn ("Fair Neck") often used by the Vaughan family.

▲ Arms of Gruffyd ap Cynan, King of Gwynedd, d1137.

IRELAND

The Irish came late to heraldry. It had little place in Gaelic culture, which had its own rich tradition of symbols. When heraldry did arrive from England, it was seen as yet another foreign import, baggage associated with the hated Anglo-Norman adventurers who managed to gain a foothold on Ireland's south-east coast during the 12th and 13th centuries. The narrow stretch of land, with its capital in Dublin, was termed "the pale": within this area the Norman lords and merchants felt secure from the native Irish who were, literally, "beyond the pale".

The arrival of heraldry in Ireland was associated with the English elite. Families such as Butler and Fitzgerald, who in time became more Irish than the Irish, spent as much time feuding against each other as they did fighting their Gaelic neighbours. The simple arms of these two families – Argent a saltire Gules for the Fitzgeralds, Or a chief indented Azure for the Butlers – reflects their early adoption.

IRISH CHARGES

In time the indigenous Gaelic nobility did become curious about heraldry, although often in a somewhat desultory fashion. Symbols that had formed part of a pre-heraldic tradition found their way on to shields of arms, where they often seem ill-placed and haphazard. Charges are cramped and squeezed into the foot of the

▲ *The arms of O'Neill, with "internal supporters", the sacred salmon and the famous red hand.*

▲ *Symbols of piety are often found in the arms of Irish Catholic families, such as those of O'Donnell.*

shield, or propped up against other main charges. A particularly Irish phenomenon is the use of animals on shields to support another charge (such as the red hand). These "internal supporters" probably started life supporting the shield in the normal way but were shifted on to the shield through a mistake on the part of the stonemason or woodcarver reproducing the arms.

Among the symbols with mystic origins favoured by the Gaelic Irish was the sacred tree, usually the oak, that grew near the

◀ *The arms of the Fitzgeralds show the simplicity of early heraldry, which arrived in Ireland with the Norman/English aristocracy.*

▼ *A knight of the Butler family looks out upon his fiefdom from 12th-century Jerpoint Abbey, in County Kilkenny. His heraldic shield is perfectly preserved.*

▼ *A knight of the Cantwell family, wearing the dress of a well-to-do military man of northern Europe in the second half of the 13th century.*

entrance to a chief's home. Its divine status was shared by the salmon. Both symbols were regarded as the insignia of royalty, and the most telling gesture a victor could make was to destroy the oak tree and despoil the salmon ponds of his defeated foe.

The salmon is closely associated with the heraldry of the O'Neills, medieval kings of Ulster who also made much use of the famous red hand, a charge found in the heraldry of many Northern Irish families. The origin of the red hand has been the cause of much speculation among Gaelic historians, but many believe it to be a symbol indicative of the bloodline of a royal house. In England the red hand of Ulster, for long associated with the province of Ulster, has gained a certain notoriety through misunderstanding of its significance, especially where it appears in the arms of baronets. Tourist guides are likely to refer to it as a mark given to families who have produced an infamous murderer.

The great beasts of the chase, the stag and the boar, were also considered noble attributes worthy to be included in the heraldry of the Irish clans. Charges commonly seen in Scottish heraldry, such as ancient ships, or religious symbols coupled to warlike symbols, can often also be found across the Irish Sea, indicating the common ancestry of many old Scottish and Irish families.

CLANS AND LINEAGE

As in Scotland and Wales, the Irish Celts placed great emphasis on a royal or noble past, especially through the medium of genealogy. But while the Welsh nobles tended to trace their lineage from many different ancestors, some legendary and others real, all Celtic Irish families traced their line back to one man, Milesius, who was believed to have brought the Celts to Ireland from Spain.

Milesius was said to have had eight sons, only three of whom produced offspring. Some of the Celtic symbols that found their way into heraldry as charges were associated with the bloodlines of Milesius' sons. For instance, it was from Eirehamon, the seventh son of Milesius,

▲ *A 19th-century copy of Charles Lynegar's genealogy of Bernard Maguire, originally drawn up in 1731.*

that the Northern Irish tribal groupings of the Ui Neill (O'Neill) and Ui Briuin sprang. While the former took the red hand as their symbol, the latter favoured the sacred oak tree.

ENGLISH RULE

Increasing English dominance over Ireland during the Tudor period meant that heraldry was increasingly adopted by the native Irish aristocracy. Having been forced by the Crown to surrender their ancient titles and territory, the Irish nobility had their lands re-granted and new English-style titles bestowed upon them. Not everyone was prepared to take advantage of this manifestation of foreign dominance. The London government encouraged an influx of English and Scots settlers who, as they were often drawn from the ranks of the gentry, wished to have heraldic recognition of their new local status. This led in 1552 to the establishment of a heraldic office in Dublin, housed for many years in Dublin Castle, the seat of the English government of Ireland. Ulster King of Arms, with his deputy, Athlone Pursuivant, headed the office.

Many Irishmen of Celtic stock saw the "Ulster Office" as yet another example of English arrogance. In time, native Irish historians with a particular interest in heraldry set themselves up as heralds in open opposition to it. One such, Cathal O'Luinnín (anglicized as Charles Lynegar), issued heraldic certificates and pedigrees to Irishmen who did not recognize the jurisdiction of the English-appointed Ulster King of Arms. To make his point more forcefully to the English, O'Luinnín styled himself King of Arms of Ulster. Whereas a patent of arms issued by the Ulster Office bore the English royal arms, the patents issued by O'Luinnín bore the arms of the head of the House of O'Neill, the ancient Kings of Ulster.

O'Luinnín's certificated pedigrees are interesting in that they were written not only in English, but also in French and Latin. This reflected the nature of many of his clients who, disaffected with English rule, had fled abroad to Catholic countries, notably France, Spain and Austria, where many acquired the aristocratic titles of those nations.

The drain of the native Irish aristocracy became more pronounced after the Battle of the Boyne in 1691, at which the Catholic monarch, James II, was defeated by the Protestant prince, William of Orange. The departure into exile of a new wave of Irish Catholics was known ever after as "The Flight of the Wild Geese". Many of them ended up at the court of the exiled James II at St Germain-en-Laye.

At the Stuart court in exile, heraldic matters were at first taken care of by James Terry, Athlone Pursuivant, who fled to Paris

To All to Whom These Presents Shall Come,
I, Fergus Gillespie, Deputy Chief Herald of Ireland, send greeting.

Whereas petition hath been made unto me by Patrick Gerard Joseph FitzGerald of Rossbrien in the County of Limerick, the son of William Joseph FitzGerald of the same place, grandson of Patrick FitzGerald also of Rossbrien, great-grandson of Michael FitzGerald of Ballysimon also in the County of Limerick and great-great grandson of William FitzGerald of the same place, setting forth that he is desirous that certain Armorial Ensigns may be duly marshalled and assigned by lawful authority unto him such as without prejudice to any other he may forever bear and advance and praying that I would grant and assign unto him and his descendants such Armorial Ensigns as aforesaid and that the Armorial Ensigns so granted and assigned may be duly ratified and recorded in the Office of the Chief Herald of Ireland to the end that the Officers of Arms there and all others upon occasion may take full notice and have knowledge thereof.

Now I, the said Deputy Chief Herald of Ireland, having taken this matter into consideration am pleased to comply with the said petition and do by these Presents, acting on behalf of and by the authority of the Government of Ireland, grant and assign unto the said Patrick Gerard Joseph FitzGerald the Arms following, that is to say:– Argent a saltire cotticed gules between in fess two ermine spots sable; and the Crest:– A boar passant argent armed and bristled gules charged on the side with an ermine spot sable; mantled gules doubled argent and with the Motto:– Ad majorem dei gloriam, the whole more clearly depicted in the margin hereof.

To have and to hold the said Arms unto the said Patrick Gerard Joseph FitzGerald and his descendants forever and the same to bear, use, shew, set forth and advance on shield or banner or otherwise according to the Laws of Arms each observing and using their due and proper differences according to the practices of this Office and without the let, hindrance, molestation, interruption, controlment or challenge of any person or persons whatsoever, always excepting the Authority of this Office.

In Witness whereof I have hereunto subscribed my Name and Title and affixed the Seal of the Office of the Chief Herald of Ireland, this tenth day of November, Two Thousand.

Volume: Y ; Folio: 96.

Fergus Gillespie
Deputy Chief Herald.

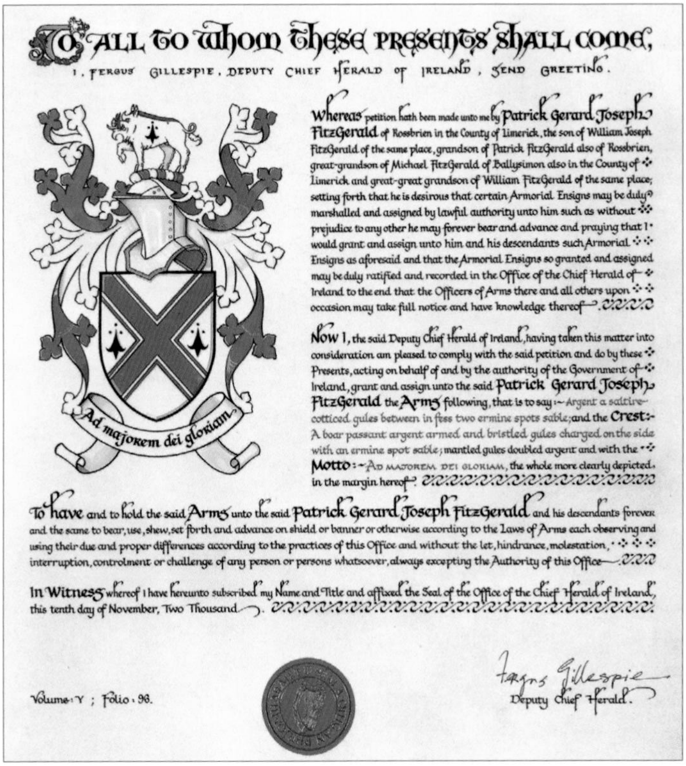

▲ *A modern grant of arms by the Office of the Chief Herald of Ireland for a Fitzgerald, based on the ancient arms of the family.*

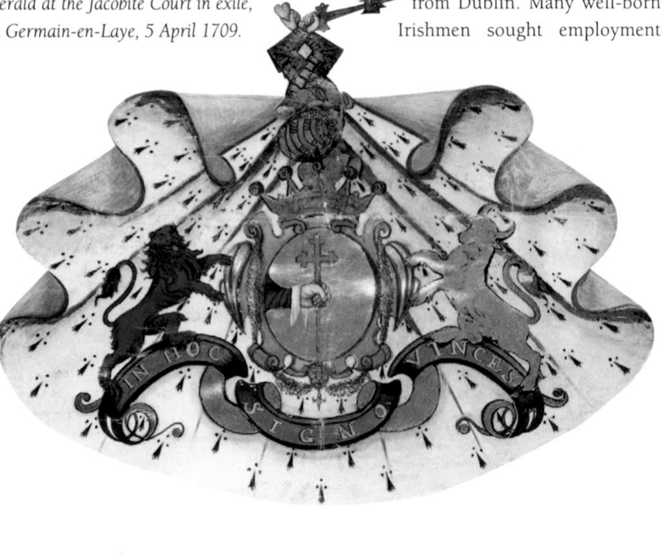

taking with him not only many documents but also the seal of the herald's office from Dublin. Many well-born Irishmen sought employment within the armed forces and government services of the Catholic monarchies of Europe, for which some proof of their nobility was required. This, together with armorial certificates, was provided by the exiled Athlone. One such patent, confirming arms from Terry to Daniel O'Donnell, is now housed in the Irish Genealogical Office in Dublin.

▼ *Confirmation of arms of Daniel O'Donnell by James Terry, Athlone Herald at the Jacobite Court in exile, St Germain-en-Laye, 5 April 1709.*

HERALDRY IN THE IRISH REPUBLIC

In 1921 the Republic of Ireland was born. Today it consists of the whole island except for the six counties of the northern province of Ulster, still under British rule.

In an agreement between the Irish and British governments, all heraldic records relating to Ireland remained under the control of Ulster King of Arms until 1943, when the Office of the Chief Herald of Ireland was established. Heraldic matters relating to British-controlled Ulster were then transferred to London, and the office

▲ *The arms recently granted to Leixlip Town by the Office of the Chief Herald. The charges on the shield reflect the complex history of the town: a Gaelic motto, a viking ship and the rose of a 16th-century English resident of Leixlip Castle.*

of Ulster King of Arms was merged with that of Norroy King of Arms, thus becoming Norroy and Ulster King of Arms.

The Office of the Chief Herald of Ireland is empowered to grant patents of arms and record pedigrees for all citizens of Ireland, others normally resident in Ireland, persons living abroad who have strong links with Ireland, ancestral or otherwise, and public authorities and other corporate bodies. The Genealogical Office (Office of the Chief Herald) is headed by the Chief Herald of Ireland, who also holds the office of Chief Librarian. Although he has the final say on heraldic matters at all levels, the day-to-day running of the office rests with the Deputy Chief Herald and the consulting heralds. Although the Irish heralds have no official uniform they do have insignia of office of the "paper" variety, with crossed batons depending on their degree placed behind a shield of their family arms.

Because of the nature of the relationship between Ireland and England, it may be that those with strong republican sympathies resident in the six counties of British Ulster will, if they aspire to arms, tend to apply to the Chief Herald's Office in Dublin. However, many organizations and individuals in Northern Ireland, Protestant

as well as Catholic, have also applied to Dublin for patents of arms. Whatever their interest or religion, all are made equally welcome by the Irish heralds, who have their offices in Kildare Street in Dublin. The Irish Heraldry Museum is housed in the same building, and has a fine collection of heraldic artefacts. From the walls hang the banners of the chiefs of the main Irish families as recognized.

In common with other national heraldic authorities, the Office of the Chief Herald has certain rules with regard to difference marks. Those of the English type are used, although this may change. Cadency marks are used by all children of the name. For example, if the eldest child is a daughter, she bears a label, the second child bears a mullet, and so on. Illegitimacy has no status in Irish law, so no marks of difference exist for it. Women may apply for a full grant of arms, including helm and crest.

That most Irish of symbols, the harp, is not often granted as a charge because it is associated with national institutions. Badges and standards are rarely given,

except to those with a "following". Similarly, supporters are reserved for special uses, such as in the personal arms of the State President.

DUBLIN CASTLE

As well as Irish family arms, Dublin Castle contains many reminders of the days of British rule, when the viceroys made it their home. It houses the banners of the former Knights of the Order of St Patrick, whose stall plates, together with a further set of banners, are displayed in the choir of St Patrick's Cathedral. Dublin Castle also houses a set of the coats of arms of the Irish presidents since independence, and the former Chapel Royal in the castle precincts has a fine display of armorial glass and wooden heraldic panels relating to the former viceroys and lord lieutenants.

▼ *A window in the Chapel Royal, Dublin Castle, bearing the arms of the viceroys of Ireland appointed from Westminster – the last viceroy's arms just happened to coincide with the last available panel.*

FRANCE

The French nobility were of course at the forefront of the heraldic story – heraldry itself is presumed to have had its origins in the area that today comprises northern France and Flanders. It is not surprising, therefore, to learn that, in common with other courtly culture, the French model of heraldry influenced that of other nations. The very language used to this day by heralds in the English-speaking world is predominantly medieval French. However, whereas in England the kings of arms were not only trusted by their monarch to set down and oversee most matters armorial, but were also entitled to grant arms on

▼ A 19th-century illustration of the arms of the leading families of France includes variants of the French royal arms, showing a variety of bends, borders and labels.

behalf of the sovereign, their French counterparts never had such a right. The granting of arms in France (as in other European powers) was the exclusive right of the monarch.

In 1616 the power of the heralds was further eroded through the appointment by the king of a judge of matters heraldic, the Juge Général d'Arms de France. The judge was expected to rule over heraldic disputes and to ensure that those persons made newly armigerous by the monarch would bear arms that conformed to the principle of the noble science. The appointment soon took on a hereditary nature, and from 1641–96 it was held by a member of the d'Hozier family.

As with the heraldry of other nations, French achievements, while keeping to a certain uniformity of rule and practice,

▲ The complete achievement of arms of the French monarchs, used at times from the reigns of Henry IV (1589–1610) to Louis XIV (1643–1715). The French fleur de lis are impaled with the arms of Navarre.

▲ *An illustration from the second half of the 15th century showing King Louis XI at a chapter of the Order of St Michael. The arms of France modern are depicted at the foot of the page.*

developed a distinctive national style. For example, during the medieval period crests were borne only by knights of "tournament rank" – those who actually participated in tournaments – and they are rarely found in later French heraldry. In most cases, when a helmet is shown above the shield it is topped by ostrich feathers – a convention that spilled over France's southern border into Spain.

Coronets of rank existed for each tier of the nobility, a unique addition to which was the title of "Vidame". Its holder acted as commander-in-chief to the military forces of a bishop, and was therefore responsible in time of war for the defence of a diocese. The coronet of a Vidame consisted of a jewelled circlet bearing four crosses, which is depicted in heraldry with one full and two half crosses.

Certain nobles, whatever their rank, bore the additional title of "Pair de France", for which they were entitled to place behind their shield a robe referred to as a *manteau* or robe of estate. This robe was at first depicted as being charged with the arms (including quarterings) of the bearer, but in later times it was coloured blue and edged in gold.

FRENCH ROYAL HERALDRY

No other emblem has had such a lasting and turbulent career as the French lily, or fleur de lis. The love affair between French royalty and its fleur de lis predated heraldry, and the flower's adaptability and obvious beauty has ensured its survival despite the fall of its latter propagator, the royal house of Bourbon. It has managed to weather revolutions and republics, flowering again after each, and may still be seen in one form or another in many French civic arms.

From the early 13th to the end of the 14th century the golden lilies were liberally strewn over a blue field (France ancient). During the Hundred Years War between England and France the number of lilies on the French shield was reduced to just three (France modern), when the English kings promptly reduced the lilies on their shield to the same number.

The many offshoots of the dynasties of Valois and Bourbon made use of both versions of the royal arms differenced in a number of ways, usually by bends, borders and labels. All these could be further dif-ferenced from a more senior branch by the addition of smaller charges. Today, many variants of the royal arms are still in use by the departments from which the branches of the royal family took their titles.

The French nobility viewed the lower classes with a certain suspicion and believed them always wanting "to emulate what hitherto they admired", from fine furs to armorial bearings. The bourgeoisie and even the peasantry did indeed start to adopt arms, and if originally this was frowned on by nobility and monarch alike, the latter took the somewhat pragmatic view that it might bring the throne some increased revenue. So it was that in 1696 Louis XIV enforced an edict whereby those of armigerous status would pay a tax on their arms. All newly granted arms had to be entered into an enormous register, the *Armorial Général*.

▼ *The elaborate arms of Napoleon I, Emperor of the French. A beautiful example of the heraldic artwork that was inspired by Napoleon's lavish court – in this case on the door of the imperial coach.*

THE *ARMORIAL GENERAL*

In November 1696, King Louis XIV called for the implementation of a French general armorial, an inventory of all blazons and coats of arms used in the kingdom. Anyone who failed to submit their declaration of rank and honours was to be fined 300 livres, and have their properties seized.

The real aims of this edict were financial rather than heraldic. A long period of warfare had emptied the state coffers and the heraldic census was one way of refilling them. Apart from threatening fines for failure to declare arms, the order also imposed charges for the registration of arms, with rates fixed according to status. So an archbishopric was expected to pay 100 livres, an abbey 50 livres, a parish 25 livres and an individual 20 livres.

The first results of the edict were disappointing, with most declarations coming only from nobles and parishes. Thus in 1697 a second edict was passed. This went further than the first, particularly in the power it gave to the Judge of Arms to identify any who had not declared themselves.

▼ *The Napoleonic system of heraldry laid down a large number of symbols to show rank and profession. This oval denoted a countess, and the sword in pale showed that she was the widow of a military officer.*

In heraldic terms, these laws were of mixed value. The armorials do remain a useful source of documentation on the French heraldic landscape of the 17th century. However, the official lists include large numbers of coats of arms that were never

▼ *Examples of Napoleon's shields denoting rank (from left to right): eagle on a chief (sovereign prince); chief semy of bees (prince grand dignitary); semy of stars (duke); quarter Azure in chief dexter (count), charged for an officer in the imperial household; quarter Gules in chief sinister (baron), charged for a mayor.*

▲ *Heraldry has long been thought a suitable medium by cartoonists – here a British caricature of Napoleon's arms incorporates the Devil and his emblems.*

actually displayed, either because their bearers did not use a coat of arms at all or because they used a different one.

From 1699, in response to issues raised by the recording of arms, particularly the complaints of those forced to pay sums higher than were justified by the revenue from their estates, many exemptions were allowed and by 1709 declarations had become little more than optional.

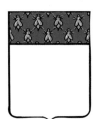

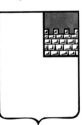

▲ Under Napoleon, towns were divided into three degrees, identified by the style of their arms and mounts. This is the pattern for the 36 major cities ("bonnes villes").

▲ The designated pattern for a town of the second degree, whose mayor was appointed by the emperor.

▲ The designated pattern for a town of the third degree, whose mayor was appointed by the local prefect.

THE NAPOLEONIC SYSTEM

By 1790 the French Revolution had swept away the notions of nobility and chivalric order, yet by 1802, Napoleon, who had already declared himself Life Consul if not yet emperor, had created a new chivalric order, the Legion of Honour. Once emperor, he went further. In 1806 he granted to his most loyal generals dukedoms of the lands conquered in Italy, and in 1808 he created a new nobility in France with six categories:

1 Sovereign prince (for those awarded sovereignty of a foreign principality)
2 Prince grand dignitary (for princes without sovereign power)
3 Duke
4 Count
5 Baron
6 Knight (with the Legion of Honour)

These six titles were hereditary, except for knights who were unable to prove an annual income of at least 3,000 francs.

Such was Napoleon's liking for control that a new set of heraldic rules was necessary for his brand new imperial nobility. Shields borne by the Napoleonic aristocracy showed the bearer's degree through a system of chiefs and cantons. Chiefs of rank were used for princes and dukes. Counts bore blue cantons in the dexter chief, barons bore red cantons in the sinister chief. Additional symbols borne on these cantons indicated the profession of the bearer. The arms of towns and cities of the empire were also designed according

▼ Under Napoleon, coronets of rank for the aristocracy were replaced by embellished caps, the detail of which signified rank. Left to right, caps for: knight, baron, count, duke and prince grand dignitary.

to set patterns indicating their size and importance. Coronets of rank were abolished and replaced by caps of dignity, called toques, of various degrees. This range of heraldic headgear bore no similarity to anything that had appeared before. The toques were not popular and were quickly forgotten after the return of the Bourbons in 1814, who promptly resurrected the pomp and ceremony of their ancestors.

Today, there is no national heraldic authority in France. The arms of towns and other municipalities are controlled and registered by the Ministry of Justice. Although no organization grants arms to individuals, this does not mean that personal arms are free to be exploited by anyone. As in other nations, there is protection of arms in French law. Anyone who finds that their arms are being used by another is entitled to seek legal redress against the usurper.

ITALY

Italian heraldry is rich with many curiosities not found in other national heraldries, making the country an armorial explorer's paradise. Many of these curiosities have their origins in the complex political and cultural history of modern Italy, a polyglot nation of former city republics and ancient family principalities and kingdoms. The separate states have been bonded together as a unified country under one ruler or government only in the last 150 years.

Since medieval times, Italian heraldry has made use of two characteristic shield shapes seldom seen in the heraldic styles of other nations: these are the teardrop shield and the horse's head shield or "chamfron". Sometimes these distinctive shapes were incorporated into the highest of art forms by the leading artists of the Renaissance in Italy, such as Brunelleschi and Donatello.

By commissioning men of such high artistic standing to execute their shields of arms, both on paper and sculpted on to the façades of their palaces and other monuments, great patrician families such as the Medicis and the Pazzis sought to outshine their rivals in heraldic statements of their wealth and power.

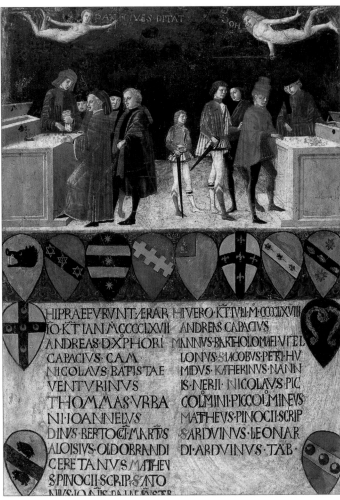

▲ The teardrop shield is popular in Italian heraldry, as seen in this display of the arms of leading figures in the city state of Siena.

▲ A seal of one of Florence's political factions, the Ghibelline party, shows the eagle of the empire stamping on a monstrous serpent that symbolizes their political opponents, the Guelfs.

POLITICAL RIVALRIES

A further statement might be made by placing a symbol associated with a political faction in the arms, normally on the capo, or chief (the band occupying the upper third of the shield). The two most famous examples were the capo d'Angio (chief of Anjou) and the capo dell'impero (chief of the empire).

From the 12th to the 15th centuries, with the German-based rule of the Holy Roman Empire extending into northern Italy, the territory was prey to the intense rivalries of two factions known as the Guelfs, who bore the capo d'Angio, and the Ghibellines, identified by the capo dell' impero. The Guelfs, supported by the papacy, advocated the independence of the powerful city states of Lombardy. The Ghibellines were the supporters of the imperial house of Hohenstaufen, most famously of Frederick I (known as

Frederick Barbarossa) who was Holy Roman Emperor from 1152–90, and his grandson Frederick II (1212–50). Both emperors struggled to consolidate their imperial power in Italy.

The *capo d'Angio* was formed by using a red label over three gold fleurs de lis on a blue chief – a simplified variation of the arms of the House of Anjou. (Sometimes the chief was "semy de lis", or scattered with small fleurs de lis). The *capo dell' impero* was gold charged with a black eagle, single- or double-headed.

This rivalry did not only express itself heraldically. It was also possible to tell the political persuasion of townspeople and ruling families from the architectural style of the upper storeys of their houses,

▲ *The fleur de lis and red label in the chief, known as the* capo d'Angio, *proclaim the Counts Guidi as Guelf supporters.*

▲ *The imperial eagle in the arms of the Venosta family, on the* capo dell'impero, *shows them to be of the Ghibelline faction.*

ITALIAN CORONETS

One peculiarity worth seeking out within the polyglot world of Italian heraldry is the usage by noblemen who bear a lesser title than the head of a family. Two coronets of rank appear in their achievement: the one that surmounts the shield is for the bearer of the achievement, while the other is placed on the helm and is for the head of the house, as shown here in this bookplate for the family of Borio de Tigliole.

churches, castles and town halls. The battlements on those erected by the Guelfs were given horizontal tops, while the Ghibellines preferred an M-shaped edge. The latter device also appeared as a charge in the arms of Ghibelline supporters.

The political nature of the chief in Italian heraldry persisted into the 20th century. Under the fascist government of Benito Mussolini (in power from 1922 to 1943), all municipal authorities were supposed to sport the *capo del littorio* in their arms. This chief included the symbol of the Fascist party, the Roman "*fasces*" – an axe surrounded by a bundle of rods – within a wreath. In fact, however, few of the authorities took up the device.

The *capo* was also used to augment the arms of supporters of the House of Savoy. The *capo di Savoia* was Gules a cross Argent. Other variants bore the dynasty's badge, the Savoy knot.

THE DUCAL CAP

In Venice the elected ruler was known as the doge (a word meaning leader that shares its derivation with the word "duke"). The doge assigned his arms with the red ducal cap or *corno dogale*. This started life as the simple conical cap of Venetian fisherfolk, but in time became a

gorgeous object, ornamented with pearls and cloth of gold. Members of families who had at some time provided a doge were also entitled to include the ducal cap in their arms. It appeared either on the shield or, more often, as a crest, combining the two forms of headgear – the cap and the helmet – in one.

▼ *Even the shape of a castle's battlements could say something about the politics of its owner. The dovetailed crenellations in the arms of the Vismara family are typical of a Ghibelline fortress.*

▲ *The* capo del littorio, *seen here in the arms of the province of Genoa, indicated allegiance to the Fascist party. It disappeared in 1945.*

ECCLESIASTICAL HONOURS

Much Italian heraldic practice devolved from the heraldry of the Roman Catholic Church. Italian families were proud to place in their arms one or more armorial devices signifying some high ecclesiastical honour bestowed on one or more of their ancestors or relatives. The noblest of these was the coupling of the crossed keys of the papacy and the pavilion or *ombrellino*

▼ *The arms of Prince Boncompagni Ludovisi and his wife Angela Maria, Duchess Altemps: within the princely robe the* ombrellino, *or pavilion, and keys show that members of the family have been Pope.*

(umbrella). This was placed either above the shield or on a chief, and indicated that a member or members of the family had been Pope. An example can be seen in the bookplate of Prince Boncompagni Ludovisi. The arms are a combination of the Boncompagni dragon (for the family of which Pope Gregory XIII was a member) and the bends of Ludovisi (the family of Pope Gregory XV).

Other great families, who had provided "gonfaloniers", or standard-bearers, to the papacy, were entitled to charge their shield with a pale – or vertical band – of the Church, which resembled in simplified form the banner or gonfalone itself. Originally the pale was red, charged with the crossed keys, one gold, the other silver, surmounted by the papal tiara or (later) the pavilion.

▲ *The horse's head shield typical of Italian heraldry is here engraved on a plate of 15th-century Murano glass. Above the shield is the distinctive red fisherman's cap of the doge of Venice.*

DEFACED ARMS

In northern Italy (and over the border into southern Switzerland) some evidence of the turbulent times that followed in the wake of the French Revolution is still apparent. In the area that was created the Cisalpine Republic for example, the zeal for reform was strong, and the urge to break the back of the old order was taken to such extremes that orders were sent out from the people's committees to the citizens to tear down and deface the heraldry of the former aristocracy. In many places through the new republic the order was ignored, but in others the order was taken seriously. Even though the republic did not survive, still visible in the region today are the stippled stonework and rough plaster-work scars that mark the walls that once bore carved and coloured shields.

REGULATION OF HERALDRY

In Italy today (in common with many other modern European nations) there is no official procedure for registering or granting arms to private individuals, although heraldic designers will provide arms for clients for a fee. The Italian government does still maintain a heraldic office of arms, the Ufficio Araldico, which approves arms for civic, district and regional authorities, and maintains certain rules specific to Italy. For instance, in the medieval period the gonfalone was held in special regard by Italian communities, and

▼ *The façade of a building in Brescia in northern Italy: the empty plaques originally bore the arms of the town's mayors and captains, which were defaced during the period of the Cisalpine Republic.*

◄ *The recently designed gonfalone of the province of Milan.*

still is to this day; the Ufficio Araldico monitors regulations regarding the colours and trappings of any new gonfalones, which may be gold in colour for a province and silver for a community.

Sadly, the grants of arms issued by the office today take the form of printed documents without any pictorial depiction of the actual arms. This has been the norm since the late 19th century, although before World War II the grants made under the rule of the house of Savoy did have finely coloured borders decorated with the badges and orders of the Kingdom of Italy and its ruling dynasty.

The pattern for armorial bearings is carefully regulated by the Ufficio Araldico. Submissions must be of a uniform style that should not suggest any local influence. Marco Foppoli, a heraldic artist from the northern city of Brescia, had his work rejected by the office as being too northern in style, in that it suggested Swiss and German influences.

SPAIN AND PORTUGAL

Many of the characteristics of early Spanish and Portuguese heraldry were shaped by the centuries of warfare known as the reconquista, or reconquest. The Iberian peninsula had been invaded from the south in 711 by the Moors, Muslim forces from North Africa, whose civilization lasted nearly eight centuries. Moorish power reached its height under the caliphs of Cordoba in the 10th and 11th centuries, but the Christian rulers of northern Spain gradually reconquered the peninsula as the Moorish empire broke up in the 13th century, and Granada alone remained Moorish. Meanwhile, the Christian rulers were unifying, a process that culminated in the marriage of Isabella of Castile and Ferdinand of Aragon in 1469. When Granada fell to the Christians in 1492, Ferdinand and Isabella became rulers of all Spain.

The presence and activity of the great military-monastic orders, such as those of Santiago, Calatrava and Alcántara, in reconquering and eventually unifying the

▼ *The quartered arms of Castile and León cover the robe of King Alfonso X of Spain in this 13th-century illustration.*

▲ *A fine stone achievement for the Pinto da Mesquito family in Yila Real, Portugal.*

whole of the Iberian peninsula, and the chivalric ideals that these knightly orders represented, must have facilitated the development and use of heraldic symbols in the late 12th century. The continual border conflict between the Moorish and Christian kingdoms in medieval Iberia helped to reinforce a sense of ethnic identity in the Christian forces. This was described as *limpieza de sangre*, or "purity of blood", and heraldry was just one outlet for this form of national expression.

There were attempts to make arms distinctive of class as well as ethnicity. In Portugal, King Afonso V (1438–81) restricted burgher arms to the use of colours only, while King Manuel I (1495–1521) forbade the use of arms to all but the titled classes. The Castilian sovereigns followed suit and the right to arms was restricted to members of the nobility.

QUARTERING

The need for social identification found a creative outlet in the marshalling of arms. The heraldic principle of quartering had its origins in Iberia: the Portuguese system aimed at representing every one of an armiger's ancestors, both heraldic heiresses and others. Moreover, since quarterings could be shown in any order, a system of differencings, or *briça*, was instituted by Manuel I to identify an armiger's grandparents. The quarters of paternal and

maternal grandfathers were identified with small charges and cantons (also sometimes charged) respectively; the quarters of paternal and maternal grandmothers were shown respectively with half cantons (*meia briça*) and cushions.

THE REGULATION OF ARMS

Spanish pursuivants, heralds and kings of arms were appointed directly by the sovereign. The junior officers had to be at least 20 years old and to be nominated by two heralds. They underwent a ceremony in which the king baptized them with water and wine, and after at least seven years they could be promoted, provided they had the blessings of two kings of arms and four heralds. New heralds and kings of arms had to take an oath of office and the latter were appointed only with the consent of every officer of arms.

Heralds, or *cronistas de armas*, were usually named after provinces and non-capital cities, such as Bethune and Cataluña, while kings of arms were named after the

▼ *King João II of Portugal (1481–95) holds his shield of arms. The bordure of castles was added by King Afonso III (1248–79).*

Spanish kingdoms, including Toledo (who bore Azure an imperial crown Or) and Granada (created in 1496 to honour the reunification of Spain). While these appointments were not hereditary, at least 15 Spanish families have produced more than one herald each in the past 500 years (compared to about the same number for England, Scotland and Ireland together).

The Portuguese King João I followed the Spanish lead in the early 15th century by appointing kings of arms, including the Englishman Arriet. The Portuguese armorial law of 1495 requiring armorial registration stimulated the production of two famous armorials, the *Livro do Rei d'Armas* and the *Livro do Armeiro-mor*.

Spanish heralds served in both palatine and private capacities, the former including diplomatic and ceremonial roles. The 17th century even saw the heralds engaged in *vistas de armas*, or visitations to the provinces and overseas colonies of Spain to locate, inspect and correct heraldic irregularities. Their regulatory powers were

such that none but the most powerful royal officials could interfere in their tours. In 1649 they castigated the Archbishop of Mexico, for irregular use of arms in the Cathedral of Los Angeles, New Spain.

The beginning of the 20th century saw many changes. The establishment of the Portuguese Republic in 1910 abolished the body of heralds in Portugal. Meanwhile, a royal decree of 1915 reformed the practice of appointing heralds in Spain. After this, heralds had to possess a degree in law or philosophy and be examined by a board of historians, notaries and archivists, while their armorial certificates were valid only if they were authorized by the Ministry of Grace and Justice.

The proclamation of the Second Spanish Republic in 1931 was soon followed by a ministerial edict abolishing the Corps of Chronicler Kings of Arms, stripping the heralds of their pensions and depositing their archives in the National Library. In Portugal, the heralds' situation improved with the founding of the Council of

▲ *Many town walls in Spain bear the imperial arms of the Habsburg monarchs, as here on a bridge in Toledo.*

Nobility by the Duke of Bragança in 1945, but in Spain it was not until 1947 that the Spanish Ministry of Justice re-established the position of the *cronista*. By ministerial decree of 1951, the heralds were allowed to apply for recognition as private professionals (the corporate body of heralds remained dormant) and four *cronistas* were permitted to continue certifying arms for the following 30 years.

A post-republican herald, Don Vicente de Cadenas y Vicent (who also served as King of Arms to Archduke Charles of Austria-Tuscany, the Carlist pretender to the Spanish throne) was appointed in 1951. In 1992 the provincial government of Castile-León appointed Don Alfonso Ceballos-Escalera y Gila, Marqués de la Floresta, Chronicler of Arms of Castile and León. Today, these Spanish heralds, along with the heraldic commission of the Associaçao dos Arqueálogos Portugueses and the Instituto Portuguese de Heraldica, continue the history of Iberian heraldry.

◀ *The Duke of Alva, governor of the Spanish Netherlands, with his family arms. Around the shield are banners taken in battle, usually from the Moors, often found in the achievements of Spanish nobles.*

GRANTS OF PERSONAL ARMS

As the Spanish heralds' palatine activities decreased, their private functions – namely the issuing of armorial certificates – grew in significance. Their monopoly on armorial certificates was confirmed in a royal order of 16 June 1802, which recapitulated an earlier order of 17 November 1749, and in the early part of the 20th century, kings of arms had their right recognized to certify the new armorial bearings of nobles in the name of the king.

On 17 July 1907, a royal order of the War Ministry authorized the Army Corps to solicit the kings of arms for armorial certificates with respect to their military units. The Spanish Ministry of Justice recognized the heralds' certificates and made the *cronistas* solely responsible for their accuracy in the reforms of 1915 and 1951, while at the same time organizing the different types of certificates into seven categories dealing with nobility, arms and genealogy. Citizens of South American republics and other countries that were formerly claimed by Spain have the same rights as Spaniards with respect to this legislation.

The practice of certifying and conferring armorial bearings to foreigners began with certificates issued to residents of the Spanish Netherlands in the 17th century. By the 18th century, Spanish kings of arms were certifying the arms of citizens of other countries, including France, Ireland and England. This practice was extended to the Americas in the 19th and 20th centuries. Even though the Spanish sovereigns reserve the right to grant new arms, and

▲ The use of charges in the form of words and phrases from prayers is characteristic of Iberian heraldry, as here in the arms of the Mendoza family.

◀ The achievement of arms of King Juan Carlos I of Spain on the cover of a modern armorial certificate.

▶ The arms of Pedro Fernandez de Andrada, c1580, include a bend engoulé (being swallowed). Such a charge being devoured by wolves or dragons is a typical feature of Spanish heraldry.

the certification of armorial bearings does not in itself constitute a new coat of arms, burgher arms (sometimes designed for a client by the *cronista*) certified by a herald are protected under Spanish law.

Today, the recipients of new Spanish titles may have armorial certificates countersigned by the king, and supporters may also be certified for those who can demonstrate a direct descent from an ennobled ancestor, or those who hold the rank of knight commander or higher in one of the dynastic or Catholic orders of chivalry.

NATIONAL HERALDIC FEATURES

Although Spanish and Portuguese arms follow rules common to all heraldry, national traits still emerge, as in the heraldry of many other European nations. Roman Catholicism is manifest through the frequent inclusion of exhortations to the saints or the Virgin Mary: often these words of prayer appear as charges on a bordure, a sub-ordinary that is much used throughout Iberian heraldry. Alternatively it may be charged with small saltires – said to be indicative of a particular battle that features in the family history.

▼ *An 18th-century viceroy of Peru, Manuel Amat de Junget, with his arms; by his time even Aztec nobility would know heraldry.*

▲ *The ceiling of the Palace of Sintra bears the arms of the Portuguese aristocracy.*

In Spain the bordure is sometimes charged with castles and lions (for Castile and León), suggesting descent or special honours from those royal families. In Portugal the *quintas*, or escutcheon, charged with five plates taken from the royal arms, performs a similar function. Another charge peculiar to Iberian heraldry is the cauldron. In ancient times this was the sign of an *hombre rico* (rich man), who was meant to keep his cooking pot filled as a duty to the poor in times of hardship.

Grandees of Spain hold a title that is set above all others within the aristocracy, and is afforded special prerogatives at court. Heraldically, the title is suggested in an achievement of arms by a robe of estate, and a coronet of rank is placed directly upon the shield, without the helmet.

▲ *In the arms of the former Portuguese overseas province of São Tome, the dexter side bears the arms of Portugal, the sinister side the provincial arms. The waves in the base signify an overseas location.*

GERMAN-SPEAKING LANDS

Through much of the period in which heraldry was in use, the German-speaking nations were loosely united under the Holy Roman Empire. Although the relationships between the emperor and the various princes, kings and other city governments were often turbulent, it was the emperor who was ultimately the fount of all honours, including arms.

The emperors delegated the granting of arms to other high-ranking personages, but they often took a keen interest in heraldic design, and kept certain honours, such as augmentation of part of the imperial arms, very much under their personal control.

Under the emperors of the house of Hohenstaufen (1138–1254), the eagle became the accepted symbol of the rulers of Germany, and through a series of embellishments was turned from a simple one-headed bird (black on a gold shield) into the glorious two-headed creature that became the symbol of the Holy Roman Emperor. From 1437 until the end of the Holy Roman Empire in 1806, the title of Emperor was held by the head of the Austrian house of Habsburg, except for the brief reign of Charles VII of Bavaria (1742–5), who placed the arms of his own family, Wittelsbach, on the eagle's breast.

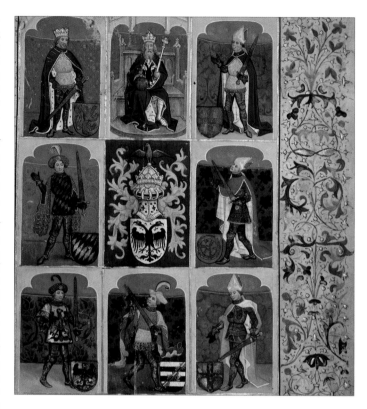

▲ *The Holy Roman Emperor (centre top) and the seven electors, each shown with his arms, from the Hausekopiar, 1484, Cologne.*

◀ *Part of the heraldic frieze in Lauf Castle, near Nuremberg, which contains an early example of an armorial hall painted in 1360.*

THE ELECTORS

For centuries it was the practice for certain great princes to elect the Holy Roman Emperor, and for much of the period the number of electors was limited to seven. They were the Archbishops of Mainz, Trier, and Cologne (who were respectively the Arch-Chancellors of Germany, Gaul and Italy) and four lay dynasts, who each enjoyed certain offices during the coronation: the King of Bohemia (Imperial Cupbearer), the Duke of Saxony (Imperial Marshal), the Count Palatine of the Rhine (Imperial Steward), and the Margrave of Brandenburg (Imperial Chamberlain). The arms of the lay electors each tended to include the symbol of their imperial offices.

Therefore the Dukes of Saxony bore an escutcheon (sometimes shown as a quarter) bearing the crossed swords of the marshalcy. The Duke-electors of Bavaria bore an escutcheon with the orb of the empire, and the Margraves of Brandenburg charged their arms with an escutcheon bearing the emperor's sceptre.

These officers of the Holy Roman Empire often delegated some of their duties, and with them the right to their insignia, to lesser members of their families. This is why the Swabian branch of the Hohenzollerns (the family of the Margraves of Brandenburg) placed in the centre of their quarters a blue escutcheon charged with crossed sceptres.

IMPERIAL DIGNITIES

In the Holy Roman Empire, the granting of arms usually went hand in hand with an act of ennoblement. Families, and even prelates of the Church, who came to hold high office within the empire, were quick to include in their shields a compartment or escutcheon devoted to their regalian rights. Among these is the splendid achievement of Franz Georg von Schönborn (1729–56), Archbishop of Trier, Prince-Bishop of Worms, Prince-Provost of Ellwangen and Prince-Abbot of Prüm, who also happened to bear the glorious title of Oberst-Erblandtruchsess (Hereditary High Steward) of Austria, a fact indicated in his shield by the imperial eagle and a crowned escutcheon of the arms of Austria. Lion supporters also held high his banners of office. In common with many other high-ranking prelates of the time, his achievement includes no sign indicating ecclesiastical rank, unless, almost as an afterthought, it is by way of the cross on his princely bonnet.

Another unusual item that has found its way on to an achievement of arms is the horse's comb borne by the (now extinct) Princes of Schwarzburg-Sondershausen, who were hereditary Masters of the Imperial Stables. Also included in their achievement is a curious device like a pitchfork, which could be mistaken for an implement used to muck out the imperial horses; in fact it is associated with other rights connected with the mining of silver in the Harz Mountains.

▼ *A show of heraldic pomp for Archbishop Franz Georg von Schönborn on the entrance to the monastery of Prüm.*

The Princes of Schwarzburg also made use of a unique crest, an allegory of a very special dignity, that of the "greater *Komitiv*", which conferred the right to grant arms, to ennoble commoners, and to install barristers. Such a right was associated with the title of Hofpfalzgraf (Count Palatine of the Imperial Court). While the right to grant arms in the Holy Roman Empire rested with the emperor, some secular and ecclesiastical princes, certain universities and persons of high standing, were granted the right of *Komitiv*. The "lesser *Komitiv*" was limited to legitimizing children and granting arms to commoners. The Counts of Schwarzburg-Sondershausen were created Hofpfalzgrafen by Leopold I on 22 December 1691. On 3 September 1697, they were raised to the degree of princes, and were then granted augmented arms that included the crest denoting the greater *Komitiv*: a knight with a sword.

▲ *The complex quarterings of the princes of Schwarzburg-Sondershausen, complete with a comb to groom the imperial horses.*

▼ *The device on the shield of Andreas Gassman of Basel, c1583, has its origins in a Swiss merchant's or house mark.*

CHARGES IN GERMAN ARMS

Germanic heraldic style combines conventional geometric charges, or ordinaries, with charges of particular charm and curiosity not found in British or southern European heraldry.

The horse head gable ends of the local houses were a favourite in the arms of communities in northern Germany, together with an even older charge – a wolf's claw – based on an implement used in German forests to drag logs (of which a variant is still used).

In Switzerland and southern Germany, burgher families made use of "house marks". These took the form of various geometric figures, often appearing as a series of lines resembling numbers, and

▲ Emperor Frederick III states his control over 95 lordships in the armorial display on the façade of the Cathedral Church of Wiener Neustadt in Austria.

they were used on property as well as market goods, often stamped alone without heraldic accoutrements. Similar marks were used by merchants on their wares. At a later date the user of such devices might place them on his shield and helmet, aping the aristocracy.

THE WAPPENSAAL

German-speaking nobles, perhaps more conscious of their lineage than any of their class elsewhere in Europe, often set aside a room in a mansion or castle as a *Wappensaal*, or armorial hall. Usually the shields were formally lined in a frieze around the walls in order of precedence, with the local rulers given prime position.

In Austria a popular theme was a family tree of the imperial family, often with figures depicting individual members accompanied by their shield of arms. Sometimes the scenes depicted were all too graphic, as in Tratzberg Castle in the Tyrol. Here, a frieze shows Albrecht of Habsburg, the King of the Romans, being stabbed to death by his nephew Johan "the Patricide" in 1308. The evil nature of the deed is expressed by showing Archduke Johan accompanied by a snake.

The Habsburgs themselves were keen to claim descent through heraldry, not only from the former ruling dynasty of Austria, the house of Babenburg, but also from legendary rulers of Austria. This theme is played out in its fullest form on the front

▼ The arms of Albrecht Dürer and his wife. Placing the helm between the two shields accolee (side by side) is typical of German marital arms.

▼ A family tree in Tratzberg Castle, Austria, showing the murder in 1308 of King Albrecht I by his nephew Johan.

of the Cathedral Church of St George, in Wiener Neustadt, where the coronation of Emperor Frederick III was commemorated in 1453 through the *Wappenwand*, a heraldic frieze representing a fantastical genealogical tree of the House of Austria through 95 lordships.

The theme of maintaining the *status quo* through heraldry is awesomely expressed in the Provincial Council House of Carinthia, Klagenfurt, where each noble family, abbey and town is represented through a baroque cartouche of arms. Not content with one *Wappensaal*, the heraldic scheme, which includes nearly 700 shields in all, also finds its way into a second, smaller chamber.

GERMAN TITLES

In the Holy Roman Empire it was usual for a family's arms to be augmented with quarters as it advanced up the social scale. The original arms were usually kept as a *Herzschild* ("heart shield"). Coronets of rank were used but often a simplified variant of the arms with a crest coronet, or the family shield and crest displayed in simple medieval style, was preferred.

One unusual form of heraldic headgear worth looking out for is the cap or bonnet of the electors of the Holy Roman Empire, a scarlet cap with a large (often scalloped) ermine brim. Such a cap can be seen in the arms borne by the Hanoverian King George III of Britain, as Prince-Elector of the Holy Roman Empire.

There is some confusion outside German-speaking lands about the prefixes attached to the title of *Graf* ("count"), such as *Burggraf*, *Pfalzgraf* or *Markgraf*. These simply designate a particular territorial responsibility and were not heraldically distinguished. A *Burggraf* ruled over a *Burg* or fortress; a *Pfalz* was a palatinate and a *Mark* was a marcher, or border, land.

The prefix *von* in a name corresponds to the French *de*, both simply meaning "of". In both German and French names, the word is followed by the place name of the family home, although as an adjunct of nobility it was common practice to add the *von* and place name to a surname after ennoblement. Families of ancient nobility

▲ *A panel depicting the complete achievement of arms of the Hungarian Dukes Batthyany, Counts Strattman.*

took their surnames from their estates. No family name was required, they were simply *von...* For those families of ancient origin still in possession of their estate, *von* was replaced by *zu* ("to"), or even *von und zu*, although this style was not so commonly used. In later centuries the use of *von* in front of a name became debased, becoming almost as common as the *van* in Dutch surnames.

Since World War I, the position of the armiger, whether a private individual or a civic authority, has proved complex and curious in German-speaking lands. Before that time, a noble title was inherited by all the legitimate children of a noble father, not just the eldest son, as is the case in the British nobility. After 1919, the bearing of noble titles was banned altogether in Austria, while in Germany the title was allowed in effect to become affixed to the family's surname. Therefore, in name if not in fact, the German aristocracy may survive long after the demise of the nobility of other nations.

This change meant that for the first time the adopted children of noble fathers, who could previously use the family name but could not inherit the noble title, were now able to call themselves, for example, "Hugo Graf von..." or "Gisela Freifrau von..." and pass the name on to their own children.

THE REGULATION OF ARMS

World War I swept away not only the German and Austrian Empires, but also various other German monarchies (those of Baden, Württemberg and Bavaria), which had each maintained their own heraldic authorities. Where once the German heralds granted arms on behalf of monarchs, their place has now been taken by a number of heraldic societies (for private individuals) and state government (for local authorities), although in both cases the certification of arms is purely a registration process, without any formal authority to grant armorial bearings.

Each federal state follows its own course with regard to the registration of arms for local authorities within its boundaries. While some, such as the administration of Lower Saxony, maintain a formal register of arms deposited within their archives and are happy to advise on good heraldic practice, others demonstrate little or no interest in such matters. This has led to the adoption of quasi-heraldic symbols or even non-heraldic logos by some municipal councils in Germany.

▼ *The arms of the Counts von Zeppelin, depicted in simple medieval style with a single charge and crest.*

NAZI HERALDRY

▲ *The ancient arms of Coburg on the left, replaced with the National Socialist-approved symbol on the right.*

Even in relatively modern times, the power of heraldry has been acknowledged, as evidenced by the interest taken in this unlikely and archaic subject by the Nazi regime in 1930s Germany. The need to manipulate and adapt heraldry to suit the ideological ideals of Hitler and his henchmen was spelt out in a decree from the Interior Ministry dated 15 December 1937. Marked "Confidential", it gave the following direction to local Nazi party leaders with regard to the approval of arms of district authorities:

▼ *The state of Thüringia saw the need to show approval and support of the new order by adding the swastika to the traditional arms of Hesse.*

▲ *The swastika, an ancient symbol taken by the Nazis as their own, dominates a rally at Nuremberg, 1933.*

In accordance with the deputy/representative of the Fuhrer, I therefore request in future, that instead of overtly ecclesiastical emblems (saints, croziers, mitres, etc) other emblems be chosen for district arms which relate to other historical events, or express the particular characters of the community at present and the current state of affairs.

The decree stated that the cross and other symbols of the confessional aroused anger in 100 per cent of National Socialists, and local leaders were encouraged to extend their control over such institutions as community centres, once dominated by the elders of the Church.

In fact, few German councils paid much notice, and most tended to favour keeping their often ancient symbols. The government of Thüringia did, however, place a swastika between the paws of the Hessian lion in its state arms, although it was almost too small to notice. At least one town council felt bound to toe the party line. Coburg had for centuries borne a Moor's head, representing St Maurice, but such an un-Aryan character rattled the

National Socialist authorities so much that in 1934 they changed the arms completely. The new shield was Per pale Sable and Or, a sword issuant from base point downwards, the pommel charged with a swastika counterchanged. In 1945 the Morenkopf of St Maurice was restored.

TEUTONIC PRIDE

Between the late 1920s and the outbreak of World War II, Germany experienced a resurgence of interest in personal heraldry. It was yet another manifestation of the Teutonic pride expounded by all members of the Nazi hierarchy, none more so than the leader of the SS, Heinrich Himmler. Though far from Aryan perfection himself, Himmler was obsessed with the cult of Germanism, and was encouraged in his

▼ *SS Brigadefuhrer Karl Maria Weisthor's Nazi arms, each part of which he endowed with its own mystic meaning.*

fantasies by such men as Karl Maria Wiligut (1866–1946) and Guido von List (1848–1919), a leader of the Ariosophy movement, which was an amalgam of nationalism and occultism. Both men claimed that the origins of heraldry were more remote than is usually agreed. In their view, it began in the world of the Teutonic gods – above all Wotan, the god of war, whom dead heroes met in Valhalla, and who knew the secrets of the runes.

RUNES AND MYSTICISM

The origin and meaning of runes obsessed many Nazi "theologians", and Wiligut, as one of the most famous exponents of this secret heraldry, saw to it that runes became the basis for the Nazis' own heraldry. It was no coincidence that the colours of the SS were also those of the

▶ *The apotheosis of Nazi heraldry, the arms of a new Teutonic Knight such as would have decorated the Knights' Chamber at Wewelsburg Castle.*

▼ *The bookplate of a Nazi party member – the eagle, which faced left for the state, faces right for the party.*

Teutonic Knights. At Schloss Wewelsburg, Himmler sought to combine the ideals of the Teutonic Knights and Teutonic mythology, together with the court of King Arthur, complete with round table, into a new "noble fraternity", who were to meet in a newly synthesized complex of rooms decorated with runic motifs.

Around the round table of solid oak would sit Himmler and his 12 senior SS commanders (the successors, so he believed, to the Teutonic Knights). Behind each officer would hang his own coat of arms, especially designed, as most of the 12 – including Himmler himself – lacked family arms. New arms were devised by the Ahnenerbe, the institution attached to the SS that dealt with racial purity and Teutonic history, using designs influenced by the runic translations of Karl Maria Weisthor (Wiligut had changed his name to what he believed was his ancient family name).

Among other odd outpourings, Weisthor/Wiligut claimed the power of "ancestral memory", which allowed him to trace his own unbroken family history back to the Teutonic peoples in the year 228,000 BC, his family springing from a coupling of the gods of water and air. He was also able to see the time when the earth was inhabited by mythological beings, including dwarves, giants and races such as the Lemurians – giant brown-skinned hermaphrodites with four arms. (Not surprisingly, after threatening to kill his wife, he was confined in a mental asylum.) Weisthor/Wiligut claimed to know the secret spells and meanings of the runes and used them in charges designed for his own family arms. He brought several of them together in one of the most fascinating objects associated with SS ritual (much of which he conceived): the Totenkopfring der SS, or SS death's head ring, which included both the swastika and the double sigrune of the SS.

The swastika was a mystical symbol of good fortune, used from ancient times by peoples from Tibet to northern Europe.

▲ *The bookplate of Hans Raven, typical of the Nazi period, with the swastika much in evidence and bearing a crest straight out of the age of the Teutonic Knights.*

In Europe it was associated with Donner (or Thor), god of adventurers, and became popular in 19th-century Germany as a symbol of racial and national unity. The latter would seem to have been the main reason for Hitler's love of the swastika, which he used as a heraldic device coupled with the German eagle.

The sigrunes of the SS symbolized victory and were first drawn side by side in 1931 by SS member Walter Heck, a graphic designer employed by the badge-manufacturing firm of Ferdinand Hoffstatter in Bonn. Both the swastika and the SS runes were among many devices chosen to decorate the new shields of arms in Wewelsburg Castle, although the outbreak of war seems to have placed the heraldic scheme there on hold. The only case of such arms being created would appear to be for SS Obergruppenfuhrer Pohl, as they appear on a ring given to him by his son in 1938.

As a postscript to this account of extraordinary quasi-heraldry, it is worth looking out for signs of "human attention" on a mountainside near Schloss Wewelsburg, for it is known that in 1945, on Himmler's orders, all the remaining Totenkopfrings (which incidentally were treated as awards, and had to be returned on the death of each recipient) were blast-sealed into a mountain, and as yet they have never been found.

RUSSIA

Heraldry came relatively late to Russia, in comparison with much of western Europe. It is generally accepted that its flowering owed much to Tsar Peter I ("the Great", 1682–1725) who during his travels in Europe saw the splendour that could be achieved by its use in such media as stained glass, carved stone and furniture. The first Vice-Master of Heraldry, appointed by Peter the Great, was an Italian who saw to it that Russian heraldic practice followed that of contemporary European nations. Not that heraldic symbolism was unknown in Russia before Peter's reign: Russian cities, such as Astrakhan with its crown and sabre, and Novgorod, with its throne and flanking bears, had used pictorial devices since the early 16th century. Some civic symbols were even older, and the most famous Russian royal devices, the double-headed eagle and the horseman slaying a dragon, had appeared on the seals of the Grand Prince of Moscow, Ivan III, in 1497.

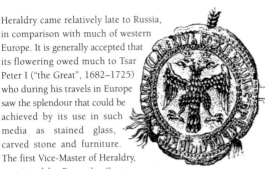

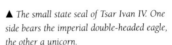

▲ *The small state seal of Tsar Ivan IV. One side bears the imperial double-headed eagle, the other a unicorn.*

EARLY HERALDRY IN RUSSIA

During his reign, Ivan IV ("the Terrible", 1547–84) required that a register of nobility was to be maintained, known – because of its cover – as the Velvet Book. At this time the Russian nobility had no titles of rank except for that of *kniaz* (prince), which was used in the main for those descended from the reigning house of Rurik. The maintenance of the Velvet Book, together with the other formal heraldic registers, was later overseen by the Heraldry Office, which was established in 1722 by Peter the Great under the control of a Master of Heraldry.

Despite Peter the Great's enthusiasm for European heraldry, Russian arms did not ape western styles and customs to the point of exactness. Indeed, Russian heraldry, like its other art forms, is a distinctive mixture of western European style and the exotic. This blend can often be observed in the official armorials of the Russian Empire, the *Obshii Gerbovnik Dvorianskikh Rodov Vserossiiskoi Imperii* (*Obschii Gerbovnik* for short) published in ten volumes between 1797 and 1840.

Peter the Great introduced the ranks of baron and count, and in 1722 decreed that all officers of the army and navy, and functionaries of the civil service above a certain rank (major in the army), were automatically entitled to enter the ranks of the aristocracy (untitled), and were thereby of armigerous status. Russian barons and

▼ *A Russian herald at the coronation in 1896 of the last tsar of Russia, Nicholas II.*

counts were entitled to coronets of their degree, in European style, while princes of Russia were entitled to bear a princely crown as well as their robe of estate. The greater part of the Russian untitled nobility were entitled to bear a crest coronet from which issued three ostrich feathers.

CHARGES AND AUGMENTATIONS

The shields of the Russian nobility are often divided into several fields, each bearing one or more charges that reflect the family history. These often refer to acts of valour and may be accompanied by a citation appearing in place of a motto, such as that of the Counts Plavtov: *For fidelity, courage and indefatigable labours.* Tartar, Cossack and Polish emblems often appear in Russian heraldry, suggesting the diverse mix of nations that made up the empire.

Many Russian arms bear some direct reference to the monarch in whose reign the family was ennobled. Often the imperial eagle appears, charged on its breast with a particular emperor's cypher, and sometimes with part of one of the orders of chivalry. A distinctive heraldic honour was created in 1741 for soldiers who had

▼ *A variant of the arms of a Leibgardets family, with the augmentation of honour appearing in the chief.*

▲ *The arms of Count Alexander Suvurov-Rymninsky (1730–1800) before his advancement to the rank of Prince; already heavily augmented, the later arms even included a map of Italy.*

led the *coup d'etat* that placed Elizabeth Petrovna on the Russian throne. They were created *leibgardets* ("life guards") to the empress, automatically raised to the rank of nobility and given an augmentation to their arms in the form of a new coat, Sable on a chevron Or between three mullets Argent as many fire bombs or grenades Proper. The augmentation was usually borne per pale with the family arms – the augmentation on the dexter side, the family coat on the sinister. Each life guard (and his descendants) was also entitled to bear a crest of a grenadier's cap with wings and ostrich feathers, and the motto (in Russian),

▼ *The arms, probably from a coach door, of Prince Michael Golenishchev-Kutuzov, Russian commander-in-chief in the country's campaign against Napoleon, 1812.*

For loyalty and zeal.

An extraordinary example of heraldic distinction for bravery must be the shield of arms borne by one Dmitry Chuvash Narbekov who, during fighting against Kazan in the 16th century, was badly injured by a spear in the back. He was then hit in an eye by an arrow, and as if this were not unfortunate enough, as he tried to extract the arrow he had his arm blown away by a cannon ball. Amazingly, he survived.

▶ *The arms of the Grand Duchy of Finland while it was under Russian rule. The Finnish lion replaces the usual warrior and dragon, and the shields on the eagle's wings are of Finnish provinces.*

Among the honours he received from his grateful monarch was a grant of arms, showing in graphic detail his various acts of heroism.

IMPERIAL ARMS

By the late 19th century, the Russian heralds had formulated rules, on the orders of the emperors, regarding armorial achievements of members of the imperial family itself. Each royal personage was entitled to bear two variants of arms, greater and lesser, and their proximity to the throne was generally designated by their heraldic supporters. The immediate family – the tsar, the tsarina, the tsarevich (the heir apparent) and his eldest son – bore as

▼ *The arms of Dmitry Chuvash Narbekov show in lurid detail the various wounds he received at Kazan.*

▲ *A postcard of the early 20th century shows the arms of the principal cities of the Russian Empire.*

supporters the Archangels Michael and Gabriel. The younger sons of the tsar had two Varangian guards as their supporters; the grandchildren by younger sons bore two unicorns Or, and so on, down to the great-great-grandsons of the tsar, who bore two griffins Sable armed Or and langued Gules. Female descendants when unmarried were entitled to the same arms and supporters as their brothers, but on a lozenge instead of a shield. There were also marks of difference other than supporters: they mainly consisted of a lessening of the number of territorial shields that accompanied the imperial arms, and the helmets, coronets and crests that were part of the territorial achievements.

CIVIC ARMS

Between the late 18th and late 19th centuries, the authorities laid down a complex series of exterior ornaments to be borne in the arms of towns and provinces. For a lesser authority the coronet might take a simple mural form, while townships of some importance had a red mural coronet with just two crenellations. The cap of Monomakh (an ancient form of jewelled fur cap) was granted to former capitals of the ancient Russian grand dukes. There were specific crowns for Kazan, Astrakhan, Poland, Finland and Georgia.

Most of these heraldic coronets date from an imperial decree of 1857, which also stipulated other ornaments to be placed on either side of the shield, such as crossed hammers for industrial cities, ears of wheat for cities in agricultural areas and vine leaves for those in wine-producing regions. Baron von Köehne, who invented the system, had intended that maritime municipalities should display crossed oars, but this was changed to anchors.

A special set of attributes was provided for "fortress cities", which were entitled not only to a special combination of coronet and imperial eagle, but also crossed flags. Those that had withstood a siege had the crossed flags charged with the cypher of the monarch in whose reign the siege had been conducted. Ribbons of the Russian orders of chivalry helped to complete these splendid achievements. By the same decree, civic shields were charged with a canton of the arms of the *guberniya*, or province, in which the city lay. Prior to 1857, the arms of the latter had been charged in chief of a shield per fess, the arms in the base being of the city itself.

POST-REVOLUTIONARY ARMS

After the revolution of 1917, heraldry was still required. A commission was set up by the temporary government to look into the matter of the national arms. It suggested that although crowns, sceptres and other symbols of monarchy should be abolished, the double-headed eagle could stay, although it vied for a time with the swastika (another popular symbol signifying eternity and prosperity). The crown was replaced by a soldier's cap.

The eagle was for a short time accompanied by soldiers and peasants, although

▼ *The arms of the town of Mohyliv-Podilsky, Ukraine as borne in the late 19th century. The grapes signify its position in a wine-producing region; the moon and cross on the canton show that the town was in the guberniya (or province) of Podillya.*

▲ *The star of communism replaced the old tsarist emblems after the fall of Emperor Nicholas II in 1918.*

by spring 1918 it was felt that the imperial bird was too symbolic of pre-revolutionary Russia, and an entirely new coat of arms was needed. The hammer and sickle were selected for use on the state seal of the Russian Federation, symbolizing the alliance between the industrial workers and the peasantry. The new arms kept the old heraldic colours of red and gold, but placed the hammer and sickle in front of the rising sun of socialism.

The first regional arms, those of the Moscow regional government (*guberniya*), were approved by the praesidium of the Moscow Soviet in September 1924. They included a five-pointed star, the Statue of Freedom erected in 1918, and the hammer and sickle. On either side were blades of cereals and at the base were the attributes of labour, including anvils, shuttles and an electric motor. The Moscow arms never had a full official description and although they were supposed to set an example to be followed by other Soviet *guberny*, the idea never really took off.

The various republics of the Soviet Union took the state arms of the USSR as their model. In these a shield was not employed; a garland of wheat instead surrounded a rising sun above which was a globe charged with the hammer and sickle. The wheat blades were bound together by a red ribbon bearing the legend *Workers of*

▶ *The star of communism in the arms proposed for Volgograd when it was declared a "hero city" in honour of its citizens' bravery during World War II.*

the world unite in the various languages of the individual republics. Above the entire design shone the red star of communism. While the arms of most of the republics were devoid of any national character, some managed to achieve a localized flavour. Kirghizia had the rising sun over a local landscape, and Azerbaijan placed an oil-well against a backdrop of the rising sun. Each was dominated by the red star.

Curiously, the pre-revolutionary civic arms granted by the tsars were not abolished by the Bolsheviks; they had meant to do so but the order was never signed. In the 1960s, when many new towns and cities were created in the Soviet Union, interest in civic arms was aroused, and this was harnessed by the authorities to encourage civic pride. Soviet deputies would instigate competitions to find new designs. The arms had to include a symbol unique to the place, encapsulating a "small motherland" that exuded its own patriotic zeal. Several hundred new civic arms were designed between the 1960s and the 1980s. The designs could be quite striking, such as that of Novokusnetsk, which had a block of coal heating the furnace of a steel works.

This arousal of interest in heraldry was not welcomed throughout the Soviet Union. In the occupied Baltic States it was seen by local communist officials as a catalyst for nationalistic fervour, and was firmly curtailed.

HERALDRY AFTER COMMUNISM

Since the collapse of the communist regime and the demise of the Soviet Union at the end of 1991, many symbols that are

▲ *The new state arms of Russia were established by a presidential decree in 1993. The traditional symbols of eagle, rider and dragon have been re-established after nearly a century.*

reminiscent of tsarist times have re-emerged, particularly the double-headed eagle, regally crowned. The crown of Peter the Great appears between the eagle's heads, and it is charged on its breast with the horseman slaying a dragon. The eagle is gold (as opposed to the imperial kind, which was black) and the horseman points to the sinister, as opposed to the dexter in the later imperial arms. The figure is simply described as a rider, and before the heraldic reform of Peter I it was thought of not so much as St George but more as an allegorical representative of the sovereign overcoming his enemies.

In today's Russia, the President as head of state executes his heraldic duties through the State Heraldic Office. The office keeps a register of all state and civic arms, flags and official insignia. It does not, however, grant arms, and at the time of writing, no legal body in Russia is entitled to do so, either for personal or civic use, although various societies and heraldic colleges exist that will advise on new heraldic designs for their members. These organizations often ally themselves to one or other member of the former imperial family, which is supposed to give them some form of quasi-official status, although the State Heraldic Office does not recognize the connection.

COMMUNIST HERALDRY

Though a leveller of class, communism still saw the need for heraldry, and understood its potential power. Therefore coats of arms could be tolerated as long as their content bore no symbols that went against the cause. For the most part this meant a ban on religious or nationalistic (other than state) motifs.

▲ *In early post-tsarist Russia the old symbols of the eagle and rider remained in favour, but were soon to be swept away.*

▼ *Workers and peasants unite around the hammer and sickle of the new Soviet Union.*

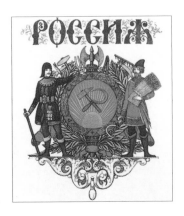

In this, as in other aspects of communism, Russia led the way. The hammer and sickle, the symbols favoured by the workers' collectives in March and April of 1918, paved the way for the designs of the arms of the Russian Federation and the various Soviet Republics.

NATIONAL TRADITIONS

At the end of World War II, nations with heraldic traditions that were centuries old came under Soviet control and influence. Most symbols associated with the old order were soon banned by the increasingly hard-line regimes installed by the Soviets in Poland, Hungary, Bulgaria and Czechoslovakia, and the red star of socialism loomed large in the rhetoric of the new order. However, certain symbols were of such an emotive nature to the individual nations that even the party apparatchiks were loathe to tamper with them, although in the German Democratic Republic, the Soviet leaders' most loyal and dependent satellite, the leadership followed Soviet symbolism to the letter.

The new national arms of the GDR were an almost exact replica of the Soviet arms, except that the sickle was replaced by a pair of compasses and the ribbon that bound the ears of corn was in the German national colours of red, gold and black. These were derived from the ancient arms of the German nation: the black eagle with its red claws and beak on a gold field.

Other nations, which did not have so much reason to forget their recent past, found that their own communist bosses approved of the most curious of heraldic alliances between the past and the post-war period, even if that past was bound up with royalty. Therefore, the twin-tailed lion of the Bohemian kings continued to appear beneath the red star, as also did that most enduring of national emblems, the white eagle of the Piast dynasty that ruled medieval Poland; in the latter case the red star that replaced the royal crown was so insignificant that it looked like a crest on the noble bird's head.

▲ *The arms of the Republic of Azerbaijan in the Soviet era show the red star of socialism set high above a Soviet dawn.*

PERSONAL ARMS

The traditional users of arms – the nobility – were now taboo, and most of those who had not fled or died languished in dingy prisons or windswept gulags. Others who had dared to follow the noble science of heraldry were viewed with suspicion by the Soviet authorities. While heraldists are today usually perceived by non-heraldists as harmless cranks hankering after a romantic and improbable past, to the hard-line Marxist-Leninists of the late 1940s and 50s, anyone who professed an interest in the plaything of the nobility was probably a supporter of the old order, who wished to see the return of feudal repression. Those who enthused about heraldry were harassed by the secret police and even thrown into prison for involvement in activities "contrary to the interests of the proletariat". Personal arms were very much a thing of the past.

CIVIC ARMS

With civic heraldry the position was not nearly so clear cut. Civic pride was allowed to exist and often nurtured, since it helped citizens to focus their thoughts firmly on the immediate locality rather than further afield. The ancient arms of Prague and Pelhrimov were retained, for example, with the addition of the republic's arms on

▲ *The arms of Baja in Hungary, designed in the 1970s, conform to the style set by the community heraldry of the Soviet era.*

▲ *The arms of the cities of Marijampole (left) and Joniskis (right) in Lithuania; both shields were banned in the 1970s by the Soviet authorities because of their religious content, and replaced with new designs.*

shield or crest. Despite the treatment that was meted out to the aristocrats themselves, the arms of many ancient lords, complete with their coronets of rank, were permitted to remain on the civic shields of their old domains.

In the German Democratic Republic, civic arms were not entirely banned, but they were not permitted to be used for official purposes. Instead, the local council was to use the state arms enclosed by an inscription stating the name of the town, city, or district.

In the Soviet Union, saints and other overtly religious symbols in civic heraldry were replaced by figures representing heroism or patriotic workers. Even the heavenly eye of providence was replaced by a golden sun. If a coat of arms was so religious as to be totally offensive to the

leadership, it had to be replaced altogether. The ancient shield of the Lithuanian city of Joniskis, which bore St Michael killing a dragon, was replaced during Soviet rule by a red shield bearing a straightened scythe, the weapon of the local peasantry, between 28 pointed golden suns.

Elsewhere in Lithuania, the city of Marijampole, which bore in its ancient arms the figure of St George and the dragon, acquired not only new arms, but a new name (Kapsunkas). The new design included a canton of revolutionary red and the flame of learning.

Even these new approved designs were banned by the Lithuanian communists after a song festival in 1970, when the participants made too much show of their city arms. From then on until the fall of the Soviet regime, in Lithuania at least, city arms, and of course the old state arms, were banned.

NEW SYSTEMS OF HERALDRY
Of all the nations that had fallen under the spell of socialism, Romania was the only one that actually developed any formal system for its civic and regional arms. The arms designed by the state committee on

▼ *During the Soviet era, new arms were devised for Krasnoznamensk in the Moscow region. The USSR's supremacy in the space race made a most suitable subject for a modern Soviet town.*

▲ *The arms of the municipality of Hunedoara, Romania, are typical of the pattern of Romanian civic arms during the years of the Ceausescu regime.*

heraldry cannot be considered beautiful. Traditional heraldic symbols long associated with the ancient rulers of Wallachia (an eagle) and Moldavia (an auroch's head), found themselves sharing a shield with images of the modern industrial world, such as petro-chemical plants, blast furnaces and weavers' shuttles. Each new shield was also charged with an escutcheon bearing the symbols and colours of the Romanian state.

In 1974, Romania's neighbour, Hungary, also attempted to impose a heraldic scheme in keeping with the new way forward, replacing the ancient arms of 83 towns and cities with those with a new socialist flavour. Whereas in communist Romania, some vestige of the heraldry of the old order had often been retained, the Hungarian regime required a clean sweep on the model of the Soviet Union, with simple, stylized figures of people reaching out towards the rising sun of a socialist dawn. Parents and toddlers replaced the symbols of the nobility, with the red star triumphant over all.

It was not heraldry as we know it, but it was heraldry, sometimes innovative though usually bland. When communism collapsed, so did most of the "heraldry" that had paid it lip service for the past 50 or more years, unloved and unlamented.

POLAND

More than any other nation, Poland has maintained a heraldic "apartness", which stems mainly from the nature of its lesser nobility, or szlachta. This social group may be thought of broadly in the same way as the English gentry.

Those who fell into the group were members of an affiliation of noble families, known as a *ród*. Before the arrival of heraldry, each *ród* had its own standard in the form of a staff bearing a unique emblem. The devices were simple figures that cannot be described in heraldic terms: most consisted of sets of lines, curves, X- and V-shapes, which have led to the popular belief that they were adapted from Viking runes. The Vikings were just one of many peoples with whom the Poles came into contact, for the Polish area of influence was a thoroughfare for traders on their way eastwards into what is now Russia.

From the east came more warlike peoples, the Tartars and later the Turks. These roving bands had their own totemic standards – staves bearing streamers, horsetails and horns. Something similar can be seen

▼ *Herb Woroniecki, showing Christian symbols defeating the Turkish crescent. These charges would have originated as simple lines and curves that were later adapted to heraldry.*

▲ *This pedigree shows tribal arms typical of Polish heraldry. Such a document was required as proof of nobility for Poles wishing to become officers in the imperial Austrian army in the late 19th century.*

today in the Turkish crescent or "jingling Johnny", a musical instrument used by German military bands, which resembles a standard hung with silver bells and horsetails. Perhaps the eastern standards and the Viking runes were married together by the Poles to make their own distinct tribal insignia.

ADAPTATIONS TO HERALDRY

In the second half of the 10th century, Poland's first ruler, Mieszko, brought Christianity to his people, and many tribal standards had their extremities made into crosses. When heraldry eventually reached Poland, other changes were made to the symbols to produce acceptable heraldic charges, such as arrowheads and crescents. The original emblem had usually been cut out of metal, so in Polish heraldry it is very rare to find a charge that is not gold or silver. The fields of shields are almost always red or blue; green and purple are virtually unknown, and heraldic furs are not used.

Each *ród* had its own rallying cry, such as *Dolega*, *Dabrowa*, or *Pilawa*, and the tribal device came to be identified by it. In effect the war cry and the device were the same entity. When, by the late 13th century, Polish *ród* started to place their old totemic emblems on shields, the practice of identifying the arms by the relevant war

cry persisted, and for this reason there has never been a need for a system of heraldic blazon in Polish heraldry.

A single coat of arms, or *herb*, was used by all members of the *ród*, no matter their position, for in effect all members were equal. However, arms were sometimes adapted through marriage. In the case of Herb Slepowron ("blind crow"), the original arms were varied after an important marriage to a lady of the Pobog clan, by placing the black crow of Herb Slepowron on the Herb Pobog, which bore a horseshoe topped by a cross.

It is rare to find more than one charge on the shield of a Polish *ród*. Ordinaries are rare, as are quarters and supporters. Some shields were credited with legendary origins: for example, that of Ogonczyk, an arrowhead issuing from a semicircle, is said to relate to an occasion when a maiden was being abducted by Tartars, and members of the tribe pursued the Tartars at the speed of an arrow. Crests are usually ostrich plumes or peacock's feathers issuing from a crest coronet. There is no set pattern for the helmet, although the barred tourney helm is mostly used.

SOCIAL ORGANIZATION

Titles such as count or baron were forbidden to Poles. Only after the partition of Poland by its neighbours in the 18th and 19th centuries did Poles take foreign titles, although this was considered unpatriotic.

A *ród* could be any size, and could number hundreds of separate families. In theory they were all related but, as with Scottish clans, other families could sometimes be taken under their wing. If a king wished to favour a subject he might ask a *ród* to take him under its name and arms.

In later centuries when members of the *szlachta* settled in towns, villages, or on their own estates, they adopted surnames by placing Z in front of the place name, in the manner of the French *de* or the German *von*. In time the Z tended to be replaced by adding *ski* or *cki* to the end of the name, and the connection with the *ród*

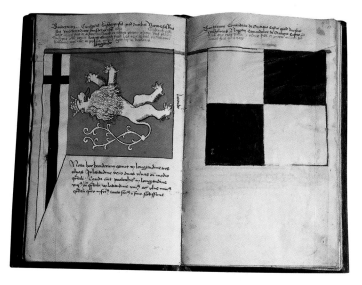

▲ At the Battle of Grunwald (Tannenberg), on 15 July 1410, a Polish–Lithuanian army decisively defeated the Teutonic knights, capturing many of the Order's standards, all of which were beautifully painted in 1448 for the Royal Archives in Krakow.

rider in pursuit of his enemy. Part of this device, the rider's armoured arm holding a sword, known to the Poles as the *pogonia*, was used as a kind of augmentation under the Polish–Lithuanian commonwealth, giving rise another *ród*; Pogon. The rider's shield was often charged with the double-armed cross of the Jagiello dynasty. Later, the dynastic arms of the Polish sovereigns were placed on an escutcheon on the quartered shield of Poland–Lithuania.

The last of the Jagiello line, Sigismund II Augustus, died in 1572. From then on, monarchs were elected by a general assembly of the nobility. Kings' powers were severely curtailed and they were closely watched by the nobility in this "royal republic". Elections were one of the great sights of Europe, with the *szlachta* making their way in groupings of *ród* to the Electoral Fields outside Warsaw. In 1573, no less than 50,000 nobles came to vote.

Many of the elected monarchs were chosen through the connivance of various factions allied to the interests of Poland's enemies and neighbours. In 1772 the first partition of Poland between its neighbours was instituted, and the kingdom of Poland–Lithuania disappeared. Both nations regained their independence following World War I.

was kept alive by placing the tribal name before the surname, as in Sas-Tarnawski or Jastrzebiec-Marikowski.

ROYAL HERALDRY

Polish culture, art and learning were greatly admired and coveted by its larger neighbours, notably Prussia, Russia and Austria. All these powers saw the Polish state as an obstacle to their territorial ambitions, but Poland had ambitions of its own.

In 1386, Jadwiga, the daughter and heiress of the Polish–Hungarian monarch, Louis of Anjou, took as her husband Grand Duke Wladyslaw Jagiello of neighbouring Lithuania, setting the scene for a period of great expansion. In 1413 the Union of Horodlo between Poland and Lithuania saw the adoption of many members of the Lithuanian nobility into the names and arms of the Polish tribes. The alliance was reflected heraldically in the arms of the Polish–Lithuanian sovereigns. The white eagle of the Poles had been borne on seals since the reign of Boleslaw V (1227–79), and is one of the most famous and enduring symbols in Europe. During the medieval period the eagle was often charged on its breast with a half moon device ending in stylized clover leaves or crosses, and from the late medieval period the eagle was crowned.

The arms of Lithuania were every bit as fascinating. They consisted of an armed

◀ An illustration from the early 16th century shows the eagle of the Polish monarchs below the mounted horseman of the Grand Duchy of Lithuania; the top right shield bears the arms of the Lithuanian Gediminas dynasty.

▼ The arms of Wroclaw (Breslau), bearing the lion of Bohemia, the eagle of Silesia and the city's patron saint, John the Baptist.

THE AMERICAS

The development of heraldry by British settlers in North America was slow, and was curtailed by the Revolution. However, the colonization of the central and western areas by the Spanish and French, in the 16th and 17th centuries, gave rise to a parallel, separate heraldic development (to say nothing of the Russian presence in the state of Alaska and the native monarchy in the state of Hawaii). The division of the continent between the major European powers fragmented the exercise of heraldic authority in what would become the United States. A comparison of the heraldic regulation exercised by the British in eastern North America, and by the Spanish in the western territories, suggests some of the differences in the colonizing methods of the two powers.

COLONIAL HERALDRY

Between Columbus's voyage in 1492 and the Declaration of American Independence in 1776, both England and Spain attempted to introduce and regulate heraldic activities in their respective

▲ The first, rejected, design for the arms of the new United States included a rose for England, a thistle for Scotland, a harp for Ireland, a fleur de lis for France, a lion for Holland and an eagle for Germany.

▲ The arms of the descendants of the Aztec Emperor Montezuma II, attributed by the Spanish heralds, are a mixture of European heraldic charges and native symbols.

spheres of authority. Among the symbols and regalia at the marriage of Philip of Habsburg and Joanna of Spain, celebrated in 1496, was a banner bearing arms for the West Indies, or the Kingdom of the Fifteen Islands. The first English grant of arms in the New World was made in 1586 to the city, governor and assistant governors of Ralegh in Virginia, while Newfoundland would receive a grant of arms about 50 years later.

These early grants made use of native scenes, wildlife and peoples, the last of which seems to have played most strongly on the heraldic imagination. Writing in 1682, Bluemantle Persuivant John Gibbon remarked on the quasi-heraldic body paint worn by Virginian natives during wardances: "The Dancers were painted some Party per pale Gu[les] and Sab[le] from forehead to foot…at which I exceedingly wondered, and concluded that Heraldry was ingrafted naturally into the sense of the humane Race."

Meanwhile, the Spanish colonizers granted titles and arms to the native aristocracy and royalty they had conquered,

as a way of excusing them from the encomienda system of forced labour imposed by the Spanish rulers during the 16th century. Native American leaders could avoid this if they could successfully claim the privileges of the Spanish nobility. One remarkable instance is the case of the descendants of the Aztec emperor Montezuma II, who ruled central Mexico from 1480 to 1520. Philip II of Spain granted the title of count to Don Pedro Tesifon Moctezuma de la Cueva in 1627, and Isabel II granted the titles of marquess and duke to other descendants in 1864 and 1865. The family bore arms blazoned Vert within an orle of five roses Argent a falcon and tiger Or in pale a bordure Gules charged with thirty coronets Or, or alternately, Azure an imperial crown Or and a falcon and tiger Argent all in pale a bordure Vert charged with thirty coronets Or.

In 1984, a claimant to the Aztec throne, Don Guillermo de Grau-Moctezuma, appointed a personal herald, the Cronista Rey de Armas de la Casa Imperial Azteca.

English and Spanish heralds attempted to establish heraldic regulation in North America during the 17th and 18th centuries. In 1705, Laurence Cromp, York Herald, also became Carolina Herald, although the office expired on his death ten years later, without any grants of arms having been made. Spanish heraldic jurisdiction in the New World was more effective: in 1649, the visiting Spanish heralds censured the Archbishop of Mexico for the inaccurate display of the Spanish royal arms in the Cathedral of Los Angeles.

AFTER INDEPENDENCE

The early leaders of the independent United States and Mexico were not opposed to the principle of bearing arms. Mexico freed itself from Spanish control not as a republic but as a short-lived empire, under the rule of the armigerous cavalry officer-cum-monarch Agustín de Itúrbide. Heraldry was also esteemed by George Washington, who wrote: "It is far from my design to intimate an opinion, that Heraldry, Coat-Armor, etc. might not be rendered conducive to public and private use with us; or that they can have any tendency unfriendly to the purest spirit of Republicanism. On the contrary, a differ-

▼ *In a splendid return to medieval heraldic design, the flag of Maryland uses the arms of its founder, George, 1st Lord Baltimore.*

▲ *The great seal of the US presidents, the main design of which dates from 1782.*

ent conclusion is deducible from the practice of Congress, and the states; all of which have established some kind of Armorial Devices, to authenticate their official instruments."

Congress set Benjamin Franklin, John Adams and Thomas Jefferson to the task of designing the arms of the new republic on 4 July 1776. In the first sketch, the shield was blazoned Quarterly of six: 1 Or a double rose Gules and Argent (for England), 2 Argent a thistle proper (for Scotland), 3 Vert a harp Or (for Ireland), 4 Azure a fleur de lis Or (for France), 5 Or an imperial eagle Sable (for the German Empire) and 6 Or a lion rampant Gules (for Holland). Fortunately, perhaps, this cluttered design did not meet with approval, and the famous arms Argent six pallets Gules a chief Azure were designed in part by Charles Thompson, Secretary of Congress, in 1782.

THE REGULATION OF ARMS

Civic heraldry prospered in the independent republic, and today such symbols are protected from misuse by legislation, but personal heraldry in the USA remains unregulated. Interest is high, however, as witnessed by the success of "bucket-shop" heraldry, and both private agencies and official bodies have sought to address the current state of affairs.

In 1928 the New England Heraldry and Historic Genealogical Society of Boston's heraldic committee began to publish the inherited and adopted arms of Americans, and in 1972 the American College of Heraldry was founded. This body has been very effective in drafting and publishing arms of adoption, with a dedication to principles of heraldic design, while the setting up of the College of Arms Foundation in the 1980s has set a good precedent.

On an official level, several European heraldic agencies have in the 20th century begun to grant and register American arms. The Office of the Chief Herald in Dublin and the Court of Lord Lyon in Edinburgh both grant arms to eminent Americans of, respectively, Irish and Scottish descent. The College of Arms in London has granted honorary armorial bearings to eminent Americans of English descent since the early 20th century, though the practice began without a general warrant from the Earl Marshal, and these documents go unrecognized by the Irish and Scottish authorities. The English College also issues devisals of arms to American corporations with the approval of their respective state governors. The Spanish Corps of Chronicler Kings of Arms issues armorial certificates recognizing the arms of citizens of American republics once claimed by the Spanish crown, including most of the USA (such certificates protect these arms under Spanish law).

These different organizations and avenues are made use of by many Americans, testifying to their heraldic interest. While there are many drawbacks to the USA's lack of a native central heraldic authority, the present unregulated situation at least allows America's plurality of heraldic traditions to develop organically.

SCANDINAVIA

The migration of heraldry from its historic centre in northern France and Flanders was rapid, and by the 13th century arms were being used by the nobility of Denmark, Sweden and Norway. Just as the nobles of Spain, Italy and England felt themselves to belong to a social group sharing a common goal that knew no borders, towns and cities throughout Scandinavia showed a common pride, taking up seals whose central motifs, such as town walls, castles and saints, could be found all over Europe.

The noble families of Finland were mainly of Swedish origin. Few were of local Finnish stock, and the indigenous families usually changed their names as they moved from estate to estate, so that sons might have different surnames from their fathers. Just one Finnish family, the Princes Menshikov, attained princely rank, a reminder of the period from 1809–1917 when the Grand Duchy of Finland was part of the Russian Empire.

The Menshikovs also reflect the polyglot nature of Scandinavian nobility in general, which assimilated into its ranks Scots, English, French and German families. Not surprisingly, the nobility of

▼ *The arms of Baron Örnsköld have the two helmets and crests accorded to a Swedish baron. The quarterings are divided by a cross throughout, in a style characteristic of Swedish heraldry.*

Scandinavia adapted the heraldic style of northern Germany, including the use of peacock feathers in crests, and arms that became increasingly augmented with quarterings as families rose to higher rank. But gradually Scandinavian heraldry took on its own flavours, and some of its charges have few equivalents elsewhere in Europe. In Denmark and Sweden, for instance, a cross throughout may divide various quarterings, and this is a practice seldom met with elsewhere, except in Scotland.

HERALDIC FUNERALS

A practice dating from the late 16th century, peculiar to Sweden, Finland and much of the Baltic coast, was the carrying of heraldic shields on poles in the funeral procession. A large achievement of the defunct's own arms, known in Sweden as the *hufvudbaner*, was carried at the head of the coffin, with smaller shields (*anvapen*) belonging to the paternal and maternal ancestors on either side.

The *anvapen* were borne separately at first, sometimes by as many as 16 bearers, but in about 1660 Queen Hedvig Eleonora decreed that such a show of pomp should be confined to the royal family. From then on just two *anvapen* were carried, but these were, if anything, more splendid: each developed into the form of a heraldic family tree, with its branches adorned with many separate shields. Both the *hufvudbaner* and the *anvapen* were carved from wood, bright with gold and silver leaf and fully coloured.

ARMORIAL COLLECTIONS

Both Sweden and Finland maintain Houses of the Nobility, in Stockholm and Helsinki respectively. Although now much reduced

▲ *A plaque for President Eisenhower of the United States, made a Danish knight of the Order of the Elephant.*

in power, they still enjoy a certain kudos and maintain splendid collections of family arms. In both cases, the arms of the nobility are grouped together through rank and chronology. Because the Finnish House of Nobility was established while Finland was under Swedish rule, it followed the Swedish system.

The Swedish Riddarhuset (the "house of nobility") contains a total of 2,320 armorial plaques, which are numbered in order of seniority. Among them is the achievement of the Counts of Wasalborg (No 5) with the curious punning charge of two crowned fish. The family was descended from Gustav Gustafsson, illegitimate son of Gustavus Adolphus, and a merchant's daughter from Gothenburg called Margareta Kabiljau (*kabelju* means "dried

▲ *The armorial plaque of the noble family of Stöltenhielm in the Riddarhuset in Stockholm. The progenitor's wooden leg appears as one of the charges.*

cod" in Swedish). The achievement includes the arms of the house of Vasa, with a bendlet sinister to show illegitimacy.

Many families have punning arms, including a troll in the arms of Trolle, and a wooden leg, or stilt, in the Stöltenhielm arms. Coats of arms of the Swedish aristocracy sometimes feature a scarlet hat, which was worn by members of the monarch's council of state. They may also include the arms of a province, if a member or members of the family had been the monarch's representative there.

ORDERS OF CHIVALRY
Many noble families of foreign extraction originated with high-ranking military officers who staffed the armies of northern Europe during the expansionist wars of the 17th and 18th centuries. They also swelled the ranks of the ancient orders of chivalry in both Denmark and Sweden.

The chapel in the Castle of Frederiksborg at Hillerød, to the north of Copenhagen, contains the armorial plaques for knights of two Danish orders: the Order of the Elephant (believed to have been founded in 1464) and the Order of the Dannebrog. The Order of the Elephant

is the senior order, and its foreign knights include Sir Winston Churchill and President Eisenhower. Its badge is a white enamelled elephant charged with a cross of five plate diamonds, guided by a mahout and bearing a golden tower. The collar of the order is charged with elephants and towers. Churchill was once seen wearing the insignia of the Elephant and when asked if it happened to be an "Order Day", he replied in the negative. He was in fact in mourning for an elephant that had just died at London Zoo.

Before 1975, Sweden maintained four orders of chivalry. The Order of the Seraphim, founded in 1748 by Fredrik I, was the highest. Each order had its own room in the royal palace in Stockholm, the wall decorations of which were taken from the collars of the orders. Today only two survive, the Order of the Seraphim and the Order of the Polar Star, but neither can be conferred on Swedish citizens other than the royal family. The Order of the Seraphim is most often conferred on foreign heads of state. Notable among non-royal knights is Nelson Mandela, whose shield bears the South African flag.

The insignia include golden seraphs, the monogram of Christ – IHS – and three nails from the Cross. Ladies of the Order and prelates have their arms within a pale

▲ *The hufvudbaner and anvapen (arms of alliance) for Diedrich Kagg (d1671) in Linköping Cathedral, Sweden.*

blue ribbon, from which the badge is suspended. Female sovereigns, like male knights, have the collar. The arms of all female members are placed on an oval. Since 1748 the Seraphim has been conferred on nearly 800 men and women, and of those over 600 have their achievements

▼ *For the memorial service of a newly deceased knight of the Order of the Seraphim, the heraldic plaque is displayed on an easel before the altar of the Riddarholmskyrka in Stockholm.*

on plaques hung, three-deep, on the walls of the Riddarholmskyrka ("Church on the Knights' Island") in Stockholm.

PERSONAL ARMS

In general the Scandinavian heraldic authorities are concerned with national, royal and military matters, rather than personal arms. Personal heraldry is usually treated like a trade mark and can be registered as such for protection, although state authorities will give advice on corporate and personal arms, especially in regard to correct blazon. Guidance can also be gained from heraldic societies and foundations. Some of the foremost heraldic experts in northern Europe collaborate under the aegis of the Societas Heraldica Scandinavica in bringing out the twice-yearly magazine *Heraldisk Tidskrift*.

Those living in Scandinavia can register their arms through the *Skandinavisk Vapenrulla*, the Scandinavian roll of arms. It has its own heraldic artists and consultants to ensure that every coat of arms is correctly treated.

CLARITY AND SIMPLICITY

While each of the Scandinavian nations enjoys its own heraldic customs and styles, during the 20th century there was a noted interaction between heraldic designers and authorities within the northern states, which provided some of the liveliest discourse and debate in the heraldic world. The most distinctive styles emanated from a handful of heraldic craftsmen and designers, notably Hallvard

Trætteberg in Norway and Gustav von Numers, Ahti Hammar and Olof Eriksson, all from Finland. Trætteberg's ideas had a profound effect not only on the civic and municipal heraldry of his own country, but also on that in neighbouring Sweden.

Norway has no state herald (the duties being undertaken by the National Archives), but Trætteberg, who worked in the Archives, may be regarded as the nearest thing to it. Between 1920 and his death in 1987, he was very much the influence behind Norwegian heraldry. His controversial stand on the matters of tincture and charges still strongly influences Norwegian military and civic heraldry.

Trætteberg advocated a number of heraldic rules, the most notable being that no more than two tinctures, one colour and one metal, should be used on a shield. He also liked the idea of one charge being used, in a singular or multiple fashion, and suggested that no shading or shadow should be applied to the charge. His theories have made modern Norwegian heraldic style the starkest and most uncompromising in use today. Those used to British arms may regard his shields as too plain, yet a Scandinavian heraldist might characterize English civic heraldry as cluttered and lacking in style.

CIVIC HERALDRY

In Finland, meanwhile, von Numers, Hammar and Eriksson were revolutionizing their nation's civic and municipal arms with a series of shields unparalleled in their symbolism and simple beauty. Taking into

▲ *Possibly the most influential of modern styles is that of Finnish municipal heraldry, with its unusual divisions of the field and combinations of charges, seen here in the arms of Liminka commune.*

account the local dialect, geographical curiosities and folklore of each place for which they devised arms, these three visionaries produced new heraldic designs that were often daring in their simplicity. Their ideas gave food for thought to the then new heraldic authorities of South Africa and Canada.

Among their innovations, ordinaries were offset in unusual fashion, sometimes combined with other charges, at other times standing alone. Among the former, the shield of the municipality of Kuivaniemi, with its single wavy flanche and seal embowed, suggests Kuivaniemi's position on the coast of the Gulf of Bothnia. Other fascinating designs include those of the municipality of Pielavesi, which features the local musical instrument – a horn made of birch bark.

Native flora and fauna are often depicted in the most unconventional forms, as in the arms of Simo in Lapland, which is one of the oldest parishes in the

1

◀ *Two civic arms exemplify the simplicity of modern Norwegian heraldry: the shield of Målselv (left) includes the district's river; for Bardu (right) a wolverine represents the area's forests.*

province, and is also famed for its salmon fishing: its twin distinctions are neatly married in a cross composed of fish tails.

Lines of partition were drawn anew by Trætteberg and the Finnish designers, with the fir trees that cover so much of the country as a favourite motif. In much modern Scandinavian heraldry, the charges, trees especially, are stylized in a simple form. This can make for a refreshing clarity, as in the arms of the Swedish border town of Haparanda: these include in their design a border post between two trees, surmounted by the midnight sun, which is enjoyed by the community for several months each year.

Inevitably, the point was eventually reached when nearly all communities, of whatever size, had had arms designed for them, and the steam went out of the innovative phase of Finnish civic heraldry. Now even this heraldic nation has started to embrace the logo. But in general Scandinavia enjoys its civic heraldry and uses it to the full. It is usual for communities to place their arms not only on buildings but also on local transport and on the boundary signs on the approaches to cities, towns and villages. In Finland, fans of civic heraldry can find plenty to spot, and are often rewarded with a two-in-one "prize", for the community arms may well be twinned with those of the local province. The latter date in the main from the 16th century, when Finland formed part of the kingdom of Sweden. Many of the provincial arms appeared on banners carried in the funeral procession of King Gustav I in 1560.

▲ *Four salmon tails in the arms of Simo in Lapland form a cross for the see of Uppsala.*

▲ *The arms of Pielavesi commune, Finland, with its birch bark horns.*

▲ *A wonderful example of a heraldic hybrid species representing forests and lakes, in the arms of the city of Zarasai in Lithuania, created in 1969.*

▲ *The arms of the Finnish municipality of Inari include an extraordinary marriage of two species raised on local farms.*

▲ *The approach to many Scandinavian towns and villages is clearly marked with heraldry, as in Haparanda in Sweden.*

▶ *The sublimely simple punning arms of the Finnish community of Sumiainen – sumu means "foggy" in Finnish.*

AFRICA

While it belongs first and foremost to the nobility of western Europe, heraldry has such an attractive character that it was bound to be taken by Europeans to the lands they invaded, subdued and settled, not the least of which were the colonial territories of Africa.

SOUTH AFRICA

Heraldry was first taken to South Africa in 1488, with the Portuguese adventurer, Bartholomew Diaz, who had stone crosses erected bearing the arms of Portugal. Although the Portuguese did not actually colonize South Africa, what was probably the first grant of arms to an indigenous armiger in this area, the Emperor Monomatapa, was made by the King of Portugal in 1569. The blazon was Gules, between two arrows Argent an African hoe barwise bladed Argent handled Or, the shield surmounted by an Eastern crown.

The Dutch ruled the land that now forms the Republic of South Africa between 1652 and 1806. They were followed by the British, who brought with them their own heraldic tradition. For much of the period of British rule, South African arms were typical of the lacklustre heraldry the British heralds of the time

▲ *The arms granted to South Africa's Emperor Monomatapa by the Portuguese king in 1569.*

were foisting on the colonies, in the fussy overladen style of the late Georgian and Victorian eras.

In 1961 the Republic of South Africa broke its ties with the British Commonwealth, incidentally cutting itself off from the authority of the British heralds. Some two years later the South African Bureau of Heraldry was established in Pretoria. The Bureau has at its head a State Herald to whom any person or corporate body may apply for grant and registration of armorial bearings. When granted, these are officially published in the Government Gazette. (Many armigers in the United Kingdom have asked for their heraldic authorities to publish such a record.)

SCANDINAVIAN INFLUENCE

The new authority looked to the Scandinavians, notably the Finnish heraldic artists, Gustav von Numers and Ahti Hammar, for inspiration. In recent years it has come up with some of the simplest and most splendid designs in modern heraldry, taking its themes from the modern Scandinavian style. In 1974 the State Herald of the time, Mr Hartman, visited Finland to meet the Finnish heraldic experts and gain insight into their local styles and design techniques. Some five years later, Hartman's successor, Frederick Brownell, followed his example.

From their time spent with their Finnish colleagues, the South African heralds decided on a fresh approach to heraldic design. Simplicity was to be the first principle, followed by new lines of partition based on the local architecture, flora and fauna. Elements of innovative Finnish design were to be incorporated into the heraldry of South Africa, where these were considered appropriate.

The marriage of the two national styles produced some strikingly simple designs. New partition lines were based on the gable ends of the Dutch-style farmhouses in the Cape and the national flower, *Protea cynaroides*, the stylized petals of which

were used to create a striking new motif reminiscent of the fir twig partition line found in Finnish and Swedish arms.

The indigenous tribes of South Africa had long marked their oval shields with a system of colour and symbol, which was not so much heraldry as armory. Such symbols were part of a "regimental" identification system, rather than a personal or family one. The South African Bureau of Heraldry has made much use of traditional native shields in the designs of arms of black townships.

HERALDRY AFTER APARTHEID

The future status of the South African Bureau of Heraldry can only be guessed at, although it is of necessity not of the first importance to the post-apartheid government. State Herald Brownell has done much to ensure that heraldry can be enjoyed by people of all creeds and colours, for in his own words, heraldry is "colourful, but colour blind".

Frederick Brownell and his fellow heralds have sought to combine English, Afrikaans and Portuguese heraldic traditions with the symbols of the indigenous African tribes. However, despite his good intentions, heraldry is bound to be viewed

▲ *Three different designs by the South African State Bureau of Heraldry based on the national flower, the protea.*

▲ *The arms of the Republic of Zimbabwe include in the crest the star of socialism and behind the shield an automatic rifle.*

▼ *In the arms of Harare, capital of Zimbabwe, heraldry finds its way on to a shield of traditional African shape.*

▲ *The arms of Soweto, a mixture of traditional African symbols and classical medieval European heraldry.*

by the vast majority of the population as yet another toy of the old European oppressors, fit to die a natural and unlamented death.

For the new national arms for the Republic of South Africa, the Bureau of Heraldry was bypassed and a design commissioned from a non-heraldic artist. The achievement was adopted in April 2000. The motto is in the now extinct Khoisan language spoken by the oldest known inhabitants of the land, and it means *Diverse people unite.* The shield is enclosed within elephants' tusks, symbolizing wisdom and strength, and ears of wheat to represent fertility and growth. The human figures are shown in an attitude of unity.

ZIMBABWE

In the neighbouring republic of Zimbabwe, the state arms have a traditional British flavour to them, and use the heater-shaped shield of medieval European heraldry.

However, this traditional shape has been married to typical Marxist-style militancy, with symbols of the workers and peasants side by side. An AK47 assault rifle, the weapon that armed many revolutionary struggles of the late 20th century, takes its place against the red star of socialism. In the arms of the capital city, Harare, the great Zimbabwe bird is used as a traditional charge, but has been placed on an African-style shield.

HERALDIC SURVIVALS

While some ex-colonial territories, such as the former Portuguese provinces of Angola and Mozambique, have wished to throw off heraldry, seeing it as an uninvited import of their former white rulers, others have taken it to their hearts. The former French territory of Gabon, for example, has employed a French heraldic designer to create (with local assistance) arms for its regions, districts and communities. In these, typically European heraldic practices are twinned with the most striking of local African fauna, flora, customs and art, creating fine examples of good heraldry.

▲ *The new coat of arms of the Republic of South Africa, a modern application of heraldry fit for the second millennium.*

CANADA

The newest of all national heraldic authorities, that of Canada, came into being in
1988 after Queen Elizabeth II, acting in
her capacity as Sovereign of Canada,
authorized the Governor General to exercise in Canada one of her Royal
prerogatives, the right to grant arms.

The Canadian Heraldic Authority,
unlike its Scottish and English counterparts, does not have a king of arms as its
chief officer. That office is exercised by the
Chief Herald of Canada. However, there
are heralds and pursuivants, as would be
found in any of the more ancient state
heraldic offices.

INDIGENOUS STYLE

The Authority grants arms to Canadian
nationals and corporate institutions after
receiving a formal petition, presented in
the same way that any English or Scots
person or corporation would do to their
own heraldic authority. But the arms

▼ *A splendid stained glass window showing
the insignia and badges of the Canadian
Heraldic Authority and its officers of arms
set against a background of the arms of the
Canadian provinces. Made by Christopher
Wallis in 1990.*

▲ *Some years ago the College of Arms in
London granted a pilot's
helmet in lieu of the
traditional medieval
warriors' helmet – a
theme taken up and
expanded by the
Canadian Heraldic
Authority. The crests of*

*these three arms are, clockwise from top
left, an Indian Shaman's
headdress for Mr Norquay, a
Maccabean warrior's
helmet for a synagogue,
and a fur parka hood for
Helen Maksagak, former
commissioner of the
Northwest Territories.*

granted by the CHA,
though they keep to
the age-old tenets of
European heraldic
tradition, often have a
very distinct flavour. Right from its beginning, as well as employing artists and
historians belonging to the European tradition in Canada (notably French, English
and Scots), the CHA has sought out those
of the indigenous peoples. All the West
Coast Indians and Inuit tribes have fascinating histories, symbols and folklore that
can be drawn from and adapted to serve
the heraldic achievement of arms.

Nowhere does this happy mixture of
native and imported traditions become
more manifest than in the achievement of
arms of the Canadian Heraldic Authority
itself. Its shield bears a maple leaf charged
with an escutcheon, the like of which
could be found on any Scots, English or
Scandinavian shield of arms, conventional

but efficient in its
effect. The supporters,
however, are wonder-
fully aboriginal in their
execution and content. They
are two fantastic creatures, half polar bear,
half raven, dancing energetically and
resembling figures that might be found at
a West Coast Indian tribal gathering or on
one of its totem poles.

This combination of "first nation" and
European symbolism allows the Canadian
heralds a wealth of charges open to no
other heraldic organization, except the
South African Bureau of Heraldry, which
has a similar blend of colonial and indigenous symbols at its disposal. Two more
creatures straight from a totem pole support a shield charged with traditional
European heraldic charges – bezants and
a pallet wavy – in the arms of the
Honourable Judy Gingell, Commissioner
of the Yukon Territory. Elsewhere, in the

arms of the city of White Rock, an iceberg can be seen along with an aboriginal representation of a killer whale.

Jewish communities are unusually well represented in Canada. While individual Jewish people have long been commemorated in the heraldry of certain European nations (notably Italy), few Jewish communities are heraldically recognized.

ACCESSIBILITY AND EQUALITY

A combination of cultures is not limited to the pictorial display of arms. In the patents issued by the Canadian Heraldic Authority, the blazon and formal declaration of the grant are written in both French and English – a legal requirement for all official Canadian documents.

The requirement to make arms known to "all and singular", whatever the reader's origin, has been taken even further by the CHA. When granting arms to the new

▲ *Cadency marks for two children of James Robson: on the left a label for an eldest son, and on the right the ermine spots in the top corners that are the mark for a second daughter in the Canadian cadency system.*

Territory of Nunavut, established on 1 April 1999, the text and motto were fully translated on the patent into the native language of the local Inuit people of that region, and the wording was first approved by local linguistic experts.

Although it may be only a babe in arms in comparison with the English College of Arms and Lord Lyon's Office in Scotland, the CHA is very much the new star of the heraldic world. It has already produced its own marks of difference for women, and

it does not discriminate between men and women in respect of helms and crests: Canadian grantees of either sex are entitled to them. Women may also use the heater-shaped shield or lozenge without any mark to differentiate their arms. As sexual equality is enshrined in Canadian law, it is considered illegal for the Heraldic Authority to treat women differently.

▲ *The shield of arms for the British Columbia Institute of Technology is charged with computer symbols.*

▼ *The patents of arms for Canadian institutions and individuals are usually worded in English and French, but native languages may also be included.*

JAPAN: THE OTHER HERALDRY

Few nations and societies outside Europe have ever maintained any system of recognition comparable with heraldry in length of service and application. There is one extraordinary exception: the crests or badges used for many centuries by the Japanese courtiers and military elite. Such devices are called mon.

THE MON

To understand the precise meaning of the word mon it is necessary to decipher the two Japanese characters that make it up: they mean "thread" and "markings". In other words, the badges originated as embroidered costume decorations. Often, as with heraldry, they employ as symbols the simplest household objects, such as fans or kitchen implements.

Various heraldic writers have been intrigued by the similarity in usage between Japanese mon and European heraldry, for the former were used by Japanese warriors on their armour and battle flags, and on the clothing they wore for formal occasions. Even so, throughout the periods during which warfare raged in both Japan and Europe, neither system can have had any influence on the other. In modern times, along with the importation into the West of so much that is Japanese, has come the triumph over heraldry of the western equivalent of the mon – the logo. Very often in recent years, corporations that previously sported full achievements of arms have shelved them in favour of a corporate emblem that in style would not have looked out of place on the battle banners of a 15th-century shogun.

As early as the 8th century, the emperors of Japan were using specific emblems associated with their dynasty. It followed that what the ruler did was aped by those who served him and formed his social circle: the courtiers and court officials. The early mon were often Chinese in flavour, with symbols such as the phoenix, cloud formations, peacocks and dragons reflecting the influence and respect felt by the Japanese court for the powerful T'ang dynasty and its court across the water.

MILITARY USE

Although in its early life the mon was primarily a feature kept firmly within the walls of the imperial court, its use was watched with envy by the other leading group in Japanese feudal society: the military, or warrior, class. As this group grew in strength it made inroads into the formal life of the court and adopted much courtly style as its own. Yet often the two classes viewed each other with mutual suspicion. The court saw the warrior caste as brutal and barbaric, while the warriors regarded the courtiers as effete and weak-willed.

Having started as a symbol that identified the courtier's possessions and costume, the mon became associated with the trappings of the military man. The three main platforms for its display were the standards or battle flags (hata), tall, narrow banners up to 3m (10ft) in length; cloth curtains (tobari) used in the military camp to partition the commander's formal enclosure; and the formal garment (hitare), made of silk brocade, which, although worn

▲ The jimbaori, the Japanese nobleman's equivalent to the tabard or jupon. This example bears the mon of the Honda clan.

▲ The marriage of two distant and distinctive symbolic traditions: a recent grant of arms to a gentleman of Japanese origin now living in Canada has placed the family mon on a European warrior's shield.

▼ Just as in Europe heralds and heraldic writers drew up rolls of armorial bearings, in Japan the history and characters of mon were studied in great detail, especially by artists. This is a page from a Japanese artist's book of mon.

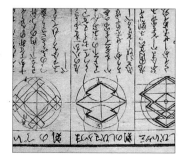

beneath armour, was visible through sleeves and leg coverings. Small flags bearing *mon* were also attached to helmets.

In time, European influence did make its presence felt in Japan and the clothes worn by Portuguese and Spanish adventurers led to the development of a Japanese version of a coat of arms. The *jimbaori* was a sleeveless garment worn over armour and often decorated with the bearer's *kaemon*, a substitute, or lesser form of, *mon*. The garment was much favoured by the *daimyo*, or feudal lords, who controlled much of Japan between 1400 and 1416. The essential difference between the *jimbaori* and the medieval western warrior's "jupon", or tabard, was that the former was removed before battle commenced.

From the late 17th century onwards, the *mon*, which had up to then been thought of as the prerogative of the courtiers and warrior classes, began to be adopted by anyone, of any status, who was in some way associated with them – such as the kabuki actors and courtesans who helped the samurai or the palace official to forget his heavy day. As in Europe, where inroads

▼ *A 17th-century battle scene shows in vivid colour and detail the use of the* mon *by the Japanese clans (in this case the Minamoto and the Taira); battle flags and standards are much in evidence.*

were made into heraldry by the merchant classes, Japanese commentators of the period bemoaned the usurpation of noble dress and insignia by those of less ancient and less honourable status.

MON MOTIFS

The *mon* of the military elite were often adapted from those of the courtiers in a way that emphasized the former's martial nature. Flowers, which were associated with a more gentle way of life, therefore had their petals interspersed with sword blades; instead of butterflies or birds, the warriors might choose axe blades and a spirited representation of the helmet horns (*kuwagata*) favoured as an adornment by Japanese warriors.

The design of the *mon* is usually very simple. Multiples of motifs are rare, as are combinations of more than two different objects. The device may be left by itself or fitted into a frame formed by a ring, square, diamond, or several-sided border (as opposed to the shield shape that is essential to heraldry).

Mon are seldom of more than one colour, and the choice of this depends on the background. Black lacquer, for example, used in Japan for many articles from furniture to armour, tends to be decorated with the family *mon* in gold. Battle flags might be of white cloth charged with the

commander's *mon* in either red or black, though if the flag was black the *mon* would probably be in white.

Whatever the nature of the motif – whether it was a bird, flower, geometric pattern or ideograph (written character) – the *mon* was designed to fill the frame in which it was used. So much of Japanese life was dominated by the symbolism of superstition that, unlike European heraldry, the *mon* might consist of a character representing an auspicious meaning, such as "good luck" or "longevity".

Many a Japanese *mon* could be translated heraldically, bars and pallets being just two devices that heraldists would recognize as directly comparable with heraldic ordinaries. But there the similarity ends, for far from being simple geometric shapes, in Japan much that is simple carries a hidden meaning through symbolism that is sometimes several millennia old.

Although formal systems of difference marks for children or branches of a family do not exist as they do in European heraldry, junior branches of a Japanese family grouping often adopted modified versions of the *mon* of the senior branch or leader. In addition to their formal mark (*jomon*), families also had several substitute symbols (*kaemon*), which might, through common practice, be granted to another family related by marriage.

THE HERALDRY OF CONFLICT

From its earliest days, heraldry has been seen as an adjunct to conflict. Just as one person's freedom fighter is another's terrorist, so also the signs and symbols of either side can promote inspiration or hatred. Heraldry grew up during a period of conflict between Christian Europe and the Islamic East, and there is some evidence that it may have had its origins in Islamic emblems. Many shields bearing crosses or crescents are said to have their origins in the Crusades, but such symbols pale beside the heraldic imagery of Hungary, whose noble families saw themselves as the last bastion of Christendom against the Turks. At least a third of all Hungarian arms bear Turkish body parts.

The clash of ideologies spilled over into the arms of other noble families of the Holy Roman Empire. The Princes of Schwarzburg, for their part in defeating a Turkish army at Raab in Hungary, were given an augmentation consisting of a Turk's head having its eye pecked out by a crow. Another augmentation, granted to the Barons Hochpied, shows the hand of a Christian freed from Turkish fetters. But heraldry can be a witness to all parties, whoever the oppressor. In the arms of the Gabonaise district of Ogooué-Lolo, broken fetters represent the countless people who were forced into slavery by Europeans.

EUROPEAN CONFLICTS

More recent struggles have been commemorated on the shields of arms of many towns, from Sweden to Serbia. The struggle for freedom from Russia by the Lithuanian townspeople of Pandorys was recorded by a rising hawk blooded in one wing, while the infamy of the Nazi concentration camp at Flossenburg in Czechoslovakia is recorded in the arms of the nearby town of Holysov, featuring a red rose rising from behind barbed wire. The division of Germany between East and West was recorded with more barbed wire in the arms of Wennerode in Lower Saxony, where the watchtowers and trip mines of the East German border zone actually passed along the edge of the parish: the heraldic Saxon stallion easily leapt the manmade absurdity.

The manipulation of symbols by men of war is of course far older than heraldry itself, but recent conflicts provide vivid examples of this use of heraldic emblems.

▲ *Heralds of the Holy Roman Empire and Hungary point to the freeing of Christian slaves in the arms of the Barons Hochpied.*

▼ *An arm patch of a Croatian Special Forces unit during the conflict in Yugoslavia. The Sahovnica, the chequered shield of Croatia, appears in the background.*

▲ *The rose of freedom throws its head above the wire of the concentration camp in the arms of Holysov.*

▼ *The Saxon horse leaps to freedom over the Iron Curtain in the arms of Wennerode.*

The break-up of the former Yugoslav Federation saw heraldry that had remained dormant for many years revived with fervour. Slovenia adopted entirely new arms, despite having a national identity many centuries old. Other states such as Bosnia-Herzegovina, Serbia and Croatia, re-adopted heraldry that each associated with a glorious past, real or imaginary.

To the Croats, the Sahovnica – their shield of white and red chequers – was a symbol of pride worn since the medieval period, but during World War II it was banned by Tito for 45 years. After 1991 it re-appeared everywhere, on flags, badges,

▲ *A Serbian military official denounces NATO bombing against a backdrop of the arms of the Yugoslav Federation, Serbia and Montenegro, Belgrade 1999.*

key rings and car stickers, and was viewed with horror by Serbs. In turn, the Serbs replaced the red star on the Serbian flag with their ancient coat of arms – a cross between four Cyrillic letter Cs – in a direct challenge to the hated Croatian chequerboard. The Cs stand for *Samo slago Srbina spasava* ("Only unity saves the Serbs").

▼ *In Northern Ireland both sides of the political divide make their presence known through heraldry. This display by a Loyalist group mixes conventional heraldic charges with local symbols such as unit numbers.*

NORTHERN IRELAND

The tempestuous twinning of symbol and sensibility has nowhere been more manifest than in Northern Ireland. Both Republicans and Ulster Unionists know equally well the power of symbols. From the 1960s to the 1990s, the most vivid by-product of the Troubles has been the development of "house art", or murals. Each side has seen this as a means of displaying the essential episodes of its history.

Heraldry has played a large part in the mural movement. The Republicans' desire to see Ireland united has often been manifested by presenting the arms of the country's four provinces – Leinster, Connacht, Munster and Ulster – on a single shield. In these cases the arms of Ulster are those of the Republic's province of that

name: a field of gold with a red cross (the arms of the de Burgh family), its centre charged with the bloody hand of the O'Neills. The British province of Ulster places the red cross on a white field, with the red hand surmounted by a crown.

Many tales are told of the origins of the red hand. It is not, as some would have it, a sign used by those who fought on the Protestant side at the Battle of the Boyne in 1690, but a charge borne in the arms of the O'Neill family. They were kings of Ireland, and the hand is said to commemorate the legend that their ancestor was part of a Viking raiding force. The Vikings had decided that whoever was first to place his hand on Irish soil would be its rightful ruler. The O'Neill ancestor, seeing that the ship of a rival would ground before his, cut off his hand and threw it on to the shore.

The hero of Protestant Loyalists is William of Orange, king of Britain 1689–1702. The Union Jack and its colours are used to decorate lampposts and kerbstones in Loyalist areas, and each Loyalist faction displays its badge combining the red hand and the crown. In murals, these may be placed beside the arms of Derry or Belfast, accompanying the portrait of a "local hero". In Republican areas, paintings of masked gunmen may be seen against a backdrop of the arms of the Republican provinces, and also of other national groups around the world.

▼ *In Republican Belfast the arms of the city of Valencia are used to express solidarity with the freedom fighters of Catalonia.*

THE CONTINUITY
OF HERALDRY

The heraldic tradition stretches back at least eight centuries, but for most of
that time no knight in armour has carried a coloured shield or worn a
helmet decorated with a crest to identify him in the thick of battle.
Heraldry has long outlived its original function on the battlefield, because it
has also served other purposes: the assertion of noble status, the declaration
of allegiance and the rallying of loyalty. Its vivid imagery and venerable
traditions still have persuasive power today, when even though few heraldic
authorities remain, coats of arms still lend grace and authority to many
products of the modern world, from cigarette packets to submarines.
Displays of the heraldry of earlier centuries are vivid reminders of our
cultural history and stability, and there are many who are proud to continue
heraldry's long tradition.

◀ *The achievement of arms of Robert Harrison,*
painted by Dan Escott.

HERALDRY'S PAST AND FUTURE

As the world enters the third millennium of Christian history, heraldry will soon be able to celebrate its first thousand years o f being. Although the exact date of its birth is, of course, unknown, perhaps 2150 might be a good time to celebrate its first millennium. Certainly by 1150 the main tenets of heraldry – as a hereditary system of colour and symbol based on the shield – were already in place. What then will heraldry look like in 2150? How might it have progressed, and will it be used in any way that resembles its original function?

Is heraldry still the preserve of the aristocracy? Britain is now possibly the only nation that continues to renew its aristocracy, by the creation of life peers. Of those who take up their seats in the House of Lords, about two thirds still apply to the English College of Arms for a grant of arms and supporters. However, the number of peers that do not bother to take up their entitlement is growing. Their attitude may be best summed up in the words of Baroness Ryder of Warsaw, better known through her charity work as Sue Ryder, who firmly rejected armigerous status:

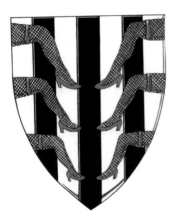

▲ In past centuries many arms featured body parts, and even a wooden leg was used as a charge. In the modern age, prison bars and six female legs grace the arms posthumously granted to a judge who often presided over cases involving prostitutes.

Those funny fellows the heralds asked me if I wanted a coat of arms. I saw how much they were asking for it and thought of how many food parcels I could send with the money. I cannot think what type of person would go for such an absurd anachronism.

Well, there are such people: they do still approach the College of Arms and feel a certain pride in a grant of armorial bearings. They may number in their hundreds in a single year, though this is unusual.

CHARGES OLD AND NEW

Those who do wish to become armigerous are taking part in a centuries' old tradition that has served and been adapted and fuelled by the fashion of the age. In heraldry's heyday, heralds compiled rolls of arms known as "ordinaries", which were catalogued according to the charges they bore. If an updated ordinary of arms were to be compiled by today's heralds, it would reflect the whole span of the history of heraldry, setting "then" alongside "now" on the same sheet.

It would be possible, for instance, to see medieval dress sense mixed with that of modern times, starting with the maunch, a medieval lady's sleeve that still graces the shields of the English families of Hastings and Cowper, just as it did in the days when such an item was actually worn some 700 years ago, and the Dutch family of van Abbenbroek still use their punning arms of a pair of breeches, in the style worn by the men of the family four centuries ago.

Beside the shields of those families might be placed that of an English judge from the late 20th century, who often had to pass sentence on the local prostitutes: he is commemorated in arms – granted (posthumously) by the English heralds – charged with pallets (representing prison bars) and six ladies' legs clad in fishnet stockings and garters.

Heraldry has shown itself to be a survivor, and will probably long continue to survive. Whereas once achievements of

▲ Trinity House, the corporation that administers English and Welsh lighthouses, had its arms granted in the Tudor period and now uses them on its helicopters.

arms could be seen on the coach panels of the aristocracy, today they are more likely to be painted on a lorry belonging to a supermarket chain, or a municipal garbage truck. Where once shields of arms were used to decorate the dinner services on noblemen's tables, today you are more likely to see a coat of arms on a china teacup on sale in a seaside souvenir shop, or on a pewter plate decorated with the arms of a German district.

SOCIAL STATUS

The longing for social recognition shows itself in many ways. The obtaining of a grant of arms is perhaps just the most blatant expression of such a need, and is not confined to the nobility.

In 17th-century France the middle classes, and even the peasantry, were encouraged to take up arms (though many of the latter were forced to accept such an honour, and were then taxed for the privilege). In Switzerland, heraldry of a domestic nature was commonly adopted by the townsfolk: builders, decorators, and even funeral directors were keen to curry favour with the middle classes. The gable ends of their houses might bear heraldic charges such as crosses, or even shields, and if the owner could make no claim to arms, his initials or the date of the house's construction could fill the space, which on

▲ *Imitation is the highest degree of flattery, and the use of heraldry always confers a certain respectability, even when it appears in a condom advertisement.*

the nobleman's house would bear his heraldic achievement. In death, the coffin fittings of the middle classes were shaped like shields or cartouches to lend an air of nobility to the funeral observances.

It is a theme carried on into our own age. Many companies associated with the leisure and pleasure industry, from playing card manufacturers to condom makers, look to an achievement of arms, real or

▼ *Arms designed by the English heralds for the Maharajahs of Jaipur appear on a plaque in Elveden Church, Suffolk, England. It commemorates the son of Duleep Singh, the Maharajah from whom Queen Victoria obtained the Koh-i-noor diamond.*

assumed, to give them a respectability associated with the traditional users of heraldry. Cigarette manufacturers notoriously commandeer coats of arms for their own ends – almost half of all popular cigarette brands are stamped with quasi-heraldic bearings in an attempt to distract attention from the message of the government health warnings prominently printed alongside.

The notion of conferring nobility through arms was behind the urge to bestow splendid achievements on those of royal or noble status who came from nations where heraldry was not known. One recipient of a regal achievement, whether he wanted it or not, was a young ward of the British Raj in India, the Maharajah Duleep Singh of Jaipur. Duly shipped off to Britain, in 1849 the Maharajah was persuaded to "present" Queen Victoria with the principal jewel of his treasury, the magnificent diamond known as the Koh-i-noor, now part of the British crown jewels. The grateful Queen, who treated the young Maharajah as one of her own family, saw to it that the coat of arms drawn up for him by the English heralds included an escutcheon of the Cross of St George – an allusion to his nominal conversion to Christianity. The Maharajah eventually moved to France, disillusioned with British control of his former realm.

LIVERIES AND SYMBOLS

Once upon a time men in armour watched over the land, bearing their personal devices on breastplates and shields. Today

▲ *In the medieval melée – the part of a tournament in which all the combatants took part together – heraldry was often the only way to identify the contestants.*

the armorial bearings they display are more likely to belong to a police force: the armoured man still exists, no longer a knight in shining armour but a member of a police anti-riot squad. Yesterday's war horse is today's battle tank or fighter bomber, though the modern German armed forces still bear the iron cross, the famed sign of the Teutonic Knights.

The medieval melée, or staged battle, with its milling knights and liveried troops,

▼ *The modern equivalent of a tournament melée can be seen on the crowded floor of the Chicago Board of Trade, where the traders identify themselves by wearing jackets in the liveries of their companies.*

▲ *The collapse of communism is vividly depicted in a Hungarian political party poster. The ancient shield of the kingdom of Hungary smashes through the arms of the communist state.*

▲ *The coat of arms of the Princes of Schwarzenberg, constructed by Franticek Rint in 1870 from human bones. It hangs in the remarkable ossuary at the monastery of Sedlec in the Czech Republic.*

has been replaced by the financial market floor, where groups of traders in coloured jackets jostle and gesticulate in a scene worthy of King René's tourney book or a painting by Uccello. A similar scene is played out in modern-day horse racing, with the jockeys wearing the liveries of the racehorses' owners, much as any household retainer might have done in the medieval period.

In Italy the great horse race of Siena, known as the Palio, takes the viewer back to medieval times. Not only does each rider wear the colour of his *contrada* (ward) but the whole day is one of medieval splendour, with each *contrada* represented by banner-bearers wearing the dress of the 15th century.

HERALDRY AS A WEAPON

While those of a certain degree have long been afforded armorial bearings, the very exclusivity of armory meant that it could be harnessed by those who wished to pour scorn on its noble and royal patrons – and this has been the case from the medieval period until the present day. Cartoonists and more formal artists have had fun with

the heraldic beast, turning even the most ferocious monsters into cuddly figures of fun at the expense of the armiger.

The political satirist has frequently turned the statement "Know by arms" on its head, poking fun at the pompous, the proud and the unpopular through their heraldic bearings, but cartoonists and poets have at times needed to tread a careful line between acceptability and prosecution, or even worse. In England in the late 15th century, the work of William Collingborne

of Bradfield Manor, Wiltshire, who chose to pen a satire on the rule of Richard III and his cronies, was just too much for the last Plantagenet monarch. Collingborne's political satire included the famous rhyme, "The Cat, the Rat, and Lovel our Dog, Rule all England under the Hog". Each name represented one of Richard's chief officials: Sir William Catesby, Sir Richard Ratcliffe, and Francis, Viscount Lovel. Sir William's crest was a cat, Lord Lovel's a dog and the King's badge was the white boar, or "hog". The author of the rhyme was seized and executed for his temerity in 1484.

ADAPTABILITY

Heraldry lends itself to a whole world of application, from the conservative to the crazy. An outstanding example of the latter can be found in the ossuary (or bonehouse) of the former Cistercian monastery at Sedlec, near Kutna Hora in the Czech Republic. Faced with a mound of up to 40,000 complete sets of human bones, the local authorities commissioned a local woodcarver, Franticek Rint, to put them in some kind of order.

Rint's original solution was to arrange them into the most bizarre decorations for the chapel, including an altarpiece and a chandelier. He started work in 1870 and,

▼ *The colours of heraldry are vibrantly rendered in a massive stained glass window displaying the arms of the Princes of Schwarzenberg in Prague Cathedral, Czech Republic.*

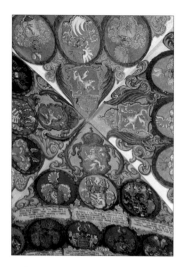

▲ *A magnificent collection of heraldry on the ceiling and walls of the chamber of the land registry court, Prague Castle, in the Czech Republic.*

▲ *Heraldry in miniature is a popular motif in jewellery. This diamond and ruby brooch, c1550, is in the shape of the imperial double eagle, the arms of Austria.*

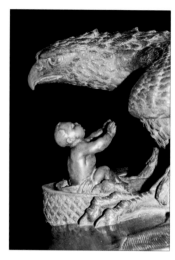

▲ *The eagle and child crest of the Stanleys appears in Liverpool's Anglican Cathedral on the monument to the 16th Earl of Derby, d1906, designed by Sir Giles Gilbert Scott.*

wishing to commemorate the new owner of the chapel, the Prince of Schwarzenberg, he used some of the bones to construct the heraldic achievement of the Prince. The eeriest part of this composition must be the augmentation granted to the family for its part in the Battle of Raab in Hungary, in which the Turkish army had been defeated. In the Sedlec ossuary, the Turk's head of the augmentation, with its eye being pecked out by a crow, is represented by a real human skull.

The Schwarzenberg arms are more traditionally depicted in stained glass in the Cathedral of St Vitus in Prague. This depiction, almost 6m (20ft) high, is kaleidoscopic in its colour, and the viewer needs to know his or her heraldry well to understand the composition.

In nearby Prague Castle, the Schwarzenberg arms also appear with many other shields of the Bohemian nobility. One of the smallest of the castle

▶ *A modern British heraldic standard, for Anthony Ryan of Bath, England. The arms are placed on the hoist (the area nearest the flag pole) and the other segments are charged with the crest (twice) and badge.*

▲ *Heraldry has been adapted to every period of its history. In this design for an IT company, the British royal arms are suggested through computer parts.*

▲ *The crest of the Stanleys, Earls of Derby: the eagle and child in its medieval form.*

chambers contains the finest collection of heraldry. The court of the land registry met here to decide matters relating to the estates of the nobility. Its high officials, the judges and their deputies, all from the aristocracy, are represented by their shields. Each term of the court's life is depicted by arranging the shields of arms of its members in hierarchical order, with the shield of the king at the head of the display, the senior judges below it and the arms of the deputies below them.

Stained glass, murals and human bones: these three examples of the ways in which it has been depicted illustrate the varied appeal of heraldry. Its adaptability and ability to evolve has been its strength.

This book shows how heraldry has used medieval fashion, the paraphernalia of war, animals, imaginary beasts, sputniks, meat hooks, mine workings and musical instruments. All are bound together and held within the world of "belonging", which is what heraldry is all about. In recent years this power to adapt has meant that it has

even taken its place in outer space. In 1992, six copies of the coat of arms of the Canadian Space Agency accompanied Dr Roberta Bondar, the Canadian astronaut, on her voyage in the space shuttle *Discovery*. Back on earth, space travel itself has featured as a motif in the arms of several Russian municipalities, reflecting the pride felt in the USSR over its lead in the 1960s space race.

The use of modern media of all kinds has also helped with heraldry's adaptation into the 21st century. A particularly striking and unusual example was to be found at the former British headquarters of the construction toy company Lego, in Wrexham, North Wales. The building's foyer was dominated by the coat of arms of the Borough of Wrexham Maelor – constructed in Lego, of course.

There was a time, not so very long ago, when the study of heraldry was considered to be the preserve of those who made most use of it – the well-to-do. Now, however, it is open to all, and heraldry societies, both national and local and all less than half a century old, are proliferating. In the age of the internet, genealogical hits on the web are said to be second in number only to pornographic sites.

USING THE FAMILY ARMS
The creativity of modern heraldic artists begs the question, how in the 21st century can one best serve heraldry while using it?

▲ *The heraldic maxim that the charge should fully fit its field was observed by A.W. Pugin when he incorporated the arms of the Talbots in his design for the doors of the Catholic church in Cheadle, England.*

There is a thin line between good and bad taste. Many people of ancient lineage would probably never be seen dead in anything as vulgar as a blazer bearing the family arms or crest; that would be associated with "new money". A discreet signet ring engraved with the family crest might be thought to be acceptable anywhere, yet, confusingly, a recently published guide to job interviews suggested leaving such a ring behind, claiming that it would suggest the wearer was attempting to show their social superiority over the other candidates for the post.

A flag bearing arms would be fine if you had a stately home to fly it from, but is not so appropriate on the average suburban house. But the hard-up owners of British stately homes, who are forced to open their crumbling piles to the public to make a living, may feel that they might as well flaunt the family escutcheon on everything from the guide book to the souvenir china mugs. In view of the declining family fortunes,

▲ *Lego bricks were used to build the local borough's coat of arms, in the foyer of the former Lego offices at Wrexham in North Wales.*

▶ *The heady delights of Amsterdam are advertised in this version of the city arms, with the traditional saltires replaced by objects reflecting the motto.*

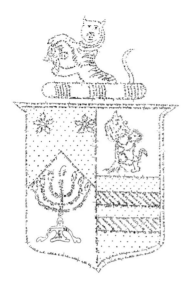

▲ *Heraldry can be adapted to suit most needs, and most creeds. Here the coat of arms of the Jewish family of Mocatta makes use of the texts of Hebrew prayers, whose letters make up the entire heraldic design.*

their noble ancestors – victorious commanders at the Battle of Agincourt or, more probably, the owners of a sugar plantation in Barbados – are probably already turning in their crested coffins within the family vault.

▼ *The helm, crest and mantling of medieval times are here adapted to the modern needs of an English football club. Southampton's halo crest reflects the team's nickname – "the Saints".*

BUCKET-SHOP HERALDRY

From the time that heraldry became established in Europe in the Middle Ages there was a constant battle between those who had a right to it and those who had not. There were many complaints from members of the aristocracy about those, such as merchants, who assumed armigerous status for themselves. In every age there have been artists ready to design and execute armorial bearings for any client, or to supply them with coats of arms that really belonged to some other family who happened to have the same surname.

The practice is still alive and well today and is usually known as "bucket-shop" heraldry. It may be as much as some people want. However, "a coat of arms for your name" will almost certainly not have the slightest connection with anyone related to you, and although it might make a pleasant decoration it would certainly be fraudulent to start using the arms on your letter heading, or in any other way that suggests it is your personal property.

For those who have a need to be noticed, there are plenty of institutions that will take their money to help them achieve this, especially bogus orders of chivalry. Such organizations offer their members the chance to take part in curious ceremonies, dress up in cloaks and funny hats and don sparkling badges and stars. They will relieve their credulous clients of even more money as they rise in rank in the "order".

Some of these bodies may be harmless, and some may even contribute to charity. Some may boast a member of an exiled royal family as their "Grand Master". Most are simply money-making enterprises, and the area is a minefield for the innocent subscriber, especially prevalent in those countries that no longer have any legitimate orders of chivalry.

In Britain, there is also the matter of lordships of the manor, which increasingly become available for sale. A lordship of the manor is a feudal title that simply concerns the ownership of land. The property in question may be perhaps no more than a small patch of turf upon which once stood an actual manor house, now long gone. Such a title gives the owner no seat in Parliament, no peerage and no automatic right to a coat of arms (though, like anyone else, he or she can apply to the College of Arms for a grant). If you are the lord of a manor you could put the title on your letter heading, but you would risk derision from those in the know, and to call yourself "Lord…" or "Lady…" would be considered decidedly beyond the pale.

▲ ▼ *In recent years the logo has often replaced the coat of arms as a more apt device, yet it needs to be designed just as carefully. In this logo for a restaurant chain the hand of the little man, seen in the original version (above) was later removed after members of the public pointed out an unfortunate interpretation – it looked as if he was trying to make himself throw up.*

A MODERN GRANT

Few nations today still retain formal heraldic authorities that grant arms to individuals. If they have heraldic institutions at all, these tend to concern themselves with matters relating to the regulation of civic and military heraldry, though those of Canada, the Republic of Ireland and Scotland often grant arms to individuals as well as to corporations. Let us take a look at how the oldest heraldic authority in the world, the English College of Arms, approaches the matter.

THE PETITION

Before an achievement of arms can be granted to an individual, he or she must formally request the right to bear them. If an attempt to prove a right to arms through descent from an earlier grantee has failed – direct male descent from the grantee being necessary in England – or if no claim to existing arms is put forward, an individual of English or Welsh nationality, and (outside Canada) of English descent, must formally petition for a patent of arms from the Crown, which is the "fount of all honour".

Patents creating and conferring the right to display armorial bearings, and to transmit them to one's heirs, are granted by the Crown through its officers, commonly called the heralds (appointed by separate letters patent from the Crown) for the purpose, upon payment of certain fees. This is the system that has existed in England since the late medieval period.

Although anybody of English nationality or descent is entitled to petition the English heralds for arms, it is not an unquestioned right that arms should be granted to them. There are certain criteria that the heralds look for when deciding if the petitioner is worthy of bearing arms. Just what these criteria are is known only to the heralds themselves, although the publicity material issued by the College of Arms makes mention of persons "eminent" in certain fields. The matter of around £3,000 ($4,200), the cost of a patent of arms at the beginning of the 21st century,

▲ The heraldic artist Andrew Jamieson works on the patent of Baz Manning.

▼ Baz Manning's patent seen in its resplendent finished state.

▲ *The patent of arms granted by Ireland's Chief Herald to the Irish Genealogical Society in March 2001. The patent is worded in both Gaelic and English.*

may also inhibit some people who might otherwise have considered the possibility of making a petition.

The whole business of payment for the patent can raise the questions, "Can arms really be considered an honour? Are they just a purchasable conceit like any other status symbol?" Whatever the answer to this conundrum, for those who do eventually decide to press forward with their petition, the business will proceed along the following lines.

The petitioner may have a particular Officer of Arms in mind when approaching the College of Arms, but it is more likely that he or she will deal with whoever is the Officer in Waiting at the initial approach. Each of the heralds takes a turn at being duty officer and will meet any casual enquirer during the period of duty. Assuming that the officer believes the petitioner to be of good character and therefore likely to be granted arms, the process can begin in earnest.

THE MEMORIAL

First, the petitioner submits a quaintly worded "memorial" to the Earl Marshal of England, His Grace the Duke of Norfolk, who on the advice of the officer of arms will officially endorse the petition. The memorial includes the following words:

The Memorial of…showeth, That your Memorialist being desirous of having Armorial Bearings duly established with lawful authority has the honour to request the favour of Your Grace's Warrant to the Kings of Arms for their granting and assigning such Arms and Crest as they may deem suitable to be borne and used by him and his descendants with due and proper difference according to the Law of Arms. And Your Grace's Memorialist will ever pray, etc.

A curriculum vitae (CV) also has to be submitted by the petitioner. All being well, once the petitioner has been found to be of good character and generally an asset to society, the business can proceed. Prompt payment of the fee helps to speed the process up, although it can still be several years before the petitioner has the finished patent in his or her hands.

The reason given by the College of Arms for the time taken from payment to patent is the number and complexity of the stages through which it passes before being signed, sealed and registered. The Officer of Arms (known as the "agent") who is assigned to the petitioner now discusses any ideas that he or she may have for a heraldic design. Before a suitable design can be finalized, the agent is required to check through the College's splendid collection of ordinaries of arms, or armorial rolls, showing all the arms already granted, to make sure the prospective design of the shield is truly unique – not only when it is displayed in full colour, but also in black and white.

The petitioner is kept fully informed about the progress of the patent, and is made welcome at the office of the agent should he or she wish to call personally

▼ *The patent of arms of the late George Messer of Bath, granted in 1992. The designs are unique, but keep to medieval simplicity and clarity.*

▲ One of the innovative recent heraldic designs from the English College of Arms, sketched by Peter Gwynn-Jones, Garter King of Arms, for Prior's Court Foundation for autistic students. The jigsaw piece is the symbol of autism. The crest reflects the love of cats of the foundation's founder, Dame Stephanie Shirley, and the unicycle is a sport much enjoyed by the pupils.

(with prior appointment) at the herald's private office in the College of Arms. The agent is always pleased to discuss the client's personal requirements for an armorial design, and once this has been approved, the agent will commission an artist to paint the arms on the patent.

DESIGNING A COAT OF ARMS

Anyone desiring their own coat of arms would do well to have some idea of what is deemed good and not good in heraldic design. It is the duty of heralds (in those countries where they are still to be found), or heraldic designers, to educate their clients, whether they are individuals or district councils. It would be easy to include a multitude of charges representing an armiger's personal cares and conceits, but it is important to remember all the different ways in which the arms might be used after the achievement is approved.

One of the most popular ways of displaying a shield or crest is on a signet ring, and it can be awkward to place a very complex design on an area this size. Charges that point in a particular direction are another problem: usually they point towards the dexter and for a seal or signet application this has to be reversed if the impression is to be correct. A non-directional charge may be preferable.

A LESSON IN DESIGN

The heraldic author and designer, Arnold Rabbow of Brunswick, Germany, is often called upon to design new arms for district or community councils in his own province of Lower Saxony. His approach to the subject of heraldic design – whether civic or individual – offers a lesson to both prospective armiger and herald.

Herr Rabbow first asks for a meeting with the client – usually a town or regional council at one of its regular sittings – during which he asks for details of the history of the community, together with any special points of interest, such as local customs, distinctive geographical features, flora, fauna and dialectic curiosities. The notes he makes on the information he is given may run to many pages, since everyone will want to have their say.

He then takes out three existing armorial designs, usually all shields of German provinces. One might be complex, such as the arms of Rheinland-Pfalz, in which four separate arms are quartered on one shield. He then shows a shield of middling complexity, with several charges, and finally a simple shield, perhaps that of his own province of Lower Saxony, which bears a single charge of a white rearing horse on a red field. Herr Rabbow takes away the three shields and asks the assembly which one they remember. The answer is usually the arms of Lower Saxony – in other words, the simplest shield.

At a subsequent meeting, Herr Rabbow's next step is to show three shields he has designed based on his discussions with the

▲ The arms of the state of Rheinland-Pfalz. A complex design that says a great deal but is difficult to recall.

▲ A slightly less complex shield for Schleswig-Holstein, combining the lions of Schleswig and the nettle leaf of Holstein.

▲ The simplicity of the German state of Lower Saxony's arms makes it the most memorable of these three designs.

assembly. The first includes all the ideas that were suggested as charges, the second features several of the most popular ideas, and the third is a simple design, often using one colour and one metal, and with very few charges, or even a single charge. After the lesson of the previous meeting, the clients choose the third design.

Herr Rabbow does not always hit the right note. Some years ago when he was asked by a community near Wolfsburg to design its arms, he came up with a shield charged with a single red water lily leaf, a design that, for several reasons, he thought appropriate to the place. However, when he showed it to the village elders it was received with a mixture of amusement and embarrassment. When he asked why, he was eventually told that the design bore an unmistakable similarity to the glowing red neon heart that hung over the entrance of the local brothel.

APPROPRIATE CHARGES

Whichever heraldic authority would-be armigers consult, they will be asked to present some form of curriculum vitae, detailing their hobbies, military service, family pedigree (if known), any knowledge of ancestors, professions, tales of bravery or, indeed, infamy. Personal paraphernalia, ranging from pets to puns on a surname – the more the merrier – all help to give the herald or heraldic artist a précis of the individual's life and likes. Yet too much knowledge can be a dangerous thing, especially on a shield of arms. It is good to remember the principle of early heraldry – that a shield of arms should be identifiable across a battlefield. Happily, most people today do not have to worry about being clubbed over the head by a knight on a charger, but the same rule can still be usefully applied. Any

▼ *The arms of the English heraldist Robert Harrison, interpreted in a medieval style by one of the greatest modern heraldic artists, the late Dan Escott.*

▲ *This lily leaf charge designed for Mörse by Arnold Rabbow caused raised eyebrows on the local council.*

▲ *The finalized arms for Mörse, reflecting its name, derived from the phrase meaning "a marshy place".*

art student knows that simplicity is the essence of good design.

Surprisingly, there are still many designs of a simple geometric nature available for a new coat of arms, and heraldic authorities are delighted to see innovations in partition lines, counterchanging and such like, so long as the designs are sufficiently different from other existing arms. Lions, unicorns, and other ancient heraldic beasts can still be made distinct through a variety of attitudes and attributes, especially when combined with other charges.

Counterchanging can lead to a refreshingly simple and unique design. The important thing is to think in medieval terms, and if possible restrict the design to two tinctures – one colour and one metal. This does not mean that modern objects cannot be included, but can a boiler flue, or a computer chip, be represented in a way appropriate to heraldry? Any charge should be recognizable to the layman and easily translated into blazon. If the charge is a creature, its characteristics should be reasonable. It might be able to hold something in its paws or claws, but would not like having another charge, such as a key or a star, pinned on its neck or wings.

A coat of arms does not stop at the shield. The crest needs to be designed in the round. The English heralds are now taught to do so, although some modern crests still appear too much like "paper heraldry" – they could never be worn on a real helmet. Real crests, as depicted in medieval scenes of the *Helmschau* ("display of helmets"), especially that in King René's tournament book, were full of imagination, and were designed to be seen from the back and front, not just from the side as in a standard heraldic painting.

In those nations that possess full heraldic authorities, the heralds are there to guide the would-be armiger in matters of design. The correspondence between herald and client is just one of the delights involved in the making of a new coat of arms. When the whole process is complete it can literally be said to be a splendid achievement, not only for the armigers themselves, but for their descendants, part of a tradition going back many centuries.

CHOOSING AN ARTIST

If you live in a country that has its own heraldic authority, you will have had your arms granted by a herald who will have a wide range of artists and craftsmen to call upon. He may put you in touch with the relevant people, or offer to organize all the work on your behalf. For the patent itself, an English herald might choose one of the herald painters at the College of Arms to execute the painting. These artists have their studios in the attic rooms at the top of the College building, reached by an ancient staircase of many flights. Many a famous name in heraldic artistry has had his studio, as befits a herald painter, in the cramped attics of the College of Arms. Once appointed they tend to stay for many years. Several have died up there, which can pose a problem as few people venture into the venerable chambers (there is no lift).

Often the herald painter is of such renown as to have a backlog of work, and the herald may decide to farm out the work to an out-of-house heraldic artist,

◀ *The arms of the Cornish heraldic artist, Dennis Endean Ivall, painted in Mr Ivall's own characteristic Celtic style.*

▲ *A bookplate by the Dutch artist Daniel de Bruin in which the lozenge of the armiger is portrayed in a surreal style.*

whom he knows to be capable of such a commission. Should the petitioner favour a particular heraldic artist, it is essential to make this preference clear at the outset. They are perfectly entitled to do so, although any delay in declaring such an interest might cause inconvenience and embarrassment if the agent has already approached an artist of his choice.

Part of the pleasure of applying for a new grant of arms, or adapting the re-discovered arms of a direct ancestor, is choosing for yourself ways in which your personal arms can be portrayed. If you live in a country without a heraldic authority you will have no option but to deal directly with an artist.

THE SOCIETY OF HERALDIC ARTS
The organization that exists as a shop window for heraldic artists in England is the Society of Heraldic Arts, based in Reigate, England. Its craft members are expected to meet a particularly high degree of craftsmanship to join, and range from stained glass artists to bookplate designers. Not only do they experiment in different media, they often have very different styles, ranging from the graphic style of the Dutch artist Daniel de Bruin, through the medievalism of Anthony Wood and Andrew Jamieson, to the swirling Celtic creations of Dennis Ivall. Associate membership, which is open to all, enables heraldists to receive the Society's journal and to rub shoulders with the artists. Clients receive a register of members whom they can contact direct, listing the items each produces and showing examples of their work.

There are very few heraldic artists in the world, so it is not surprising that a trawl through the telephone directory will not often produce a result, although a heading does exist for them in the British Yellow Pages. It is more productive to join a heraldry society, as their journals carry advertisements from a wide variety of artists, many of whom do not belong to the SHA and may only otherwise be found by word of mouth.

HERALDIC STYLES
The painting of a coat of arms on the patent is by no means the only way in which it can be portrayed. Heraldry is always open to interpretation, and the re-visualizing of a coat of arms by a number of different artists can be a stimulating and enjoyable experience.

No two artists will draw in the same way. The house style of the English College of Arms differs markedly from that of the Scottish Lyon Court, and the personal styles of British artists can be remarkably varied and often instantly recognizable, while bookplates executed by a Dutch artist and a Canadian one will be refreshingly different from each other. Artists as far apart as Russia, Sweden and Zimbabwe may all be keen to execute private

commissions and all will produce distinctive interpretations of arms.

For every occasion a coat of arms is used, it can be rendered in a different way. Slaveish copies of the grant painting do not do justice to the creative skills of heraldic artists, and can look appalling in the wrong situation. A large colour painting to hang on a wall can have a great deal of detail added to it, while a small bookplate should be drawn quite differently. An engraver will want to draw a design suitable for cutting, while monochrome artwork for stationery will be rendered with clarity of line and small-scale printing in mind.

A large number of shield shapes have been used over the last 850 years of heraldry, and each will give a different feel to the arms. The charges and the crest may all have a variety of possible designs, all heraldically accurate yet each distinctive and often unusual.

▼ *The bookplate of the English heraldic author Stephen Friar shows the versatility of the modern artist, Andrew Jamieson.*

GLOSSARY OF HERALDIC TERMS

abatement: mark of dishonour

accolée: descriptive term for two coats of arms set side by side, to indicate marriage, with the charges on each facing each other

achievement: the complete display of armorial bearings

addorsed: of beasts, back to back

affronty: of a *charge*, facing the viewer

ailettes: "little wings", shoulder plates bearing arms of the wearer

alwyte: bright steel armour from the late medieval period

Argent: silver

armed: of a human being, clothed in armour; of a beast, having teeth, beak or claws in a separate colour

armiger: a person who is entitled to bear arms

arming cap: a padded cap worn under a helmet

arming doublet: a long-sleeved, hip-length tunic worn as an undergarment for armour

armorial bearings: the symbols borne by an *armiger* to distinguish him or her from others

armorial: a roll or book listing *armorial bearings* arranged alphabetically by the names of the bearers

armory: the study of *coats of arms*, heraldry

at gaze: of deer, looking towards the viewer

attainder: the extinction of civil rights, including the right to bear arms or titles, following conviction for treason or felony

attitude: of a beast or human being, posture

attribute: of a beast or human being, a characteristic with which it is represented

attributed arms: arms devised posthumously for individuals who lived before the age of heraldry

augmentation: an addition to the arms that reflects the gratitude of the donor (usually a sovereign)

aventail: a chain mail neck guard

Azure: blue

bachelor: a knight of the lower order

badge: a heraldic device belonging to an *armiger*, worn by retainers

banner: a square or oblong flag bearing a knight's arms

bar: a narrow horizontal stripe

baron: heraldic term for a husband; also the lowest rank of the peerage

bascinet: a lightweight, close-fitting domed helmet

Bath, Order of the: a British chivalric order

▲ *Arms of Sigismondo Malatesa, Lord of Rimini and his lady, Isotta.*

baton: a narrow diagonal band which does not reach the edges of the shield

bedesman: or beadsman, someone who was employed to pray for another person or group of people

bend: a diagonal stripe on a shield, from *dexter* chief to *sinister* base

bend sinister: a diagonal stripe on a shield, from *sinister* chief to *dexter* base, often used as a mark of illegitimacy

bendlet: a narrow *bend*

bezant: a gold *roundel*

billet: a small rectangular *charge*

billetty: covered all over with *billets*

blazon: the verbal description of *armorial bearings*

Bleu celeste: sky blue

bonacon: a mythical heraldic beast

bordure: a narrow band around the edge of the shield

boss: a circular protruding central knob on a shield

brizure: a difference mark used in *cadency*

cadency: a system of small alterations and additions to differentiate the arms of children in a family from those of its head

canting: of arms, with a design that alludes to the name of the bearer, also known as punning arms

canton: a square section, smaller than a *quarter*, in the top *dexter* or *sinister* corner of a shield

chamfron: a horse's head-guard

chapeau: a hat with a turned-up fur lining, symbolizing dignity

charge: a device on a shield or other item

chequey: covered all over with squares of equal size, in two alternating colours

chevron: an inverted V-shaped stripe on a shield

chevronel: a small *chevron*, or bent *bar*, on a shield

chief: the upper third of the shield

cinquefoil: a stylized flower with five petals

cipher: a monogram

coat armour: a quilted linen garment worn over armour and emblazoned with *armorial bearings*

coat of arms: the common term for the heraldic shield

cockatrice: a mythical heraldic monster, part serpent and part cockerel

cognizance: a distinguishing *badge*

compartment: the representation of the ground or other surface on which the *supporters*, shield and motto stand

coronel: blunted, crown-shaped lance tip used in jousting

couchant: of a beast, lying down with head erect

counterchanged: descriptive of a partitioned shield where the disposition of *tinctures* on one side of the partition line is reversed on the other side

counterermine: see *ermines*

couped: of a *charge*, such as an arm or branch, clean cut

couter: armour worn to protect the elbow

crest: a three-dimensional object adorning the top of the helmet

cross crosslet: a cross with the end of each limb itself crossed

cuir-bouilli: leather boiled in oil to make it malleable

cuirass: plate armour for the torso

cuisse: leg armour

cushion: a *charge* in the shape of a cushion with tassels at the corners

dancetty: "dancing", of a *line of partition*, a zigzag with large indentations

degradation: demotion from knighthood

delf: a square geometric *charge*

dexter: right (from the point of view of the shield bearer)

diaper: an all-over pattern resembling designs woven into damask fabric

difference mark: a *charge* added to a shield to differentiate a branch of a family

dimidiated: an early form of *marshalling* arms by halving them

dovetailed: of a *line of partition*, like a joint in carpentry

embattled: of a *line of partition*, like battlements

engrailed: of a *line of partition*, scalloped, with the points facing outwards

ensign: to place a crown, coronet, cap, helmet or cross above, and touching, a *charge*

erased: of a *charge* such as a limb, torn off

ermine: one of the *furs*, white with black tails (the stoat's winter coat)

ermines or counterermine: one of the *furs*, black with white tails

erminites: like *ermine*, with a red spot on each side of the black tail

erminois: one of the *furs*, gold with black tails

escarbuncle: a wheel-like device with spokes radiating from the centre of the shield

escutcheon: a small shield

escutcheon of pretence: a small shield bearing the wife's family arms set in the centre of her husband's shield

estoile: star with wavy points

femme: heraldic term for a wife

fess: a horizontal stripe across the middle of the shield

field: the background *tincture* of the shield

fimbriated: of a *charge*, edged with a narrow band of another *tincture*

fitched: usually of a cross, pointed at the foot

flanches or flaunches: a pair of curved segments on each side of the shield

fleur de lis: a stylized heraldic lily

formy: of a cross, having triangular limbs wide at the ends and narrow at the centre

fountain: a *roundel* bearing blue and white wavy bars

fraise: a white *cinquefoil* representing the strawberry flower

fret: a *voided lozenge* interlaced with a *bendlet* and a *bendlet sinister*

fretty: covered all over with a grid of diagonal lines

fur: a *tincture* representing an animal pelt

fusil: an elongated *lozenge*

gambeson: a quilted undergarment worn with chain mail

gambs: animals' paws

garb: a sheaf (usually of wheat)

Garter King of Arms: the most senior English herald

Garter, Order of the: the senior order of knighthood in England

golpe: a purple *roundel*

gonfalone: a large flag often hung from a cross-beam

gonfalonier: a standard-bearer of the Church

gore: a portion of the shield cut off by a curved line, like a *flanch*, but ending in a point

gouttes: small *roundels* or droplets

goutty: covered all over with *gouttes*

great helm: a helmet made with a series of hammered plates rising to a gradual point

greaves: leg-guards

griffin or gryphon: a mythical monster with the forepart of an eagle and the hindquarters of a lion

guardant: of a beast or human being, looking out of the shield at the viewer

guidon: a long flag used in battle as a marker or standard

guige: a strap to hold a shield when not in use

Gules: red

gusset: a side portion of the shield, cut off at top and bottom by diagonal lines

gyron: a wedge-shaped *charge*

gyronny: covered with *gyrons*, arranged around the centre of the shield

harness: a suit of armour

hatchment: a diamond-shaped board painted with a *coat of arms* to indicate the death of the bearer

heater shield: shield shaped like the base of a flatiron

heraldic heiress: the daughter of an *armiger*, who inherits his arms in the absence of any sons

hoist: the area at the top of a flag near the pole

honour point: the upper middle point of a shield

hurt: a blue *roundel*

imbrued: bloodied

impalement: the placing of two *coats of arms* side by side on a single shield

impress or impresa: a personal *badge* incorporating a motto

in chase: of deer, running

indented: of a *line of partition*, with small saw-like points

inescutcheon: a small shield borne in the centre of another shield

invected: as *engrailed*, with points facing inwards

jupon: a short, close-fitting quilted coat, usually decorated with the bearer's arms

king of arms: a senior herald

▲ *Arms of the Polish tribe Boncza..*

knight banneret: 1 a high-ranking knight in command of a body of men; 2 a square or oblong banner denoting his presence in battle

label: a difference mark across the *chief* of the shield applied to the arms of a son, usually the heir

langued: of a beast, with a tongue in a separate colour

line of partition: a line delineating a division of the shield

lists: a jousting enclosure at a tournament

livery: the uniform worn by a lord's retainers, made in his colours

livery collar: a chain of office indicating allegiance

lodged: of a deer, lying down

lozenge: 1 a diamond-shaped *charge*; 2 a diamond-shaped device used to display the arms of women

Lyon, Lord: the chief herald in Scotland

mantling: material protecting the back and sides of the helmet and the wearer's neck

marshal: to combine two or more coats of arms on one shield

mascle: a *lozenge* with its centre removed

matriculation of arms: the updating of family arms in Scotland

maunch: a medieval sleeve with a hanging pocket

melée: a battle staged as a tournament event

mullet: a five-pointed star

mural coronet: a circlet of stone with battlements or columns

Murrey: mulberry, a purplish-red

nebuly: of a *line of partition*, shaped like the edges of clouds

nombril or navel point: the lower middle point of a shield

officer of arms: a herald

ogress: a black *roundel*

Or: gold

ordinary: 1 a basic geometric *charge* on a shield; 2 a *roll of arms* in which *coats of arms* are catalogued according to the charges they bear

orle: a narrow band following, but set in from, the edge of the shield

pageant helmet: a helmet with ornamental bars across the face

pairle: a division of the *field* into three sections radiating from the centre

pale: a vertical band down the middle of the shield

pall: a Y-shaped band on a shield

panache: a feathered *crest*

paper heraldry: a derogatory description of accessories, such as *crests*, designed after heraldry ceased to have a practical function, which could not have been used for their ostensible purpose

partition lines: see *lines of partition*

▲ *Arms of Mary, Duchess of Bedford.*

passant: of a beast, walking across the shield

patty: of a cross, having triangular limbs which are wide at the ends and narrow at the centre

pean: one of the *furs*, black with gold tails

pellet: a black *roundel*

pencil: a small *pennon*

pennon: a personal flag, long and tapering, with a rounded or divided end

peytrel: a horse's chest-plate

pheon: an arrowhead

pile: an *ordinary* consisting of a triangular wedge with one side along the top of the shield

plate: a silver *roundel*

point: the base of the shield cut off by a horizontal line

point champain: the base of the shield cut off by a shallow concave line

pomme: a green *roundel*

potent: in the shape of a crutch

proper: shown in natural colours or form

punning arms: see *canting*

Purpure: purple

pursuivant: a junior herald

quarter: 1 a *sub-ordinary* occupying the top *dexter* quarter of the shield; 2 to divide a shield into any number of divisions each bearing a different *coat of arms*

quatrefoil: a stylized four-petalled flower, similar to a clover leaf

queue fourchy: a forked tail

raguly: of a *line of partition*, like battlements but set obliquely

rampant: of a beast, rearing up to fight

recursant: usually of an eagle, displayed with its back towards the viewer

reguardant: looking backwards

respectant: of two beasts or human beings, looking at each other

reversed: upside-down

roll of arms: a herald's catalogue of *coats of arms*

roundel: a circular *charge*

rustre: a *charge* like a *lozenge* with a hole in the middle

Sable: black

saltire: a diagonal cross on a shield

Sanguine: blood red

segreant: of a *griffin*, rearing up

sejant: of a beast, sitting upright facing *dexter*

semy: covered all over with small *charges*

sinister: left (from the point of view of the bearer of the shield)

springing: of a deer, leaping

stain: a heraldic colour that is not one of the primaries

standard: a long tapering flag in *livery* colours bearing the national emblem, usually placed at the commander's tent

statant: of a beast, standing facing *dexter*

sub-ordinary: one of the smaller, less frequently used geometric *charges*

supporters: figures supporting the shield of arms

surcoat: a quilted linen garment worn over armour and emblazoned with *coats of arms*

tabard: a short tunic emblazoned with *coats of arms* worn by heralds

talbot: large hunting dog, extinct

targe: a shield

Tenny: tawny orange

Thistle, Order of the: the senior order of knighthood in Scotland

tierced in pairle: of a shield, divided in three in the form of a Y

tilt: a wooden jousting barrier

tincture: the generic term for heraldic colours, stains, metals and furs

torse: see *wreath*

tourney shield: a small rectangular shield, with a notch for a lance

tourteau: a red *roundel*

trapper: a development of the saddle-cloth which covered the horse entirely, decorated with *armorial bearings*

tressure: a narrow band following, but set in from, the edge of the shield, narrower than the *orle* but often doubled

tricking: a method of noting a *blazon* in shorthand

trippant: of deer, walking or trotting across a shield

vair: one of the *furs*, represented as a pattern of blue and white

Vert: green

visor: the opening front of a helmet

voided: of a *charge*, represented in outline only

vulned: of a beast, wounded and bleeding

wreath, torse: a twisted cord of material around the top of the helmet, below the crest

wyvern: a heraldic winged dragon with two feet and a serpentine tail

yale: a heraldic beast resembling an antelope with tusks and curved horns, always shown parted

GLOSSARY OF FLAG TERMS

armed forces flags: special flags for each part of the armed forces (army, navy, air force, marines) which are used to mark military garrisons and quarters; also used for parades and ceremonies

armorial banner: a flag that consists of the *field* and *charges* of a *coat of arms*

badge: a heraldic emblem, different from a *coat of arms* in that it does not employ a shield

banner: (i) a square or rectangular flag fastened to a *staff* or attached to a *crossbar*, with an armorial or other elaborate design and made of costly material, often hand-painted and/or embroidered; (ii) any flag designed to hang vertically from a *crossbar*, with the design arranged accordingly

battle honour: a mark added to a *colour* or to a flag of a branch of the armed forces to show its military service

becket: a loop at the end of a *hoist* rope that fastens to a *toggle* at the end of the *halyard*, making it easier to *bend on a flag*

bend on a flag: to fasten a flag to a *halyard* in order to hoist it

bicolour: a flag whose *field* is divided horizontally, vertically or diagonally into two equal parts in two different colours

border: a wide band surrounding a *field* of different colour

break out a flag: to unfurl a flag that has been rolled and tied in such a way that a sharp tug on the *halyard* will cause it to open out

broad pennant: a tapering descate or *swallow-tailed* flag, mostly used by navies as the flag of the head of state; in British and American naval and yachting usage, it is the rank flag of a commodore

bunting: a traditional all-wool fabric used for making flags from the 17th century to the present day

burgee: a small distinguishing flag of a club or individual yachtsman, usually either triangular or tapering *swallow-tailed*

calico: a plain-woven cotton fabric of Indian origin used in the 17th

and 18th centuries in Europe for some flags

canton: the area of the upper *hoist* corner of a flag; also a square or rectangular *field* covering that area

charge: an object placed on the *field* of a flag; unlike the *badge*, a charge is not used separately

checky: a *field* bearing squares of alternating colours

civil ensign: a flag designating national identity, flown on commercial or pleasure vessels; formerly called a *merchant flag*

civil flag: a flag designating national identity, flown by private citizens on land

cleat: a metal device with two arms, attached to the lower part of a *staff*, to which the *halyards* are made fast

club pennant: a triangular flag to be hung vertically, usually charged with the emblem and *livery colours* of a sporting club

coat of arms: the common term for a heraldic shield

colour: the flag of a military unit (regiment, battalion or company), usually *fringed* and with different designs on the *obverse* and *reverse*

command pennant: a flag identifying the commander of a particular navy formation (flotilla, squadron, group etc) or an individual ship, usually triangular or tapering *swallow-tailed*

commission pennant: a very long, narrow flag, flown on a warship to indicate its commissioned status; the term *masthead pennant* is synonymous

consecration: the dedication ceremony of a *colour* or other flag

cord: a decorative, flexible string or rope made from several twisted strands, usually of gold or silver thread, or in national *livery colours*

counterchanged: having two colours alternating on each side of a line drawn through a flag

courtesy flag: the civil *ensign* of a country being visited by a merchant vessel or yacht of a different nationality, which is hoisted on entering a foreign port

cravat: a wide ribbon attached to a *staff* below the *finial*, used as a distinction or as a mark of honour with a military *colour* or flag

cross: a *charge* in the form of a cross concentric with the field, its arms extending to the edges of the flag; see also *Greek Cross*, *Scandinavian Cross*

crossbar: a rod bearing a flag (usually a *pennant*, *banner* or

▲ *Soviet Union (1924–1935).*

gonfalon), attached to a *staff*

damask: a reversible fabric, usually silk or linen, with a pattern woven into it

deface: to add a *badge* or crest to a flag

desecration: disrespectful treatment of a flag, such as public burning, which is punishable in many countries of the world

dip a flag: the custom of lowering a flag briefly and temporarily in salute to honour the national anthem, an important person or another vessel

disc: a circular device of a single colour used as a *charge*

distinguishing flag: a flag identifying a branch of government, military or naval service, or an official

drape a flag: the custom of attaching a black *cravat* to a *staff* as a sign of mourning

dress ship: to decorate a vessel with all *signal flags* for a holiday or special occasion

drum-banner: a small flag decorating a parade drum

eagle: (i) a *vexilloid* with a representation of an eagle on the top of the *staff*; (ii) the name of the French *colour* during the Napoleonic era

ensign: (i) a flag used to indicate the nationality of civil, government and naval vessels, flown by ships at or near the stern; (ii) in the United States, the lowest commissioned officer in the navy; (iii) in the 17th and 18th centuries, the usual term for a military *colour* and the colour-bearer

ensign-banner: a rectangular flag with a *field* and *fringe* of *livery colours*, charged with the full *coat of arms*

false colours: an *ensign* worn by a ship not entitled to it

fan: a semi-circular patriotic decoration made of *national flags* or fabric in *livery colours*

fanion: (i) a small *bicolour* used for marking a position in surveying; (ii) a small *pennon* in the *regimental colours*, used on military vehicles for marker purposes

ferrule: a metal ring at the top end of the *staff*, just below the *finial*

field: the whole area of a flag

fimbration: a very narrow border of a simple geometric *charge*, usually in a contrast colour

finial: a three-dimensional ornament on the top of a *staff*, usually made of metal

flag of convenience: the *civil ensign* of a country with low taxation and without stringent maritime regulations, used by a ship owner who is not a citizen of that country, but who registers the vessel there to avoid high taxes and in order to hire cheap labour

flag officer: a naval officer entitled to use a *rank flag*, usually above the rank of captain

flagpole: a pole made of wood, metal or glass fibre on which a flag is hoisted; it may be upright or projecting at an angle from a wall

flagstaff: see *flagpole*

flammule: a flame–shaped edge to a flag, often used in the past in the Far East

fly: the second half of the flag, the opposite end to the *staff*

fold a flag: a ceremony performed after a flag is taken down from a flagpole or removed from a coffin

frame: a wood or metal device designed to hold the top edge of a flag

fringe: a decoration made of twisted thread or metal (gold or silver), usually attached to the edges of the flag on the three free sides

gaff: a spar set diagonally on the aft side of a ship's mast from which a flag is hoisted

gonfalon: a long flag with a square or triangular tail, displayed from a *crossbar*, and originating in medieval Italy (a *gonfaloniero* being the person who carried such a flag)

gonfanon: a large lance flag with a square or rectangular *field*, and two to five squared long tails (the name deriving from the Norse *gunn-fane*, or "war flag"); in pre-heraldic and medieval times it was the flag of a ruler which was carried on

▲ *Romania (1921–1948).*

horseback

government flag: see *state flag*

Greek Cross: a *charge* in the form of a *cross* with arms of equal length

grommet: a metal eyelet reinforcing a hole near both ends of the *heading*, through which clips are attached to a *halyard*

guidon: a small military flag, usually *swallow-tailed* or with a fly descate or cloven-descate, serving as a guide to troops

gyronny: a *field* divided into eight or twelve triangles whose apexes meet at the centre

half-mast: to fly a flag at a point much below its normal position, usually as a sign of mourning

halyard: the rope to which a flag is bent in order to be hoisted; see *bend on a flag*

heading: a piece of canvas into which the *hoist* edge of a flag is sewn

hoist: the half of a flag nearest to the *staff*

honour a flag: a ceremony performed to signify an award to a military unit or civil organization, where the order ribbons are attached to the *staff* of the *colour* or *banner* by the head of state or his or her deputy

house flag: the flag of a commercial firm flown at sea, and from its headquarters or branches on land

inglefield clips: interlocking metal clips used to attach a flag securely to the *halyard*; their quick-release mechanism makes it possible to *bend on a flag* easily

jack: a small flag flown from a special jack-staff set in the bow of a warship, usually hoisted when a warship is in harbour

Jolly Roger: the popular term for a black pirate flag with a skull and crossbones design

lance pennon: a small flag, usually triangular or *swallow-tailed*, attached to the end of a lance

lay up colours: to deposit old *colours* ceremoniously in a church or museum

livery colours: the principal colours of a *coat of arms*

masthead pennant: see *commission pennant*

merchant flag: see *civil ensign*

mourning ribbon: a long black ribbon tied in a bow and attached to the *staff* just above the flag as a sign of mourning

national flag: (i) a flag of a nation-state, or formerly independent state, or of a non-independent national group that has its own government; (ii) in the case of an independent state, a flag and *ensign* used by the government authorities, general public and the navy

naval ensign: see *war ensign*

naval reserve ensign: a flag used as a *civil ensign* on a merchant vessel commanded by a retired naval officer

obverse: the more important, front side of a flag located to the observer's right from the *staff*; the opposite of *reverse*

pall flag: a flag laid over a coffin, hearse or tomb, used mainly at government and military funerals

parade flag: a flag carried outdoors by a marcher

parley flag: a plain white flag displayed by combatants to request a ceasefire and to indicate the desire to negotiate terms of surrender

paying-off pennant: the *commission pennant* of a vessel returning home after a long period of service; it has up to 75 m (82 yd) of extra material added to the length

pendant: see *pennant*

pennant: a flag that is tapering, triangular or *swallow-tailed* in shape, originally flown from a *crossbar* and in modern times also flown from a vertical *staff*

pennon: in medieval times, the small personal flag of an arms-bearer below the rank of knight banneret, intended for use on a lance borne by a mounted warrior

pilot flag: a flag flown by a vessel requiring or carrying a pilot

pinsil: a Scottish triangular flag used as a rallying point by a clan captain in the absence of the clan chief

pipe-banner: a small flag attached to the drone pipes of bagpipes

quarantine flag: a yellow flag flown by a ship that has not yet received medical clearance on arrival and which requires a certificate of good health

quarterly: a *field* divided into four equal parts in a crosswise fashion

rank flag: a distinguishing flag indicating the rank of an officer of the navy (commodore to fleet admiral), army or air force (generals)

regimental colour: see *colour*

reverse: the less important rear side of a flag located to the observer's left from the *staff*; the opposite of *obverse*

roundel: a circular emblem of nationality employed on military aircraft and air force flags, usually consisting of concentric rings of national colours

saltire: a *charge* in the form of a diagonal *cross* whose arms extend to the edges of a flag; known also as a St Andrew's Cross

salute the flag: the custom of saluting a flag when it is being hoisted, lowered or passed in a parade review; civilians stand at attention, men remove their headgear and military personnel perform a prescribed salute

Scandinavian Cross: a *charge* in the form of a Latin *cross* positioned on the *field* of a flag horizontally, with the vertical arms in the *hoist* portion of the flag

schwenkel: a rectangular or triangular tail extending from the upper *fly* corner of a flag, or a strip along the top edge of a flag, with a dependent tail; can also refer to a whole flag with a schwenkel

sendal: a fabric with a linen warp and silk weft used in north Europe since the 13th century and suitable for painted heraldic *banners*

serrated: a jagged division line or edge

service ensign: a flag designated to identify a vessel, providing a particular service for customs, mail, fishery inspection, lighthouse service, environmental protection, and so on

signal flag: a flag used to transmit messages, especially at sea

sleeve: the tube of material along the *hoist* of a flag through which the *staff* is passed

staff: the cylindrical piece of wood to which the flag is fastened; see also *crossbar*, *flagpole*, *gaff*

standard: (i) a *vexilloid* used by an army; (ii) a long tapering descate flag of heraldic design originally borne by a king or high-ranking noble; (iii) a rectangular flag of heraldic design which is not an *armorial banner*; (iv) a flag of a head of state

state ensign: a flag designating national identity, flown on non-military vessels in government service; also called a government ensign

state flag: a flag designating national identity, used by government authorities and institutions on land; also called a government flag

streamer: (i) a long ribbon attached to the *staff*, which is used mainly in the form of *battle honours*;

(ii) a long, narrow *pennant* used until the 17th century as a decoration on vessels

swallow-tailed: a flag with a triangular section cut out from the *fly* end

tab: a small piece of leather sewn inside the *sleeve* at either end, fastened to a screwhead to prevent the flag from slipping on the *staff*

tangle rod: a metal device attached to a *staff* projecting at an angle from a wall, to clasps a flag and stop it from wrapping around the staff

tassel: a tuft of loosely hanging twisted threads or metal hanging from a cord attached to the *staff*, used with a *colour*, or other ceremonial or decorative flag

toggle: a device at the end of a rope sewn into the *heading*, consisting of an oval-shaped wooden or plastic crosspiece that fastens to a *becket* at the end of the *halyard*, making it easier to *bend on a flag*

tricolour: a flag whose *field* is divided horizontally, vertically or diagonally into three parts in three different colours

triple swallow-tailed: a flag with two symmetrical triangular sections cut out from the *fly* end

truck: a circular metal cap fixed on the head of a flagpole below the *finial*, containing a pulley over which the *halyard* passes

trumpet-banner: a small flag to decorate a ceremonial trumpet, usually a proper *armorial banner*

union mark: a symbol expressing the political unification of two territories, used in the *canton* of other flags

vexilloid: a wooden or metal *staff* topped by an emblem made of animal bones, feathers, hide, wood or metal and serving the same purpose as a flag

vexillum: a square piece of cloth fastened to a *crossbar*, the standard of the Roman cavalry

war ensign: the naval flag of a nation, also called a naval ensign, carried by warships at the stern

yardarm: a bar attached horizontally to the mast of a ship or to a flagpole on shore to increase the number of flags that may be hoisted

▼ *Japan (since 1889).*

BIBLIOGRAPHY

Much of the data in the flags section of this book is based on official government publications and flag specifications from the 19th and 20th centuries, preserved in the files of the Flag Design Center, established and managed by A Znamierowski. The following also includes important sources of vexillological knowledge or contains information on particular flags used in this book:

Barraclough, E.M.C. and Crampton, William G., *Flags of the World* (Frederick Warne, London – New York, 1978)

Barber, Richard and Barker, Juliet *Tournaments: Jousts, Chivalry and Regents in the Middle Ages* (Boydell Press, Woodbridge, 1989)

Bascape, G.C. and Del Piazzo, M. *Insegne e simboli* (Ministero per i beni culturali e ambientali, Rome, 1983)

Bedingfield, Henry and Gwynn-Jones, Peter *Heraldry* (Magna Books, Leicester, 1993)

Brownell, F.G., *National and Provincial Symbols and flora and fauna emblems of the Republic of South Africa* (Chris van Rensburg Publications (Pty) Ltd, Melville, 1993)

Bruckner, A. and B., *Schweizer Fahnenbuch* (Zollikofer & Co. Verlag, St. Gallen, 1942)

Calvo Peréz, José Luis and Grávalos González, Luis, *Banderas de España* (Silex, 1983)

Campbell, Gordon and Evans, I.O., *The Book of Flags* (Oxford University Press, London, 1974)

Campbell, Una *Robes of the Realm, 300 years of Ceremonial Dress* (Michael O'Mara, London, 1989)

Cannon, Devereaux D. Jr., *The Flags of the Confederacy* (St. Lukes Press and Broadfoot Publishing, Memphis 1988)

Carek, Jiri Mestské *Znaky v Cesk'ych Zemich* (Academia, Prague, 1985)

Casas, R. D. *Arte y Etiqueta do los Reyes Catolicos* (Editorial

Alpuerto, Madrid, 1993)

Cascante, Ignacio Vincente *Heraldica General y Fuestes de las Armas de Espana* (Barcelona, 1956)

Ceballos-Escalera y Gila de, A *Heraldos y Reyas de Armas en la Corte de España* (Prensa y Ediciones Iberoamericanas, Madrid, 1993)

Colangeli, Oronzo, *Simboli e Bandiere nella Storia del Risorgimento Italiano* (Casa Editrice Prof. Riccardo Patron A.S., Bologna, 1965)

Collectible Stamps of the Arms of German Districts and Towns (Kaffee Hag, 1900–1930s)

Corswant-Naumburg, Inga von Huvudbaner och anvapen under stormaktstiden (Ödin, Stockholm, 1999)

Coss, Peter *The Knight in Medieval England 1000-1400* (Alan Sutton Ltd, 1993)

Crampton, William, *Flags of the World* (Dorset Press, New York, 1990)

Crouch, David William Marshal (Longman, Harlow, 1990)

Csáky, Imre A Magyar királyság vármegyéinek címerei a XVIII–XIX (Corvina, Budapest, 1995)

D'Acosta, Lino Chaparro *Heraldica de los Apellidos Canarios* (Estudios Tecnicos del Blason, 1979)

De-la-Noy, Michael *The Honours System* (Allison & Busby, London, 1985)

Dennis, Mark D. *Scottish Heralds: An Invitation* (Heraldry Society of Scotland, 1999)

Dower, John W. and Kawamoto, Kiyoshi *The Elements of Japanese Design* (Walker/Weatherhill, New York, 1971, revised 1979)

Dlugosz, JAN, *Banderia Prutenorum* (manuscript, 1448, reprint by PWN, Warszawa, 1958)

Ferro, Carlos A., *La Bandiera Argentina* (Ministerio de Cultura y Educacion, Buenos Aires, 1970)

Flaggenbuch (Oberkommando der Kriegsmarine, Berlin, 1939);

▲ *Arms of the Visconti family of Italy.*

Flags of the Native Peoples of the United States (Raven, Volumes 3–4, 1996-1997)

Flags of the World (The National Geographic Magazine, Special Edition, 1917)

Foppoli, Marco Gli stemmi dei comuni di Valtellina e Valchiavenna (Alpinia Editrice, 1999)

Foss, Michael *Chivalry* (Michael Joseph, London, 1975)

Friar, Stephen *A New Dictionary of Heraldry* (Alphabooks, Sherborne, 1987)

Friar, Stephen and Ferguson, John, *Basic Heraldry* (Herbert Press, London, [1993])

Furlong, William Rea and McCandless, Byron, *So proudly we hail, the History of the United States Flag* (Smithsonian Institution Press, Washington D.C., 1981)

Gall, Franz, *Österreichische Wappenkunde* (Verlag Hermann Böhlaus, Wien – Köln, 1977)

Gallupini, Gino, *La Bandiera Tricolore nella Marina Sarda* (Ufficio Storico delle Marina Militare, Roma, 1971)

Gallupini, Gino and Gay, Franco, *Insegne Bandiere Distinctive e Stemmi della Marina in Italia* (Rivista Maritima, 1992)

Gayre of Gayre and Nigg, Robert, *Heraldic Standards and other Ensigns* (Oliver and Boyd, Edinburgh – London, 1959)

Gerard, R., *Flags over South Africa* (Technical College, Pretoria, 1952)

Ghisi, E., *Il Tricolore Italiano*

1796-1870 (Milano – Torino – Roma, 1912)

Gittings, Clare *Death, Burial and the Individual in Early Modern England* (Croom Helm, London, 1984)

Given-Wilson, Chris and Curteis, Alice *The Royal Bastards of Medieval England* (Routledge & Kegan Paul, London, 1984)

Godlo i Barwa Polski Samorzadowej (Instytut Wzornictwa Przemyslowego, Warszawa, 1998)

Gonzalez-Doria, Fernando *Diccionario Heraldico y Nobiliaria de los Reinos de España* (Bitacora, Madrid, 1987)

Gordon, W.J., *Flags of the World, Past and Present, Their Story and Associations* (Frederick Warne & Co., London - New York, 1915)

Guerra y Villegas, J. A. de Discurso Histórico Político Sobre el Origen y Preheminencias de el Oficio de Heraldos, Reyes de Armas, Feciales y Caduceadores (Mateo de Llanos y Guzmán, Madrid, 1693)

Hayes-McCoy, G.A., *A History of Irish Flags* (G.K. Hall & Co., Boston, 1979)

Heim, Bruno *Heraldry in the Catholic Church* (Van Duren, Gerrards Cross, 1978, revised 1981)

Hesmer, Karl-Heinz, *Flaggen und Wappen der Welt* (Bertelsmann Lexikon Verlag, Gütersloh, 1992)

Hildebrandt, Adolf M. Wappenfibel, *Handbuch der Heraldik* (Degener, Berlin, 1967)

Hopkins, Andrea *Knights* (Collins & Brown, London, 1990)

Horstmann, Hans, *Vor- und Frühgeschichte des Europäischen Flaggenwesens* (Schünemann Universitätsverlag, Bremen, 1971)

Hupp, Otto *Deutscher Wappenkalender* (1900s–1930s)

Innes of Learney, Sir Thomas *Scots Heraldry* (Oliver & Boyd,

Edinburgh, 1934, revised 1956)

Ivanov, K.A., *Flagi gosudarstv mira* (Transport, Moscow, 1971)

Janácek, Josef and Louda, Jirí Ceské erby (Albatros, Prague, 1974, revised 1988)

Kannik, Preben, *The Flag Book* (M. Barrows & Company Inc., New York, 1957)

Kartous, P., Novak, J. and Vrtel, L., *Erby a vlajky miest v Slovenskej republike* (Vydavatelstvo Obzor, Bratislava, 1991)

Kieboom, Jaques van den, *La connaissance des Pavillons ou Bannieres Que la plûspart des Nations arborent en mer* (La Haye, 1737)

Kissane, Noel, ed. *Treasures from the National Library of Ireland* (Boyne Valley Honey Co, 1994)

Laars, T. van der Wapens, *Vlaggen en Zegels van Nederland* (van Campen, Amsterdam, 1913)

Leaf, William and Purcell, Sally *Heraldic Symbols: Islamic Insignia and Western Heraldry* (Victoria & Albert Museum, London, 1986)

Libro del conocimiento de todos los reinos, tierras y señoríos que son por el mundo (manuscript c.1350)

Litten, Julian *The English Way of Death: the Common Funeral since 1450* (Robert Hale, 1991)

Littlejohn, David, *Foreign Legions of the Third Reich,* vols. 1–4 (R. James Bender Publishing, San Jose, 1987)

Lupant, Michel R., *Drapeaux et Insignes de Gendarmerie et de Police,* Vol. 1, 2 (Centre Belgo-Européen d'Etudes des Drapeaux, Ottignies 1993, 1995)

Mandich, Donald R. and Placek, Joseph A. *Russian Heraldry and Nobility* (Dramco Publishers, Florida, 1991)

Meuss, J.F., *Die Geschichte der Preussichen Flagge* (Mittler & Sohn, Berlin, 1916)

Mühlemann, Louis, *Wappen und Fahnen der Schweiz* (Bühler Verlag AG, Lengnau, 1991)

NAF Veibok 2001 (NAF, Oslo, 2001)

The National Flag of Canada (Department of Canadian Heritage, Ottawa, 1998)

Neubecker, Ottfried, *Fahnen und Flaggen* (L. Staackmann Verlag, Leipzig, 1939)

Niesobski, Mariusz *Popularny herbarz rodzin i radów polskich* (Tychy, Kadem, [1991])

Nordenvall, Per Kungliga *Serafimerorden (Armorial Plaques of the Knights of the Seraphim),* 1748–1998 (Swedish Royal Orders, Stockholm, 1998)

Nyulászíné Straub, Eva Ôt évszázad címerei a Magyar Országos Levéltár címereslevelein (Budapest, Corvina, 1987)

Over, Keith, *Flags and Standards of the Napoleonic Wars* (Bivouac Books Ltd, London, 1976)

Pastoureau, Michel *Heraldry: An Introduction to a Noble Tradition* (Abrams, New York, 1997)

Pedersen, Christian Fogd, *The International Flag Book in Colour* (Blandford Press, Dorset, 1971)

Perrin, W.G., *British Flags* (University Press, Cambridge, 1922)

Pinches, J. H. *European Nobility and Heraldry* (Heraldry Today, Ramsbury, 1994)

Platts, Beryl *Origins of Heraldry* (Procter Press, London, 1980)

Preble, Geo. Henry, *Origin and History of The American Flag* (Nicholas L. Brown, Philadelphia, 1917)

Rabbow, Arnold, *dtv-Lexikon Politischer Symbole* (Deutscher Taschenbuch Verlag GmbH & Co. KG, München, 1970)

Richardson, Edward W., *Standards and Colors of the American Revolution* (The University of Pennsylvania Press, 1982)

Rietstap, J. B. *Armorial General.* Originally published in the 19th century, reprinted several times since, and can be obtained through the services of Heraldry Today, Ramsbury, England.

Rothero, Christopher *Medieval Military Dress, 1066–1500* (Blandford Press, Poole, 1983)

Scheffer, C.G.U. Svensk vapenbok fôr landskap, län och städer (Generalstabens litografiska anstalt, Stockholm, 1967)

Schultz, Karl, *Die Deutsche Flagge* (Mittler & Sohn, Berlin, 1928)

Siegel, R., *Die Flagge* (Dietrich Reimer (Ernst Vohsen) Verlag, Berlin, 1912)

Smith, Whitney, *Flags Through the Ages and Across the World* (McGraw-Hill Book Co., Maidenhead, 1975)

Smith, Whitney, *The Flagbook of the United States* (William Morrow & Company, Inc., New York, 1975)

Strickland, Adrian, *A Look at Malta's Insignia* (Cyan Ltd, Balzan, 1992)

Styring, John S., *Brown's Flags and Funnels* (Brown, Son & Ferguson, Glasgow, 1971)

Symbols of Canada (Department of Canadian Heritage, Ottawa, 1995)

Uden, Grant *A Dictionary of Chivalry* (Harmondsworth, Kestrel, 1977)

Urquhart, R.M. *Scottish Burgh and County Heraldry* (Heraldry Today, Ramsbury, 1973)

Urquhart, R.M. *Scottish Civic Heraldry* (Heraldry Today, Ramsbury, 1979)

Wappen und Flaggen der Bundesrepublik Deutschland und ihrer Länder (Bundeszentrale für politische Bildung, Bonn,

1994)

Die Welt im bunten Flaggenbild (Kosmos Sammelbilder, Memmingen, 1950)

Wilson, Timothy, *Flags at Sea* (Her Majesty's Stationery Office, 1986)

Wise, Terence, *Military Flags of the World* (Blandford Press, Dorset, 1977)

Woodcock, Thomas and Robinson, John Martin *The Oxford Guide to Heraldry* (Oxford, OUP, 1988)

Znamierowski, Alfred, *Stworzony do chwaly* (Editions Spotkania, 1995)

Zieber, Eugene *Heraldry in America, 1895* (New York, Greenwhich House, 1984)

Further valuable information has been extracted from articles published in the *Reports* from the International Congresses of Vexillology and in the following vexillological journals:

The Flag Bulletin (Winchester, Massachusetts, U.S.A.); *Das Flaggenkabinett informiert* (Berlin, Germany); *Vexillinfo* (Bruxelles, Belgium); *Vexillologie* (Praha, Czech Republic); *Banderas* (Spain); *Vexilla Italica* (Torino, Italy); *Vexilla Helvetica* (Zollikon, Switzerland); *Vexillologia* (Paris, France); *Vexilla Belgica* (Bruxelles, Belgium); *Raven* (Trenton, U.S.A.); *SAVA Journal* (Pinegowrie, South Africa); *Der Flaggenkurier* (Berlin, Germany); *Flagmaster* (Chester, England) *Znak* (Lviv, Ukraine).

▼ *Mali Federation (1959–1961)*

ACKNOWLEDGEMENTS

▲ *Battle flag of the Confederacy States of America (1861–1865).*

While every attempt has been made by the publishers to credit picture sources correctly, any further information would be welcome. Thanks to the following agencies and individuals for the use of their images.

28b Bruno Barbey/Magnum; 37br Beata Gierblinska; 44br Miroslaw Stelmach; 45m NASA; 47tl Chad Ehlers/Tony Stone Images, tr Ron Sherman/Tony Stone Images; 49tr Ron Sherman/Tony Stone Images; 51m Raghu Rai/Magnum; 54b Hulton Getty; 101b National Geographic Society; 235tl.tm,m Der Flggenkurier (Achim); 237br Instytut Wzornictwa Przemyslowego (Warsaw); 239tr Alex Majoli/ Magnum, bl James Nachtwey/ Magnum, br Robert Van Der Hilst/ Tony Stone; 252bl A. Hornak/ Westminster Abbey; 253tr Bruno Barbey/Magnum.
AKG London: pp288bl, Erich Lessing; 292t; 294b, British Library, from Rothschild Bequest; 302bl, Erich Lessing, Warsaw Museum; 306tr, Erich Lessing; 310br, Domingie Museo Nazionale del Bargello, Florence, Italy; 356tr, British Library; 358b, British Library, Froissart's Chronicle; 393t; 397b; 399tr; 443t; 454t; 467t&br; 479. **Ancient Art & Architecture Collection**: pp263br, 265tl, R. Sheridan; 359br; 398t; 453t. **Anness Publishing Ltd**, courtesy Daniel de Bruin, photography Jos Janssen; pp290t&btl; 318b; 332tr&bl; 340tl; 363tr; 376 all; 377; 378 all; 379; 395b. Anness Publishing Ltd/ Stephen Slater, photography Mark Wood: pp262b; 273b; 274t; 284t; 284bl, King René's Tourney Book; 290t; 301t; 305t; 310t&bl; 312bl,bm &br; 313bl&tr; 314ml; 316t; 318& 337tl; 322tr; 336bl; 338ml; 339tl; 340tr; 350t&bl; 360tr; 361 all; 362bl; 363ml; 368b; 369br; 384b; 385; 386; 389b; 390bl; 392bl&bm; 403t; 408tl, tm&tr; 409tr,mr&br; 410t; 411t&b; 414m&t; 416bl; 417mr; 418t; 442t&b; 452br; 460bl&br; 461t; 464

all; 465ml; 467bl; 470b; 478br; 480 all; 485tr. Anness Publishing Ltd/ unattributable: pp304tr&br; 305m; 307bl. Archive of Stato di Massa, Ministero peri Beni le Attivita Culturali, photograph Progra Immagini, Massa: p339br. **Art Archive**: pp265tr, Manesse Codex, University Library Heidelberg/Dagli Orti; 272t British Library; 268t, Musée des Art Décoratifs, Paris/Dagli Orti; 271b, engraving by Hogenberg, Dagli Orti; 272t, British Library, from Roman de Petit Jean de Saintre; 274b, Musée de Versailles/Dagli Orti, copy of anonymous painting at Hampton Court, Friedrich Bouterwick; 276bl, British Library; 291t, Bibliothèque Nationale, Paris; 292br, College of Arms/John Webb, designed by Maximilian Colt, the King's Carver; 387t; 402t; 403b; 404b; 434t; 450br. **Associated Press**: p481t. **Bridgeman Art Library**: pp267t, British Library, Froissart's Chronicle; 270t, British Library; 270b, British Library, Book of Hours; 286br, William Henry Pyne, Herald, from Costume of Great Britain, William Miller, 1805; 291b, Victoria & Albert Museum, T. Rowlandson and A. C. Pugin; 293b, Bibliothèque Nationale, Paris, Chronicle of Charles VII of France; 404t; 406b; 419t, courtesy St Bride's Church; 420tr. **British Association of Urological Surgeons, London**: pp400, 425tl. **Camera Press**: p388 all. **Collections**: pp424t, 435br, Oliver Benn. **The College of Arms, London**: p286bl. **Corbis**: pp289t; 407b.**Sylvia Cordaiy**: p412tl. **DERA**, Boscombe Down: p415br. **Ede & Ravenscroft Ltd**: p389t. **Edifice**: p463tl, Sarah Jackson. **Edimedia**: pp264t, Chronicle of William of Tyr; 264b, British Library; 266b; 272b; 304tl. **Eglinton County Park/North Ayrshire Council**: pp263br, 265tl. **Tim Graham**: p405b. **Sonia Halliday Photography**: pp267bl, Church of St Chad, Prees, England, Laura

Lushington; 346t, Laura Lushington; 396t; 451t. F.H.C. Birch. **Hulton/Getty**: pp311tr; 458t; 485br, Stone. **Irish Heraldic and Genealogical Office, Dublin**: pp439; 440 all. **The Jewish Museum, London**: p489tl. **Willem Jörg**: pp282; 296bm. **A.F. Kersting**: p273, Temple Church, London. **Leixlip Town Clerk**: p441t. **Gordon Lockie**: p433b. **Lothian & Borders Police photographic unit**: p417tl. **Maltese Tourist Board**: p399b. **Maryland Office of Tourism**: p469b. **Det Nationalhistoriske Museum på Frederiksborg**: p470t. **Peter Newark's Pictures**: pp268m; 303tr, Codex Balduineus; 382br, from Froissart manuscript; 394t; 412tr; 444t; 469t. **Northern Territories of Australia Government**: p315tr. **Novosti** (London): pp288br; 460t; 461m; 462tl; 463tr. **Orlogsmuseet/ Copenhagen**: p412b. **University of Padua**: p422bl&br. **Press Association**: p387b; 406t. **Resianische Militara-kademie, Wiener Neustadt**, Austria: p456t. **Photo RMN**, Paris, France: p443b, Arnaudet. **Royal Armouries**: p268bl, IV600. **Royal Palace of Stockholm/Alexis Daflos**: p471b. **Salisbury and South Wiltshire Museum**: p276tr. **Scala**: pp265b; p268br; 271t; 280t; 351tl; 426bl; 446 all; 448tr; 453bl; 456bl. **Scottish Viewpoint**: pp430b; 432b. **Mick Sharp**: p435t. **Stephen Slater**: pp258; 261b; 262tr; 276br; 277b, Priory Church, Abergavenny, Wales; 278br; 289bl,bm&br; 293tl, Brunswick Cathedral, Germany; 293tr; 294t, Harefield Church, Middx, England; 295t&b, courtesy the Earl of Rothes and Clan Leslie; 296t, Bruges, Belgium; 296bl, Boyton Church, Wilts, England; 300 all; 304bl, Salisbury Cathedral, England; 307tl; 312t, Trowbridge Church, Wilts, England; 314tl&tr; 316bl; 321bm; 335bl, Salisbury Cathedral, England; 338bl; 339bl, Abbey of St Denis, Paris; 342tm; 347m&bl; 357tl; 360bl, 360br, West Lavington Church; 362tm; 363tl&bl; 364tr; 364bl, Harefield Church, Middx, England; 365ml, Westbury Church, Wilts, England; 365bl; 369bl; 371tl; 372tr; 373tl; 374t; 375tl,tr,ml&bl; 380; 382t; 383bl; 390t&br; 391; 392r; 393b; 394b; 395t; 397tl; 408b; 410bl,bm&br; 413bl&bm; 416tr&br; 417tr&br; 418t; 419b; 420bl&br; 421 all; 422t; 423tl&tr; 424b; 425br; 426br; 427br; 428&476tr; 430tr; 431tr,mr,br; 432t; 434b; 436bl&bm; 441b; 448bl;

449b; 451b; 452bl; 453br; 454b; 455 all; 457 all; 465tl, tr&b; 471tl; 475 br; 481bl&br; 485tl&bl; 486 all; 487tl,tr,mr; 488 all; 489mr,bl&br. **Stockczech**: p335bm, Karla Koruna. **Swiss National Museum**, Zurich: p269tl. **Victoria & Albert Museum**: pp288t, Daniel McGrath; 313br; **Zeiner, Josef**: p334br.
Private Collections: pp459tr & 495t, Daniel de Bruin; 450t, Mr Jim Constant; 423br, Eton College; 337bl, Marco Foppoli; 495b, Stephen Friar; 492t, Peter Gwynn-Jones; 314tr, Lord Hanson; 365t, 472t, 473bl & 493br, Robert Harrison; 307tr, Jan Van Helmont Publishing Company, Belgium/a European Noble Gentleman; 357bl & 494 Denis E. Ivall; 435bl, Tony Jones; 475tr, Mike Mailes; 369bm, 414b, 415t&bl, 490 all, 491 all, Baz Manning; 433t, William Naesmyth of Posso; 471tr, Mr Naumberg; 277tl, Collection of the Duke of Northumberland; 427br, Les Pearson; 366, private collection; 461br, Risto Pÿÿkko; 452t, 487b, Tony Ryan; 466t, Malina Sczieskowska; 354br, Carl Stiernspetz; 425br, Peter Taylor; 322bl, Derek Walkden.
Unattributable: pp260tm&b; 261tl, from John of Worcester's Chronicle; 261r; p263t&rml; 266t&rm; p269b; 277tr; 278t&bl; 279tl; 279b; 280br&bl; 280m, Matthew Paris, Chronicle Majora; 281t, Sir Thomas Wriothesley's Book of Standards; 285 all; 286t, Thomas Jenyns' Ordinary; 288ml; 290br; 292br; 296br; 301b; 302t,bm&br; 306bl; 308t; 308b, Biblioteca Trivulziana; 309bl; 311bl; 315br; 317bl; 321br; 327bl&br; 334tr, Zurich Roll; 334bl; 336tl, Ripon Cathedral, Yorks; 340tl; 341tl&tr; 343br; 344bl; 350br, Buckland Abbey, Devon; 352tr; 354bl; 359tr; 360m; 371tm; 372bl&br; 373tr,ml&bl; 374b; 375br; 382ml&bl; 384t; 396bl; 405t; 407t; 412bl; 417bl; 425m; 431bl; 436t; 438bl&bm; 447bl; 450bl; 456br; 458bl; 459m&bl; 466b; 476 all; 477t&b; 478t&bl; 484t; 487tm&rm.

▼ *Oerlese, Germany.*

▼ *Russia, c.1700–1858.*

ALFRED ZNAMIEROWSKI wishes to dedicate the flag section of this book to the memory of his late teacher and friend Dr Ottfried Neubecker, and to extend thanks for encouragement, help and support to Beata Gierblinska (Warsaw), Whitney Smith (Winchester, Massachussetts), Roman Klimes (Bonn) and Jacek Skorupski (Warsaw). Thanks also to: The Flag Design Center, Warsaw, for use of images from the archive; and to Judy Cox; John Clarke; and Dr Lawrie Wright of Queen Mary and Westfield College, University of London.

STEVE SLATER wishes to dedicate the heraldry section of this book to Ma, the dogs, and the Gang of Four, and acknowledge the help of the following. For making this book possible and for the hospitality always shown to me, Steve and Kate Friar. For the inspiration to follow the project through, Arnold Rabbow of Braunschweig. To Arnaud Bunel, Sebastian Nelson and Peter Taylor for help with parts of the text. Thanks to William and Mrs Sybil O'Neill for the kindness in allowing me at all times to make use of Terry's library. Joan Robertson, Karen and John Say, and Margaret Smith for their companionship in the many hours I have bored them silly over escutcheons and hatchments. Baz Manning, without whose help and kindness I would have been unable to complete such a project. Mikhail Medvedev of St. Petersburg for his answering my many questions on Russian heraldry. Alice Hall for her translating letters to foreign locations. Roland Symons for his delightful and unfailing assistance. Sr Marco and Sra Lia Foppoli for their long and happy friendship. James and Mrs Cathy Constant for the refuge they so often afford me. Robert Harrison for his unstinting encouragement. Sebastian Nelson, a true friend of heraldry from the United States. The Officers of Arms, College of Arms, London for their kindness and expertise in answering many a curious and obscure question. David Hubber with many thanks for his kindness and his artwork. The staff at QinetiQ Larkhill, most especially Andy Pike for his patience and understanding. Joanne Rippin of Anness Publishing, whose patience and tenacity have largely been responsible for making sure this work became a reality and Beverley Jollands for her excellent copy editing. Russ Fletcher for the use of his library. Mrs Manning for her excellent deciphering of my scatty notes. Daniel de Bruin for his kindness in giving me access to his splendid collection of grants/patents of arms.

Thanks also to the following people and organizations for their help: Peter Trier of Warpool Court Hotel, St David's; Lt Colonel Herbert A. Lippert (Retd); Mrs Malina Sieczkowska; Michael Messer; Anthony Ryan; the Staff of HM Security Service; The Central Intelligence Agency of the United States, John Uncles; HH the Prince of Oettingen; Herr Willem Jorg; Herr Gunter Mattern; Anthony Jones; Colonel Carnero, Military Attache, Spanish Embassy, London; Risto Pyykko; Keith Lovell; Gordon and Jean Ashton; Bruce Patterson, Saguenay Herald and the Canadian Heraldic Authority; Micheal O'Comain, Consulting Herald, Office of the Chief Herald of Ireland; Fergus Gillespie, Deputy Chief Herald of Ireland; Elisabeth Roads, Lyon Clerk and the staff of the Court of Lord Lyon, Edinburgh; Andrew Martin Garvey; Jennifer Marin, Curator,

▲ *Hokkaido, Prefecture of Japan.*

The Jewish Museum, London; Dr Adrian Ailes; Mrs Marian Miles OBE; Distributed Technology Ltd, Robin Lumsden; Dame Stephanie Shirley DBE, and the staff of the Prior's Court Foundation; Adjutant Luc Binet and the staff of the Service Historique de l'Armee de Terre, Vincennes; Dr. Jan Erik Schulte, Kultur/Kreismuseum, Buren; Bruce Purvis; Martin Davies; David Phillips; Dr Malcolm Golin; The staff of the Haermuseet, Oslo; Lt. Colonel Nick Bird OBE, RA (Retd) and staff of the Royal School of Artillery; Kevin Fielding; Per Nordenval, Riddarhuset, Stockholm; Anna Lilliehöök, KMO. And finally, to all bonacons, wherever they may be.

▼ *A melee at a tournament.*

INDEX

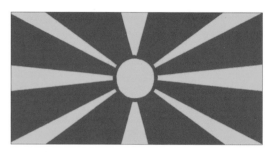